Plutarch and the *Persica*

EDINBURGH STUDIES IN ANCIENT PERSIA

Dealing with key aspects of the ancient Persian world from the Achaemenids to the Sasanians: its history, reception, art, archaeology, religion, literary tradition (including oral transmissions), and philology, this series provides an important synergy of the latest scholarly ideas about this formative ancient world civilization.

SERIES EDITOR
Lloyd Llewellyn-Jones, Cardiff University

EDITORIAL ADVISORY BOARD
Touraj Daryaee, Andrew Erskine, Thomas Harrison, Irene Madreiter, Keith Rutter, Jan Stronk

TITLES AVAILABLE IN THE SERIES

Courts and Elites in the Hellenistic Empires: The Near East After the Achaemenids, c. 330 to 30 BCE
By Rolf Strootman

Greek Perspectives on the Achaemenid Empire: Persia through the Looking Glass
By Janett Morgan

Semiramis' Legacy: The History of Persia According to Diodorus of Sicily
By Jan P. Stronk

ReOrienting the Sasanians: East Iran in Late Antiquity
By Khodadad Rezakhani

Sasanian Persia: Between Rome and the Steppes of Eurasia
Edited by Eberhard W. Sauer

Plutarch and the Persica
By Eran Almagor

FORTHCOMING TITLES

The Bactrian Mirage: Iranian and Greek Interaction in Western Central Asia
By Michael Iliakis

Scholasticism in Late Antique Iran: The Pahlavi Version of the Yasna Haptaŋhāiti
By Arash Zeini

Visit the Edinburgh Studies in Ancient Persia website at
edinburghuniversitypress.com/series/esap

Plutarch and the *Persica*

Eran Almagor

EDINBURGH
University Press

Edinburgh University Press is one of the leading university presses in the UK. We publish academic books and journals in our selected subject areas across the humanities and social sciences, combining cutting-edge scholarship with high editorial and production values to produce academic works of lasting importance. For more information visit our website: edinburghuniversitypress.com

© Eran Almagor, 2018

Edinburgh University Press Ltd
The Tun – Holyrood Road
12(2f) Jackson's Entry
Edinburgh EH8 8PJ

Typeset in 11/13pt Sabon by
Servis Filmsetting Ltd, Stockport, Cheshire,
and printed and bound in Great Britain.

A CIP record for this book is available from the British Library

ISBN 978 0 7486 4555 8 (hardback)
ISBN 978 0 7486 4556 5 (webready PDF)
ISBN 978 1 4744 3718 9 (epub)

The right of Eran Almagor to be identified as the author of this work has been asserted in accordance with the Copyright, Designs and Patents Act 1988, and the Copyright and Related Rights Regulations 2003 (SI No. 2498).

Contents

Preface

In more ways than one, the production of this book has been encouraged by many friends and scholars. Above all, I would like to express my profound and heartfelt thanks to Lloyd Llewellyn-Jones, the editor of this series, for his comments, his kind assistance and for guiding my approach to Edinburgh University Press. I am also grateful for the helpful suggestions and useful feedback received during fruitful discussions over the years on various forms of some of the ideas presented here. Special thanks go to Fred Brenk, Edward Dąbrowa, Ken Dowden, Joseph Geiger, Thomas Harrison, Amelie Kuhrt, John Marincola, Christopher Pelling, Tim Rood, Jacek Rzepka, Donald Russell, Nicholas Sekunda, Joseph Skinner, Rex Stem, Rolf Strootman, Christopher Tuplin, Luc Van der Stockt, Tim Whitmarsh and Alexei Zadorojnyi. I am also indebted to the many colleagues and friends who heard presentations of my methodology on various occasions and responded with inspiring remarks and observations.

As the distant origins of this book lie in my PhD dissertation ('Plutarch's *Artaxerxes*: Historical and Literary Commentary', the Hebrew University), I would also like to convey my deepest and continuous gratitude and appreciation to my supervisors, Deborah Gera and Doron Mendels, for their help and support, for reviewing that version and for their valuable comments on it. The errors that remain in this version are, of course, entirely my own. I am deeply grateful to Carol Macdonald for her aid and encouragement during the stages of composition and preparation of the text, and to Camilla Rockwood and James Dale. I would like to thank Nili for helping me put ideas into comprehensible and communicative phrases, and Hilly for her patience and loving care – and for being there.

Series Editor's Preface

Edinburgh Studies in Ancient Persia focuses on the world of ancient Persia (pre-Islamic Iran) and its reception. Academic interest with and fascination in ancient Persia have burgeoned in recent decades, and research on Persian history and culture is now routinely filtered into studies of the Greek and Roman worlds; Biblical scholarship too is now more keenly aware of Persian-period history than ever before; while, most importantly, the study of the history, cultures, languages and societies of ancient Iran is now a well-established discipline in its own right.

Persia was, after all, at the centre of ancient world civilizations. This series explores that centrality throughout several successive 'Persian empires': the Achaemenid dynasty (founded c. 550 BCE) saw Persia rise to its highest level of political and cultural influence, as the Great Kings of Iran fought for, and maintained, an empire which stretched from India to Libya and from Macedonia to Ethiopia. The art and architecture of the period both reflect the diversity of the empire and proclaim a single centrally constructed theme: a harmonious world order brought about by a benevolent and beneficent king. Following the conquests of Alexander the Great, the Persian Empire fragmented but maintained some of its infrastructures and ideologies in the new kingdoms established by Alexander's successors, in particular the Seleucid dynasts who occupied the territories of western Iran, Mesopotamia, the Levant and Asia Minor. But even as Greek influence extended into the former territories of the Achaemenid realm, at the heart of Iran a family of nobles, the Parthian dynasty, rose to threaten the growing imperial power of Rome. Finally, the mighty Sasanian dynasty ruled Iran and much of the Middle East from the third century CE onwards, proving to be a powerful foe to Late Imperial Rome and Byzantium. The rise of Islam, a new religion in Arabia, brought a sudden end to the Sasanian dynasty in the mid-600s CE.

These successive Persian dynasties left their record in the historical, linguistic and archaeological materials of the ancient world, and Edinburgh Studies in Ancient Persia has been conceived to give scholars working in these fields the opportunity to publish original research and explore new methodologies in interpreting the antique past of Iran. This series will see scholars working with bona fide Persian and other Near Eastern materials, giving access to Iranian self-perceptions and the internal workings of Persian society, placed alongside scholars assessing the perceptions of the Persianate world from the outside (predominantly through Greek and Roman authors and artefacts). The series will also explore the reception of ancient Persia (in historiography, the arts and politics) in subsequent periods, both within and outwith Iran itself.

Edinburgh Studies in Ancient Persia represents something of a watershed in better appreciation and understanding not only of the rich and complex cultural heritage of Persia, but also of the lasting significance of the Achaemenids, Parthians and Sasanians and the impact that their remarkable civilisations have had on wider Persian, Middle Eastern and world history. Written by established and up-and-coming specialists in the field, this series provides an important synergy of the latest scholarly ideas about this formative ancient world civilisation.

Lloyd Llewellyn-Jones

List of Abbreviations

BM	British Museum
BMC	*Coins of the Roman Empire in the British Museum, volume III: Nerva to Hadrian* (ed. H. Mattingly, 1936, London: British Museum)
BNJ	*Brill's New Jacoby* (ed. I. Worthington, 2006–)
FGrH	*Die Fragmente der griechischen Historiker* (ed. F. Jacoby, Berlin, Leiden, 1926–58)
IG	*Inscriptiones Graecae* (1873–)
Jastrow	Jastrow, M. (1886–1903), *Dictionary of the Targumim, the Talmud Babli and Yerushalmi, and the Midrashic Literature* (New York: G. Putnam's Sons)
LCL	Loeb Classical Library
LGPN	*Lexicon of Greek Personal Names* (ed. P. M. Fraser and E. Matthews, M. J. Osborne and S. G. Byrne, T. Corsten, Oxford, 1987–2010)
LSJ	*Greek–English Lexicon* (ed. H. G. Liddell, R. Scott and H. S. Jones, Oxford, 1940–96)
ML	*A Selection of Greek Historical Inscriptions to the End of the Fifth Century* BCE (ed. R. Meiggs and D. Lewis, rev. edn, 1988)
MPer.	Middle Persian
MT	Massoretic Text
OLD	*Oxford Latin Dictionary* (ed. P. G. W. Glare, Oxford, 1982)
OPer.	Old Persian
OT	Old Testament
PF	*Persepolis Fortification Tablets* (Hallock 1969)
PFS	*Persepolis Fortification Seals* (cited according to Garrison and Root, 1998)

POxy	*The Oxyrhynchus Papyri* (ed. B. P. Grenfell, A. S. Hunt and others, London, 1898–)
RIMA	*Royal Inscriptions of Mesopotamia, Assyrian Period Volumes 1–3* (ed. A. K. Grayson, Toronto, 1987–96)
SEG	*Supplementum Epigraphicum Graecum* (1923–)
SIG	*Sylloge Inscriptionum Graecarum* (ed. W. Dittenberger, 3rd edn, 1915–24)

PERSIAN INSCRIPTIONS

DPd	Darius I, Persepolis
DB	Darius I, Behistun
DSe, DSf, DSp	Darius I, Susa
DNa, DNb	Darius I, Naqsh-I Rustam
XPh	Xerxes I, Persepolis

ANCIENT AUTHORS AND WORKS

Plutarch	*Plut.*

Lives

Aemilius Paulus	*Aem. Paul.*
Agesilaus	*Ages.*
Agis	*Ag.*
Alcibiades	*Alc.*
Alexander	*Alex.*
Antony	*Ant.*
Aratus	*Arat.*
Aristides	*Arist.*
Artaxerxes	*Art.*
Brutus	*Brut.*
Caesar	*Caes.*
Camillus	*Cam.*
Cato Maior	*Cat. Mai.*
Cato Minor	*Cat. Min.*
Cicero	*Cic.*
Cimon	*Cim.*
Cleomenes	*Cleom.*
Coriolanus	*Cor.*

Crassus	*Crass.*
Demetrius	*Demetr.*
Demosthenes	*Dem.*
Dion	*Dion*
Eumenes	*Eum.*
Fabius Maximus	Fab.
Flamininus	*Flam.*
Gaius Gracchus	*Gai. Gracch.*
Galba	*Galb.*
Lucullus	*Luc.*
Lycurgus	*Lyc.*
Lysander	*Lys.*
Marcellus	*Marc.*
Marius	*Mar.*
Nicias	*Nic.*
Numa	*Num.*
Otho	*Otho*
Pelopidas	*Pelop.*
Pericles	*Per.*
Philopoemen	*Phil.*
Phocion	*Phoc.*
Pompey	*Pomp.*
Publicola	*Publ.*
Pyrrhus	*Pyrrh.*
Romulus	*Rom.*
Sertorius	*Sert.*
Solon	*Sol.*
Sulla	*Sull.*
Themistocles	*Them.*
Theseus	*Thes.*
Tiberius Gracchus	*Tib. Gracch.*
Timoleon	*Tim.*
Comparatio	Comp.

Moralia (in the conventional order)

On the education of children [*De liberis educandis*]   *De lib. educ.*
On reading the poets [*De audiendis poetis*]   *De aud. poet.*
On listening to lectures [*De audiendo*]   *De aud.*
On friends and flatterers [*Quomodo adulator ab amico internoscatur*]   *Quomodo adulat.*
On progress in virtue [*De profectibus in virtute*]   *Prof. in virt.*

How to profit from your enemies [*De capienda
    exinimicis utilitate*]   *De cap. ex inim.*
On having many friends [*De amicorum multitudine*] *De am. mult.*
On fortune [*De fortuna*]   *De fort.*
On virtue and vice [*De virtute et vitio*]   *De virt. et vit.*
Consolation to Apollonius [*Consolatio ad
    Apollonium*]   *Cons. ad Apoll.*
Advice on health [*De tuenda sanitate praecepta*] *De tuenda sanit.*
Advice on marriage [*Coniugalia praecepta*]   *Con. praec.*
Symposium of the seven sages [*Septem sapientium convivium*] *Sept.*
On superstition [*De superstitione*]   *De sup.*
Sayings of kings and commanders [*Regum et
    imperatorum apophthegmata*]   *Reg. et imp. apophth.*
Spartan sayings [*Apophthegmata Laconica*]   *Ap. Lac.*
Virtues of women [*Mulierum virtutes*]   *Mul. virt.*
Roman questions [*Quaestiones Romanae*]   *Quaest. Rom.*
Greek questions [*Quaestiones Graecae*]   *Quaest. Graec.*
Minor parallels [*Parallela Graeca et
    Romana*]   *Parall. Graec. et Rom.*
On the fortune of the Romans [*De fortuna
    Romanorum*]   *De fort. Rom.*
On the fortune and virtue of Alexander the Great [*De
    Alexandri Magni fortuna aut virtute*]   *De Alex. fort.*
On the glory of Athens [*De gloria Atheniensium*] *De glor. Athen.*
On Isis and Osiris [*De Iside et Osiride*]   *De Is. et Os.*
On the 'E' at Delphi [*De E apud Delphos*]   *De e*
On the Pythia's prophecies [*De Pythiae oraculis*]   *De Pyth. or.*
On the decline of oracles [*De defectu oraculorum*]   *De def. or.*
Whether virtue can be taught [*An virtus doceri possit*] *An virt. doc.*
On moral virtue [*De virtute morali*]   *De virt. mor.*
On the control of anger [*De cohibenda ira*]   *De coh. ira*
On tranquility of mind [*De tranquillitate animi*]   *De tranq. an.*
On brotherly love [*De fraterno amore*]   *De frat. am.*
On the love of offspring [*De amore prolis*]   *De am. prol.*
Is vice a sufficient cause of misery? [*An vitiositas ad
    infelicitatem sufficiat*]   *An vitiositas*
Ills of the body and ills of the mind [*Animine an
    corporis affectiones sint peiores*]   *Animine an corp.*
On talkativeness [*De garrulitate*]   *De gar.*
On curiosity [*De curiositate*]   *De cur.*
On the love of wealth [*De cupiditate divitiarum*]   *De cup. div.*
On harmful scrupulousness [*De vitioso pudore*]   *De vit. pud.*

On envy and hatred [*De invidia et odio*]	*De inv. et od.*
On inoffensive self-praise [*De laude ipsius*]	*De se ipsum laud.*
On god's slowness to punish [*De sera numinis vindicta*]	*De sera*
On fate [*De fato*]	*De fato*
On the sign of Socrates [*De genio Socratis*]	*De gen.*
On exile [*De exilio*]	*De exilio*
Consolation to my wife [*Consolatio ad uxorem*]	*Cons.ad ux.*
Table Talk [*Quaestiones Convivales*]	*QC*
Dialogue on love [*Amatorius*]	*Amat.*
Love stories [*Amatoriae narrationes*]	*Am. narr.*
On the fact that the philosopher ought most of all to converse with leaders [*Maxime cum principibus philosopho esse disserendum*]	*Max. cum princ.*
To an uneducated ruler [*Ad principem ineruditum*]	*Ad princ. iner.*
Whether old men should engage in public affairs [*An seni respublica gerenda sit*]	*An seni*
Political precepts [*Praecepta gerendae reipublicae*]	*Praec. ger. reip.*
On monarchy, democracy, and oligarchy [*De unius in republica dominatione, populari statu, et paucorum imperio*]	*De unius*
That we ought not to borrow [*De vitando aere alieno*]	*De vit. aer.*
Lives of the ten orators [*Decem oratorum vitae*]	*Dec. or. vit.*
Summary of a comparison between Aristophanes and Menander [*Comparationis Aristophanis et Menandri epitome*]	*Comp. Ar. et Men.*
On the malice of Herodotus [*De Herodoti malignitate*]	*De Herod. malig.*
Doctrines of the philosophers [*Placita philosophorum*]	*Plac. philos.*
Natural questions [*Quaestiones naturales*]	*Quaest. nat.*
On the face in the moon [*De facie quae in orbe lunae apparet*]	*De fac.*
On the first cold [De primo frigido]	*De prim. frig.*
Which is more useful, fire or water? [*Aqua an ignis utilior sit*]	*Aqua an ignis*
On the intelligence of animals [*De sollertia animalium*]	*De soll. anim.*
Gryllus [*Gryllus/Bruta animalia ratione uti*]	*Brut. anim.*
On the eating of meat [*De esu carnium*]	*De esu*
Platonic questions [*Quaestiones Platonicae*]	*Quaest. Plat.*
On the Creation of the Soul in the *Timaeus* [*De animae procreatione in Timaeo*]	*De anim. proc.*

On Stoic contradictions [*De Stoicorum repugnantiis*]   *De Stoic. rep.*
Stoic paradoxes are stranger than poets [*Stoicos
   absurdiora poetis dicere*]   *Stoic. absurd. poet.*
Against the Stoics on common conceptions [*De
   communibus notitiis adversus Stoicos*]   *De comm. not.*
It is not possible even to live pleasantly according
   to Epicurus [*Non posse suaviter vivi secundum
   Epicurum*]   *Non posse*
Against Colotes [*Adversus Colotem*]   *Adv. Col.*
On living unknown [*De latenter vivendo*]   *De lat. viv.*

OTHER AUTHORS

1 Maccabees		1 Macc.
Aelian		Ael.
De natura animalium	*NA*	
Varia Historia	*VH*	
Aeneas Tacticus		Aen. Tac.
Aeschylus		Aesch.
Agamemnon	*Ag.*	
Persae	*Pers.*	
Septem contra Thebas	*Sept.*	
Agathias		Agath.
Ammianus Marcellinus		Amm. Marc.
Andocides		Andoc.
Anthologia Palatina		*AP*
Apuleius		Apul.
Apologia	*Apol.*	
Aristophanes		Aristoph.
Acharnenses	*Ach.*	
Aves	*Av.*	
Ecclesiazusae	*Ecc.*	
Equites	*Eq.*	
Ranae	*Ran.*	
Vespae	*Vesp.*	
Aristotle		Arist.
De generatione animalium	*GA*	
Ethica Nicomachea	*EN*	
Historia animalium	*HA*	
Poetica	*Poet.*	
Politica	*Polit.*	

Arrian	Arr.
Anab.	*Anab.*
Epicteti dissertationes	*Diss. Epict.*
Athenaeus	Athen.
Aulus Gellius	Aul. Gell.
Noctes Atticae	*NA*
Callimachus	Callim.
Hymns	*Hymn.*
Cicero	Cic.
De divination	*De div.*
De legibus	*De leg.*
De Oratore	*De Or.*
Epistulae ad familiars	*Ad Fam.*
Epistulae ad Quintum fratrem	*Ad. Quint.*
Clemens Alexandrinus	Clem.
Protrepticus	*Protr.*
Stromateis	*Strom.*
Curtius Rufus	Curt. Ruf.
Demosthenes	Dem.
Dio Cassius	Dio Cass.
Dio Chrysostomus	Dio Chrys.
Diodorus Siculus	Diod.
Diogenes Laertius	Diog. Laert.
Dionysius Halicarnassensis	Dion. Hal.
Antiquitates Romanae	*AR*
De Thucydide	*Thuc.*
De compositione verborum	*De comp. verb.*
Epistula ad Pompeium	*Ad Pomp.*
Epistula	*Ep.*
Eunapius	Eun.
Vitae sophistarum	*Vit. Soph.*
Euripides	Eur.
Phoenissae	*Phoen.*
Eusebius	Eus.
Chronica	*Chron.*
Praeparatio evangelica	*PE*
Excerpta historica iussu Imp. Constantini	
Porphyrogeniti	Porph.
Excerpta de insidiis	*Exc. de Insid.*
Excerpta de virtutibus et vitiis	*Exc. de Virt.*
Gorgias	Gorg.
Helena	*Hel.*

Herodotus		Hdt.
Hesychius		Hesych.
Hippocrates		Hippoc.
De aera, aquis, locis	*Aer.*	
Homer		
Iliad	*Il.*	
Odyssey	*Od.*	
Horace		Hor.
Odes	*Od.*	
Hyginus		
Fabulae	*Fab.*	
Isocrates		Isoc.
Aeropagiticus	*Areop.*	
Evagoras	*Evag.*	
Ad Philipum	*Phil.*	
Panathenaicus	*Panath.*	
Panegyricus	*Paneg.*	
Josephus		Jos.
Antiquitates Judaicae	*AJ*	
Contra Apionem	*CA*	
Lucian		Luc.
Philopseudes	*Philops.*	
Quomodo historia conscribenda sit	*Quom. hist. consc.*	
De saltatione	*Salt.*	
Verae historiae	*VH*	
Lysias		Lys.
Marcus Aurelius		Marc. Aur.
Nepos		Nep.
Alcibiades	*Alc.*	
Chabrias	*Chab.*	
Conon	*Con.*	
Datames	*Dat.*	
De Regibus Exterarum Gentium	*De Reg.*	
Themistocles	*Them.*	
Nicander		Nicand.
Theriaca	*Ther.*	
Orosius		Oros.
Ovidius		Ov.
Ars amatoria	*Ars Am.*	
Pausanias		Paus.

Philo
   De specialibus legibus   *Spec. leg.*
Photius
   Biblotheke   *Bibl.*
Pindar   Pind.
   Pythian odes   *Pyth.*
Plato   Plat.
    Alcibiades 1   *Alc. 1*
    Gorgias   *Gorg.*
    Leges   *Leg.*
    Phaedo   *Phaed.*
    Phaedrus   *Phaedr.*
    Politicus   *Polit.*
    Protagoras   *Prot.*
    Respublica   *Rep.*
    Sophista   *Soph.*
    Symposium   *Sym.*
    Timaeus   *Tim.*
Pliny the Elder   Plin.
   Naturalis historia   NH
Pliny the Younger   Plin.
   Panegyricus   *Paneg.*
Polyaenus   Polyaen.
Porphyry   Porphyr.
   De abstinentia   *De abst.*
   Vita Pythagorae   *Vit. Pyth.*
Propertius   Propert.
Pseudo Aelius Aristides   Ps.-Ael. Arist.
Pseudo Apollodorus   Ps.-Apoll.
Pseudo Aristotle   Ps.-Arist.
   De Mundo   *Mund.*
Pseudo Demetrius   Ps.- Demetr.
   De Elocutione   *De eloc.*
Pseudo Lucian   Ps.-Luc.
   Macrobii   *Macr.*
Polybius   Polyb.
Pompeius Trogus   Trog.
   Prologus   *Prol.*
Quintilian   Quint.
   Institutio oratoria   *Inst.*

Sallust   Sall.
  Bellum Jugurthinum   *Bell. Jug.*
  Historiae   *Hist.*
Scholia   Schol.
Scriptores Historiae Augustae   SHA
  Avidius Cassius   *Av. Cass.*
  Lucius Verus   *Ver.*
  Marcus   *Marc.*
Seneca   Sen.
  De beneficiis   *De benef.*
  Apocolocyntosis   *Apoc.*
Sophocles   Soph.
  Oedipus Tyrannus   OT
Statius
  Thebais   *Theb.*
Stephanus Byzantius   Steph. Byz.
Suetonius   Suet.
  Nero   *Ner.*
Tacitus   Tac.
  Historiae   *Hist.*
  Annales   *An.*
Tertullianus   Tert.
  De testimonio animae   *De anim.*
Theognis   Thgn.
Theophrastus   Theophr.
  Characteres   *Char.*
Thucydides   Thuc.
Tzetzes   Tzetz.
  Historiarum Variarum Chiliades *Chil.*
Valerius Maximus   Val. Max.
Velleius Paterculus   Vell. Pat.
Vergilius   Verg.
  Georgics   *Georg.*
Vitruvius   Vitruv.
Xenophon   Xen.
  Agesilaus   *Ages.*
  Anabasis   *Anab.*
  Cyropaedia   *Cyr.*
  Hellenica   *Hell.*
  Memorabilia   *Mem.*

To my parents, Nili and Uri

'. . . all the great historians, Herodotus, Plutarch, Livy, were poets'
(Percy Bysshe Shelley, *A Defence of Poetry*)

1. *Introduction*

It is the aim of this book to build a bridge between two worlds or two branches of scholarship which have been sadly separated in research: the historically oriented Achaemenid/Persian Studies and the historically or literary-oriented studies of Greek imperial literature, in particular the studies of the biographer and essayist Plutarch of Chaeronea (c. 45–c. 120 CE).[1] The book intends to provide a better understanding of the character of the (now lost) fourth century BCE portrayals of ancient Persia, as well as of the manner of the reception and adaptation of these works nearly five hundred years later. Understanding these two sets of texts will allow us, on the one hand, to appreciate the information given on Persia within the extant texts of Plutarch, and on the other, through a study of several of Plutarch's texts, in particular his *Artaxerxes*,[2] to offer scholars insight into the way he composed his works in general.

More often than not, Greek authors are our only guide to ancient Persia.[3] This is true for any Greek text describing Persia besides Herodotus, including the extant *Artaxerxes* and his sources, the lost fourth century BCE works called by future generations *Persica* (= 'Persian Matters'). In order to evaluate the historical descriptions of the political and social reality of the period in Plutarch's works,

---

[1] For the date of Plutarch, see Ziegler (1951: 639–41).

[2] The form used in this volume will be 'Artaxerxes', in conformity with the form seen in the MSS of many ancient authors, including Thucydides, Xenophon, Diodorus, Josephus, Polyaenus, Aelian and Athenaeus, and certain of Plutarch's works. This is despite the fact that the MSS of Plutarch's biography of the king (apart from N), some MSS of Photius' epitome of Ctesias' work, Herodotus and Arrian all use 'Artoxerxes'.

[3] Cf. Momigliano (1990: 5–6) on Herodotus.

we have to address two historiographic questions. The first concerns Plutarch, the other concerns the works he employed. In our case:

(1) What do we know about Plutarch's work method?
(2) What do we know of the *Persica* works?

In general, one might begin to answer the first query by comparing extant works of other authors with Plutarch's use of them.[4] We could have said something more accurate on the second question had we known that Plutarch's work method is constantly the same throughout his entire oeuvre.[5] But it is not. We do not, therefore, tread on solid ground when we attempt to answer either of these two questions. Indeed, absolute certitude in the matter of the intriguing problem of *Quellenforschung* (source criticism) is beyond expectation, and especially in the case of Plutarch.[6] Some of my proposals below are, therefore, conjectural.

Since these questions are two great unkowns, it would seem apt to apply here the old puzzle of a comparison of black hats in a dark room.[7] Such a discussion, however, is not without its value, as it promotes a better appreciation of Plutarch's methods of adapting and modifying the original versions of his stories. In what follows, an attempt is proposed to allow the answers to reflect one upon the other. I will try to show that the two great mysteries – namely, the content and character of the now lost *Persica* works and Plutarch's method of work in using them and composing his biographies – shed light on each other. I will attempt to show how dealing with both issues simultaneously is the most appropriate way to approach the two knotty problems.

---

[4] See Pelling (1985: 314) on Sallust, Pelling (2002a) on Thucydides, Pelling (2007: 150–62) on Herodotus, Shipley (1997) on Xenophon.

[5] A step towards determining Plutarch's technique is provided by Pelling (1980: 127–30; cf. 2011: 56–7), who ascribes to him several devices of abridging the material (like the conflation of similar items, chronological compression or chronological displacement, transference of an item from one character to another, expansion of material or fabrication/creation of a context).

[6] For criticism of the very scholarly pursuit of *Quellenforchung* see Millar (1964: viii): '... source criticism is mere speculation and its results often no more than the product of the assumptions with which the examination of a text was begun'. Cf. also Stadter (1989: lix): 'The modern reader is forced to steer an uneasy and often dangerous path between the Scylla of speculative reconstruction and the Charybdis of Skeptical agnosticism.'

[7] See McDonald (1953: 163).

PLUTARCH

The Greek imperial author Plutarch produced an impressive amount of written work. The editor of the Byzantine lexicon the *Suda* even succinctly characterised him with the brief depiction 'he wrote a lot' (ἔγραψε δὲ πολλά: s.v. 'Plutarch', π 1793 Adler). It is conventional, ever since the medieval manuscript tradition after Maximus Planudes (Paris gr. 1672, fourteenth century), and, more importantly, since the fifteenth century, to divide his literary output into two parts: (a) the *Moralia* section ('moral treatises'), which is a miscellaneous assortment of seventy-eight works, including rhetorical pieces and moral/philosophical essays and dialogues;[8] and (b) the biographies, or *Lives* (*bioi*).[9] Indeed, Plutarch obviously *read* a lot too, though not all the works he does refer to were read by him at first hand.[10]

It is customary to believe that an ancient author would generally write with one single scroll open (on a book-rest or held by a slave) – a work that would form the basis of the narrative[11] – occasionally turning to other sources for additional items or different accounts. Plutarch admits using written notes (ὑπομνήματα: *De tranq. an.* 464f) as well, in an interim stage, presumably after a preliminary reading was involved.[12] Following the methods of Christopher Pelling (1979: 94–5) for historical narratives,[13] and Luc Van der Stockt (1999, esp. 580) and his colleagues for philosophical works, these *hypomnemata* could be considered as more detailed notes, in the form of rough draft 'clusters' of data. While it is very profitable to compare these 'clusters' of details or ideas, we propose a different method. Let

---

[8] On the manuscript tradition see Manton (1949); at least nine works may be spurious. On the *Moralia* see Ziegler (1951: 313–14), Russell (1968: 132–40), Harrison (1991), Geiger (2008).

[9] The word biography, Βιογραφία first appeared only in Damascius, *Life of Isidorus* (Photius, *Bibl.* cod. 181 p. 121 a 5, cod. 242 p. 335 b 14). There were two arrangements of the *Lives* dated to the ninth and eleventh centuries CE: in two volumes, known as the *editio bipartita* (ordered according to the chronology of the Greek heroes), used by Photius (cod. 245, p. 398b–399a), and the three volumes, or *editio tripartita* (following the geographical origins of the Greek heroes). See Ziegler's introduction to the 1957 Teubner edition, I.1, v–xx; Pade (2007: 1.57–8).

[10] A glimpe at the number of authors and works cited explicitly by Plutarch is in the volume of Helmbold and O'Neil (1959). Not at first hand: cf. Hamilton (1969: xlix–lii) on the *Alexander*; Jones (1971: 85); cf. Russell (1973: 42–3, 46, 54). There were surely many texts which Plutarch consulted and does not mention. See Pelling (2011: 38–40).

[11] See Westlake (1938) on Plutarch's *Timoleon*, Russell (1963: 21) on the *Coriolanus*, Pelling (2002a: 119) on *Nicias* 12–29. See Pelling (1979: 94–5; 2011: 39–40). Luce (1977: 199–203) discusses this method for Livy.

[12] Doubtless the content of the *hypomnema* regarding self-love (φιλαυτία: 468e, 471e, 472c) has to do with Plutarch's claim that he wrote this note for *himself* (ἐμαυτῷ πεποιημένος ἐτύγχανον).

[13] Cf. Luc. *Quom. hist. consc.* 47–8. See App. II.

us not study the way these notes became the core of their respective works, but rather begin from the extant text and work our way back to Plutarch's presumed notes.

The first point in our interpretive method is thus to treat Plutarch's works, especially the biographies, as complete artistic artefacts, works of literature and rhetoric aimed to highlight certain moral or philosophical ideas. This is significant first and foremost against the image of Plutarch's biographies, embraced by outdated scholarship, as simply a combination of sections taken from previous authors.[14] Under no circumstances did Plutarch identify his works as supplanting his sources, nor indeed did he ever envisage his oeuvre to outlast the texts he consulted. Plutarch's biographies should therefore not be regarded merely as a mine to quarry fragments from lost historians. Since Plutarch is seen as a highly original author, with his own agenda, ethical outlook and unique methods of narration, it entails that he adapted his sources and sometimes transformed – not to say manipulated – them, to suit his literary aims and moral goals. Furthermore, when we dismantle Plutarch's narrative into anecdotes or clusters of ideas, we sometimes lose sight of the artistic merit found in them. This is especially true of the *Lives*. Apparently, Plutarch himself left open the question of the generic type of his *Lives*, blurring the boundaries of fact and fiction, history and literature.[15]

This brings us to the second point – the moral aspect of history. In his *Lives*, Plutarch's heroes provide good or bad examples for readers to imitate or shun.[16] In his philosophical work *De virtute morali* (*On Moral Virtue*, 441d–443d), Plutarch shows his conformity[17] with the Platonic internal partition of the soul (Plat. *Rep.* 4.439e–440d;

---

[14] See Van der Stockt (1992: 10): 'one must be careful not to disintegrate Plutarch and simply reduce him to his sources. For contrary to the attitude of nineteenth century *Quellenforschung*, Plutarch's striving to develop personal views is now receiving growing acknowledgement.' Cf. Pelling (2011: 38).

[15] Following the neat compartmentalisation of Aristotle (*Poet.* 9.1451b1–8) between history and poetry, the first telling us 'what happened' (τὰ γενόμενα λέγειν) and the latter 'what might happen' (οἷα ἂν γένοιτο), Plutarch's *Lives* should ostensibly be placed more in the realm of history, for they relate what Alcibiades did or suffered. However, despite the famous *Alex.* 1.2 (οὔτε γὰρ ἱστορίας γράφομεν, ἀλλὰ βίους, 'for I do not write histories, but *Lives*', cf. Nepos, *Pelop.* 1.1), in many other places Plutarch treats his work as history (*Cim.* 2.4–5: τῇ ἱστορίᾳ; *Dem.* 2.1: τῷ . . . σύνταξιν ὑποβεβλημένῳ καὶ ἱστορίαν; cf. *Aem. Paul.* 1.1; *Thes.* 1.2; *Lyc.* 1.1; *Tib.-Gai. Gracch.* 1.1). In *Galb.* 2.5, the relation of the biography with history is presented as more subtle. See Beck (2007: 397): '[Plutarch's] awareness includes the perception that his is a different form of historical writing.' See Duff (1999: 13–51), Pelling (2011: 13–16, 22–5).

[16] See *Per.* 2.4; *Aem. Paul.* 1.4–6; *Demer.* 1.1–7. Cf. *Prof. in Virt.* 84b–85b.

[17] Cf. Dillon (1977: 194), Duff (1999: 72–6). Vander Waerdt (1985: 295 n. 31).

442a–c),[18] which separates the rational (λογιστικόν) aspect – desiring knowledge (Plat. *Rep.* 4.435e, 9.581b) and the Good[19] – from the irrational element. The latter, or passionate part, is divided in turn between (a) the spirited (θυμοειδές), interested in honour, success and standing (Plat. *Rep.* 4.442bc, 9.581ab) and (b) the appetitive (ἐπιθυμητικόν), endeavouring to gratify physical needs such as thirst, hunger and sexual urges (Plat. *Rep.* 4.435e–436a, 437de, 439d, cf. 436a, 440a) as well as love of money (*Rep.* 8.580e–581a).[20] When the rational part guides and restrains these irrational passions (Plat. *Rep.* 4.440a–441e, 442c), the soul becomes controlled and is at one, and the person is morally virtuous (Plat. *Rep.* 4.443c–444a, 444d, 431de, 422cd, cf. *Phaedr.* 284a–c).[21]

This thought is related to Plutarch's belief of two principles in the world, derived from an interpretation of Plato. The autonomous, primeval, shapeless, chaotic matter (cf. Plat. *Tim.* 52d–53c. cf. *Polit.* 273bc), upon which the divine craftsman (the Demiurge) works, has the origin of alteration and movement within itself (cf. Plat. *Tim.* 37bc, 77c, 89a), and hence is seen to be an embodied soul.[22] This soul is thus the principle of erratic and undiscipline movement. When orderliness was forced upon it, the world was created (in the sense that it received reason, order and form, cf. *De anim. proc.* 1015f–1016c, 1017ab. 1024a, 1027a).[23] Individual souls are part of this World Soul and parallel to it in structure (*De virt. mor.* 441f), they all possess rational and irrational elements (*De virt. mor.* 452b), oscillating between order and disorder (as we saw above) due to this irrational unruly constituent. In conformity with this Platonic scheme, as well as with Aristotle's principle that virtue (ἀρετή) lies in

[18] See also Plat. *Rep.* 10.602c–606d; *Leg.* 1.644e–645c; *Tim.* 41e–44c, 69b–72d (with Robinson, 1990); *Phaedr.* 246a–249d, 253c–254e, 255e–256d, and *Phaed.* 68c, 82c, *Symp.* 205d. See Saunders (1962) on the *Leg.* Cf. Stocks (1915), Miller (1998), Gerson (2003: 99–147), Lorenz (2006: 14–52), Ferrari (2007).

[19] See Kahn (1987: 84, 86–91).

[20] See Arist. *EN* 2.1104b30 on the three motives of choice (or avoidance): the noble (the base), the expedient (the harmful), and the pleasant (the painful), and his threefold division of the desiderative part (*EN* 2.3.7.1104b30).

[21] See *Gorg.* 503d–504d. On vice as consisting of psychic disorder, see the first of the two evils of the soul in Plat. *Soph.* 227d–228e (internal conflict, like a disease of the body); the other kind is evil out of ignorance/error (cf. *Gorg.* 468ab, 509d–510a, *Meno*, 77b–78b, *Tim.* 86d, *Leg.* 5.731c, 9.860d–861d, 863cd, 864d, 908e), comparable to deformity of the body, a certain lack of excellence (cf. Plat. *Rep.* 1.353c–e). See Cherniss (1954), Guthrie (1978: 93–4), Cooper (1984: 13–17), Wood (2009, esp. 354–6, 361, 381–3).

[22] On the soul as principle of movement: Plut. *De anim. proc.* 1015e. See Cherniss (1976: 196–7 n. d.).

[23] Cf. *De Is. et Os.* 47.370c–48.371a, *De anim. proc.* 1014e, 1016b, *Quaest. Plat.* 2.1001c, 4.1003a. Cf. Plat. *Polit.* 272e–273c, Baltes (2000: 248–50), Opsomer (2004: 143, 149).

the realisation of the right 'mean' between two extreme passions,[24] Plutarch displays his belief that a moral character (ἦθος) is good when it is educated by reason (*De virt. mor.* 443d), and is bad when formed by the habitual choice of the soul to follow an excessive passion, failing to find the right balance (*De virt. mor.* 444c–445a, 451de).[25]

Plutarch's *Lives*, where the moralistic tendency is pronounced, have, therefore, an aim beyond telling a (historical) story, or employing previous volumes in order to narrate an account. In order to achieve the moralistic goal, Plutarch focuses on characterisation, which is thus central to the process of encoding the text of the biography. Thus, while the subject matter of a Plutarchan *Life* may appear to be a historical figure (like Alcibiades), in actual fact it concerns his character or *type* of character, as exemplified in the historical person. For the achievement of this goal, certain exemplary sayings and actions of the protagonist are reported.[26] Moreover, contrary to Aristotle (*Poetics* 6.1450a20–38), who views characters in tragedy as subordinate to the action,[27] it appears that Plutarch sees the hierarchy between these elements as reversed. Unlike the Stagirite (*Poetics* 8.1451a15–36), Plutarch appears to believe that the plot revolves not around an action but around a character. This focus seems to govern his own initial reading of the sources, the selection of the parts intended for use, and the modifications and alterations of the material that he introduces. The chosen texts are made to fit the portrayal of a multifaceted character, to present the changes it undergoes or the complexity it reveals.

Yet, even as compositions possessing moral aims, the *Lives* are not straightforward in the examples and lessons they present. Plutarch invites readers to reflect upon the content, to investigate, draw their own conclusions, explore the different virtues and vices presented, and reassess the relation between them and political success and failure. Plutarch's moralism has been depicted as 'exploratory' (descriptive) rather than 'expository'.[28] It has no direct injunction on how to behave. Plutarch gives the reader an active role in thinking about the right path he or she should take. The result is a text that is

---

[24] See Hardie (1964–5), Urmson (1973), Losin (1987).
[25] Dillon (1977: 195–6), Opsomer (2012: 328). Cf. Plat. *Leg.* 1.644b, 6.782d.
[26] Ziegler (1951: 903–5), Pelling (2011: 15–25).
[27] See House (1956: 68–81), Will (1960), Else (1965: 259–86), Lucas (1968: 103–12, 115–17), Lord (1969), Belfiore (2009: 631–2).
[28] Pelling (1995: 207; cf. 2011: 17, 24). Cf. Duff (1999: 390; cf. 37–42, 68–71). See Stadter (2000: 493, 503–5), Verdegem (2010: 19–27). Cf. Whitmarsh (2001: 54–6).

not as clear-cut as might be assumed on first reading, but is rather in need of an in-depth interpretation.

This intricate presentation is related to another feature. Plutarch's stories in the *Lives* might contain contradictions, illogical inferences and unbelievable items, and at times display different competing versions presented alongside each other. If we envisage Plutarch's aims to be solely directed at telling a historical story, we might seriously call into question his sound judgement, let alone the merit of his works for historians.[29] If, however, we understand that Plutarch's interest lies elsewhere, on the moral plane, we realise why Plutarch does not present a simple picture of historical reality. The episodes are given in a way that forces the readers to evaluate the data. In order to provide them with different points of view to judge the heroes, the text has to allow sufficient diversity of interpretations and a range of different versions. In other words, it must have different layers of significance; it must show us one thing and tell us another.[30] This implies that some discrepancy within the description is needed in order to enhance this feature.[31]

As a literary written work, one cannot avoid the realisation that Plutarch employs the *persona* of a narrator to communicate the story and his ideas. This is our third point. While admittedly ancient literary criticism did not formulate a comprehensive distinction between author and narrator,[32] ancient rhetorical practice employed a very similar variance between the orator and the *persona* he adopts in the delivery of a speech.[33] Acknowledging that the real author (e.g. the flesh-and-blood Plutarch) is forever hidden from us, Wayne Booth, in his seminal work *The Rhetoric of Fiction* (1961), further develops this differentiation. Booth distinguishes the narrator, who tells the story and has a voice in the narrative world, from the *implied author*, i.e., the ideal image of the real writer, and his set of values or norms; the implied author's presence is crucial for the story and

---

[29] See Bosworth (1992: 80), Binder (2008: 23–6), Stronk (2010: 92–103). Cf. Gomme (1945: 57); cf. Stadter (1989: xlviii–ix).

[30] See Duff (2011: 61–8) on what Plutarch's text 'tells' and 'shows' us.

[31] This can be seen as one of the functions of the formal comparisons or *Synkriseis* after a pair of *Lives*, which encourage the reader to contrast and evaluate the two figures and which contain a new arrangement of features and events as opposed to the biographies themselves. See Erbse (1956), Pelling (1986), Larmour (1992), Duff (1999: 243–86).

[32] Nünlist (2009: 132–3). The distinction between narrator and his characters is also not discernible, yet may appear as it suits the argument; cf. Hunter and Russell (2011: 197), on *De aud. poet.* 35a.

[33] Cf. Quint. *Inst.* 6.3.85, 9.1.29 on *simulatio* (pretence of having a certain opinion) and *dissimulatio* (feigning not to understand). See 12.1.12 (*simulatio*), cf. 6.1.36 (*persona*); cf. Lausberg (1998, § 582–5, 902–4). See Anderson (2000: 39–40).

text as its creator and unifier, but he lacks a voice in it.[34] Thus, the real Plutarch is veiled by the person transmitting the story (cf. the simplified diagram 1).

The analytical difference between the persons of the author and the narrator explains the employment of what is termed as 'figured speech', namely, the devices of allegory, irony and innuendo, which display a gap between the meaning the author intends to convey to the reader and the explicit words of the narrator. In these cases, the narrator's depictions and comments are made to communicate one (overt) meaning, while the author is understood to transmit quite a different, implicit one through his narrator. The narrator *tells* us one thing while he is *showing* us something completely different, which we construe as the author's real intent. We notice this gap when we realise the narrator is not what we expect him to be. He seems to be aiming at the truth and appears to have reasonable judgements; he presents himself as omniscient, as one who knows the innermost thoughts of characters, their motives and the consequences of their actions.[35] This image, however, is repeatedly shattered and the narrator emerges as fallible and unreliable.

From the questionable details inserted in the stories of Plutarch and from the contradictory versions which his narrator is made to include in the accounts, we can see the scepticism of the implied author towards the reports as they are presented. The scepticism also affects the texts the narrator mentions as the ones being used. There is, however, no room for surprise, for this uncertainty reflects Platonic doubts on the possibility of attaining true knowledge through writing. Particularly in the *Phaedrus*,[36] we find that the written text should not be taken so seriously or literally: it is there only to remind us of what we know, that is, of justice and beauty and goodness.[37] This is because words, when written, are twisted about (*Phaedr.* 275cd). While comprehending the implied author's uncertainty with regard to the text, the reader is made to think about the written biography he or she is just reading, about

---

[34] Cf. Booth (1983 [1961]: 74–5): 'The "implied author" chooses, consciously or unconsciously, what we read; we infer him as an ideal, literary, created version of the real man; he is the sum of his own choices.' Cf. 73: '"Narrator" is usually taken to mean the "I" of a work, but the "I" is seldom if ever identical with the implied image of the artist.' Cf. 151. See the ongoing debate whether the person of the 'implied author' is needed at all in Genette (1988 [1983]: 93–107), Rimmon-Kenan (1983: 86–7), Kindt and Müller (2006). The scheme was elaborated by Chatman (1978: 148–51), to include an 'implied reader'.

[35] Fludernik (2009: 92–3).

[36] See *Phaedr.* 274b–278b. Cf. *Ep.* 7.341c–342a, 344 1c–e and *Ep.* 2.314bc.

[37] Cf. Ferrari (1987: 204–24).

truth and falsehood and about the use of texts as an educational tool.

Plutarch's narrator uses references to other authors and works.[38] This feature is ostensibly in accordance with the ancient practice, especially in historiography.[39] In historical writing, sources are usually cited to strengthen the account or lend authority to the story.[40] The mention of these sources in Plutarch's biographies is not systematic, nor is it found in cases where we would expect them to be. The reason for their inclusion is certainly not evident to modern historians dealing with source criticism, who sometimes take it as a mere indication of Plutarch's scholarship and erudition.[41] Yet these indications of reading do not aim to give references or supply foot-notes to the readers, but rather to fulfil entirely different purposes. Along the lines we suggest here, these references are present because they have literary importance relevant to characterisation and the moral purpose of the work. It is suggested here that this approach should be systematic and should cover the interpretation of all content conveyed in Plutarch's works and biographies. The inclusion of asides such as unrelated historical information, philosophical and moral comments, historiographic references and critiques, scientific data, etymological explanations, anthropological or ethnographic observations, descriptions of animals, plants and scenery, instances of *ekphrasis*, personal reflections and even autobiographical notes, is conducive to characterisation.[42]

One of the facts related to the perception of Plutarch's works as fictional literature is that they contain a narrative world. This narrative world is called *diegesis* in so far as it is the actual 'spatio-temporal universe designated by the narrative'[43] (the fictional world), and *exegesis* in so far as it is the level of narration and of the 'narrator's

---

[38] On Plutarch's habit of citation in the *Lives*, cf. Bowie (2008), who claims it to be an extension of techniques developed in philosophical and miscellaneous writings.

[39] On the relatively insignificant role of references in ancient historiography see Schepens (1977: 100–18). On the ancient literary code that allowed large sections of previous authors to be absorbed without credit see Barrow (1967: 153), Jones (1971: 84). Cf. Russell (1973: 54): 'Fortunately, the literary conventions of the *Lives* admit, or indeed require, a certain amount of reference to sources and "problematic" discussion of different views.'

[40] In some cases, historians mention certain writers to remove responsibility for an outlandish account. Cf. Barrow (1967: 153): 'When he diverged from his main authorities, or added an alternate version, [Plutarch] tended to name the source. Or he might name its main authority when he wished to assert its superior credibility as against other versions, named or implied ...' Cf. Russell (1973: 55).

[41] Stronk (2010: 96). Scholarship: cf. Stadter (1965: 128–32; 1989: lxxxv).

[42] Almagor (2013a: 153–4, 165); cf. Pechter (1975: 81–2). For a different view, see Russell (1966: 153) or Wardman (1974: 174); cf. Verdegem (2010: 81).

[43] Genette (1980 [1972]) 2 n. 2, 94 n. 12; Genette (1988 [1983]) 17–18.

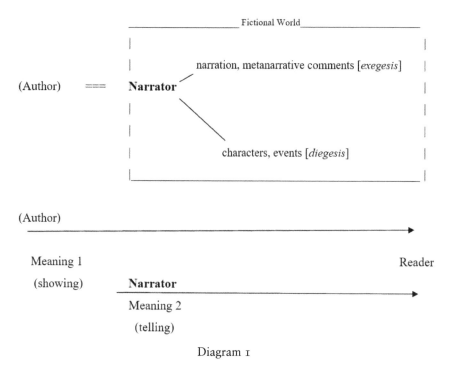

Diagram 1

comments, explanations, reflections and metanarrative remarks that accompany a story'[44] (the fictional story). This narrative world includes the narrator as much as it comprises the characters and the narrative.[45] In the case of Plutarch's biographies or ceratin other works, the narrator is not part of the *diegesis* or the story, but he is just as fictional as the *exegesis*.[46] As such, the narrator can sometimes be presented as resembling or mimicking other characters within the fictional world.[47] Plutarch uses this device often, displaying the narrator or the authors he mentions as imitating the fictional figures, thereby highlighting some character traits or features of the narrative.

For the sake of convenience, we shall not employ the technical terms of 'narrator' and '(implied) author', but rather use Plutarch's

---

[44] Schmid (2010) 6; cf. 68. Cf. Coste and Pier (2009) 300. See Fludernik (1996) 250–60.

[45] Schmid (2010) 32–3, 35.

[46] As de Jong (2004: 45) mentions with respect to the Homeric poems, the narrator is 'a *creation* of the poet like the characters'. Rabel (1997: 19) goes on to make the poet treat the narrator as another character.

[47] The idea that a dramatised narrator can be similar to the characters in the narrative world is another insightful proposal made by Booth (1983 [1961]: 155).

name for both. The differentiation should, however, be kept in mind, so that when we say that Plutarch 'tells', 'describes', etc., it is the narrator who is made to do so by Plutarch the author. Similarly, when 'Plutarch' is singled out as mimicking the figures in the fictional world, it is the narrator occupying the narrative world who is referred to and not the author.[48]

It is the assumption of the current discussion that in order to arrive at the historical significance of Plutarch's descriptions, we have to pass through this literary terrain. The method broadly proposed in this volume consists of two stages:

(1a) **Appreciation of the literary aspect of Plutarch's works.** This applies mainly to the *Lives*, but is also relevant to other works of Plutarch. What is meant is that the literary aspects of the works (including the presence of a narrator, what he elects to tell us and the existence of the fictional world) have to be recognised before any evaluation of their historical merit or before any discussion of source criticism. This involves understanding the plot or the narrative, comprehending the context of the reference to an author within the story, and grasping the way the reference stands in relation to the content of the scene and parallels the relations of the figures themselves.

(1b) A further element in this approach would be the examination of the **attitude of Plutarch's narrator towards the authors or historians he mentions and refers to;** this might tell us something about the way these authors were known and received by Plutarch and his audience. If the attitude is not consistent with other passages in the same work, we should associate it rather with the limited literary purposes of the passage in question and attempt to understand its relation to the overall message in the work.

In other words, the method of analysis adopted here is that when a name of an author is mentioned by Plutarch in a narrative (mostly in the *Lives*), this author is treated as a person within the narrative world, and Plutarch's attitude towards him is also considered part of the narrative world, echoing or mimicking the action described.

Stage (2) is designed to set a check on the conclusions arrived at in stage (1). Since Plutarch did not invent every detail in his narratives,

---

[48] Another mark would be the use of the present tense mostly for Plutarch's narrator and the past tense mostly for the author.

how are we to disentangle the content of the original sources on which he relied and which served as a basis for his artistic elaboration?

(2a) When the external sources referred to are available and present themselves, **a detailed comparison between these texts and Plutarch's version** will show the extent of Plutarch's literary manipulation of the original that was imposed on the material.

(2b) When such external sources are lacking, as in our case, a check on the text will be made through **a study of parallel sections in extant texts that refer to the same sources** or the same events/ figures, with the aim of proposing a method by which Plutarch used these lost works.

(2c) Alternatively, when no extant texts can offer us a definite solution as to the identity of Plutarch's sources, the only way to arrive at an answer would be **a study of internal coherence in the narrative Plutarch presents.** When a passage does not cohere with other items or the rest of the *Life*, this may be indicative of a different literary source being used, especially when it has its own logic and thematic unity. When it lacks even that internal coherence of itself, the passage may betray an adaptation by Plutarch of that other source, the assumption being that Plutarch's work is a new creation, containing at least several distinct components in its making – the sources on the one hand, and Plutarch's own vision, vocabulary and arrangement of the text on the other.

Again, a *caveat* should be noted that absolute certainty in this matter cannot be expected. It is my wish that at least the method, used here for the test case of the *Persica* works, will appear sound and valid, and will prove to be valuable for a further study of Plutarch.

PERSICA

Labelling certain volumes composed by Greek authors of the fifth to the fourth centuries BCE with Persia as their subject matter under the name 'Persian Matters' (*Persica*) is derived from the recognition that these works were similar not only in terms of content, but also with respect to form, structure and mode of presentation. Modern studies view these works as close to forming a literary genre of their own,[49] perhaps even displaying unique linguistic features (cf. *Suda*,

---

[49] Stevenson (1997: 1–22, 45–8, 80–1, 157–61).

s.v. 'Διονύσιος', δ 1180 Adler: Περσικὰ Ἰάδι διαλέκτῳ, 'Persica in the Ionic dialect'). When these works included narratives, they contained a so-called *Petite histoire*,[50] stories of the king's court, his family and his staff, including the characteristically eastern eunuchs and concubines, debauchery of the Achaemenid court, royal luxury, royal sexual decadence, royal brutality, court machinations among members of the royal family and courtiers. Furthermore, they were occupied with strange items – like unusual animals and plants and peculiar practices (similar to the *thomata* [= 'wondrous things'] or paradoxographic literature), including luxury court items (e.g. the royal golden egg-shaped cup or the royal golden footstool). All these elements are discernible in Herodotus, whose court stories are balanced by the inclusion of political narratives.

The *Persica* works are in fact not easy to define as a genre. Lloyd Llewellyn-Jones and James Robson (2010: 4, 6–7, 66–79, 86) variously define the *Persica* style as something more than straightforward 'history' writing, a melding of 'the legendary aspects of Eastern history' with personal observations of recent events, a 'court history', a 'novella' combined with history, a 'creative dramatic history' and a 'melange of history, gossip, fantasy, and (tragic) poetry'.[51] In structure they were probably a string of short episodes (Ctesias, *FGrH* 688 T 13: διηγημάτων), aptly called by Llewellyn-Jones and Robson (2010) 'tales'. Dominique Lenfant (2014) sees the *Persica* works as displaying 'a kind of political ethnography', where the political entity (the Persian Empire) counts more than the ethno-cultural reality, and where an *explanation* is provided about the court practices, as opposed to the popular caricaturistic and hostile portrayal of the Great King's *tryphe* (cf. Lenfant, 2009: 322–3).

At least eight important authors are listed in Felix Jacoby's *Die Fragmente der griechischen Historiker* (1923–58, commonly abbreviated *FGrH*) as belonging to the *Persica* group of works: Athenaeus (*FGrH* 681), Zenon (?) (*FGrH* 684), Dionysius of Miletus (*FGrH* 687), Ctesias of Cnidus (*FGrH* 688), Heracleides of Cyme (*FGrH* 689), Deinon of Colophon (*FGrH* 690), Diogenes (*FGrH* 692), Diocles (*FGrH* 693). Two other authors closely affiliated with this genre and interests are Charon of Lampsacus (*FGrH* 262 F 3ab = 687b F 1ab) and Hellanicus of Lesbos (*FGrH* 4 T 12, 24, F 59–63, 132, 167, 178–184 = 687a T1–3, F 1–11). According to Jacoby

---

[50] Drews (1973: 106, 116, 200 n. 93). Cf. Stevenson (1997: 45–6), Lenfant (2009: 74), Stronk (2010: 69).
[51] Cf. Waters (2017: 14).

(1921: 622–4), the *Persica* works are said to have disappeared in the wake of Alexander's campaign.

Not everyone agrees with Jacoby that ethnography was the second historiographic genre, and that in this genre, the first full-scale work was the *Persica* of early fifth century BCE author Dionysius of Miletus (*FGrH* 687 F1).[52] Yet Karl F. Lehmann-Haupt (1902) believes that Dionysius was the principal source for both Herodotus' and Xenophon's depictions of Persian history (especially for Xerxes' reign).[53] Plutarch does not mention Dionysius and apparently made no use of his works. Hellanicus was among Herodotus' (younger?) contemporaries (*Suda*, s.v. ε 739 Adler),[54] and is occasionally mentioned together with him (Strabo 1.2.35, 11.6.2–3; Dion. Hal. *Ad Pomp.* 3.7),[55] although his style was deemed more antiquated compared to the Halicarnassian.[56] All his works are lost. A work called *Persica*, consisting of at least two books,[57] is attributed to him, but may have been a part of another work. It probably included the mythic origins of the Persians,[58] ethnography, and an early history of the Assyrians and Medes,[59] besides a (concise?) narrative of the Persian Wars.[60] Hellanicus apparently supplied a different version from some of Herodotus' stories, whether his descriptions antedated the Halicarnassian or not.[61] Plutarch refers to Hellanicus several times,[62] but only once and very briefly (*De Herod. malig.* 36.869a) in a Persian context (the Naxian contribution to the Battle of Salamis), and would therefore hardly fit the genre of works we are dealing with here.

---

[52] Cf. Marincola (1999: 297). See Jacoby (1909: 90–2).

[53] See Lenfant (2007: 201). Cf. Moggi (1972). For his date, see Drews (1973: 20–22), Lenfant (2009: 10–13).

[54] Although see Dion. Hal. *Thuc.* 5.2, *Ad Pomp.* 3.6 (contradicted in *Thuc.* 9.3), Aul. Gell. *NA* 15.23.2. See Jacoby (1913a: 107–10), Pearson (1939: 208), Drews (1973: 22, 99), Toye (1995), Lenfant (2009: 22–4), Fowler (2013: 682–3).

[55] See *FGrH* 687a T 2 = 4 F 184 ~ Hdt. 3.16. On Hellanicus see Pearson (1939: 203–9), Schreiner (1984), Lenfant (2007: 202), Pownell's entries 4 and 687a for the *BNJ*.

[56] Dion. Hal. *Thuc.* 5.2, Diod. 1.37.3, Cic. *De Or.* 2.12.53.

[57] Steph. Byz. s.v. Ἀρταία, Τυρόδιζα and Χαλδαῖοι and Harpocration, s.v. Στρέψα.

[58] Cf. *FGrH* 687a F 1ab = 4 FF 59–60 ~ Hdt. 7.61. Strabo 11.6.2–3 seems to be more on Ctesias than on Hellanicus.

[59] Cf. *FGrH* 687a F 2a = 4 F 63a on Sardanapallus, 687a F 5a = 4 F 132 and 687a F 5b = 4 F 179, fuller versions than Hdt. 7.62 on the Arians and Medea, 687a F 7 = 4 F 178, 687a F 8 = 4 F 180,

[60] 687a F 11 = 4 F 183, possibly Harpocration, s.v. Στρέψα.

[61] In Hellanicus' *Aegyptiaca*: *FGrH* 608a F 2 = 4 F 55 ~ Hdt. 2.161–2, 687a F 10 = 4 F 182 vs. Hdt.7.2.2 (Darius' eleven vs. seven sons, but this may be a misreading, counting the four sons Darius had with Atossa twice, so probably no divergence there), 687a F 11 = 4 F 183 vs. Hdt. 8.46. See Drews (1973: 23–4).

[62] *Thes.* 17.3, 25.5–7, 26.1–2, 27.1–2, 31.1–5, *Alc.* 21.1, *De Is. et Os.* 34.364d, *Dec. or. vit.* 834bc.

Charon is considered by some to have been Herodotus' predecessor,[63] but he is more likely his younger contemporary.[64] To Charon is attributed a work called *Persica* in two books (*Suda*, s.v. χ 136 Adler: Περσικὰ ἐν βιβλίοις β', Athen. 9.394e); yet, as in the case of Hellanicus, this may have been part of another work, or even a later excerpt of his work on Lampsacus (Περὶ Λαμψάκου).[65] It presumably treated the political event of the Persian Wars.[66] One late source informs us that Charon also wrote court tales of Median and Persian history (Tert. *De anim.* 46: the dream of Astyages), similar to Herodotus (1.107–8), and if this is true, it would appear that Charon described not only events related to Greek history. Plutarch's use of Charon is sparse. On two occasions (*De Herod. malig.* 20.859ab, 24.861ad), his main concern is the Persian Wars, and so not suitable to the genre we are exploring, and on a third occasion he appears to indicate that Charon wrote on an event which took place in the Persian court, namely, Themistocles' interview with the Great King (*Them.* 27.1). Since we deal lengthily with this passage twice in this book, in the context of Deinon and Heracleides, we shall not repeat it again. Nevertheless, since a few words are in order, we will address this passage very briefly as an excursus within Chapter 6.

Unfortunately, all the works known as *Persica* are lost, so that the impression we have of their subject matter and arrangement, based merely on the interests, work methods and style of the late authors who employed them, may well be misleading. We may never know the degree of political narrative contained in the original works, as opposed to ethnographic descriptions. Moreover, most of these authors are obscure to the point of uncertainty: Zenon may in fact be a corrupted form of Deinon, Athenaeus may be that of Naucratis (cf. *FGrH* 166 F 1), inserted as a hypercorrection by a later reader from the margins of the text, Diogenes may be Laertius (cf. Diog. Laert. 1.6), following the same logic. Lastly, Xanthus of Lydia (*FGrH* 765) does not belong to this group, because of his Lydian focus, and since a work of this kind was never attributed to him in antiquity. The attribution to Xanthus of certain stories told

[63] See Dion. Hal. *Ad Pomp.* 3.7, *Thuc.* 5.2, and consequently Pearson (1939: 140), Drews (1973: 25–6), Moggi (1977), Fowler (1996: 67; 2006: 40), Parker (2005). See Lenfant (2009: 14–16).

[64] See Jacoby (1938; 1940: 6 n. 11), Momigliano (1958: 5), Chaniotis (2005), Rengakos (2011: 336), and see Ceccarelli's entry 262 for the *BNJ*.

[65] See Schwartz (1899a: 2179). See Pearson (1939: 140–1).

[66] Athen. 9.394e on Mardonius' expedition, 392 BCE ~ Hdt. 6.43–5; Plut. *De Herod. malig.* 20.859ab on Cyrus and the Ionians vs. Hdt. 1.156–61; Plut. *De Herod. malig.* 24.861ad vs. Hdt. 5.99–102. Drews (1973: 30–2).

by Nicolaus of Damascus concerning Cyrus the Great is without real evidence.[67]

Of all the *Persica* authors, the most cited and influential was Ctesias, and to a lesser degree Deinon and Heracleides. This volume will address all three in relation to Plutarch's use of them as extensively as possible, given the limitations of our knowledge. Plutarch is one of the most important authors who preserves fragments from Ctesias and Heracleides, and his text is thus indispensable for the study of the Achaemenid era. The present book claims that one cannot remove references to the *Persica* works from their original venue (as in Plutarch's works). It is therefore important to understand Plutarch's aims and presentation before we can appreciate the sections he conserves.

PLUTARCH AND PERSIA

As a child of the Imperial period, Plutarch is greatly interested in Persia.[68] Eleven of his extant Greek *Lives* (*Themistocles, Alcibiades, Aristides, Lysander, Cimon, Agesilaus, Alexander, Pelopidas, Demosthenes, Pericles and Nicias*) have heroes contemporary with the Achaemenid Empire, or even clashing with it. The lost *Epaminondas* would make it more than half of the Greek biographies of the *Parallel Lives*. The extant *Artaxerxes* (below) is a unique case. The great divide between East and West was now, in the Roman era, once again ostensibly definitely marked. The great literary output of this period in comparison with earlier times, and the high survival rate of literature from this period, would lead to the conclusion that the image we have today of the Greek impression of Persia is largely influenced by the texts from this period.

The eastern power that existed and was contemporaneous with the Greek writers during most of this period was that of the Arsacid Parthians, while the Achaemenid Persians belonged to the distant past.[69] The Greek association of the Achaemenids and the Parthians[70]

---

[67] For instance, it is related (*FGrH* 90 F 68.11–12) that when Croesus was saved from burning on the pyre, the people remembered 'the Sibyl's oracles and Zoroaster's *logia* (Ζωροάστρου λόγια)'. There is no observable ground to attribute this aetiological story, meant to explain why the Persians do not burn bodies, with Xanthus; see, however, Boyce (1982: 183). See Drews (1973: 100–3).

[68] Cf. Bowie (1970: 7, 14, 27), Anderson (1993: 56, 179), Swain (1996: 95–6), Whitmarsh (2011: 50, 51–8). See Almagor (2017a: 340; 2017c: 124–33).

[69] On the Arsacids see Debevoise (1938), Colledge (1967), Bivar (1983), Wolski (1993).

[70] For instance, the title 'King of Kings' (βασιλεὺς βασιλέων), used of the Great King and of the Parthian king: compare Darius' letter to Gadates (*ML* 12 with Briant, 2002a: 491), echoing Achaemenid practice (cf. DNa 1.1–3) and Plut. *Pomp.* 38.2. See the comparison between the nomadic practices of the Achaemenid and Parthian kings: Strabo 15.1.16, Athen. 12.513f.

was contemporary with the Roman presentation of the clash of East and West as a revival of the Persian Wars, in particular the expedition of Alexander the Great.[71] This notion was conveyed, for instance, by the designation 'Persae' to the eastern kingdom, even though Persis (Pārsa/Fārs) was not the base of the Parthian Empire.[72] The interest of second century CE Greek authors in Parthia was therefore enhanced in the wake of Roman fascination with Parthia, reaching its climax in the campaigns of the Emperor Trajan (114–117 CE) against Osroes I,[73] and of the co-Emperor Verus (161–165 CE), a generation later, against King Vologesus (Vologaeses) IV.[74] Among the works inspired by these political developments were Arrian's *Parthica* (*FGrH* 156 F 30–53), treatises by anonymous writers (*FGrH* 203–206),[75] by Antiochianus (*FGrH* 207), Crepereius Calpurnianus (*FGrH* 208),[76] Demetrius of Sagalassus (*FGrH* 209) and Callimorphus (*FGrH* 210).[77] One outcome of this trend was to confuse references to the past with the present Roman–Parthian clash.[78] Some of the historians Lucian alludes to term the Parthians 'Persians'.[79]

Moreover, the attitude prevalent among Greek writers and men of letters towards the previous period was nostalgic. Events and occasions known from the period of the Persian Wars were very popular in the oratorical schools as well as in public presentations, performed before large groups of spectators, where Greek character

---

Clothes: ἀναξυρίδες or ἀναξυρίς, Hdt. 5.49 and Luc. *Quom. hist. consc.* 19. Cf. an inscription from the Parthenon at Athens in honour of the Emperor Nero (dated to 61/2 CE), *IG* 2² 3277 = Sherk (1988), no. 78. Cf. Spawforth (1994: 237).

[71] See Seager (1980), Rosivach (1984: 2–3), Spawforth (1994, especially 237–43) and Hardie (1997) on Augustan appropriation of fifth-century images of the Persian Wars. Cf. Isaac (2004: 375–80); Jung (2006).

[72] For this identification see Cic. *Pro domo sua* 60; Verg. *Georg.* 4.290; Propert. 2.13.1–2, 3.3.11.21; Horace, *Od.* 1.2.22, 51; 1.21.14; 2.2.17; 3.3.44; 3.5.4; 4.14.42; Ov. *Ars Am.* 1.225; Sen. *Apoc.* 12.

[73] On this war cf. Statius *Silvae* 5.1; Dio Cass. 68.17.1–3, 19–23, 26–30; Arrian, *Parthica* F 37–48. See Longden (1931), Debevoise (1938: 213–39), Lepper (1948).

[74] On this war cf. Dio Cass. 71.2. See Luc. *Quom. hist. consc.* 20–1, 30; *SHA Av. Cass.* 6.5; *Marc.* 9.1; *Ver.* 7.1–2. See Mitford (1980: 1203), Birley (2000: 160–5).

[75] See Strobel (1994) and Georgiadou and Larmour (1994: 1448–78).

[76] See Baldwin (1978) and von Möllendorf (2001).

[77] Anderson (1994: 1433–4) claims these works and historians were not real. Cf. Homeyer (1965: 20–3); MacLeod (1991: 284–6). See also Anderson (1976: 79–80); Hall (1981: 314–21) and Jones (1986: 161–5), MacLeod (1994: 1362–79).

[78] See Almagor (2011: 4–5). This is evidenced, for instance, by the fascination with Alexander's campaign or references to Xenophon's march. For example, Lucian, dealing with historians of the Parthian Wars, also cites *Anabasis* 1.1.1 (*Quom. hist. consc.* 23).

[79] They also use Herodotean allusions; e.g. Luc. *Quom. hist. consc.* 18 (ἔδεε γὰρ Πέρσῃσι γενέσθαι κακῶς, 'for the Persians had to fare badly'). Cf. Hdt. 1.8.2: χρῆν γὰρ Κανδαύλῃ γενέσθαι κακῶς, 'it was destined that evil should happen to Candaules'. Cf. 2.161 [Psammis]; 4.79 [Scyles]; 9.109 [Artaunte].

was explored.[80] Greek men of letters were also fascinated with the Imperial idea and endeavoured to examine it through the reading of earlier texts dealing with imperial models and paradigms. The Greek twist for this examination of court reality was the description of the Roman Imperial institutions in terms used by classical authors to describe the Persian organisation, such as 'satraps' or 'Great King'. Many joined this trend, as can be seen by the choice of terminology and use of the literary devices of analogy and juxtaposition. Some, like Plutarch, employed the word 'up' (ἄνω) to refer to going to Rome (*Praec. ger. reip.* 814C), just as the writers of old would denote the travel to Persia (Cf. Arr. *Diss. Epict.* 1.10.2).

An offshoot of this interest in empires was the revival of the idea of a sequence of world dominations, the so-called *translatio imperii* (from the Assyrian Empire onwards, this series included four or five items).[81] In this scheme, Rome was to become the heir of Persia, a portrayal which ultimately made all references to the Achaemenid Persians operate in a subtle way as implicit allusions to Rome. This interpretation was unique to Greek readers. Awareness of the potentially delicate subtexts of the Persian kingdom in the contemporary Roman Empire and of the fact that these examples might have volatile political potential in stirring up the Greek masses may be detected in Plutarch's writings.[82] It can be seen in his advice to a local politician to refrain from mentioning the past glories of the Persian Wars (*Praec. ger. reip.* 814B–C): Plutarch would rather have the orators deal with this explosive material, presumably since their performances are construed as detached from any political import.[83]

In Plutarch's period, therefore, the representation of Persia was coloured by the realities of Roman rule, the demise of the Republic, the political weakness of contemporary Greece, and the conflict between the Roman and Parthian empires.

Plutarch's historical attention is focused on the petty stories of Persia, as he seems to find moral significance in tales of Achaemenid oriental court decadence. He is not interested in the political and

---

[80] See Kohl (1915): topics related to the expeditions of Darius and Xerxes (nos. 28–47), or related to Miltiades, Aristides, Themistocles (nos. 48–71). Cf. Anderson (1989: 146–52); Swain (1996: 87–9).
[81] A scheme of four empires appears in the OT book of Daniel (2:1–40; cf. 7:2–3), variously interpreted, and one of five successive kingdoms is found in authors from the Roman period (e.g. Polyb. 38.22.1–3; Dion. Hal. *AR* 1.2.1–4; Vell. Pat. 1.6.6 [Aemilius Sura]; Tac. *Hist.* 5.8; Appian, *Praef.* 9). See Swain (1940) and Mendels (1981); cf. Alonso Núñez (1983), Clarke (1999: 15–16, 226–8).
[82] Cf. Pelling (2011: 11).
[83] Cf. Jones (1971: 113–14); Spawforth (1994: 245–6); Whitmarsh (2005: 66–7).

administrative units of the Persian Empire, the various social groups and the interaction between the kings and the local aristocracy; similarly, he barely refers to the army or manpower issues of the Empire.[84] He includes anecdotes related to the Achaemenid kings of the fifth century BCE, but is more concerned with the general and moral theme of the decline and fall of the Persian Empire in the following century. In Greek conception, the fourth century BCE reigns of the last Persian kings were seen as a period of decay and decadence in comparison with those of former sovereigns, especially Cyrus the Great and Darius I.[85] This picture was not accurate, yet it had a lasting impact in antiquity. For these details, Plutarch consulted mostly Herodotus, Xenophon and some later works, as well as the *Persica* authors. Plutarch combines this stereotype with the image of the Persians as the eternal enemy engaged in a continuous clash with the Greeks. In this image, the Greeks are set as a sort of a boundary to Persian ambition and brutality, and the existence of Greek civilisation beyond the Persian Empire curbs barbarian passion. This can be seen as a reversed variation on the *metus hostilis* idea known in Rome.[86]

At the basis of Plutarch's treatment rest Greek stereotypes of the Persians, going back to classical literature, and reflecting two commonplaces of the barbarians as overly (decadently) civilised, or exceedingly wild and uncivilised. As a special case in classical literature, both 'types' of barbarity – that is, both boldness (θυμός), usually associated with the northern/western nations, and softness (μαλακία), the mark of the eastern/southern nations – are applied to them.[87] They are presented as submissive slaves, but also uninhibited, especially the Great King. All the ethnographic depictions of the Persians found within Plutarch's writings fit into these two moulds.

Instances of inhibitions, timidity and effeminate demeanour to the point of slavery appear in the following references: Persians fulfil orders only if they are from the king (*De sup.* 168e); Plutarch claims that the king's table provides food for everyone, including dogs, implying the Persians are tamed like canines (*QC* 7.4.703de). The Persian kings themselves are no kings in the eyes of Plutarch:

---

[84] Almagor (2011: 19). For Plutarch's similar simplified historical understanding of Roman politics of the people against the few, see Pelling (2002c: 211–17, 220; 2011: 58–64); cf. de Blois (1992).

[85] Plato, *Leg.* 3.693c–698a, Xen. *Cyr.* 8.8.15–16 and Isocrates' *Panegyricus* (150–2). Cf. Briant (2002b: 193–6).

[86] Cf. Sall. *Bell. Jug.* 41.2–3, *Hist.* I.11–12 concerning Carthage. Cf. Livy 2.39.7 and Lintott (1972: 632–3); cf. Plut. *Cat. Mai.* 27.4 (Scipio Nasica).

[87] Cf. Arist. *Polit.* 1327b18–33l; cf. Hippoc. *Aer.* 22; Almagor (2017c: 133–6).

he mocks Darius I's rise to power (*De Alex. fort.* 340b ~ Hdt. 3.84), portrays them as pawns at the hands of eunuchs (*De Alex. fort.* 326f, 337e, 340b; cf. Diod. 17.5.3-6, Ael. *VH* 6.8, 12.43, Strab. 15.3.24, Arr. *Anab.* 2.14.5), depicts them as having no power over their wives (*Max. cum princ.* 780c), highlights the fact that the kings do not fight – like Xerxes at Salamis (*Them.* 13.1) – and indulge in luxury (*Them.* 16.2, cf. *Ages.* 14). Royal Persian depravity is symbolised by the gesture of prostration, or *proskynesis* (*Them.* 27.2–5; *Alex.* 54.2–4, 74.1–2; *Art.* 22.4–6, *Pelop.* 30.1–3), that is, the act of bowing in reverence.[88] For the Greeks, it was a sign of servitude.[89]

Contrary to the general servility of Persian subjects, the Persian kingship is depicted as absolute and limitless. Persian lack of restraint is seen in stereotypical royal cruel behaviour, which Plutarch is fond of repeating: Xerxes notoriously kills Pythius and divides up his corpse (*Mul. virt.* 263a-b ~ Hdt. 7.38–9); Amestris the queen mother buries alive twelve persons (*De sup.* 171d, a conflation of Hdt. 7.114 and 3.35); the king is made to praise Ahreman, the dark or evil spirit (*De Is. et Os.* 369e), for having Themistocles in his possession (*Them.* 28.6). Another instance of unrestrained behaviour is the disregard of divine omens, designed to limit action (dream of Darius: *Alex.* 18.4–5, which the Magi misinterpret ~ cf. Hdt. 7.134–5, 9.64); the Persians cannot control their jealousy for their wives (*Them.* 26.3–4) or concubines (*Art.* 27.1).

Plutarch toys with both stereotypes in two other cases. One is his adaptation of Herodotus' famous description that among the Persians the worst thing is lying (1.138), that is, an example of a behaviour which has no restraint, and being in debt is the second worst. Plutarch reverses the order of the two vices and makes being in debt the worst thing among the Persians, before lying (*De vit. aer.* 829c), in a manner which would make the Persians believe that limitations on behaviour are worse than no constraints.[90] The second case is the Persian banquet. On the one hand, Plutarch is pleased

---

[88] See Aesch. *Pers.* 499. On the eastern gesture see Gruber (1980: 1.169–71). On the Achaemenid court protocol of honour paid to the Great King see Hdt. 3.86, 7.14.1, 7.136.1, 8.118.4, Xen. *Cyr.* 4.4.13, 5.3.18, 8.3.14, Dem. 21.106, Nep. *Con.* 3.3 [*venerari*]; Plut. *Them.* 27.4–5, *Art.* 22.8; Ael. *VH* 1.21. See Horst (1932: 22), Sachsen-Meiningen (1969), Frye (1972: 102–3), Gabelmann (1984), Briant (2002a: 223).

[89] Aristoph. *Vesp.* 515–17. Cf. Xen. *Ages.* 1.22, 1.34. Cf. Esther 3:2. It was also an impious gesture, with the connotation of paying reverence to man that should be given to god. See Hdt. 7.136.1, Isoc. *Paneg.* 151, Xen. *Anab.* 3.2.13, Jos. *AJ* 11.6.8.230. But see Brown (1949: 241: '[i]t implied servility rather than impiety') and Bowden (2013: 60).

[90] By altering Herodotus' picture, Plutarch would ironically not appear as completely worse from the Persian perspective, since he is not in debt to Herodotus' description (although he is not being truthful to Herodotus' text).

that it is restricted in many aspects: there are customary questions for debate (as in the Greek manner, QC 1.2.629d–630e, Xen. *Cyr.* 5.2.18), the consumption of the king is limited and the ideal is to hold the wine.[91] On the other hand, there is a certain excessive license which Plutarch notes and sometimes praises. For instance, the practice of deliberating on important questions while intoxicated (QC 7.9.714a, d ~ Hdt. 1.133; Strabo, 15.3.20) is commended; while the wives are excluded from the banquet, the concubines are brought in (1.1.613a). Limitations are forced on particular participants, but not on all invitees.[92] The two stereotypes thus co-exist in the Persian banquet, a symbol of the two features of Persian society.

Plutarch was fascinated with Zoroastrian religious tenets.[93] It is not surprising to find that he was interested in religious matters, bearing in mind that he was a priest of Apollo in Delphi.[94] But leading the way was his philosophical inclination, his metaphysical dualism, that is, the belief that reality essentially consists of two entities, two *kinds* of things, independent of each other and irreducible one to another.[95] His admiration of the teaching of Zoroaster on the two principals at work in the world can be seen in several works (*De Is. et Os.* 369e, cf. *De anim. proc.* 1026b). The Plutarchan dualistic system was perhaps even inspired by the interpretation of Zoroastrian religion.[96] In the Zoroastrian sacred writing the *Avesta*, the world is divided between *drug* (the Lie, or disorder) and its opposite principle, *aša* (Old Persian *Arta*, Indo-Iranian *ṛtá-*), Truth, or cosmic, social and ritual order. The *drug* relates to the evil spirit Ahreman (Angra Mainyu) and the *aša* is supported by the good spirit Ohrmazd (Ahura Mazda), who will ultimately triumph.[97]

---

[91] As Cyrus the Younger stresses in his bid to become king: QC 1.4.620c, *Art.* 6.3. Cf. *Reg. et imp. apophth.* 173e and Appendix II.

[92] Cf. the descriptions of the wreaths on the sympotic participants (cf. Thgn. 1001, Aristoph. *Ach.*1091, 1145, *Eq.* 844, Athen. 15.669c), highlighting equality.

[93] Cf. Dillon (1977: 191) for the suggestion that Plutarch's knowledge of Persian religion came to him from his teacher Ammonius.

[94] See Ziegler (1951: 659–62). He was initiated into the mysteries of Apollo, fulfilled the function of the senior of the two priests of the Greek god at the Oracle of Delphi (Plut. *An seni* 792f, cf. QC 7.2.700e) and was an *epimelete* of the Amphictyonic Council in that city, not far from his Chaeronea. Cf. *SIG*³ 843. See Swain (1991), Lamberton (2001: 52–9), Stadter (2004). See Brenk (1987: 330–6) on Plutarch's religion and philosophy; cf. Russell (1968: 133–5). See Brenk (1977: 274) and Froidefond (1987: 233) on Plutarch as essentially a philosopher; yet he was not viewed as such at some point in antiquity; see Dillon (1977: 230).

[95] On Plutarch's dualism see Dillon (1977: 202–8), Froidefond (1987: 215–17), Bianchi (1987), Alt (1993), Chlup (2000), Bos (2001).

[96] Cf. Dillon (1977: 203, 218). Cf. Brenk (1987: 281). On Zoroastrian influence on Platonic dualism, Dodds (1945: 21, 24–5) claims: 'Not proven.'

[97] Cf. *Yasht* 19.92–6; Cf. Boyce (1975: 200–1, 283; 1982: 120–1). In the *Gathas*, the oldest stratum of the Avesta, *drug* appears more frequently than the evil spirit itself. See Boyce (1975:

Plutarch's most important passages on Persian religion are an interlude on Zoroastrian dualism and on the eschatological defeat of the evil spirit within the work *On Isis and Osiris*. This philosophical work addresses an Egyptian myth, and proposes that only the Greek (Platonic) philosophical interpretation leads the way to grasp the divine beneath the barbaric myth and ritual.[98]

Another dualism observed in Plutarch's works concerning Persian religion is the variance between doctrine and cult. Plutarch rejects the religious practices but appreciates the religious precepts. This ambivalence ironically corresponds to the said dualistic thought, the hallmark of Zoroastrian religion.[99] Among the Persian rituals Plutarch disapproves of are the killing of water-mice by the Magi (*De Inv. et Od.* 3.537a, cf. *QC* 4.2.670d; cf. Agath. 2.24), the sacrilege committed by Cambyses (*De Is. et Os.* 44.368f ~ Hdt. 3.29) and Ochus (*De Is. et Os.* 11.355c, 31.363c ~ Ael. *VH* 4.8) against the Bull Apis, or the destruction of temples (*Them.* 1.3; *Arist.* 20.4)[100] and plunder of statues (*Them.* 31.1).[101] In the *On Superstition* (166a), Plutarch also notes the gesture of prostration as a typical barbarian superstition.[102]

Plutarch's own era was attentive to real or invented Persian Magi.[103] He himself seems to be part of the Platonic tradition interested in the Zoroastrian religion as seen in the *Alcibiades I* or *Alcibiades Major* attributed to Plato.[104] 'Socrates' in that dialogue describes an

---

123). However, the belief that the two spirits are of an equal power is later than Plutarch, and is associated with the Zurvanite dualistic belief, the official one in fifth and sixth centuries CE. This belief was influenced by a scholarly exegesis of *Yasna* 30.3; Boyce (1982: 232). See Christensen (1944: 150–5), Zaehner (1955: 275–418, 419–46). Cf. Boyce (1957, 1982: 180, 231–41, 1990, 1996), Frye (1959), Rezania (2010: 12–24).

[98] *De Is. et Os.* 2.351e, 3.352c, 9.354b, 11.355d, 67.377f–378a. See Richter (2001: 198–200, 206–8), Petrucci (2016:227–9). On the work see Hopfner (1940), Griffiths (1970), Froidefond (1988).

[99] See a similar discrepancy between Persian opinions and practice in Diog. Laert. 1.6–9.

[100] Cf. Diog. Laert. 1.9, finding this plausible. Herodotus (1.131) claims that the Persians do not have temples, alongside the absence of statues and altars. Cf. Strabo 15.3.13. See Boyce (1982: 221–3) and Boyce and Grenet (1991: 235–8). See, however, Berossus *FGrH* 680 F 11, Cic. *De leg.* 2.10.26 and de Jong (1997: 92–4, 343–52). There is evidence for Persian open-air altars. See Olmstead (1948: 61) and Schmidt (1970: 11) on two isolated square stone stuctures in Pasargadai (cf. Stronach, 1978: 138–45: altars for the worship of fire).

[101] Cf. Hdt. 1.183 (golden statue from Babylon), 8.53.2 (Athens), Cic. *De Leg.* 2.10.26, Paus. 8.46.3. Diod. 1.46.4.

[102] Theophr., *Char.* 16.5 also notes the kneeling down as a mark of the superstitious ('When he passes one of the smooth stones set up at crossroads he anoints it with oil from his flask, and will not go his ways till he have knelt down and worshipped it,' Edmons trans., Loeb Classical Library series).

[103] See Dio Chrys. 36.39–54. Cf. Paus. 5.27.5.

[104] For the question of the authenticity of *Alcibiades* I see Schleiermacher (1836: 328–36), Shorey (1933: 415) and Smith (2004) on the one hand and Friedländer (1964), Benveniste (1929: 16) and Gershevitch (1964: 37) on the other. See Denyer (2001: 14–26) and Pangle

ideal Persian educational system, in which four chosen royal tutors (βασίλειοι παιδαγωγοί) convey Socratic virtues to the heir apparent (*Alc. I* 121c–122a). Among these, the wisest one teaches him the magian lore (μαγεία) of 'Zoroaster, son of Horomazes', that is, 'the worship of the gods' (θεῶν θεραπεία) and 'what pertains to a king' (τὰ βασιλικά).[105] In antiquity, the dialogue was considered authentic,[106] and Plutarch apparently employed it elsewhere.[107] Plutarch may have also regarded his turn to Zoroastrian precepts in his works as entirely within the Platonic tradition, although the exact particulars of his precursors' attraction to this faith are not entirely certain. He appears to allude to this Platonic dialogue in the description of the education of Cyrus the Younger in the *Artaxerxes* (6.4: μαγεύειν), adapted from Ctesias' story (*FGrH* 688 F 16.59),[108] leaving readers to decide whether the prince's teacher/Magos succeeded in imparting justice and truth or not.[109] To this biography we now turn.

THE *ARTAXERXES*

Until recently, Plutarch's *Artaxerxes* was seldom visible in scholarly publications concerning Plutarch.[110] The intriguing problem of its sources was dealt with sporadically,[111] as were some of its themes,[112] and only brief critical and linguistic remarks on the text were

---

(1987: 1–18), Gribble (1999: 260–1), Archie (2015: 36–44). See de Jong (1997: 448–9). Plato's authentic writings do not refer to Zoroastrian beliefs. In the *Politicus* 270a Plato rejects the existence of two opposing gods. See Leisegang (1950: 2519) for the opposite view. The Magi admittedly appear in another dialogue (*Rep.* 9.572e) but their traits are pejoratively portrayed, as hedonistic tyrant makers (τυραννοποιοί). Plato was probably inspired here by the stories of Herodotus and Ctesias. Cf. Plat. *Ep.* 7.337a.

[105] Cf. Diog. Laert. 1.6, Dio Chrys. 36.41, 49.7, Porphyr. *De Abst.* 4.16. See de Jong (1997: 213).

[106] Diog. Laert. 3.37, although his insistence on its being the earliest dialogue indicates that the ancients also observed its peculiarities. Cf. Apul. *Apol.* 25–6, Amm. Marc. 23.6.32; cf. Philo, *Spec. leg.* 3.100–1, Cic. *De div.* 1.41.91. See Annas (1985: 112–13), de Jong (1997: 252).

[107] In particular *Alc.* 1.3, *Lyc.* 16.6. See Verdegem (2010: 55–6, 64, 100–1, 106–7, 109, 117, 127, 137–8, 140, 148–9, 170, 399).

[108] Almagor (2012: 28–31).

[109] The Magian lore was compared to rhetorical manipulation by Gorgias (*Hel.* 10) as pointed out by Horky (2009: 72–3); cf. Plat. *Polit.* 291c.

[110] Some of the exceptions are Leo (1901: 157–8), Hirzel (1912: 27, 62), Weizsaecker (1931: 77, 81), Ziegler (1951: 898n.1, 912), Wardman (1971: 258–9), Pelling (1990: 226, 232), Duff (1999: 29–30, 304 n.53). The following comments on the biography appear in fuller form in Almagor (2014b: 278–9, 282–5).

[111] E.g. Haug (1854: 87–98), Schottin (1865), Smith (1881), Mantey (1888), Krumbholz (1889), König (1972: 106–9), Marasco (1994: 658–69), Stevenson (1997: 24–9).

[112] E.g. Buckler (1977) on Antalcidas' embassy to Persia (*Art.* 22), Orsi (1979–80) on the propaganda against Cyrus the younger (*Art.* 1–19) and Orsi (1988) on the representation of Persian kingship in *Art.* 3.1–2, 6.3–4.

made.[113] Several commentaries have been written on the biography, one in French by Flacelière and Chambry (1979), another in Italian by Manfredini, Orsi and Antelami (1987: 267–308), and a brief annotation by Gabriele Marasco (1994: 657–70). A recent commentary in German by Carsten Binder (2008) is historical in character and limited in the way it addresses Achaemenid context.[114] Judith Mossman (2010) is to be commended for a literary treatment – albeit brief – of the *Life*. This scholarly neglect may well result from the fact that the *Artaxerxes* is a solitary *Life*,[115] and its hero is a barbarian.[116]

Ever since the ancient period, the *Artaxerxes* has been joined with the *Aratus*, the biography of the distinguished Achaean politician (271–213 BCE).[117] These two works are outside Plutarch's *paralleloi bioi (Parallel Lives)* series or any other larger composition, and most likely were written and presented discretely.[118] The association of the two separate *Lives* may be seen in the Lamprias Catalogue, that is, the register of Plutarch's works in a library, presumably made in the early fourth century CE.[119] The catalogue attests that the pairing of the *Aratus* and the *Artaxerxes* perhaps occurred close to its composition. The catalogue has the two biographies paired at number 24, but has a solitary *Aratus* as number 40, like other four non-extant *Lives*, which are not associated with a project.[120] Thus, it may well be the case that

---

[113] See Bähr (1819). Other critical notes on the MSS are provided by van Herwerden (1880: 541–2), Richards (1903: 335–7), Hartman (1911: 323–6), Poutsma (1912), Kronenberg (1927: 76; 1933–4: 172).

[114] See the reviews of Kuhrt (2009) and Lenfant (2011).

[115] The other three extant biographies not included in this project are those of Aratus, Otho and Galba. The latter two were part of a series of biographies devoted to the Caesars (see below).

[116] Mossman (2010: 145, 147) claims that no Greek context could be used as parallel to the *Artaxerxes*. Stronk (2010: 99) proposes Nero as a Roman counterpart.

[117] On the *Aratus* see Porter (1937); Manfredini, Orsi and Antelami (1987: ix–xxvii, 193–266) and in general Almagor (2014b: 278–82).

[118] On the date of the *Artaxerxes* see below. The *Aratus* is dedicated to Polycrates, who may be the same person mentioned in *De Pyth. Or.* 409c. This work has to be dated after 95 CE and before Hadrian (Jones, 1966: 63–5, 72). This same person is also mentioned in *QC* 4.4–5.667c–671b.

[119] The catalogue was allegedly written by Plutarch's son; see *Suda* s.v. 'Lamprias', λ 96 Adler. For the Catalogue see Treu (1873), Ziegler (1908: 239–44), Ziegler (1927: 20–1), Ziegler (1951: 696–702), Barrow (1967: 193–4), Sandbach (1969: 3–29), Irigoin (1986) and Stronk (2010: 90).

[120] Ziegler (1951: 895) believes this appearance of a similar title indicates two different biographies of two different *personae*, that is, the Achaean statesman and his namesake, the Greek poet (c. 315–240 BCE), author of the *Phaenomena*. Although Plutarch indeed shows interest in Aratus' *Phaenomema* (the work is cited in two places: *Quaest. Nat.* 912d ~ *Phaen.* 946–7 and *De soll. anim.* 967f ~ *Phaen.* 956), and although the Lamprias Catalogue (no. 119) lists a commentary (now lost) on Aratus' other known poem, the *Weather Signs*, there is no evidence that Plutarch wrote a *Life* of the poet. The other two biographies Plutarch wrote of poets, i.e., Hesiod and Pindar, have Boeotian background, which is absent in Aratus of Soli's case.

the identical biography was listed twice, once as originally planned by Plutarch, and once in an arrangement which paired it with another solitary *Life*. As Plutarch's format of pairs of biographies was a famous and successful layout,[121] these two were thus joined together, although they lacked any connection between them. It would appear that the Achaean and the Achaemenid were paired merely because of the alphabetical order of the names of the two statesmen.

Basing their conclusions on subject matter, Friedrich Leo (1901: 157–8), Maurice Croiset (1899: 5.2.26) Sergei Averincev (1965: 57) and Binder (2008: 44, 57 + n. 226) maintain that the *Artaxerxes* is an early composition. Yet the biography could just as well have been written at a later stage in Plutarch's career. Judged by its technique and subtlety, it seems to be produced by a mature author.[122] Interestingly, a reference to one of the *Persica* authors, Deinon, in the *De Iside et Osiride* (*On Isis and Osiris*, 31.363c), presumably one of Plutarch's late works,[123] might be instrumental in placing the biography as falling at a later stage of Plutarch's work. Like the *Parallel Lives*, the *Artaxerxes* would belong to the period between the reigns of Nerva (96–98 CE) and Trajan (98–117 CE), as shown in the study of Christopher Jones (1966).[124] It may have been ispired by the preparations for Trajan's Parthian campaign (114–17 CE).[125] It would be difficult to assume that the work was composed and circulated immediately after the short-lived presence of Rome in Babylon, as the work insinuates the moral breakdown and the imminent political collapse of the East. Moreover, hinting at the inevitability of the failure of eastern campaigns by reference to Cyrus the Younger *after* the termination of Trajan's campaign would have been problematic, while such an allusion before the campaign would have been instructive.

Only rarely does Plutarch reveal his motives for choosing the heroes of his biographies,[126] and in this *Life* he does not supply any such explanation. Plutarch's choice of Artaxerxes II as a protagonist for a *Life* is fascinating and probably resulted from several reasons.

---

[121] Cf. Agathias in *AP* 16.331.

[122] *Pace* Stronk (2010: 101–2). It is later than some biographies. The mention of the *Skytale* at *Art.* 6.5 shows that Plutarch assumes his audience's acquaintance with it, and hence that it follows the composition and publication of *Lysander* 19.8. In the *Pericles* (24.2–11) Plutarch mentions our Aspasia, but does not refer to the Persian king by name; this fact, together with the justifications Plutarch provides for the inclusion of Aspasia there, apparently show that he has not written yet the *Artaxerxes*.

[123] See Jones (1966: 72): 'c. 115 AD'; cf. Griffiths (1970: 16–18).

[124] Cf also the notes of Ziegler (1951: 708–19, 899–903).

[125] Cf. Pelling (2011: 203) on the *Alexander–Caesar* as inspired by Trajan's triumphant return from his wars against Dacia (101–7 CE).

[126] For instance, in the case of the Hellenistic heroes. See Geiger (1981: 90).

In fact, three questions are involved: (a) Why did Plutarch elect a barbarian hero? (b) Why did he opt for a Persian king? (c) Why did he choose Artaxerxes II Mnemon?

Greek preoccupation with the traditional ethnic and cultural 'others', namely the barbarians, did not disappear in the imperial literature. On the contrary, this was still a prevalent theme and a constant concern. Hence it is not surprising to find an extensive mention of the barbarians in Plutarch's comprehensive corpus.[127] Plutarch writes from a Greek point of view,[128] and a pan-Hellenistic approach can be identified in his writings.[129] At times, he makes use of the traditional, mutually exclusive antithesis between Greeks and barbarians (e.g. *QC* 3.2.649e) and deems the Hellenic civilisation superior to any non-Greek way of life. From this Hellenocentric perspective, Rome is viewed as a foreign power,[130] even if the Romans are not explicitly described as barbarians.

This approach is set alongside another one, which sees Romans and Greeks alike as culturally affiliated advanced nations.[131] Plutarch values the affinity between the Greek and Roman cultures, and it can be said that the *Parallel Lives* project, with its choice of Roman and Hellenic heroes, essentially treated as equal, and its intended audience of both types of readers, signifies this link between the two societies.[132] He was himself a Roman citizen (*SIG*³ 829a: Mestrius Plutarchus),[133] and had friends among the Roman elite,[134] such as L. Mestrius Florus (cos. between 73 and 76),[135] who probably procured the citizenship for him, and Q. Sosius Senecio (cos. 99, 107),[136] the dedicatee of his *Parallel Lives* (*Thes.* 1.1, *Dem.* 1.1, *Dion* 1.1) and the *Table Talk* (*Quaestiones Convivales*, 1.612c etc.) – where both are regular participants.[137] Plutarch belonged to this social and cultural

---

[127] The most comprehensive discussion to date is Schmidt (1999); see also Nikolaidis (1986); Mayer (1997); Pelegrín Campo (1997); Strobach (1997: 47–54, 115–41, 142–70); Brenk (2005); Schmidt (2002), (2004).

[128] Aalders (1982: 20), Swain (1996: 86–7).

[129] See *Cim.* 19.3–4; *Tim.* 29.5; *Them.* 6.5; *Ages.* 15.4.

[130] Cf. *Flam.* 2.5, 11.7: ἀλλόφυλοι. Cf. *Pyrrh.* 16.7: βαρβάρων.

[131] See Jones (1971: 122–3).

[132] See Swain (1996: 137–45).

[133] Cf. *SIG*³ 844a (the philosopher Mestrius Autobulus, Plutarch's son); Jones (1971: 11).

[134] See Flacelière (1963: 43–4), Jones (1971: 22–3), Puech (1992), Stadter (2002). See Pelling (2011: 8–9).

[135] Jones (1971: 44), Puech (1992: 4860). Mentioned in *Otho* 14.2–3, 18.1–2.

[136] Ziegler (1951: 657–8), Jones (1971: 28–9, 54–7), Puech (1992: 4883). Cf. Dio Cass. 68.16.2.

[137] Sosius Senecio: *QC* 1.4–5.622c–623d, 2.3.635e–638a; Mestrius: *QC* 1.9.626e. 5.7.680c, 5.7.684e, 4.3.650a, 4.4.651ac, 4.5.652b, 5.7.860c, 5.10.684ef–685f, 7.1.698e, 7.4.702df, 7.6.707c–710a, 8.1.717d–2.720c, 8.10.734cd.

milieu of the Imperial elite, which included Romanised Greek pro-vincials.[138] According to the ninth-century chronographer Syncellus (659 Dindorf), Plutarch was even part of the imperial administration, as he was assigned by Hadrian to act as a procurator of Greece.[139] He certainly ostensibly praises the advantages of Roman rule (*Praec. ger. reip.* 824C, *De Pyth. or.* 408bc; *De tranq. an.* 469e; *An seni* 784f).[140] In this world view, the Barbarians are thus regarded as outsiders, beyond the limits of the empire and of civilisation.[141]

However, a third taxonomy can be seen in Plutarch's works, namely, a threefold division of humanity, in which Romans are placed between Greeks and barbarians.[142] It seems that in their cruelty and uninhibited ambition they share some of the unsavoury traits of the latter, though they are also capable of adhering to the same set of values as the Greeks. Choosing a barbarian hero would indicate the state of savagery Romans might lapse into without the restraining impact of a proper Hellenic education.[143]

Within the biographies, the barbarian adversaries shed light on the character of Plutarch's heroes. Plutarch's ethical interests require the depiction of foils, individuals or collectives, against whom the hero is examined. Incidentally, this is the role of some Persian figures: Artaxerxes I for Themistocles, Cyrus the Younger and Pharnabazus for Lysander, Tissaphernes for Alcibiades and Pharnabazus for Agesilaus. The choice of a barbarian as a hero entails a different kind of biography.[144] A precedent of a work dedicated to a barbarian hero was, of course, known to Plutarch. The immediate predecessor of Plutarch in this respect was prob-ably the Latin biographer Cornelius Nepos (c. 110–24 BCE), who composed the *Lives* of Hamilcar, Hannibal and Datames, and it

---

[138] Cf. Pelling (2011: 10–11) on *De tranq. an.* 470cd.

[139] See Flacelière (1963: 45–6), Swain (1991), Bowie (1997).

[140] One needs to be wary that some passages are ironic (e.g. *Flam.* 11.3–7, *pace* Bremer 2004: 262).

[141] Cf. *Cat. Mai.* 12.2, *Luc.* 29.6, *Aem. Paul.* 4.3, *Mar.* 14.1, *Pomp.* 70.3–4; cf. *Amat.* 768b, *Flam.* 5.6, *Pyrrh.* 16.7.

[142] See Jones (1971: 124–5), who notes a lost *Quaestiones barbaricae* (*Barbarian Questions*) in Lamprias Catalogue no. 139, alongside the Greek and Roman ones. On similar threefold divisions in post-classical authors, cf. Almagor (2005: 44–8) on Strabo. This approach stems from two sources: the Greek practice of allotting a special place to nations who received the Hellenic culture but were still considered foreign, and the Roman reluctance to be regarded as either Greeks or barbarians.

[143] See Russell (1966: 145 n.1, 1973: 132), Pelling (1989: 206–7), Swain (1996: 140–4).

[144] Although Plutarch uses comparisons to highlight the character of Artaxerxes. For instance, as compared with his mother Parysatis (*Art.* 6.8, 14.9–10) and with his son Artaxerxes III, the king seems less cruel. Yet, in contrast to the caution of the executioner (*Art.* 29.9) in killing Darius the royal heir, Artaxerxes appears merciless. See Almagor (2016a: 76; 2017c: 151).

is possible that he inspired Plutarch in making this 'barbarian' choice.[145]

The previous models of such a biography were Persian kings. Xenophon's *Cyropaedia*,[146] fictionally describing the life and career of Cyrus the Great, was one of the first instances of such a tradition. We should add here the Socratic habit of depicting the Persian king as a standard in moral thought and as the person to exhibit injunctions for the right monarchic behaviour. This tradition is known from the works of Antisthenes (several books called *Cyrus*: Diog. Laert. 6.16, 18; cf. Arr. (*Diss. Epict.*) 4.6.20; Marc. Aur. 7.36), Xenophon's *Oeconomicus* (4.16–25: Cyrus the Younger; cf. 4.4), *Anab.* 1.9 (Cyrus the Younger) and Plato's *Menexenus* 239–40, *Laws* 694–5 (Cyrus the Great).[147] A work in this tradition,[148] most pertinent to our discussion, is the *Artaxerxes* of Demetrius of Phaleron (Diog. Laert. 5.81). It is most likely that the work dealt with Artaxerxes Mnemon: given Xenophon's interest in Cyrus the Younger, Demetrius probably wrote on the real monarch, the victor of the war between the two brothers. It is unclear whether Demetrius' *Artaxerxes* was a historical work or whether it was a collection of sayings and deeds (of the character of his *Sayings of the Seven Sages* or *Aesop's Fables*.[149]

Indeed, the genre of biography may be closely related to the Imperial idea centred on the authority of one great person. It is only natural that it would develop in Persia, the first all-encompassing Empire.[150] This period saw the culmination of the genre of biographical inscriptions (e.g. Darius' Behistun inscription,[151] whose copies disseminated throughout the Empire).[152] If this is true, it is not surprising that the earliest nearly comprehensive work to endure from antiquity in the genre of biography is the *Cyropaedia* of Xenophon, relating the account of the upbringing and career of Cyrus the Great. It has all we seek in a biography – context, schooling, rise, *acme* and

---

[145] Nepos' influence on Plutarch is stressed by Geiger (1981: 95–6, 1985: 117–120, 1988).

[146] See Gera (1993: esp. 8–11 on the choice of the Persian hero), Due (1989), Tatum (1989), Nadon (2001).

[147] Cf. *Soph.* 230d on the Great King where he is a bad paradigm. On Cyrus as one of the Cynic heroes see Höistad (1948).

[148] Hirzel (1895: 1.337 n.1).

[149] See Diog. Laert. 5.80–81 with Perry (1962).

[150] See Momigliano (1971: 36–7).

[151] This inscription was written in the genre of the Near Eastern royal inscriptions and conveyed to the Greek-speaking world. Among the Greeks, it made fashionable the first-person authorial voice and perhaps contributed to the stress on the person, inducing a return to archaic paradigms of the mythic heroes, although altered.

[152] See DB 4.91–2 on spreading the message 'to every province'. See Cowley (1923: 249–50), Seidl (1976: 125–7, pls. 34–7; 1999) and von Voigtlander (1978: 63–6). Herodotus' account (3.61–79) may have been influenced by a Greek version; see Lewis (1997).

decline; however, the work is completely imaginary, and has no claim to being a true account.[153] It would thus appear almost inevitable that Persian items would find their way into the *Lives*. This 'imperial' background would provide a suitable explanation for the revival of the genre during the Roman Empire.

The *Artaxerxes* is fundamental in presenting the latter-day Hellenic viewpoint concerning the barbarians of old, and in particular Plutarch's understanding of a different, distant culture. Worthy of special notice here are the repeated portrayals of excessive violence (e.g. *Art.* 2.2, 25.3, 29.11), beastly cruelty (e.g. *Art.* 14.9, 16.3–7, 17.7, 19.9, 30.3), unbridled sexual behaviour (e.g. *Art.* 23.5, 27.2), the effeminate conduct and frailty of powerful men (e.g. *Art.* 14.9–10, 17.4, 18.5), and, conversely, the dominant influence of women (e.g. *Art.* 4.1, 6.7–9, 17.3, 18.6, 19.1). The *Life* is also essential in preserving many facts not attested elsewhere, such as rituals and court protocol (e.g. *Art.* 3.1–2, 5.5, 10.3, 26.5, 29.9–10), common customs (e.g. *Art.* 4.5, 17.4–5, 27.4) and distinct political events (e.g. *Art.* 5.2, 8.2, 24.2–9).

Plutarch almost certainly did not compile a series of biographies of the Persian kings – similar to that of Roman emperors[154] – of which the *Artaxerxes* could be supposed to be a part. There is no evidence for such a series in the Lamprias Catalogue, nor does our biography suggest that the idea was ever contemplated. But if the biography was meant to be solitary, why did Plutarch choose Artaxerxes II and not, for instance, Cyrus, Darius or Xerxes? These latter kings would seem to be more obvious candidates because of their renown to any Greek reader of Herodotus. The decisive reasons for Plutarch's choice seem to fall into several categories: (a) his sources, (b) his historical perspective and (c) the complex and intriguing character of the prospective protagonist.

(a) Artaxerxes II was known to educated readers in Plutarch's time as the king against whom his brother, Cyrus the Younger, launched his failed campaign – the familiar subject matter recounted in the first book of Xenophon's *Anabasis*[155] – as well as the Achaemenid ruler who succeeded in imposing his will on Greece. Nepos' influence again

---

[153] See Cic. *Ad Quint.* 1.1.23. Momigliano (1971: 55–6).

[154] On this series, see Jones (1971: 72–80), Georgiadou (1988), Ash (1997). The assumption of its composition is mainly based on the existence of the lost biographies of Augustus, Tiberius, Claudius, Nero, Gaius and Vitellius (numbers 26–31, 33 in the Lamprias Catalogue). The date of writing the series has been suggested as the reign of Vespasian (Stadter 2015a), Domitian (Jones 1971: 72–3) or Nerva (Geiger 1975). See Pelling (2002c: 253; 2011: 2).

[155] On the popularity of the *Anabasis* in the Roman period, see Münscher (1920: 78–9), Breitenbach (1967: 1903–5).

appears essential. In the short section entitled *De Regibus Exterarum Gentium* (*On the Kings of Foreign Nations*, 1.4),[156] Nepos includes two brief statements on kings Artaxerxes I and II. The statement dealing with our hero proclaims that although his mother murdered his wife, Artaxerxes treated her with due filial piety (*cum matris suae scelere amisisset uxorem, tantum indulsit dolori, ut eum pietas vinceret*). In all likelihood, Plutarch's decision to write a biography on Artaxerxes II resulted from reading this concise positive judgement. The central place he assigns to the murder of queen Stateira in his biography (announced in *Art.* 6.8–9 and 18.6 and fully described in *Art.* 19) may be seen as evidence of the impact of Nepos' statement on Plutarch.[157]

(b) The fourth century BCE attracts Plutarch, among other reasons, probably because of two significant developments that took place during that period: the rise and hegemony of Boeotian Thebes (a theme prominent in the *Pelopidas* and the lost *Epaminondas*),[158] which was dear to his heart,[159] and the decline of Greece,[160] which assisted the rise of Macedonia and ultimately of Rome; this decline was hastened by the enforced implementation of the Persian settlement known as the King's Peace. The *Artaxerxes* includes, albeit briefly, these two major historical events (*Art.* 21–2).

(c) The biography can be neatly divided into four parts:[161] (1) *Art.* 1–11, in which the two brothers Cyrus and Artaxerxes clash, a confrontation which culminates in the Battle of Cunaxa (401 BCE); (2) *Art.* 12–19, which narrates the aftermath of the fighting and Artaxerxes' triumph, including scenes of vicious court machinations; (3) *Art.* 20–2, displaying the high point of Artaxerxes' career, with the Battle of Cnidus (394 BCE) and the settlement he enforced on Greece; (4) *Art.* 23–30, which shows the political and moral failure of the king, who weds his own daughter (or two daughters, according to one version), kills his commanders and slays his own son Darius. In

---

[156] See Geiger (1979), who succinctly demonstrates that the *De Regibus* is not a mere abridgement of a series of biographies, but the original work itself. For other views, see his references.

[157] It may be that this case of Artaxerxes and Parysatis is implicitly meant by Plutarch to be compared with Nero's matricide (Plut. *Galb.* 14,19; cf. Suet. *Ner.* 34). On Plutarch's usually negative attitude towards Nero, see Flacelière (1963: 38–40), Brenk (1992: 4356–63).

[158] Number 7 in the Lamprias Catalogue, a life parallel to that of Scipio. On the importance of the Boeotian aspect in the choice of heroes for the solitary lost *Lives*, see Ziegler (1951: 895–6). Cf. Aalders (1982: 14–16).

[159] Cf. Stadter (2015b: 123).

[160] On Plutarch's interest in fourth-century Greece, see Mossé (1996). On the possibility of implicitly paralleling the decline of Greece with the downfall of the Republic, see Swain (1996: 139).

[161] See Almagor (2014b: 283).

the last section Artaxerxes seems to have completely lost power in his court, displaying feebleness which is abused by his son Ochus.

Views of the character of Artaxerxes as portrayed in the biography vary.[162] It is no surprise that there is no agreement on how to understand the biography. In what is perhaps one of his most sophisticated works,[163] Plutarch presents the *psyche* of the Persian monarch as comprising two incompatible parts, one of which is seemingly contained and moderate, and another that is uninhibited and cruel. The true character of Artaxerxes is not entirely clear to the reader. Up to a certain point, Artaxerxes never inflicts pain or executes anyone. This behaviour contradicts the readers' expectations, nurtured by tales of the brutality of the king's father Darius (*Art.* 2.2) and the Herodotean account of the Persian monarchs.[164] Artaxerxes appears rather mild (*Art.* 4.4), especially to his brother Cyrus the Younger, who is blamed for planning an assassination attempt (*Art.* 3.5–6),[165] and to deserters during the military clash (*Art.* 14.3–4). Later on, he savagely punishes one of his men for daring to espouse a different version of the occurrences (*Art.* 16.2–7), revealing Artaxerxes as a callous, despotic sovereign. In the end, he executes his own son (*Art.* 29.11). The initial mild image of Artaxerxes is alluded to, rather than shown, by the narrator, and the reader may justly wonder whether it has any basis in reality. If, however, the two conflicting traits are real, there remains the question of whether the biography depicts an actual change from a moderate to brutal character.[166] Artaxerxes' fascinating character as depicted by diverse sources presumably drove Plutarch to write this king's biography.

PLUTARCH AND THE *PERSICA*

The following chapters are devoted to the known *Persica* authors, two for Ctesias, two for Deinon and one for Heracleides. Chapter

---

[162] Positive: Manfredini, Orsi and Antelami (1987: xxvii xxviii), Kuhrt and Sancisi-Weerdenburg (1997: 48), negative: Hood (1967: 68–85), Binder (2008: 40–2) and in Stronk (2010: 102 n. 46), balanced approach: Schmidt (1999: 318–24).

[163] *Pace* Flacelière and Chambry (1979: 14), Binder (2008: 44–9 [49]): 'Als ein Meisterstuck Plutarchs . . . ist sie nicht zu werten' (as a masterpiece of Plutarch . . . is it not to be considered), Stronk (2010: 101–2). Cf. Mossman (2010: 147): 'the real star of this life is the Persian court and its luxury and cruelty'.

[164] See Almagor (2009: 138).

[165] According to Xenophon (*Anab.* 1.1.3) and Plutarch (*Art.* 3.6), Parysatis the queen mother intervened for Cyrus, and managed to send him back to his region. After Ctesias (cf. *FGrH* 688 F 16.59 and Almagor 2012: 30–1).

[166] Cf. Mossman (2010: 157): 'his [Artaxerxes'] character is consistent rather than internally contradictory'.

2 addresses Plutarch's explicit references to the physician Ctesias of Cnidus and his *Persica*. It discusses the presentation of Ctesias in Plutarch's work and how it compares with what we know about him from other sources, exploring how Plutarch uses Ctesias' name and reputation to serve his literary aims. Chapter 3 studies passages from other authors (mostly Photius' epitome) and compares them with Plutarch's sections which either refer to Ctesias explicitly, or refrain from mentioning his name. In this manner, Plutarch's work method and literary technique are explored. Chapter 4 concerns the work of the enigmatic Deinon of Colophon and its nature as can be gleaned from Plutarch's employment of his *Persica*. The chapter deals with Plutarch's explicit references to Deinon by comparing them to what we know of this author from other sources. This comparison is helpful for uncovering the character of Deinon's work and the literary use made of it by Plutarch. Chapter 5 deals with passages which form the last third of the *Artaxerxes* and are probably to be ascribed to Deinon. Here the nature of Plurach's source is examined and the reasons for attributing it to Deinon are presented after analysing Plutarch's method of using it. Chapter 6 focuses on the third author, Heracleides of Cyme, and the relatively small use made of his work by the biographer in the *Artaxerxes* and elsewhere. The presumed character of Heracleides' work is discussed, and a proposal concerning Plutarch's work method is made. In the Conclusion we describe the main features of the content and structure of the *Persica* works as gathered in this study, and outline Plutarch's method of employing these sources.

The translations in this volume are my own, unless specified otherwise. The Greek text used for the passages (including the division into sections) of Plutarch's *Lives* is mostly the Teubner edition edited by Konrat Ziegler (*Plutarchi: Vitae Parallelae*, Munich/Leipzig, 1959–72). Passages from the *Moralia* mostly follow the Teubner edition edited by Max Pohlenz, William R. Paton, Wilhelm Sieveking, Wilhelm Nachstädt, John Bradford Titchener, Curt E. H. Hubert, Jürgen Mau, Berthold Häsler, Johannes Wegehaupt, Hans Drexler and others (*Plutarchi Moralia*, Leipzig, 1925–74). Without any claim to being comprehensive in this regard, I listed some of the more interesting and relevant variants in brief critical apparati appended to certain of the passages. By convention, the *Moralia* are referred to by their Latin title and the Stephanus page number (of the edition of Frankfurt, 1599). Attempt was made to adopt the conventional Latinized forms of Greek names throughout. The text of Greek and Latin authors is that of standard editions. The text used for Photius' *Bibliotheke* is that of Immanuel Bekker (Berlin, 1824). Again, I have noted down some variants in the text, including the emendations of Felix Jacoby (in his *Die Fragmente der griechischen Historiker: Teil 3, Bd. 1. Aegypten–Geten [Nr. 608a–708]*, Leiden, 1958).

SIGLA

B	cod. Marcianus 450	saec. X
C	cod. Marcianus 451	saec. XII
N	cod. Matritensis 4685	saec. XIV
U	cod. Vaticanus 138	saec. X, XI
M	cod. Marcianus 385	saec. XIV, XV
A	cod. Parisinus 1671	AD 1296
Y	consensus codicum UMA	
G	cod. Coislinianus (vel Sangermanensis) 319	saec. X–XI
G^{1-2}	scriptura codicis G primae vel secundae manus	
L	cod. Laurentianus 69, 6	saec. X
L^{1-2}	scriptura codicis L primae vel secundae manus	
P	cod. Palatinus 283	saec. XI, XII
R	cod. Vaticanus Urbinas 97	saec. X, XI
R^{1-2}	scriptura codicis R primae vel secundae manus	
Π	consensus codicum RP	
S	cod. Seitenstettensis	saec. XI, XII

EDITIONS AND NOTES REFERRED TO:

Bongars = Bongars, J. (1581), *Editio Iustini* (Paris).

Graevius = Graevius, J. G. (1683), *Iustinus* (Leiden).

Hartman = Hartman, J. J. (1913), 'Ad Plutarchi *Moralia* Annotationes Criticae', *Mnemosyne* 41: 64–110, 209–32, 333–7, 341–81.

Hercher = Hercher, R. (1866), *Claudii Aeliani De natura animalium libri xvii, Varia historia, Epistolae, Fragmenta, Vol 2* (Leipzig).

Korais = Korais, A. (1809–14), *Πλουτάρχου βίοι παράλληλοι* (Paris).

Olson, S. D. (2007), *Athenaeus: The Learned Banqueters* (Cambridge, MA).

Reiske = Reiske, J. J. (1774–9), *Plutarchus* (Leipzig).

Schäfer = Schäfer, G. H. (1826–1830), Vitae. *Plutarchus*, vols. 1–5 (Leipzig).

Schweighäuser = Schweighäuser, J. (1801–7), *Athenaei Naucratitae Deipnosophistarum libri quindecim* (Strassburg: Bipontium).

2. *Ctesias (a)*

The most important writer of the group of authors who are said to have composed *Persica* works is Ctesias of Cnidus (*fl.* 400–390 BCE). Of all the authors treated in this book, Ctesias the physician is the only one about whom we have relatively secure information concerning his life and work, even though it all appears to ultimately come from his own descriptions, and despite the fact that certain issues are still unclear. Contrary to other scholarly treatments of Plutarch's use of Ctesias, we shall divide the discussion here into two chapters: the first is the group of passages in which Ctesias' name is explicitly stated as a source by Plutarch, and the second is the class of sections which can be attributed to Ctesias with a high degree of probability. In this chapter, after an analysis of the passages in Plutarch's work, we shall combine our observations with what is known of Ctesias from other sources, to infer Plutarch's work method and his purpose of using Ctesias in the *Artaxerxes* and mentioning this source.

PLUTARCH AND CTESIAS

Apart from one instance, all the explicit references to Ctesias in Plutarch's corpus come from the *Artaxerxes*. This fact leads to the most likely conclusion that Ctesias' work was only read and used by Plutarch for this biography, even though abridged sections from his *Persica* may have been encountered by the biographer in other works and collections of which we have no possibility of knowing. The first passage comes from the beginning of the *Artaxerxes* and seems to imply that the intended readers are familiar with Ctesias' name and reputation (*Art.* 1.4):

Artaxerxes was originally called Arsicas, but Deinon says his name was Oarses. Ctesias, however, even if he includes fanciful tales and nonsense in his books, is not likely to be ignorant of the name of the king, in whose house he lived and whom he treated, together with the king's wife, mother, and children.

ὁ δ᾽ Ἀρτοξέρξης Ἀρσίκας πρότερον ἐκαλεῖτο· καίτοι Δείνων φησὶν ὅτι Ὀάρσης. Ἀλλὰ τὸν Κτησίαν, εἰ καὶ τἆλλα μύθων ἀπιθάνων καὶ παραφόρων ἐμβέβληκεν εἰς τὰ βιβλία παντοδαπὴν πυλαίαν, οὐκ εἰκός ἐστιν ἀγνοεῖν τοὔνομα τοῦ βασιλέως, παρ᾽ ᾧ διέτριβε θεραπεύων αὐτὸν καὶ γυναῖκα καὶ μητέρα καὶ παῖδας.

The opening of Plutarch's biography includes many of the themes that are to appear later in the biography. One of these themes is a certain duality in the character of Artaxerxes, as can be seen in the contrast between the grandfather of the hero, called Artaxerxes I (ὁ πρῶτος Ἀρτοξέρξης), who is mentioned in the first words of the *Life*, and the protagonist's sons (παῖδας), among them his future successor, the later Artaxerxes III Ochus (cf. *Art.* 30.9). Plutarch's ingenuity enables this presentation to place Artaxerxes II between the two extremes of his namesakes: the mild character of Artaxerxes I (1.1: τῶν ἐν Πέρσαις βασιλέων πραότητι καὶ μεγαλοψυχίᾳ πρωτεύσας, 'among the Persians foremost in mildness[1] and greatness of soul') and the cruel nature of his son (30.9: ὠμότητι καὶ μιαιφονίᾳ, 'brutality and bloodthirstiness'). This duality appears through a set of oppositions within *Art.* 1, all designed to shed light on the king's complex *psyche*: there are two Artaxerxes, there are two brothers, Artaxerxes II and Cyrus,[2] there are two Cyruses (the Younger and Cyrus the Great) and two versions of Artaxerxes' original name (Arsicas/Oarses) related respectively in two sources (Ctesias and Deinon). The difference between Ctesias and Deinon, which exemplifies this inner conflict of traits, recurs in the biography (*Art.* 6.9, 10–11, 19.2–6) and is dealt with below.[3]

The first piece of knowledge concerning Ctesias is thus the assertion that his account supplies only one version, or one part, of reality, and is contrasted with another, in analogy to the Persian world, which is made up of binary dichotomies. To this trait Plutarch adjoins the popular negative impression of Ctesias' descriptions as being lengthy tall stories. The word Plutarch uses, παράφορος, is 'mad, frenzied' (LSJ I.3) from παραφέρω ('deviate'), hinting at Ctesias' tendency to digress outside the narrative's main road.[4]

---

[1] On this trait see Martin (1960), Duff (1999: 77–8).
[2] The structure of *Art.* 1 shifts between them: 1.1 [A] – 1.2 [C] – 1.3 [C] – 1.4 [A].
[3] See also Almagor (2013b: 22, 25).
[4] Note the tongue-in-cheek effect of the alliteration ἐμβέβληκεν . . . βιβλία.

What is the advantage of Ctesias' version over the other? Deinon's variant of Artaxerxes' original name (on which we shall say more in Chapter 3) is disqualified by Plutarch because the author Deinon was not present at the royal court, while the information Ctesias provides is accepted on the grounds that he was there, even though he allegedly tends to falsify. Both the emphasis on Ctesias' presence at court and the question of a truthful account seem to be a playful comparison between the writer Ctesias and the Persian king, and to foretell the main plot of the *Life*. As we shall see below, in Ctesias' account, during the great battle, Artaxerxes was injured and was taken away from the scene; Cyrus lost his life, but not by the monarch. Yet after the clash Artaxerxes strove to appropriate the glory for the killing of his brother and to have his false version circulated as true, even though he was not present (*Art.* 14.5, 16.2). By contrast, Plutarch tells us, Ctesias was there at the Persian court and therefore can be trusted.

Or can he? Plutarch's whole argument is clearly a *non sequitur*. If Ctesias is generally lying, he could also have fabricated the fact that he was present at court, not to mention the name of the king.[5] Indeed, Marco Dorati (1995) questions Ctesias' very presence in Persia.[6] Yet even Ctesias' presence does not guarantee the truthfulness of what he says. The atmosphere conveyed in *Art.* 1 appears to reflect a world closed to the external eye. It is a world in which only Ctesias or a person who is there can gain access to royal secrets and know the real name of the king. It is therefore a world in which truth is a tricky business, since assertions cannot be validated by external readers. Ctesias' very sojourn in Persia may thus be the reason his work is characterised as untrustworthy. In this case, Ctesias could have been lying *because* he was present at the scene and not free to express his mind while residing in court; and he was able to do so because his words could never be scrutinised by others outside the court.

The healing of the Persian king during the Battle of Cunaxa (401 BCE, below) may be the first real event Ctesias referred to in his work with himself as an active historical agent. Yet the relationship between historical reality and agency in court on the one hand and historical writing on the other is slippery when it comes to Ctesias. For instance, there is a striking resemblance between the life and

---

[5] Cf. Russell (1973: 57): '[Plutarch's] "probability"... includes considerations which we should regard as dubious and subjective ... his criteria are unfamiliar and unconvincing.'

[6] Cf. Jacoby (1922: 2046–7). See, however, Lenfant (2009: 28 n. 1).

career of Democedes, as known from Herodotus (3.129–37), and those of Ctesias, including Democedes' eventual escape to Croton after a period of service in the royal court.[7] We are thus not sure whether Ctesias' report reflected historical reality or imitated Herodotus' art.

The debate surrounding Artaxerxes' real given name reflects the theme of appearance vs. reality and the problem of grasping Artaxerxes' true nature. The fact that Artaxerxes had a given name and a throne name relates to the issue of a person's character: does it change during adult life, or is it supposed to have been established and be fixed from birth? If we perceive a change in one's demeanour, does it imply a revelation of an innate nature or rather a transformation of his or her character? In particular, was Artaxerxes' cruel side concealed and only occasionally exposed during his lifetime? Or, on the contrary, was his moderate nature only a mask fabricated in fictitious descriptions by courtiers or the Greek sources?[8] These open questions, which are not made clearer throughout the biography, are presented already at the outset by this ostensible historiographic debate.

The historiographic argument itself is made to mimic the conflict of the brothers, which becomes evident in the next section of the biography. Arsicas and Cyrus the Younger compete for the Persian throne and desire to succeed their father, Darius II (*Art.* 2.3–5). Plutarch's decision in favour of Ctesias' version is like Darius' choice of Arsicas over Cyrus. Ctesias' variant, like Arsicas, is the older one, while Deinon's account is clearly the 'younger'. One may note that Deinon is brought in as someone who challenges Plutarch's version, almost subversively. Moreover, Ctesias was *there*, like Arsicas, as readers of Xenophon's *Anabasis* will surely recall (*Anab.* 1.1.2: ὁ μὲν οὖν πρεσβύτερος παρὼν ἐτύγχανε, 'the elder chanced to be there', i.e., at Darius' death-bed); by implication, Deinon was not – like Cyrus. It is not for internal qualities of the author or his work that Ctesias' version is chosen – for his account is admittedly flawed and unreliable – but simply because the physician was present, and thus was already integrated in court life. The same may go for Arsicas, who does not strike one as kingly when set against Cyrus, who has a royal name and supposedly royal virtues from the start.

The next passage in the *Artaxerxes* in which the Greek physician

---

[7] On the resemblance, see Griffiths (1987: 48). Lenfant (2004: X–XI n. 19) rejects the scepticism based on this comparison.
[8] See Almagor (2014b: 284). Cf. Mossman (2010: 149).

is mentioned tackles the same motifs, and once again draws a contrast between Ctesias and Deinon (*Art.* 6.9):

> For Deinon says the plot was accomplished during the war, while Ctesias puts it later. And it is not likely that the latter would be unaware of the time, since he was present during the events, and would not willingly have a reason to take the event out of its temporal context, while describing how it happened, however often his narrative diverts from truth to the mythical and dramatic, so the place he gave to the event will be adopted.
>
> ἐπεὶ δὲ Δείνων μὲν ἐν τῷ πολέμῳ συντελεσθῆναι τὴν ἐπιβουλὴν εἴρηκε, Κτησίας δ᾽ ὕστερον, ὃν οὔτ᾽ ἀγνοεῖν τὸν χρόνον εἰκός ἐστι παρόντα ταῖς πράξεσιν, οὐθ᾽ ἑκὼν αἰτίαν εἶχεν ἐκ τοῦ χρόνου μεταστῆσαι τὸ ἔργον, ὡς ἐπράχθη διηγούμενος – οἷα πάσχει πολλάκις ὁ λόγος αὐτοῦ πρὸς τὸ μυθῶδες καὶ δραματικὸν ἐκτρεπόμενος τῆς ἀληθείας – τοῦτο μὲν ἦν ἐκεῖνος ἀπέδωκε χώραν ἕξει.
>
> μυθῶδες: θυμῶδες GRL¹ μυθῶ supra scr. PL² ‖ μὲν οὖν GP ‖

Plutarch refers to the assassination of the queen Stateira by the queen mother Parysatis. If Ctesias and Deinon differed with regard to the timing of this event, the former's position obviously appears more probable, and placing the death of the queen Stateira before that of Cyrus the Younger is undoubtedly erroneous. Moreover, Ctesias was there, so it is inconceivable that he would not know the correct order.[9] Nonetheless, the core of the plot in both writers seems to have been the same, with the exception of slight differences (see below in this chapter and in Chapter 4). The two similarly described the antagonism of Parysatis and Stateira and the murder of the latter by poisoning; the two depicted the same dish (a certain bird) and even the identical method. There are some divergences, however, between the two authors, the major one being that of the arrangement of details (on the probable thematic organising principle of the materials in Deinon's work, see Chapter 4). Plutarch's promise to follow Ctesias' sequence and not Deinon's order is ironic: by the very act of making his promise Plutarch breaks it, since he already mentions the murder not in its proper place.[10] Plutarch thus appears to be following Ctesias, but in fact lets Deinon's description into his account. By this presentation he appears to be mimicking Parysatis, who is ostensibly loyal to Artaxerxes and resides in the court, but secretly supports Cyrus.

   Art. 6 in its entirety plays upon the variation of being present and being absent, emphasising the movement from one condition to the other. Thus, Cyrus relies on people who are far away in the heartland (*Art.* 6.2: τοῖς ἄνω πιστεύων) no less than on those who are present in

---

[9] Note the **οὔτ᾽ ἀγνοεῖν** τὸν χρόνον **εἰκός** ἐστι, which echoes *Art.* 1.4: **οὐκ εἰκός** ἐστιν **ἀγνοεῖν**.
[10] Cf. Almagor (2013b: 22).

his immediate surroundings[11] and enlists the distant Spartans to help him (*Art.* 6.3). The introduction of the figure Clearchus, an exile who was sentenced to death *in absentia* (Xen. *Anab.* 2.6.2–4), is related to the theme of not being present.[12] Clearchus is remote from Sparta and can only be reached by messengers (*Art.* 6.5). Both Cyrus (*Art.* 6.5: ἀνέβαινεν ἐπὶ βασιλέα, 'going up to the king') and Tissaphernes[13] move towards the king: the latter in order to warn him (*Art.* 6.7).[14]

Overall, the theme of movement, so prominent in *Art.* 6, is related to that of finding a place. One notes the taunt of Stateira at Parysatis (*Art.* 6.7: '**Where** are your promises now?', ποῦ νῦν αἱ πίστεις ἐκεῖναι), as well as Plutarch's play with the order of words of the text to convey this feature of place: at first Stateira is angry at Parysatis (*Art.* 6.7: ἠνία τὴν **Παρύσατιν** ἡ <u>Στάτειρα</u>), and then reciprocally, Parysatis is said to be hateful of Stateira (μισοῦσα τὴν <u>Στάτειραν</u> ἡ **Παρύσατις**). This theme appears in Cyrus' depiction of Artaxerxes' failure to preserve his position on his horse (*Art.* 6.4). Since this picture has relevance to some of the scenes of Ctesias which Plutarch presents, it may be discussed here, even though the attribution of this passage to Ctesias is not entirely certain (see Chapter 3):

> [Cyrus said that] he [Artaxerxes] because of his timidity and softness could not sit on his horse during the hunt nor sit on the throne in face of danger.
>
> ἐκεῖνον δ᾽ ὑπὸ δειλίας καὶ μαλακίας ἐν μὲν τοῖς κυνηγεσίοις μηδ᾽ ἐφ᾽ ἵππου, ἐν δὲ τοῖς κινδύνοις μηδ᾽ ἐπὶ τοῦ θρόνου καθῆσθαι.

Is Cyrus better than his brother? It would appear that in one respect there is no great difference between the two. Cyrus' letter to the Spartans conveys the surprising message that *not* holding to one's own place is the key to greater success. Cyrus promises to provide the Spartans a better place (*Art.* 6.3: ἐὰν δ᾽ ἀγροὺς ἔχωσι, κώμας· ἐὰν δὲ κώμας, πόλεις, 'if they had farms, he would give them villages; if they had villages, cities').[15] Plutarch soon follows suit by mimicking

---

[11] See Farrell (1961), Briant (2002a: 626–7). Cf. Xen. *Anab.* 1.1.5 and Isoc. *Paneg.* 145.

[12] Clearchus son of Rhamphias, one of the famous commanders of the Peloponnesian War (Thuc. 8.8.2, 39.3, 80.1–3; Diod. 13.40.6), did not obey the Ephors to return from his mission against the Thracians. Diodorus (14.12.2–47) claims that he controlled Byzantium as a tyrant and was expelled by the Spartans from the city. See Binder (2008: 169).

[13] Tissaphernes was satrap of Sardis and perhaps also the commander-in-chief of the king's forces in Asia Minor (Thuc. 8.5.4). After being replaced by Cyrus the Younger, Tissaphernes retained the position of the satrap of Caria alone (Xen. *Hell.* 3.2.12, *Anab.* 1.1.2, 1.9.7). See Lehmann-Haupt (1921: 125), Olmstead (1948: 358–64), Lewis (1977: 119 n. 78), Ruzicka (1985).

[14] Cf. Xen. *Anab.* 1.2.4–5. Cf. Diod. 14.11.1–4, 14.22.1 and Nepos, *Alc.* 9.4–5 [Pharnabazus in 404 BCE]. See Rahe (1980: 94), Briant (2002a: 618). Xenophon may have derived this version from Ctesias, as Tissaphernes was the villain in the accounts of both authors.

[15] By promising to provide chariots to Spartan horsemen (*Art.* 6.3), Cyrus in effect promises to unhorse them. See Almagor (2014a: 7).

Cyrus in promising readers to move them to a better place in the narrative.[16] Like Cyrus, who pledges for lands (*Art.*6.3: κώμας, πόλεις),
Plutarch vouches for a place (*Art.*6.9: χώρα), the same place which
Ctesias gave to the subject matter; similarly to Cyrus, who relies
on people far away up country, so does Plutarch point to a place
far away in the text, in which he will depict Stateira's murder (*Art.*
6.8–9).

Once again Ctesias is preferred over Deinon because he was
present at the court during the time of events. Once again the entire
argument is a *non sequitur*, and for the same reason: Ctesias could
easily have diverted from the truth with regard to his actual presence
in court. By the use of the spatial imagery of ἐκτρεπόμενος ('diverting'), Plutarch again plays upon a distinct feature of Ctesias' work,
namely, his digression or deviation from the route of the narrative,
as well as on his notoriety for being unreliable (as in 'diverting from
truth'), to anticipate the behaviour of Artaxerxes and his appropriation of a false version, despite the fact that he was not present.

Artistically, the historiographic debate again reflects on the actual
political clash, with both belligerent sides resembling the two brothers. On the one hand, Deinon wishes to include the murder of Stateira
here and now; he appears impetuous, almost like Cyrus (cf. *Art.* 2.1:
σφοδρὸν). By contrast, Ctesias seems cautious or hesitant, preferring
to wait for a further point in the future; in this he resembles the
image of the king drawn by Cyrus, namely, one who decides not to
give battle at once but rather wait in Persia till all his forces gather
from all parts of the empire (cf. *Art.* 7.1). On the other hand, Deinon
seems to prefer dealing with the death of Stateira at the very point
that the issue of the relationship of Stateira and Parysais comes up,
and not surrender the topic; in this he appears to be like the king,
trying to preserve the throne and power he already has. By transfer-
ring the murder of Stateira to the future Plutarch makes Ctesias
appear, on the contrary, to be setting a distant goal for himself,
aiming for something which he does not posses now; in this Ctesias
is, of course, very similar to the attitude of Cyrus on his way to attain
the power he never actually holds. The fact that each author is made
to imitate both brothers is an indication of the apparent changes that
the belligerent siblings would soon undergo; for instance, Artaxerxes
surprises Cyrus with an uncharacteristic speed and determination
(*Art.* 7.4–5).

Strictly speaking, the next passage attributed to Ctesias concerns

---

[16] Cf. Almagor (2013b: 26).

only a minor detail, but it comes within a section that is most probably taken in its entirety from him (*Art.* 9.1):

> Cyrus, riding on a high bred but difficult horse (Pasacas was his name, according to Ctesias) came face to face with Artagerses, the leader of the Cadusians ...
>
> Κύρῳ δὲ γενναῖον ἵππον ἄστομον δὲ καὶ ὑβριστὴν ἐλαύνοντι, Πασακᾶν καλούμενον, ὡς Κτησίας φησίν, ἀντεξήλασεν ὁ Καδουσίων ἄρχων Ἀρταγέρσης ...

In Persian royal and aristocratic contexts, the steed was highly significant.[17] Horsemanship was part of the royal ideology and, reflecting physical strength and bravery in war, it was regarded as a proper justification for holding the crown.[18] The name of the stallion, Pasacas,[19] may remind the reader of the horse through whose help Darius I became the king. Herodotus relates (3.84) how the seven conspirators' method of electing the new king was based on horsemanship: they agreed that he whose horse neighed first in the day should have the throne.[20] Herodotus mentions (3.88) that upon the accession of Darius I, a monument was erected of a man on horseback 'mentioning the name' of the horse (τὸ οὔνομα λέγων).[21] Herodotus does not specify this name. It may be that drawing on his readers' acquaintance with Herodotus, Plutarch presents Ctesias as wishing to surpass his predecessor by supplying the name of Cyrus' stallion.[22] In the historiographic sphere, this desire may mimic the political ambitions of Cyrus: both historian and prince use the horse for their own purposes.

At the end of *Art.* 9, immediately after Artagerses, the royal cavalry

---

[17] See Darius (DPd.8): 'This country... which Ahuramazda bestowed upon me, good, possessed of good horses (*uvaspâ*), possessed of good men'. Cf. DSf, 11; DSp, 3: 'possessed of good charioteers, of good horses'. Almagor (2014a: 5).

[18] In the Platonic *Alc.* I (121e–122a), the military education among the Persians included horsemanship and hunt (for seven-year-old boys), and was also aimed to induce courage. Cf. Xen. *Cyr.* 1.4.14. See the way Darius presents himself in the Naqsh-i-Rustam inscription (DNb, 41–4): 'As a horseman I am a good horseman (*asabâra uvâsabâra amiy*). As a bowman I am a good bowman both afoot and on horseback.' Cf. Xen. *Anab.* 1.7.9, 1.8.12. See Briant (2002a: 90, 227–8). On the notion of linking (or exchanging) kingdom for a horse see the episode of Cyrus and the Sacian (Xen. *Cyr.* 8.3.35–50) with Gera (1993: 174–5).

[19] The name might signify 'mane' (MPer. *pās*); see Justi (1895: 244–5). Alternatively, this name might be a distortion of *Nasakas*, 'wild and disobedient' (MPer. *nā-sāz*). Cf. Binder (2008: 191).

[20] Cf. 3.85–8 on the ruse employed by Darius. Cf. Ctesias' version in Photius' summary FGrH 688 F 13.17.

[21] See Briant (2002a: 217).

[22] The horse appears as a *dramatis persona* of Ctesias' account. See Lonsdale (1990: 74) on the presence of horses in the *Iliad*: 'The horse is a ubiquitous and indispensable actor in the plot. ... Homeric horses are flesh and blood creatures with a will and a way of their own, individuals [with] a rich system of epithets and sometimes accorded names and lineage.' See Almagor (2014a: 14).

commander, is killed at the hands of Cyrus, Plutarch states he will provide two different versions of Cyrus' death, departing from this same juncture (*Art.* 9.4):

> Almost everyone agrees that Cyrus killed Artagerses. On the (matter of) death of Cyrus himself because Xenophon relates it simply and briefly, since he was not there, perhaps nothing prevents me from relating what Deinon says and then Ctesias.
>
> τὸν μὲν οὖν Ἀρταγέρσην ἀποθανεῖν ὑπὸ τοῦ Κύρου σχεδὸν ἅπαντες ὁμολογοῦσι· περὶ δὲ τῆς αὐτοῦ Κύρου τελευτῆς ἐπεὶ Ξενοφῶν ἁπλῶς καὶ συντόμως, ἅτε δὴ μὴ παρὼν αὐτός, εἶπεν, οὐδὲν ἴσως κωλύει τὰ Δείνωνος ἰδίᾳ καὶ πάλιν τὰ Κτησίου διελθεῖν.

In this passage, Xenophon's account is said to be problematic, and therefore unusable; since the Athenian historian was not present near the king during the battle, Plutarch prefers the versions of Ctesias and Deinon. The irony of this claim is enhanced against the background of the earlier assertion that Deinon was not present during these historical events. He is now implicitly made out to be someone who witnessed the occurrences (which he most probably did not, if we follow the logic of *Art.* 1.4), while Xenophon is relegated to being someone who was not present (but of course, he was there). Furthermore, the Athenian historian is said to present such a vivid story that the reader almost becomes a witness to the events (*Art.* 8.1, quoted in Chapter 3). Yet, on the other hand, in the following section (*Art.* 9.4), we see Plutarch claiming that he will *not* use Xenophon on the grounds that the Athenian historian was not present.[23] The combined ironic impact of these two descriptions of Xenophon reflects on Plutarch's verdict on Ctesias: it is the pursuit of glory that made Xenophon attempt to give a lively picture (at the expense of certain significant details, such as the name of the battle site), even though he was not present at several points. This playful presentation has a bearing on the issue of Artaxerxes' later version of his brother's death and the fact that he was not there, as said above.

The stories of Ctesias and Deinon run parallel to each other in the next two sections (*Art.* 10–11). The two variants are portrayed as forking out of one situation, in the typical image of a crossroad from which two tracks diverge. This road imagery (κακὴν ὁδόν, 'evil path': *Art.* 9.2), portraying two alternative routes, echoes the story of Heracles' moral choice between virtue and vice, attributed to Prodicus (cf. Xen. *Mem.* 2.1.21–33).[24] For the third time in the biog-

---

[23] Stadter (2012: 45 n. 12) does not see the irony in the combination of the passages.
[24] See Kuntz (1994), Sansone (2004).

raphy, Plutarch appears to believe Ctesias (or to follow his account) because he was there. A subtle insinuation of the future behaviour of the king is implied by the fact that 'almost everyone' (preseumably especially Xenophon and Deinon) appropriated the description of Ctesias, apparently without giving him due credit, exactly as Artaxerxes did with relation to the killing of Cyrus.

The second variant branching out of this situation is that of Ctesias (*Art.* 11.1–3):

> The narrative of Ctesias, given here in a concise and abbreviated version, is as follows: after killing Artagerses, Cyrus directed his horse against the king, and the latter towards him, both rode in silence. Ariaeus, a friend of Cyrus, made the first throw, but failed to hit. The king threw his spear, missed Cyrus but hit Satiphernes, loyal and noble friend of Cyrus, and killed him. Cyrus then threw his spear and hit him through the breastplate in the chest, causing a wound of two fingers deep, and knocked him off his horse. As men around him were fleeing and in disorder, he (Artaxerxes) stood up and with several men, including Ctesias, occupied a small hill quietly.
>
> Ἡ δὲ Κτησίου διήγησις, ὡς ἐπιτεμόντι πολλὰ συντόμως ἀπαγγεῖλαι, τοιαύτη τίς ἐστι. Κῦρος ἀποκτείνας Ἀρταγέρσην, ἤλαυνεν εἰς αὐτὸν βασιλέα τὸν ἵππον, καὶ αὐτὸς εἰς ἐκεῖνον, ἀμφότεροι σιωπῇ. φθάνει δὲ βαλὼν Ἀριαῖος ὁ Κύρου φίλος βασιλέα, καὶ οὐκ ἔτρωσε. (2) Βασιλεὺς δ' ἀφεὶς τὸ δόρυ Κύρου μὲν οὐκ ἔτυχε, Σατιφέρνην δὲ πιστὸν ἄνδρα Κύρῳ καὶ γενναῖον ἔβαλε, καὶ κατέκτεινε. Κῦρος δ' ἐπ' αὐτὸν ἐξακοντίσας διὰ τοῦ θώρακος ἔτρωσε τὸ στῆθος, ὅσον ἐνδῦναι δύο δακτύλους τὸ ἀκόντιον, πεσεῖν δ' αὐτὸν ὑπὸ τῆς πληγῆς ἀπὸ τοῦ ἵππου. (3) Φυγῆς δὲ καὶ ταραχῆς τῶν περὶ αὐτὸν γενομένης, ὁ μὲν ἀναστὰς μετ' ὀλίγων, ἐν οἷς καὶ Κτησίας ἦν, λόφον τινὰ πλησίον καταλαβὼν ἡσύχαζε.

Like Plutarch, who begins his narrative trying to impose textual limits on his source by way of abbreviation, but eventually ends up yielding to it,[25] Ctesias is not able to contain the historical reality in his text, and becomes absorbed in it. It is as if the boundaries between story and reality are blurred for him, thereby engrossing the writer in the historical experience he sets out to describe: first, in the act of saving the king's life as a historical agent, and then by the sardonic quip (below) making Ctesias the one who actually 'kills' Cyrus. Ultimately, this development echoes the progression noticed in the king, who, in claiming to have killed Cyrus, is absorbed in the fiction he has created, assuming the role of a historical agent he did not really play in actual time. Thus, Plutarch's failure to abide by his

---

[25] Plutarch makes a comment similar to the opening *Alex.* 1.1, in which he is asking the reader's forgiveness for abbreviating the material (ἐπιτέμνοντες τὰ πλεῖστα). Both in the *Alexander* and in *Art.* 11 this claim is made to be ironic, since Plutarch does dwell on many details as he progresses and does not seem to abbreviate the material, as can be seen at the end of *Artaxerxes* 11 (cf. *Alex.* 77.1).

own restrictions reflects on the understanding of both Ctesias and the protagonist Artaxerxes.

Plutarch presents Ctesias the physician as having a dual, almost contradictory, role in the scene: as a physician he saves the king's life; as the historian who writes about it, he destroys the king's image. If Joan Bigwood (1983: 348) is right to note that Ctesias the royal physician had an interest in exaggerating the injury of Artaxerxes,[26] then Ctesias the Greek author would ironically also appear to 'inflict a wound' on the Persian king in his depiction.

We shall return to this description momentarily, in the context of comparison between *Art.* 11 and the text of Xenophon, but in the meantime it is important to note Plutarch's picture of the death of Cyrus (*Art.* 11.5-11):

> And a young Persian by the name of Mithridates ran toward him and hit him in the temple near the eye, without knowing who he was. Much blood was let from the wound, and Cyrus fell, from dizziness and torpor. The horse turned and escaped, but the blood-soaked saddle cloth was carried by the assistant of the man who hit Cyrus. Cyrus was struggling to recover from the blow, and barely some eunuchs who were present tried to put him on another horse and save him. They helped him, as he was weak and wished to walk.
>
> Drowsy and trippling, Cyrus thought he had won, since he heard people fleeing and calling him 'king' and begging for mercy. In this group were lowly and poor Caunians, who followed the king's army to carry out tedious tasks, and happened to mix with Cyrus' men as if they were friends. They were barely able to recognise purple tunics, and since all the royal troops wore white tunics, they understood that those were enemies. One of these people was so bold as to hit Cyrus from his rear with a spear. As the blow split the vein near the knee, Cyrus fell and hit his wounded temple on a rock and died. Such is the account of Ctesias who barely kills the man (Cyrus), as if using a blunt sword.
>
> (5) Καὶ παρατρέχων νεανίας Πέρσης ὄνομα Μιθριδάτης ἀκοντίῳ βάλλει τὸν κρόταφον αὐτοῦ παρὰ τὸν ὀφθαλμόν, ἀγνοῶν ὅστις εἴη· πολὺ δ' αἷμα τοῦ τραύματος ἐκβαλόντος, ἰλιγγιάσας καὶ καρωθεὶς ὁ Κῦρος ἔπεσε. (6) Καὶ ὁ μὲν ἵππος ὑπεκφυγὼν ἐπλάζετο, τὸν δ' ἐφίππειον πῖλον ἀπορρυέντα λαμβάνει τοῦ τὸν Κῦρον βαλόντος ἀκόλουθος αἵματος περίπλεω. (7) Τὸν δὲ Κῦρον ἐκ τῆς πληγῆς ἀναφέροντα χαλεπῶς καὶ μόλις εὐνοῦχοί τινες ὀλίγοι παρόντες ἐπεχείρουν ἐπ' ἄλλον ἵππον ἀναθέσθαι καὶ σῴζειν. (8) Ἀδυνάτως δ' ἔχοντα καὶ δι' αὐτοῦ προθυμούμενον βαδίζειν ὑπολαβόντες ἦγον, τῷ μὲν σώματι καρηβαροῦντα καὶ σφαλλόμενον, οἰόμενον δὲ νικᾶν, ἀκούοντα τῶν φευγόντων ἀνακαλουμένων Κῦρον βασιλέα καὶ φείδεσθαι δεομένων. (9) Ἐν δὲ τούτῳ Καύνιοί τινες ἄνθρωποι, κακόβιοι καὶ ἄποροι καὶ ταπεινῶν ὑπουργημάτων ἕνεκα τῇ τοῦ βασιλέως στρατιᾷ παρακολουθοῦντες, ἔτυχον συναναμειχθέντες ὡς φίλοις τοῖς περὶ τὸν

---

[26] She draws attention to the fact that in Ctesias, the king's behaviour does not seem compatible with a serious injury: he leaves his post to see his brother's body, gathers supporters and so forth.

Κῦρον. Ὡς δὲ μόλις συνεῖδον τὰ ἐπιθωρακίδια φοινικᾶ, λευκοῖς χρωμένων τῶν βασιλικῶν ἁπάντων, ἔγνωσαν πολεμίους ὄντας. (10) Εἷς οὖν ἐκείνων ἐτόλμησεν ἀγνοῶν ἐξόπισθεν βαλεῖν τὸν Κῦρον ἀκοντίῳ· τῆς δὲ περὶ τὴν ἰγνύαν φλεβὸς ἀναρραγείσης, πεσὼν ὁ Κῦρος ἅμα παίει πρός τινι λίθῳ τὸν τετρωμένον κρόταφον, καὶ ἀποθνῄσκει. (11) Τοιοῦτος μὲν ὁ Κτησίου λόγος, ᾧ καθάπερ ἀμβλεῖ ξιφιδίῳ μόλις ἀναιρῶν τὸν ἄνθρωπον ἀνῄρηκεν.

ἰγνύην L

Cyrus' aspirations for kingship are openly portrayed as delusional, stemming from his physical condition after the blow he receives.[27] Like Cyrus, a historical agent who thinks he has the ability to describe reality correctly, but actually maintains false beliefs and is subtly mocked for it, so is Ctesias the historian, who professes in his own account to have been a historical agent, is sardonically mocked by Plutarch. Ctesias' claim to have acted in the real world, since he was present there, seems to be ridiculed by Plutarch as almost a sort of a literary *metalepsis*, a violation of the narrative levels, when Ctesias the author is ironically presented as 'killing' Cyrus, a figure in the narrative world. Ctesias' intervention in the scene is now consigned to be a virtual impossibility, paralleling Cyrus' delusion. This can be seen also in the correspondence of the fact that Ctesias hardly kills Cyrus (*Art.* 11.11: **μόλις** ... ἀνῄρηκεν) and the fact that Cyrus barely recovers to mount a horse (*Art.* 11.7: ἀναφέροντα χαλεπῶς καὶ **μόλις** ...).

Yet there is an indication that this impression of a *metalepsis* was insinuated by Ctesias himself through his *metapoetic* innuendos. In this case, Plutarch was almost inevitably led to an ironic interpretation of his predecessor's text by the original presentation of the *Persica*.

Ctesias introduced the figure of a Carian, said to have been responsible for the death of Cyrus.[28] Since Ctesias himself was a Carian, he had some relationship with the person who finally slayed Cyrus; indeed, Ctesias 'kills' Cyrus through him. His ultimate role as an author describing the event is in the final elimination of the

---

[27] On the nature of the injury inflicted to Cyrus, see Bassett (1999: 480–3).

[28] Although several authors differentiated between the Caunians and the Carians (Hdt. 1.171–2; Thuc. 1.116.3), Caunus was a city in Caria (Strabo, 14.2.2). See Smith (1881: 34), Mantey (1888: 14), Bürchner (1921a), Lenfant (2004: 281 n. 685). Addressing the person who delivered the fatal blow to Cyrus, Plutarch tends to shift between Carian (*Art.* 14.6, *Art.* 10.3) and a Caunian (*Art.* 11). Similarly, there is a Caunian in Plut. *Art.* 12.5 (14.2). In Photius he is called a Carian (*FGrH* 688 F 16.67), and this presumably was Ctesias' version. Plutarch's alteration between Carian and Caunian is perhaps done for artistic purposes, as highlighting two sides of this person's character, indirectly reflecting on the complex nature of the king. There is no need to emend the text, as suggested by Means (1947/8); cf. Binder (2008: 212, 234).

prince in writing, regardless of who performed the deed in reality. Cyrus' death thus has a double aspect: as a real event and as a literary depiction. It is replicated. Plutarch appears to duplicate reality as much as Ctesias did in his own account. Corresponding to the two persons who in Ctesias' account were jointly responsible for Cyrus' death (i.e. Mithridates[29] and the Carian), Plutarch brings the variants of both Deinon (*Art.* 10, see Chapter 4) and Ctesias (*Art.* 11) to the slaying of Cyrus. Moreover, as Ctesias used the Carian by giving him a spear (ἀκοντίῳ) to kill Cyrus, Plutarch employs Ctesias by giving him a 'dagger' (ξιφιδίῳ) to 'kill' Cyrus.

Another point to consider may be a certain intertextual play by Ctesias with the introduction of Mithridates. This is the name of the person who, according to Herodotus (1.110: τῷ οὔνομα ἦν Μιτραδάτης), saves the life of Cyrus the Great and becomes his adoptive father (1.112–15). By making this Mithridates kill Cyrus the Younger, Ctesias forms a literary closure with Herodotus, hinting at both his indebtedness to his predecessor – his own literary father, as it were – and also at the way he is able to turn his story upside down. Ctesias is thus conscious of his act of 'literary parricide', if you please.

The end of *Art.* 11 thus marks a certain break from the previous appearances of Ctesias in Plutarch's *Life*. His presence in Persia is no longer simply taken at face value, but is rather seen to be logically problematic as involving a *metalepsis*. Building upon Ctesias' absence from the battle scene (together with the king) and from Cyrus' death scene, Plutarch makes the physician virtually absent from other aspects of the war and its aftermath, although this was not necessarily true. In Plutarch's following depictions, the doubt concerning Ctesias' claims to be a historical agent comes to the fore. If the assertion in *Art.* 11.10, according to which Ctesias the author interferes in the story level to 'kill' Cyrus, sounds absurd, the next reference to the historiographic debate involving the strength of the royal army (*Art.* 13.3) is similarly tongue-in-cheek. Ctesias is reported to have claimed that Artaxerxes led 400,000 men into battle, but to have been contradicted by 'the followers of Deinon and Xenophon' (οἱ δὲ περὶ Δείνωνα καὶ Ξενοφῶντα), who maintain

[29] Mithridates is a theophoric name (OPer. **Miθra-dāta*, 'given by Mithra'); see Justi (1895: 209–10), Mayrhofer (1973: 203 [8.1126]), Hinz (1975: 167), Schmitt (2006: 110–13); cf. Ezra 1:8. If the association between Mithras and the sun (Strabo 15.3.13, de Jong, 1997: 286–7) was known in Ctesias' time (cf. Gnoli 1979, Briant 2002a: 251–2), we observe his subtle play on Mithridates' name as the one who kills Cyrus (= sun, according to the Persians; see Chapter 3).

that the number was larger. The historiographic argument parallels the historic clash between the king and his brother: like people wavering between the sides (*Art.* 13:2: ἀμφιδοξοῦσιν), the historians disagree (*Art.* 13.4: διαμφισβήτησιν). The political or military language (see also Chapter 4) colours the historiographic debate, as if taking Ctesias' claim to be present at the battle scene *ad absurdum*. Like Cyrus the Younger, Ctesias is historiographically outnumbered by the two authors Xenophon and Deinon. One outcome of this numerical disadvantage, as it were, is that Ctesias' claims are discredited by comparison to Xenophon's account – including the very claim to have engaged in a diplomatic activity (below). Thus, ironically, Ctesias' claim to have been present, taken at face value, and making the author a real belligerent party, ultimately renders this very statement false.

The absurdity of Ctesias' claim to be present is echoed through a parallel with the monarch. In *Art.* 13.1, the king is encouraged by the fact that many have rejoined his camp (πλήθει τῶν συντρεχόντων πάλιν πρὸς αὐτὸν καὶ συνισταμένων ἐθάρρει) following his victory. Artaxerxes thus describes the situation as if he were a historian, and appears as a mirror image of sorts of Ctesias the historian, who is 'outnumbered' by the 'followers' of Xenophon and Deinon as if he were a historical agent.

Plutarch voices his disbelief in Ctesias' claim to have been a diplomatic envoy (*Art.* 13.5–7):

> The account of Ctesias is a glittering lie, as saying that he was sent to the Greeks with Phaullus of Zacynthus and several others. Xenophon knew that Ctesias was living with the king. For he mentioned him and had evidently come across his books. Xenophon then would not have passed over someone who came and was an interpreter of these important talks as anonymous, but rather named Phaullus of Zacynthus. In fact, Ctesias, it would seem, was marvellously ambitious, and no less biased towards Sparta and Clearchus, always giving himself places in his narrative in which he will mention many fine things about Clearchus and the Spartans.
> (5) ἐκεῖνο δὲ τοῦ Κτησίου λαμπρὸν ἤδη ψεῦσμα, τὸ πεμφθῆναι φάναι πρὸς τοὺς Ἕλληνας αὐτὸν μετὰ Φαλλύνου[30] τοῦ Ζακυνθίου καί τινων ἄλλων. (6) Ὁ γὰρ Ξενοφῶν ἠπίστατο συνδιατρίβοντα βασιλεῖ Κτησίαν· μέμνηται γὰρ αὐτοῦ καὶ τοῖς βιβλίοις τούτοις ἐντετυχηκὼς δῆλός ἐστιν· οὐκ ἂν οὖν ἐλθόντα καὶ λόγων τοσούτων ἑρμηνέα γενόμενον παρῆκεν ἀνώνυμον, Φαλῖνον δὲ τὸν Ζακύνθιον ὠνόμαζεν. (7) Ἀλλὰ δαιμονίως ὁ Κτησίας, ὡς ἔοικε, φιλότιμος ὤν, καὶ οὐχ ἧττον

---

[30] Phalinus' name is given as Φαλῖνος or Φαλύνος in the MSS of Xenophon's *Anabasis* (F). The form Φάϋλλος (as in G¹R²) is attested across the Greek world. See Fraser and Matthews (1987: 456A), (1997: 444), (2000: 417), Osborne and Byrne (1994: 443) and Plut. *Amat.* 76oab. On the other hand, only two Φαλῖνος are known (Boeotia: Fraser and Matthews, 2000: 416; Dodona: Fraser and Matthews, 1997: 444).

φιλολάκων καὶ φιλοκλέαρχος, ἀεί τινας ἐν τῇ διηγήσει χώρας ἑαυτῷ δίδωσιν, ἐν
αἷς γενόμενος πολλὰ καὶ καλὰ μεμνήσεται Κλεάρχου καὶ τῆς Λακεδαίμονος.
Φαλλύνου: Φαλλύνου PLG²R¹ | Φαύλλου G¹ R² ‖ Φαλῖνον Ziegler: Φάυλλον GΠ
Φάυλον L

Ctesias' claim to have participated in a delegation headed by Phaullus
(Phalinus?) and dispatched to negotiate with the Greek mercenaries
in the morning after the Battle of Cunaxa is doubted by Plutarch on
the grounds of a well-known section in Xenophon's work (*Anab.*
2.1.7–23) and Ctesias' unreliable character, as seen in his writing.
This was Ctesias' second major activity as a historical agent in his
original work, and he apparently presented himself as an important
part of this delegation.

Xenophon says nothing about Ctesias being involved in any activity, although he acknowledges that there was a delegation to the
Greeks, and may have witnessed the diplomatic mission to the Greek
generals. Readers were probably familiar with Xenophon's depiction
of the aftermath of the war (*Anab.* 2.1.7): in the morning, heralds
from the king and Tissaphernes arrived, all being barbarians with the
exception of one Greek, called Phalinus. The latter is presented as
the one who in fact demanded that the mercenaries surrender their
arms. After he delivered the king's request, a debate ensued among
the Greek commanders which resulted in refusal.[31]

Inventively, Xenophon's account and the readers' acquaintance with it are used by Plutarch to underscore his point. In that
version, Xenophon does not mention Ctesias at all, and this fact
is employed by Plutarch to infer that Ctesias is lying (*Art.* 13.6).
Ctesias' assumption of a central role in his own accounts is made
by this comparison to look like an 'ostensible lie', thereby foreshadowing the lie of Artaxerxes, who appropriates the honour for the
death of Cyrus. The slipperiness of truth and lie becomes evident as
Xenophon, who was discarded earlier in the biography (*Art.* 9.4)
for not being present, is now preferred over Ctesias, whose version
of the events was previously favoured because he was described as
being there.

So influential has Plutarch's presentation been that some scholars agree with this claim.[32] The inference, however, is unnecessary.
Xenophon may have chosen to remove Ctesias from his depiction of
the embassy for his own reasons, or for the sake of literary arrangement. The fact that Xenophon relied on Ctesias' *Persica* for many

---

[31] Cf. Xen. *Anab.* 2.1.10–14 and Diod. 14.25.4–6.
[32] See Schottin (1865: 2), Bigwood (1983: 346).

details,[33] hinted by Plutarch's reference to his acquaintance with Ctesias' work, shows that Xenophon really thought Ctesias to be reliable. This would make Xenophon's downplaying of Ctesias' involvement in the action while emphasising his own role a case of φιλοτιμία no less manifest than that of Ctesias.[34]

Ctesias' love of honour was presumably known in antiquity.[35] This image probably originated in his own writings, as Plutarch soon makes very clear (*Art.* 14.1):

> After the battle, the king gave gifts to the son of Artagerses, who was killed by Cyrus, and honoured Ctesias together with a few others.
>
> Μετὰ δὲ τὴν μάχην δῶρα κάλλιστα μὲν ἐξέπεμψε καὶ μέγιστα τῷ Ἀρταγέρσου παιδὶ τοῦ πεσόντος ὑπὸ Κύρου, καλῶς δὲ καὶ Κτησίαν καὶ τοὺς ἄλλους ἐτίμησε.
>
> ἐτίμησε Reiske: ἐπετίμησε GLΠ

Yet the attribution of the quality of φιλοτιμία (*Art.* 13.7), or honour-seeking, to Ctesias appears to ascribe to the writer a trait earlier specifically associated with the political sphere (*Art.* 6.1: τὸ μέγεθος τῆς ἡγεμονίας βασιλέως δεῖσθαι φρόνημα καὶ φιλοτιμίαν ἔχοντος, 'the magnitude of the empire needed someone who possessed a kingly spirit and ambition'), following his own assumption of both roles as historian and historical agent. It serves to liken him to the king. This can also be seen in the mention of the honours given to the anonymous son of Artagerses, whose very existence comes as a surprise. The honours to Artagerses' son bear upon the question of unjust awards.[36] The description anticipates the unjust award given to the king in the case of killing Cyrus, which he did not accomplish, but still took credit for.

The next appearance of Ctesias in the *Artaxerxes* is related to his third claimed activity in the real world, in a section that is divided between Ctesias as a historical agent and Ctesias as a writer (*Art.* 18.1–4):

> After he deceived Clearchus and other generals and after he broke his oaths, Tissaphernes arrested them and sent them bound in chains; Ctesias says that

---

[33] See Almagor (2012: 28–36).

[34] If Ctesias did participate in the delegation, this service might have been asked of him, since as a Greek on the spot he was most suited to converse with the mercenaries. It does not necessarily mean that Ctesias was loyal to Tissaphernes; on the contrary, the king wanted another Greek in the delegation, to balance the person loyal to his shady satrap. Cf. Lenfant (2004: XII).

[35] Diodorus (2.32.4), relying on a description that ultimately came from Ctesias' own account, claims the physician was honoured (τιμώμενος) by the king.

[36] Typical in a Persian context is the fact that the title and status of benefactor is inherited. Cf. Hdt. 6.30, 8.85; DB 4.80–8 and esp. 86–8 and Hdt. 3.84 on the benefits for the family of Otanes.

Clearchus asked him where he might find a comb. After attaining it, he took care of the hair on his head. After he enjoyed this service, he (Clearchus) gave him a ring as a symbol of friendship (to show) his relatives and members of his household in Sparta. The ring had a seal of Caryatids dancing. The soldiers chained together with Clearchus seized and consumed the food sent for him, and left little for Clearchus. Ctesias treated this problem and made sure that provisions would be sent to Clearchus, and other supplies separately to the soldiers. He performed and produced (these provisions) out of favour to Parysatis and in her knowledge. Since a piece of swine thighbone was sent to Clearchus in his daily provisions, he asked him and instructed him that a small knife should be inserted inside the meat and sent to him hidden, so as not to allow his end to be given to the king's cruelty. Yet, he (Ctesias), out of fear did not wish (to abide).

Ἐπεὶ δὲ Κλέαρχον καὶ τοὺς ἄλλους στρατηγοὺς Τισσαφέρνης ἐξηπάτησε, καὶ παρεσπόνδησεν ὅρκων γενομένων, καὶ συλλαβὼν ἀνέπεμψεν ἐν πέδαις δεδεμένους, δεηθῆναί φησιν αὐτοῦ τὸν Κλέαρχον ὁ Κτησίας, ὅπως κτενὸς εὐπορήσειε. (2) Τυχόντα δὲ καὶ τημελήσαντα τὴν κεφαλήν, ἡσθῆναί τε τῇ χρείᾳ, καὶ τὸν δακτύλιον αὐτῷ δοῦναι σύμβολον φιλίας πρὸς τοὺς ἐν Λακεδαίμονι συγγενεῖς καὶ οἰκείους· εἶναι δὲ γλυφὴν ἐν τῇ σφραγῖδι Καρυάτιδας ὀρχουμένας. (3) Τὰ δὲ πεμπόμενα σιτία τῷ Κλεάρχῳ τοὺς συνδεδεμένους στρατιώτας ἀφαιρεῖσθαι, καὶ καταναλίσκειν, ὀλίγα τῳ Κλεάρχῳ διδόντας ἀπ᾽ αὐτῶν. ἰάσασθαι δὲ καὶ τοῦτό φησιν ὁ Κτησίας, πλείονα τῷ Κλεάρχῳ πέμπεσθαι διαπραξάμενος, ἰδίᾳ δ᾽ ἕτερα τοῖς στρατιώταις δίδοσθαι· καὶ ταῦτα μὲν ὑπουργῆσαι καὶ παρασχεῖν χάριτι καὶ γνώμῃ τῆς Παρυσάτιδος. (4) Πεμπομένου δὲ καθ᾽ ἡμέραν τῷ Κλεάρχῳ κωλῆνος ἐπὶ τοῖς σιτίοις, παρακαλεῖν αὐτὸν καὶ διδάσκειν ὡς χρὴ μικρὸν εἰς τὸ κρέας ἐμβαλόντα μαχαίριον ἀποκρύψαντα πέμψαι, καὶ μὴ περιιδεῖν ἐν τῇ βασιλέως ὠμότητι τὸ τέλος αὐτοῦ γενόμενον· αὐτὸν δὲ φοβούμενον μὴ ἐθελῆσαι.

Τισσαφέρνης *Π*: Τισσαφέρνης GL‖ ἰάσασθαι L²: ἰᾶσθαι G*Π*L¹

The episode in which Ctesias assists Clearchus must have been an important scene in the *Persica* and one that connected the composition of his work with the activity of the real Ctesias. If the physician did participate in the embassy of Phaullus/ Phalinus, then perhaps that was the first occasion on which he met Clearchus.[37] If this is true, the physician's participation in that delegation was crucial to the rest of the story, in which the connection between the two continued during the Spartan commander's captivity. Plutarch seems to be suspicious, and the indirect speech form of most of this passage allegedly alludes to this doubt; nevertheless, he relates both scenes.[38]

The image of the Caryatid girls is a powerful one, and has to do with their double representation of movement and frozen stability. On the one hand, they were known as dancers. Each year they

[37] Indeed, Plutarch's employment of the term φιλοκλέαρχος in *Art.* 13.5–6 might imply that the original story at that point had something to do with Clearchus.

[38] Plutarch's playful use of the word ἰάσασθαι ('treated'), said of Ctesias' assistance, is a token of this sceptical tone, alluding to Ctesias' profession.

danced for Artemis in the Peloponnesian city of Caryae, at the border of Laconia and Arcadia, which at some point was under Spartan rule.[39] On the other hand, they gave their name to static columns in the form of women. Most famous are those of the Athenian *Erechtheum*.[40] The presence of the image of the dancing girls within a ring[41] has again to do with the tension between movement and immovability, and may well be another *metapoetic* image, referring to Ctesias' two roles as a historian and a historical agent, and symbolising the relationship between the fixed written historical text and the historical changes it is meant to capture (more below).

The plea to hide a knife in the dish, done at the request (or knowledge) of Parysatis,[42] surely anticipates the poison hidden in Stateira's meal, handed to her with Parysatis' knowledge (below) and administered through a knife. Ctesias (the agent) apparently does not wish to provide Clearchus the means to kill himself as much as Ctesias (the author) does not wish to deliver a negative image of Clearchus. However, in his description, Ctesias (the author) will provide a knife to Parysatis to kill Stateira later on for her part in the killing of Clearchus, as the story continues (*Art.* 18.5–8):

> The king agreed not to kill Clearchus in response to his mother's pleading, and promised this. He was convinced, however, by Stateira to kill everyone except Menon. Because of this Parysatis plotted against Stateira and prepared the poison to be used against her, but what he says is unlikely and is illogical concerning the motive, if Parysatis did such a terrible deed and venture because of Clearchus and dared to kill the lawful wife of the king, and the spouse who raised his children to inherit the throne. Rather, it is obvious that he (Ctesias) overdramatised this in memory of Clearchus. For he says that after the generals were killed, the bodies of the rest were torn by dogs and birds, but to the corpse of Clearchus a squall of wind brought a great pile of earth, covering and hiding his body. Shortly afterwards, a few scattered dates created an amazing grove, and a shady place, so that the king regretted very much that he had killed a man dear to the gods, Clearchus.
> (5) Βασιλέα δὲ τῇ μὲν μητρὶ παραιτουμένῃ μὴ κτεῖναι τὸν Κλέαρχον ὁμολογῆσαι, καὶ ὀμόσαι· πεισθέντα δ᾽ αὖθις ὑπὸ τῆς Στατείρας ἀποκτεῖναι πάντας πλὴν Μένωνος. (6) Ἐκ δὲ τούτου τὴν Παρύσατιν ἐπιβουλεῦσαι τῇ Στατείρᾳ καὶ συσκευάσασθαι τὴν φαρμακείαν κατ᾽ αὐτῆς, οὐκ εἰκότα λέγων ἀλλὰ πολλὴν

---

[39] On the dance see Luc. *Salt.* 10. On the city see von Geisau (1919). Cf. Paus. 3.10.7, 4.16.9; Pollux 4.104. For literary representations see Plin. *NH* 36.4.23, 34.19.92; Pollux 5.97.

[40] These columns were first called by this name by Lincaeus (*ap.* Athen. 6.241d). See the explanation of Vitruvius, 1.1.5 together with Fiechter (1919), Rowland and Howe (1999: 136). For another explanation see Plommer (1979: 100). See Homolle (1917), Vickers (1985) and Rykwert (1996).

[41] For an example see Boardman (1970: n. 718); cf. Bigwood (1995: 140).

[42] Some historians accept that Ctesias treated Clearchus at Parysatis' request: Stevenson (1997: 73); Briant (2002a: 265, 238), Lenfant (2004: XII–XIII).

ἀλογίαν ἔχοντα τῆς αἰτίας, εἰ δεινὸν ἔργον οὕτως ἔδρασε, καὶ παρεκινδύνευσεν ἡ
Παρύσατις διὰ Κλέαρχον, ἀνελεῖν τολμήσασα τὴν γνησίαν βασιλέως γυναῖκα καὶ
τέκνων κοινωνὸν ἐπὶ βασιλείᾳ τρεφομένων. (7) Ἀλλὰ ταῦτα μὲν οὐκ ἄδηλον, ὡς
ἐπιτραγῳδεῖται τῇ Κλεάρχου μνήμῃ. Καὶ γὰρ ἀναιρεθέντων φησὶ τῶν στρατηγῶν,
τοὺς μὲν ἄλλους ὑπὸ κυνῶν σπαράττεσθαι καὶ ὀρνέων, τῷ δὲ Κλεάρχου νεκρῷ
θύελλαν ἀνέμου γῆς θῖνα πολλὴν φέρουσαν ἐπιχῶσαι καὶ ἐπικρύψαι τὸ σῶμα.
(8) Φοινίκων δέ τινων διασπαρέντων, ὀλίγῳ χρόνῳ θαυμαστὸν ἄλσος ἀναφῦναι,
καὶ κατασκιάσαι τὸν τόπον, ὥστε καὶ βασιλεῖ σφόδρα μεταμέλειν, ὡς ἄνδρα θεοῖς
φίλον ἀνῃρηκότι τὸν Κλέαρχον.

Plutarch delivers a picture in which truth and falsehood/fiction are
blended together in a series of *metalepses*. In the first half of *Art.* 18,
Clearchus (the real figure) fears the cruel image of the king which
Ctesias (the author) has created (*Art.* 18.4), and therefore would
rather kill himself; the image is so powerful that even Ctesias (the
agent) believes it, and would not smuggle a knife into the food
provided for Clearchus. Similarly, in the second half, the king falls
for the image of Clearchus as beloved by the gods, another fiction
created by Ctesias the author (*Art.* 18.8), and therefore regrets
having killed him. One may note that while Ctesias does not wish to
hide (ἀποκρύψαντα: 18.4) the dagger out of fear of the king, the gods
do hide (ἐπικρύψαι: 18.7) Clearchus' body and save it from the fate
the king destined for it. The description of Clearchus' body is very
close to the Homeric report on the preservation of Hector's corpse:
the expression θεοῖς φίλον ('dear to the gods') here is close to *Il.*
24.66-67: Ἕκτωρ φίλτατος . . . θεοῖσι ('Hector dearest to the gods').[43]
Hector's body is saved from the dogs (*Il.* 23.184-6), and Apollo lets
a black cloud cover it (*Il.* 23.188–191; cf. 24.18–21 on the golden
Aegis).[44] Making the king fear this divine intervention would make
him understand the Greek significance of this image as a reader of
the (Greek) text of Ctesias.

Like the lie of the official version (claiming that Artaxerxes has
killed Cyrus himself) – which assumes a life of its own and becomes
real – the fictional stories of Ctesias become factual. The literary
device Plutarch uses to display these ideas is the employment of indirect speech, the mode in which most of *Art.* 18 is written. This device
aptly captures the intricate relation between the fixed written historical text and the historical movement, as in the image of dancing girls
in the ring above; it epitomises the relationship between Ctesias
the author and Ctesias the historical agent. It is no wonder that the
biographer also inserts the detail concerning the shadowy grove of

[43] Cf. Plut. *Sert.* 20.5. Cf. Konrad (1994: 171–2).
[44] See Segal (1971: 57–8).

palm trees, with the Platonic connotations of shadows,[45] presumably hinting at the fictionality of the scene. Similarly, the two allegedly external signs connected with Clearchus, namely the ring as a token for friendship (*Art.* 18.2: φιλίας) and the palm trees as a token that he is loved by the gods (*Art.* 18.8: θεοῖς φίλον) are only present within the text.

After mentioning the murder of Stateira twice before its actual occurrence, Plutarch turns to the assassination (*Art.* 19.1–10). The repetition stresses that he accepts the temporal sequence of Ctesias but not the motive the physician attributes to Parysatis in executing it. Since this scene refers both to Ctesias and Deinon as authors who described it, part of the discussion will be found in Chapter 4 below:

> So Parysatis, who hated Stateira from the start, and since there was a deep jealousy involved, with her seeing her power based on the king's respect and honour, while that of (Stateira), based on love and trust, was stable and strong. She aimed at what she thought were greater things. She had a trusted and highly able servant girl called Gigis, whom Deinon claims prepared the poison, but Ctesias (says) only knew of it unwillingly; he names the giver of the poison Belitaras, while Deinon calls him Melantas. After their previous suspicion and disagreement, they now began to frequent each other and to dine together, so that together with their fears and remaining on guard, they used the same dishes and from the same portions. There is a small bird in Persia, which has no excrement and is completely filled from the inside with lard, and they think that the animal feeds on wind and dew. It is called *rhyntaces*. Ctesias says that Parysatis cut it in two with a small knife smeared with poison on one side, and wiped dry the poison from the other side. The undefiled and pure (half) she took into her mouth, and gave to Stateira the poisoned one. Yet Deinon (says) not Parysatis but Melantas had cut with the knife and served the poisonous parts of the meat before Stateira.
>
> Ἡ δ' οὖν Παρύσατις, μίσους τε πρὸς τὴν Στάτειραν ἐξ ἀρχῆς ὑποκειμένου καὶ ζηλοτυπίας, ὁρῶσα τὴν μὲν αὐτῆς δύναμιν αἰδουμένου βασιλέως καὶ τιμῶντος οὖσαν, τὴν δ' ἐκείνης ἔρωτι καὶ πίστει βέβαιον καὶ ἰσχυράν, ἐπεβούλευσεν ὑπὲρ τῶν μεγίστων ὡς ᾤετο παραβαλλομένη. (2) Θεράπαιναν εἶχε πιστὴν καὶ δυναμένην παρ' αὐτῇ μέγιστον ὄνομα Γίγιν, ἣν ὁ μὲν Δείνων ὑπουργῆσαι τῇ φαρμακείᾳ φησί, συγγνῶναι δὲ μόνον ἄκουσαν ὁ Κτησίας· τὸν δὲ δόντα τὸ φάρμακον οὗτος μὲν ὀνομάζει Βελιτάραν, ὁ δὲ Δείνων Μελάνταν. (3) Ἐκ δὲ τῆς πρόσθεν ὑποψίας καὶ διαφορᾶς ἀρξάμεναι πάλιν εἰς τὸ αὐτὸ φοιτᾶν καὶ συνδειπνεῖν ἀλλήλαις, ὅμως <διὰ> τὸ δεδιέναι καὶ φυλάττεσθαι τοῖς αὐτοῖς σιτίοις καὶ ἀπὸ τῶν αὐτῶν ἐχρῶντο. (4) Γίνεται δὲ μικρὸν ἐν Πέρσαις ὀρνίθιον, ᾧ περιττώματος οὐδέν <ἐν>εστιν, ἀλλ' ὅλον διάπλεων πιμελῆς τὰ ἐντός, ᾗ καὶ νομίζουσιν ἀνέμῳ καὶ δρόσῳ τρέφεσθαι τὸ ζῷον· ὀνομάζεται δὲ ῥυντάκης. (5) Τοῦτό φησιν ὁ Κτησίας μικρᾷ μαχαιρίδι κεχρισμένῃ τῷ φαρμάκῳ κατὰ θάτερα τὴν Παρύσατιν διαιροῦσαν, ἐκμάξαι τῷ

---

[45] For the Plutarchan habit of inserting shadows into his adaptation of his sources cf. Xen. *Hell.* 4.30 and Plut. *Ages.* 12.1. On shadows in Plato see the cave parable (Plat. *Rep.* 7.515a–e), cf. *Rep.* 6.510a, *Phaedr.* 229ab.

Table 1

	Ctesias	Deinon
Time of the murder	ὕστερον (6.9)	ἐν τῷ πολέμῳ (6.9)
The one who prepares the poison	Παρύσατιν . . . συσκευάσασθαι τὴν φαρμακείαν (18.6)	Γίγιν, ἣν . . . ὑπουργῆσαι τῇ φαρμακείᾳ (19.2)
The one who gives the poison (τὸν δὲ δόντα τὸ φάρμακον: 19.2)	Βελιτάραν (19.2)	Μελάνταν (19.2)
The one who slices the bird	Παρύσατιν διαιροῦσαν (19.5)	Μελάνταν τέμνοντα τιθέναι κατὰ τὴν Στάτειραν (19.6)
The one who serves the dish	Παρύσατιν . . . δοῦναι δὲ τῇ Στατείρᾳ (19.5)	Μελάνταν . . . τιθέναι κατὰ τὴν Στάτειραν (19.6)

ἑτέρῳ μέρει τὸ φάρμακον· καὶ τὸ μὲν ἄχραντον καὶ καθαρὸν εἰς τὸ στόμα βαλοῦσαν αὐτὴν ἐσθίειν, δοῦναι δὲ τῇ Στατείρᾳ τὸ πεφαρμαγμένον. (6) Ὁ δὲ Δείνων οὐ τὴν Παρύσατιν ἀλλὰ τὸν Μελάνταν τέμνοντα τῷ μαχαιρίῳ τὰ φαρμασσόμενα τῶν κρεῶν τιθέναι κατὰ τὴν Στάτειραν.

<διὰ> add. Ziegler | τὸ GL¹: τῷ *ΠL*² <ἅμα> τῷ Jacoby || <ἐν>εστιν add. Ziegler: ἐστιν GL*Π*

There are several variances in detail between the two authors, also mentioned in *Art.* 6, 18 and 19 (see Table 1). In Ctesias' account, the person who administered the poison is called Belitaras; Deinon gives him a Greek name, Melantas (*Art.* 19.2), and has him cutting the bird with the poisoned knife (*Art.* 19.6). Ctesias, however, claims that Parysatis is the one who slices the bird. Ctesias seems to implicate the queen mother in the murder, while Deinon appears to exonerate her from the charges.

The recurrent theme in *Art.* 19 is duality, displayed through the pairing of characters (Parysatis/Stateira, Parysatis/Gigis, Parysatis/Melantas). The figure of the poison provider is called by two different names, as if presenting two persons (*Art.* 19.2). The most obvious example is the splitting in two of the bird used for the poisoning (*Art.* 19.4). This duplication creates some problems of understanding, as the difference between the person who gives the poison and the one who serves the dish is not clear.[46] In this debate, Plutarch no longer prefers one variant since its author was present. Such consideration is completely absent from the depiction of the historiographic debate. The impression is that Plutarch refrains from adopting one version as

---

[46] See Stevenson (1987: 27 n. 2; 1997: 67–8).

correct, but rather leaves the two without commenting on the validity of either. This is in contrast to his usual practice earlier, in which Ctesias' version is accepted or rejected. In fact, Plutarch takes this theme of duality and transfers it to the historiographic plane, making the differences between Ctesias and Deinon appear as if the section is also virtually torn asunder at several points.

The final mention of Ctesias in Plutarch's *Artaxerxes* refers to his last diplomatic mission at the service of the king (*Art.* 21.2–4):

> Seeing that he was in need of a force to pursue his own plans while the king's army needed a good leader, he [sc. Conon] sent a letter to the king disclosing his plans. He ordered the letter-carrier to deliver it to the king through Zenon the Cretan dancer or Polycritus the Mendaean physician, and if these men were not present, then Ctesias the physician. It is said that Ctesias, after receiving the letter, added to Conon's instructions the request that he be sent to Conon, to assist him on matters concerning the sea. Ctesias, however, says that the king enforced this service on him of his own will.
>
> (2) Ὁρῶν δὲ καὶ τοὺς ἑαυτοῦ λογισμοὺς δυνάμεως καὶ τὴν βασιλέως δύναμιν ἀνδρὸς ἔμφρονος δεομένην, ἔπεμψεν ἐπιστολὴν βασιλεῖ περὶ ὧν διενοεῖτο. (3) Καὶ ταύτην ἐκέλευσε τὸν κομίζοντα μάλιστα μὲν ἀποδοῦναι διὰ Ζήνωνος τοῦ Κρητὸς ἢ Πολυκρίτου τοῦ Μενδαίου· τούτων δ' ἦν ὁ μὲν Ζήνων ὀρχηστής, ὁ δὲ Πολύκριτος ἰατρός· ἂν δ' οὗτοι μὴ παρῶσι, διὰ Κτησίου τοῦ ἰατροῦ. (4) Λέγεται δ' ὁ Κτησίας τὴν ἐπιστολὴν λαβὼν παρεγγράψαι τοῖς ὑπὸ τοῦ Κόνωνος ἐπεσταλμένοις, ὅπως καὶ Κτησίαν ἀποστείλῃ πρὸς αὐτόν, ὡς ὠφέλιμον ὄντα ταῖς ἐπὶ θαλάσσῃ πράξεσιν· ὁ δὲ Κτησίας αὐτὸν ἀφ' ἑαυτοῦ βασιλέα φησὶ προσθεῖναι τὴν λειτουργίαν αὐτῷ ταύτην.

The Athenian general Conon, who resided in Cyprus after the disaster in the sea Battle of Aegospotami (405 BCE),[47] sent messages to the king to request help in defeating the Spartans.[48] Plutarch begins *Art.* 21 with the king's employment of Conon to expel Sparta from the Aegean Sea, and continues in the latter half (*Art.* 21.5–6) with Artaxerxes' use of the Spartan Antalcidas to regain control of the Greek cities in Asia Minor. The recurrent idea is that the internal division among the Greeks worked in the Great King's service. Like Artaxerxes, who used mediators, so did Conon himself (Zenon and others). The Persian king is portrayed as enjoying the success of others, Conon and Antalcidas (both are the grammatical subjects of *Art.* 21.1, 21.3, 21.6). Even the only action that Artaxerxes is seen to instigate in one version, namely, requesting Ctesias to join Conon, comes in indirect speech quoted by Ctesias.

---

[47] On the battle see Ehrhardt (1970), Wylie (1986), Strauss (1983). On Conon reaching Cyprus see Xen. *Hell.* 2.1.28–9, Isoc. *Phil.* 62, Diod. 13.106.6, Plut. *Lys.* 11.5, *Alc.* 37.4. Asmonti (2015: 104–14).

[48] Letters to the king's commanders: cf. Isoc. *Phil.* 63, *Evag.* 55.

The juxtaposition of the King's Peace and the changes Ctesias introduced to the letter addressed to the king is not accidental. Like Ctesias, who inserted into the epistle the request that he be sent on a diplomatic mission and made it look like it originated from Conon, the king dictated a peace settlement to Greece which looked like it came from the Greeks themselves. Ctesias echoes the king's demeanour, in that handing over responsibility to others seems to explain his success.

Plutarch includes two accounts of the eventual release of Ctesias from his service to the king. In the first, it is the physician himself who takes a letter from Conon and inserts in it a request to be sent away; the second portrays it as the idea of the monarch. Here we see two sides of Artaxerxes, as either passive or actively taking the initiative. The two facets of the king are foregrounded: the passive man, relying on others to do the work for him, or the honour-seeking monarch, acting to preserve his throne. When the king is active Ctesias is passive, and vice versa. The tension between Ctesias the historian and the historical agent gives way now to a certain mixture of the two. In a very clever presentation, Ctesias is made to claim, as a historian, that he was merely *acting* on the order of the king. As a historical figure, Ctesias is made to insert items in a *written* text.

The only reference to Ctesias outside the *Artaxerxes* comes from the work *De sollertia animalium* (*On the Cleverness of Animals*), a dialogue on the question of whether land animals or sea animals are cleverer. The somewhat artificial division into these two groups as well as the absence of a conclusion[49] may indicate that apart from the aim of discrediting the Stoic refusal to admit reason to all animals (cf. *De soll. anim.* 1–8.959b–965e),[50] Plutarch is being playful in the arguments of this work, their order and the use of anecdotal examples. Near the end of the argument in favour of the terrestrial animals comes this passage within the argument of the interlocutor Aristotimus (*De soll. anim.* 21.974e):

> Less marvellous, although still incredible, are the things done by those beings which have a grasp of number and the ability to count, like the bovine near Susa. They water the royal park there by buckets [elevated by] wheels, whose number is defined. Each cow carries one hundred buckets each day. More than that is not possible. Not unawares, and not even if someone forces them. When often, for the sake of experiment, they add to the number, [the

---

[49] See Newmyer (2014: 224, 226–31).
[50] See Babut (1969: 54), Newmyer (1992: 44–8), Becchi (2000: 207–8; 2001: 123–4).

cow] resists and will not proceed after she gives the regular amount. So closely she adds and remembers the principal amount – as Ctesias of Cnidus reported.

Ἧττον δὲ ταῦτα θαυμαστά, καίπερ ὄντα θαυμάσια, ποιοῦσιν αἱ νόησιν ἀριθμοῦ καὶ δύναμιν τοῦ ἀριθμεῖν ἔχουσαι φύσεις, ὥσπερ ἔχουσιν αἱ περὶ Σοῦσα βόες. Εἰσὶ γὰρ αὐτόθι τὸν βασιλικὸν παράδεισον ἄρδουσαι περιάκτοις ἀντλήμασιν, ὧν ὥρισται τὸ πλῆθος· ἑκατὸν γὰρ ἑκάστη βοῦς ἀναφέρει καθ᾽ ἡμέραν ἑκάστην ἀντλήματα· πλείονα δ᾽ οὐκ ἔστιν οὔτε λαθεῖν οὔτε βιάσασθαι βουλόμενον· ἀλλὰ καὶ πείρας ἕνεκα πολλάκις προστιθέντων ὑφίσταται καὶ οὐ πρόεισιν, ἀποδοῦσα τὸ τεταγμένον· οὕτως ἀκριβῶς συντίθησι καὶ καταμνημονεύει τὸ κεφάλαιον, ὡς Κτησίας ὁ Κνίδιος ἱστόρηκε.

Immediately after this section, Plutarch claims that the Libyans laugh (καταγελῶσι) at the Egyptians for recounting a marvellous story on the oryx: that it cries when the Dog Star (Sirius) rises. This juxtaposition may insinuate that these stories are not to be taken in earnest. The examples may be brought tongue in cheek, as if showing that the argument for considering animals as rational beings involves the contrary thought of seeing some men as irrational (or gullible) creatures. In fact, when we reach the second part of the debate, the speaker Phaedimus promises (*De soll. anim.* 22.975d) not to employ 'Egyptian fables or unattested tales of Indians or Libyans' (οὔτ᾽ Αἰγυπτίων μύθους οὔτ᾽ ἀμαρτύρους Ἰνδῶν . . . ἢ Λιβύων διηγήσεις); at the end of his argument (*De soll. anim.* 36.985c), however, Phaedimus apologises for using examples from the realm of myth (μῦθον) to 'a point furthest from the credulous' (πορρωτέρω τοῦ πιθανοῦ). The context would thus make the reference to Ctesias not entirely sincere, so that the speaker may not even believe it himself.[51]

Not all the details Plutarch provides in this work are explicitly attributed to authors. The ascription to Ctesias, therefore, may be significant in instilling some uncertainties, bearing in mind his reputation as a paradoxographer.[52] Noteworthy is the fact that, since the two arguments are meant to parallel each other, the counterpart for this anecdote in the realm of the water animals (*De soll. anim.* 26.977e) is another Persian example derived from Herodotus (the use of a net: Hdt. 6.31), but is uncredited, as if the readers/listeners should know its original venue.[53] In all, Herodotus is alluded

[51] Cf. Newmyer (2008: 118, 122) on the cattle's 'relative numerousness judgements' rather than absolute numerosity.

[52] Among authors mentioned in that work, the only other famous paradoxographer is Myrsilus of Lesbos (*De soll. anim.* 36.984e).

[53] The fact that this example anthropomorphises animals, and is made to ascribe reason to fish by the analogy it makes between the fishermen's use of the net and its employment by the Persians against men, reverses Herodotus' allegory in an ironic way.

to several times in the water animals section (e.g. *De soll. anim.* 31.980d ~ 2.68, 33.981f ~ 2.93, 36.984d ~ 1.24) but not even once in the terrestrial animals part, as if Plutarch is subtly utilising the association of the two authors, current in his time, in order to set them as an opposing pair in the two groups of animals.[54]

CTESIAS AND PLUTARCH'S CTESIAS

Let us examine now the way in which what we know or can reasonably say of Ctesias and his writing, gathered from other sources, compares with the impression given in Plutarch's explicit references to Ctesias as seen in the first part of this chapter.

Ctesias the author and the historical agent

As in Plutarch's allusions, Ctesias was famous in antiquity mainly for two things: his writings and his soujourn in the court of Artaxerxes II as a physician (*Suda*, s.v. Κτησίας, κ 2521 Adler ~ Tzetz. *Chil.* 1.82–6). His *Persica* (*Persian Matters*) was a very ambitious project, covering the period from the legendary Assyrian king Ninus (*FGrH* 688 F 1 = Diod. 2.1.4–2.7.1) to the contemporary days of Artaxerxes II in twenty-three books. The year 398/7 BCE was the last year mentioned in his work (Diod. 14.46.6), terminating with the story of the departure of Ctesias himself from Persia.

One may wonder whether Ctesias' *Persica* was ever read in its entirety soon after publication or at all. First, because it was so voluminous, it seems to have been preserved only in summaries, which eventually doomed the original work to oblivion. Second, at an early stage, the work was divided into several parts. Books 1–6, dealing with pre-Persian history and sometimes called *Assyriaca* (Strabo 14.2.15), are largely known to us via Diodorus (1.56.5–6, 2.1–28, 2.31.10–2.34.6) and most probably some fragments of Nicolaus of Damascus.[55] The books were further divided into three volumes of Assyrian history (books 1–3) and three of Median history (books 4–6).

We know the essential content of books 7–23 from the summary of the Byzantine patriarch and scholar Photius (810–c.893 CE). In his

---

[54] When Herodotus also fell out of favour as an unreliable prose author, the two were often denigrated together. See Strabo, 1.2.35, 11.6.3; Luc. *VH* 2.31, *Philops.* 2; see Lenfant (2007).

[55] *Exc. de Insid.* p. 3.24 de Boor = *FGrH* 90 F1, *Exc. de Virt.* p. 329.16 Büttner-Wobst = *FGrH* 90 F2, *Exc. de Insid.* p. 4.23 de Boor = *FGrH* 90 F3, *Exc. de Virt.* p. 330.5 Büttner-Wobst = *FGrH* 90 F4, *Exc. de Virt.* p. 335.20 Büttner-Wobst = *FGrH* 90 F5, *Exc. de Insid.* p.23.23 de Boor = *FGrH* 90 F66. On the *Assyriaca* see Lenfant (2004: XXXIX–LIV).

composition Βιβλιοθήκη (*Bibliotheca, Library*), Photius summarised the *Persica* as well as Ctesias' book *Indica* (*Indian Matters*, below) and included both epitomes in codex 72 of his work.[56] This is what Photius says of Ctesias' work (*Bibl.* cod. 72, p. 35 b 35–36 a 6):

> I read the work of Ctesias of Cnidus, the *Persica* in 23 books. But in the first six books he deals with Assyrian matters and anything that happened before the Persian matters. From the seventh book he goes through Persian affairs. In the seventh, eighth, ninth, (tenth), eleventh, twelfth and thirteenth books he expounds the deeds of Cyrus, Cambyses, the Magus, Darius and Xerxes. In almost all points he posits different versions from those of Herodotus, and refutes him as a liar in many points and calls him writer of myths. He is after all younger than Herodotus. Ctesias claims that he himself was an eye-witness for a large part of what he narrates or became an ear-witness from the Persians themselves when he was not able to see them for himself. In this manner he wrote his history. He does not only relate the contradictory things from Herodotus, but also disagrees with Xenophon son of Gryllus on several matters.
>
> Ἀνεγνώσθη βιβλίον Κτησίου τοῦ Κνιδίου τὰ Περσικὰ ἐν βιβλίοις κγ'. Ἀλλ᾽ ἐν μὲν τοῖς πρώτοις ς' τά τε ᾽Ασσύρια διαλαμβάνει καὶ ὅσα πρὸ τῶν Περσικῶν, ἀπὸ μέντοι τοῦ ζ' τὰ Περσικὰ διεξέρχεται. Καὶ ἐν μὲν τῷ ζ' καὶ η' καὶ <θ' καὶ> ι' καὶ ια' καὶ ιβ' καὶ ιγ' διέξεισι τὰ περὶ Κύρου καὶ Καμβύσου καὶ τοῦ μάγου, Δαρείου τε καὶ τοῦ Ξέρξου, σχεδὸν ἐν ἅπασιν ἀντικείμενα Ἡροδότῳ ἱστορῶν, ἀλλὰ καὶ ψεύστην αὐτὸν ἀπελέγχων ἐν πολλοῖς, καὶ λογοποιὸν ἀποκαλῶν· καὶ γὰρ νεώτερος μέν ἐστιν αὐτοῦ. Φησὶ δὲ αὐτὸν τῶν πλειόνων ἃ ἱστορεῖ αὐτόπτην γενόμενον ἢ παρ᾽ αὐτῶν Περσῶν, ἔνθα τὸ ὁρᾶν μὴ ἐνεχώρει, αὐτήκοον καταστάντα, οὕτω τὴν ἱστορίαν συγγράψαι. Οὐχ Ἡροδότῳ δὲ μόνῳ τἀναντία ἱστορεῖ, ἀλλὰ καὶ πρὸς Ξενοφῶντα τὸν Γρύλλου ἐπ᾽ ἐνίων διαφωνεῖ.
>
> <θ' καὶ> add. Jacoby

Photius seems to imply that the work was based on a division to hexads. The first six books (*Assyriaca*) dealt with affairs prior to the Persians. The next six books addressed the history of Persia till the death of Darius. It would seem that Xerxes' accession marked book 13 (*FGrH* 688 F 13.24), and this hexad continued till the death of Darius II in book 18 (see *FGrH* 688 F 15.56). The last section (books 19–23), narrating events during the reign of Artaxerxes II, do not form a hexad. This may imply that the project was unfinished by Ctesias.[57]

---

[56] This work is dedicated to Photius' brother Tarasius, and contains 279 codices in which are summarised the essential points in the books which the dedicatee did not read. For the date of its composition see Mango (1975: 38, 40–2), Wilson (1983: 85, 93–4), Lemerle (1986: 38), Treadgold (1980: 30). On his work method see Hägg (1973: 213–18), Wilson (1983: 95–6), Lemerle (1986: 39–40, 223–4). Photius claims to have edited the summaries with a secretary (*hypographeus*: *Bibl.* Intr. cf. Treadgold 1977, 1980: 24), relying on memory/note (*mneme*). That is, they were either dictated from notes or from memory. Some parts betray memory slips (cf. *Bibl.* cod. 189 p. 146 a 13). See Stronk (2010: 130–46).

[57] Cf. Smith (1881: 28 n. 2), König (1972: 28). The division into books is Ctesias'; see, however, Jacoby (1922: 2049–3), Lenfant (2004: XXVII n. 79), Waters (2017: 10).

The medical treatment of the king was presumably not the main reason for Ctesias' presence at court: Photius (*Bibl.* 72 p. 44 a 31= *FGrH* 688 F 27.69) claims that Ctesias was the physician of Parysatis (ἰατρὸς ὢν Παρυσάτιδος). As we mostly hear of Greek physicians treating Persian royal women (Democedes and Atossa: Hdt. 3.133–4; Apollonides of Cos and Amytis: *FGrH* 688 F 14.44), one might not be off the mark in presuming that Ctesias was largely employed to attend to Parysatis. All the Greek doctors in Persia we know of are reported to be saving a male noble (Democedes treats Darius I: Hdt. 3.132 and Apollonides of Cos rescues Megabyzus: *FGrH* 688 F 14.34) and employed at the service of women.[58] Ctesias' assistance to the king occurred when he happened to be at the scene of battle, probably escorting the royal entourage.[59]

Plutarch does not seem to know that Ctesias was a captive in Persia. Diodorus (2.32.4) is the only source that mentions the circumstances that brought Ctesias to the Great King's service and the only one who mentions captivity:

> Ctesias of Cnidus lived at the time of the expedition of Cyrus against his brother Artaxerxes. He was taken as prisoner; because of his medical knowledge, he was taken up by the king, and for seventeen years was held in continuous honour by him.
> Κτησίας δὲ ὁ Κνίδιος τοῖς μὲν χρόνοις ὑπῆρξε κατὰ τὴν Κύρου στρατείαν ἐπὶ Ἀρταξέρξην τὸν ἀδελφόν, γενόμενος δ᾽ αἰχμάλωτος, καὶ διὰ τὴν ἰατρικὴν ἐπιστήμην ἀναληφθεὶς ὑπὸ τοῦ βασιλέως, ἑπτακαίδεκα (?) ἔτη διετέλεσε τιμώμενος ὑπ᾽ αὐτοῦ.

It does not seem probable that Ctesias was captured during the Battle of Cunaxa.[60] Truesdell Brown (1978a: 7–10) proposes that Ctesias was captured during Pissouthnes' revolt (414 BCE). Jan Stronk (2004–5: 102–4, 2010: 8) and Llewellyn-Jones and Robson (2010: 14) suggest that it occurred during the revolt of Amorges (begun c. 413 BCE). All these explanations are speculative,[61] and assume too long a hiatus between Ctesias' alleged captivity and the service at the king's court (mostly spent at the service of the satrap

---

[58] On Ctesias' contemporary Greek gynaecological knowledge and practice, found in the Hippocratic texts, see Hanson (1991) and King (1998). On the role of the physician in the Achaemenid court, see Xen. *Cyr.* 8.2.24. See Briant (2002a: 264–6), Llewellyn-Jones and Robson (2010: 15). Other physicians were Egyptians (cf. Hdt. 3.129). See Almagor (2015: 83–5).
[59] On the manner in which royal women travelled with the court during military campaigns or the seasonal migration of the king see Brosius (1996: 84, 87, 90–3). Cf. Curt. Ruf. 3.3.22–5, Plut. *Alex.* 43.2.
[60] *Pace* Bähr (1824: 13–15), König (1972:17 n. 1) or Gardiner-Garden (1987: 1); cf. Jacoby (1922: 2033–5).
[61] Smith (1881: 28). See the equally unconvincing attempt of Stevenson (1997: 4–6).

Tissaphernes, according to one version). In fact, it might be that Ctesias never claimed to have been captured: one would assume this sort of story to have been found in some form in Photius' epitome had the physician dwelled on these circumstances.

The vocabulary Diodorus mentions is completely his own: the phrase γενόμενος αἰχμάλωτος ('taken prisoner') and variants appear elsewhere in his work (2.44.2, 9.2.3, 9.33.4, 12.p.1.64, 12.57.1, 12.72.6, 17.68.5).[62] One may safely presume that given the absence of any other information concerning the incarceration of Ctesias, and given Diodorus' interest in prisoners of war observable elsewhere, this picture of Ctesias the prisoner of war was the outcome of his own interpretation. If this is true, it would imply that Diodorus had no more reliable information than we do on the circumstances that brought Ctesias to Persia. Diodorus' guess, however, may seem to be founded on certain similarities between Ctesias and Herodotus' account of Democedes of Croton, as noted above.[63] Pierre Briant (2002a: 264) is most probably correct in assuming that Ctesias was contracted, invited to the king's court because of his medical skills. Ctesias was not only a contemporary of Hippocrates of Cos (fl. 420 BCE),[64] but also related to him by being Asclepiads (*FGrH* 688 T4 = F 67 and Plat. *Phaedr.* 270c; *Prot.* 311b).[65]

The MSS of Diodoros have 'seventeen years' (ἑπτακαίαδεκα) for the number of years Ctesias spent in Persia.[66] It might be that this number of years is a fabrication originating from the physician, allegedly to show his superiority over any other predecessor in his sojourn in Persia.[67] Yet it could be that neither Ctesias nor Diodorus employed this figure. The emendation of the text to 'seven years' (ἑπτὰ ἔτη), as proposed by Karl Müller (1844: 2) and followed by Robert Drews (1973: 103) and Bigwood (1978: 19) might be in place. This would mean that Ctesias began his sojourn corresponding to Artaxerxes' rise to power (405/4 BCE).[68] It might even be the case that another ancient reader, of Diodorus or of the source he used, assumed that Ctesias' stay in Persia was longer, and had begun

---

[62] The following argument also appears in Almagor (2012: 11–13).

[63] Based on Ctesias' own presentation. Cf. Brosius (2011: 74–5).

[64] Cf. Lenfant (2004: VIII).

[65] For the fact that the difference between the Coan and Cnidian schools of medicine were not that great, see Penfield (1957), Smith (1973) and Jouanna (1974). See Kollesch (1989), Lonie (1978).

[66] This figure appears also in Tzetzes (*Chil.* 1.85–9 = 1.82–6 Kiessling), who is known to have read Diodorus.

[67] See Jacoby (1922: 2033). Cf. Bigwood (1964: 177).

[68] Even Brown (1978a: 8–10) or Eck (1990: 431–2), who accept the figure of 'seventeen', maintain that Ctesias began the *actual* service to the king in that year of accession.

in the reign of Darius II.[69] Consequently, he erroneously changed the figure to 'seventeen'.

Ctesias certainly left Persia on the seventh *regnal year* of Artaxerxes (398/7 BCE), a detail that may have been present in the work itself. A reader may have misunderstood this to mean that he had spent seven years in court. Yet all the events which Ctesias describes relating to his own personal presence in Persia, and which are seen in Plutarch's account, are set between 401 and 398/7 BCE, i.e., less than seven years. It would appear that Diodorus and the ancients were not sure about the length of Ctesias' stay in Persia (see the variance between *FGrH* 688 F 27.71 and *Art.* 18.8 discussed below).

Ctesias' unreliablity

As we see in Plutarch's account, Ctesias appears to have had a very bad reputation in antiquity in terms of the reliability of his reports. Yet most of the criticism was directed at his *Indica*.[70]

As we learn from our sources, and Photius' summary in particular, the *Indica* had a unique character of description, more in line with paradoxographic literature, recounting ethnographic, geographic, botanical and zoological aspects of India (*FGrH* 688 F 45–52). It included some fictional stories about exotic people and creatures, like the dog-headed tribe (Κυνοκέφαλοι: *FGrH* 688 F 45.37) or unicorns (*FGrH* 688 F 45.45, cf. F 45q) besides descriptions of real animals, like the elephant (*FGrH* 688 F 45.7, 15) or the parrot (*FGrH* 688 F 45.8). Ctesias may have included more factual ethnographic material in the *Indica*, but this was of less interest to Photius or any other excerptor.

Elsewhere I considered the possibility that the *Indica* was originally part of the *Persica*.[71] An interesting passage mentioned by Diodorus (2.16.2–4) seems like an introduction to India, within the context of a report told to Semiramis about this area and the people that convinced her to attack the country. If Diodorus does in fact give an abridged version of Ctesias here, there are two possible conclusions to be drawn: the *Persica* at this point intentionally alluded to Ctesias' other work. Alternatively, the *Indica* was in fact this very digression, a self-contained book along the lines of Herodotus' book 2. Furthermore, if the section on India – which later on was separated

---

[69] Perhaps close to the reading made by the modern historian Syme (1988a: 139). See also Bigwood (1978: 20 n.3).

[70] See Llewellyn-Jones and Robson (2010: 32–5).

[71] Almagor (2012: 19–20). Cf. Lenfant (2004: CLVII). On the *Indica* see also Bigwood (1989, 1993a, 1993b, 1995), Nichols (2011).

from the rest of the work – was written even before the *Persica* to form a single standalone work, it was soon incorporated into the *Persica*. Nevertheless, it still maintained its own distinct place within this work, presumably as a digression, again like Herodotus' book 2.

As a fascinating and a closed unit on its own, the *Indica* was soon to achieve popularity that would eclipse the rest of Ctesias' *Persica*. The depictions in this volume were to become Ctesias' most famous scenes, as evidenced by the number of ancient references to them. Unfortunately, this popularity served to cast Ctesias in a negative light as an author, which probably led to the *Persica*'s disappearance and to its author's disrepute.

Aristotle (*HA* 8.606a8) is the earliest writer to claim that Ctesias is not very reliable (οὐκ ὢν ἀξιόπιστος). Aristotle refers to Ctesias' *Indica*, apropos of his notoriously incorrect statement that there are no swine in India.[72] Yet, like Plutarch, while casting doubts on Ctesias' depictions, Aristotle nevertheless refers to his predecessor's work on more than one occasion.[73] Similarly, in the imperial period, Lucian's challenge to Ctesias' claim to autopsy (*VH* 1.3, below) refers to the *Indica*. In one of the following scenes in his own work (*VH* 2.31), Lucian mocks both the genre of travellers' tales and mythic narratives, and portrays Herodotus and Ctesias as being everlastingly punished for their lies.[74] Aulus Gellius (*NA* 9.4.1–12) includes Ctesias in his depiction of some Greek books 'full of wonders and tales, unheard of, incredulous stories' (*miraculorum fabularumque pleni, res inauditae*), which he saw in Brundisium; after an initial enthusiasm, Gellius soon acknowledges them to be worthless writings that contribute nothing useful to life.[75] It is clear that Ctesias was identified in antiquity with paradoxographic writing.

Aristotle (*Polit.* 5.8.14.1312a) alludes to a scene known from Ctesias' *Persica* concerning the effeminacy of the last Assyrian king, Sardanapallus, and discredits it as well (εἰ ἀληθῆ ταῦτα οἱ μυθολογοῦντες λέγουσιν, 'if the things told by the story tellers are true').[76] Lucian, too (in *Quom. hist. consc.* 39), extends his mistrust

---

[72] Cf. *FGrH* 688 F 45.27; F 45kβ; F 45kγ; F 45kδ; F 45kε; F 45dα; F 48.

[73] Cf. also Arist. *HA* 2.1.501a on the *Martichora*. Cf. Aristotle's judgement of Ctesias' incorrect conclusions about the sperm of elephants (*HA* 3.523a, *GA* 2.736a). See Bigwood (1993a).

[74] = Lenfant T 11hβ. Lucian is preoccupied with the mythic lies of Ctesias and Herodotus also in *Philops.* 2 (= Lenfant T 11hγ). See Lenfant (2007) on ancient attitudes to Ctesias and Herodotus.

[75] Some scholars doubt whether this story is in fact true. It may be a sophisticated allusion to Pliny, *NH* 7.2.9–28, for it is in the same sequence and deals with similar content. See Holford-Strevens (1982: 67, 1988: 50–1).

[76] This may be an authentic passage of Aristotle, since the philosopher may have known the *Persica* as well. Cf. Lenfant (2004: 250 n. 314).

of Ctesias to the *Persica*. In his view, Ctesias was pressed by his
position at the court of the Great King and was, allegedly, reduced
to flattery out of fear, violating his duty as a historian to report the
truth (cf. Tac. *Hist.* 1.1.1, *An.* 1.1.2). While Lucian does not mention
Ctesias specifically, it is obvious that he is the one referred to:

> '[the historian] would not be able to [say the truth] if he was terrified of
> Artaxerxes whom he served as a physician, or wished to obtain a purple
> clothing, a gold chain or a Nisaean horse as fee for exalting the king'.[77]
> Τοῦτο δ' οὐκ ἂν δύναιτο ἄχρι ἂν ἢ φοβῆται Ἀρταξέρξην ἰατρὸς αὐτοῦ ὢν ἢ ἐλπίζῃ
> κάνδυν πορφυροῦν καὶ στρεπτὸν χρυσοῦν καὶ ἵππον τῶν Νισαίων λήψεσθαι
> μισθὸν τῶν ἐν τῇ γραφῇ ἐπαίνων.

From the summaries of Photius of books 7–23, it seems that the
Persica was a straightforward and candid work which did not
portray Artaxerxes II (or any Persian king) in a wholly favourable
light. Following Lucian's logic, the *Persica* was probably written in
a Greek country, outside of the monarch's reach and control.[78] The
date of its publication is hard to ascertain with precision, but it had to
precede Xenophon's use of it in his *Anabasis*;[79] that is, the late 380s
or early 370s BCE.[80] On the other hand, the *Indica*, with its insinua-
tions and ambiguities clad in the exotic and the fantastic, may have
been composed in Persia – if we continue to follow Lucian's logic.[81]
Indeed, certain contemporary scenes at court included in the later
books of the *Persica* are alluded to in the *Indica* fragments by way of
innuendo.[82] The *Indica* may have been written during Ctesias' stay
in Babylon (400–398 BCE).[83]

---

[77] = Lenfant T11hδ. See Lenfant (2004: 229 n. 48). One may argue whether it does indeed
describe Ctesias' work or attitude. See Stronk (2010: 51) for an opinion that Lucian's jeer
against Ctesias is unfounded.

[78] Cf. Lenfant (2004: XVII, XXIII). Cf. Jacoby (1922: 2046–7) and Smith (1881: 30).

[79] See Almagor (2012: 28–36).

[80] See MacLaren (1934), Delebecque (1957), Breitenbach (1967: 1641–2), Stevenson (1997:
8 n.11).

[81] Cf. Llewellyn-Jones and Robson (2010: 33) and Stronk (2010: 34) for the possibility of
Ctesias taking notes in Persia.

[82] For instance, *Art.* 19.4, taken from the *Persica*, relates a small bird called *rhyntakes* which
has no excrement (γίνεται δὲ μικρὸν ἐν Πέρσαις ὀρνίθιον, ᾧ περιττώματος οὐδέν ἐστιν) and is the
size of an egg (F 27.70), used as an instrument in the assassination of Stateira. This description
parallels the elements found in one depiction of the *Indica* (F 45.34). It describes a small bird
called *dikairon*, the size of a partridge egg, which buries its excrement so it cannot be found
(καὶ ὄρνεόν φησιν ἐπικαλούμενον δίκαιρον ... τὸ μέγεθος ὅσον πέρδικος ᾠόν. τοῦτο τὸν ἀπόπατον
κατορύσσει, ἵνα μὴ εὑρεθῇ). Cf. Aul. Gell. *NA* 4.41. Similarly, the depiction of the beverage
used by the king in interrogation (F 45.31) evokes the use of wine in *Art.* 15.4. See the conflation in Diogenianus, 7.28: Οἶνος καὶ ἀλήθεια· Εὔανδρος παρὰ τοῖς Πέρσαις φησὶν οὐ βασάνοις
ἐξετάζεσθαι, ἀλλὰ μεθυσκομένους, 'Wine and Truth: Evander says that among the Persains they
do not interrogate by torture, but they intoxicate.'

[83] There are several arguments for this venue: the *Martichora*'s description (*FGrH* 688 F
45dαβγ) evokes Marduk's dragon (*mušḫuššu*) portrayed on the Ishtar Gate and Processional

The statements of Plutarch and Lucian have largely influenced the negative way modern scholarship has valued Ctesias' work. Leading the way was Jacoby (1922: 2033, 2045–7: 'gleich Null', 'worthless').[84] On the other hand, another contemporary view now attempts to appreciate Ctesias' historical descriptions and to rehabilitate his reputation as a historian.[85]

Ctesias' verbose style

Plutarch indicates Ctesias' propensity for lengthy reports (especially with respect to the death of Cyrus). Ctesias' notoriety for verbosity is mentioned in several ancient jugements. Ps.-Demetrius (*De eloc.* 209–212) claims that some 'accuse Ctesias of babbling because of his employment of repetition (διλογία)'; he admits that sometimes, but not always, those censors may be accusing him with justice.[86] As an example, he brings the scene of breaking the news of the death of Cyrus the Younger to Parysatis (216). The brief example shows that Cteisas' dialogues were lengthy, in accordance with the method of conveying information slowly.[87] Ctesias' dialogues did not have Socratic goals of revelation. Another manifestation of this in the fragments of Ctesias is *FGrH* 688 F 13.13 (Photius): Cambyses asks Tanioxares' eunuch about the pretender/Magus, and is given an evasive answer ('who else shall we think it is?'), which does not reveal the truth or the identity of the Magus. According to Ps.-Demetrius, the messenger is not expressing outright the tragic fate of Cyrus, but rather keeps the internal audience (Parysatis) as well as the external audience (the reader or listener, τὸν ἀκούοντα) in suspense, with the purpose of creating a dramatic effect. The effect on the reader is one of ἐναργεία, or 'vividness', since the discovery of what happened

Way at Babylon; see Nichols (2011: 105). Ctesias claims to have seen an elephant displace a date-palm tree in Babylon (*FGrH* 688 F 45bα); there is a contrast between the palms in India and those that grow in Babylon (*FGrH* 688 F 45.29). See Almagor (2012: 19–20).

[84] Cf. Burn (1962: 12), Momigliano (1975: 134), Cook (1983: 22), Sancisi-Weerdenburg (1987: 35, 43), Briant (2002a: 7, 265), Lenfant (2004: CXXIV–VII). Cf. Drews (1973: 103–16). See references in Gardiner-Garden (1987: 2 n. 7).

[85] For a high opinion of Ctesias' account of the revolt of Inarus see the references in Bigwood (1976: 1 n. 2). Cf. Cawkwell (1972: 39–40). See also Stevenson (1997: 72): 'basic honesty in the description of contemporary events in which he was not personally involved' (cf. 1997: 75, 81); cf. Murray (2001: 42 n. 57), Lenfant (2004: CXXIII), Llewellyn-Jones and Robson (2010: 53, 81–2), Stronk (2010: 54), Almagor (2012: 11). For a view that sees Ctesias as faithfully transmitting local traditions see Momigliano (1931); cf. Lenfant (1996).

[86] Cf. Lenfant (2004: CLXIII). The repetitions, as well as other elements construed as tedious by ancient readers, may even imply that the *Persica* as circulated was not finalised and polished.

[87] See Gera (1993: 207) and cf. Plut. *Art.* 15.4.

has to be built upon the suffering and misery of Parysatis.[88] Ctesias'
presentation was seen as highly loquacious.

Poetic myths or historical autopsy?

Plutarch's censure of the 'mythical' (τὸ μυθῶδες) element in Ctesias'
writing is paralleled by other sources. Photius chastises Ctesias (*Bibl.*
cod. 72 p. 45 a 5) for not keeping away 'from mythic stories' (τῶν
... μύθων ... οὐδ' οὗτος ἀφίσταται), especially in the *Indica*. He also
mentions 'a character close to a mythic tale' (τὸ ἐγγὺς τοῦ μυθώδους).
Strabo (2.1.35) refers to Ctesias (and others) as 'weaving in myths
intentionally ... through an intentional invention of the impossible'
(μύθους παραπλέκουσιν ἑκόντες ... πλάσει τῶν ἀδυνάτων). Elsewhere,
an account of Theopompus (*FGrH* 115 F 267) on ravens is preferred over Ctesias' similar story (688 F 36). Despite the insistence
of Timothy Peter Wiseman (1993: 131) that Ctesias displayed the
category of lies associated with travellers' tales, it is clear that Ctesias
is also linked with the lies of physical impossibility displayed in myths.

Applying this element to Ctesias' account entails viewing him as a
kind of poet. This is indeed how Ps.-Demetrius (*De eloc.* 215) treats
him: 'this poet – and poet one may call him with reason' (Καὶ ὅλως δὲ
ὁ ποιητὴς οὗτος – ποιητὴν γὰρ <ἂν> αὐτὸν καλοίη τις εἰκότως).[89] Ctesias
is made by Strabo to resemble poetry (11.6.3) or to deal with myth
in the guise of history (2.1.35); one would recall that the famous
scene of the Indian 'dogheads' was part of a poetic tradition.[90]

Strabo (11.6.2–3) criticises authors who wrote on the old matters
of Persia, Media and Syria, because of their love of fable (φιλομυθίαν).
The label would suit Ctesias, as would the division into Persian,
Median and Syrian (i.e., Assyrian) matters. It is of importance that
Strabo claims that these authors, in the fashion of the mythogra-
phers, sought to entertain:

> 'if they would say in the form of history what they never saw nor heard (not
> even from people who saw).'
> ἐὰν ἐν ἱστορίας σχήματι λέγωσιν ἃ μηδέποτε εἶδον μήτε ἤκουσαν (ἢ οὐ παρά γε
> εἰδότων).

---

[88] Cf. Llewllyn-Jones and Robson (2010: 73–4).
[89] ἂν added in the MS Marcianus gr. 508 (fourteenth century). See Stronk (2010: 36–42,
47, 2011). See Drews (1973: 116) on the *poiesis* in the *Persica* works. Cf. Lenfant (2009: 316
n. 2). Cf. Jacoby (1922: 2045).
[90] These appear as Κυνοκεφάλους in Aeschylus and Ἡμίκυνες in Hesiod, according to Strabo.
See *FGrH* 688 F 45.37–43, F 450β; F 45ρα; F 45ρβ; cf. Aul. Gell. *NA* 9.4.9. Herodotus uses
the same image (4.191).

Strabo's description is echoed in Lucian's criticism of Ctesias in *VH* 1.3, that he wrote on the lands of India and its population, things that he had not seen himself nor heard about from truthful persons (συνέγραψεν περὶ τῆς Ἰνδῶν χώρας καὶ τῶν παρ' αὐτοῖς ἃ μήτε αὐτὸς εἶδεν μήτε ἄλλου ἀληθεύοντος ἤκουσεν). The claims resemble each other so closely that a reversal of Ctesias' original autopsy statement (above) is most likely implied in both.[91]

Photius, in the passage above, differentiates between Ctesias as an eye-witness or an ear-witness. This distinction may go back to the Herodotean distinction between the reliability of the ear and the eye (Hdt. 1.8).[92] One may suspect, however, whether this formulation is strictly the one Ctesias used. Most of the *Persica* (book 1– the middle of book 18) recounts stories which Ctesias could not have witnessed himself. Thus, the claim that the physician witnessed *most* of what he related (τῶν **πλειόνων** ἃ ἱστορεῖ αὐτόπτην) is not accurate, and is more relevant to a historian writing his own period.[93] It may be Photius' own addition and emphasis.

This stress on autopsy in Ctesias' work echoes the importance placed on it by Plutarch (above, *Art.* 1.4) and the fact that the physician was present. Yet, according to one passage, Ctesias seems to have mentioned reliance on written documents as well. Diodorus (2.32.4) asserts that Ctesias claimed to have inquired into the royal archives 'in which the Persians arranged their ancient accounts according to a certain custom', and by examining them, he conveyed the information to the Greeks (οὗτος οὖν φησιν ἐκ τῶν βασιλικῶν διφθερῶν, ἐν αἷς οἱ Πέρσαι τὰς παλαιὰς πράξεις κατά τινα νόμον εἶχον συντεταγμένας, πολυπραγμονῆσαι τὰ καθ' ἕκαστον, καὶ συνταξάμενος τὴν ἱστορίαν εἰς τοὺς Ἕλληνας ἐξενεγκεῖν). It is hardly imagineable that Ctesias would write the same general assertion twice, once describing his method as relying on autopsy and hearsay, and another as relying on written evidence. It appears, therefore, that Diodorus and Photius refer to the same original passage, each rendering it differently. It was probably taken from the beginning of the *Persica* and repeated in Photius' edition. It would seem that something had gone wrong with Diodoros' depiction.[94] Moreover, the existence of these royal

---

[91] Both references also echo Thucydides. See Bartley (2003).

[92] Cf. Marincola (1997: 63–86).

[93] From Thucydides (1.22) to Josephus (*CA* 1.55) and in others. Cf. Polyb. 12.4c.4–5 and Luc. *Quom. hist. consc.* 47.

[94] Furthermore, the criticism of Lucian (above) that Ctesias' lies were the inevitable result of his position at the court of the Great King does not appear to go along with Ctesias' claim to have consulted written works. In *BNJ* 696 I have written also on the potentially two relevant passages in Diod. 2.22.5 (probably a distorted rendering of Hdt. 2.106) and Agath.

archives of documents is suspect,[95] and hence some scholars doubt the very existence of Ctesias' reliance on them.[96]

Ctesias thus emphasises autopsy, and this is the impression we have from Plutarch as well. To be sure, Ctesias claims autopsy in both the *Persica* and the *Indica* (*FGrH* 688 F 8, 15.51, 45.24, 45g),[97] even with regard to fantastical creatures (*FGrH* 688 F 45.15, 45dβ, 45dγ: the *Martichora* (man-eating beast)). Most of his facts seem to be have been derived, however, from informants (possibly soldiers, merchants, officials, courtiers).[98] Ctesias' greatest informant was Parysatis, whose physician he probably was (above). Photius asserts (*FGrH* 688 F 15.51), 'the author claims to have learned this from Parysatis herself' (φησιν ὁ συγγραφεὺς αὐτὸς παρ' αὐτῆς ἐκείνης τῆς Παρυσάτιδος ταῦτα ἀκοῦσαι).

Partisanship, pursuit of honours and overstatements of his own role

Ctesias' bias for Sparta may be seen in the peculiar arrangement which placed the scenes of the Battles of Plataea and Salamis in reverse order (*FGrH* 688 F 13.28–30), a structure which would ostensibly give the Spartans greater credit in expelling the Persians. Cnidus, his homeland, was a Dorian city, and member of the Dorian *pentapolis* in Asia Minor (Hdt. 1.144). Citizens of the city saw themselves as *apoikoi* of Sparta (Hdt. 1.174), and from the end of the fifth century BCE Cnidus served as the naval basis of the Spartans. After departing from Persia, Ctesias is said to have returned to Cnidus and Sparta (*FGrH* 688 F 30.74).[99]

Ctesias' seemingly overstated responsibility for his role in saving the king's life is presumably reflected in the story of the fatal injury of Cyrus the Great (*FGrH* 688 F 9.7), who was also carried outside the battlefield. Ctesias may have invented this story to highlight the fact that it was a physician now who saved Artaxerxes' life rather than Cyrus' men, who could not. Following the suggestion made

---

2.26 (probably taken from Diod. 2.32.4). One may note that the Sassanian practice of keeping records (and decrees) in archives was influenced by foreign habits and not from local traditions, as evidenced by the use of the MPer. *daftar* (*dptl*) 'book, account book', from the Greek word for leather (διφθέρα). Rajabzadeh (1993): 563.

[95] See Briant (2002a: 6): 'there is not another shred of evidence of such Persian historical archives, aside from a late and suspect tradition that attributes their destruction to Alexander'. Cf. Drews (1973: 111). See, however, Stronk (2010: 15–25), Waters (2017: 16–19).

[96] See Rettig (1827), Jacoby (1922: 2047–9) and Lenfant (2004: XXXVI–XXXIX).

[97] See Marincola (1997: 87, 107).

[98] Cf. Drews (1973: 107).

[99] Cnidus and Sparta: See Lewis (1977: 97); cf. Cook (1961: 67–72). Ctesias' pro-Spartan position: see Tuplin (2004: 308).

by Bigwood (1995: 137), Ctesias' rewards for this deed may have included the gift of a sword from the king, mentioned in the *Indica* (*FGrH* 688 F 45.9), alongside a sword from Parysatis. If this is true, then Ctesias referred to these honours twice: in the *Indica* section and in the *Persica* proper. Ctesias thus included a reference to himself (and indeed to Artaxerxes and Parysatis) at a relatively early part of the work, and within a digression (if the assumption that the *Indica* was part of the *Persica* is true), long before the actual point in time when that event took place in the narrative.[100]

Abridgement of Ctesias

Plutarch's need to shorten Ctesias' description is matched by the fate of his work. Aside from its dissemination in three books, Strabo also attests to a division of two (14.2.15), which would mean that the *Indica* circulated separately (see the passage of Gellius above). For instance, we know (*Suda*, s.v. Παμφίλη, π 139 Adler) that Pamphile of Epidaurus (*fl.* mid-first century CE) made an *Epitome of Ctesias* in three books ('Ἐπιτομὴν τῶν Κτησίου ἐν βιβλίοις γ'). Even though not stated, the three sections of Pamphile's epitome, one would imagine, corresponded to the three divisions of *Assyriaca*, *Persica* and *Indica*.[101] If any of these epitomes (either the one made by Pamphile or similar to it) reached Photius, it is more probable that it was that of the *Indica*. Pamphile's method of epitomising influenced Photius, who mentions it in *Bibliotheca* cod. 175.[102] Stronk (2010: 34–5, 144–5) believes that the patriarch did not read an epitome of the *Persica*, because he would have said so, and because he used Ctesias' original text for his *Lexicon*. Yet both assumptions are not necessary. If it is true that Photius held a version that had been worked on by another reader, this might explain his dismay at the abrupt change in registers and his comment on the inconsistent use of the Ionic forms. Moreover, Photius reports that the pleasure from Ctesias' history is in the elaboration of the plots, which has the 'unexpected' element (ἀπροσδόκητος) in it. It may be that this component of unforeseen

---

[100] Cf. the way Herodotus mentions his sojourn in Egypt (2.13, 28–9) before he even recounts Cambyses' campaign.

[101] See Regenbogen (1949), Plant (2004: 127–9); Lenfant (2004: XXVII, XXXIX–XL). See, however, König (1972: 30–3).

[102] This is why von Christ (1912: 1.523) suggests that this epitome was used by Photius also in his summary of the *Persica*. Cf. also Lesky (1971: 698) and Grant (1980: 115). Cf. *FGrH* 688 F 14a = Steph. Byz. s.v. κυρταία (mention of Megabyzus' exile in book 3 (sic!) of the *Persica*: γ Περσικῶν) with Lenfant (2004: 270 n. 583). Stronk (2010: 34–5, 141) rejects this proposal.

turns of events was made to look even more dramatic in a skeletal abbreviation of the *Persica*.[103]

Furthermore, Photius continues to claim (*Bibl.* cod. 72 p. 45 a 20) that in the *Indica*, Ctesias tends to use the Ionic dialect frequently (ἐν οἷς μᾶλλον ἰωνίζει). The validity of this statement may be proved by the fact that in emulation of his Cnidian predecessor, Arrian wrote his own *Indica* in the Ionic dialect, even calling Ctesias by the form Κτησίης (3.6).[104] The claim that Ctesias employed Ionisms more frequently in the *Indica* probably strengthens the assumption that this work circulated independently once separated. Photius' copy of the *Indica* thus had a different tradition of transmission which kept many of the original Ionisms, as opposed to his *Persica*, which was reworked to some extent till it reached Photius.[105] If this is true, it may be the case that the *Persica* Photius had at his disposal was an epitome or an abbreviated form of the original.

Ctesias and his narrative world

Plutarch's playful use of certain images of Ctesias as *metapoetic* is not explicitly matched in our other sources concerning the work of the physician. One passage, however, is potentially relevant. This is the depiction of Ctesias writing letters to Evagoras and Conon (*FGrH* 688 F 30.72–3). In Plutarch's version (*Art.* 21.2–4), Ctesias appears as amending Conon's letter. His involvement with real historical figures through writing (of a letter) corresponds to his dealing with historical figures through his composition. If at the outset of his work he asserted that in his writing he would convey 'to the Greeks' (Diodorus) what he heard 'from the Persians' (Photius), here his intermediate role becomes apparent: he delivers letters from the court to messengers, and a letter from the king to Conon.

Furthermore, the relevance of his written historical work to his own generation may be seen in another feature of his *Persica*. Like Herodotus, Ctesias used historical scenes to echo future events in

---

[103] See Bigwood (1989: 311) that Photius was more interested in the content and less in the form of the descriptions. Stronk (2010: 35) admits that 'Photius actually did use a complete, but transmitted and therefore *potentially* altered, copy of Ctesias' work.'

[104] Cf. Lenfant (2004: 11 n. 39); cf. the spelling in Arr. *Anab.* 5.4.2 (Κτησίας).

[105] *POxy* XXII 2330 (second century CE, = F 8b*), depicting the letter of Stryangaeus to Zarinaea, is considered as reflecting the *ipsissima verba* of the physician, based on a phrase found in Ps.-Demetrius (*De eloc.* 213). See Biltcliffe (1969), Bigwood (1986: 406), Stronk (2007; 2010: 2–3). On the other hand, there are reasons to believe that the papyrus may be a reworking of Ctesias: Giangrande (1976: 31–41), Gardiner-Garden (1987: 14). If it is a genuine fragment, Ctesias apparently wrote in the Attic dialect or less rigorous Ionic. See Del Corno (1962: 128).

his own lifetime. Ctesias did so by duplicating names of historical contemporary figures and transmitting them to persons of the
distant past.[106] He also let an early scene allude to a later one.
For example, in their revolt against Athens (*FGrH* 688 F 14.45)[107]
the Caunians are willing to give themselves to a Persian, Zopyrus,
but refuse to surrender to the Athenians. One of the city members,
Alcidas, kills Zopyrus with a stone thrown at his head, and is cruci-
fied by the king's mother (and Zopyrus' grandmother). The existence
of many similarities between that episode and the one involving
Cyrus the Younger (Caunian, lethal stone, and punishment by the
queen mother, see above and *Art.* 14.9–10) leads to the inevitable
conclusion that Ctesias intended them to echo each other.

Reading Ctesias' text with other authors

Plutarch's constant comparison of Ctesias with other authors is
repeatedly found in antiquity. It is evidenced in the contrast Photius
(*FGrH* 688 F 16.62) draws between Ctesias and Herodotus concerning the Persian treatment of corpses; this assertion is matched by
Diodorus (2.15.1–2).

If Ctesias did not include an explicit reference to Herodotus,
then these mentions of his predecessor are an example of a reader's
response to his text, inserted as a way to understand his descriptions.[108]
The reader's acquaintance with Xenophon can also be seen in the
ancient reception of Ctesias, as we noticed above in Plutarch's case.
First, the date of Ctesias' *acme* is established by Eusebius (*Chron.*:
Olymp. 95.1) and Photius (*Bibl.* cod. 72 p. 36 a 6) via Xenophon.
Photius claims that Ctesias flourished 'at the time of Cyrus, son
of Darius and Parysatis, who was the brother of Artaxerxes, to
whom the Persian kingdom was handed' (ἤκμασε δὲ ἐν τοῖς χρόνοις
Κύρου τοῦ ἐκ Δαρείου καὶ Παρυσάτιδος, ὃς ἀδελφὸς Ἀρτοξέρξου, εἰς
ὃν ἡ Περσικὴ βασιλεία κατῆλθεν, ἐτύγχανεν). The description here of
Cyrus' relation with his parents echoes *Anab.* 1.1.1 (Δαρείου καὶ
Παρυσάτιδος γίγνονται παῖδες ...) and the depiction of the βασιλεία
handed to Artaxerxes evokes the description of *Anab.* 1.3.1. The fact
that Cyrus the Younger died in 401 BCE, while Artaxerxes went on to
rule for a very lengthy period, makes the first chronological indicator

---

[106] Cf. Jacoby (1922: 2049), Bigwood (1976: 19–20).
[107] In 440 BCE: Hornblower (1982: 28 + n. 176); between 430 and 425 BCE: Eddy (1973: 255 + n. 81).
[108] On Ctesias' relation to Herodotus see Bichler (2007). See also Lenfant (2004: XXVIII–XXXII). On Ctesias' text as demanding audience engagement see Waters (2017: 12).

more definite. Second, Dionysius of Halicarnassus (*De comp. verb.*
10) joins the two authors together not only in terms of chronology
but also in aesthetic evaluation: the style of both is agreeable, but
lacks beauty (ἡδέως . . . οὐ μὴν καλῶς).

*

This chapter saw Plutarch's references to Ctesias in his texts (mainly
in the *Artaxerxes*) within two contexts: (1) the literary importance
of these historiographic allusions for the artistic goals of his work,
for the presentation of the story or argument (that is, by the narrator or speaker), and ultimately for the characterisation of the protagonist; (2) the image of Ctesias and his work in antiquity, and by
implication, in Plutarch's time and among his readers. We observed
interesting matches between the stereotypical picture of Ctesias and
what Plutarch makes of it, while also noticing some insightful new
ways in which Plutarch connected this image of the author and his
work with the content of Plutarch's own work (for instance, in the
question of the truthful account). Our next chapter will examine
more thoroughly Plutarch's emendation of Ctesias' report, based
on comparison with other texts, and the way he highlights certain
features in it by promoting this very comparison.

3. Ctesias (b)

Sadly, the text of Ctesias is lost. Given the disappearance of Ctesias' work, this chapter proposes to check Plutarch's adaptation of the physician's work in the following three parts. The first compares Plutarch's confirmed use of Ctesias (mostly in the sections of the *Artaxerxes* where he is explicitly mentioned and which are given in the previous chapter) with the same stories or details as they appear in the works of other ancient readers, mainly in Photius' epitome. The second explores Plutarch's employment of the differences between Ctesias' work and other texts (mainly Xenophon's *Anabasis*) as part of his method of characterisation, building on his readers' expectations. The third part studies Plutarch's probable use of Ctesias in cases where the physician's name is not explicitly mentioned; these passages (from *Art.* 1–4, 9, 12–17 of the biography) are usually included as fragments of Ctesias (e.g. by Jacoby, Lenfant, Stronk and Llewellyn-Jones/Robson). This part advances a cautious approach with regard to these sections, and suggests a way to locate them in the original work.

USE OF CTESIAS

This is what Photius relates of the corresponding sections in the *Persica* (*FGrH* 688 F 15.47, 51 = *Bibl.* cod. 72 p. 41 b 42–42 a 8, 42 b 3–15):

(47) ... Artaxerxes had seventeen illegitimate sons, amongst them Secyndianus (= Sogdianus) by Alogyne the Babylonian, Ochus and Arsites by Cosmartidene, also a Babylonian. Ochus would afterwards become king. Besides these, the king also had children named Bagapaeus and Parysatis by Andria, also a Babylonian. This Parysatis would later be the mother of Artaxerxes and Cyrus ...

73

(51) Ochus, also known as Dareiaeus, became the sole ruler. Three eunuchs were most influential with him, Artoxares was the greatest, Artibarzanes second and Athoos third. However, for advice he listened to his wife, by whom he had two children before his accession, a daughter called Amestris, and a son named Arsacas who would later be called Artaxerxes. As queen, she gave birth to another son named Cyrus, after the sun. Then she bore him Artostes and nine other children, to the number of thirteen. Ctesias claims to have learned this from Parysatis herself. The rest of these children died early, and the ones whose names were mentioned, as well as a fourth son named Oxendras, survived.

(47) ... Ἑπτακαίδεκα δὲ νόθους υἱοὺς ἔσχεν ὁ Ἀρτοξέρξης, ἐξ ὧν ἐστι καὶ Σεκυνδιανὸς ὁ ἐξ Ἀλογούνης τῆς Βαβυλωνίας, καὶ Ὦχος, καὶ Ἀρσίτης ὁ ἐκ Κοσμαρτιδήνης καὶ αὐτῆς Βαβυλωνίας· ὁ δὲ Ὦχος ὕστερον καὶ βασιλεύει. Ἔτι δὲ παῖδες αὐτοῦ πρὸς τοῖς εἰρημένοις καὶ Βαγαπαῖος καὶ Παρύσατις ἐξ Ἀνδρίας καὶ αὐτῆς Βαβυλωνίας· αὕτη ἡ Παρύσατις Ἀρτοξέρξου καὶ Κύρου μήτηρ ἐγένετο ... (51) Βασιλεύει οὖν μόνος Ὦχος ὁ καὶ Δαρειαῖος. Εὐνοῦχοι δὲ τρεῖς ἠδύναντο παρ' αὐτῷ, μέγιστον μὲν Ἀρτοξάρης, δεύτερος δὲ Ἀρτιβαρζάνης, καὶ τρίτος Ἀθῶος. Ἐχρῆτο δὲ συμβούλῳ μάλιστα τῇ γυναικί· ἐξ ἧς πρὸ τῆς βασιλείας δύο ἔσχε τέκνα, Ἀμῆστριν θυγατέρα καὶ **Ἀρσάκαν** υἱόν, ὃς ὕστερον μετωνομάσθη Ἀρτοξέρξης. Τίκτει δὲ αὐτῷ ἕτερον υἱὸν βασιλεύουσα, καὶ τίθεται τὸ ὄνομα αὐτοῦ ἀπὸ τοῦ ἡλίου Κῦρον· εἶτα τίκτει Ἀρτόστην, καὶ ἐφεξῆς μέχρι παίδων δεκατριῶν. καί φησιν ὁ συγγραφεὺς αὐτὸς παρ' αὐτῆς ἐκείνης τῆς Παρυσάτιδος ταῦτα ἀκοῦσαι. Ἀλλὰ τὰ μὲν ἄλλα τῶν τέκνων ταχὺ ἀπεβίω, οἱ δὲ περιγεγονότες οἵ τε προρρηθέντες τυγχάνουσι, καὶ ἔτι τέταρτος υἱὸς Ὀξένδρας ὠνομασμένος.

Ἀνδρίας Bekker, Jacoby: Ἀνδίας BC

We can see that the physician originally noted the king's personal name. However, the forms used by Photius are not consistent: he has Arsacas in F 15.51 and Arsaces (Ἀρσάκης) in the Ionic form in F 15.55 (below). The differences may stem from copyist errors,[1] or from emendation in the process of abbreviation, causing Ionic forms to disappear almost entirely. This variance was presumably found in Ctesias' text as it was at Photius' disposal. If it was present in the version of the *Persica* that Plutarch read as well (perhaps also some abridgement), then the biographer may have spotted an interesting feature concerning Artaxerxes' original name in his text which he soon utilised for his literary purposes. The introduction of Deinon to supply a different variant of the name would thus accentuate this textual discrepancy already found in the MSS of Ctesias' *Persica* (or the abridgement of it). Thus, the discrepancy is taken by Plutarch to highlight a certain duality in the protagonist's character.

As suggested by Friedrich Wilhelm König (1972: 89 n. 4), the form

---

[1] See Bigwood (1976: 6–10, 21–3) for other examples of distortion of names in Photius' *Bibliotheca*. For convincing arguments that the Plutarchan version should be accepted see Schmitt (2006: 75–7).

that appears in Photius' text may be influenced by the common name Arsacas.[2] The most famous person of this name was the semi-legendary founder of the famous Parthian dynasty the Arsacids (c. 250 BCE – 226 CE). Strabo (15.1.36) informs us that the Parthian kings were all named Arsacas (Ἀρσάκαι γὰρ καλοῦνται πάντες), a detail which is not true (and is probably derived from some misunderstanding of the meaning of the *Arsacids*), but is repeated in Justin, 41.5.8 (*omnes reges suos hoc nomine* [scil. Arsacas] … *cognominavere*, 'all of their kings are called by this name'), comparing them with the Roman dynasty in which all rulers are called 'Caesars' and 'Augusts' (*sicuti Romani Caesares Augustosque*). This piece of information probably comes from a confused comment conflating the personal given name and the throne name, as Diodorus (15.93.1) has a very similar view of the Persians: 'since the first Artaxerxes had ruled well and was seen as amiable and prosperous, the Persians altered the names of those who followed him as rulers and ordered that they should be called the same'. Plutarch seems to have been familiar with this conflation of the personal name and the throne name among Greek readers, and to have utilised this confusion to instil unclarity about the character of the hero, whether he was born with kingly traits or not.

The version given by Plutarch (*Arsicas*) has the suffix *-ica*, which is the hypocoristic ending.[3] This form was presumably heard by Ctesias as it was constantly employed by members of the royal family, especially Parysatis.[4] Photius asserts that Ctesias claimed to have heard these details from Parysatis herself (αὐτὸς παρ' αὐτῆς ἐκείνης τῆς Παρυσάτιδος ταῦτα ἀκοῦσαι). This indication of the physician's independent autopsy, related in Photius' summary to the number and names of the sons, seems to be adopted by Plutarch. The biographer maintains (*Art.* 1.4, above) that the physician is reliable with respect to Artaxerxes' name because he treated the king and family and stayed in his house. It may be that the biographer borrowed this justification for his information from Ctesias, yet transferred it narrowly only to the topic of the king's original name.

Plutarch ignores Amestris, the sister of Artaxerxes, both in *Art.* 1 and in the subsequent plot. She is also neglected in Xenophon's story, so that Plutarch's presentation may be influenced by the familiarity of his readers with Xenophon's account, and from the wish to keep

[2] Cf. Thuc. 8.108; Polyaen. 1.30.4; Curt. Ruf. 8.3.17; Arr. *Anab.* 5.29.4 for other bearers of this name.
[3] See Schmitt (1977: 423, 1982: 92). Cf. Kent (1953: 55 n. 164).
[4] See the proposal of Lenfant (2004: 275 n. 632; cf. 272 n. 607).

the number of the children not greater than four, corresponding to the number of Artaxerxes' own children mentioned at the end (*Art.* 29–30).

Photius did not preserve much of Ctesias' account of the Battle of Cunaxa, except for two details (*FGrH* 688 16.64, 67 = *Bibl.* cod. 72 p. 43 b 34–5, 44 a 12–14):

> (64) Cyrus attacked the king's army, won a victory, but died in the battle when he failed to follow the advice of Clearchus . . .
> (67) He [Artaxerxes] gave rewards to the man who carried off Cyrus' saddle-cloth and he honoured the Carian who was thought to have killed Cyrus . . .
> (64) Προσβολὴ Κύρου πρὸς τὴν **βασιλέως στρατιάν**, καὶ **νίκη** Κύρου· ἀλλὰ καὶ θάνατος Κύρου ἀπειθοῦντος Κλεάρχῳ . . .
> (67) Ὡς Ἀρτοξέρξης δῶρα ἔδωκε τῷ ἐνέγκαντι τὸν Κύρου **πῖλον**· καὶ ὡς τὸν Κᾶρα τὸν δοκέοντα Κῦρον **βαλεῖν** Ἀρτοξέρξης ἐτίμησε . . .

Despite the very slim grounds for comparing Plutarch with Photius, there are still some interesting similarities clearly in evidence. In Plutarch's account as well, Cyrus senses victory (*Art.* 11.4: ἐπαιρόμενος δὲ τῇ **νίκῃ**). Plutarch accentuates this detail to display Cyrus' character trait of love of honour (or love of victory, i.e., φιλονικία). Moreover, Cyrus is presented by Plutarch as left without his Greeks and lacking any external or internal constraints to his vanity. This roughly corresponds to Photius' picture, in which the prince is seen as rejecting Clearchus' advice. The phrase 'king's army' actually appears in Plutarch's version (*Art.* 11.9: **βασιλέως στρατιᾷ**). The mention of the saddle-cloth appears as well (*Art.* 11.6: τὸν δ' ἐφίππειον **πῖλον**), and the verb used of the Carian is the same and in the same form (*Art.* 11.6: ἐξόπισθεν **βαλεῖν**). Most interesting of all is that Photius also refers to an anonymous person who picked up the blood-soaked saddle-cloth of Cyrus after he was hit, and not to the fact that it was an attendant of Mithridates (*Art.* 11.6), who is later to play a significant role in the next scenes, as can be inferred from Plutarch (*Art.* 11.5, 14.5, 15–16) and from Photius' subsequent reading (F 16.67). It would seem that it was Ctesias himself who toyed with the motif of a person not receiving his due credit (for Mithridates is officially rewarded for this: *Art.* 14.5), and therefore left in anonymity.[5]

Diodorus (14.23.5) sees the clash of the brothers as similar to a famous mythic contest:

---

[5] The proposal of Binder (2008: 233–4, cf. 230–1, 240) that somehow Plutarch's source was 'contaminated' is not sustained.

Fate, it would seem, turned the strife of the brothers over power to assume the form of a duel, imitating the ancient recklessness of Eteocles and Polyneices depicted in tragedy.

ἡ τύχη τὴν ὑπὲρ τῆς ἡγεμονίας τοῖς ἀδελφοῖς ἔριν εἰς μονομαχίαν καθάπερ εἰς ἀπομίμημα τῆς παλαιᾶς ἐκείνης καὶ τραγῳδουμένης τῆς περὶ τὸν Ἐτεοκλέα καὶ Πολυνείκην τόλμης.

The example may be illuminating in that it is a real ancient reader's response to the portrayal of Ctesias. While Diodorus may have relied on both Ephorus (cf. 14.22.2) and Xenophon for the story of the Ten Thousand, the comparison may be Diodorus' own.[6] What is of interest is that this particular well-known mythic clash ended up with the death of *both* siblings.[7] What Diodorus may have sensed, Plutarch accentuates in his portrayal of the king as he emerges from his victory in Cunaxa. One of the main ideas seen in Plutarch's story is the complete personal change which the king undergoes after the battle, from mild to cruel, as if the old Arsicas/Arsaces dies in Cunaxa. The interpretations of Plutarch and Diodorus may be based on hints in Ctesias' original depiction.

There was probably something highly unbearable in Ctesias' over-statement of his own role in the delegation to the mercenaries after Cunaxa to have elicited Plutarch's reaction to this assertion as 'a glaring lie'. The response of Xenophon, insisting that there was only a *single* Greek delegate (*Anab.* 2.1.7: οἱ μὲν ἄλλοι βάρβαροι, ἦν δ' αὐτῶν Φαλῖνος εἷς Ἕλλην), now looks like an oblique polemic directed against Ctesias' contention that he was a member of this group.[8] Referring to Xenophon's denial, Plutarch notes that Xenophon men-tions Ctesias 'and evidently came across his books' (μέμνηται γὰρ αὐτοῦ καὶ τοῖς βιβλίοις τούτοις ἐντετυχηκὼς δῆλός ἐστιν). Indeed, there are two utterances in the *Anabasis* that specifically refer to Ctesias as a source and seem to present Xenophon as citing the physician. Thus, it would appear that Plutarch is alluding to the two literary references.

These two references in Xenophon's text, however, are almost certainly not genuine.[9] The first (*Anab.* 1.8.26) tackles Artaxerxes' wound, which was caused by Cyrus and Ctesias' medical treatment of it. It appears in the text immediately next to the report of Cyrus' rash onslaught against his brother and the injury he inflicts on the

[6] See his version of the myth earlier in his work: Diod. 4.64.4–65.8.
[7] See Aesch. *Sept.* 804–11, Eur. *Phoen.* 1356–1424, Ps.-Apollod. 3.6.1–8, Paus. 9.5.12, Hyginus, *Fab.* 71, Statius, *Theb.* 11.524–73.
[8] See Lendle (1995: 92–3), and cf. Dorati (1995: 39–40), Cawkwell (2004: 50 n. 7).
[9] The following is a brief summary of the argument in Almagor (2012: 33–5).

king. Breaking the dramatic episode by an interlude is a comment to the effect that Cyrus incapacitated the king past the breastplate:

> He went to hit him in the chest and wounded him through the breastplate, as Ctesias the physician says, and this wound he had treated, so he says.
> καὶ παίει κατὰ τὸ στέρνον καὶ τιτρώσκει διὰ τοῦ θώρακος, ὥς φησι Κτησίας ὁ ἰατρός· καὶ ἰᾶσθαι αὐτὸς τὸ τραῦμά φησι.

Xenophon then goes back to Cyrus, who is melodramatically portrayed as being hit at the very instant he is giving the strike (παίοντα δ᾽ αὐτὸν . . .). The second reference to Ctesias occurs almost immediately, after the account on the subsequent skirmish of the associates of Cyrus and Artaxerxes (*Anab.* 1.8.27):

> Many men stationed near the king died, Ctesias says (for he was by his side).
> ὁπόσοι μὲν τῶν ἀμφὶ βασιλέα ἀπέθνῃσκον Κτησίας λέγει (παρ᾽ ἐκείνῳ γὰρ ἦν).

While it is asserted that Ctesias gave the number of the fallen among the king's men, strangely no figure is specified. After this note Xenophon relates Cyrus' end together with eight of his courageous confidants.

Both references seem to be incoherent: the first has 'he says' twice: ὥς **φησι** Κτησίας . . . τὸ τραῦμά **φησι**. The second is grammatically incorrect. The description is definitely coherent without these words. Furthermore, the second allusion to Ctesias would be more understandable as a gloss on the margin, affected by Ctesias' version of the clash of the followers of the two brothers that was placed in the inappropriate spot in Xenophon's text. As to the first reference, Xenophon's description would be clearer without it. The deletion of these words would also render the depiction stronger, in that Cyrus' end would be more dramatic.

More than one hundred years ago, the scholar Félix Dürrbach (1893: 363 n.1) suggested that these two mentions of Ctesias were in reality later interpolations in the *Anabasis* and were not Xenophon's own remarks. Somewhat revised, Dürrbach's three claims are as follows:

(1) The references are uncomfortably injected in the text and seem foreign to it.
(2) Generally, Xenophon never mentions the sources he uses;[10] there is no ostensible cause why he should do so – twice – in this specific passage.
(3) The allusion to the Great King's injury refutes the account in

---

[10] Cf. Marincola (1997: 227).

Xenophon's work, in which Artaxerxes is highly energetic in the ensuing clash (see above).

Dürrbach's proposition was not generally accepted by scholars, and the two allusions are even now deemed by many as authentic.[11] Dürrbach's claims, however, have not been thoroughly considered.[12] The awkward allusions to Ctesias in the *Anabasis* have been supported as genuine, once by arguing that through these references Xenophon is conveying his misgiving concerning Ctesias' descriptions,[13] and once by arguing that Xenophon alludes to Ctesias to strengthen his own portrayal.[14] Both lines of argument have to be rejected. Arguing for Xenophon's distrust is not persuasive, given that the allusions seem to reinforce the particulars specified (the king's injury or the number of the fallen on the Great King's side), and therefore would not be considered doubtful by Xenophon. In contrast, the employment of the physician to assure Xenophon's depiction is similarly objectionable. In the second case it is not even comprehensible why Ctesias' account should be alluded to if the numbers are not provided. The rhetorical aim of this allusion is not transparent, in view of the absence of any figure, and in comparison with the precise number of eight men falling on the body of Cyrus, which closely follows. For the first case, why must Xenophon allude to a negligible injury (as one can assess by the king's quick recuperation) at all, if it is to be omitted as rapidly as it is introduced? Xenophon's account is entirely coherent without it.

It is doubtful whether these allusions to Ctesias are genuine. It goes against Xenophon's unwillingness to allude to his precursor, all the more so in circumstances where he should mention him. Overt allusion to Ctesias or to the king's injury would require acknowledgement of many details told by Ctesias: the physician's service at court and on the spot during battle, the narrative in which he saved the king, who was debilitated and could not take part in the conflict, and the fact that Ctesias' numbers were reliable. Eventually, Xenophon's mistrust of Ctesias would then cast doubt on his own version. Other ancient writers did not recognise Ctesias' role as a

---

[11] See Jacoby (1922: 2067): 'natürlich sind das keine Interpolationen' ('obviously these are no interpolations'). Cf. Cawkwell (1972: 17), Bigwood (1983: 347), Wylie (1992: 132), Stronk (2010: 185, 368–9), Tuplin (2011: 468–70), Gray (2017: 232), Marincola (2017: 107), Vlassopoulos (2017: 364). See, however, Stevenson (1997: 88) and Binder (2008: 194).
[12] See Lenfant (2004: 226 n. 12). Dürrbach was preceded by Reuss (1887: 1–3).
[13] See Bigwood (1983: 348 + n. 39). Cf. Dorati (1995: 38).
[14] See Gray (2003: 119). Cf. Tuplin (2004: 155).

historical agent without hesitations. There is no reason to believe Xenophon would admit it, twice, within the same brief passage. But most important of all, the claim that the allusions (the second in particular) are authentic would require that Xenophon be dependent on his readers' familiarity with Ctesias' *Persica* to appreciate the reference, which is not likely and completely in conflict with his habit of refraining from mentioning other texts.[15] An allusion of the type that forces the reader to turn to another text is typical of a librarian from a later period, not the writer Xenophon.

Dürrbach's suggestion deserves to be adopted. It would indeed appear that at some point the notes were inserted from the margins of the *Anabasis* text into its body. In an earlier formulation of this proposal, I accepted Dürrbach's suggestion that Xenophon's MSS had already incurred an interpolation at some stage before Plutarch read the work for his biography – that is, sometime between the end of the fourth century BCE and the first century CE. This needs to be reconsidered now.

Is it sheer coincidence that the two references to Ctesias in Xenophon's MSS are found in Plutarch's *Artaxerxes* as two explicit references to Ctesias in the same sequence? First Plutarch mentions (*Art.* 11.3) that the king, wounded through his corselet (διὰ τοῦ θώρακος), was assisted by several men including Ctesias, and then (*Art.* 13.3) Ctesias is mentioned as discussing the number of the dead (ἀριθμὸν δὲ νεκρῶν). One may observe that a clear number is given neither by Plutarch nor in the note within Xenophon's MSS. One option would be to assume that these two scenes in Ctesias' original description were so powerful that any reader would remember them (i.e., Plutarch and the interpolator of Xenophon's *Anabasis*). Another option would be that these interpolated notes were *inspired* by the reading of Plutarch's *Artaxerxes*, and were recalled by a later reader of Xenophon's text.

If all this is true, then Plutarch's μέμνηται γὰρ αὐτοῦ is an utterly ironic statement, not based on any real reference, but rather directed at Xenophon's practice of appropriating sections from his predecessor without even crediting him. This suggestion would be in keeping with the general theme of these sections in the biography, emphasising vain pursuit of honour and unjust appropriation of glory.

---

[15] Xenophon both borrows details from Ctesias and implicitly argues against the account of the *Persica*, while being cautious never to mention his precursor. Such conduct is also typical of Xenophon with relation to Plato. See Stokes (2012: 248–59, at 259): 'Xenophon . . . toning down Plato's flights of fancy even while making use of them'.

Plutarch's use of Ctesias in *Art.* 18 is evident in the verbal similarities of his account with Photius' epitome. Photius writes (*FGrH* 688 F 27.68 = *Bibl.* cod. 72 p. 44 a 21–3) of Tissaphernes' deception of the generals at the beginning of book 21 of Ctesias' *Persica*:

> Tissaphernes was plotting against the Greeks ... (he captured) Clearchus and the other commanders through the use of deception and (false) vows ὡς Τισαφέρνης ἐπιβουλεύει τοῖς Ἕλλησι ... **Κλέαρχον καὶ τοὺς ἄλλους στρατηγοὺς** ἀπάτῃ καὶ ὅρκοις ἐχειρώσατο.

This is somewhat close to Plutarch's version (*Art.* 18.1: ἐπεὶ δὲ **Κλέαρχον καὶ τοὺς ἄλλους στρατηγοὺς** Τισσαφέρνης ἐξηπάτησε, καὶ παρεσπόνδησεν ὅρκων ... 'after Tissaphernes deceived Clearchus and the other generals, and broke his vows ...'). The description is also similar, and there are some verbal resemblances (deception: ἀπάτῃ/ ἐξηπάτησε; vows: ὅρκοις/ὅρκων) appearing in the same sequence.[16] Even Photius' depiction of the commanders sent to Babylon is close to the phrasing of the biographer. Note the similarity between Photius' text (*FGrH* 688 27.69 = *Bibl.* cod. 72 p. 44 a 29: ὡς εἰς Βαβυλῶνα πρὸς Ἀρτοξέρξην Κλέαρχον καὶ τοὺς ἄλλους ἀπέστειλεν **ἐν πέδαις**, '[Tissaphernes] sent Clearchus and other generals in chains to Artaxerxes in Babylon') and Plutarch's words (καὶ συλλαβὼν ἀνέπεμψεν **ἐν πέδαις** δεδεμένους, 'and having arrested them he sent them tied in chains').[17]

The correspondence between Photius and Plutarch continues in several other instances: (1) Photius claims that Ctesias treated Clearchus on behalf of Parysatis (*FGrH* 688 F 27.69 = *Bibl.* cod. 72 p. 44 a 33: πρὸς ἡδονὴν καὶ θεραπείαν δι᾽ αὐτῆς ἔπραξε, 'for her pleasure and service'), and Plutarch includes a close description, according to which he acted to please Parysatis and at her suggestion (*Art.* 18.3: χάριτι **καὶ** γνώμῃ τῆς Παρυσάτιδος). The structure is roughly the same, although paraphrased. Plutarch gives Parysatis more responsibility in his version. He conveys the impression that Ctesias (the agent) is Parysatis' creature, while at the end of *Art.* 18 Plutarch criticises the depiction and the manner in which Parysatis is made to be the (fictional) creature of Ctesias (the author).

(2) Both Plutarch and Photius assert that Menon was kept alive for a certain period of time – and in roughly the same phrases. Compare Photius (*FGrH* 688 F 27.69 = *Bibl.* cod. 72 p. 44 a

---

[16] In fact, the theme of breaking of promises constantly appears in Ctesias (F 14.35, 14.38–9, 15.52–3).

[17] One should compare Diodorus' account in 14.27.2, close to both: Τισσαφέρνης δὲ τοὺς στρατηγοὺς **δήσας ἀπέστειλε** πρὸς Ἀρταξέρξην ('Tissaphernes sent the generals in chains to Artaxerxes').

39–40: Ἀνῃρέθησαν δὲ καὶ οἱ σὺν αὐτῷ ἀναπεμφθέντες Ἕλληνες **πλὴν Μένωνος**, 'Together with him were killed the Greeks sent (to the king) except Menon') and Plutarch's words (*Art.* 18.5: πάντας **πλὴν Μένωνος**, 'everyone except Menon'). This would indicate that the original probably contained exactly the same phrase. The singling out of Menon rather than Clearchus is not explained, and the deed of saving his life seems completely arbitrary. Yet it is hardly surprising to Xenophon's readers. Menon is said to have been kept alive for a longer time by Xenophon (*Anab.* 2.5.38, 2.6.29; cf. Diod. 14.27.2) because of his treason (*Anab.* 2.5.28). Plutarch engages in a play with the readers: he is not violating their anticipations in this regard, and now has the king, who broke his earlier promise to Parysatis to save Clearchus (*Art.* 18.5), ironically acting as expected.

(3) The first peculiar occurence surrounding Clearchus' corpse, namely the great mass of earth covering his body (*Art.* 18.7: τῷ δὲ Κλεάρχου νεκρῷ θύελλαν **ἀνέμου** ...) is very close to Photius' account (*FGrH* 688 F 27.69 = *Bibl.* cod. 72 p. 44 a 38: μεγίστου πνεύσαντος **ἀνέμου** ... , 'a strong wind blew'). The form is exactly the same, pointing at the probable original text of Ctesias. In both versions, the wind is not in the nominative case and is not the grammatical subject of the sentence. Plutarch hints at an external agent responsible (the divine, or Ctesias the author). Similarly, in Plutarch's description of the second strange phenomenon occurring near Clearchus' tomb, some dates fall on the ground and in a short time a wonderful grove of trees springs up (*Art.* 18.8: **φοινίκων** δέ τινων διασπαρέντων ...); Photius (*FGrH* 688 F 27.71 = *Bibl.* cod. 72 p. 44 b 16–17) has the same phenomenon occurring after eight years (δι' ἐτῶν ὀκτὼ μεστὸν ἐφάνη **φοινίκων**).

In Photius' sequence, the second odd event on Clearchus' tomb happens after Stateira's death, in an order of events which was probably the original one, altered by Plutarch for literary purposes. Photius' summary treats the two miraculous events in the following manner (*FGrH* 688 F 27.69–71 = *Bibl.* cod. 72 p. 44 a 36–41, 44 b 16–19):

(69) ... Clearchus was killed, and a marvel happened over his body. Suddenly on his corpse a strong wind blew and a large raised mound was formed. Together with him were killed the Greeks sent (to the king) except Menon.
(70) Insults of Parysatis towards Stateira and (the latter's) death ...
(71) The mound of Clearchus, after eight years, was full of palm trees which after he died Parysatis had secretly planted through her eunuchs.

(69) ... καὶ ἀνῃρέθη Κλέαρχος, καὶ τέρας ἐπὶ τῷ σώματι συνέστη· αὐτομάτως γὰρ ἐπ' αὐτῷ τάφος, μεγίστου πνεύσαντος ἀνέμου, ἐπὶ μέγα ἠρμένος ἐπισυνέστη. ἀνῃρέθησαν δὲ καὶ οἱ σὺν αὐτῷ ἀναπεμφθέντες Ἕλληνες πλὴν Μένωνος.

(70) λοιδορία Παρυσάτιδος πρὸς Στάτειραν, καὶ ἀναίρεσις . . .
(71) καὶ τὸ χῶμα δὲ τοῦ Κλεάρχου δι᾽ ἐτῶν ὀκτὼ μεστὸν ἐφάνη φοινίκων, οὓς ἦν κρύφα Παρύσατις, καθ᾽ ὃν καιρὸν ἐκεῖνος ἐτελεύτησε, διὰ εὐνούχων καταχώσασα.

More than Plutarch, Photius explicitly presents the first occurence as miraculous (and note the word τέρας).[18] Photius also uses the term αὐτομάτως to indicate the lack of external intervention.[19] This would probably be the impression Ctesias wanted to convey. Conversely, for the second event, Plutarch does not mention Parysatis' intervention, and implicitly presents it as another miracle. Parysatis allegedly wished to insinuate that the gods created this garden without any human interference. By the phrase 'dear to the gods' Plutarch enhances this impression, although it was probably absent from the *Persica*; Ctesias did not present the palm trees as divinely created, and, from what can be gathered from the fragments, it seems that explicit divine agency was absent from his account altogether.[20] It is Plutarch who creates this impact. Nevertheless, again, he seems to enhance a feature that was already in the work. Plutarch transposed Ctesias' idea of a man-made result from the palm trees (planted by Parysatis according to Ctesias) to their textual depiction; he took a creation which appeared to be real and natural, devoid of any trace of human intervention, and attributed its impact onto another. Plutarch transferred the effect of the trees on the king to the impact of the *description* of the trees on the monarch. While capturing the idea of the original passage, Plutarch succeeded in creating a new and sophisticated account.

One may entertain the thought that the presence of Ctesias (the agent) in this section was indeed found between the two miraculous events, namely in the story of the assassination of Stateira (below). On her deathbed, Stateira's accusation against the queen mother is similar to the earlier case of Amytis the queen, who persuades her mother Amestris that Apollonides the physician is responsible for her deadly condition (*FGrH* 688 F 14.44). It could be that Ctesias, the physician attending to Stateira, heard these accusations. If so, Ctesias probably toyed with the same three types of court members (queen, queen mother, physician), and thus inserted his own person (and implicitly, himself as an author) into the account.

---

[18] Another corpse-saving miracle in Ctesias is in *FGrH* 688 F 9.6 (lions preserving Oebaras' corpse); cf. *FGrH* 688 F 14.48; both passages come from Photius' epitome.
[19] Cf. his similar use throughout the *Bibliotheca*: cod. 47 (11 a 36), cod. 221 (177 b 32), 223 (209 b 18, 212 a 26, 212 b 9), cod. 234 (298 b 24), cod. 235 (303 b 29), cod. 240 (322 b 13), cod. 249 (440 a 5), cod. 250 (458 a 16), cod. 251 (461 a 4), cod. 278 (528 a 9).
[20] Yet, cf. *FGrH* 688 F 13.29 (from Photius).

Plutarch criticises the motivation of Parysatis as presented by Ctesias as improbable (*Art.* 18.6). We find in Photius' summary of the *Persica* similar motivation in the case of Megabyzus' revolt after the execution of Inarus by the queen mother Amestris (*FGrH* 688 F 14.40). Readers of Ctesias would have been accustomed to this sort of motivation and perhaps anticipated it. They would also not put anything beyond Parysatis. Plutarch's argument is presumably brought forward in order to make the ensuing lenient treatment of the king towards Parysatis after the murder understandable. By highlighting the absurdity of the motive, Plutarch partially exonerates her. It is thus an abrupt change of attitude on Plutarch's part.[21]

According to Photius, palm trees grew on the grave of Clearchus and this spectacle was seen eight years after Clearchus' death (δι' ἐτῶν ὀκτὼ μεστὸν ἐφάνη φοινίκων). Yet Plutarch claims that this was observed 'shortly afterwards' (*Art.* 18.8: φοινίκων ... διασπαρέντων ὀλίγῳ χρόνῳ ...). How are we to understand this discrepancy? Jacoby's two attempts to emend the text in order to reconcile Plutarch and Photius are clearly wrong and needless: the first (1922: 2034) was to propose 'during two years', changing the η into β (similarly, Krumbholz, 1889: 4 proposed 'three years'), and the second (1958: 481) was διὰ μηνῶν ὀκτώ ('eight months'). The two attempts are not compatible with each other, and both seem awkard. Date palm trees (*Phoenix dactylifera*) bear fruit four to eight years after planting; hence Jacoby's suggestions – as well as Plutarch's phrase 'short time afterwards' (ὀλίγῳ χρόνῳ) – are wrong. It might be that the original indication of time was not sufficiently clear in the text Plutarch and Photius read.

Photius' remark concerning the date trees is usually employed to shed light on the *date* of publication of Ctesias' *Persica*, which is otherwise hard to ascertain. Since the execution of Clearchus took place c. 401/0 BCE, the year 393/2 BCE is usually given as the *terminus post quem* for the work.[22] Yet this interpretation is not necessary if the figure of 'eight' comes not from Ctesias, but is Photius' own phrasing. It must be remembered that Ctesias did not profess to have seen the trees.[23] He could therefore have used a general statement of the

---

[21] This attitude is almost as surprising as the abrupt miraculous events which are brought in without a comment. On Parysatis' motives see Lenfant (2004: 162 n. 733) and Binder (2008: 268–9). For the example of Inarus' revolt see Bigwood (1976: 19).

[22] See Brown (1978a: 6), Eck (1990: 433–4), Stevenson (1997: 6), Lenfant (2004: VIII, XXIV n. 72, 159 n. 728), Stronk (2010: 11), Binder (2008: 266).

[23] See Smith (1881: 28), Stevenson (1997: 4) and Lenfant (2004: 159 n. 728). Cf. the

sort of καὶ νῦν ('and is now') at this point. If this is true, then it is easy to comprehend the divergence between Plutarch and Photius. Both interpreted Ctesias' phrase according to their own understanding. The 'eight years' may come from Photius' misunderstanding of the 'seven years' mentioned at the beginning of the work (above), as if the work was written in the eighth year (starting from the beginning of Ctesias' sojourn? from the beginning of Artaxerxes II's reign?).[24] Plutarch was not clear as to the date of the καὶ νῦν and left it vague. Incidentally, if this constraint is removed, the *Persica* could just as well have been written later than the 390s BCE.[25]

In between the two miraculous occurrences, Photius brings in the murder of Stateira (*FGrH* 688 F 27.70 = *Bibl.* cod. 72, p. 44 a 40–44 b 9):

(70) Insults of Parysatis towards Stateira and the latter's death through a poison prepared in this fashion: Stateira was constantly on her guard (lest what actually did happen would not occur). For she (Parysatis) smeared one side of a knife with poison, and the other unpolluted. With it she cut a small bird the size of an egg. The Persians call this small bird *Rhyndake*. It was cut in two, one half was pure of the venom which Parysatis herself took and ate, the other associated with the poison she handed to Stateira. After she (Stateira) saw the giver eat her half, she was not able to sense (the plot), and ate the poison of death.

(70) Λοιδορία Παρυσάτιδος πρὸς Στάτειραν, καὶ ἀναίρεσις διὰ φαρμάκου τοῦτον διασκευασθέντος τὸν τρόπον (**ἐφυλάττετο** γὰρ Στάτειρα λίαν μὴ παθεῖν ὃ πέπονθε)· **μαχαιρίου** τὸ ἓν **μέρος** ἐπαλείφεται τῷ φαρμάκῳ, τὸ δὲ λοιπὸν οὐ μετεῖχε. Τούτῳ τέμνεται **ὀρνίθιον μικρόν**, μέγεθος ὅσον ᾠοῦ· ῥυνδάκην **Πέρσαι** τὸ ὀρνίθιον καλοῦσι. τέμνεται δὲ δίχα, καὶ τὸ μὲν **καθαρεῦον** τοῦ ἰοῦ ἥμισυ αὐτὴ λαβοῦσα Παρύσατις **ἐσθίει**, τὸ δὲ προσομιλῆσαν τῷ φαρμάκῳ ὀρέγει Στατείρᾳ· ἡ δὲ ἐπειδὴ ἐσθίουσαν τὴν ἐπιδοῦσαν ἑώρα τὸ ἥμισυ, μηδὲν συνιδεῖν δυνηθεῖσα, καὶ αὐτὴ συνεσθίει τοῦ θανάτου τὸ φάρμακον.

Photius' depiction bears verbal resemblances to Plutarch's account (see Chapter 2): the use of the knife (*Art.* 19.5: μικρᾷ **μαχαιρίδι**), the smearing of one side with poison (ἑτέρῳ **μέρει**), the fact that one side is left pure (**καθαρὸν**) and the detail that Parysatis is the first to consume the bird (αὐτὴν **ἐσθίειν**). Presumably these similarities echo the original. Plutarch has Parysatis and Stateira both standing on guard (**φυλάττεσθαι**). The name of the small bird (*Art.* 19.4: **μικρὸν**

---

far-fetched assumption of König (1972: 26 nn. 13, 29; also Eck 1990: 425–6) that the physician returned to Persia, rightly rejected by Lenfant (2004: XXII). Cf. the equally implausible suggestion (cf. Rettig 1827: 16), according to which Ctesias did not leave Persia before 394/3 BCE.

[24] Cf. the question put by Brown (1978a: n. 23): 'can he be counting the eight years from 398 instead of 400 BCE?'

[25] Cf. Eck (1990: 434), Lenfant (2004: XXIII–XXIV, 2009: 26).

ἐν **Πέρσαις ὀρνίθιον**) is roughly the same (*Art.* 19.4: ῥυντάκης).[26] We shall return to this scene at the end of this chapter.

The final mention of Ctesias by Plutarch corresponds to the last sections of his own *Persica* and to the end point of the work in the year 398/7 BCE (*FGrH* 688 F 30.72–5 = *Bibl.* cod. 72, p. 44 b 20–41):

(72) The reasons why the king quarrelled with Evagoras king of Salamis. Evagoras sent messengers to Ctesias in order to receive letters from Abuletes. Ctesias wrote a letter to him on his reconciliation with Anaxagoras the king of Cyprus. Evagoras then sent envoys to Cyprus, and Ctesias sent letters to Evagoras. (73) Conon, meanwhile, spoke to Evagoras about coming to the king. Evagoras sent a letter on matters he thought he merited from the king. Conon sent a letter to Ctesias; Evagoras paid tribute to the king. Letters were sent to Ctesias. Ctesias spoke with the king about Conon and wrote a letter to the latter. Evagoras sent gifts to Satibarzanes. Messengers were sent to Cyprus. A letter was sent from Conon to the king and Ctesias. (74) Messengers sent from the Spartans to the king were watched; the king sent a letter to Conon and to the Spartans which Ctesias personally carried. Conon was appointed as commander of the fleet by Pharnabazus. (75) Ctesias went to his homeland Cnidus and Sparta. There was a trial at Rhodes for the Spartan envoys and an acquittal.[27]

(72) Αἰτίαι δι᾽ ἃς Εὐαγόρᾳ βασιλεῖ Σαλαμῖνος βασιλεὺς Ἀρτοξέρξης διηνέχθη. καὶ ἄγγελοι Εὐαγόρα πρὸς Κτησίαν ὑπὲρ τοῦ λαβεῖν παρὰ Ἀβουλήτου τὰς ἐπιστολάς· καὶ Κτησίου πρὸς αὐτὸν ἐπιστολὴ περὶ τοῦ διαλλαγῆναι αὐτὸν Ἀναξαγόρᾳ τῷ Κυπρίων βασιλεῖ. Τῶν παρὰ Εὐαγόρα ἀγγέλων εἰς Κύπρον ἄφιξις, καὶ τῶν παρὰ Κτησίου γραμμάτων ἀπόδοσις Εὐαγόρα. (73) Καὶ Κόνωνος πρὸς Εὐαγόραν λόγος ὑπὲρ τοῦ πρὸς βασιλέα ἀναβῆναι· καὶ Εὐαγόρα ἐπιστολὴ περὶ ὧν ἠξιώθη ὑπ᾽ αὐτοῦ· καὶ Κόνωνος πρὸς Κτησίαν ἐπιστολή· καὶ βασιλεῖ παρὰ Εὐαγόρα φόρος· καὶ τῶν ἐπιστολῶν Κτησίᾳ ἀπόδοσις. Κτησίου λόγος πρὸς βασιλέα περὶ Κόνωνος· καὶ ἐπιστολὴ πρὸς αὐτόν. Τῶν παρὰ Εὐαγόρου δώρων ἀπόδοσις Σατιβαρζάνῃ· καὶ τῶν ἀγγέλων τῶν εἰς Κύπρον ἄφιξις· καὶ Κόνωνος ἐπιστολὴ πρὸς βασιλέα καὶ Κτησίαν. (74) Ὡς ἐτηρήθησαν οἱ παρὰ Λακεδαιμονίων ἄγγελοι πεμφθέντες πρὸς βασιλέα. Βασιλέως ἐπιστολὴ πρὸς Κόνωνα καὶ πρὸς Λακεδαιμονίους, ἃς Κτησίας αὐτὸς ἐκόμισεν. Ὡς ὑπὸ Φαρναβάζου ναύαρχος Κόνων ἐγένετο. (75) Κτησίου εἰς Κνίδον τὴν πατρίδα ἄφιξις καὶ εἰς Λακεδαίμονα· καὶ κρίσις πρὸς τοὺς Λακεδαιμονίων ἀγγέλους ἐν Ῥόδῳ, καὶ ἄφεσις.

Ἀβουλήτου B: Ἀβουλίτου C, Jacoby ‖ ἐν Ῥόδῳ B: ἐν λόγῳ C

---

[26] Cf. Hesychius, s.v. ῥυνδάκη ρ, 503 Schmidt. Arnott (2007: 303): 'It is uncertain whether Rhyndakē and Rhyntakēs are one and the same bird, and impossible to make any plausible guess at its or their identity.' Despite the fact that the identification of the bird is difficult, one should mention that MPer. *Rund* is the name of the Ricebird. See Vullers (1864: 54): *Avis, quae in Oryzetis frequens est.* Cf. Steingass (1963 [1892]: 588), Johnson (1952: 633). See Benveniste (1966: 485).

[27] The last episode was often interpreted as meaning that Ctesias was himself tried and acquitted. Yet as Lenfant (2004: XXI) points out, the Greek makes possible another understanding, i.e., that the trial mentioned was in fact not of Ctesias, but of the Spartan delegates. Cf. Jacoby (1922: 2036), Brown (1978a: 18), Eck (1990: 423–4). Cf. Llewellyn-Jones and Robson (2010: 17).

While the account may be garbled (note 'Evagoras then sent envoys to Cyprus'), the overall picture is clear. Conon, who was received by Evagoras I, king of Salamis, in Cyprus (in 405 BCE),[28] used that base in order to assist Athens and weaken Sparta. In order to achieve these aims, a fleet had to be established, and this needed the support of the Great King; hence a reconciliation between Evagoras and the Great King was needed (399/8 BCE).[29] Several sources report different lines of communication with the king, mostly emphasising the role of Pharnabazus, the satrap of Dascylium.[30] Ctesias' account may be true, in that this link with Pharnabazus only came later. One may note that the general trend in antiquity was to suppress Ctesias' own involvement in the talks: Isocrates omits his role altogether (*Evag.* 55–6; cf. *Philip* 62).[31]

Photius' summary includes a description of correspondence between Evagoras, Ctesias and the king, but it is very sketchy and vague, proving that near the end of the work, the patriarch presumably lost interest in the details. There are three stages in this correspondence:[32]

(1) Evagoras and Ctesias play a role.
(2) Conon is added; at this stage, a discussion takes place (probably appearing in a dialogue format in the original text) between Evagoras and Conon.
(3) The king appears as participant; there is a discussion between the king and Ctesias.

Conon is at the centre of the last two stages, and the entire correspondence is presented by Photius between two sentences. The

---

[28] See Chapter 2, cf. Xen. *Hell.* 2.1.28, Diod. 13.106.6, 14.39.1, Justin 5.6.10; Athen. 12.532b. See Ruzicka (2012: 45).

[29] See Costa (1974: 49). See Diod. 14.39.1. But cf. Lewis (1977: 141), who sees it as too early a date. Cf. Nepos, *Con.* 2.2, Philochorus *FGrH* 328 F 144–5. It was the creation of this fleet that prompted Agesilaus to campaign in Asia Minor. Lewis (1977: 141 n. 41) sets the date at 397 BCE. In that year Conon moved with forty ships to Cilicia (Diod. 14.39.4) and from there to Caunus in Caria. According to Isocrates (*Paneg.* 142), the king had not invested in the fleet for three years; it would appear that Artaxerxes found the threat from Agesilaus to be more serious; alternatively, he could have been suspicious of Conon. See March (1997: 265–8).

[30] See Xen. *Hell.* 5.6.24, 7.8.25. Nepos (*Con.* 2.1) has Conon arriving to Pharnabazus first. Cf. Justin, 6.1.4–9. See Barbieri (1955: 83). Stevenson (1997: 115 n. 2) explains this discrepancy by a possible confusion with Evagoras. See Lenfant (2004: 286 n. 744), Asmonti (2015: 120–5).

[31] Total rejection of Ctesias' testimony, however, may not be justified. See Stevenson (1997: 116, 140), who believes in the account of the last diplomatic mission of Ctesias as he had no obvious reason to exaggerate his role.

[32] Cf. Stevenson (1997: 114).

first speaks of the reason Artaxerxes and Evagoras quarrelled, presumably making use of the literary device of flashback/*analepsis*.
The second relates how Conon was appointed as an admiral by
Pharnabazus. The appearance of this detail after the mention of the
letters leads us to conclude that Conon's new appointment was part
of the reconciliation between the Great King and Evagoras.

There can be two instances in which Plutarch's letters fit the correspondence mentioned in *FGrH* 688 F 30: (I) the first letter of
Conon to Ctesias,[33] dispatched after a discussion the Athenian has
with Evagoras concerning a visit to the Persian king; (II) the king's
answer to Conon (*FGrH* 688 F 30.72: Κτησίου πρὸς αὐτὸν ἐπιστολὴ),
which is sent after a discussion in which Ctesias and Artaxerxes
participate. In Photius' summary Conon sends another letter to the
king, to which Artaxerxes replies.

Some scholars believe that Plutarch's references to Ctesias as inserting elements to Conon's letter come from a different author, presumably Deinon, who is allegedly mocking the physician.[34] Yet this is
unwarranted. There was hardly any author referring to Ctesias as a
historical agent in antiquity. Moreover, there is no factual difference
between the versions: the additions of Ctesias to the letter of Conon
influence the king to send him away. It is perfectly plausible that
Ctesias described how he escaped from Persia through this clever
ruse.[35]

Furthermore, Plutarch's passage relating Ctesias' manipulation
of the letter mentions Zenon the Cretan dancer and Polycritus the
Mendaean physician. We know that Ctesias referred to Zenon the
dancer from a passage in Athenaeus' work (1.22c = *FGrH* 688 F
31):[36]

> The famous dancers ... Zenon the Cretan was the most agreeable to
> Artaxerxes according to Ctesias.
> ὀρχησταὶ δὲ ἔνδοξοι ... Ζήνων δὲ ὁ Κρὴς ὁ πάνυ ᾿Αρταξέρξῃ προσφιλέστατος
> παρὰ Κτησίᾳ.

What about the other person? There was a historian by the name
Polycritus (*FGrH* 559), of Mende, whose lost works concerned Sicily:
F 1 (Diog. Laert. 2.63) on Aeschines at the court of Dionysius the

---

[33] *Pace* Stevenson (1997: 117), it is assumed that the physician was only an intermediate.

[34] Flacelière and Chambry (1979: 12), Dorati (1995: 45), Stevenson (1997: 25, 118), Lenfant (2004: 227 n. 20), Binder (2008: 264–6, 288–9). Smith (1881: 3, 16) suggested Polycritus as a source, rightly refuted by Krumbholz (1889: 5).

[35] For folkloristic parallels see categories K 511, 1851 in Thompson (1957).

[36] Interestingly, Ziegler (1972: 214) does not mention this passage. See Briant (2002a: 787–8, 293–4), on dancers and players. Cf. the wedding feast of Alexander: Athen. 12.539a.

Younger of Syracuse, F 2 (the Peripatetic *De mirabilibus ausculta-tionibus* 112), a description of remarkable water in Sicily, and F 3 (Diod. 13.83.3) on the wine cellar of a rich person in Acragas. Konrat Ziegler (1952) tends to identify the historian with the physician mentioned by Plutarch, based on chronology (the event in the first fragment refers to the year 357 BCE).[37] But this is completely unnecessary: we do not know the date of Polycritus the historian; the dramatic date does not inform us of the time of composition. The reference to this author in the Peripatetic paradoxographic work *De mirabilibus auscultationibus* (*On Marvellous Things Heard*) may place him before the third or second centuries BCE, but there are sections in that work which are rather late, so the dating is inconclusive.[38]

A clue may be provided in that Polycritus related a story (*FGrH* 559 F 2) about a lake that would throw those who bathed in it up in the air, after reaching the number of fifty people.[39] Indeed, this story is told of a lake in India by a physician – Ctesias himself (*FGrH* 688 F 45.47: 'there is a spring in India . . . when they [the bathers – E.A.] leap into it, the water hurls them out', ὅτι κρήνην ἐν Ἰνδοῖς φησιν . . . ὅταν δὲ εἰσπηδῶσιν, ἐκβάλλει αὐτοὺς τὸ ὕδωρ ἄνω).[40] The similarity between the two descriptions is so remarkable[41] that a certain link between them was made in ancient times. The association of the Indian and Sicilian lakes is noticed by Callimachus, as quoted in the book of marvels *Rerum mirabilium collectio* (*Collection of Wonders*), attributed to the third century BCE Antigonus of Carystus, 150: 'Ctesias writes about one of the lakes in India, which does not accept whatever is cast in it, like the ponds in Sicily and Media . . .').[42] If the two lakes were connected, the two authors may have been joined as well.

A plausible explanation for the strange appearance of the

---

[37] Also Auberger (1991: 9). Jacoby (1955: 516), multiplying entities, speaks of two figures which are grandfather and grandson. Luraghi (*BNJ* 559) makes 'Polykritos the Younger' another physician-historian; cf. Lenfant (2010). Cf. Tuplin (2004: 318–19).

[38] Its nucleus goes back to the third century BCE. See Ziegler (1949a: 1149–52), Vanotti (2007). For ancient evidence, see Athen. 12.541ab.

[39] . . . τὸ δὲ πέρας ἕως εἰς πεντήκοντα ἀνδρῶν . . . ἐπειδὰν δὲ τοῦτον τὸν ἀριθμὸν λάβῃ, ἐκ βάθους πάλιν ἀνοιδοῦν **ἐκβάλλειν** μετέωρα τὰ σώματα τῶν λουομένων ἔξω ἐπὶ τὸ ἔδαφος ('its limit is up to fifty men. . . . When it receives this number, it swells up from the bottom and throws the bodies of the bathers out onto the land').

[40] The anecdote recurs in the MS of the anonymous authors, called the *Paradoxographus Florentinus*, 3: 'there is a spring in India which throws out those who jump in it on to dry land like a catapult, in accordance with the history of Ctesias' (κρήνη ἐν Ἰνδοῖς, ἣ τοὺς κολυμβῶντας ἐπὶ τὴν γῆν **ἐκβάλλει** ὡς ἀπ' ὀργάνου, ὡς ἱστορεῖ Κτησίας).

[41] Cf. Lenfant (2004: XXXV n. 117).

[42] περὶ δὲ λιμνῶν Κτησίαν μὲν ἱστορεῖν λέγει (scil. Καλλίμαχος) τῶν ἐν Ἰνδοῖς λιμνῶν τὴν μὲν τὰ εἰς αὐτὴν ἀφιέμενα <μὴ> καταδέχεσθαι, καθάπερ τὴν ἐν Σικελίᾳ καὶ Μήδοις.

Mendaean historian in a story of Ctesias would be a stray marginal gloss made by a reader of Ctesias who was acquainted with Polycritus, a gloss that may have entered the text. It may be the case that Plutarch encountered this awkward reference to Polycritus in a manuscript he read, concerned with marvels, presumably a text unrelated to the material he consulted for the *Artaxerxes*. It would not be far-reaching to assume that Plutarch amusingly inserted this late historian into the Persian court, harping again on the theme of being present where one should not be, very closely related to the image of Ctesias manipulating his own text by inserting the names of another person (that is, himself). One may be tempted to think that a physician called 'Polycritus of Mende' did not appear in Ctesias' original account at all – if ever such a physician existed. Polycritus should probably be cast out of this scene like the bathers from the fabulous lake. This duplication of physicians, as well as the duplication of the story, may also be Plutarch's literary presentation of the division within Ctesias' story between himself as an author and as an agent.

Let us turn now to the last of Plutarch's explicit references to Ctesias, in the *De sollertia animalium*. In his work *Nature of Animals* (*De Natura Animalium*, Περὶ Ζῴων Ἰδιότητος), which is a series of examples of exotic animal behaviour, Claudius Aelian writes (*NA* 7.1 = *FGrH* 688 F 34a):

I have learned that the oxen in Susa are not without knowledge of arithmetic. As evidence that this assertion is not only boasting, is the story that in Susa the king has oxen which can each draw one hundred buckets of water to the arid places in the parks. Indeed, they do this duty with great solemnity whether it was forced upon them or they were raised to do it and you would never observe one avoiding it. Yet, if you attempted to force them to draw up even one pitcher more than the mentioned hundred, you could neither sway nor coerce them, neither with thrashing nor with or charming words. This says Ctesias.

Πέπυσμαι δὲ ἄρα καὶ ἀριθμητικῆς τὰς βοῦς οὐκ ἀμοίρους εἶναι τὰς Σουσίδας. καὶ ὡς οὐκ ἔστιν ἄλλως κόμπος τὸ εἰρημένον, μάρτυς ὁ λόγος ὁ λέγων ἐν Σούσοις τῷ βασιλεῖ βοῦς εἰς τοὺς παραδείσους πολλὰς εἰς τὰ ἧττον ἐπίρρυτα ἀντλεῖν ἑκάστην κάδους ἑκατόν. Οὐκοῦν ἢ τὸν ἐπινηθέντα αὐταῖς ἢ τὸν συντραφέντα ἐκ πολλοῦ μόχθον προθυμότατα ἐκτελοῦσι, καὶ οὐκ ἂν βλακεύουσάν τινα θεάσαιο· εἰ δὲ πέρα τῆς προειρημένης ἑκατοντάδος ἕνα γοῦν προσλιπαρήσειας κάδον ἀνιμήσασθαι, οὐ πείσεις οὐδὲ ἀναγκάσεις, οὔτε παίων οὔτε κολακεύων. λέγει Κτησίας.

προσλιπαρήσειας Hercher: προσλιπαρήσαις codd.

It seems that both Plutarch and Aelian convey the same note and hardly change its skeletal structure; even the attribution to Ctesias comes at the end in both variants. Theoretically, Aelian could have relied on Plutarch for this passage, or else the section could have been interpolated in Aelian's work by a later reader of Plutarch's work. Indeed, many of the examples given in both works parallel each other and even seem to roughly follow the same order. For instance, the examples in Aelian's work which find parallels to *De soll. anim.* 12.968e to 14.970c alternate between the sixth and seventh book of the *NA*,[43] the section *De soll. anim.* 20.974bc corresponds to Aelian's *NA* 6.3–4, and the section *De soll. anim.* 23.976a–b follows almost exactly the sequence of *NA* 8.4–6. Yet the differences between the two works, as well as the fact that in Aelian some of the anecdotes are fuller, would make it probable that both authors relied independently on the same source (or sources), whether directly or indirectly, relying on some other work which culled the references to animals from Ctesias' *Persica* (esp. *Indica*). Aelian cites Ctesias elsewhere in his work, and he never relies on Plutarch in the other instances.[44] One of the compilers who could be considered the common source for Aelian and Plutarch is Ctesias' fellow Carian, Alexander of Myndus (first century CE), in his own work *On Animals* (Περὶ Ζῴων; Athen. 9.392c, cf. 5.221b), known to both authors.[45]

The fact that Plutarch includes only a single reference to Ctesias in his work on animals, although there were probably other examples he could have added, indicates that Plutarch perhaps had no deeper acquaintance with the *Persica* at the stage he wrote *De sollertia*,[46] or else wished to keep the mention of Ctesias minimal, being aware of his reputation.

The anecdote is analogous to the curious story from Ctesias, told by Photius (*FGrH* 688 F 15.58 = *Bibl.* cod. 72, p. 42 a 17–19), according to which the mules pulling the wagon with the corpse of Artaxerxes I refused to move, 'as if they were waiting' for the body of his son Xerxes II, and only when it soon joined them did they leave (αἱ γὰρ ἄγουσαι τὴν ἁρμάμαξαν ἡμίονοι, ὥσπερ ἀναμένουσαι καὶ τὸν τοῦ παιδὸς νεκρόν, οὐκ ἤθελον πορεύεσθαι· ὅτε δὲ κατέλαβε, σὺν προθυμίῃ ἀπῄεσαν). See also the fifty bathers limit in the lake (above).

---

[43] Ael. *NA* 6.52, 7.15, 6.59, 7.10, 7.13, 6.49, 6.25, 7.40.

[44] Aelian's citations of Ctesias can be classed in two groups: one is mainly in book 4 (*NA* 4.21, 4.26, 4.27, 4.32, 4.36, 4.41, 4.46, 4.52) with two occurrences in book 3 (3.3) and book 5 (5.3); the second group is in books 16–17 (16.2, 16.31, 16.37, 16.42, 17.29, 17.34).

[45] Ael. *NA* 3.23, 4.33, 5.27, 10.34; Plut. *Mar.* 17.6, although strictly speaking, this is most likely a reference to Alexander's *On Birds* (Περὶ Πτηνῶν): cf. Athen. 2.64b, 65ab, 9.387f, 9.388d, 9.389c, 9.390f, 9.391bc, 9.392c, 9.393ab, 9.393d, 9.394d, 9.395c–e, 9.398c. See Wellmann (1892), Arnott (1987). These works may have been sections of a book called *Collection of Marvels* (Θαυμασίων Συναγωγή), attributed to an 'Alexander' by Photius (*Bibl.* cod. 188 p. 145 b 9–15, cf. cod. 189, p. 145 b 35–9, cod. 190 p. 147 b 23–6).

[46] Cf. Binder (2008: 21).

XENOPHON REVERSED (*ART.* 11, 18)

A text with which Plutarch's readers in the know would probably compare his description is Xenophon's *Anabasis*. Plutarch seems to assume this comparison, and even to promote it.[47] Through this comparison, Plutarch is able to convey a further message needed for characterisation. For instance, in Chapter 1, Ctesias' depiction of the Battle of Cunaxa was quoted (*Art.* 11.1), relating that Ariaeus, a friend of Cyrus, made the first throw, but failed to hit. Xenophon also mentions Ariaeus and calls him 'the satrap (ὕπαρχος) of Cyrus' (*Anab.* 1.8.5), especially honoured by the prince (*Anab.* 3.2.5).[48] In the picture Plutarch presents, Ctesias apparently had Ariaeus play an important role at the battlefront, but according to Xenophon, Ariaeus was not anywhere near Cyrus during the clash, and was placed at the head of his left wing (*Anab.* 1.8.5). Furthermore, Xenophon claims that Ariaeus differed from all the other friends of Cyrus surrounding him in that he alone did not die in the course of the war (*Anab.* 1.9.31) or near his corpse (*Oec.* 4.19). When he heard about the death of Cyrus, he fled with his soldiers and reached the last station held before the battle (*Anab.* 1.10.1, 2.1.3). Even Diodorus (14.24.1), who calls him Aridaeus (Ἀριδαῖος ὁ Κύρου σατράπης), describes him as one who was not near Cyrus. Diodorus has Aridaeus initially clashing with the barbarians positioned against the left flank, where he was located (cf. 14.22.5). Several scholars assume that because of the surprise attack by the king, Ariaeus did not even have time to reach the front.[49] Moreover, the fact that Ariaeus did not participate in the battle (as well as his later betrayal of the Greeks)[50] may explain the king's clemency in his case.[51]

Rather than merely noting this difference, or assuming that the difference stems from a misunderstanding on the part of Ctesias or Plutarch,[52] it would be simpler to propose that Ctesias invented

---

[47] Cf. Shipley (1997: 48) on the *Agesilaus*.

[48] His description as φίλος, 'friend', by Plutarch, implies a position parallel to a real honour at the royal court. See Briant (2002a: 308–9).

[49] Cf. Xen. *Anab.* 1.8.14. See Anderson (1974: 106–7, 111), Tuplin (2011: 471–2, 477), Wylie (1992: 125 n. 17), Bigwood (1983: 343, 347, 355) *pace* Tarn (1933: 9).

[50] Xen. *Anab.* 2.4.1–2, 5. 9–10, 2.5.28, 35–42, 3.2.2, 5, 17, 3.5.1.

[51] He may have continued to be the satrap of Great Phrygia in the 390s (based on Diod. 4.80.8: διὰ Ἀριαίου σατράπου; cf. Judeich (1895) and Lewis (1977: 119 n. 78). Yet Hornblower (1994: 78–9) convincingly shows that he was not a satrap himself, but acted at the service of others (see *Hellenica Oxyrhynchia* 19.3, where he is subordinate to Tithraustes, and cf. Diod. 14.80.6–8 and Polyaen. 7.16.1; cf. Xen. *Hell.* 4.1.27). Cf. Bruce (1967: 90–1), Occhipinti (2016: 36).

[52] Cf. Lenfant (2004: 281). Manfredini, Orsi and Antelami (1987: 282) propose the existence of two persons called Ariaeus at the scene.

this description, in the same manner he used the name Ariaeus for the character of the Arabian king who was the ally of the legendary Ninus in another dramatic scene (Diod. 2.1.5 = *FGrH* 688 F 1b 1.5). Plutarch employs this depiction to highlight his main theme: Ariaeus is made to appear as if he were present in the clash between the brothers, while almost all the other evidence shows that he was not. This portrayal anticipates the king's false claim to have been present at the scene of his brother's death.

If this is so, and this is the impression Plutarch's readers would get from this scene, then there is significance in the depiction of the spears thrown. It may be the case that Plutarch cleverly uses the image of the spear missing its mark to indicate Ctesias' fallacious tall stories where truth is lacking. Truth signifies correspondence with reality, like a spear hitting the mark, not missing it. One would recall the meaning of the archaic word νημερτής, denoting truthful, as something not missing, or not failing to strike, the target.[53] In that case, Ariaeus' failure alludes to Ctesias' blatant fiction, while the king's failure to hit Cyrus anticipates his later false version concerning the prince's death. That Artaxerxes nevertheless hit someone else shows there may have been a grain of truth in the story, in anticipation of the blurring of fact and fantasy in the royal version. The fact that Cyrus succeeds in hitting Artaxerxes and throwing him off his horse implies that Cyrus' words concerning his brother earlier on were accurate (and self-fulfilling): the king cannot hold his place on his horse after all.

Furthermore, readers note that Cyrus is not the first to throw the spear. According to Xenophon (*Anab.* 1.8.26), the prince caught sight of the king and with the cry 'I see the man,' he rushed upon him and struck him through his breastplate. Diodorus (14.23.6) follows suit. This presentation would show Cyrus' bravery (albeit also his ill-advised rashness) in the face of danger, and his impulsive desire for glory. Ctesias' version as Plutarch brings it robs Cyrus of the honour of the first throw. A similar story in Ctesias, which may have been familiar to Plutarch's readers,[54] was the premature throw of Megabyzus, the courtier of Artaxerxes I during their joint hunt (*FGrH* 688 F 14.43);[55] the king was justly infuriated, even though this throw may have saved his life. As Ariaeus almost appropriates Cyrus

---

[53] Cf. Cole (1983:13–16).
[54] On its appearance in the collection of sayings *Regum et Imperatorum Apophthegmata* (*Sayings of Kings and Commanders*) attributed to Plutarch (173d), see Appendix II.
[55] Cf. Curt. Ruf. 8.6.7.

of the glory of killing the king, Artaxerxes would later on arrogate the reputation for killing his brother from the ones who actually did it.

Those who read Plutarch's *Artaxerxes* against the background of Xenophon's *Anabasis* would probably find another element odd. Ctesias' description, as presented by Plutarch, and similar to Diodorus' account (14.23.6), has Artaxerxes falling down and being rushed out of the battlefield.[56] Diodorus even gives the impression that the king's injury prevented him from remaining in the battlefield; Tissaphernes appears as assuming command in the ensuing clash,[57] while the king is still recovering from the wound several days later (14.26.1). But the story told by Xenophon has the king highly active in the battle, leading his men to the camp of Cyrus (*Anab.* 1.10.1, 2, 4), organising his forces to attack the Greek army (*Anab.* 1.10.5), moving down to their rear (*Anab.* 1.10.6), joining forces with Tissaphernes (*Anab.* 1.10.6, 8) and negotiating with the Greeks through messengers (*Anab.* 2.1.7, 2.3.1). It was crucial to Ctesias' version that the king was not present, in view of the following narrative. Thus, the image Plutarch's readers would form of the king here is the opposite of that which they would make of Ariaeus: while Ariaeus should not be present at the battlefield but is there, Artaxerxes should be present (as in Xenophon's account) but is now absent.

A section from Plutarch's description has been withheld from Chapter 2 and is appropriate to our discussion here (*Art.* 11.3–4):

> Cyrus' horse carried him with passion to the enemy's front for a great distance, and as it was already in the dark, he was unrecognised by his enemies while his friends were looking for him. Elated by his victory and filled with anger and boldness, he rode and cried 'Get out of the way, you wretched men!' And this he shouted in Persian many times; some people stepped aside and bowed. Then the tiara (cap) fell from the head of Cyrus.
>
> (3) Κῦρον δὲ τοῖς πολεμίοις ἐνειλούμενον ὁ ἵππος ἐξέφερεν ὑπὸ θυμοῦ μακράν, ἤδη σκότους ὄντος ἀγνοούμενον ὑπὸ τῶν πολεμίων καὶ ζητούμενον ὑπὸ τῶν φίλων. (4) Ἐπαιρόμενος δὲ τῇ νίκῃ καὶ μεστὸς ὢν ὀργῆς καὶ θράσους, διεξήλαυνε βοῶν 'ἐξίστασθε πενιχροί'· τοῦτο δὲ περσιστὶ πολλάκις αὐτοῦ βοῶντος, οἱ μὲν ἐξίσταντο προσκυνοῦντες, ἀποπίπτει δὲ τῆς κεφαλῆς ἡ τιάρα τοῦ Κύρου.
> ὀργῆς G : ὁρμῆς R

The bold and overconfident character of Cyrus is insinuated by Xenophon's portrayal,[58] but comes out clearly in this description of

---

[56] Cf. Tuplin (2011: 472–3). The description may be reliable; Persian kings seldom participated in battles (see Briant, 2002a: 227), and Artaxerxes may have taken the opportunity to step out of the armed conflict.

[57] But this is very Diodoran, see Bigwood (1983: 352–4).

[58] Despite his overt attempt to claim otherwise: *Anab.* 1.9.5 (αἰδημονέστατος ... τῶν ἡλικιωτῶν, 'Cyrus was the most modest of his fellows').

Ctesias, as Plutarch brings it. In both versions, Cyrus sees the Greeks as defeating the troops opposite them, and chooses to make a plunge forward (*Anab.* 1.8.21–4). The development which Xenophon charts from the characterisation of Cyrus as 'not tempted to join the chase' (*Anab.* 1.8.21: οὐδ' ὡς ἐξήχθη διώκειν) to the constrasting 'could not contain himself' (*Anab.* 1.8.26: εὐθὺς οὐκ ἠνέσχετο) is made more dramatic in Plutarch's description, as Cyrus completely loses control of the situation. While Xenophon gives Cyrus a rational basis for this transition (δείσας μὴ ὄπισθεν γενόμενος κατακόψῃ τὸ Ἑλληνικὸν ('feared lest [the king] might outflank the rear of the Greeks and massacre them'), in Plutarch's use of Ctesias' account, only passion plays a part in his action. Thus, against Xenophon's picture, Cyrus' impudence becomes even more stressed and prominent.[59]

Plutarch thus seems to be using Ctesias' description in an implicit contrast with that of Xenophon, presumably known to his readers, to emphasise the ostensible sudden change in the prince's discretion. One element of Ctesias' story is that of Cyrus' horse; the use of this picture is as an ironic reversal of Xenophon's obituary (*Anab.* 1.9.5), where the prince is said to be the most devoted to horses and the best in handling horses, φιλιππότατος καὶ τοῖς ἵπποις ἄριστα χρῆσθαι). Cyrus is then made to utter different words than Xenophon gives him: instead of shouting 'I see the man' (Τὸν ἄνδρα ὁρῶ), he commands his men to get out of his way. This presentation displays him in a different, unflattering and vain light.[60] The impression a reader acquainted with Xenophon would have now is that Cyrus does *not* see clearly, and that, furthermore, there are obstacles in his way (which he wishes to remove).

An interpretation according to which Cyrus' real self is now revealed is suggested by the addition that he shouts in Persian (bereft as he is of his Greek mercenaries), and by the important detail, that a headdress worn by him, now drops. Readers of Xenophon who would remember that Cyrus goes into battle bareheaded (*Anab.* 1.8.6)[61] would find in Plutarch's mention of the tiara Cyrus' attempt to cover and disguise.

---

[59] A similar response to that described here appears in the account of Diodorus, who relates Cyrus' elated feeling in his attack (14.23.7: Κῦρος **ἐπαρθεὶς** τῷ προτερήματι . . .). Cf. Plut. *Art.* 8.6 (τὸ τὸν Κύρου θράσος . . . 'the boldness of Cyrus'). Cf. Tuplin (2011: 474–5).

[60] See similar scenes and utterances in Plutarch's biographies: *Gai. Gracch.* 13.2, *Galb.* 26.5.

[61] Xenophon certainly does not give the impression that Cyrus wears a helmet when he was struck; cf. Bassett (1999: 476–7). In the MSS of Xenophon's *Anabasis* the next sentence states that the other Persians had their heads exposed (λέγεται δὲ καὶ τοὺς ἄλλους Πέρσας ψιλαῖς ταῖς κεφαλαῖς ἐν τῷ πολέμῳ διακινδυνεύειν), but this seems to be a late interpolation, based on the image of the bare head as suiting warriors (cf. Strabo 11.13.9) and a misunderstanding of Hdt. 3.12 or 7.61.

It is as if Plutarch's Cyrus tries to cover his head and disguise his real barbarian and arrogant personality. Of course, the confusion increases at night.[62] Sherylee R. Bassett (1999: 477) is probably right in claiming that Cyrus looked like his brother because of the tiara, the headdress which covers the face, neck, ears and chin.[63] The upright tiara was the privilege of the king,[64] and it may be that Cyrus' cap was worn in the royal manner.[65] It is presumably because of this cover that people prostrated themselves before him,[66] before the cap fell down.[67]

The theme of identity, reflecting on the obscure character of Cyrus, is seen in the figure of Mithridates. A reader coming to Plutarch's rendition of Ctesias' account, acquainted with Xenophon's picture, is surprised to note that the killer of Cyrus has a name. Xenophon merely writes that 'someone hit Cyrus' with a spear (*Anab.* 1.8.27: αὐτὸν ἀκοντίζει τις παλτῷ). Diodorus makes him 'one of the occassional Persians' (14.23.7: ὑπό τινος τῶν τυχόντων Περσῶν). The experience of Plutarch's readers is thus one of discovery when encountering the person's real name, Mithridates. Plutarch appears to be employing this feature further to enhance the issue of uncredited glory, which will soon occupy the rest of the narrative. Indeed, when Plutarch mentions the assistant of Mithridates who picked up the soaked saddle-cloth, he merely refers to this person now as 'the man who hit Cyrus' (τοῦ τὸν Κῦρον βαλόντος ἀκόλουθος).

The fact that Cyrus falls off his horse and prefers to walk even though another steed is offered may highlight those very negative traits that the prince pointed out in his brother, and shows him to be unkingly. Bearing in mind the abovementioned well-known association of the horse with royalty in Persia, this portrayal of Cyrus is in direct contrast to the picture the readers would know from Xenophon ('most kingly', βασιλικώτατος: *Anab.* 1.9.1).

---

[62] Xenophon places sunset at a much later stage of the battle (*Anab.* 1.10.15) than Ctesias and may be correct. Cf. Wylie (1992: 126): Cyrus made his attack at about two or three p.m. Cf. Stevenson (1997: 89), who opts for four p.m. Cf. Hewitt (1919: 86–8). Diodorus (14.24.3) appears closer to Xenophon's version here.

[63] On this cap see Strabo, 15.3.15; see the figure of Darius III in the Alexander mosaic; see Hinz (1974), Calmeyer (1977).

[64] See Xen. *Anab.* 2.5.23, Sen. *De Benef.* 6.31.12, Plut. *De frat. am.* 488d, Hesych. s.v. τιάρα T, 836 Schmidt (s.v. κυρβασία· ὀρθὴ τιάρα K, 4662 Latte). The others wore theirs in the regular manner (cf. Aristoph. *Av.* 1486–7, Hdt. 7.61, 3.12, Xen. *Cyr.* 8.3.13, Plut. *Reg. et imp. apoph.* 173d, *De sera*, 565a). See Tuplin (2007).

[65] See the theory of Weiser (1989: esp. 281), who claims that Cyrus coined already in the summer of 401 BCE currency of himself with the upright royal tiara.

[66] Cyrus appears surrounded by enemies also in Justin, 5.11.8–9; cf. Oros. 2.18.2.

[67] Cf. Hdt. 3.12, 7.61. Cf. Lenfant (2004: 281 n. 687–8) who believes Xenophon's version and argues that Cyrus was bareheaded in order to look like a Greek mercenary. But this again plays on the theme of masking identities, which goes back to Ctesias' account.

To readers familiar with Xenophon's very brief account (*Anab.* 1.8.26–27), Plutarch's presetation of Ctesias' version may indeed seem to be lengthy and tedious, as Plutarch seems to imply himself. The significant difference between Ctesias and Xenophon is that the latter implies that Cyrus died instantaneously during the clash with his brother, while Ctesias prefers to postpone the death till later.

Turning to *Art.* 18, we may observe the following. Xenophon's readers would find two depictions surprising. First, the description of Clearchus and the generals as remaining in prison goes against the information given in Ariaeus' account very close to the capture of the commanders (*Anab.* 2.5.38: Κλέαρχος ... τέθνηκε), according to which Clearchus, Agias and Socrates died instantly. It also goes against the impression Xenophon conveys (*Anab.* 2.6.1) that they did not survive long in prison.[68] Again, persons are present when we would expect them not to be.

Second, the dismay readers might feel at the generals' behaviour towards Clearchus in Plutarch's account may be enhanced against the reading of Xenophon's obituary of the generals in *Anab.* 2.6. In particular, the latter's description of Agias and Socrates, with whom no one has found any fault in terms of friendship (*Anab.* 2.6.30: οὐδεὶς κατεγέλα οὔτ' εἰς φιλίαν αὐτοὺς ἐμέμφετο), does not lead us to expect this demeanour in Plutarch's passage. Cleverly, Plutarch lets the frustration of readers' anticipation almost echo Tissaphernes' breach of the generals' expectations (cf. the story in Xen, *Anab.* 2.5.25–32, cf. Diod. 14.26.6–7) mentioned in the same section of the *Artaxerxes*. Yet, ironically, Tissaphernes' perfidy in arresting and killing Clearchus and the others was notorious in antiquity,[69] so that readers would expect this breach of expectations.

PROBABLE USE(S) OF CTESIAS

Let us examine Plutarch's probable use of Ctesias in the *Artaxerxes*, and what we can learn from it about the original *Persica* and about Plutarch's method of adaptation. The problematic nature of Plutarch's source analysis is evident from the start of the biography, since it appears that the biographer handles his material as he pleases. We saw above that in Photius' summary of Ctesias, there

---

[68] See Bigwood (1983: 356), Stevenson (1997: 73).
[69] Cf. Dio Chrys. 74.14. Polyaen. 7.18.1. The author of the end of the *Cyropaedia* (8.8.3) deems Tissaphernes' breaking of promises as a watershed, signalling the beginning of the deterioration of Persian morality.

were four royal brothers. Plutarch seems to follow Ctesias, yet this is
Ctesias in a completely new garb (*Art.* 1.2–3):

> Darius and Parysatis had four children: the eldest was Artaxerxes, after him
> Cyrus, and the younger ones were Ostanes and Oxathres. Cyrus was named
> after Cyrus the ancient, and the latter was given his name from the sun, as
> they say; for the Persians call the sun 'Cyrus'.
>
> Δαρείου γὰρ καὶ Παρυσάτιδος παῖδες ἐγένοντο τέσσαρες· πρεσβύτατος μὲν
> Ἀρτοξέρξης, μετ' ἐκεῖνον δὲ Κῦρος, νεώτεροι δὲ τούτων Ὀστάνης καὶ Ὀξάθρης.
> Ὁ μὲν οὖν Κῦρος ἀπὸ Κύρου τοῦ παλαιοῦ τοὔνομα ἔσχεν, ἐκείνῳ δ' ἀπὸ τοῦ ἡλίου
> γενέσθαι φασί· Κῦρον γὰρ καλεῖν Πέρσας τὸν ἥλιον.

The opening line of Xenophon's *Anabasis* (1.1.1) is alluded to by
Plutarch, though the author is not mentioned explicitly.[70] Readers
have no reason to be given a particular reference in order to identify
it.[71] The biographer omits Xenophon's historic present, advances
the name (παῖδες) in front of the verb, and abandons the rhetorical
opposition of πρεσβύτερος – νεώτερος in favour of a more complex
structure: now Artaxerxes is the πρεσβύτατος, followed by Cyrus,
while the νεώτεροι are the last two brothers. The reason for this
change is fairly clear: whereas in Xenophon's account Cyrus is the
hero, contrasted with his brother, for Plutarch, Artaxerxes is the
main character. Plutarch almost deliberately works to make Cyrus
disappear amidst his brothers. His sophisticated change can hardly
be defined merely as 'correction'.[72] Corresponding to the recurrent
theme of the biography, the surprising appearance of two royal
brothers who were not present in the familiar account of Xenophon
is meant to anticipate the problematic royal version which would
insert persons into the narrative where they were not supposed to
be, and yet claim to be truthful. It also introduces the question of
whether written texts can ever arrive at the truth, for Plutarch is not
faithful to Xenophon's text, yet is still truthful.

That Plutarch took from Ctesias the derivation of the name 'Cyrus'
from the sun[73] seems to be firmly established.[74] Plutarch says φασί,

---

[70] Plutarch did not find it in Deinon's work, as curiously maintained by Smith (1881:1, cf.
15, 38). See Morris (1881: 237), in a review of Smith's dissertation and Mantey (1888: 13–14).
Cf. Krumbholz (1889: 19).

[71] The *Anabasis*' opening was very well known among writers of the second century CE.
Lucian (*Quom. hist. consc.* 23) sees in it a model to be followed. Cf. Ps.-Ael. Arist. *Ars Rhet.*
2.12.6. Cf. Rutherford (1998: 143).

[72] See Stadter (2012: 45) for a different view.

[73] The word for 'sun' in OPer. was presumably *hwar, modern Persian *Khwur* or *Hur*.
There was a certain connection of the radiance of the sun and the Persian notion of royal glory
or (good) 'fortune', the Avestan *Khvarenah* (or xᵛarənah, OPer. *farnah*–). See Gnoli (1963),
Boyce (1982: 17 n. 23), Jacobs (1987). The link of the sun to the name Cyrus is not accepted
by all scholars. See Schmitt (2002: 59–60, 2006: 104). According to Strabo (15.3.6), this was

which probably refers to Ctesias and his informant(s) as rightly proposed by Lenfant (2004: 274, n. 630). One should note the hiatus ἀπὸ τοῦ ἡλίου, which appears in Photius' epitome as well (above),[75] and thus probably echoes Ctesias' original words (or an epitome of Ctesias used by all authors). Plutarch tends to avoid the hiatus.[76] A comparison with Photius' account shows that the explicit association of Cyrus the Younger with Cyrus the Great is Plutarch's own, and was not present in Ctesias' work. Yet the link between these two persons and its overtones was obviously clear to Ctesias' readers.[77]

Photius' account (see *FGrH* 688 F 15a = *Bibl.* cod. 72, p. 42 b 10, 15) has different names for the remaining brothers: Artostes (Ἀρτόστης) for the third and Oxendras (Ὀξένδρας) for the youngest. These are not different persons,[78] since both Photius and Plutarch report the same sequence of descendants.[79] It is rather an error in the transmission of the MSS of Photius or of the text of Ctesias (or his epitome) at Photius' disposal.[80] This is clearly so with regard to the last name mentioned by Photius (Ὀξένδρας), which makes no sense,[81] as opposed to Plutarch's Oxathres (Ὀξάθρης).[82] Ostensibly, it would seem that Plutarch is using some other source for these names, since the figure of Ostanes appears later (*Art.* 22.11), in a section which could not possibly have come from Ctesias.[83] If this is indeed the case and Plutarch is relying on an unknown author, then his overt claim to be dependent on Ctesias (*Art.* 1.4) may be interpreted as ironic,

---

not Cyrus' original name. For an interpretation of the name as Elamite see Henkelman (2011: 585 n. 25).

[74] See Haug (1854: 91), Mantey (1888: 3), Krumbholz (1889: 10).

[75] It also appears in Hesychius, s.v. 'Kuros' (K 4700 Latte).

[76] See Ziegler (1951: 932–3), Russell (1973: 18–41). On hiatus in the *Artaxerxes* see Schottin (1865: 14–16).

[77] For a suggestion that the name of Cyrus the Younger reflects a nostalgic yearning for an earlier time see Sancisi-Weerdenburg (1983a: 151).

[78] *Pace* Justi (1895: 398–9), cf. Schmitt (2006: 227).

[79] See Lenfant (2004: 274 n. 629).

[80] See Krumbholz (1889: 13), who assumes that the -αν of Ὀστάνης dropped, thereby making the incomprehensible Ὄστης, which was afterwards hypercorrected with the addition of the prefix Ἀρτ- . Lenfant (2004: 274 n. 629) also believes the Plutarchan version to be closer to the original reading of Ctesias. Cf. Bigwood (1976: 6–10, 21–3; 1978: 27 n. 30). See Binder (2008: 91–4; 2011: 64–5).

[81] See Justi (1895: 492), Lenfant (2004: 272 n. 608); Schmitt (1979: 123, 128; 2006: 177).

[82] It probably echoes OPer. *Hu-xšaθra*, 'with good rule'; cf. Schmitt (2006: 177). Cf. Justi (1895: 232, 500), Hinz (1975: 123).

[83] Cf. Smith (1881: 7). According to Mantey (1888: 3), the names of the brothers in Plutarch's version were taken without doubt from Deinon, and the biographer accepted, intentionally or unknowingly ('bewusst oder unbewusst') this historian's tradition in his work. Stevenson (1985: 19) justly opposes this contention, but seemingly for the wrong reason, namely, that Plutarch would have stated it explicitly if he had switched to Deinon at this stage. One should note that the name Ostanes is found as the grandfather of Darius III in Diodorus (17.5.5), and Oxathres as his brother (17.34.1). Cf. Krumbholz (1889: 12).

given his actual endorsement of a competing account. It would, however, be more probable that Plutarch does exclusively employ Ctesias for the names of the brothers. The appearance of Ostanes in *Art.* 22 may be explained by Plutarch's transference of some details to this person – who became important as the middle brother of the three remaining siblings after Cyrus' death – indeed, by Plutarch's imaginative addition.[84]

Plutarch abridged much of Ctesias' long description of an important event which followed in the original sequence of book 18 of the *Persica*; its details are preserved by Photius (F 15.55–56 = *Bibl.* cod. 72, p. 43 a 11–43 b 2):

(55) Arsaces, the king's son, who later changed his name to Artaxerxes, married Stateira, daughter of Idernes. At the same time, Teritouchmes, son of Idernes, married Amestris, the king's daughter, and after the death of his father, became satrap in his place. However, Teritouchmes had a half-sister by the same father named Rhoxane, who was beautiful and skilled with bow and spear. He fell in love with her, had an intimate relationship with her, and hated Amestris his wife. Eventually, he planned to throw her in a sack and to have 300 men, with whom he intended to rebel (against the king), pierce her. However, a certain Oudiastes, who had some influence on Teritouchmes, received letters from the king, promising that if he saved his daughter, he would be generously rewarded. Therefore, he attacked and killed Teritouchmes, although the latter fought boldly, killing many people. It is said he killed thirty-seven men.

(56) Mithridates, the son of Oudiastes, a shield bearer of Teritouchmes, was away. When he learned of the situation, he cursed his father, seized the city of Zaris and kept it for Teritouchmes. Parysatis then ordered Teritouchmes' mother, his brothers Mitrostes and Helicus, and his sisters (there were two in addition to Stateira) to be buried alive, and this was done. Rhoxane was cut into pieces while still alive. The king told Parysatis to give the same treatment to Stateira, his son's wife, but Arsaces, in tearful supplication, begged his parents and moved Parysatis to mercy. After she agreed, Ochus, also called Darius, told Parysatis that she would be sorry for this decision. This is the end of book 18.

The involvement of three hundred men in the endeavour to kill Amestris,[85] the battle where Teritouchmes fell, the letters from the king to Oudiastes, the capture of the city of Zaris[86] – all these imply some major occurrences and not merely court machinations. Darius'

---

[84] Cf. Pelling (2002c: 57; 2011: 57–8) on this feature in Plutarch's writing. See more below.

[85] One may find equivalence to the three hundred Greek mercenaries escorting Cyrus to his father: Xen. *Cyr.* 1.1.2, or the three hundred men accompanying Tissaphernes to Phrygia: Polyaen. 7.16.1; were they all bodyguards? Cf. Lenfant (2004: 140 n. 624).

[86] Zaris could be Zranka or Drangiana, modern Seistan in east Iran. Cf. Cook (1983: 255, 278). Note that a place called Zaranda is known from the inscriptions of Sargon II, in his eighth campaign against Urartu; see Chapter 5 below. Cf. Gardiner-Garden (1987: 17).

desire to execute Stateira of course foreshadows future events. It does not necessarily imply that Stateira is involved in the revolt, but it is an indication of the fear that she might act to promote her own family's interests, which are assumed to be opposed to those of her husband.[87] Parysatis' future regret for saving Stateira is echoed later in Artaxerxes' regret for listening to Stateira and executing Clearchus and the Greek generals (above).[88]

Out of the lengthy depiction of Teritouchmes' revolt, Plutarch abbreviates and preserves only Darius' desire to kill Stateira and her rescue by Arsicas (*Art.* 2.2):

> [Arsicas] married a beautiful and virtuous woman at the command of his parents and protected her despite their reluctance, for when the king had killed her brother he wished to do the same to her. However, by entreating his mother and by lamenting much, Arsicas just barely persuaded [her] not to execute his wife and not to separate them.
> Γυναῖκα δὲ καλὴν καὶ ἀγαθὴν ἔλαβε μὲν τῶν γονέων κελευόντων, ἐφύλαξε δὲ κωλυόντων. τὸν γὰρ ἀδελφὸν αὐτῆς ἀποκτείνας ὁ βασιλεὺς ἐβουλεύετο κἀκείνην ἀνελεῖν· Ὁ δ' Ἀρσίκας τῆς μητρὸς ἱκέτης γενόμενος καὶ πολλὰ κατακλαύσας, μόλις ἔπεισε μήτ' ἀποκτεῖναι μήτ' αὐτοῦ διαστῆσαι τὴν ἄνθρωπον.

Like Plutarch, Photius also has Arsicas pleading for the life of his spouse, yet the phrase is different. Photius describes the future king as addressing both of his parents and persuading them in tearful supplication not to kill Stateira (**πολλὰ** τὴν μητέρα καὶ τὸν πατέρα δάκρυσι καὶ κοπετοῖς ἐξιλεωσάμενος). Plutarch, on the other hand, makes Arsicas turn to his mother alone, in a picture which shows him as barely succeeding in convincing her not to execute his wife. Both authors, however, give the impression that Darius' change of heart and the relief of Stateira come after Parysatis is won over. Note Plutarch's use of the word **πολλὰ**, which may go back to Ctesias' text, as it is also found in Photius' version (F 15.56). Plutarch condenses the entire episode and makes it correspond to the immediate scene in the biography, the attempt of Parysatis to put Cyrus on the throne. Thus, Darius' frustrated wish (*Art.* 2.2: ὁ βασιλεὺς ἐβουλεύετο) is echoed later in Parysatis' unfulfilled desire to see Cyrus as king (*Art.* 2.3: βουλομένη βασιλεύειν). While Arsicas barely persuades his mother (*Art.* 2.2: μόλις ἔπεισε) to save Stateira, Parysatis is not able to have her way (*Art.* 2.5: οὐ . . . ἔπεισεν).

Cyrus' claim for the throne (*Art.* 2.4) on account of his birth

---

[87] Cf. the story of Intaphernes' wife (Hdt. 3.119) or that of Artaunte (Hdt. 9.108–10). See Sancisi-Weerdenburg (1983b: 30), Lenfant (2004: 273 n. 626).
[88] Cf. Mossman (2010: 160): 'one is left with Stateira as the only positive influence in his [Artaxerxes'] life'.

'in the purple' seems to perfectly suit Photius' portrayal of Cyrus as a person born after his mother became queen (cf. *FGrH* 688 F 15.51: τίκτει δὲ αὐτῷ ἕτερον υἱὸν βασιλεύουσα, above). Moreover, the sentiment of Parysatis towards Cyrus, 'But his mother had more love for Cyrus, and wished that he should succeed to the throne' (*Art.* 2.3: Ἡ δὲ **μήτηρ ὑπῆρχε** τὸν Κῦρον **μᾶλλον φιλοῦσα** καὶ βουλομένη βασιλεύειν ἐκεῖνον) probably appeared in Ctesias' narrative, judging by the affectionate feelings of Parysatis for Cyrus, both as an ambitious young prince and after his death – elements portrayed by the physician throughout the latter books.[89] Nevertheless, the phrasing is made to resemble Xenophon's original words (*Anab.* 1.1.4: Παρύσατις μὲν δὴ **ἡ μήτηρ ὑπῆρχε** τῷ Κύρῳ **φιλοῦσα** αὐτὸν **μᾶλλον** ἢ τὸν βασιλεύοντα Ἀρταξέρξην, 'for she had more love for him than for Artaxerxes who sat upon the throne').[90] The assertion is taken out of its context in Xenophon's *Anabasis*, namely, at the point of the delivery of Cyrus from the death sentence through the help of Parysatis (below). Plutarch introduces the special relations of the queen and her son at an earlier stage in the narrative, and thus enhances the picture of Cyrus as a prince whose ambition is fuelled by his mother's aspirations, presumably insinuated by Ctesias.

Plutarch's allusion to Xerxes' *porphyrogenesis* argument ('being born in the purple'), however (*Art.* 2.4), seems to point directly at Herodotus' report (Hdt. 7.2–3). According to the latter, Xerxes contends that he was born when Darius was already king (γένοιτο Δαρείῳ ἤδη βασιλεύοντι καὶ ἔχοντι τὸ Περσέων κράτος), whereas the birth of Artobazanes, his elder half-brother, occurred when Darius was still a *privatus* (ἔτι ἰδιώτῃ ἐόντι Δαρείῳ). Herodotus states that the person who counsels Xerxes to voice this claim is the exiled Spartan king Demaratus, son of Ariston. The appearance of these two items in the *Artaxerxes* is probably Plutarch's own addition, stemming from a recollection of the account of Herodotus; he was not influenced by a different source.[91] Ctesias was apparently not employed for the item concerning Demaratus. Contrary to Herodotus (6.61–70), the physician (*FGrH* 688 F 13.27) seems to have related that Demaratus first (πρῶτον) met the Persian monarch in Abydus, on the eve of

---

[89] See Manfredini, Orsi and Antelami (1987: 270), Lenfant (2004: 279 n. 664). It may be the case that in his report, Xenophon tries to tone down Parysatis' involvement in Cyrus' quest for the crown as part of his oblique dispute with Ctesias.

[90] *Pace* Stevenson (1985: 18), who notices the verbal resemblance, yet assumes all the same that Plutarch does not follow Xenophon's text directly.

[91] See Smith (1881: 8–9). But cf. Manfredini, Orsi and Antelami (1987: 270) for a contrary approach. It would seem that there is no need to suppose, like Mantey (1888: 5), that the reference to Xerxes and Demaratus comes from an interim source (i.e., Deinon).

the departure of the great campaign to Greece.[92] Plutarch presumably insinuates that in his account of Cyrus' argument regarding the Persian royal succession after Darius II, Ctesias borrowed from Herodotus' depiction of Xerxes' argument, concerning the succession after Darius I.

Parysatis succeeds in assisting one son, Artaxerxes, to preserve what he already has (Stateira), but fails to aid another son in achieving what he does not have (kingship). The first item comes from Ctesias, the second from Xenophon. Pertinent to our discussion here is the ironic manner in which the content is at odds with Plutarch's work method as it is seen in this instance. While describing Arsicas' success in safeguarding what he has, the biographer does the opposite: he abbreviates the original account of Ctesias and omits most of it. Conversely, by misplacing Xenophon's statement regarding Parysatis' support of Cyrus and putting it out of its original context, Plutarch produces an entirely novel picture concerning the involvement of the queen mother in her son's bid for power. While describing Cyrus' inability to bring about an unprecedented state of affairs, it is Plutarch who achieves this by changing his original source.

Photius begins his summary of *Persica* book 19 with this assertion (*FGrH* 688 F 16.57 = *Bibl.* cod. 72, p. 43 b 3–5):

> In the nineteenth book of his history, Ctesias describes how Dareiaeus Ochus died of illness in Babylon after ruling for thirty-five years, and then Arsaces became king, changing his name to Artaxerxes.
>
> Ἐν δὲ τῇ ιθ' ἱστορίᾳ διαλαμβάνει, ὡς Ὦχος ὁ Δαρειαῖος ἀπέθανεν ἀσθενήσας ἐν Βαβυλῶνι, ἔτη βασιλεύσας λε', βασιλεύει δὲ Ἀρσάκης ὁ μετονομασθεὶς Ἀρτοξέρης.

In Xenophon's account, Darius II falls ill during his war with the Cadusians (*Hell.* 2.1.13: ἐπεὶ αὐτῷ παρὰ τοῦ πατρὸς ἧκεν ἄγγελος λέγων ὅτι ἀρρωστῶν ἐκεῖνον καλοίη, ὢν ἐν Θαμνηρίοις τῆς Μηδίας ἐγγὺς Καδουσίων, ἐφ' οὓς ἐστράτευσεν ἀφεστῶτας, 'an envoy had arrived to him [to Cyrus – E.A.] from his father announcing that he was ill and bid him to come, for he was in Thamneria, Media, near the land of the Cadusians, against whom he campaigned, after they revolted'). If this depiction comes from the physician's work, as indeed proposed by Ronald Syme (1988a: 139), then it would be reasonable to suppose that the beginning of Xenophon's *Anabasis* (1.1.2), which Plutarch follows (*Art.* 3.1), also comes from him. According to this

---

[92] In his edition, Jacoby attempts to emend the text and suggests the form πρότερον, contrary to the MSS, in order to adjust it to Herodotus' story. This proposal, however, appears uncalled for, as the two accounts may have been different after all.

portrayal, Darius lies sick and sends for Cyrus from the Satrapy. One should note, however, that according to Photius, Darius II dies in Babylon, and not in Thamneria, as Xenophon has it. One option to resolve this discrepancy would be to suppose that Ctesias' original text was not clear, so that while Darius fell ill in Media, his deathbed was in Babylon, so that Xenophon got it wrong; alternatively, Photius could be mistaken, influenced by passages like Xen. *Cyr.* 8.6.22, which locates the Persian palace in Babylon for most days of the year.

Another indication that *Art.* 3.1 ultimately comes from Ctesias is a passage of Athenaeus (12.548e), in which a dying Persian monarch named Ochus advises his eldest son (πρεσβύτατος) on how to preserve the kingdom. Since Ochus/Artaxerxes III is known to have been poisoned and to have died instantaneously (Diod. 17.5.3–4), it seems more probable that this king has to be Ochus/Darius II, and the elder son is Artaxerxes.[93] It is feasible to suppose that this description is related to Ctesias' story of Darius' death (assuming indeed there was such a depiction), which also influenced Xenophon in the *Cyropaedia* (8.7.5–28: the final words of 'Cyrus' to his two sons at his deathbed).

The following scene in the biography alludes to the coronation ceremony in a temple (*Art.* 3.2–4):

> Shortly after the death of Darius, the king (Artaxerxes) went to Pasargadae in order to take part in the coronation ceremony performed by Persian priests. There was a temple of a warrior goddess, which might be comparable to Athena. The initiate had to go to the temple, cast aside his robes and take on the clothes worn by Cyrus the ancient before he became king, eat cake of figs, chew terebinth, and drink a cup of sour milk. If they did something else, it remained hidden from others. As Artaxerxes was about to perform the ritual, Tissaphernes came up to him with one of the priests, who had instructed Cyrus in his youth and taught him the skills of the Magi, and who had seemed to be upset more than any Persian when (Cyrus) had been denied inheritance of the crown. As a result, his charge against Cyrus was reliable. He claimed that Cyrus was preparing an ambush in the temple and was going to attack and kill the king when he took off his cloak.
>
> Ὀλίγῳ δ᾽ ὕστερον ἢ τελευτῆσαι Δαρεῖον ἐξήλασεν εἰς Πασαργάδας ὁ βασιλεύς, ὅπως τελεσθείη τὴν βασιλικὴν τελετὴν ὑπὸ τῶν ἐν Πέρσαις ἱερέων. (2) Ἔστι δὲ <ἐκεῖ> θεᾶς πολεμικῆς ἱερόν, ἣν Ἀθηνᾷ τις <ἂν> εἰκάσειεν· εἰς τοῦτο δεῖ τὸν τελούμενον παρελθόντα τὴν μὲν ἰδίαν ἀποθέσθαι στολήν, ἀναλαβεῖν δ᾽ ἣν Κῦρος ὁ παλαιὸς ἐφόρει πρὶν ἢ βασιλεὺς γενέσθαι, καὶ σύκων παλάθης ἐμφαγόντα τερμίνθου καταγαγεῖν, καὶ ποτήριον ἐκπιεῖν ὀξυγάλακτος· εἰ δὲ πρὸς τούτοις ἕτερ᾽ ἄττα δρῶσιν, ἄδηλόν ἐστι τοῖς ἄλλοις. (3) Ταῦτα δρᾶν Ἀρτοξέρξου μέλλοντος, ἀφίκετο Τισσαφέρνης πρὸς αὐτὸν ἄγων ἕνα τῶν ἱερέων, ὃς ἐν παισὶ

---

[93] But cf. Briant (2002a: 615).

Κύρου τῆς νομιζομένης ἀγωγῆς ἐπιστάτης γενόμενος καὶ διδάξας μαγεύειν αὐτόν, οὐδενὸς ἧττον ἐδόκει Περσῶν ἀνιᾶσθαι, μὴ ἀποδειχθέντος ἐκείνου βασιλέως· διὸ καὶ πίστιν ἔσχε κατηγορῶν Κύρου. (4) Κατηγόρει δ᾽ ὡς μέλλοντος ἐνεδρεύειν ἐν τῷ ἱερῷ, καὶ ἐπειδὰν ἐκδύηται τὴν ἐσθῆτα ὁ βασιλεύς, ἐπιτίθεσθαι καὶ διαφθείρειν αὐτόν.

ἐκεῖ add. Ziegler ‖ Ἀθηνᾶν GL*Π*: Ἀθηνᾷ Reiske | Ἀθηνᾶν <ἄν> τις Korais: Ἀθηνᾷ <ἄν> τις Schäfer | Ἀθηνᾷ τις <ἄν> Ziegler ‖ Τισσαφέρνης: Τισαφέρνης RLG

Unlike the view expressed by Charles Smith (1881: 9) and Peter Calmeyer (1976: 70 n. 146), the mention of the temple of Athena does not seem to derive from Deinon's account.[94] It probably came from Ctesias' work, as argued by Martin Haug (1854: 91) and followed by Schottin (1865: 3) Jacoby (1958: 473 = F 17) and Heleen Sancisi-Weerdenburg (1983a: 148).[95] Plutarch's admission that no one else knows what is happening during the ceremony (ἄδηλόν ἐστι τοῖς ἄλλοις) echoes the sort of claims an author who attributes great importance to autopsy would make. Ctesias is this kind of author (see above). Among the dishes mentioned in the coronation ceremony, the sour milk is significant. It was known in antiquity for its medicinal therapeutic value, as we can see in medical treatises.[96] It may have been of special interest to a physician, who discussed sour milk in India (*FGrH* 688 F 45.50). Similarly, the mention of the terebinth (τερμίνθος) appears as a typical food among the Persians in a fragment of Nicolaus of Damascus (*FGrH* 90 F 66.34 = *Exc. de Insid.* p.31.13 de Boor), probably adapted from Ctesias.[97] Most important of all, there is an internal link between the description of the ceremony in the temple and the accusation against Cyrus.

Ctesias can certainly be regarded as the source for this dramatic accusation. Nevertheless, all that is given in Photius' epitome is a brief mention (*FGrH* 688 F 16.59 = *Bibl.* cod. 72, p. 43 b 10–15):

> Before his brother Artaxerxes, Cyrus was denounced by Tissaphernes. He fled to his mother Parysatis, and was cleared from the allegations. Slighted by his brother, Cyrus departed for his own satrapy and planned a revolt.
>
> Διαβάλλεται Κῦρος ὑπὸ Τισαφέρνους πρὸς Ἀρτοξέρξην τὸν ἀδελφόν, καὶ καταφεύγει Παρυσάτιδι τῇ μητρί, καὶ ἀπολύεται τῆς διαβολῆς. Ἀπελαύνει

---

[94] Mantey (1888: 7) is of the opinion that *Artaxerxes* 3 in its entirety is taken from Deinon, since it relates that Cyrus was released by Parysatis in exchange for vows which were later violated, and because this breach of trust is described elaborately in *Art.* 6, which according to this scholar also derives from Deinon. Both claims may not be correct. Cf. Binder (2008: 111–13).

[95] Cf. Hood (1967: 134), Wiesehöfer (2001: 31–2), Lenfant (2004: 279 n. 664).

[96] E.g. Galen, *De alimentorum facultatibus* 518, 689, 692–3 Kühn; Pseudo-Galenus, *De remediis parabilibus* 420, 465 Kühn.

[97] Cf. Jacoby (1926: 251–2), Lenfant (2000).

Κῦρος ἠτιμωμένος παρὰ τοῦ ἀδελφοῦ πρὸς τὴν οἰκείαν σατραπείαν, καὶ μελετᾷ ἐπανάστασιν.

The patriarch does not provide the content of Tissaphernes' allegation, yet his summary clearly asserts that there was an accusation in the physician's report. Plutarch's description is richer than any of our extant texts, including Xenophon's (*Anab.* 1.1.3), which, like Photius', merely states the fact of the accusation against Cyrus, but not its content (Τισσαφέρνης διαβάλλει τὸν Κῦρον πρὸς τὸν ἀδελφὸν ὡς ἐπιβουλεύοι αὐτῷ, 'Tissaphernes falsely accused Cyrus to his brother of plotting against him'). One may safely deduce that Ctesias is the source for most of the details of the false charge found in Plutarch's *Artaxerxes*, such as the involvement of the priest and the substance of the charge. Xenophon only claims that the king is persuaded (πείθεται), and it would seem reasonable that Artaxerxes is swayed because of the priest, Cyrus' former tutor in the wisdom of the Magi, as mentioned by Plutarch (*Art.* 3.3).

Xenophon's report thus seems secondary and derivative, as it merely mentions an accusation but does not provide its substance. It is much more feasible to assume that Xenophon deliberately omitted a number of elements than to speculate that these items were only later added to the story in the *Anabasis* and were not known to him. It is hard to imagine, bearing in mind the physician's fondness for fanciful fictions and extended stories, that he would not have expanded on the content of the accusation of the plot and on Cyrus' incarceration, and instead would have considered a brief mention to be sufficient. Ctesias' narratives are abundant in fabricated accusations (cf. *FGrH* 688 F 13.11–12, 14.32–3, 16.60) and he does not shy away from relating the participation of priests in machinations and intrigues (cf. *FGrH* 688 F 13.11, 19) of precisely the type that we find in Tissaphernes' charge. These details may be deemed as some of the characteristic features of his tales of court. Andrew Nichols (2008: 188) argues convincingly that the appearance of the words διαβάλλω and διαβολή in Photius' summary shows that his version was not far from that of Xenophon or Plutarch in depicting the accusation as a false allegation.[98]

Moreover, a dark image of the Magi appears in the story of the usurper found in the Behistun Inscription (DB 1.26–71), Herodotus (one Magus: 3.67–73, two: 3.61–6, 74, 76–9) and Ctesias (*FGrH* 688 F 13.11–18).[99] Xenophon portrays a much more positive image

[98] Cf. Lenfant (2004: 276 nn. 641–2).
[99] The association of the Magi with secret conspirative political plots can also be seen

of the Magi (as he does for the eunuchs),[100] almost as if deliberately opposed to Ctesias' image. Thus, contrary to Ctesias, Xenophon omits the content of the allegation brought by the Magus against Cyrus the Younger. Correspondingly, in Xenophon's *Cyropaedia*, the Magi are important as performing acts of worship, sacrifice and setting aside war booty to the gods,[101] and as experts in interpreting the will of the gods.[102]

Plutarch continues (*Art.* 3.5–6):

> Some say that the ensuing arrest was because of this allegation; others claim that Cyrus really went to the temple and was betrayed by the priest while he was hiding. As (the king) was about to execute (Cyrus), his mother hugged him, threw her curls around him, pressed his neck against her own, and by lamenting and wailing profusely she successfully pleaded for his life. He was sent back to the shore, but was not satisfied with his post, nor did he remember the pardon, but only the arrest, and, driven by rage, he was keen more than before to obtain the kingship.
>
> (5) Οἱ μὲν <οὖν> ἐκ ταύτης τῆς διαβολῆς τὴν σύλληψιν γενέσθαι φασίν, οἱ δὲ καὶ παρελθεῖν τὸν Κῦρον εἰς τὸ ἱερὸν καὶ παραδοθῆναι κρυπτόμενον ὑπὸ τοῦ ἱερέως. (6) Μέλλοντα δ᾽ αὐτὸν ἤδη ἀποθνήσκειν, ἡ μήτηρ περισχοῦσα ταῖς ἀγκάλαις καὶ τοῖς βοστρύχοις περιελίξασα καὶ συλλαβοῦσα τὸν ἐκείνου τράχηλον πρὸς τὸν αὐτῆς ὀδυρομένη πολλὰ καὶ ποτνιωμένη παρῃτήσατο· καὶ κατέπεμψεν αὖθις ἐπὶ θάλατταν, οὐκ ἀγαπῶντα τὴν ἀρχὴν ἐκείνην οὐδὲ μεμνημένον τῆς διέσεως ἀλλὰ τῆς συλλήψεως, καὶ δι᾽ ὀργὴν σπαργῶντα μᾶλλον ἢ πρότερον ἐπὶ τὴν βασιλείαν.
>
> <οὖν> add. Ziegler ‖ ἀποθνήσκειν GL*Π*: [ἀπο]θνήσκειν em. Ziegler

In order to enhance the dilemma Artaxerxes faces in the story, whether to believe the allegation against Cyrus or discard it, Plutarch emulates the situation on the historiographic plane by citing two alleged views. Plutarch gives the impression that he has two versions of the incident before him.[103] Some even assume that one of them is derived from Ctesias' work, while the other is from Deinon's report.[104] In fact, there is no great difference between the versions, as they do

---

in Soph. *OT* 385–9; see Rigsby (1976), Asheri, Lloyd and Corcella (2007: 460). Cf. Beck (1991: 514) that from the Greek perspective, the religious system of the Magi was not only dangerous and inimical to the established Greek ritual, but also inferior because it was defeated.

[100] On the eunuchs' fidelity see Xen. *Cyr.* 7.5.60–5. Cf. 5.2.28, 7.5.24–32, 8.3.17, 8.4.2. See Briant (2002a: 270–2). Cf. Waters (2017: 28–39).

[101] Xen. *Cyr.* 4.5.14, 4.5.51, 4.6.11, 5.3.4, 7.3.1, 7.5.35, 7.5.57, 8.3.24, Gera (1993: 56, 59).

[102] Cyrus institutes the college of Magi: *Cyr.* 8.1.23. Cf. 8.3.1. Cf. Boyce (1982: 213–14). It would appear that Xenophon had some influence on the picture depicted in *Alcibiades 1* attributed to Plato. One should note the similarity to Xen. *Cyr.* 1.2.6–7 (cf. 8.8.13).

[103] Briant (2002a: 616) believes the second version was invented later as part of the royal propaganda to mar the memory of the rebel.

[104] Cf. Stevenson (1985: 20; 1997: 26). There is no need to suppose, like Mantey (1888: 7), that the debate between the versions is found already in Deinon's account.

not contradict each other: the arrest and imprisonment may have been the result of the false accusation brought by the priest. In the second variant we have the content of the slander, only mentioned in the first. The single apparent difference is that according to the second version, Cyrus is actually made to have been *present* in the temple. The first variant suits Xenophon's abridgement, with the mention of the libel and imprisonment (*Anab.* 1.1.3: καὶ συλλαμβάνει Κῦρον, 'he arrested Cyrus'), and with the omission of the priest.[105] The assumption that the second version comes from Ctesias' account may seem probable given the content of the libel. There seems to be no reason to seek for other accounts beyond the storyline of Ctesias.

It would be interesting to consider the possibility that the second version came not from any author or historian Plutarch may have read, but was rather a version told by a character in Ctesias' narrative world; most reasonably, Tissaphernes. In this case, Plutarch took the voice of one of the fictional figures and treated it as an *independent voice*. That the ancient readers and critics sometimes blurred the boundaries between the different voices of the narrator (speaking for the author/poet) and the character is known. Athenaeus suitably remarks (4.178d) that 'if something is said *in* Homer, this is not said *by* Homer' (οὐ γὰρ εἴ τι λέγεται παρ' Ὁμήρῳ, τοῦθ' Ὅμηρος λέγει). As noted by René Nünlist (2009: 131–3), 'Ancient critics often write "the poet says X" when in fact they should have written something like "the poet has his character A say X".' This confusion was probably used by Plutarch, in making Ctesias 'say' what one of his figures says.

With regards to the *Artaxerxes*, the outcome is ironic, related to the questions of being present and of the ensuing truthfulness of the account. The second version depicts Cyrus as actually present in the temple, but this may have been claimed by a figure from the fictional world of the narrative. Thus, lending an independent voice to this figure is tantamount to rendering it factual and present in the real world. Moreover, readers of Xenophon, acquainted only with the libel version, would surely see the second variant as patently false, and conclude that a forced attempt is being made to make Cyrus appear where he probably was not. Plutarch undermines Xenophon's well-known version, and makes the libel against Cyrus approximate reality as if it has an equal claim to being truthful. Plutarch thus anticipates what Artaxerxes will eventually do, when he would claim glory for Cyrus' death by pretending to be present at the scene.

---

[105] Cf. Binder (2008: 112). Justin 5.11.4 is a confused narrative based mainly on Xenophon.

Jacoby includes the beginning of the next section of the biography as part of fragment 17 of Ctesias (*Art.* 4.1):

Some say that he revolted because he had not enough for his daily meals, but they are talking nonsense ...

Ἔνιοι δέ φασιν οὐκ ἀρκούμενον οἷς ἐλάμβανεν εἰς τὸ καθ᾽ ἡμέραν δεῖπνον ἀποστῆναι βασιλέως, εὐήθη λέγοντες ...

The attribution to Ctesias may be correct, though not in a straightforward manner. Material causes are never used to explain Cyrus' decision to begin the campaign.[106] Theoretically, of course, other competing reports of Cyrus' expedition by obscure lost historians are perfectly possible, and one of them might have introduced this cause as a genuine motive. But perhaps there is no need to assume such a phantom author, used only for this specific detail. Instead, there are signs that Plutarch again uses the text of Ctesias,[107] and lets a character in his narrative assume an independent voice in describing the events. This character may be the figure of Artaxerxes himself.

From Photius we know that in Ctesias' *Persica* the two brothers addressed their respective troops (*FGrH* 688 F 16.63 = *Bibl.* cod. 72, p. 43 b 25–6): 'how Cyrus and Artaxerxes encouraged each his own army' (Ὅπως τε Κῦρος τῇ ἰδίᾳ στρατιᾷ καὶ Ἀρτοξέρξης πάλιν τῇ οἰκείᾳ παρήνεσαν). Attributing such crude material motives to Cyrus rather than principled or honourable ones was made from a derogatory perspective, which would perfectly fit Artaxerxes' speech, mocking his opponent. Moreover, attributing such motivation to Cyrus insinuates that the prince is not able to pay his soldiers; this would make sense in an address to the army in a propaganda war designed to dissuade them from defecting to the other side. *Art.* 4 ends with a saying of the king to a commoner called Omisus that were he

---

[106] The statement that Cyrus planned the rebellion because he deemed his daily provided meal as insufficient can be interpreted in two ways. The first is to understand the phrase 'daily meal' as a term referring to taxes or grants that the locals were required to pay, partially to cover the costs of the satrap. See Briant (2002a: 403) and Frye (1962: 114) on the additional taxes imposed by governors. Cf. Nehemiah 5: 14–18 with Batten (1913: 244–7) and Fensham (1982: 196–9). In other words, Cyrus revolted because the territory given to him was reduced, and was not enough to collect large amounts of taxes. The statement, however, can also be read literally: the payment in kind which Cyrus received from the court was not enough for his daily dinner. See Lewis (1977: 4–5) followed by Stevenson (1997: 27, 144). The main evidence for this system is the Elamite Persepolis tablets (of the fortification), dated to the reign of Darius (509 to 494 BCE) discovered in 1933/4 and partially published (mostly by Hallock, 1969). These documents record transference of food products and animals as rations on a daily or monthly basis to certain groups, differentiated according to age, gender, status and profession. See Briant (2002a: 422–71), Wiesehöfer (2001: 9–10, 67).

[107] Cf. Krumbholz (1889: 19).

entrusted a small city, he would speedily make it great (οὗτος ὁ ἀνὴρ καὶ πόλιν ἂν ἐκ μικρᾶς ταχὺ ποιήσειε μεγάλην πιστευθείς); it may be the case that *Art.* 4 also begins with an (implicit) address of the king.

Plutarch rejects the explanation of Cyrus' material urgency by mentioning Parysatis' assistance to the prince. One would imagine that whoever voiced this material explanation was unaware of Parysatis' help to Cyrus. Artaxerxes is a notable candidate to be that person. In the same section, the queen mother is depicted as alleviating the king's suspicions, so that he does not notice the amassing of Cyrus' army (*Art.* 4.3). Cyrus is portrayed as giving false motives for the enlisting of the Greek mercenaries (*Art.* 4.3: ἐπὶ πολλαῖς προφάσεσι, 'on many pretexts', cf. Xen. *Anab.* 1.1.6–11). Corresponding to these false pretexts, the motive noted at the beginning of *Art.* 4 can also be seen as a fabricated reason given to the troops. Indeed, one of the themes of *Art.* 4 is deception: Cyrus deceives his soldiers and the king, Parysatis deceives the king; similarly, Plutarch may be misleading his readers to think there is another historical account here, when there is none. If all this is true, Plutarch subtly and ironically introduces the king here as a historian trying to depict and understand the events, the exact same role he would later on assume in his royal version (in *Art.* 13.1).[108]

A probable use of Ctesias may be assumed in the depiction of Cyrus' letter to the Spartans (*Art.* 6.3–4), mentioned in Chapter 2.[109] Xenophon (*Hell.* 3.1.1) and Diodorus (14.19.4) – most likely relying on Xenophon[110] – mention messengers from Cyrus to the Spartans, but do not refer to any written letter; in their account, the request is minimally phrased and merely calls for the Spartans to aid the prince as allies. Yet surely there was some more detailed demand and a certain promise on Cyrus' part. Letters are mentioned in the diplomatic activity of Conon, Evagoras and the king. It stands to reason that Xenophon downplays any problematic content a letter may have contained, potentially pointing at Spartan knowledge of Cyrus' real rebellious intentions. If this is so, it is certainly probable that Xenophon used Ctesias' account but removed unconfort-

---

[108] Xenophon may have been influenced by Ctesias' portrayal in his own description of the complaint of Pharnabazus, the satrap of Phrygia, claiming to be so impoverished from the Greek raids on his area that he cannot even have a meal on his land (Xen. *Hell.* 4.1.33).

[109] As opposed to my belief in Almagor (2014a: 6 n. 21). The thematic similarity I noted between this letter and that of Glos to the Spartans (Diod. 15.9.4), which may originate from Deinon (see Chapter 5), may be due to an adaptation of this letter by Deinon, and thus attest to the fact that it was earlier. Cf. Descat (1995: 103), Tuplin (1999: 344), who believe the origin is Ctesias. *Pace* Binder (2008: 164).

[110] But cf. Westlake (1987: 242).

able elements from it. Sparta chose to assist Cyrus by instructing the naval commander Samius (*Hell.* 3.1.1 or Pythagoras in *Anab.* 1.4.2, cf. 1.2.21; Diodorus, 14.19.4 has Samus)[111] and Cheirisophus heading 700 (or 800) hoplites (see *Anab.* 1.4.3). The clear status of Clearchus the Spartan exile in relation to the authorities in his country is not clear,[112] especially in Ctesias' account,[113] yet surely the prominent place of Clearchus in the campaign would not have been seen favourably by Sparta had there not been some special link between her and the commander.[114] Plutarch's transference of Xenophon's words from Samius (*Hell.* 3.1.1: Σαμίῳ ... ἐπέστειλαν ὑπηρετεῖν Κύρῳ) to Clearchus (*Art.* 6.5: σκυτάλην πρὸς Κλέαρχον ἀπέστειλαν ὑπηρετεῖν Κύρῳ), although not faithful to Xenophon's text, is nevertheless more truthful, and may go back to Ctesias' description as well.

Did Plutarch invent the content of Cyrus' letter? Readers familiar with Xenophon's encomium of the prince (*Anab.* 1.9) would tend to believe that the biographer's description is an answer to his predecessor,[115] and as we saw repeatedly in this chapter, Plutarch builds on the detection of inverted images by his readers for added effect. However, what if it is the other way around, and Xenophon was reversing the images of his own forerunner? We saw this practice of Xenophon in this chapter as well. If this is true, Xenophon would seem to be eagerly attempting to portray a positive picture of Cyrus in response to the image Ctesias was circulating. Furthermore, if Plutarch invented this picture for the *Artaxerxes*, it would not seem probable that he would cite part of it elsewhere (*QC* 1.4.620c), using it as a known quote. This part is the section where Cyrus claims he can carry wine better than his brother. The fact that some version of this citation is found in the collection *Regum et Imperatorum Apophthegmata* (*Sayings of Kings and Commanders*), 173ef, implies that it must come from an external source,[116] presumably Ctesias.

---

[111] The reason for this change is not clear. Was Xenophon trying to hide something? Or is it a case of an unclear interpolation in the text? See Hartman (1887: 34), Schwartz (1899b: 193), Meyer (1902: 5.185). The name Samius was more common in Sparta: Poralla (1913: 112), Jacoby (1930: 349).

[112] Lenschau (1921: 576). Cf. Isoc. *De Pace* 98, *Panath.* 104.

[113] See Stevenson (1997: 28, 85–6).

[114] Cf. Meyer (1902: 5.185), Lewis (1977: 151 n. 100).

[115] Mossman (2010: 151): 'Plutarch has picked up some themes of this passage (the greater energy, the horsemanship, the sheer talent), and transferred them from the narrative voice to Cyrus' own, while rather undercutting Cyrus' claims (perhaps particularly the claim to philosophy) by introducing this self-praise as "talking big" (μεγαληγορῶν) – a contrast to Xenophon's "most respectful"'. Cf. Mantey (1888: 9).

[116] See Appendix II.

Xenophon (*Anab.* 1.7.3–4) adopted some of the content of this letter to his own depiction of Cyrus' address to the Greeks.[117]

Another subtle reference to Ctesias may appear in a different passage of the biography (*Art.* 8.1-2 ~ *FGrH* 688 F 18):

> Since many have related this battle and Xenophon shows it to view the action not as it happened long ago but as if standing present while it happens ... it would not make sense to tell it in detail, except the things worth mentioning he skipped over. For instance, the place where the armies clashed was called Cunaxa. ... Before the battle, when Clearchus urged Cyrus to stay behind the warriors and put himself out of harm's way, he reportedly replied, 'What do you mean, Clearchus? Do you support that I, who aim at the kingship, am not worthy of kingship?'
>
> Τὴν δὲ μάχην ἐκείνην πολλῶν μὲν ἀπηγγελκότων, Ξενοφῶντος δὲ μονονουχὶ δεικνύοντος ὄψει καὶ τοῖς πράγμασιν, ὡς οὐ γεγενημένοις ἀλλὰ γινομένοις ἐφιστάντος ... οὐκ ἔστι νοῦν ἔχοντος ἐπεξηγεῖσθαι, πλὴν ὅσα τῶν ἀξίων λόγου παρῆλθεν εἰπεῖν ἐκεῖνον. (2) Ὁ μὲν οὖν τόπος ἐν ᾧ παρετάξαντο Κούναξα καλεῖται ... Κῦρον δὲ πρὸ τῆς μάχης Κλεάρχου παρακαλοῦντος ἐξόπισθε τῶν μαχομένων εἶναι καὶ μὴ κινδυνεύειν αὐτόν, εἰπεῖν φασι· 'τί λέγεις ὦ Κλέαρχε; σὺ κελεύεις με τὸν βασιλείας ὀρεγόμενον ἀνάξιον εἶναι βασιλείας;'

It would seem that *Art.* 8 has two parts. In the first, a contrast is set between the impulsive behaviour of Cyrus and the restrained/hesitant conduct of Clearchus. While the biographer has only Clearchus counselling Cyrus not to fight but rather to stay behind the warriors, Xenophon (*Anab.* 1.7.9) depicts all the commanders discussing the issue with Cyrus as advising the same. In this presentation, Plutarch appears to follow Ctesias, as can be seen from Photius' summary (*FGrH* 688 F 16.64: 'Cyrus ... died in the battle when he failed to follow the advice of Clearchus', above). By using a detail from Ctesias' account to check Xenophon's report, Plutarch cleverly mimics the confrontation of the two historical figures Cyrus and Clearchus on the historiographic plane. The imagery Plutarch employs here portrays Xenophon as pushing forward, as it were, creating gaps in the description (note the spatial metaphor 'skips over', παρῆλθεν), which Plutarch tries to fill in. This corresponds to the contrast of the impulsive behaviour of Cyrus and the restrained/hesitant conduct of Clearchus in *Art.* 8. The said detail that has to be filled in is the name of the battle site, which Xenophon neglects to mention, but which most certainly comes from Ctesias.[118] It may derive from an Aramaic form. However, not all follow the persuasive conclusion of Jacob Obermeyer (1929: 73 n. 1, 249) that the name

---

[117] Cf. the structure of *Cyr.* 6.2.36.
[118] See Bigwood (1983: 344), Lenfant (2004: 280 n. 676). Cf. Mantey (1888: 12)

Cunaxa is a distorted Greek form of *Kenishta*, namely, (Jewish) synagogue.[119] Ctesias' informants were Aramaic speakers, familiar with the place and most likely inhabiting it. He probably gathered the information during his presumed sojourn in Babylon.

In the second part of *Art.* 8 Plutarch switches sides, as it were, and by emulating Cyrus, who discarded the advice of Clearchus, he seems to ignore the account of Ctesias and follow Xenophon, to balance the impact of his reliance on the other text in the first part.[120] Now Clearchus is blamed for being too cautious and for not obeying Cyrus (*Art.* 8.3). Indeed, Xenophon relates (*Anab.* 1.8.13) that Cyrus ordered Clearchus to redeploy against the enemy's centre, where the king was, but the Spartan commander refused for fear of being encircled.[121]

Some historians accept Xenophon's account and blame Clearchus for the disaster.[122] Others acquit him and blame Cyrus.[123] Both views are found in *Art.* 8. The inconsistency is evident when Plutarch says of Clearchus, 'he had marched ten thousand stadia up from the sea-coast under arms, with no compulsion upon him' (*Art.* 8.4: ὁ δὲ μυρίους σταδίους ἀπὸ θαλάσσης ἐν ὅπλοις ἀναβεβηκώς, μηδενὸς ἀναγκάζοντος), a clear departure from his own previous account in *Art.* 6.5 (based on Ctesias?), according to which the Spartans ordered Clearchus to aid Cyrus.[124] By changing his mind in the course of *Art.* 8 – which is made apparent by his attitude towards his sources – Plutarch is being as erratic as Cyrus.

It is most probable that the rest of *Art.* 9, besides the detail of the name of Cyrus' stallion, comes from Ctesias (*Art.* 9.2–3). This is the episode of the confrontation of Cyrus and Artagerses, and the latter's lethal wound from Cyrus' spear. The exact location of the wound (9.3: διήλασε παρὰ τὴν κλεῖδα διὰ τοῦ τραχήλου τὴν αἰχμήν, '[Cyrus] driving his spear through the neck at the collarbone') fits the depiction of a physician.[125]

---

[119] The Jewish community was probably that of 'Kenishta de Safyatib' (= *Shaf*, 'moved', *Yatib*, 'settled'), built, according to Jewish tradition, from the very stones of the temple in Jerusalem. Cf. Talmud, Megilah Tractate 29a. See Barnett (1963: 16–17), Lendle (1986: 198 n. 10), Gasche (1995: 201 n. 1).

[120] *Pace* Schottin (1865: 9) and Stevenson (1997: 28, 85). See Bigwood (1964: 43 n. 99), Binder (2008: 181). Cf. Tuplin (2011: 468).

[121] *Art.* 8.8 ~ Xen. *Anab.* 1.8.13. Cf. Manfredini, Orsi and Antelami (1987: 280). Cf. Krumbholz (1889: 21).

[122] See Grote (1884: 9.43–4), Bury (1913: 507), Gugel (1971: 243). Cf. Shannahan (2014: 76).

[123] See Anderson (1974: 104–5), Rahe (1980: 83) and Wylie (1992: 125–6, 130–1). Cf. Tarn (1933: 9): Cyrus charged 'to retrieve as a soldier the battle he had lost as a general'.

[124] See Zeitz (1854: 23).

[125] Bigwood (1964: 170), Stevenson (1997: 28–9), Bassett (1999: 476 n. 10). *Pace* Binder (2011: 58).

Within *Art.* 10, devoted to Deinon's version of the death of Cyrus (on which see Chapter 4 below) we find Ctesias' Carian as well as the honours awarded him (*Art.* 10.3):

> Thus Cyrus fell, as some say, by a wound he received from the king, but as others have it, from the blow of a Carian, who was rewarded by the king for this deed with the privilege of always carrying a golden rooster upon his spear in front of the line during a campaign; Persians call the Carians roosters, because of the crests with which they decorate their helmets.
>
> (3) Πίπτει δ' ὁ Κῦρος, ὡς μὲν ἔνιοι λέγουσι, πληγεὶς ὑπὸ τοῦ βασιλέως, ὡς δ' ἕτεροί τινες, Καρὸς ἀνθρώπου πατάξαντος, ᾧ γέρας ἔδωκε τῆς πράξεως ταύτης ὁ βασιλεὺς ἀλεκτρυόνα χρυσοῦν ἐπὶ δόρατος ἀεὶ πρὸ τῆς τάξεως ἐν ταῖς στρατείαις κομίζειν· καὶ γὰρ αὐτοὺς τοὺς Κᾶρας ἀλεκτρυόνας οἱ Πέρσαι διὰ τοὺς λόφους οἷς κοσμοῦσι τὰ κράνη προσηγόρευον.

These details are ultimately derived from Ctesias (above). Ernst Herzfeld (1931: 59–61) and Wilhelm Eilers (1935; 1940: 189–92, 225–7) are the first to suggest that the Carians are found in the royal Persian inscriptions as OPer. *Karkā* (DNa.30, DSe.30, DSf.33–4, XPh.28). As a significant corroboration to this theory, Eilers (1940: 211) points out this passage from Plutarch and the fact that the OPer. (onomatopoetic) name of the rooster was **Karka* (Avestan *Kahrka*, and Pahlavi *Kark*). Thus, it would appear that a 'Carian' in Old Persian was indeed called by a name that resembled that of a rooster. If this detail indeed comes from Ctesias, we have some evidence here that his text may have contained a wordplay in Persian.[126]

During the battle, and immediately after Cyrus' death, Plutarch includes the following scene, which is probably taken from Ctesias (*Art.* 12.1–3):

> When Cyrus died, Artasyras, the 'King's Eye', happened to ride his horse nearby. He recognised the eunuchs mourning the dead, and asked the most trustworthy: 'Pariscas, who is it that you mourn for?' The eunuch replied: 'Artasyras, can you not see that Cyrus is dead?' Artasyras was surprised and asked the eunuch to be brave, and to guard the body. He himself went to Artaxerxes, who had already given up, and was suffering thirst and from his wound. He [Artasyras] informed him that he personally saw the dead Cyrus. He [Artaxerxes] hurried to leave at once, and ordered Artasyras to lead him to the place. Since there were plenty of rumours about the Greeks, and there was fear that they were chasing and winning and strong, he decided to send a large party to see, and sent thirty men with torches.
>
> Ἤδη δ' αὐτοῦ τεθνηκότος, Ἀρτασύρας ὁ βασιλέως ὀφθαλμὸς ἔτυχεν ἵππῳ παρεξελαύνων. Γνωρίσας οὖν τοὺς εὐνούχους ὀλοφυρομένους, ἠρώτησε τὸν

---

[126] This designation is even more complicated, as the reason Plutarch gives for this similarity is the crest on the Carian helmet, with the likeness of the rooster's comb. There was in fact a literary tradition for this identification. See Strabo 14.2.27, quoting Alcaeus (fr. 22 Bergk); cf. Hdt. 1.171; Aristoph. *Av.* 290–3.

πιστότατον αὐτῶν· 'τίνα τοῦτον, ὦ Παρίσκα, κλαίεις παρακαθήμενος;' ὁ δ' εἶπεν· 'οὐχ ὁρᾷς, ὦ 'Αρτασύρα, Κῦρον τεθνηκότα;' (2) Θαυμάσας οὖν ὁ 'Αρτασύρας τῷ μὲν εὐνούχῳ θαρρεῖν παρεκελεύσατο, καὶ φυλάττειν τὸν νεκρόν, αὐτὸς δὲ συντείνας πρὸς τὸν 'Αρτοξέρξην, ἀπεγνωκότα μὲν ἤδη τὰ πράγματα, κακῶς δὲ καὶ τὸ σῶμα διακείμενον ὑπό τε δίψης καὶ τοῦ τραύματος, χαίρων φράζει ὡς αὐτὸς ἴδοι τεθνηκότα Κῦρον. (3) Ὁ δὲ πρῶτον μὲν εὐθὺς ὥρμησεν αὐτὸς ἰέναι, καὶ τὸν 'Αρτασύραν ἄγειν ἐκέλευσεν ἐπὶ τὸν τόπον· ἐπεὶ δὲ πολὺς ἦν λόγος τῶν 'Ελλήνων καὶ φόβος, ὡς διωκόντων καὶ πάντα νικώντων καὶ κρατούντων, ἔδοξε πλείονας πέμψαι τοὺς κατοψομένους, καὶ τριάκοντα λαμπάδας ἔχοντες ἐπεμφθησαν.

αὐτὸς om. GR ‖ τοὺς κατοψομένους: τοὺς om. G

The image of the king reflected in the following passage is that of an isolated ruler, cut off from the surrounding world and helped by others, such as the 'King's Eye' (*Art.* 12.1) and his eunuchs (*Art.* 12.4). The king's two concerns in *Art.* 12 are finding the place where Cyrus' body lies and securing water to revive himself. Accordingly, two men are sent to fulfil these missions: Artasyras is told to lead him to the place (12.3: τόπον), and Satibarzanes is assigned the search for water, a beverage (12.4: ποτόν). In Platonic fashion, these two concerns reflect two different passions, namely, honour and bodily pleasures. If Ctesias is indeed the origin for this image, they presumably reflected in his work an ironic take on the famous Persian demand for 'Earth and Water' representing admission of subservience to the Great King.[127] Similarly, one might imagine that the play on the 'King's Eye' who does not see Cyrus' corpse was also found in the original and was not lost on Plutarch.

Two central figures in *Art.* 12 appear elsewhere in Photius' summary of Ctesias. The first, Artasyras, appears to be the same person who is sent with an army to crush the rebellion of Arsites, the full brother of Darius II (*FGrH* 688 F 15.52 = *Bibl.* cod. 72, p. 42 b 18–19).[128] The second is Satibarzanes, who in Photius' epitome (*FGrH* 688 F 16.60 = *Bibl.* cod. 72, p. 43 b 15) falsely accuses Orontes of an intrigue with Parysatis, and causes his execution. Later on, according to Photius (*FGrH* 688 F 30.73 = *Bibl.* cod. 72 p. 44 b 33; circa 398 BCE), Satibarzanes receives presents from Evagoras.[129] In the collection *Sayings of Kings and Commanders* (*Reg. et imp. apoph.* 173e), Satibarzanes is described

---

[127] On which see Kuhrt (1988), Rung (2015). See Hdt. 4.126–32, 5.18, 5.73, 6.48–9, 7.32, 7.131, 7.133, 8.46, 8.136.

[128] Shortly before 417 BCE. See Cook (1983: 129). Not in Puchstein (1895) or Osborne (1973: 521). Artasyras was the father of Orontes, who married Rhodogyne, Artaxerxes' daughter (*Art.* 27.7, cf. Xen. *Anab.* 2.4.8). See the inscriptions at Nemrut-Dagh noting the forefathers of Antiochus I of Commagene (*OGIS* 391.7–10, 392.10–15). Cf. Reinach (1890: 365).

[129] A very influential man, it would appear. See Lenfant (2004: 276 n. 644).

as the κατακοιμιστής (chamberlain) of Artaxerxes I. This should most probably be Artaxerxes II. Themistius (8.117b) describes an episode in which Artaxerxes and Satibarzanes are the main characters. It is quite possible that all these details are derived from Ctesias. The concern with eunuchs and their important role at court is a prominent feature in the physician's stories.[130] Moreover, the interest in corpses of the royal family members appears in Ctesias' work.[131] One may recall the example of Bagapates, who sits near the tomb of Darius for seven years and guards it (and dies while doing so: *FGrH* 688 F 13.23)[132]. Another literary motif observed in Ctesias' depiction is that of Cyrus not being recognised in the dark, whether alive or dead.[133]

The story continues (*Art.* 12.4–6):

> Satibarzanes the eunuch went around looking for a beverage for him (Artaxerxes) who was nearly dying from thirst, but there was no water in the area, and the camp was far away. Then he came across one of those lowly Caunians who had eight Cotylai of polluted and putrid water in a a poor wineskin, and he brought it to the king. When he (Artaxerxes) drank it all, (Satibarzanes) asked him if he had found the drink disgusting, but he vowed to the gods that he had never had sweeter wine or water clearer and purer, 'so that' (he said) 'if I cannot find the person who gave you this water, I pray the Gods to make him blessed and rich.'

> (4) Αὐτῷ δὲ μικρὸν ἀπολείποντι τοῦ τεθνάναι διὰ τὸ διψῆν Σατιβαρζάνης ὁ εὐνοῦχος περιθέων ἐζήτει ποτόν· οὐ γὰρ εἶχε τὸ χωρίον ὕδωρ, οὐδ' ἦν ἐγγὺς τὸ στρατόπεδον. (5) Μόλις οὖν ἐπιτυγχάνει τῶν Καυνίων ἐκείνων τῶν κακοβίων ἑνός, ἐν ἀσκίῳ φαύλῳ διεφθαρμένον ὕδωρ καὶ πονηρὸν ἔχοντος, ὅσον ὀκτὼ κοτύλας· καὶ λαβὼν τοῦτο καὶ κομίσας τῷ βασιλεῖ δίδωσιν. (6) Ἐκπιόντα δ' ἅπαν ἠρώτησεν εἰ μὴ πάνυ δυσχεραίνει τὸ ποτόν· ὁ δ' ὤμοσε τοὺς θεοὺς μήτ' οἶνον ἡδέως οὕτως πώποτε πεπωκέναι μήθ' ὕδωρ τὸ κουφότατον καὶ καθαρώτατον, 'ὥστ'' ἔφη 'τὸν δόντα σοι τοῦτ' ἄνθρωπον, ἂν ἐγὼ μὴ δυνηθῶ ζητήσας ἀμείψασθαι, τοὺς θεοὺς εὔχομαι ποιῆσαι μακάριον καὶ πλούσιον'.

---

[130] Ctesias described each of the Persian kings as surrounded by one eunuch or more, who are very influential: for instance, Petesacas and Bagapates during Cyrus' reign (*FGrH* 688 F 9.6, 13.9); Izabates, Aspadates and Bagapates again around Cambyses (F 13.3, 9), N/Matacas and Aspamitres with Xerxes (F 13.24, 31, 33); Artoxares and Bagorazus during Artaxerxes I's reign (F 14.42–3, 47); Artoxares, Artibarzanes and Athoos around Darius II (F 15.51). See Guyot (1980: 181–2), Briant (2002a: 168–72), Lenfant (2012).

[131] For instance, Cambyses sent the corpse of Cyrus the Great to be buried in Persepolis (F 13.9); Astyages' corpse remained intact in the sands (F 9.6); Bagorazus carried the bodies of Artaxerxes I and Damaspia to Persia (F 13.47); Achaemenides' corpse was sent from Egypt (F 14.36).

[132] Some eunuchs attend the corpse of the king and its arrival at the royal tombs: Bagapates took care of the body of Cyrus (F 13.9) and Izabates that of Cambyses (F 13.15). Cf. the assertion of 'Cyrus' (Xen. *Cyr.* 7.5.64) that the loyalty of eunuchs is revealed after the death of their masters. See Waters (2017: 40–4).

[133] Lenfant (2004: 282 n. 691) rightly points this out. It may be a tongue-in-cheek allusion to the fact that the name Cyrus is allegedly derived from the sun.

This would seem to be the most significant grounds for attribution to Ctesias: another passage assigned to the physician from Athen. 2.45b (= *FGrH* 688 F 37), describes water from the Choaspes River:

> 'The king of the Persians', as Herodotus claims in his first book, 'takes with him water from the river Choaspes, which flows near Susa. He drinks only this water. A great number of four-wheeled waggons drawn by mules follow him, laden with silver vessels containing this water, which is boiled.' And Ctesias the Cnidian reports also how this royal water is boiled, and how it is put into the vessels and conveyed to the king, saying that it is the lightest and sweetest of all waters.
>
> Ὁ Περσῶν βασιλεύς, ὥς φησιν ἐν τῇ α' Ἡρόδοτος, 'ὕδωρ ἀπὸ τοῦ Χοάσπεω πιεῖν ἄγεται τοῦ παρὰ Σοῦσα ῥέοντος, τοῦ μόνου πίνει ὁ βασιλεύς. Τοῦ δὲ τοιούτου ὕδατος ἀπεψημένου πολλαὶ κάρτα ἅμαξαι τετράκυκλοι ἡμιόνειαι κομίζουσαι ἐν ἀγγείοις ἀργυρέοισιν ἔπονταί οἱ'. Κτησίας δὲ ὁ Κνίδιος καὶ ἱστορεῖ, ὅπως ἕψεται τὸ βασιλικὸν τοῦτο ὕδωρ, καὶ ὅπως ἐναποτιθέμενον τοῖς ἀγγείοις φέρεται τῷ βασιλεῖ, λέγων αὐτὸ καὶ ἐλαφρότατον καὶ ἥδιστον εἶναι.

Since the reference to Herodotus (1.188) is fairly accurate, we can assume that the one concerning Ctesias is reliable as well. One can see that the description assigned to Ctesias is in fact none other than the one referring to Artaxerxes in the aftermath of the Battle of Cunaxa. There is a perfect fit.[134] The same use of the superlative form describing the water (ἐλαφρότατον καὶ ἥδιστον) is used, corresponding to those we find in *Art.* 12.6 (κουφότατον καὶ καθαρώτατον). Athenaeus is surely not dependent on Plutarch, for he mentions Ctesias as a source; moreover, he includes material which is not in Plutarch's biography: the water is boiled, and it is from the Choaspes River in Susiana.[135] On the pleasure gained from the Choaspes water see Curt. Ruf. 5.2.9 (*delicata aqua*), which may be derived from the same Ctesian tradition.[136] Aelian (*VH* 12.40) has a similar story:

> Amongst the supplies full of splendour and display which were in Xerxes' train, was water from the River Choaspes. When they were thirsty in a desolate place, and nothing was of service, a call was made in the camp, that if anyone had water of the Choaspes, that he should provide it to the king to drink. There was found one who had a little [water], and it was rotten. Xerxes drank it, and considered the provider as his benefactor, in that he would have died of thirst if he had not been found.

---

[134] Jacoby, however, merely includes this passage as 'Aus den Persika', and in Lenfant's edition (2004: 168) it is merely 'Divers sur l'empire perse'.

[135] Cf. Strabo 15.3.22. Briant (1994: 56–60) explains these restrictions as security measures, designed to safeguard the king for fear of poisoning.

[136] See Bequignon (1940: 23). Cf. the story of David and the three heroes (2 Samuel 23: 15–17: 'Oh, that someone would get me a drink of water from the well near the gate of Bethlehem'; cf. 1 Chronicles 11: 17), presumably influenced by Persian stories; but note that David does not drink the water; cf. Plut. *Alex.* 42.7–9.

Τά τε ἄλλα ἐφόδια εἵπετο τῷ Ξέρξῃ πολυτελείας καὶ ἀλαζονείας πεπληρωμένα, καὶ οὖν καὶ ὕδωρ ἠκολούθει τὸ ἐκ τοῦ Χοάσπου. ἐπεὶ δ᾽ ἔν τινι ἐρήμῳ τόπῳ ἐδίψησεν, οὐδέπω τῆς θεραπείας ἠκούσης, ἐκηρύχθη τῷ στρατοπέδῳ, εἴ τις ἔχει ὕδωρ ἐκ τοῦ Χοάσπου, ἵνα δῷ βασιλεῖ πιεῖν. Καὶ εὑρέθη τις βραχὺ καὶ σεσηπὸς ἔχων. ἔπιεν οὖν τοῦτο ὁ Ξέρξης, καὶ εὐεργέτην τὸν δόντα ἐνόμισεν, ὅτι ἂν ἀπώλετο τῇ δίψῃ, εἰ μὴ ἐκεῖνος εὑρέθη.

This story has some striking resemblances with the Ctesian one; note especially the putrid water (σεσηπὸς) and the fact that the king drank it and awarded the giver as benefactor (cf. *Art.* 14.2). It would seem that these stories relate the *same* story.[137] During the transmission from Ctesias' *Persica* to some collection of stories used by Aelian, Artaxerxes became 'Xerxes', as so often happened.[138] The minor variances can be seen as different adaptations, and indeed, one can observe the details Plutarch chooses to omit, like the fact that the king needed a special kind of water (from the Choaspes River), and that there was stress on the soldier's obligation. By uniting all three fragments together, we can assume that the depiction of the River Choaspes (Athenaeus) was a lengthy digression in the original picture, presumably serving to increase suspense. Athenaeus thus skipped over the entire passage which mentioned Artaxerxes.

The conclusion of the battle appears in the next section of biography (*Art.* 13.1–3):

Meanwhile, the thirty men rode back glowing with rejoice, and they informed him of his unexpected good fortune. He felt filled with courage when he saw the many fighting men who were coming back to him and joining the ranks, and he went down the hill surrounded by great light. (2) He stood by the corpse and, in accordance with the custom of the Persians, the right hand and head were removed from the body; he then ordered the head to be brought to him and he grabbed him by the hair, that was thick and bushy, to show those who still doubted and fled. (3) They were amazed and prostrated themselves, so he soon had 70,000 people with him who entered the camp along with him.

Ἐν δὲ τούτῳ προσήλαυνον οἱ τριάκοντα λαμπροὶ καὶ περιχαρεῖς, ἀναγγέλλοντες αὐτῷ τὴν ἀνέλπιστον εὐτυχίαν. Ἤδη δὲ καὶ πλήθει τῶν συντρεχόντων πάλιν πρὸς αὐτὸν καὶ συνισταμένων ἐθάρρει, καὶ κατέβαινεν ἀπὸ τοῦ λόφου, φωτὶ πολλῷ περιλαμπόμενος. (2) Ὡς δ᾽ ἐπέστη τῷ νεκρῷ, καὶ κατὰ δή τινα νόμον Περσῶν ἡ δεξιὰ χεὶρ ἀπεκόπη καὶ ἡ κεφαλὴ τοῦ σώματος, ἐκέλευσε τὴν κεφαλὴν αὐτῷ κομισθῆναι· καὶ τῆς κόμης δραξάμενος, οὔσης βαθείας καὶ λασίας, ἐπεδείκνυε τοῖς ἀμφιδοξοῦσιν ἔτι καὶ φεύγουσιν. (3) Οἱ δ᾽ ἐθαύμαζον καὶ προσεκύνουν, ὥστε ταχὺ μυριάδας ἑπτὰ περὶ αὐτὸν γενέσθαι, καὶ συνεισελάσαι πάλιν εἰς τὸ στρατόπεδον.

---

[137] See Briant (1994: 62–3; 2015: 306) for a different view.
[138] Cf. Alpers (1969).

Although Photius in his summary says that the king himself cut off Cyrus' body (F 16.64 = *Bibl.* cod. 72, p. 43 b 36–8: καὶ αἰκισμὸς τοῦ σώματος Κύρου **ὑπὸ τἀδελφοῦ 'Αρτοξέρξου**· τήν τε γὰρ κεφαλὴν καὶ τὴν χεῖρα, μεθ' ἧς τὸν 'Αρτοξέρξην ἔβαλεν, **αὐτὸς ἀπέτεμε**, καὶ ἐθριάμβευσεν, 'His body was mutilated by his brother Artaxerxes. He himself cut off the head and the hand which [Cyrus] used to wound Artaxerxes and he displayed them'), the rest of the narrative and the comparison with Plutarch (*Art.* 17.1) make it clear that Ctesias had a eunuch do it on behalf of the King. Indeed, Photius corrects himself later on and attributes the act to Bagapates (see below). It would seem that Ctesias' original depiction was initially vague at this point (cf. *Art.* 12.3: at first the king wishes to see Cyrus' corpse himself but then sends a company).[139]

Cyrus' body was probably mutilated in the king's presence. The following scene evokes the image of the seven conspirators displaying the heads of the Magi (Hdt. 3.79), and pertinent here is the self-image of Cyrus as versed in the teachings of the Magi (*Art.* 6.4: μαγεύειν βέλτιον). The picture of the mutilation of Cyrus' body is associated with Ctesias' account and presumably comes from his text. It would seem that Xenophon did not see Cyrus' severed head and hand. As it is presented in the *Anabasis*, this description itself seems disconnected from the rest of the text. Plutarch (*Art.* 13.2) has the mutilation of Cyrus' body taking place at night. The head of the prince was held aloft by the king, a move designed to encourage those combatants in the field who were still wavering in their support to rally back to Artaxerxes (*Art.* 13.2). Xenophon includes none of this. When he presents himself as addressing Proxenus' officers (*Anab.* 3.1.17), he refers to the act of removing Cyrus' head and hand and nailing them to a cross as items familiar to the soldiers. Yet it is not at all clear when Xenophon and the others would have had the opportunity to see the severed body parts. It was not in the hours of darkness following the battle itself, since the Greeks were not yet aware of Cyrus' death (*Anab.* 1.10.16, 2.1.1), and on the subsequent night they were already far from the king's camp (*Anab.* 2.2.3). Two options, therefore, remain: either the soldiers viewed this sight in the morning following the battle, when they were looking for food (*Anab.* 2.1.6), or they never saw it at all. It is more probable that Xenophon learned of this act for the first time while reading Ctesias' account and then incorporated it in the story with no indication of

---

[139] Cf. Schottin (1865: 4). This seems like another instance of the king gaining undue credit for a deed.

background or reason for the deed, nor with a claim to have seen Cyrus' body (*Anab.* 1.10.1). Xenophon inserts this information just before Artaxerxes' attack on the Greek camp and in the speech he himself supposedly delivered to his comrades. One would assume that this detail was too powerful and familiar to any reader of Ctesias for Xenophon to leave it out.

The question 'who killed Cyrus?' probably permeated most of the rest of Ctesias' narrative. In Plutarch's rendition we see that gradually all those who defy Artaxerxes' glory for the deed find their deaths in brutal executions. The official version eventually prevails, although it is false. All these scenes appear in Photius' summary (*FGrH* 688 F 16.66–67 = *Bibl.* cod. 72, p. p. 44 a 6–19):

> (66) Matters concerning Bagapates, the man who had cut the head from Cyrus' corpse on the order of the king. The queen mother played a game of dice with the king which she won and seized Bagapates as agreed. He was flayed and crucified by Parysatis and then she stopped her excessive mourning for Cyrus at the request of Artaxerxes. (67) He gave rewards to the man who carried off Cyrus' saddle-cloth and he honoured the Carian who was thought to have killed Cyrus. Parysatis tortured and killed the Carian who had been honoured. Artaxerxes handed Mithridates over to Parysatis at her request, for he boasted at the table that he killed Cyrus. She took him and killed him cruelly. This is the summary of books 19–20.
>
> Τὰ περὶ Βαγαπάτου τοῦ ἀποτεμόντος προστάξει βασιλέως τὴν κεφαλὴν ἀπὸ τοῦ σώματος Κύρου, ὅπως ἡ μήτηρ μετὰ βασιλέως κύβοις ἐπὶ συνθήκαις παίξασα καὶ νικήσασα ἔλαβε Βαγαπάτην, καὶ ὃν τρόπον τὸ δέρμα περιαιρεθεὶς ἀνεσταυρίσθη ὑπὸ Παρυσάτιος· ὅτε καὶ τὸ πολὺ ἐπὶ Κύρῳ πένθος αὐτῇ ἐπαύσατο διὰ τὴν πολλὴν τοῦ Ἀρτοξέρξου δέησιν. (67) Ὡς Ἀρτοξέρξης δῶρα ἔδωκε τῷ ἐνέγκαντι τὸν Κύρου πῖλον· καὶ ὡς τὸν Κᾶρα τὸν δοκέοντα Κῦρον βαλεῖν Ἀρτοξέρξης ἐτίμησε, καὶ ὡς Παρύσατις τὸν τιμηθέντα Κᾶρα αἰκισαμένη ἀπέκτεινεν. Ὡς Ἀρτοξέρξης παρέδωκεν αἰτησαμένη Μιτραδάτην Παρυσάτιδι, ἐπὶ τραπέζης μεγαλαυχήσαντα ἀποκτεῖναι Κῦρον, κἀκείνη λαβοῦσα πικρῶς ἀνεῖλε. ταῦτα ἡ ιθ' καὶ ἡ κ' ἱστορία.

The sequence in Photius' summary has the punishment of Bagapates (F 16.67, *Art.* 17), then the story of the Carian (F 16.67, *Art.* 14) and finally, the story of Mithridates (F 16.67, *Art.* 15–16). Presumably this was the original order, which showed an escalation in the cruelty of Artaxerxes. Plutarch changes the sequence presumably to play on the dual nature of Artaxerxes' character: his brutality on the one hand and compliance with Parysatis' cruelty on the other hand, anticipating *Art.* 18–19.

The entire following section in Plutarch's biography (*Art.* 14–17) is devoted to the rewards and punishments given by Artaxerxes to the persons who have either assisted or harmed him. It begins with two alleged defectors (*Art.* 14.3–4):

There was some care concerning the punishments of the people who did wrong. Arbaces, a Mede who fled to Cyrus during the battle, but changed his mind, when the latter died, he (Artaxerxes) convicted of cowardice and softness, not of treason or ill will, and ordered him to carry around a naked prostitute astride on his neck for the entire day in the market. When another person, in addition for changing sides, lied about having killed two of the enemy's men, he (Artaxerxes) ordered to pierce his tongue with three needles.

(3) Ἦν δέ τις ἐπιμέλεια καὶ περὶ τὰς τῶν ἐξαμαρτόντων δικαιώσεις· Ἀρβάκην μὲν γάρ τινα Μῆδον ἐν τῇ μάχῃ πρὸς Κῦρον φυγόντα καὶ πάλιν ἐκείνου πεσόντος μεταστάντα, δειλίαν καὶ μαλακίαν καταγνούς, οὐ προδοσίαν οὐδὲ κακόνοιαν, ἐκέλευσε γυμνὴν ἀναλαβόντα πόρνην περιβάδην ἐπὶ τοῦ τραχήλου δι᾽ ἡμέρας ὅλης ἐν ἀγορᾷ περιφέρειν. (4) Ἑτέρου δὲ πρὸς τῷ μεταστῆναι ψευσαμένου καταβαλεῖν δύο τῶν πολεμίων, προσέταξε διαπεῖραι τρισὶ βελόναις τὴν γλῶτταν.

Arbaces is accused of cowardice and softness; the second man is accused of telling a lie – claiming to have killed two people from the enemy's side – and is penalised more severely by a certain distortion of his body. An implicit comparison to the king shows the irony involved in these punishments: the mild penalty to Arbaces displays the king's own softness (as we saw above, this is exactly Cyrus' charge against him in *Art.* 6.4), while the harsher punishment to the liar overlooks the lie of Artaxerxes, who wishes others to acknowledge that he killed Cyrus (*Art.* 14.6). One notes the irony of leaving anonymous the person who claims glory for killing. From Xenophon we know that Arbaces was one of the king's commanders, who (like Abrocomas, Tissaphernes and Gobryas) commanded 300,000 men (*Anab.* 1.7.12). The description of his defection cannot be true.[140] In the list of satraps at the end of the *Anabasis* (7.8.25), describing the state of the empire in the year 401/0 BCE, there is an Arbaces as satrap of Media. It is probably the same person, whom Plutarch also calls 'Median'.[141] Moreover, to assume that such a senior person would be so mildly punished for defection would be hard to imagine.[142] In fact, it might be the case that this person's imaginary absence provides a fictional counter-example to the king's false presence at the scene during the killing of Cyrus. It would thus seem that the allusion to

[140] Justi (1895: 20–1) believes it is not the same person. Cf. Binder (2008: 231).

[141] See Manfredini, Orsi and Antelami (1987: 285). The authenticity and value of the list are questionable. Lehmann-Haupt (1921: 113) accepts them while Ehtecham (1946: 168–78) is in doubt; Bivar (1961: 121–3) finds reliable information in it, but Briant (2002a: 988) expresses mistrust. Ctesias gave this name to another Mede, a person who fought against Sardanapallus (*FGrH* 688 F 1b.2.24.1).

[142] Elsewhere in Photius' summary (F 16.63), Artaxerxes is said to cruelly punish Ar<ta>barius, who considered defecting to Cyrus. The prince himself executed Orontas, who wished to defect to the king (Xen. *Anab.* 1.6).

the king's behaviour through this character was already intended by Ctesias.

Ctesias probably included a play on the king's lies. The emphasis on avoidance of lying goes back to the known description in Herodotus, with its emphasis on telling the truth as a key concept in the Persian education of the young (Hdt. 1.136; Strabo 15.3.18), and with the depiction of lying and dishonesty as being the most despicable of evils in Persia (Hdt. 1.138; cf. 7.102, 7.209). In the royal Achaemenid ideology, especially in the inscriptions of Darius I, the Lie (*drauga*) is considered a serious offence against the king.[143] The supposed pretenders in the Behistun inscription are presented as liars (DB 1.39, 1.78, 3.80).[144] The Lie is tantamount to rebellion, as 'those following the Lie' are regarded as lawbreakers. These depictions echo one of the principles of the Zoroastrian faith.[145] Earlier in Ctesias' work (*FGrH* 688 F 9.1), liars are punished (cf. Hdt. 3.27). Yet, as in Herodotus' account (Hdt. 3.72: ἔνθα γάρ τι δεῖ ψεῦδος λέγεσθαι, λεγέσθω, 'for where it is necessary that a lie be spoken, let it be spoken', ironically put in the mouth of the future king Darius), in this story too the monarch (Artaxerxes) endorses a lie, and executes the Carian who challenges his official version by speaking the truth (*Art.* 14.5–7).

According to the royal ideology repeated in the inscriptions, the king is supposed to hit the enemy himself (see DB 1.57, 1.59, 1.73, 1.83, 2.5, 2.69, 5.13, 5.27; the recurring word is *avājanam*, 'I killed'). Ctesias' story seems to be a sardonic dismantling of this ideal, where the Carian's punishment is given not by the king, but by his mother, thereby rendering the monarch passive while others act for him (*Art.* 14.8–10):

> ... [the Carian] complained by bringing witnesses and shouting that no one else but him had killed Cyrus, and that he was deprived unjustly from his fame. Hearing this, the king was furious and ordered his head to be cut off. His mother, who was present, said, 'Oh king, you set the wretched free, but with me he will receive the worthy reward for what he dared to say.' When she received him from the king, Parysatis ordered the executioners to take the person and for ten days to stretch him on the wheel and then to gouge out his eyes and then pour molten bronze into his ears until he died.

---

[143] Cf. DB 4.33–5: 'Darius the King says: These are the provinces which became rebellious. The Lie made them rebellious, so that these (men) deceived the people'; cf. DB 4.36–9: 'Darius the King says: You who shall be king hereafter, protect yourself vigorously from the Lie; the man who shall be a Lie-follower, him do you punish well' (trans. by Kent). Cf. DB 1.34, 4.63; Cf. DNb.12.

[144] See Briant (2002a: 126–7, 138).

[145] See the introduction. On the centrality of this opposition between truth and lie in the Indo-Iranian religious setting prior to the emergence of the Zoroastrian belief see Lommel (1930: 40–52), Stausberg (2002: 1.91–5).

(8)... ἠγανάκτει μαρτυρόμενος καὶ βοῶν, ὅτι Κῦρον οὐδεὶς ἕτερος ἀλλ᾽ αὐτὸς ἀπεκτόνοι, καὶ τὴν δόξαν ἀδίκως ἀποστεροῖτο. (9) Ταῦτα δ᾽ ἀκούσας ὁ βασιλεὺς σφόδρα παρωξύνθη, καὶ τὴν κεφαλὴν ἐκέλευσεν ἀποτεμεῖν τοῦ ἀνθρώπου· παροῦσα δ᾽ ἡ μήτηρ 'μὴ σύ γε' εἶπεν 'οὕτω τὸν Κᾶρα τοῦτον, ὦ βασιλεῦ, τὸν ὄλεθρον ἀπαλλάξῃς, ἀλλὰ παρ᾽ ἐμοῦ τὸν ἄξιον ἀπολήψεται μισθὸν ὧν τολμᾷ λέγειν'. (10) Ἐπιτρέψαντος δὲ τοῦ βασιλέως, ἐκέλευσε τοὺς ἐπὶ τῶν τιμωριῶν ἡ Παρύσατις λαβόντας τὸν ἄνθρωπον ἐφ᾽ ἡμέρας δέκα στρεβλοῦν, εἶτα τοὺς ὀφθαλμοὺς ἐξορύξαντας εἰς τὰ ὦτα θερμὸν ἐντήκειν χαλκόν, ἕως ἀποθάνῃ.

According to Plutarch's rendition of Ctesias' story, the king wishes all people to think and say that he killed Cyrus himself (*Art.* 14.5: οἰόμενος δὲ καὶ βουλόμενος δοκεῖν καὶ λέγειν πάντας ἀνθρώπους ὡς αὐτὸς ἀπεκτόνοι Κῦρον). Xenophon (*Anab.* 2.1.8) testifies that this was indeed the official version after the battle (ἐπεὶ νικῶν τυγχάνει καὶ Κῦρον ἀπέκτονε, 'since victory had fallen to him and he had slain Cyrus'; cf. Diod. 14.25.1). Artaxerxes thus had to remove the Carian. At the beginning, Mithridates, the other person responsible for Cyrus' death, is silent (*Art.* 14.7), but his disaster soon follows (*Art.* 15) when he discloses at a banquet the truth of Cyrus' death and thus contests the official royal version. Photius' summary of this dramatic episode is very brief, yet he mentions one word which Plutarch surprisingly does not: 'table' (ἐπὶ τραπέζης). By ignoring this word and downplaying the Persian setting, Plutarch, like the host of this event, Sparamizes, the eunuch of Parysatis, creates the impression that the banquet is more Greek in character; but, of course, it is not.[146] It is in fact an incongruous union of the Greek symposium and Persian environment. Of note is the notion of truth, which is set in the context of the Greek symposium (*Art.* 15.4: ἐπεὶ δέ φασιν Ἕλληνες οἶνον καὶ ἀλήθειαν εἶναι, 'as the Greeks say "Wine and there is Truth"'), markedly different from the Persian notion of truth as the embodiment of the cosmic/social/political order. Again, Artaxerxes' own version is presented as a lie and the subversive one of Mithridates as truthful.[147] This presentation seems to derive from Ctesias. Cleverly, it is enhanced by Plutarch with his portrayal of Ctesias' presentation itself as a lie we can still believe in, as hinted at the beginning of the biography.

After Mithridates divulges everything, the host, assuming again one of the key functions of a Greek *symposiarch*, tones down emotions by urging the participants to keep their differences within bounds as they eat and drink, and to prostrate themselves before the King's *daimon* (*Art.* 15.7):

---

[146] See Almagor (2009: 133–5). On Persian feasts see Hdt. 1.207, 3.22, 3.34, 1.133; cf. Persian banquets in Esther 1:3, 9, 2:18, 5:4, 7:1–10.

[147] See Lincoln (2007: 94), Almagor (2009: 135–6).

'my dear friend Mithridates, let us drink at present and eat, and bow before the *daimon* of the king, and let us leave these words which are beyond us'.
'ὦ τᾶν' ἔφη 'Μιθριδάτα, πίνωμεν ἐν τῷ παρόντι καὶ ἐσθίωμεν, τὸν βασιλέως δαίμονα προσκυνοῦντες, λόγους δὲ μείζους ἢ καθ' ἡμᾶς ἐάσωμεν.'

Some scholars believe that this is Ctesias' portrayal echoing a Persian phrase with 'the king's *daimon*'.[148] The expression may not be Ctesias'.[149] The physician may have used a phrase approximately similar to the expression θεὸς βασίλειος (see Hdt. 3.65; cf. 5.106, Plut. *de Alex. fort.*, 338f, *Alex.* 30.12), and may have referred to the god Ahura Mazda – rather than any other deity, including the *Xvarenah* (OPer. *farnah*), i.e., divine royal glory/fortune – since the close and unique association of the king to the supreme Iranian divinity appearing in the royal inscriptions (DSk.3–5: 'mine is Ahura Mazda, of Ahura Mazda am I') matches the Greek phrase.[150] By mentioning the *daimon*, usually an interim deity between god and man, Plutarch leaves the description vague.[151] He is also able to reintroduce the king as present in the scene while he is not really there (the words τῷ παρόντι are telling), thus exactly matching the debate on the question of Artaxerxes' presence at Cyrus' death and his responsibility for the killing.

Under the necessity to turn his fabricated version of the events into the factual one, Artaxerxes has therefore to resort to unprecedented cruelty for the misbehaviour of Mithridates, as Plutarch relates in the following section (*Art.* 16.2–6):

He ordered that Mithridates would be killed by the torture of the boats. The boats torture is something as follows: two boats are matched together, to the one they make the convict lie down on his back. Then they bring on another and fit them, so that the head and arms and feet are protruding, and the rest of the body is covered. Then they make the person eat. If he does not want to, they force him by pricking his eyes. After eating, they pour into his mouth blended honey and milk to drink, and smear the same on his face. Then his eyes are always turned against the sun, and swarms

[148] See Brenk (1977: 151), Swain (1989: 299). See Almagor (2010) for discussion.
[149] Cf. Schottin (1865: 4).
[150] See Almagor (2017b: 32–8, 46–7).
[151] In the *On the Decline of Oracles* (*De def. or.* 415b), the character Cleombrotus speaks of *daimones* as occupying a place between gods and men – and praises the Magi for this notion. Plutarch can be ironic here, in showing the problematic nature of an interim deity. See Brenk (1987: 278, 291): Cleombrotus is ridiculed for his gullibility and ignorance. Cf. de Jong (1997: 166). On Plutarch's daimonology see Soury (1942), Dillon (1977: 216–24), Babut (1983), Brenk (1987: 275–94). See Dillon (1977: 223): 'It does seem as if there is an incoherence here in Plutarch's thought, resulting, perhaps, from a clash of Persian (and popular) influences with more purely Platonic ones.' On the doctrine of *daimones* populating the sublunary world as developed by Xenocrates see Dörrie (1967: 1524–5), Dillon (1977: 31–2), Schibli (1993).

of flies settle and cover his face. Since inside he does what people who eat and drink have to do, maggots and worms break out from the decay and putrefaction of the excrement; by these as they penetrate the body, it is wasted. (2) Ἐκέλευσεν οὖν τὸν Μιθριδάτην ἀποθανεῖν σκαφευθέντα. (3) Τὸ δὲ σκαφευθῆναι τοιοῦτόν ἐστιν· σκάφας δύο πεποιημένας ἐφαρμόζειν ἀλλήλαις λαβόντες, εἰς τὴν ἑτέραν κατακλίνουσι τὸν κολαζόμενον ὕπτιον· (4) εἶτα τὴν ἑτέραν ἐπάγοντες καὶ συναρμόζοντες, ὥστε τὴν κεφαλὴν καὶ τὰς χεῖρας ἔξω καὶ τοὺς πόδας ἀπολαμβάνεσθαι, τὸ δ᾽ ἄλλο σῶμα πᾶν ἀποκεκρύφθαι, διδόασιν ἐσθίειν τῷ ἀνθρώπῳ· κἂν μὴ θέλῃ, προσβιάζονται κεντοῦντες τὰ ὄμματα. φαγόντι δὲ πιεῖν μέλι καὶ γάλα συγκεκραμένον ἐγχέουσιν εἰς τὸ στόμα, καὶ κατὰ τοῦ προσώπου καταχέουσιν. (5) Εἶτα πρὸς τὸν ἥλιον ἀεὶ στρέφουσιν ἐναντίον τὰ ὄμματα, καὶ μυιῶν προσκαθημένων <ὑπὸ> πλήθους πᾶν ἀποκρύπτεται τὸ πρόσωπον. (6) Ἐντὸς δὲ ποιοῦντος ὅσα ποιεῖν ἀναγκαῖόν ἐστιν ἐσθίοντας ἀνθρώπους καὶ πίνοντας, εὐλαὶ καὶ σκώληκες ὑπὸ φθορᾶς καὶ σηπεδόνος ἐκ τοῦ περιττώματος ἀναζέουσιν, ὑφ᾽ ὧν ἀναλίσκεται τὸ σῶμα διαδυομένων εἰς τὰ ἐντός.
<ὑπὸ> add. Korais ‖ πλήθους GL²R: πλῆθος L¹ et ante corr. R

Ctesias is justly perceived to be the source of this image.[152] Photius' epitome (*FGrH* 688 F 16.67 = *Bibl.* cod. 72, p. 44 a 16–17), asserting that the king handed the young Persian to Parysatis to be tortured (ὡς Ἀρτοξέρξης παρέδωκεν αἰτησαμένη Μιτραδάτην Παρυσάτιδι), is probably an error, stemming from a hasty note or an inaccurate recollection.[153] It is clear that Photius conflates the fates of three characters: he attributes to the Carian what happened to the eunuch and to Mithridates the fate of the Carian. It should be mentioned that Photius refers to an identical scene earlier, where the same torture, the 'Punishment of the Boats',[154] is administered by Artaxerxes I to Aspamitres, convicted of plotting against Xerxes and his son Darius (*FGrH* 688 F 14.34 = *Bibl.* cod. 72, p. 40 a 14–15: σκαφεύεται ... οὕτως ἀναιρεῖται).[155] Photius' mistake was perhaps caused by a break in his reading of the *Persica* at this point, seen also in Plutarch's version. Bearing in mind that Aspamitres' story was told in book 17 of Ctesias' work and that of Mithridates in books 19 or 20, it is hardly likely that the physician provided a fully detailed description of the punishment a second time, and we may reasonably assume

---

[152] See Smith (1881: 34), Mantey (1888: 14–15), Krumbholz (1889: 16), Stevenson (1997: 12–14).
[153] Bigwood (1976: 4 n. 13), argues that Photius' mind was distracted by the punishment of the Carian 'eunuch'. It could be that Photius misread a phrase to the effect that Parysatis was given the information (cf. *Art.* 16.1). It need not imply the use of a different source by Plutarch, *pace* König (1972: 106–7) and Binder (2008: 241–2).
[154] The cruel mode of torture is also mentioned (but not described) by Eunapius, *Vit. soph.* 7.4.15 and Tzetzes, *Chil.* 10.359.676, as being typical of the Persians (as Περσῶν σκάφευσις).
[155] On the direct involvement of the monarch in this punishment see Lincoln (2007: 89).

that only in the earlier book did he elaborate on this torment. Both Plutarch and Photius were presumably interrupted in their reading by a backward reference (perhaps even one mentioning Aspamitres), causing Photius to turn back and incur a memory slip, and making Plutarch describe the punitive procedure as general, without a clear connection to this story's characters. Incidentally, if this is true, then this is an indication that Ctesias included internal references in his *Persica*.[156]

If Ctesias did not include a description of the punishment at this particular juncture, and the readers had to discover it in a distant and hidden part of the original work, this would accentuate the feature of revelation of Artaxerxes' character by the reader. Correspondingly, the length given by Plutarch to this horrid torment testifies to the significance it has in the biography for the unfolding of the story and the presentation of the hero's character and moral development. The ghastly scene is tucked away in Plutarch's presentation between two depictions of punishments (to the Carian and to the eunuch) in which the king's cruelty is not pronounced, as compared with that of his mother. Plutarch therefore artistically stresses a trait that was probably present in Ctesias' original description. Inventively, the placement of this gruesome torture between the other two scenes emulates the punishment of the boats itself, in a way that brings out Ctesias' intention better than it perhaps was in the original.

The final person to incur punishment for his treatment of Cyrus is mentioned in the next section of the biography (*Art.* 17.1–9). It can be attributed to Ctesias with some certainty, by the similarity with Photius' epitome (above):

> (17) The remaining part of Parysatis' aim was the king's eunuch Masabates, who cut off Cyrus' head and hands. As he gave her no opportunity to get him, Parysatis devised the following scheme: she was an able woman and skilled with dice; because of this she often played dice with the king before the war. After the war ... she took Artaxerxes once as he started to be fretful with his leisure, and invited him to play dice for one thousand Darics. And when he played she made sure he would win and gave him the gold. She pretended to be troubled and contentious and requested to play dice again, for a eunuch, and he concurred. After they made an agreement, each party put aside five most trusted persons, and from the rest the winner would choose and the loser would give. And on these terms they played

---

[156] Cf. an indication of an internal reference backwards in Herodotus (7.8.a: Xerxes on his predecessors). It may be that the MSS of Ctesias even included a forward reference to 'Mithridates' in the Aspamitres' passage (perhaps as a marginal gloss), for Diodorus (11.69.2) calls Aspamitres 'Mithridates' and obviously relied on a source that conflated the two (cf. *POxy* XIII.1610, *FGrH* 70 F 191.16, Bigwood, 1976: 23 n. 89).

dice. Parysatis, very much absorbed in the act and serious in the game, did well as the dice fell, won and took Masabates (he was not among those set aside). Before the king had misgiving of the deed, she handed the eunuch to the executioners and ordered to flay him alive, place his body athwart on three poles and stretch his skin separately. When the king heard what happened, he took it hard and was furious at her, she said in irony and with a smile, 'How sweet and blessed you are that you are irritated by a miserable old eunuch while I am silent and content with the one thousand Darics I lost in the game of dice.' The king repented having been deceived and was quiet, but Stateira resisted her in public and was displeased at this, how because of Cyrus she had destroyed cruelly and illegally loyal and trusted men of the king.

Λοιπὸς δ' ἦν τῇ Παρυσάτιδι σκοπὸς ὁ τὴν κεφαλὴν ἀποτεμὼν καὶ τὴν χεῖρα τοῦ Κύρου Μασαβάτης βασιλέως εὐνοῦχος. (2) Ὡς οὖν αὐτὸς οὐδεμίαν καθ' ἑαυτοῦ λαβὴν παρεδίδου, τοιοῦτον ἐπιβουλῆς τρόπον ἡ Παρύσατις συνέθηκεν. (3) Ἦν τά τ' ἄλλα θυμόσοφος γυνὴ καὶ δεινὴ κυβεύειν· διὸ καὶ βασιλεῖ πρὸ τοῦ πολέμου πολλάκις συνεκύβευε. (4) Μετὰ δὲ τὸν πόλεμον... (5) Λαβοῦσα δή ποτε τὸν Ἀρτοξέρξην ὡρμημένον ἀλύειν σχολῆς οὔσης, προὐκαλεῖτο περὶ χιλίων δαρεικῶν κυβεῦσαι· καὶ κυβεύοντα περιεῖδε νικῆσαι, καὶ τὸ χρυσίον ἀπέδωκε. Προσποιουμένη δ' ἀνιᾶσθαι καὶ φιλονικεῖν, ἐκέλευσεν αὖθις ἐξ ἀρχῆς περὶ εὐνούχου διακυβεῦσαι· κἀκεῖνος ὑπήκουσε. (6) Ποιησάμενοι δὲ συνθήκας, πέντε μὲν ἑκάτερον ὑπεξελέσθαι τοὺς πιστοτάτους, ἐκ δὲ τῶν λοιπῶν ὃν ἂν ὁ νικῶν ἕληται, δοῦναι τὸν ἡττώμενον, ἐπὶ τούτοις ἐκύβευον. (7) Σφόδρα δὴ γενομένη πρὸς τῷ πράγματι καὶ σπουδάσασα περὶ τὴν παιδιάν, εὖ δέ πως αὐτῇ καὶ τῶν κύβων πεσόντων, νικήσασα λαμβάνει τὸν Μασαβάτην· οὐ γὰρ ἦν ἐν τοῖς ὑπεξῃρημένοις. Καὶ πρὶν ἐν ὑποψίᾳ γενέσθαι βασιλέα τοῦ πράγματος, ἐγχειρίσασα τοῖς ἐπὶ τῶν τιμωριῶν προσέταξεν ἐκδεῖραι ζῶντα καὶ τὸ μὲν σῶμα πλάγιον διὰ τριῶν σταυρῶν ἀναπῆξαι, τὸ δὲ δέρμα χωρὶς διαπατταλεῦσαι. (8) Γενομένων δὲ τούτων, καὶ βασιλέως χαλεπῶς φέροντος καὶ παροξυνομένου πρὸς αὐτήν, εἰρωνευομένη μετὰ γέλωτος 'ὡς ἡδύ' ἔφασκεν 'εἴ καὶ μακάριος, εἰ χαλεπαίνεις διὰ γέροντα πονηρὸν εὐνοῦχον, ἐγὼ δὲ χιλίους ἐκκυβευθεῖσα δαρεικοὺς σιωπῶ καὶ στέργω'. (9) Βασιλεὺς μὲν οὖν ἐφ' οἷς ἐξηπατήθη μεταμελόμενος ἡσυχίαν ἦγεν, ἡ δὲ Στάτειρα καὶ πρὸς τἄλλα φανερῶς ἠναντιοῦτο, καὶ τούτοις ἐδυσχέραινεν ὡς ἄνδρας εὐνούχους καὶ πιστοὺς βασιλεῖ διὰ Κῦρον ὠμῶς καὶ παρανόμως ἀπολλυούσης αὐτῆς.

εὐνούχους codd.: εὐνοϊκοὺς Ziegler

A game of chance is involved in the preservation of this poor man's name. It is true that Plutarch and Photius use different name forms for the eunuch. It is also true that Photius' version (Bagapates) is better attested.[157] Yet this does not necessarily mean that Plutarch follows a different source than Ctesias and different from the one he followed so far.[158] Photius could have been led astray by his memory (or his notes?) of the name of the eunuch who took care of the corpse of Cyrus the Great (*FGrH* 688 F 13.9). Alternatively,

[157] Schmitt (2006: 163–4); see, however, Lenfant (2004: 274 n. 629).
[158] Cf. Binder (2008: 73, 253–4).

Plutarch's text had the same form but was corrupted at this point. The original name form was most likely composed with the ending -*(a)pates*, which ironically lost its 'head', or first stem.[159] There was certainly some deceit (ἀπάτη, ἐξηπατήθη: 17.9) as well as a horrible torture (διαπατταλεῦσαι: 17.7) involved, introduced by Plutarch with a play on the form of the eunuch's name he used.

Ctesias may have presented Parysatis as creating reality through the game, a deed at once comparable to the king's creation of reality through his royal version and subversive of his authority. It is not clear how the game between Parysatis and Artaxerxes was decided, except that it included dice.[160] It is possible that the word σπουδάσασα ('serious') suggests the game involved some effort on Parysatis' part. The game may have been some form of board game as well.[161] The fact that the game of Artaxerxes and Parysatis results in the removal of the king's confidants may sardonically refer to a variant of back-gammon, a game that entails the removal of pieces – or rather, persons, treated as pieces or pebbles on a board.[162] Ctesias may have envisaged his own narrative of the game as equally subverting the authority of the king. In this case, it is the turn of Plutarch to have the last word, as he rearranges Ctesias' three scenes and moves about the persons involved (the Carian, Mithridates and the eunuch) as pieces on the board of his own story. Like Parysatis, who reserves Masabates for last (*Art.* 17.1: λοιπός), and like the king, who sets him aside (*Art.* 17.6: ἐκ δὲ τῶν λοιπῶν), so does Plutarch prefer to keep this scene as the final episode out of the three.

The last passage we treat here concerns the aftermath of the assassination of Stateira (*Art.* 19.7–10), which does not specifically mention Ctesias:

> The woman (Stateira) died in great pain and convulsions, and was aware of the evil done and conveyed her suspicion to the king against his mother, and he knew her brutal and hard-to-satisfy character. He rushed therefore to investigate, and arrested the servants and table waiters of his mother and tortured them; Parysatis kept Gigis for a long time in her house with her, and though the king asked for her, she would not give her. Later, however,

---

[159] The form we have in Plutarch's text is perhaps based on a hypercorrection of a mixture of ὀνομάσας/ὀνομάσαι ('naming') and a corrupt form (–βαπάτης?).

[160] See Lamar (1927: 1934–89). Cf. Held (1935: 264–77) on a similar game in the great Indian epic *Mahābhārata* (composed between the fourth century BCE and the fourth century CE), where a game in which the stakes are raised higher with every defeat (2.51.1–52.35) is described. See Stevenson (1997: 74–5). It may be that the story was also inspired by Herodotus (3.128), who relates that Darius has his courtiers cast lots, a method by which Bagaeus is chosen.

[161] Cf. Daryaee (2002: 282–3).

[162] See Polyb. 5.26.12–13; cf. Diog. Laert. 1.59.

when she asked to be freed to go home during the night, he learned of this, arranged an ambush, seized her and sentenced her to death. In Persia, poisoners are killed by law in this manner: on a flat stone they place the head, and with another stone they strike and press till they crush the face and the head. Gigis died this way, but to Parysatis Artaxerxes said and did nothing bad, and sent her to Babylon, as she wanted, saying that as long as she was there, he would not see Babylon. So far are the affairs of the royal house.

(7) Ἀποθνήσκουσα οὖν ἡ γυνὴ μετὰ πόνων μεγάλων καὶ σπαραγμῶν, αὐτή τε συνῃσθάνετο τοῦ κακοῦ, καὶ βασιλεῖ παρέσχεν ὑποψίαν κατὰ τῆς μητρός, εἰδότι τὸ θηριῶδες αὐτῆς καὶ δυσμείλικτον. (8) Ὅθεν εὐθὺς ἐπὶ τὴν ζήτησιν ὁρμήσας, τοὺς μὲν ὑπηρέτας καὶ τραπεζοκόμους τῆς μητρὸς συνέλαβε καὶ κατεστρέβλωσε, τὴν δὲ Γίγιν ἡ Παρύσατις πολὺν χρόνον εἶχεν οἴκοι μεθ᾽ αὑτῆς, καὶ βασιλέως ἐξαιτοῦντος οὐκ ἔδωκεν, ἀλλ᾽ ὕστερον αὐτῆς δεηθείσης εἰς τὸν οἶκον ἀφεθῆναι νυκτός, αἰσθόμενος καὶ λόχον ὑφεὶς συνήρπασε καὶ κατέγνω θάνατον. (9) Ἀποθνήσκουσι δ᾽ οἱ φαρμακεῖς ἐν Πέρσαις κατὰ νόμον οὕτως· λίθος ἐστὶ πλατύς, ἐφ᾽ οὗ τὴν κεφαλὴν καταθέντες αὐτῶν ἑτέρῳ λίθῳ παίουσι, καὶ πιέζουσιν ἄχρι οὗ συνθλάσωσι τὸ πρόσωπον καὶ τὴν κεφαλήν. (10) Ἡ οὖν Γίγις οὕτως ἀπέθανε, τὴν δὲ Παρύσατιν ὁ Ἀρτοξέρξης ἄλλο μὲν οὐδὲν οὔτ᾽ εἶπε κακὸν οὔτ᾽ ἐποίησεν, εἰς δὲ Βαβυλῶνα βουλομένην ἐξέπεμψεν, εἰπὼν ἕως ἐκείνη περίεστιν, αὐτὸς οὐκ ὄψεσθαι Βαβυλῶνα. Τὰ μὲν οὖν κατὰ τὴν οἰκίαν οὕτως εἶχεν.

That this section comes from Ctesias can be seen from a comparison with Photius' epitome (*FGrH* 688 F 27.70 = *Bibl.* cod. 72, p. 44 b 9–16):

The king was furious at his mother because of these things and imprisoned her eunuchs, tortured them and killed them. He arrested Ginge, who served Parysatis, brought her to trial, and when she was acquitted he reversed the verdict. He tortured Ginge and killed her. Parysatis was angry at her son, and he was furious at her.

Ὀργὴ διὰ ταῦτα τοῦ βασιλέως πρὸς τὴν μητέρα, καὶ σύλληψις τῶν εὐνούχων αὐτῆς καὶ αἰκισμὸς καὶ ἀναίρεσις. Καὶ ἔτι σύλληψις Γίγγης, ἣ ᾠκείωτο Παρυσάτιδι· καὶ κρίσις ἐπ᾽ αὐτῇ, καὶ ἀθώωσις μὲν παρὰ τῶν κριτῶν, καταδίκη δὲ παρὰ βασιλέως· καὶ αἰκισμὸς Γίγγης καὶ ἀναίρεσις· καὶ ὀργὴ διὰ τοῦτο Παρυσάτιδος πρὸς τὸν υἱόν, κἀκείνου πρὸς τὴν μητέρα.

In Photius' account as well, the king arrests and tortures his mothers' men (Plutarch: servants and table waiters, τοὺς μὲν ὑπηρέτας καὶ τραπεζοκόμους τῆς μητρός) and then her servant girl. The name is different in Photius' version and may involve a copyist error in Plutarch's variant (from the genitive form Γίγγης, conflated with the well-known Herodotean form Γύγης, Giges?).[163] Let us use Plutarch's form for the sake of convenience. The mention of Gigis at this late point in Photius' summary may imply that her name only appeared

---

[163] Cf. Schmitt (2006: 236–7). This may be an Iranian (Justi, 1895: 116) or a Babylonian name: König (1972: 25 n. 14: Gigit(um)). Cf. Stevenson (1987: 28).

during the interrogation of Parysatis' servants and not earlier in the narrative. If this is true, Plutarch's presentation of Gigis at an earlier point is meant to cast the king's verdict as a real choice between alternatives rather than as an inevitable decision which is necessitated by the evidence amassed during the inquiry of the other servants. Photius defines the role of Gigis as ἣ ᾠκείωτο Παρυσάτιδι (*FGrH* 688 F 27.70) while Plutarch relates that later on τήν δὲ Γίγιν ἡ Παρύσατις ... εἶχεν οἴκοι ('Parysatis kept Gigis ... in her house'). Both terms probably reflect Ctesias' original οικ- stem. Plutarch's phrase δυναμένην παρ᾽ αὐτῇ ('highly able', 'powerful', see Chapter 2) evokes other phrases in the summary of Photius concerning the power of eunuchs on kings (see above). It would seem that Ctesias' original depiction maintained some vague labels, if we compare Photius' ἐσθίουσαν τὴν ἐπιδοῦσαν ἑώρα τὸ ἥμισυ ('she saw the giver eating her half') and Plutarch's δόντα τὸ φάρμακον (*Art.* 19.2: 'the provider of the poison').

The king decides to investigate and, after hearing testimonies, comes to the conclusion that Gigis is responsible for the murder. It is the king's version of what happened that gains the force of truth, because it is the king's version – exactly as in the case of the death of Cyrus. As earlier, when Artaxerxes executes the people who killed Cyrus (Mithridates and the Carian) in order to make his version the only truthful one, his killing of Gigis lends force to the account in which she is mainly responsible for the murder of Stateira. Readers are now left, as they were in the case of the official version of Cyrus' death, with the feeling that truth is a slippery thing and is determined by the powerful.

In the previous sections (*Art.* 6, 18), Plutarch gives the impression that it is Parysatis who kills Stateira. By anticipating the murder of Stateira in the biography, Plutarch suggests that Parysatis is really guilty. Ctesias himself may have similarly directed the reader to doubt the king's decision in earlier sections of the work; a hint that Parysatis was chiefly responsible for Stateira's death was probably found in an earlier book (book 19 in his *Persica*), in the depiction that Parysatis poisoned the son of Teritouchmes (*FGrH* 688 F 16.61).

Plutarch makes the king have the last say on the matter, as does Photius, but he cleverly makes Artaxerxes' verdict appear even more arbitrary and contrary to the facts related by Ctesias than was presumably presented in the original description. By making the king decide against the readers' impression, Plutarch enhances the literary impact that was already present in Ctesias' text, namely, that the king dictates the interpretation of reality in his reversal of the judges' verdict.

We mentioned in the previous chapter the theme of duality in *Art.* 19. This duality reaches its main manifestation in the twofold response of Artaxerxes after the murder of Stateira: the brutal execution of Gigis (*Art.* 19.9) on the one hand, as opposed to the mild punishment of the queen mother (*Art.* 19.10) on the other. A duality between mildness and cruelty is one of the main features of the king's character. The stress on the cruel side seems to portray the king as different from the lenient image he had earlier, and the moment Gigis is made to lose her face and identity, the king appears to cast off his. By contrast, Plutarch displays the king as weak before the queen mother in that he does not dare punish her. Although Artaxerxes may have a choice whether to follow the Persian custom of not killing one's elders (Hdt. 1.137), he nonetheless seems to have no authority, as witnessed by his failure to procure Gigis from his mother and his resort to the means of an ambush.

Plutarch is made to artistically mimic the king: this form of presentation allegedly shows Plutarch's power to control the course of the story's action and to decide the 'life' and 'death' of his characters; when he postpones the recounting of the death of Stateira from *Art.* 6 to 19 he apparently temporarily 'spares' the life of the queen, exactly like the king initially pardons Cyrus (*Art.* 3.6) only to clash with him later, and as Parysatis saves the life of Stateira (*Art.* 2.2), only to kill her afterwards.

Yet, in fact, the presentation shows Plutarch's position as weak, like the king confronting Parysatis. Plutarch merely follows the proper chronological order of the events and accepts Artaxerxes' decision concerning the assassination of Stateira. By inserting the competing account of Deinon he casts doubt on the responsibility of Parysatis. Moreover, it is only when the king sets a boundary to Parysatis by confining her to Babylon that Plutarch decides to draw a line of his own and discard domestic affairs – and basically to abandon Ctesias as a source. Yet he returns to Ctesias again in *Art.* 21, a reliance which anticipates the return of Parysatis to the scene in *Art.* 23.

SOME CONCLUSIONS

Let us briefly review the main points we learn of Plutarch's work method in his dealing with Ctesias.

Reading

1. It seems clear that Plutarch needed only the last six volumes of Ctesias' *Persica* (books 18–23), and it might be safe to say that of the earlier volumes he read very little, if at all. This corresponds to the assumption above that Ctesias was especially read by Plutarch only for the *Artaxerxes*, that is, the lifetime of Artaxerxes II. It would probably not be far-fetched to presume that Plutarch formed the initial idea for a biography of Artaxerxes before he began reading, and did not draw inspiration for the *Life* from an incidental reading of Ctesias.

2. The only passage we may reasonably assume was read outside books 18–23 of the *Persica* is Aspamitres' story in book 17, concerning the punishment of the boats. Given the rarity of such a note, we may presume that Plutarch was led there by an explicit internal reference in the text.

3. It is not possible to know whether Plutarch had access to the original long version of the *Persica*, or whether he read just an abbreviated one. Judging by the several verbal correspondences with Photius' text, he may have had roughly the same version that the patriarch had, the texts at their disposal probably being adapted versions. On the other hand, given Plutarch's implicit criticism of Ctesias' verbosity, the biographer may have had a slightly lengthier account.

4. Regardless of the length of the work, the quality of Ctesias' MS which Plutarch read was better than that of Photius. This can be seen by the forms of the names which were not distorted in the text Plutarch read.

5. Plutarch presumably had a collection of stories relating to animals in which Ctesias was alluded to at least once. It may be the case that this compendium was in Plutarch's hands before he began reading for the *Artaxerxes*.

6. While reading, Plutarch probably culled certain elements from the text, like notable sayings and actions. Judged by his reference to the original order of the scenes, Plutarch was aware of this sequence later on.[164]

---

[164] Cf. Stadter (2014: 681) on summaries of historical narratives made by Plutarch.

Writing

7. As revealed by a comparison with Photius' version, within each scene Plutarch seems to have preserved many phrases in their original cases and even in the original word order of the text in his possession.

8. Yet when it comes to the scenes themselves, Plutarch's alterations seem considerable. He omitted entire episodes, altered their order[165] and added competing versions. The result, however, highlighted elements and sentiments that were probably already in the original. So, paradoxically, Plutarch proved faithful to the spirit of the text by deviating from its literal reading.

9. Plutarch presumably used the voice of the characters in the narrative world and presented it as an independent rendition of the events, in order to compensate for the fact that when he wished to show historiographic diversity, for literary purposes, he mainly had Ctesias' version at his disposal. The other variants Plutarch had were most likely derivative; indeed, to the variant of Deinon we shall now turn.

---

[165] This roughly corresponds to Pelling's (1980: 127–8; 2011: 56–7) techniques of *alteration of sequence, chronological compression*.

4. *Deinon (a)*

Next among the *Persica* authors in terms of importance and of the extent of his employment by Plutarch is Deinon, one of the most obscure authors from antiquity, and certainly one of the most mysterious writers in the corpus of lost Greek historians. Plutarch's employment of Deinon can be divided into passages in which the ascription is explicit or plausible, and those which are implicit and conjectured. Correspondingly, the present chapter will treat the first type of references, and the next will attempt to substantiate the attribution of sections of Plutarch's text to Deinon. It can be seen that Plutarch uses Deinon mostly in the *Artaxerxes* (he is mentioned in 1.4, 6.9, 9.4, 10.1, 13.3, 19.2, 6, 22.1), but also refers to his work in the *Themistocles* (27.1), *Alexander* (36.4) and *De Iside et Osiride* (31.363c). This means that Plutarch's employment of Deinon or knowledge of his text was more widespread than his use of Ctesias, and may have even spanned several periods of his writing. As in the study of Ctesias, let us commence with an analysis of Plutarch's passages, and explore what we can learn of Deinon from these sections, proceed to compare them with what can be said of Deinon and his work in general from other sources, and then present some ideas on Plutarch's adaptation of Deinon's work.

PLUTARCH AND DEINON

The references to Deinon in the *Artaxerxes*, as well as in the other three works of Plutarch mentioned, treat themes related to the Achaemenid monarch. Specifically, Plutarch quotes Deinon for matters of court protocol (especially in the reign of Artaxerxes II) or the behaviour of Artaxerxes III Ochus in Egypt. It would not be far-fetched to claim that Deinon's work appears thus to have had the Great King and matters of court as its focus, and perhaps was chosen by Plutarch for this reason.[1]

In the beginning of the *Artaxerxes*, Deinon is contrasted with Ctesias on the issue of the monarch's original name (1.4):

> Artaxerxes was at first called Arsicas; although Deinon gives the name as Oarses.
>
> Ὁ δ᾽ Ἀρτοξέρξης Ἀρσίκας πρότερον ἐκαλεῖτο, καίτοι Δείνων φησὶν ὅτι Ὀάρσης.
> Ὀάρσης PL: Ὁ ἄρσης GR

Deinon's version is brought as the alternative version, and is quickly discarded on the grounds that the author was not present at court. We have seen how the issue of the historian's presence at the scene is connected to one of the central topics of the *Artaxerxes*, namely, the false claim of the king to be responsible for the death of Cyrus even though he was absent from the battlefield at that crucial moment. Plutarch, who uses some versions of both texts, and is in a position to compare between the respective writings, thus implies at the outset of the *Life* that Deinon's work is in some ways less reliable, because no autopsy was involved. In other words, Deinon seems not to have conducted independent research. Plutarch in effect is suggesting that Deinon's details are fanciful creations.

There may be something more to this presentation, which involves another facet of the characterisation of Artaxerxes. The only element supporting the alternative of 'Oarses' is the authority of Deinon. The form 'Arsicas' seems to gain the (admittedly problematic) authority of Ctesias, but also the presence of the latter in court, alongside Artaxerxes' family (wife, mother and children). While Ctesias' version appears to place Artaxerxes in the context of the court, in the company of the persons who would have so detrimental an influence upon him in the course of the biography, Deinon displays the alternative of independence. Deinon himself was not part of the court and he was not present there at that time and place. His account offers, as it were, release from the court and those figures, but also a certain liberation from Ctesias' narrative, which (as we saw) portrays the king in an unfavourable light. At the very beginning of the biography, Plutarch cleverly presents Artaxerxes as a different kind of Persian king, not wholly conforming to the (Herodotean or even the Ctesian) stereotype, thus lending his figure depth and complexity. The historiographic dispute therefore shows the (Persian)

---

[1] Drews (1973: 116), Stevenson (1997: 40–3).

protagonist's complicated relationship with (Greek) images. Is his true self a brutal and licentious person waiting to be freed from the shackles of morality and surrounding society, or is he a mild and gentle spirit absorbed in the gruesome atmosphere of his court life? Deinon's alternative is rejected, and this dual aspect of Artaxerxes' character is set aside till the next appearance of the author.

The second explicit reference to Deinon in the biography (6.9) deals with the proper chronological place of the murder of Stateira the queen:

> For Deinon says the plot was accomplished during the war, while Ctesias puts it later.
> Ἐπεὶ δὲ Δείνων μὲν ἐν τῷ πολέμῳ συντελεσθῆναι τὴν ἐπιβουλὴν εἴρηκε, Κτησίας δ᾽ ὕστερον . . .

Again Plutarch creates the impression that Deinon is independent of Ctesias' account. But if Deinon placed the murder of Stateira *during* the war between Cyrus and the king, he appears to have been misguided. Thus, in his wish to be original and autonomous as an author, Deinon does not seem to be responsible. Interestingly, this reluctance to follow Ctesias involves flouting characterisation and motivation, and breaking away from the logic of probability. It also involves killing. If in *Art.* 1 Deinon's independence seems to reside in his autonomy from figures of the court in terms of sources for his information, here he actually appears to be impetuously removing one of these court figures ahead of time. Deinon's presentation as if this feud involves only Stateira and Parysatis removes any responsibility to this state of affairs from the king, in a perfect correspondence between Artaxerxes and Deinon. We find later on in *Art.* 18.5–6 that in fact Ctesias involved the monarch in the sequence of events that led to this murder, by having him kill Clearchus at Stateira's request. Here he seems to stand outside of this main event in court. Again Plutarch discards Deinon's version and prefers to follow that of Ctesias, and similarly, Artaxerxes is imbibed again in court intrigues and machinations.

We do note, however, that if Ctesias and Deinon agree on the fact of the assassination, they differ on the issue of arrangement. Combined with the fact noted in *Art.* 1, that Deinon was not at the scene, both of these references imply that Deinon's version is later than Ctesias' and may be responding to it. This has bearing on two aspects:

(a) Rearrangement as a sign of autonomy. This trait actually connects all figures in *Art.* 6, in a way that completes what we said in Chapter 2. In the political sphere, Cyrus promises to rearrange lands in his would-be kingdom and to allot them to the Spartans; his movement creates a commotion. On the historiographic plane, Deinon rearranges the temporal sequence, forcing Plutarch to revert back to Ctesias' original order after this disruption and thus to appear free not to follow Deinon. In this way, Plutarch connects form (Deinon's creative arrangement) with content (the political upheaval he describes).

(b) The price of continuity. This theme is related to the one of preservation. By responding to Cyrus' threat and the need to protect his seat, Artaxerxes takes measures which will eventually change him. Similarly, by choosing to stick to Ctesias' temporal sequence of events, Plutarch appears to be maintaining the same course, but the introduction of Deinon here and Plutarch's assertion that he prefers to follow Ctesias' order make him step outside the story into the metanarrative, a position which he is to occupy occasionally in the following sections. Thus, Plutarch preserves (the core of the plot) while changing (the character of the presentation), as the king appears to be doing – and by implication, Deinon as well, as we shall soon see.

The next mention of Deinon in the *Artaxerxes* (9.4–10.3) constitutes a seemingly lengthy continuous reliance on this author. It concerns the actual Battle of Cunaxa and the death of Cyrus:

(9.4) Almost everyone agrees that Cyrus killed Artagerses . . .
(10) Deinon, then, says that after Artagerses fell, Cyrus charged forcibly against those drawn up in front of the king, and wounded his (the king's) horse, so that he fell off. Tiribazus, however, quickly mounted him on a different horse, and said: 'O King, remember this day, for it is unworthy of forgetfulness.' Cyrus then attacked again and dismounted Artaxerxes. But at the third assault, the king grew impatient, and saying to those present that ceasing to live was better, rode against Cyrus, who was sweeping headlong and incautiously through the missiles confronting him. He (the king) himself hurled a spear, and his attendants hurled theirs. Thus Cyrus fell, as some say, hit by the king, but as others relate, when a Carian man hit him . . .
(9.4) Τὸν μὲν οὖν Ἀρταγέρσην ἀποθανεῖν ὑπὸ τοῦ Κύρου σχεδὸν ἅπαντες ὁμολογοῦσι . . .
(10.1) Φησὶν οὖν ὁ μὲν Δείνων ὅτι τοῦ Ἀρταγέρσου πεσόντος εἰσελάσας βιαίως ὁ Κῦρος εἰς τοὺς προτεταγμένους τοῦ βασιλέως κατέτρωσεν αὐτοῦ τὸν ἵππον, ὁ δ' ἀπερρύη· Τιριβάζου δ' ἀναβαλόντος αὐτὸν ἐπ' ἄλλον ἵππον ταχὺ καὶ εἰπόντος· 'ὦ βασιλεῦ, μέμνησο τῆς ἡμέρας ταύτης· οὐ γὰρ ἀξία λήθης ἐστί', πάλιν ὁ Κῦρος ἐνσείσας τῷ ἵππῳ κατέβαλε τὸν Ἀρτοξέρξην. (2) Πρὸς δὲ τὴν τρίτην ἐπέλασιν δυσανασχετήσας ὁ βασιλεὺς καὶ εἰπὼν πρὸς τοὺς παρόντας ὡς βέλτιόν ἐστι μὴ ζῆν, ἀντεξήλαυνε τῷ Κύρῳ, προπετῶς καὶ ἀπερισκέπτως εἰς ἐναντία βέλη

φερομένῳ. Καὶ βάλλει μὲν αὐτὸς ἀκοντίῳ, βάλλουσι δ' οἱ περὶ αὐτόν. (3) Πίπτει δ' ὁ Κῦρος, ὡς μὲν ἔνιοι λέγουσι, πληγεὶς ὑπὸ τοῦ βασιλέως, ὡς δ' ἕτεροί τινες, Καρὸς ἀνθρώπου πατάξαντος …

As noted above, Ctesias related that Cyrus came face to face with Artagerses, the leader of the Cadusians and head of the king's advance guard, who hurled his spear at him. Plutarch explicitly says that Ctesias' description of the killing of Artagerses by Cyrus was accepted by 'almost everyone'. Xenophon mentions the end of Artagerses in a brief but heroic passage (*Anab.* 1.8.24)[2] and we may suppose that the other author that Plutarch has in mind here is Deinon. If so, this is a hint that at this point Deinon's account was somewhat derivative. Deinon thus presumably simplified Ctesias' account, similar to what Xenophon attempted to do (*Anab.* 1.8.27).[3]

In the next scene coming specifically from Deinon's account, the king clashes with Cyrus in single combat (*Art.* 10.2–3). Deinon's story was probably simple and dramatic: the king clashed with Cyrus, was unhorsed, and attacked his brother again (and presumably killed him). We do not find any such description in Ctesias' version, and here is perhaps another example of his autonomy. On the historiographic plane, this trait corresponds to the content of the scene, when the king attempts to assert his authority without relying on any of his men. However, both Deinon and the king do not succeed: Plutarch immediately presents an obscure picture, in which a person aids the king in killing, and in the next section turns (*Art.* 11) to Ctesias' portrayal. Indeed, when we read Ctesias' version (on which see Chapter 2), we find that the Carian is a figure associated with his account as sharing the responsibility for the death of Cyrus with Mithridates. In fact, Plutarch does to Deinon's report what the latter presumably did to Ctesias' depiction, and so actually does out-Deinon Deinon, as it were. Plutarch rearranges the material out of sequence, by having Cyrus die in *Art.* 10 and then bringing him to life again in *Art.* 11, or by relating the Carian's honour before recounting his deed. The tension between the display of a new portrayal and the preservation of an earlier one is relevant to Deinon (concerning the extent of Ctesias'

---

[2] In his *Cyropaedia*, a fictional work, Xenophon is known to have occasionally appropriated names of historical figures and relocated them in the past. This happens in the case of the cavalry commander in Cunaxa, Artagerses, who is made into the leader of the Cadusian infantry in the entourage of 'Cyrus' (*Cyr.* 6.3.31, 33, 7.1.27–8); the phrase Καδουσίων ἄρχων actually reappears in *Cyr.* 5.4.15–23. *Pace* Tuplin (2011: 478 n. 57).
[3] See Almagor (2012: 31). Cf. Stevenson (1997: 86–93), Lenfant (2009: 180).

description that he preserved in his work), to Plutarch (regarding the extent of Deinon that he preserves in his biography), and the king (the extent to which he retains his old self in his attempt to maintain his throne).

The fourth passage from the *Artaxerxes* concerns the size of the king's army (*Art.* 13.3):

> He (Artaxerxes) set out for battle, according to Ctesias, with four hundred thousand men, but with many more committed to battle according to the followers of Deinon and Xenophon.
>
> Ἐξεληλάκει δ᾽, ὡς ὁ Κτησίας φησίν, ἐπὶ τὴν μάχην τεσσαράκοντα μυριάσιν. οἱ δὲ περὶ Δείνωνα καὶ Ξενοφῶντα πολὺ πλείονας γενέσθαι λέγουσι τὰς μεμαχημένας.

Again, Plutarch posits Deinon against Ctesias. We have seen above how this tongue-in-cheek presentation depicts the historiographic dispute as a real military one. The reader cannot fail to note the artistic display of correspondence between form and content, when by being historiographically outnumbered, Ctesias' claims concerning the lower *numbers* of the king are discredited. Deinon is grouped together with Xenophon. This is not the first time such a combination is mentioned. Earlier, in the depiction of Artagerses' death scene, the other descriptions are taken together, implying that they all imitate Ctesias' portrayal and are derivative. Here, however, they seem to be innovative in showing a different number of soldiers. It is insinuated that breaking away from Ctesias' narrative can only be achieved by a combination of forces (or sources). It is perhaps through this combination that Deinon's account gains some credence for the first time in the biography. Earlier on, both Deinon and Xenophon are presented as less credible since the authors were not present at the scene. Now, the innovative feature of their reports is what gives their accounts its truthful character. This ironic reversal of approach on Plutarch's part is especially relevant to what the king will do in the following sections: he will promote a story which does not follow what Ctesias recounts as the true occurrences, yet claim it is truthful.

As promised, Plutarch brings the death of Stateira at the place allotted to it by Ctesias (*Art.* 19). Plutarch's depiction is split between Deinon and Ctesias, as noted above, and our discussion is accordingly split between several chapters. The description appears to suggest a great variance between Ctesias and Deinon, to such a degree that Drews (1973: 117) even claims: 'Dinon corrected Ctesias just as often as Ctesias corrected Herodotos, but since Ctesias' subject matter was inconsequential, Dinon's "corrections" seem less grotesque.'[4] However, the core of the plot in both writers seems to have been the same, with the exception of slight dissimilarities. As shown in Chapter 2 (see Table 1), in Ctesias' version, the main character carrying out the plot is Parysatis. She is the one who prepares the poison, slices up the bird, and serves the poisoned half to Stateira. In Deinon's version, Parysatis does not appear at any stage. Gigis' involvement is greater in Deinon's story,[5] but she is not absent from Ctesias' account: not only does she know about the poisoning, but she probably also acts in some way, as the word ἄκουσαν, 'unwillingly', might indicate.[6] Moreover, the term συσκευάσασθαι with the prefix συν/σ- implies that Parysatis does not act alone but with an accomplice in Ctesias' version. It may be the case that Plutarch stresses the elements in Deinon's account which distance Parysatis from the poisoning, and thus explains why she is not severely punished.

As we saw in Chapter 3, Photius includes the fact that Gigis is acquitted by the judges, but then convicted by the king. Plutarch omits this detail, but seems to reflect the divergence of opinion on the historiographic level. The king now has to decide, as it were, between the version of Ctesias (which places greater responsibility on Parysatis) and that of Deinon (which tends to acquit Parysatis of the crime). The fact that Artaxerxes 'chooses' to believe Deinon's version completes his own liberation from Ctesias' narrative and from the unfavourable image of the king that the physician draws. It also finally marks Deinon's account as superior to that of Ctesias and more believable, with the implication that what Ctesias said concerning the death of Cyrus may be wrong. If Ctesias' report regarding Parysatis' responsibility is false, then the version of the king, in particular that recounting his presence at the death of his brother, may be correct after all.

The next reference to Deinon in the *Artaxerxes* marks the last occasion where Plutarch explicitly mentions him in the biography. Its context is the Great King's attitude towards Antalcidas the Spartan (*Art.* 22.1):

> For this reason, although Artaxerxes always loathed other Spartans, and thought them, as Deinon says, the most shameless of all humanity, he liked Antalcidas very much when he made the journey up country to the Persians.

---

[4] Cf. Lenfant (2004: 275, n. 632).

[5] Stevenson (1997: 72) believes that Deinon presented a description which reflected the official royal position, because the king found Gigis guilty and killed her, and eventually forgave his mother.

[6] *Pace* Stevenson (1997: 67).

Διὸ καὶ τοὺς ἄλλους Σπαρτιάτας ἀεὶ βδελυττόμενος ὁ Ἀρτοξέρξης, καὶ νομίζων, ὥς φησι Δείνων, ἀνθρώπων ἁπάντων ἀναιδεστάτους εἶναι, τὸν Ἀνταλκίδαν ὑπερηγάπησεν εἰς Πέρσας ἀναβάντα.

Jacoby includes the whole section of Plut. *Art.* 21.5–22.1 as a fragment of Deinon (*FGrH* 690 F 19), but it should really be restricted to 22.1, relating that Artaxerxes thought the Spartans the most shameless of men. The reference in the biography is to the King's Peace, which Antalcidas accomplished together with Tiribazus in 387/6 BCE (Xen. *Hell.* 5.1.6, 25, Diod. 14.110.2–4). The rest of *Art.* 22 relates the changed position of the Great King towards the Greek states, as it recounts stories of three Greek delegates at the Persian court: Antalcidas the Spartan, Ismenias the Theban and Timagoras the Athenian (see Chapter 6 below). This mention comes from a period Ctesias did not deal with, and it gives the correct impression that Deinon's work continued to describe events taking place after the dramatic time in which Ctesias' *Persica* ended.

Indeed, this is the only time Deinon is mentioned without a historiographic counterpart, either Ctesias or Xenophon. It is as if Deinon has the last say on historiographic matters. This portrayal implies that Deinon is left without any other version to balance its one-sided picture. The allegedly glorifying depiction of the Spartans by Ctesias has now been abandoned in favour of another, attributed to Deinon, which stresses the shamelessness of the Spartans. If we follow the same thread of tracing parallelism between the historiographic and historical planes, we can note that after dictating his will to Greece, the king is similarly left without any real foes in the international arena. On the level of characterisation, there is virtually no restraint now within his *psyche*, beautifully symbolised by the solitary mention of Deinon. Indeed, in the next episodes, his licentiousness will know no bounds.

Pertinent here is Agesilaus' quip, to someone who claimed that the Spartans are Medising, 'No, rather the Persians are Laconising' (*Art.* 22.4: Ὁ μὲν γὰρ Ἀγησίλαος ὡς ἔοικε πρὸς τὸν εἰπόντα· 'Φεῦ τῆς Ἑλλάδος ὅπου μηδίζουσιν ἡμῖν οἱ Λάκωνες', 'οὐ μᾶλλον', εἶπεν, 'οἱ Μῆδοι λακωνίζουσι'). Within the biography, we see how the Spartans quickly turn from enemies to allies of the Persians (*Art.* 21.5). In *Art.* 5.2 we have the impression that a Spartan, Eucleidas, stays in the retinue of the king;[7] it is said that he would often say bold and impudent things to him (Εὐκλείδᾳ δὲ τῷ Λάκωνι πολλὰ παρρησιαζομένῳ πρὸς αὐτὸν

---

[7] This Eucleidas is not known. See Poralla (1913: 305), Fraser and Matthews (1997: 167). Niese (1907) believes he was 'Gesandter bei Artaxerx' ('An envoy at Artaxerxes' [court]'), which is plausible.

αὐθαδῶς) and the πολλὰ surely indicates a lengthy stay in Persia. This anecdote, clearly taken out of chronological sequence, is placed before the Spartans join the plans of Cyrus to oust him. The fickle nature of the Spartans, who change sides in accordance with their interests and collaborate with the party that seems promising at the time,[8] is shown, through Agesilaus' jest, to apply to the ('Laconised', as it were) Great King himself; it is he who now appears to switch sides between the Greeks. Similarly, Plutarch himself now selects Deinon as the source to follow. Matching the transition from Ctesias to Deinon is the political shift in dominance over Greece from Sparta to Thebes (and Athens). As this change in the political plane has no obvious termination, the preference given to one Greek source is also theoretically not constant. In fact, a new source, Heracleides, is mentioned in *Art.* 23.6 (see Chapter 6 below).

The next passages we treat here come from three other works (one in each). The reference in the *Alexander* (36) is within the context of the mention of the treasures captured by the Macedonians in Susa (= *FGrH* 690 F 23b):

> After taking Susa, Alexander got hold of forty thousand talents of minted money in the palace, and of indescribable other possessions and riches. In this they say was revealed five thousand talents' weight of purple from Hermione, which, although laying there for two hundred (minus ten) years, preserved its brilliance fresh and new. The cause of this, they say, is the use of honey in the purple dyes, and white olive oil in the white dyes; for these substances, and the brightness of these, for the same length of time, is seen to be pure and gleaming. Deinon reports that the Persian kings had water from the Nile and the Ister (Danube), and together with the other items store them with their treasures, as if confirming the greatness of their empire and the fact that they are masters of all.
>
> Ἀλέξανδρος δὲ Σούσων κυριεύσας, παρέλαβεν ἐν τοῖς βασιλείοις τετρακισμύρια τάλαντα νομίσματος, τὴν δ' ἄλλην κατασκευὴν καὶ πολυτέλειαν ἀδιήγητον. (2) Ὅπου φασὶ καὶ πορφύρας Ἑρμιονικῆς εὑρεθῆναι τάλαντα πεντακισχίλια, συγκειμένης μὲν ἐξ ἐτῶν δέκα δεόντων διακοσίων, πρόσφατον δὲ τὸ ἄνθος ἔτι καὶ νεαρὸν φυλαττούσης. (3) Αἴτιον δὲ τούτου φασὶν εἶναι τὸ τὴν βαφὴν διὰ μέλιτος γίνεσθαι τῶν ἁλουργῶν, δι' ἐλαίου δὲ λευκοῦ τῶν λευκῶν· καὶ γὰρ τούτων τὸν ἴσον χρόνον ἐχόντων τὴν λαμπρότητα καθαρὰν καὶ στίλβουσαν ὁρᾶσθαι. (4) Δίνων δέ φησι καὶ ὕδωρ ἀπό τε τοῦ Νείλου καὶ τοῦ Ἴστρου μετὰ τῶν ἄλλων μεταπεμπομένους εἰς τὴν γάζαν ἀποτίθεσθαι τοὺς βασιλεῖς, οἷον ἐκβεβαιουμένους τὸ μέγεθος τῆς ἀρχῆς καὶ τὸ κυριεύειν ἁπάντων.

No apparent inherent connection exists between the coins, the dye and the water containers apart from their seemingly acciden-

---

[8]   It is a playful allusion to the Spartans in Thermopylae, as described by Herodotus (7.210: ἀναιδείη).

tal presence in Susa treasury.[9] Yet, in relating how the items are transferred from Persian to Macedonian ownership, Plutarch insinuates the transience of the two kingdoms, foreshadowing the fall of Alexander: just as the Persian Empire has fallen, so will that of Alexander dissolve in due course.[10] The repetition of the words in a chiastic structure at the beginning and end of the section seems to make it clear (Σούσων κυριεύσας ... κυριεύειν ἁπάντων). There is a hint of the rule of Alexander in Asia in the mention of two hundred years taking out ten (ἐξ ἐτῶν δέκα δεόντων διακοσίων); Alexander's campaign was approximately ten years, and his rule was short, compared to that of the Persians (more than two hundred years), despite its virtual splendour. The three items mentioned (coins, dye, water) transcend the period in which they were collected. It seems that in order to stress this theme of ephemerality, Plutarch has to resort to the use of a source which described the Persian Empire and was associated with it by being its contemporary. That Deinon is singled out as such a source would allow us to assume that this author belonged to the period before Alexander or at least was considered as such by Plutarch. The implication is that Plutarch has a broader perspective of time, while Deinon did not.

Deinon is one of several historians mentioned in a passage from *Themistocles*, dealing with the meeting of Themistocles and the Persian king in 465 BCE (27.1 = *FGrH* 690 F 13):

> Thucydides and Charon of Lampsacus claim that after Xerxes' death, Themistocles had an interview with his son; Ephorus and Deinon and Cleitarchus and Heracleides and very many others (assert) that he arrived to see Xerxes. Thucydides appears to conform more with the chronological records, although these are not composed in an immutable manner themselves.
>
> Θουκυδίδης μὲν οὖν καὶ Χάρων ὁ Λαμψακηνὸς ἱστοροῦσι τεθνηκότος Ξέρξου πρὸς τὸν υἱὸν αὐτοῦ τῷ Θεμιστοκλεῖ γενέσθαι τὴν ἔντευξιν· Ἔφορος δὲ καὶ Δείνων καὶ Κλείταρχος καὶ Ἡρακλείδης, ἔτι δ' ἄλλοι πλείονες πρὸς αὐτὸν ἀφικέσθαι τὸν Ξέρξην. τοῖς δὲ χρονικοῖς δοκεῖ μᾶλλον ὁ Θουκυδίδης συμφέρεσθαι, καίπερ οὐδ' αὐτοῖς ἀτρέμα συντατττομένοις.
>
> αὐτοῖς Y ‖ συντατττομένοις Y : συντεταγμένος S

It would appear that this section at the beginning of *Them.* 27 dealing with the identity of the Persian king closely corresponds to its final part, when the Chiliarch Artabanus asks Themistocles for

---

[9] For other depictions of the Susa treasures cf. Diod. 17.65–6; Strabo, 15.3.9; Curt. Ruf. 5.2.8–14; Arr. *Anab.* 3.16.6; Justin 11.14.9.

[10] His mention of the Ister, no longer held by the Persians, stresses this point. Cf. Lenfant (2009: 208–9).

his identity (τίνα δέ ... Ἑλλήνων ἀφῖχθαι φῶμεν; 'Which ... of the Greeks shall I say has arrived?'). Exactly as (Greek) readers are left in the dark as to the king's real name, so is Artabanus confounded concerning the name of the Greek person, when the Athenian hero refuses to disclose it before his direct audience with the monarch. Incidentally, the name of Artaxerxes is missing from this passage – and from the entire biography.

If the first and last part of the *Them.* 27 can be aptly described by the question 'What's in a name?', the central part of the section may be paraphrased as 'What's in a *nomos?*' This dialogue between Themistocles and Artabanus relates to this question, opening with Artabanus' claim: 'Men's practices vary; different men see different habits as good; but for everyone their own particular customs are good to honour and maintain' (νόμοι διαφέρουσιν ἀνθρώπων· ἄλλα δ' ἄλλοις καλά· καλὸν δὲ πᾶσι τὰ οἰκεῖα κοσμεῖν καὶ σῴζειν: *Them.* 27.3).[11] Whereas the Greeks valorise liberty and equality, the Chiliarch asserts, the Persians regard honouring the king and paying him obeisance as the fairest thing (*Them.* 27.4). Themistocles is presented with the choice of whether to accept Persian ways and prostrate himself before the king, or to observe his own customs and employ messengers and mediators instead of communicating with him directly. Themistocles selects the former option and thus appears to be neglecting Greek ways.[12]

A special Greek practice is alluded to in *Them.* 27. In keeping with the stereotype of Greek loquacity and litigency is the Greek habit of debating.[13] The trait is illustrated in the section through the historiographic plane, where as many as eight authors (including Deinon) are mentioned. Apparently, all the names of the historians had to be included in order to elucidate this feature of Greek squabbling, an element highlighted when a comparison with the parallel passage in Nepos' description (*Them.* 9.1) is made.[14] The impression the readers get from this bickering is disturbing, and might even justify Themistocles' choice of a different, non-Greek way of life.

---

[11] Almost a commonplace in Persian narratives since Hdt. 3.38.
[12] I have written more on this for the *BNJ* entry 690.
[13] On Plutarch's tendency to display this feature among the Greeks see Almagor (2014b: 284).
[14] *Scio, plerosque ita scripsisse, Themistoclem, Xerxe regnante, in Asiam iransisse. Sed ego potissimum Thucyclidi credo, quod aetate proximus, qui illorum temporum historiam reliquerunt, et ejusdem civitatis fuit* ('I know most authors have written that Themistocles went to Asia in the reign of Xerxes, but I believe Thucydides better than others, because he was closest in time to Themistocles of all those who left a written history of that era, and was of the same city'). See Frost (1980: 213).

Yet it would seem that as much as Themistocles requests a direct conference with the Great King, he is hindered from doing so or else is removed from him by intermediaries. This is where Plutarch cleverly confuses the historical and historiographic realms in his account. Not only Artabanus acts as a go-between. The effect of the enumeration of four different historians who associate Themistocles with Xerxes is to make these authors alleged mediators between them. They all act as courtiers in the king's service, as it were. Thus, by acting in accordance with Greek customs (i.e., the constant wrangling), they inadvertently abide by the laws of protocol employed in the king's court, like Themistocles himself. The fact that all the authors mentioned were rough contemporaries of the Persian Empire also makes their 'service' to the king ironically plausible.

The last reference to Deinon treated here appears in the work *On Isis and Osiris*, the only one outside Plutarch's biographies.[15] The relevant section concerns the grounds for the Egyptians' behaviour towards Artaxerxes III (31.363c = *FGrH* 690 F 21):

> Because of this, since they reviled Ochus more of all the Persian kings because he was a contaminated and repulsive ruler, they named him 'the Ass'. He in turn commented, 'This Ass, however, will feast upon your Bull,' and sacrificed Apis, as Deinon has recounted.
>
> Διὸ καὶ τῶν Περσικῶν βασιλέων ἐχθραίνοντες μάλιστα τὸν Ὦχον ὡς ἐναγῆ καὶ μιαρόν, ὄνον ἐπωνόμασαν. Κἀκεῖνος εἰπὼν 'ὁ μέντοι ὄνος οὗτος ὑμῶν κατευωχήσεται τὸν βοῦν', ἔθυσε τὸν Ἄπιν, ὡς Δείνων ἱστόρηκεν.

The passage clearly builds upon Herodotus' description of Cambyses in Egypt and his slaying of the bull Apis (3.27–9), while slightly altering it. Deinon describes Ochus as experiencing the Egyptian mockery in reality, while Herodotus' Cambyses only imagines it. Ochus' behaviour is also a sophisticated take on Herodotus. Cambyses incidentally strikes the bull's thigh and proves to the priests that the creature is not divine (3.29). Later on, Cambyses dies (3.64) by incidentally injuring the same part he had struck Apis, namely, his thigh, with his sword. This image is a playful insinuation (to the external audience) that the Great King himself is not divine, a reversal of Persian belief and ideology, as the Greeks understood it.[16] When

---

[15] On this treatise see the Introduction.

[16] As I have tried to show in Almagor (2017a), the Greek image of the Persians giving the Great King almost divine honours is partially based on real elements seen in the royal inscriptions and the adjoining iconography of the reliefs, circulating through the empire. These display the Achaemenid king and the divine as intimate, hint at some reciprocal relation between them and show the king as acting in some way in the divine sphere.

Ochus assumes the figure of the ass,[17] he also adopts the person of the evil deity Typhon. The two are said to be associated by the Egyptians[18] because of the ass's stupidity or arrogance and colour. Deinon's Ochus thus mockingly displays himself as a deity (albeit evil) in killing the bull, while Cambyses, who is severely punished for committing the same act, is denied that status. Ochus adopts the Egyptian framework (the opposition of good and bad and his own association with the ass/Typhon), but turns it on its head. He, who is disparagingly called 'the Ass' by the Egyptians, furiously accepts this part, and in an inversion of the Egyptian dichotomy, kills Apis.[19] Plutarch appears to be indicating that what Deinon is doing in his narrative parallels his figure Ochus: Deinon also accepted a framework (the Herodotean one) and worked within it to undermine it. Again we see the tension between the two traits of Deinon's work as being derivative on the one hand and innovative on the other; in the *On Isis and Osiris* this duality is linked to the aspect of a binary opposition, which forms this treatise's motif.

DEINON AND HIS WORK ACCORDING TO OTHER SOURCES

What do we actually know about Deinon? Does it fit with the impression we receive from Plutarch? The fact that so little is said about Deinon by the editor of the *Suda* suggests that he was an enigma in ancient time as well. Firstly, there was no consensus in antiquity with respect to the form of his name: either Δείνων (the form that appears, e.g. in Athenaeus, Clement or in Plutarch's *Artaxerxes* and *Them.* 27.1)[20] or Δίνων (v.l. in some MSS of Plut.

---

[17] The ass is said to be valued by alien cultures: the Persian and supposedly the Jewish. The belief that the ass was revered by Jews is known from antiquity. E.g. Jos. *CA* 2.7, 2.9; Plut. *QC* 4.5.670e; Tac. *Hist.* 5.2–4; *Suda*, s.v. 'Damocritus', δ 49 Adler. On the 'ass libel', see especially Bar-Kochva (2010: 226–31).

[18] Cf. 30.362f–363a. Cf. 22.359e. On this association see Griffiths (1970: 409–10), Lenfant (2009: 198–200).

[19] That Herodotus lies at the back of this description is obvious and can be seen earlier, in *De Is. et Os.* 31, where Plutach analyses the Egyptian notion of sacrifice. Evoking Herodotus (2.38–9) without mentioning him explicitly, Plutarch depicts how in Egypt the head of the victim incurs curses and is severed. Plutarch asserts that in a previous period the Egyptians used to cast the head into the Nile, but currently they trade it to foreigners. This detail may come from the first century BCE writer Castor, for he is cited in the next item, with regard to the mark (cf. Griffiths, 1970: 416–17) on the sacrificial animal, considered profane; here again Herodotus (2.38) is suggested, but his name is not mentioned. Castor thus may be the origin for the two items. Cf. Schwartz (1949: 69), Lenfant (2009: 195).

[20] Cf. the name of the Spartan polemarch (Xen. *Hell.* 5.4.33, 6.4.14).

Alex. 36.4).[21] It may be that at a certain period, the form circulating in the MSS was even Δίων. This may explain the presence of Deinon, Dio of Prusa (40–115 CE = Dio Cocceianus)[22] and the historian L. Dio Cassius (164–229 CE) under the same *Suda* heading 'Dio' (δ 1239 Adler):[23]

> [Dio], identified as Cassius, and labelled Cocceius – still some [call him] Coccieanus. Of Nicaea, historian, lived in the era of Alexander [Severus] . . . He wrote a *History of Rome* in eighty books; they are divided into groups of ten. [He also wrote] *Persica, Getica, Omens, Events of Trajan's Rule*, [and a] *Life of Arrian the Philosopher.*

Deinon was not fortunate enough to have his work summarised by Photius. Hence, little is known of his writings, and even less of his life. All that is said about him is that he was an author of a *Persica* (*Suda*), was the father of the popular Alexander historian Cleitarchus (Plin. *NH* 10.70.136: *Clitarchi celebrati auctoris pater*), and was an inhabitant of Colophon, if indeed he is the individual mentioned in the list of references to the *Historia Naturalis*, with a somewhat dissimilar name (1.10: *Dione Colophonio*). On the basis of other references in the indices to Pliny's work (for books 12–13: *Dinone* and for books 14–15, 17–18: *Dinone Colophonio*), it is unclear whether Pliny meant this person.[24] This is admittedly very thin ground to tread upon.

Plutarch never refers to Deinon as a Colophonian. An argument in favour of the historian's ascribed provenance as well of the accuracy of the relatively rare name form Δείνων might be the fact that another Deinon is known from Colophon from the second/first century BCE (*LGPN* Va, 119 = *SEG* XXXVI 1063).[25] Some familial relationship may subsist between the two, even if it is not the same individual. The Ionian centre Colophon (Strab. 14.1.27–8; Paus. 7.3.1–4) was the hometown of renowned literary persons, nearly all of them poets (Xenophanes, Mimnermus, Antimachus, Nicander, Theopompus the Epic poet, Gorgus, who

---

[21] On both forms see Schwartz (1903b), who prefers the second one.

[22] The *Suda* dedicates other entries to Dio Chrysostom: δ 1240 Adler deals with 'Dio, son of Pasicrates; of Prusa' and defines him as 'a sophist and philosopher' with the epithet 'Golden Mouth' (Χρυσόστομος, *Chrysostomos*). Another item is devoted to the name Cocceianus (κ 1914 Adler), clarified as a 'proper name' (ὄνομα κύριον).

[23] See Gowing (1990).

[24] See Pearson (1960: 226 n. 36) for the difficulties of the MSS. Cf. Stevenson (1997: 10–11), Lenfant (2009: 80–8). Complicating matters are the references to an unknown Dio of Colophon by Varro (*De Re Rustica* 1.1.8) and Columella (*De Re Rustica* 1.1.9).

[25] The same lexicon lists our own Deinon as Δίνων (*LGPN* Va, 130). See four bearers of the name Δείνων in Caria: *LGPN* Vb, 98.

collected stories from the poets,[26] Hermesianax, Phoenix). Of course, the two traits ascribed to Deinon may be wrong.[27] The ancients themselves were not certain about the author of these stories; indeed, some were not even sure whether the work was composed by one person or by several. Arguably, a notable feature of this work caused this uncertainty, namely, its fragmentary nature, the division into scenes and sections with no perceived connection (below).

One of the subtle implications of Plutarch's mention of Deinon in the *Alexander*, as we saw above, is that this author preceded the Macedonian king's campaign, or at least was silent about it, in a way that contrasts with Plutarch's broader perspective and ability to observe the aftermath of the Persian Empire. If true, this is an important piece of information that could shed light on the question of Deinon's date. The issue, it would seem, is hard to ascertain. The latest known event mentioned in Deinon's work is Artaxerxes III Ochus' conquest of Egypt in 343/2 BCE, as we saw above. This may have been the latest event that Deinon recounted. In all probability, the *Persica* (or at least its ultimate part) was not written immediately in the same year, but at least some time afterwards. Jacoby (1921: 622–4) believes that Deinon's work was composed during the time of Alexander, since *Persica*, as a genre, was not written after the end of the Achaemenid period. This argument, however, is circular, as it presupposes that Deinon did not live later.

There is indeed no mention of Alexander in the extant fragments of Deinon's work, and no evidence of the author's familiarity with him. Although this is an *argumentum ex silentio*, if the fact is given weight, it might indicate that Deinon's work was written shortly before (or even during) the Macedonian campaign against Persia. If it was written afterwards, Deinon may have simply chosen to ignore Alexander.[28] We know that at least the generation immediately following Alexander saw some interest in Persian history and in particular events in the Persian court. For instance, Phaenias the Peripatetic (late fourth century BCE) was interested (see Chapter 6) in Themistocles (cf. Plut. *Them.* 27).

---

[26] *Athen. Mitt.* XI 428 (= FGrH 17 T 1).

[27] Could it be that his name was derived from a misapprehension of a marginal attribution to 'δείνων', the Genitive Plural form of δεῖνα (LSJ, s.v.; see Dem. 20.106), 'of so-and-so', viz., 'nameless/indeterminate, indefinite' (authors)? This is undeniably a hypothetical suggestion, but it might explain certain doubtful traits characterising this author, including the fact that his personality is obscure.

[28] Cf. Hamilton (1969: 96): 'Dinon's interest in Cunaxa scarcely proved that he wrote after Gaugamela.' Cf. Stevenson (1997: 10), Lenfant (2009: 31).

Another important clue as to Deinon's date is his relationship with Cleitarchus, one of the Alexander historians, said by Pliny (Plin. *NH* 10.70.136) to be Deinon's son. If Deinon indeed preceded Cleitarchus by a generation, and if Cleitarchus' date could be approximately fixed, then the impression Plutarch conveys may be corroborated.

Ironically, little is known about the life and work of the 'famous' (*celebratus*: Pliny *NH* 10.70.136) Cleitarchus.[29] His *Histories* recounted the reign and the campaign of Alexander the Great to his death in at least twelve books.[30] We cannot be certain when Cleitarchus lived and wrote. The prevailing view prefers a 'high' dating, i.e., that he lived at the end of the fourth century or the beginning of the third century BCE.[31] But there is little evidence for this assertion. Indeed, what evidence there is seems to favour a later date for Cleitarchus.[32] A 'low' dating for Cleitarchus, i.e., in the 280s BCE and even later, is perhaps to be accepted. This is also the recent conclusion of Andrew Chugg (2009: 34–9), using probability calculations and conjectural arguments. If Cleitarchus did study under Stilpo of Megara in c. 310–308 BCE (Diog. Laert. 2.113 = *FGrH* 137 T 3), he could have been born in c. 330 BCE or slightly later, which would make him write his work at a relatively later age in life (but still younger than Aristobulus when he published his account).[33] If Deinon was indeed Cleitarchus' father, this would place the *floruit* of the author of the *Persica* in the 330s, making all the evidence fit into place.

If Deinon did live in Colophon, and Cleitarchus was in fact his offspring, this piece of information may clarify why the latter is not linked with that city, but rather with Alexandria.[34] After Lysimachus conquered Colophon in c. 302 BCE, he compelled most of its

---

[29] The extent of its use by Diodorus (book 17) and Curtius Rufus is unclear as well, and it would be unsafe to conclude on its character based on the latter authors' portrayals. In antiquity, Cleitarchus' work was obviously widely read, especially in late republican and early imperial times, but not valued. Quintilian, 10.1.74 approves Cleitarchus' talent, but not his accuracy. Cicero *Brutus*, 42–3 accuses the historian of false details concerning the death of Themistocles. Cf. Curt. Ruf. 9.5.21. For criticism of his style see Ps.-Demetr. *De eloc.* 304. Cf. Cic. *De leg.* 1.7.

[30] Book 12: Diog. Laert. 1.6. 13–15 books in all: Pearson (1960: 213), Bosworth (1997: 216), Chugg (2009: 5). See on his work Jacoby (1921); Prandi (1996); Parker (2009).

[31] Cf. Jacoby (1921: 625–6); Hamilton (1961); Badian (1965). Baynham (2003: 10–11); Zambrini (2007: 20); Heckel (2008: 7–8). For previous bibliographical references, see Prandi (1996: 69–71 and 77–9).

[32] See Tarn (1948: 5–29); Pearson (1960: 226–7); Hazzard (1992: 52–6); (2000: 7–17); Ravazzolo (1998).

[33] Who did it, so P.-Luc. *Macr.* 22, tells us, at the age of eighty-four.

[34] That is, if Ἀλεξανδρεύς in *FGrH* 137 T 12 (Philodemus) indeed describes him. Cf. *POxy* LXXI 4808: Cleitarchus as tutor (διδάσκαλος) of Ptolemy IV Philopator ([Φ]ιλοπάτορος; reigned 222/1–205 BCE). Prandi (2012: 23) is certainly right that the author apparently conflated the rulers. He might have meant Philadelphus (Ptolemy II).

population to evacuate the city and be relocated at Ephesus (see Paus. 1.9.7); even though the city was restored after Lysimachus' death in 281 BCE, many of its previous residents never returned.[35]

Deinon and Cleitarchus were associated or even confused in antiquity (Plutarch, *Them.* 27.1; Plin. *NH* 10.70.136, possibly Diod. 2.7.3 and Schol. Aristoph. *Av.* 487).[36] This may cast some doubt on the ascription of a familial connection between them. Nevertheless, this has no bearing on the fact that Deinon may have preceded Cleitarchus by a generation. At some point, the works of Deinon and Cleitarchus may have circulated together (while also being circulated apart). This is no wonder, as they complemented each other: joining together a brief book on Achaemenid Persia in front of a book on Alexander, and perhaps linking the end point of one with the start point of the next, would indeed be plausible.[37]

The narrative of Darius III Codomannus' assumption of power was connected to an occurrence that happened in the reign of Artaxerxes III Ochus, that is, an expedition against the Cadusian tribe (Justin 10.3.2). In this campaign, Codomannus won a duel. Since the king triumphed through Codomannus, the latter was given the satrapy of Armenia as an award. It might not seem probable that two great pictures of a clash between a Persian monarch and the Cadusian nation would be duplicated by the same author. Since there is some likelihood that the Cadusian Campaign of Artaxerxes II, portrayed by Plutarch (*Art.* 24–5), was derived from Deinon (see Chapter 5), the source for Justin's account of Ochus' expedition, therefore, was probably not Deinon, but rather some author who followed in his footsteps. The break in Diodorus between 16.52.8 (finishing with the reward to Mentor for his acts in the course of Ochus' war in Egypt) and 17.5.3–8 (the shift from Ochus to Arses and Darius) in his treatment of the situation in Persia is perhaps related to this change of sources. If all this is true and Cleitarchus was following Deinon, he could have been pursuing his narrative from the very point Deinon finished his *Persica*. Thus, Codomannus' story was inserted as a digression in the campaign narrative of Alexander.[38] If Cleitarchus was Deinon's son, his continuation of his father's story

---

[35] See Bürchner (1921b).

[36] Steele (1921) already proposed that Pliny confused the two authors. Cf. Pearson (1960: 221, 230), Lenfant (2009: 54–5).

[37] What we know of the structure of Cleitarchus' work is that the first four books dealt with events up to the Battle of Issus and the fifth with Phoenicia; the Indian campaign (*FGrH* 137 F 6) comes from the twelfth book (see Jacoby, 1921: 638–40).

[38] Cf. Chugg (2009: 12), who assumes there was such a digression in the third book of Cleitarchus.

of Ochus would then be similar to the state of Ephorus' text, said to be finalised by his son, Demophilus, who completed the work by the inclusion of the Sacred War at its proper place (*FGrH* 70 T 9a = Diod. 16.14.3), perhaps in book 30.

Deinon's Persica *and other authors*

The work of Deinon, simply termed *Persica* (*Persian Matters*), was apparently divided into at least three parts (συντάξεις), each one containing several books. This can be gathered from a reference to 'the fifth book of the first part' (ἐν τῇ πέμπτῃ τῶν Περσικῶν τῆς πρώτης συντάξεως, Athen. 13.609a) and 'the first book of his third part' (ἐν τῷ πρώτῳ τῆς τρίτης συντάξεως, Schol. Nicand. *Ther.* 612–3).

The logic of the sequence of scenes in Deinon's work is not entirely clear, if we follow a chronological order. The reference to the first part already mentions a Persian king (MS read 'Xerxes' but should be emended to 'Artaxerxes': see below). The fact that Xerxes (or rather Artaxerxes I) was presented so prematurely in Deinon's *Persica* encouraged Müller (1848: 2.93) to alter the text into τρίτης in his version, conforming to his idea of the threefold division.[39] One may imagine, however, that the future kings were part of an aside, or, otherwise, that the work was organised thematically according to topics and not chronologically. If this is true, then the assignment of references to the Assyrians (Ael. *VH* 7.1: Semiramis), to Cyrus the Great (Athen. 14.633ce, Cic. *De div.* 1.23.46) and to Cambyses (Athen. 13.560de) need not necessarily be to the first part. The third part mentioned Median diviners. The original context in Deinon's work cannot be fathomed: it may relate to his account of the usurper Magus, but we cannot be certain.

The fragments do give the impression that Deinon's descriptions were derivative, and that this author has substantially borrowed scenes from his predecessors Ctesias and Herodotus.[40] Some examples will suffice. The story attributed to Deinon and quoted by Athenaeus (13.609a) on the wife of Baga<ba>zus,[41] who was a sister of Xerxes by the same father, Anoutis by name, who was the most unbridled of women (ἀκολαστοτάτη) in Asia, is actually the tale of Amytis (Ἄμυτις), wife of Megabyzus (Μεγάβυζος).[42] The latter fact

---

[39] See also Binder (2008: 60). Cf. Lenfant (2009: 63, 66).
[40] See, however, Drews (1973: 117), Binder (2008: 65), Lenfant (2009: 67–8).
[41] The MS reading rightly corrected by Rühl, following Justin 3.1.5, *Baccabasum*. See Lenfant (2009: 90).
[42] On the change *baga-/mega-* see Justi (1895: 56), Benveniste (1966: 79, 108), Schmitt

is known from Ctesias' work (*FGrH* 688 F 13.24, 26, 32, 14.34). If this is true, then the name of the king should be Artaxerxes,[43] and the portrayal of Amytis' promiscuous behaviour perfectly corresponds to Ctesias' depiction (*FGrH* 688 F 13.32, 14.34).

Deinon's story of Cyrus the Great (Athen. 14.633ce) is said to have related that Cyrus was at the head of the corps of rod-bearers (ῥαβδοφόροι) of Astyages the Mede, later in charge of his arm bearers (ὁπλοφόροι) and then asked to depart for Persia (**ᾐτήσατο τὴν εἰς Πέρσας**).[44] Deinon is reported as describing that while Astyages was feasting with his friends, a man named Angares, an illustrious singer, was summoned, and sang of a large beast let loose in the marshes, that would soon grow stronger; when Astyages enquired of this animal, Angares replied that this was Cyrus the Persian. Astyages was then said to conclude that he rightly suspected Cyrus. This version is very close to that of Nicolaus of Damascus (*FGrH* 90 F 66 = *Exc. de Insid.* p.23.23 de Boor), according to which Cyrus was a son of a robber and a goatherd who gradually rose to power as a lamp-carrier and a cupbearer, and revolted against Astyages.[45] Here Cyrus asks the king's permission to visit Persia (F 66.21: **ᾐτήσατο** βασιλέα **τὴν εἰς Πέρσας** πορείαν) and, as in Deinon's account, Astyages is suspicious of Cyrus (F 66.25). The greatest similarity is revealed in the mention of a song. Nicolaus (F 66.26) has one of Astyages' concubines sing about the beast, that becomes stronger, and would conquer the most powerful. The differences apparently result from artistic licence taken by Nicolaus or from a faulty summary of Deinon's account by Athenaeus' source (or Athenaeus himself).[46] Since Nicolaus' passage is rightly treated by Lenfant (2000: 304–14; 2004: F 8d, pp. 93–108) as a fragment of Ctesias, Deinon seems to have repeated this story of Ctesias with some variation.[47] It should be noted that 'Angares'

(1967: 130), Mayrhofer (1973: 134 [8.187]; cf. other examples there: 135 [8.196], 136 [8.207], 137 [8.210]). See Schmitt (2006: 107).

[43] See Lenfant (2009: 92–3). For a different view, see Briant (2002a: 265, 282; see the different entries at 1149). Cf. Kuhrt (2007: 309 n. 3).

[44] ᾐτήσατο corrected by Kaibel. See Lenfant (2009: 135–45). Cf. Ael. *VH* 12.43: Darius was the δορυφόρος (spear carrier) of Cambyses; see Asheri, Lloyd and Corcella (2007: 518), Henkelman (2003: 120), cf. Hdt. 7.3.

[45] Cf. Drews (1974: 387–93) on Sargon II; cf. Kuhrt (2003: 355–6). This portrayal differs from that of Herodotus' version (1.107–130), where Cyrus is presented as the grandchild of Astyages through his daughter Mandane. Cf. Xen. *Cyr.* 1.2.1. On the different versions see Pyankov (1971), Müller-Goldingen (1995), Lenfant (2004: LVII–LX); cf. Hdt. 1.95.

[46] Cf. C. Jacoby (1874); cf. Tietz (1896: 10–11) and Lenfant (2000: 309–11).

[47] In both Ctesias and Nicolaus, Cyrus is not related to Astyages (*FGrH* 688 F 9.1; he is only linked with the Medes through marriage to the last king's daughter, Amytis). In both accounts, Astyages is defeated and has to flee (*FGrH* 90 F 66.46; *FGrH* 688 F 9.1, 6). Yet the strongest arguments are the facts that Spitamas (*FGrH* 90 F 66.8), the husband of Astyages'

was probably not a personal name, but a reference to an official. The riding-post in the Persian relay system is termed by Herodotus *angareion* (ἀγγαρήιον, 8.98).[48] For this word used as meaning 'messenger', see some MSS of Hdt. 3.126.[49] The word could have had larger semantic scope, associated with service given.[50]

A depiction of Deinon (Cicero, *De div.* 1.23.46), in which Cyrus dreams that the sun is at his feet, attempts in vain to seize it with his hands and is given the interpretation by the Magi that he would rule for thirty years, seems to be heavily influenced by both Herodotus and Ctesias. The threefold repetition of an action in relation to Cyrus is Herodotean (Croesus on the pyre, Hdt. 1.86), as well as are the dream of Cyrus (Hdt. 1.209) and the depiction of the Magi as interpreters of dreams (Hdt. 1.107–8, 120, 128, cf. 7.19). The portrayal of Cyrus as an outsider who climbs his way up to the throne of Astyages is surely Ctesian (above). The dream Ctesias related,[51] if Nicolaus is any guide (*FGrH* 90 F 66.8, 11, 17, 24–5), was that of Cyrus' mother, interpreted by a Babylonian to mean that Cyrus would rule Asia.[52] The imagery of the sun perhaps appeared in Ctesias' account (see *FGrH* 688 F 15.51, Plut. *Art.* 1.2 and above). The attribution of thirty years to Cyrus' reign by Deinon is definitely Ctesian (*FGrH* 688 F 9.7, and Justin 1.8.14).[53]

---

daughter, is repeated by Photius' summary of Ctesias (*FGrH* 688 F 9.1) and Oebaras, one of Cyrus' closest men, is mentioned in both accounts (*FGrH* 90 F 66.13–29, 32, 34–5, 38–9 and *FGrH* 688 F 9.1, 4–6) and is displaying similar character traits. Photius' summary begins with the reign of Cyrus, in book 7 of Ctesias' *Persica* (*FGrH* 688 F 9), and hence Ctesias must have written about these episodes in his *Assyriaca*. Apropos of the steps Cyrus clims in both accounts, they are complementary and not contradictory (*pace* Stevenson, 1987: 28, 1997: 70). It is the same story.

[48] Cf. Xen. *Cyr.* 8.6.17; Hesychius s.v. See Huyse (1990: 96–7); Brust (2005: 17–19).

[49] See Theopompus *FGrH* 115 F 109; Jos. *AJ*. 11.203 (probably through Nicolaus, *FGrH* 90 F4.4–6 = *Exc. de Virt.* p. 330.5 Büttner-Wobst). Cf. Aesch. *Ag.* 282 (ἄγγαρον πῦρ, signal fire). The relation between the concept and the Greek Ἄγγελος (messenger) is not clear. See Frisk (1960: 8: 'unbekannten Wegen aus dem Orient eingedrungen') and, on the other hand, Shrimpton (1991b: 78) on *angaros* as a Persian mispronunciation of *angelos*.

[50] Menander (FF 349, 353 K–T) perhaps implies a functionary in general; cf. LSJ s.v. A.2 and Tuplin (1996: 148). The origin of the word is most probably the Akkadian word *agru(m)* (LÚ.ḪUN.GÁ; LÚ.A.GAR], pl. Old Babylonian *agrū*, New Babylonian *agrūtu*), 'a hired man, hireling', in relation with *igru(m)*, 'hire, rent, wage' (cf. Arabic: 'gīr أجير 'employee, hired man'). It would seem that with time, this worker was conceived of a 'compulsory worker', i.e., of the king, or a 'conscription', 'requisition', well observed in the later Greek (Arr. *Epict. Diss.* 4.1.79; cf. the verb ἀγγαρεύειν, Matthew 5:41, 27:32, Mark 15.21; Jos. *AJ* 13.52 ~ 1 Macc. 10.30) and the Latin (cf. Ulpian *Digest* 49.18.4, Paulus *Digest* 50.5.10.2, reflected in the Talmud, Gutmann and Sperber, 1971; Sperber, 1969). It is a category broad enough to include the royal mounted postal couriers.

[51] Cf. the dream of Amytis, *FGrH* 688 F 9.6, concerning Oebaras plotting with Petesacas to abandon Astyages.

[52] Yet, this may be rather Nicolaus' own reworking of Ctesias to suit Herodotus (1.107) for artistic reasons (*pace* Jacoby, 1922: 2057). See Lenfant (2009: 147).

[53] Herodotus: twenty-nine years (1.214). In reality twenty years: Cyrus' death is said to be

Deinon's description (Ael. *NA* 17.10) of one-horned birds in Ethiopia (ἐν Αἰθιοπίᾳ γίνεσθαι τοὺς ὄρνιθας τοὺς μονόκερως) and sheep which have the hair of camels instead of wool (πρόβατα ἐρίων μὲν ψιλά, τρίχας δὲ καμήλων ἔχοντα) may also echo both Herodotus and Ctesias, although the picture as transmitted to us may contain errors. Deinon's beasts may have been fashioned out of Herodotus' one-horned serpents in Libya (Hdt. 4.192: καὶ ὄφιες μικροί, κέρας ἓν ἕκαστος ἔχοντες), his celebrated winged serpents of Arabia (2.75, 3.107–9, ὑπόπτεροι ὄφιες), and the monstrous snake (οἱ ὄφιες οἱ ὑπερμεγάθεες, 4.191). Ctesias, according to the second century BCE author Apollonius (*Historiae Mirabiles* 20), described certain camels, whose hair was similar to Milesian wool with respect to its softness (καμήλους τινὰς ἐν τῇ χώρᾳ γίγνεσθαι, ἃς ἔχειν τρίχας πρὸς Μιλήσια ἔρια τῇ μαλακότητι); he may have claimed that these live in the Caspian (cf. Aelian *NA* 17.34 = *FGrH* 688 F 10b). It is the exact opposite picture of what is assigned to Deinon, and this contrast may have to do with a certain misinterpretation by some reader, based on the Herodotean manner in which Libya was presented as the utter reversal of the northern areas.[54]

Athenaeus (2.67ab) asserts that neither Deinon nor Ctesias mention pepper or vinegar (οὔτε πεπέρεως μέμνηται οὔτε ὄξους) as prepared for the king at his dinner. Ctesias' fascination with pepper may have been focused only on its medicinal uses (cf. *FGrH* 688 F 63, if authentic); the physician may have been uninterested in its presence in meals. Deinon could have been following Ctesias here. Athenaeus joins Ctesias and Deinon together in another passage (4.146c), again related to the king's dinner, which is said to be sufficient for 15,000 men. The precise number of people dining at the king's table perhaps did not appear in the original works of either Ctesias or Deinon, and may be an interpretation made by a reader of a certain fact that is also found in a fragment of Heracleides (*FGrH* 689 F 2), namely, that the king was feeding the *doryphoroi* (spear-bearers) and the light-armed troops. The former group numbered 10,000 men according

in 530 BCE (Parker and Dubberstein,1956: 14), and accession c. 550. Thus, the higher figure may include his reign as 'king of Anšan', his title in the *Nabonidus Chronicle* (= Grayson, 1975: 7 II.1, dated to 550/49 BCE; cf. *Cyrus Cylinder* 21–2); see Gilmore (1888: 143), Briant (2002a: 16–18), Lenfant (2004: LXVI).

[54] The third type of beasts attributed to Deinon's description, 'boars with four horns' (ὗς τετράκερως), may be Aelian's own, since creatures with four horns are a favourite of Aelian (*NA* 11.40, 12.3, 15.14), and this number may be his own interpretation. Herodotus (4.192) mentions horned asses (ὄνοι οἱ τὰ κέρεα ἔχοντες), and the conflation with boars perhaps stems from a wrong interpretation of ταῦτά τε δὴ αὐτόθι ἐστὶ θηρία καὶ τά περ τῇ ἄλλῃ, πλὴν ἐλάφου τε καὶ ὑὸς ἀγρίου ('these are the wild animals on the spot, as well as the animals that are found elsewhere, except the stag and the wild-boar'). Cf. Lenfant (2009: 201).

to Xenophon (*Cyr.* 7.5.68: μυρίους δορυφόρους), and the light-armed troops were roughly half of this number (cf. Hdt. 7.40–1: 3,000 men in three groups, a thousand horsemen and another thousand out of 10,000).[55] So this piece of information, traced to Ctesias, was apparently also present in Deinon's work.

Deinon claims (Athen. 13.560de) that it was Cyrus to whom Neitetis was sent by the Pharaoh Amasis and that Cambyses, born from her, made his expedition against Egypt to avenge his mother (τὴν Νειτῆτιν Κύρῳ πεμφθῆναί φασιν ὑπὸ Ἀμάσιδος, ἐξ ἧς γεννηθῆναι τὸν Καμβύσην, ὃν ἐκδικοῦντα τῇ μητρὶ **ἐπ᾽ Αἴγυπτον ποιήσασθαι στρατείαν**). Both assertions go back to the three explanations Herodotus provides (3.1–3) for the Persian war against Egypt. Deinon's version (cf. Polyaen. 8.29) may be a garbled summary of Herodotus' two explanations: the third – in which Cambyses was the son of Cassandane, and promised to avenge Egypt (Hdt. 3.3.3: **ποιήσασθαι τὴν ἐπ᾽ Αἴγυπτον στρατηίην**) for the insult given to his mother – and the second, in which Cambyses was born of Neitetis. Ctesias (Athen. 13.560de = *FGrH* 688 F 13a) follows Herodotus' first version, in which Neitetis was sent to Cambyses. That this confusion would appear among Herodotus' readers is not so surprising, since his intention in setting these variant accounts side by side was perhaps to confound, and to cleverly convey the impression that Neitetis, Cambyses' wife (in the first version) is also his mother (in the second); in that manner, Herodotus perhaps signals that Cambyses is already involved in an incestuous relationship (with his mother). As a reader of Herodotus, Deinon thus seems to display this expected sort of mixture.

The story (Athen. 14.652bc) that dried Athenian figs were brought to the king's table and were the reason for the Persian campaign, especially the last element in it, that the person who brought it to his table did this intentionally, to remind the king of the expedition against Athens, may strike one as an echo of Herodotus (5.105), where Darius requests one of his servants to remind him of Athens every day. Athenaeus mentions in his version Darius' claim that it does not befit kings to use any foreign food or drink, and this may hark back at Herodotus (1.188) on the king's exclusive consumption of water from the Choaspes or meals ready made at his home (σιτίοισι εὖ ἐσκευασμένος ἐξ οἴκου). It also has some relation with Mardonius' saying (Hdt. 7.5) that Europe has all kinds of fruit bearing trees, and

---

[55] Cf. Ctesias *FGrH* 688 F 9.5. See Stevenson (1997: 17) on the matching of the detail in Heracleides' fragment concerning the thousand beasts slaughtered and the descriptions of Ctesias and Deinon. Cf. Lenfant (2009: 212).

that the king alone of all mortals is worthy to possess it (ὡς ἡ Εὐρώπη περικαλλὴς εἴη χώρη, καὶ δένδρεα παντοῖα φέρει τὰ ἥμερα, ἀρετήν τε ἄκρη, βασιλέι τε μούνῳ θνητῶν ἀξίη ἐκτῆσθαι).The inclusion of figs may stem from an interpretation of Herodotus' tale of the slander of the Peisistratids against the Athenians (6.94), with a rather too literal understanding of the word 'denounce', συκοφαντέω (LSJ s.v.).[56]

Similarly, Deinon's depiction (Scholion on Nicander's *Theriaca* (=*Venomous Animals*) 612–13) of Median diviners who are able to predict from sticks of tamarisk (Μήδους <μυρίκης> ῥάβδοις μαντεύεσθαι) may be grounded in Herodotus 4.67 (also cited by Nicander) on the Scythian practice to divine by willow rods (**μαντεύονται ῥάβδοισι**).[57]

Lastly, Deinon asserts (Clem. *Protr.* 4.65.1) that the Magi sacrifice beneath the open sky, believing fire and water the only icons of the gods (**θύειν** ἐν ὑπαίθρῳ τούτους . . . θεῶν **ἀγάλματα** μόνα τὸ **πῦρ** καὶ **ὕδωρ** νομίζοντα).[58] This sentiment goes back to Herodotus 1.131 and in fact may be repeating it: **ἀγάλματα** μὲν καὶ νηοὺς καὶ βωμοὺς οὐκ ἐν νόμῳ ποιευμένους ἱδρύεσθαι . . . **θύουσι** δὲ ἡλίῳ τε καὶ σελήνῃ καὶ γῇ καὶ **πυρὶ** καὶ **ὕδατι** καὶ ἀνέμοισι ('images and temples and altars they do not account it lawful to erect . . . they sacrifice to the Sun and the Moon and the Earth, to Fire and to Water and to the Winds . . .').[59]

Deinon was grouped together with Herodotus and Ctesias in the work of the second century CE historian Cephalion (*ap.* Eusebios, *Chron.*, p. 28, Karst = Syncell. p. 315, 6, *FGrH* 93 F 1a) as authors describing Semiramis' walls of Babylon. The sixth century CE[60]

---

[56] This Herodotean passage also mentions the servant reminding the king of the Athenians. Cf. Lenfant (2009: 154–9). We shall never know if a version of Deinon's story inspired Cato the Elder in 153 BCE to use African figs in order to persuade the senate to attack Carthage (Plut. *Cat. Mai.* 27.1, Plin. *NH* 15. 20.74–5 with Meijer, 1984 for the story).

[57] See Asheri, Lloyd and Corcella (2007: 630). Presumably the branches were set alight; it was a good omen if the leaves crackled while burning, and a bad one if they did not. This practice implies that divine will manifests itself in inanimate things, like rods or wood. See Iamblichus, *Theurgia or On the Mysteries of Egypt*, 3.7 and Taylor (1821: 161 n.). Cf. also the divination method used in Ezekiel 21.21 (with arrows and *teraphim*); cf. Hosea 4.12. Cf. Lenfant (2009: 99–102).

[58] The Greek and Roman image of the Persians was that they worshipped fire or regarded it as a deity (Hdt. 1.132, 3.16; cf. Basil, *Ep.* 258.4). See references in Bidez and Cumont (1938: 1.74; 2.67–70), de Jong (1997: 100, 111, 133–5, 148–50, 158, 250, 284, 305, 439, 441). Fire is at the main attention of Zoroastrian ritual practices (see *Yasna* 35–41, esp. 36; *Vendidad* 8.81–96). Cf. Boyce (1975: 454–65). On the early link of Zoroaster and fire see Dio Chrys. (36.40–1) and de Jong (1997: 321–2). In Zoroastrian religious faith, fire must be kept pure and unpolluted (cf. Hdt. 3.16). On the association of the *Magi* and the sacred fire see Strabo 15.3.15; Vitruv. 8. praef. 1; Amm. Marc. 23.6.34; Procopius *De bello Persico* 2.24.2; Agath. 2.25 (for divination). Cf. Lenfant (2009: 246–51).

[59] Cf. Lenfant (2009: 240–6).

[60] Karst (1911: XXXVI–VIII); cf. Petermann (1866 [1865]: 458–9). Drost-Abgarjan (2006: 255–62) thinks that the Armenian version dates to the fifth century CE.

Armenian translation of Eusebius has the name 'Zenon', but this form should most probably be corrected to 'Deinon'.[61]

This examination of Deinon's fragments reveals the extent of his reliance on his precursors, corresponding to the impression Plutarch gives on Deinon's relation with Ctesias. Bearing in mind the verbal echoes we encountered, one might reasonably conjecture further that some parts of Deinon's work may have been adapted passages of Ctesias and Herodotus. Others were probably interpretations of them.

The significance of Deinon's work

What can we make of these features? One scholarly opinion (Drews, 1973: 117–18) tends to highlight Deinon's creativity and to see him as a fabricator of facts:[62]

> In short, Dinon's 'history' of Assyria, Media, and early Persia seems to have been an entertaining pastiche of Ctesias' account. But unlike Ctesias, Dinon intentionally falsified history in order to make it more dramatic. . . . The 'tragic' historiography of Duris and the Peripatetics merely adapted to *Zeitgeschichte* the techniques which Dinon had used in his *Persica*.

At some points, Rosemary Stevenson (1997) finds the reason for Deinon's fabrications in his tendency to serve contemporary royal propaganda:[63]

> If Deinon effected this change to make his account reflect more closely the king's view, then it is likely that other alterations of Ctesias' account by Deinon were made for the same reason. His account will therefore reflect official feeling . . . (72)[64]
> Deinon's range is wider [than Ctesias' – E.A.]. . . but it also has limitations. He chooses not to describe any of the Persian defeats in Egypt in the fourth century . . . (160)

Yet even Stevenson (1997: 77, 80, 159) occasionally appreciates Deinon as a serious historian who gives fairly reliable details on Persian life. Indeed, this comes across when we disregard the Hellenic colouring of the stories attributed to him.[65]

The biographer Cornelius Nepos praises Deinon's trustworthiness (*Con.* 5.4) while recounting that after Conon's victory at the Battle of Cnidus (394 BCE), the Athenian general secretly attempts to restore

---

[61] Müller (1849: 3.174) and Jacoby. Cf. *FGrH* 684 F 1.
[62] See Schottin (1865: 6–7), Stevenson (1987: 29).
[63] See Kaemmel (1875: 681), Smith (1881: 51), Hood (1967: 73–4), Bassett (1999: 475). Cf. Orsi (1979–80: 127), Lenfant (2009: 70–1, 181).
[64] Cf. Stevenson (1987: 29–30, 1997: 90–5).
[65] Cf. Stevenson (1987: 35).

Ionia and Aeolia to the Athenians,[66] but his intention is detected by Tiribazus, the satrap of Sardis, who summons Conon under the pretence of wishing to send him on a matter of great importance to the king (see Chapter 5). When Conon arrives, he is incarcerated:[67]

> After that, some have recorded that he was taken off to the king, and died there. Contrary to these accounts, Deinon the historian, whom we believe most on Persian matters, wrote that he escaped. He expresses his doubts whether he did so with the knowledge of Tiribazus or whether he was unaware.
>
> *inde nonnulli eum ad regem abductum ibique [eum] periisse scriptum reliquerunt. contra ea Dinon historicus, cui nos plurimum de Persicis rebus credimus, effugisse scripsit; illud addubitat, utrum Tiribazo sciente an imprudente sit factum.*

Other sources relate that Conon was detained by Tiribazus.[68] However, supporting Deinon's account that Conon escaped is the item found elsewhere (Lys. 19.39–41), according to which he perished in Cyprus. If we follow Nepos and see Deinon as a reliabile historian, as is also evidenced by some of the material explored in this chapter and the fragments ascribed to him, we can attribute this fact to his reliance on good written sources or reports of his forerunners.

Two traits are thus seen in Plutarch's portrayal of Deinon's stories or their arrangement, and noticeable in other passages affiliated with this author:

(a) Deinon's accounts appear to rely on material originally found mainly in Herodotus and Ctesias. That **his stories are derivative** in this sense does not mean that Deinon merely copied the accounts of his precursors, although the brief summaries of his work might give this impression. His originality presumably lay in his new (thematic or simplifying) arrangement, in transposing depictions from one historical character to another, or in new combinations of items originally found in various scenes.

Deinon's modes of adaptation can be seen in the following fragments: Ochus' slaughter of the Apis bull is reminiscent of Herodotus' account of Cambyses' demeanour in Egypt (3.27). The mention of water prized by the king (also in Plut. *Alex.* 36) evokes the portrayal of Hdt. 1.188 and Ctesias *FGrH* 688 F 37, both discussing the

---

[66] See Xen. *Hell.* 4.3.10–12, Diod. 14.83.5–7. This image reflects the Athenian point of view (e.g. Dem. 20.68–70, Andoc. 3.22, Isoc. *Paneg.* 154, *Phil.* 63–4, *Evag.* 56, 68, *Areop.* 12, 65, cf. Diod. 14.83.4 and Nepos, *Con.* 4.4), which highlighted this clash as a landmark in the history of Greece. See Seager (1967: 99, 115), Strauss (1986: 107, 130, 153–4).

[67] See Swoboda (1922: 1319), Barbieri (1955: 186–7), Ruzicka (2012: 62–4), Asmonti (2015: 166–73).

[68] See Xen. *Hell.* 4.8.16, Diod. 14.85.4, Isoc. *Paneg.* 154.

water of the Choaspes River used for consumption by the king; it is no wonder they are all collected together in Athenaeus 2.45ab. One may assume, therefore, that Deinon transferred a Herodotean episode from one Achaemenid king (Cambyses) to another (Ochus), and transposed the description concerning stored water from the Choaspes to the Nile (and the Ister). These changes can be accounted for by assuming that Deinon largely worked with written sources (in particular Herodotus and Ctesias).[69]

Deinon's work can be compared to the way Xenophon appropriated material from Ctesias in his *Anabasis* (above). As part of the first wave of the reception of the *Persica*, Xenophon employed his forerunner's depiction of the military clash, its backdrop and its direct outcome in his own description.[70] For instance, Xenophon took from Ctesias those sections of the *Persica* that offered the setting to Cyrus' rebellion, like Tissaphernes' libel against Cyrus, which would have caused the prince's death if the queen mother Parysatis had not pleaded with the king to release him (Xen. *Anab.* 1.1.3 ~ *FGrH* 699 F 16.59, Plut. *Art.* 3.2–4). Xenophon omitted a number of elements (like the content of the libel) and simplified the account. It is my claim here that Deinon did a similar thing to the stories of Herodotus and Ctesias.

(b) There is, however, another trend in Deinon, which may be comparable to Xenophon in his *Cyropaedia*,[71] that is, **the writing of fictional narrative based on some historical facts.** Deinon is different from Xenophon in that we have no knowledge of his presence in Persia and no sign of an autopsy conducted by him. In fact, Plutarch indicates (and almost assumes that his readers have this impression as well) that Deinon is not considered to have been present at the scene. This creative/imaginative aspect will be explored mostly in the next chapter (assuming the passages discussed there really come from Deinon), but it is discernible in certain of the cases in this one as well.

Xenophon appropriates certain details from Ctesias and presents them in a format which he found in his predecessor: the novella form interwoven between historical narratives.[72] Among the features

---

[69] Note the possible verbal echoes of Ctesias' ὕδατος ἀπεψημένου and ὅπως ἐναποτιθέμενον (*FGrH* 688 F 37) in Deinon's μεταπεμπομένους εἰς τὴν γάζαν ἀποτίθεσθαι... (*FGrH* 690 F 23b).

[70] Cf. Reuss (1887: 3–5), Neuhaus (1901: 279). Cf. Jacoby (1922: 2067), Momigliano (1971: 57) and Bigwood (1983: 347 n. 33).

[71] Or, indeed, to the Book of Esther.

[72] Llewellyn-Jones and Robson (2010: 69–70) mention four episodes: (a) Panthea the Lady of Susa (*Cyr.* 5.1.1–30; 6.1.30–55; 6.4.1–20; 7.3.3–17), (b) King Croesus (*Cyr.* 7.2.1–29), (c) Prince Gobryas (*Cyr.* 4.6.1–12; 5.2.1–14; 5.4.41–51), and (d) Gadatas the chieftain (*Cyr.* 5.3.15–4.51). See Gera (1993: 115–18, 199–215, 240–1). Cf. Jacoby (1922: 2067).

Llewellyn-Jones and Robson (2010: 69–70) indicate as characteristic of this format are: (1) episodic presentation, (2) a link with the work's main narrative framework, not as isolated digressions, (3) scenes of emotional intensity and (4) dialogues. As Drews (1973: 119–21) shows, Xenophon introduces items he found in Herodotus or Ctesias; he them merges them into one whole.

One example (not mentioned by Drews) we can bring is the following: Xenophon claims (*Cyr.* 8.5.28) that while Cyrus was in Media, he married the daughter of Cyaxares, who 'to this day there is a story of her wonderful beauty' (ἧς ἔτι καὶ νῦν λόγος ὡς παγκάλης γενομένης), but then also mentions that 'some of the story-tellers say that he married his mother's sister'. Xenophon contends that 'that girl must have been a very old woman'.

Cyaxares, Cyrus' fictional father-in-law, is the son of Astyages the Mede (*Cyr.* 1.2.1, 1.4.7, 1.5.2); these figures are an adaptation of Herodotus' Astyages, son of Cyaxares (Hdt. 1.107–9).[73] The marriage alliance appears like an elaboration of Herodotus' story (1.73–4) of the marriage alliance between Alyattes of Lydia, through his daughter, and Cyaxares the Mede, through his son.[74] The peaceful transfer of the Median kingdom to the Persians, however, goes against Herodotus' story (1.127, 1.130), in which the last king Astyages is defeated in battle. This may be the result of oral traditions concerning Cyrus,[75] but more probably builds on Ctesias (*FGrH* 688 F 9.1), who asserts that Cyrus married Astyages' daughter after his victory.[76] We noted above that Nicolaus of Damascus' version of the rise of Cyrus may have been derived from Ctesias. Indeed, Nicolaus (*FGrH* 90 F 66) mentions the beauty of Astyages' daughter (Ἦν δὲ Ἀστυάγῃ θυγάτηρ πάνυ γε γενναία καὶ εὐειδής), which corresponds to Xenophon's depiction of Cyaxares' daughter.[77]

Yet, most importantly, Xenophon mentions 'story-tellers' who say that Cyrus married his mother's sister. This is obviously a conflation of Herodotus (who describes Mandane as Astyages' daughter and Cyrus' mother: 1.107) and Ctesias (who depicts Amytis as Astyages' daughter and later Cyrus' wife: *FGrH* 688 F 9.1). In Xenophon's

---

[73] See Kuhrt (2007: 45).
[74] Cf. Helm (1981), Sancisi-Weerdenburg (1994).
[75] Cf. Hdt. 1.95. See Tuplin (1997).
[76] On the different versions see Pyankov (1971), Lenfant (2004: LVII–LX).
[77] Nicolaus' Astyages gives his daughter, Amytis, in marriage to Spitamas, her first husband before Cyrus, along 'with all of Media as a dowry' (δίδωσι ἐπὶ προικὶ πάσῃ Μηδίᾳ), a phrasing which corresponds to the saying of Cyaxares to Cyrus in Xenophon's *Cyropaedia* (8.5.19: ἐπιδίδωμι δὲ αὐτῇ ἐγὼ καὶ φερνὴν Μηδίαν τὴν πᾶσαν). Admittedly, of course, Nicolaus could have been influenced here by Xenophon.

creative combination, Mandane and Amytis became sisters and Cyrus married his aunt.[78]

If we follow the close parallel of Xenophon, we can examine the worth of Deinon's accounts. We could either trace the original core of his descriptions to the literary accounts of Herodotus or Ctesias; in the latter case this would make Deinon's fragments serve as a gateway to the lost text of Ctesias as well as to an early interpretation of Herodotus. Alternatively, we could acknowledge the fictional and imaginative character of Deinon's setting and content as an adaptation and transformation of historical reality, which we observe in the descriptions of Herodotus and Ctesias (and others). Plutarch seems to be following the second route. He mostly displays the sections in which Deinon dealt with topics already covered by his forerunners, and he generally presents Deinon's portrayals as fantasy. Yet, this is true up to a certain point, and this is Plutarch's *artistic* representation of Deinon, a deliberate presentation of his text for literary means. When read carefully, we may see that Plutarch appreciates the great value of Deinon's work, which he probably used for the last third of the biography (see next chapter).

Let us pursue then the first route in understanding Deinon's text and its content. I choose a difficult example to explore this method. It comes from part of a papyrus known as the Oxyrhynchus Glossary (*POxy* XV 1802, fr. 3 col. II 45; first century BCE/CE century), which survives in twenty-six fragments, preserving about 200 lines of text, and incorporating lemmata of terms ordered alphabetically and clarified by an allusion to a source. The specific line under question here reads:

> *Menemani.* (is) water among the Persians. Deinon i[n Book * of the *Persi*]*ca*
> μενεμανι· τὸ ὕδωρ παρὰ τοῖς Πέρσαις· Δείνων ἐ[ν * Περσι]κῶν.

The papyrus in fact reads Ζείνων, and the modification to Δείνων, endorsed by Jacoby, seems perfectly credible. The term found here, μενεμανι, has no comparable word with the identical significance in Persian or any other Iranian language (in which the root for 'water' is *ap*-).[79]

Based on an image of Deinon as sojourning in the east, and conducting some research there, Francesca Schironi (2009: 27) suggests:

> [W]e might imagine D(e)inon, the source of the gloss, asking some local Persians for their word for water by pointing at a basin containing water and

---

[78] Concerning Amytis' old age, we notice that Ctesias asserts that 'for a while' Cyrus honoured Amytis like his mother (πρότερον μὲν μητρικῆς ἀπολαῦσαι τιμῆς) before marrying her.
[79] Schironi (2009: 89).

asking what they called it. The Persians might have thought that they were being asked about the name of the container, the basin, and not the content, the water. Thus their reply would have been the word used to indicate basin or that particular kind of container, rather than the word used for water.[80]

There would thus have been no way for Deinon, according to this interpretation, to realise his mistake.[81] If we see Deinon, however, not as receiving information from local informants himself but rather as an author who adapted material he found in other written sources (most likely Ctesias), we might be able to find a path to better comprehend these obscure references. The word seems to come from a different language. Schironi (via Stephanie Dalley) suggests Akkadian (*me* = water). However, it would appear that the word comes from Aramaic,[82] the official *lingua franca*, and probably the main language in which information was communicated to Ctesias or his interpreter. Ctesias almost certainly received information on foreign words in Aramaic, including Persian loanwords (see *FGrH* 688 FF 15.49, 15.50, 15.51, F 45.15, 45dβ, 45dγ and F 18).

If this is true, then the word has a striking resemblance to the biblical book of Daniel, especially to the so-called 'court tales' section (2–6).[83] Verse 5:25 (the writing on the wall) reads 'Mene, Mene, Teqel (and) Pharsin (מנא מנא תקל ופרסין)', which are interpreted (5:26–28) as 'the numbered (days of Belshazzar's kingdom) he (God) has weighed and divided'. Two wordplays are ostensibly involved. The three items can mean nouns, denoting monetary weights (respectively, *Mina* = 60 Shekels, *Shekel* and *Halves* (of a Mina or a Shekel), whether in the plural or dual forms).[84] They can also mean nominal verbs, passive participles from the verbs 'count', 'weigh', 'divide', the latter introducing another play on *Paras* (= Persians [and Medes]). The repetition of the first word *mene* is usually taken to be a scribal error, involving dittography, as this duplication is not referred to in the following interpretation.[85] Yet, following the MT reading,[86] one may note that the recurrence of the first word (*mene mene*) is

---

[80] Schironi attributes this idea to Oktor Skjærvø.
[81] The image almost evokes Wittgenstein's thought experiments concerning meaning (*Philosophical Investigations*, 1.669–70).
[82] See Grenfell and Hunt (1922: 161).
[83] See Montgomery (1927: 90).
[84] Clermont-Ganneau (1886). Cf. Porteous (1965: 82).
[85] Three words, rather than four, are found in the versions of LXX, the Vulgate, Jos. *AJ* 10.11.3 and Theodotion's translation. See Lacocque (1976: 103).
[86] Instone-Brewer (1991: 311): 'By the principle that the most difficult text is the best, the MT is probably nearest to the original.' Cf. Goldingay (1989: 102).

amazingly close to the word μενεμανι. Judging by the evidence of the Greek papyrus, the text of Daniel may betray a certain expression, composed from the noun *mene* (= *Mina*) and the verb *mani*. The 3 sg. pers. perfect form *mani* ('he has counted, delivered, appointed, ordained, set over', Jastrow s.v. 'מני, מנא') appears in Daniel 2:24 (with an infinitive) and 2:49 (with the construction 'to' (*le-*) a person 'over' (*al*) a thing). There was clearly a penchant for alliterations in expressions concerned with these elements, as we find in the Talmud, Shevuot Tractate 34a: *mane manitikha* (34b: *mane maniti lekha*). ('I counted/delievered to thee a *Mina* [as a loan]' etc.: here it is the 1 sg. pers. perfect). It would appear that the original had someone counting/delivering a *Mina* (or a passive participle, something 'numbered', 'weighed').

A probable candidate for a story connecting weighted money and water would be the prize one Carian received from the king (Plut. *Art.* 14.2, see Chapter 3) in return for providing the monarch with some water (Plut. *Art.* 12.6). This story came from Ctesias, who may have incorporated some form of this Aramaic expression, as it was told to him. Another version is recounted by Plutarch in *Art.* 5.1 (cf. Ael. *VH* 1.32), and may be Deinon's rendition of the same story, for it has most of the same elements. The expression was presumably taken by Deinon from Ctesias as well, but perhaps because it was somehow taken outside of its original context, or was abbreviated, some confusion set in, either in Deinon's text, or, more probably, in the summary of his work.

PLUTARCH'S USE(S) OF DEINON

If all this is true, we may be in a better position to understand Plutarch's method of work in his adaptation of Deinon. Let us examine the cases we noted earlier.

Some of the MSS of the *Artaxerxes* (GR) have the form ὁ Ἄρσης for the alternative of Artaxerxes' given name. This may have been the original reading of Plutarch's text, corresponding to the name of Artaxerxes II's grandchild, the Persian king Arses (338/7–336/5 BCE), as found in the Greek form Ἄρσης, and in the Babylonian astronomical documents (*Ar-šu*).[87] This may also have been the original reading of Deinon and thus not very different from that of

---

[87] Sachs and Hunger (1988: nos. 381, 382). For the Persian tradition of naming a child after one's father, cf. Schmitt (1977: 423, 2006: 76), Lenfant (2009: 167–8). *Pace* Stevenson (1997: 76–7) on the prefix *Hu* denoting 'good' and cf. Justi (1895: 231).

Ctesias; it is not as fanciful as might be imagined from Plutarch's intentional presentation. Ἄρσης and Ἀρσίκας both probably reflect the name **R̥šā* derived from the Old Iranian root **r̥šan-* 'hero'.[88] It may therefore be the case that the form Ἄρσης was already found in Ctesias' work alongside the hypocoristic Ἀρσίκας.

One may wonder whether Plutarch in effect attempts here to create a bigger gap between the versions of Ctesias and Deinon than there really was in their respective texts. The biographer prefers to overlook the similarities of the names and to highlight the differences of the two versions, indicating the uncertainty concerning the king's character and the two possible different readings of his personality.

In the case of Stateira's murder, since, broadly speaking, Deinon's version mostly resembles that of Ctesias, the difference with regard to the timing of the events need not mean that Deinon purposefully altered the facts, or that this was done in accordance with his literary or even political agenda.[89] One may assume a different and much simpler explanation. Following what we said above about the possible places of Semiramis, Cyrus the Great or Cambyses as side stories in the overall scheme of the work, the organising principle of the materials in Deinon's *Persica* may not have been chronological at all but rather thematic.[90]

The *Persica* may have been arranged along a principle guiding the work of one of Deinon's rough contemporaries,[91] Ephorus, who is reported to have written κατὰ γένος (*FGrH* 70 F 11 = Diod. 5.1.4), that is, 'according to type/group'.[92] The segments written by Deinon were probably not presented in the form of books like Ephorus' text, but appeared as sections within his larger work *Persica*. In accordance with this presumed thematic design, Stateira's murder was placed by Deinon within the framework of her relationship with Parysatis. Starting with the upheaval in court resulting from the rumours regarding Cyrus' uprising, the section proceeded to describe

---

[88] See Hinz (1975: 131).

[89] Cf. Stevenson (1997: 71–2), Lenfant (2009: 172–3).

[90] *Pace* Stevenson (1997: 14): 'There is no evidence that Deinon's version was not also chronological.' I have written on this idea for the *BNJ* entry of Deinon (690).

[91] On Deinon's presumed date, see above.

[92] Schwartz (1907: 4) believes that each book of Ephorus appeared with a proem which outlined its specific unity. According to Jacoby (1926: 26), this approach involved a classification by principal geographical areas. Cf. Drews (1963), (1976) and Schepens (1977: 115–18). Barber (1935: 13–18) assumes that the phrase implies that the events were assembled in different books reflecting various parts of the world; he presupposes a chronological order in the works of Ephorus. Stylianou (1998: 85–6) proposes the significance to be a thematic unity of each book, but strongly denies (90–2) that separate books were devoted to Greek and Persian affairs.

the mutual hostility of the two women, and ended with Stateira's death at the hands of the queen mother. After completing this topic, Deinon probably moved on to the next part of his work, i.e., relating the war between Cyrus and Artaxerxes. By assuming a thematic order in Deinon's *Persica*, this author's alleged 'error' may thus be explained.

Deinon's work can be compared to other approximate contemporary texts from the fourth century BCE, the biblical Masoretic books of Ezra and Nehemiah, comprised in the great work I Esdras. The sequence of the reigns of the Persian kings is problematic,[93] for after relating Cyrus' edict to rebuild the temple (I Esdras 2:1–14/ Ezra 1:1–11), there is a flashforward (*prolepsis*) to Artaxerxes I (I Esdras 2:16–30a/Ezra 4:7–16) and then a return to Darius' second regnal year (I Esdras 3:1–8, 5–6/Ezra 4:1–5, 5–6). This sequence is not chronological, and may be considered thematic, bearing in mind the affinities between Cyrus' letter and Artaxerxes' epistle. Just as Plutarch seems to have read Deinon's sequence chronologically, so does the first century CE writer Josephus apply a chronological scheme onto the biblical text, thereby altering the reading of I Esdras 2:16/Ezra 4:7 from 'Artaxerxes' into 'Cambyses' (*AJ* 11.21–30), according to the order of the kings listed in Herodotus.[94] After Darius, Josephus changes the original 'Artaxerxes' into 'Xerxes' (*AJ* 11.120–183), once again in accordance with Herodotus' sequence of the reigns of the Persian kings.[95] Josephus and Plutarch may have been inspired by chronological writing (of, say, the Roman annalistic tradition). It is interesting to consider that Plutarch may not have even been aware of the organising principle in Deinon's work. If this is true, it might mean that the acts of reading Deinon and selecting stories from his text to abridge were perhaps not done by himself (maybe by his assistants?).

Jacoby includes *Art.* 10 in its entirety as a fragment of Deinon, and prints it in large spaced letters, as if all of it was his *ipsissima verba*. If true, this would mean that Deinon's picture was unclear and confused, referring to Ctesias' figure of the Carian and mentioning his award of having the privilege of carrying a golden rooster upon his spear in front of the line during a military campaign. This is, however, unlikely. As Stevenson (1997: 92) rightly claims, it is not clear why Deinon would leave open the question of the part played

---

[93] This example is mentioned in Almagor (2016b: 92).
[94] See Tuland (1966: 178, 183).
[95] See Tuland (1966: 178); cf. Marcus (1937: 324, note b).

by the king in the death of Cyrus, creating doubt by mentioning two versions.[96] More plausibly, it was Plutarch who combined Deinon's version with the account of Ctesias concerning the Carian with the intention of obscuring the portrayal. The depiction of the Carian in *Art.* 10.3 seems to be compatible with Plutarch's presentation of Ctesias' version (*Art.* 14.6) – where the awards given to him are mentioned, though not elaborated – and therefore completes it.[97] One should also especially note the similar structure of Plut. *Dem.* 4.6:

> Batalus, **some say**, was an effeminate flute-player, and Antiphanes composed a comedy in which he mocked him for this. **Some**, however, mention Batalus as a poet who wrote sensual rhymes and drinking songs.
> (6) Ἦν δ' ὁ Βάταλος, **ὡς μὲν ἔνιοί φασιν**, αὐλητὴς τῶν κατεαγότων, καὶ δραμάτιον εἰς τοῦτο κωμῳδῶν αὐτὸν Ἀντιφάνης πεποίηκεν. **ἕτεροι δέ τινες** ὡς ποιητοῦ τρυφερὰ καὶ παροίνια γράφοντος τοῦ Βατάλου μέμνηνται.
> ἕτεροι N: ἔνιοι Y

This is the exact same construction as *Art.* 10.3. In the biography of Demosthenes it is clear that there are at least two sources referred to. For artistic reasons, Plutarch blurred Deinon's account by combining it with elements from Ctesias' version. Again, Plutarch lets the historiographic plane reflect on the historical one in order to allow a better literary representation of the characters. Thus, the king's indecisiveness in battle is mirrored by the lack of determination on the part of Plutarch, who hesitates which version to adopt (Deinon's or Ctesias').[98] In Deinon's variant (*Art.* 10.1–2), the king is unhorsed twice before he rises again to attack Cyrus. Plutarch likewise undercuts this description twice, obscures it by attributing its source to 'some', and then presents an anonymous account originating with 'others'.[99]

As we have seen above, Plutarch voices his opinion that Ctesias' position is problematic because of his pro-Spartan stance. It may be the case that by lowering the total number of the men the king led into battle, the physician increased the percentage of the fallen to

[96] Her answer, though (namely, that Tiribazus is the ultimate source for both versions in *Art.* 10), is untenable. The last sentence of Plut. *Art.* 10 addresses the manner in which Persians name the Carians roosters. This would especially seem to characterise Ctesias and his interest in Persian words and nomenclature (cf. *FGrH* 688 F 15.51, F 19, *Art.* 9.1).
[97] One should note that Photius explicitly mentions *honours* to the Carian (*FGrH* 688 F 16.67: τὸν Κᾶρα ... Ἀρτοξέρξης **ἐτίμησε**; καὶ ὡς Παρύσατις τὸν **τιμηθέντα** Κᾶρα ...). The honours received by the Carian tally with the privilege of carrying a golden rooster upon his spear. *Pace* Tuplin (2011: 471). Similarly, the awards to Mithridates mentioned generally in *Art.* 14.5 are specified in *Art.* 15.2.
[98] Although the 'spoiler' he introduces in 10.3 with the Carian hints at his preference.
[99] See Almagor (2013b: 26).

flatter the Spartans.[100] This does not necessarily mean that Deinon, by choosing another figure, was predominantly pro-Artaxerxes. In fact, we have no idea what Deinon's figure was. Plutarch gives the impression that it was close to that of Xenophon,[101] which incidentally is not given here, but only in *Art.* 7.4. According to Xenophon (*Anab.* 1.7.12) the figure was 1,200,000 men nominally, but the actual fighting force was lower (900,000), since Abrocomas and his men were late to arrive.[102] This number is schematic. Xenophon seems to have a large ratio between the armies (approximately one to ten): Artaxerxes' nominal 1,200,000 soldiers are opposed to Cyrus' 115,000; similarly, Artagerses' 6,000 horsemen (*Anab.* 1.7.11) are set against Cyrus' 600 (*Anab.* 1.8.6). Diodoros gives a rough ratio of one to five: in 14.22.6, Cyrus is said to have 10,000 soldiers vs. the king's 50,000; in 14.22.1 he adopts (through Ephorus) Ctesias' figure of 400,000 men against Cyrus' army of 86,000 men (14.19.6). Actually, if this is the ratio adopted by Ctesias as well, the king's army should have contained slightly more than 400,000 combatants (430,000, to be exact). For all we know, Deinon could have given this schematic number, which is higher than Ctesias' but still far from that of Xenophon. We cannot, however, be certain one way or the other. Deinon could have echoed Ctesias' story, but Plutarch chooses here to group him with Xenophon for artistic reasons.

The mention of Deinon in the *Alexander* concerns items in the Great King's possession. The very mention of water from the Nile and Ister, meant to display the greatness of the Persian Empire, is a probable allusion to the Imperial demand for 'Earth and Water' as a token for unconditional acceptance of Persian dominance.[103] Ironically, this item eventually outlives the empire. Similarly, the dye, coming from a different location (Hermione in Argolis, Greece),[104] suggests that survival may depend on extraction from the place of

---

[100] Xenophon does not number the fallen in the king's camp, but simply states that no Greek has died (*Anab.* 1.8.20). Diodorus mentions more than 15,000 (14.24.5–6). This figure is almost one tenth of the king's force, if we follow Xenophon's nominal numbers, but 26.6 per cent if we follow that of Ctesias. Bigwood (1983: 351 n. 49) stresses that the number used by Diodorus is the exact middle point between the two figures given – 9,000 as the number given to the king, and 20,000 as Ctesias' estimate.

[101] See Smith (1881: 5–6).

[102] This number seems improbable (yet cf. Lendle, 1995: 59). See Wylie (1992: 123) for the logistical and tactical implications of the implausible number 400,000. A realistic estimate would put the number at 60,000 men; cf. Anderson (1974: 100), Bigwood (1983: 341–2, 347) and Tuplin (2011: 456, 467–8).

[103] See Chapter 3 above.

[104] See Alciphron (3.10.4) on the purple from Hermione.

origin, on being removed from the original context.[105] Reflecting
on the protagonist of the *Life*, it may suggest that Alexander could
become 'Great' only once he is outside his original habitat, as his
success in procuring their treasures proves. Indeed, this is precisely
what happened to Deinon's passage, which survives only because it
was cut from its original work and put in a new context, namely, the
story of Alexander. It is, perhaps, no coincidence. If this fact bears
upon what Plutarch knew of Deinon at that point, it might mean
that the biographer received the passage as an already detached
fragment, perhaps in some sort of collection of data (on Persia?), and
that Deinon at the time the *Alexander* was composed was a name
associated with such fragmentary collections.[106]

This conclusion may be implied in the mention of Deinon in the
Themistocles. Plutarch appears to play with some of the Greek
names mentioned in *Them.* 27.[107] In particular, the depiction αὐτὸ
τὸ δεινόν ('the dreadful thing', probably the act of prostrating before
the king) calls to mind the historian's name (Δείνων). This play raises
the question whether during the composition of the *Themistocles*
Deinon was for Plutarch the author of a text avaialable to him or
merely a name of a historian.

These two sections outside the *Artaxerxes*, in which Plutarch mentions Deinon, do not appear thus to betray any thorough familiarity
of the biographer with the work of his predecessor. This is different
with the reference in the *On Isis and Osiris*. The fact that Plutarch
is aware of Deinon's adaptation of Herodotus and actually might
allude to this feature of his work in his treatment of the clash of
Persian and Egyptian beliefs may suggest a direct knowledge of
Deinon's *Persica* – whether the biographer read it himself, or read a
summary of it made by someone else. This impression that Plutarch
knew something of the content of Deinon's work is reinforced by a
seemingly continuing employment of Deinon's text in the *Isis and
Osiris*.

In another passage of that work (11.355c), Plutarch relates the
brutal behaviour of Ochus in killing many, slaughtering the Apis
bull and feasting on it, which caused him to be called 'the Knife'
(μάχαιραν) by the locals. Admittedly, this passage is not attributed to

---

[105] The river reference may evoke Callimachan imagery of the contrast between a pure
and undefiled stream of spring and a huge polluted river (*Hymn.* 2.105–13). See Jones (2005:
54–5).

[106] An interest of Deinon in water is testified in *FGrH* 690 FF 28–9.

[107] Throughout *Them.* 27 the names seem to reverberate (e.g. Θεμιστο<u>κλεῖ</u>... <u>Κλεί</u>ταρχος καὶ
Ἡρα<u>κλεί</u>δης; Ἐρατοσθένης ... Ἐρετρικῆς; cf. Κλεί<u>ταρχος</u> ... χιλί<u>αρχος</u>, etc.).

Deinon, but it would make perfect sense to assume that it does come from this author's work, cited for this very incident later on, and conveying the same sentiment. If this is so, when Plutarch composed the *On Isis and Osiris*, he was conscious of the content of Deinon's work, if only the sections of it pertaining to Artaxerxes II and the following period. This may indicate that material gathered for the *Artaxerxes* was used in the period of composition of this late work.

Two more passages should be mentioned here. The story of the Persian king and the Athenian figs (Athen. 14.652bc) mentioned above also appears in the collection *The Sayings of Kings and Commanders* (173c): Ἀττικὰς δ᾽ ἰσχάδας οὐκ ἂν ἔφη φαγεῖν ὠνίους κομισθείσας, ἀλλ᾽ ὅταν τὴν φέρουσαν κτήσηται χώραν ('[Xerxes] said he would not eat Attic figs brought (for him), but only when he conquered the land producing them').[108] The fact that the same story is brought in Athenaeus,[109] shows the relative popularity and circulation of this story, presumably outside of its original context.

Similarly, the story of the rise of Semiramis to power, attributed to Deinon by Aelian (*VH* 7.1) and mentioned by Diodorus (2.20.3), also appears in a parallel version in Plutarch's treatise *Amatorius* (753de):

> The Syrian Semiramis was the servant and concubine of a domestic slave of the king. When Ninus the Great while reigning fell in love with her, she gained so much power and felt so much disrespect for him that she requested of him to allow her to be seated on the throne, wear the diadema and direct affairs for one day. When he agreed to this and commanded everyone to serve and obey her as they would himself, in her first orders she used moderation, to make trial of her guards. But after she saw that they were not opposed or hesitant, she instructed Ninus to be arrested and chained, and lastly executed. After all this was done, she reigned over Asia conspicuously for a long time.

> ἡ δὲ Σύρα Σεμίραμις οἰκότριβος μὲν ἦν βασιλικοῦ θεράπαινα παλλακευομένη· Νίνου δὲ τοῦ μεγάλου βασιλέως ἐντυχόντος αὐτῇ καὶ στέρξαντος οὕτως ἐκράτησε καὶ κατεφρόνησεν, ὥστ᾽ ἀξιῶσαι καὶ μίαν ἡμέραν αὐτὴν περιιδεῖν ἐν τῷ θρόνῳ καθεζομένην ἔχουσαν τὸ διάδημα καὶ χρηματίζουσαν. δόντος δ᾽ ἐκείνου καὶ κελεύσαντος πάντας ὑπηρετεῖν ὥσπερ αὐτῷ καὶ πείθεσθαι, μετρίως ἐχρῆτο τοῖς πρώτοις ἐπιτάγμασι, πειρωμένη τῶν δορυφόρων· ἐπεὶ δ᾽ ἑώρα μηδὲν ἀντιλέγοντας μηδ᾽ ὀκνοῦντας, ἐκέλευσε συλλαβεῖν τὸν Νίνον εἶτα δῆσαι, τέλος δ᾽ ἀποκτεῖναι· πραχθέντων δὲ πάντων, ἐβασίλευσε τῆς Ἀσίας ἐπιφανῶς πολὺν χρόνον.

---

[108] See Appendix II. This is not to be confused with 174a.

[109] The Scholion to Theocritus (1.147–8) appears to refer to another anecdote (Plut. *Reg. et imp. Apoph.* 174a). '... that dried Attic figs are the sweetest, Di<n>on also says'. (ὅτι δὲ αἱ Ἀττικαὶ ἰσχάδες ἥδισται, καὶ ὁ Δί<ν>ων μαρτυρεῖ).

All these sections should really be seen as ultimately derived from the same story of Deinon, despite the minor differences.[110] The tale's popularity appears to indicate again that it spread independently from the work of Deinon. Moreover, the fact that Diodorus (or his reader) attributes it to an obscure author called 'Athenaeus' may point out that it was a 'floating anecdote' with no clear author. The Athenaeus referred to may in fact be Athenaeus of Naucratis (as was proposed by Jacoby) in his work *On the Kings of Syria* (*FGrH* 166 F 1 = Athen. 5.211a). Athenaeus definitely refers to Deinon in his extant work (*FGrH* 690 F 1, 4, 9, 11, 12a, 23a, 24, 25a, 26, 27), and hence it seems plausible that he also alluded to him and to this story in his other writings. This 'Athenaeus' may have therefore entered the text from a note of Diodorus' reader at the margins of the text and substituted an original 'Deinon'.[111] There are indeed verbal echoes between the variant of Diodorus and Aelian's version.[112]

Because these two stories thus circulated independently, they do not necessarily show a direct acquaintance of Plutarch with Deinon's text at the stage they were composed. More probably, they predate such an acquaintance, if their isolated appearance and the fact that both are unattributed are any guide.

As the sections from the *Artaxerxes* plainly show, Deinon wrote a work of history, containing narratives, historical events and historical figures with their own motives and aims. The work may have included ethnographic digressions, but was mainly one in which historical plots could be found, as was the case of the work of Ctesias (and Herodotus). Before we conclude our findings concerning Plutarch's work method with regard to Deinon's *Persica*, let us turn to the continuous stories of this kind which may have appeared in his work.

[110] For instance, the name of Assyrian King is not given by Aelian, but Plutarch rightly calls him Ninus. Plutarch has a crown (τὸ διάδημα) instead of sceptre and the royal dress, and one day instead of five.

[111] Cf. Müller (1848: 2.89).

[112] ἐχρῆτο τῷ κάλλει in Aelian and Diodorus' διὰ τὸ κάλλος; Aelian's τὴν βασίλειον στολὴν λαβεῖν and Diodorus' τὴν βασίλειον στολήν; both versions speak of five days.

5. *Deinon (b)*

The present chapter deals with sections of Plutarch's *Artaxerxes* which may be ascribed to Deinon with a certain degree of likelihood, although they are not explicitly attributed to him. In assigning these passages to Deinon, the chapter follows a cautious course, progressing from sections that are more probable to ones that are less so. We shall start with a literary understanding of these sections, and then proceed to assumptions concerning their original internal organisation based on Plutarch's passages and external material. Most of the episodes here, which Plutarch presumably adopts from Deinon but does not ascribe to him explicitly, belong to the period after the conclusion of Ctesias' *Persica* (that is, events after 398 BCE).

SECTION (I): PLUTARCH, *ARTAXERXES*, 26–30

The first section we shall examine is the unit consisting of the last five sections of the biography, all taking place in the royal court and revolving around the same court figures. The story has an internal unity of plot, which indicates that it came from the same source.

The section begins with the bestowal of the title of heir to the king's eldest son Darius (26.4: ἀνέδειξε τὸν Δαρεῖον βασιλέα) and not to his youngest child Ochus. This is said to take place while the king is still alive, and is intended to shatter Ochus' hopes already at this stage, to prevent the recurrence of the course of action adopted by Cyrus the Younger in instigating revolt and war. Since according to a Persian custom, the heir apparent usually has his wish granted, Darius asks for Aspasia, a Greek concubine of Artaxerxes who was formerly of Cyrus' retinue (26.5: ἤτησεν Ἀσπασίαν ὁ Δαρεῖος τὴν μάλιστα σπουδασθεῖσαν ὑπὸ Κύρου, τότε δὲ τῷ βασιλεῖ παλλακευομένην). Plutarch then uses the device of flashback (*ana-lepsis*) to return to the first encounter between Cyrus and Aspasia (26.6–9). Artaxerxes is offended by Darius' request (27.1: ἠνίασε τὸν πατέρα), and gives Aspasia the choice to decide whether she agrees (27.3: λαμβάνειν ἐκέλευσε βουλομένην). Since she chooses Darius (27.3: παρ' ἐλπίδας τοῦ βασιλέως ἑλομένης τὸν Δαρεῖον), the king is forced to oblige, and indeed does so, but soon changes his mind and takes Aspasia back, making her a priestess of Artemis (Anaitis), and celibate for life (27.4: ἱέρειαν ἀνέδειξεν αὐτήν, ὅπως ἁγνὴ διάγῃ τὸν ἐπίλοιπον βίον). Darius, who is deeply insulted by this, is soon manipulated by Tiribazus the courtier, who incites him into action against the king (28). At this point, Plutarch once again digresses and relates how Artaxerxes offended Tiribazus twice in the past by promising him his daughters Amestris and Atossa, both of whom the monarch sequentially married himself (27.7–9).

A great number of men have joined in the conspiracy, but the plot to assassinate the king is disclosed to him by a eunuch (29.1: εὐνοῦχος ἐδήλωσε τῷ βασιλεῖ τὴν ἐπιβουλὴν καὶ τὸν τρόπον). Artaxerxes manages to escape from his would-be assassins after seeing them clearly (29.4: οὐκ ἐξανέστη πρότερον ἢ τῶν ἐπ' αὐτὸν ἐρχομένων τὰ πρόσωπα κατιδεῖν καὶ γνωρίσαι σαφῶς ἕκαστον). The conspirators flee, but Tiribazus is hit by a spear and dies (29.7). Darius' verdict is given by the royal judges (29.8–9). Plutarch provides two versions of Darius' death: in one, he is beheaded by the executioner, who initially hesitates (29.9–10: ἰδὼν [scil. ὁ δήμιος] δὲ τὸν Δαρεῖον ἐξεπλάγη καὶ ἀνεχώρει πρὸς τὰς θύρας ἀποβλέπων, ὡς οὐ δυνησόμενος οὐδὲ τολμήσων αὐτόχειρ γενέσθαι βασιλέως ... ἀναστρέψας καὶ τῇ ἑτέρᾳ χειρὶ δραξάμενος τῆς κόμης αὐτοῦ καὶ καταγαγών, ἀπέτεμε τῷ ξυρῷ τὸν τράχηλον), and in the other, the king himself smites him with a dagger (29.11: τὸν δ' ὑπ' ὀργῆς ἀναστάντα καὶ σπασάμενον τὸν ἀκινάκην τύπτειν ἕως ἀπέκτεινεν). Artaxerxes is then said to step out into the courtyard and prostrate himself before the sun (29.12). The final section describes Ochus' schemes to eliminate his two brothers, Arsames and Ariaspes. Ochus succeeds, by using false reports, in driving the latter to take his own life (30.5: τοσαύτην ἐνέβαλον πτοίαν αὐτῷ καὶ ταραχὴν καὶ δυσθυμίαν εἰς τοὺς λογισμούς, ὥστε φάρμακον σκευάσαντα τῶν θανασίμων καὶ πιόντα τοῦ ζῆν ἀπαλλαγῆναι). Through the help of Arpates, the son of Tiribazus, Ochus then kills Arsames (30.8: ἀπέκτειναν δι' ἐκείνου τὸν ἄνθρωπον). When he learns of the tragic fate of his sons, Artaxerxes is said to die of grief (30.9: οὐδ' ὀλίγον ἀντέσχεν, ἀλλ' εὐθὺς ὑπὸ λύπης καὶ δυσθυμίας ἀπεσβέσθη).

One of the definite features of this part as a unit is that of closure, a return to images and motifs depicted in *Art.* 1–2.[1] The key images are associated with Cyrus the Younger. *Art.* 26 begins with a competition for the throne among the king's sons, evoking that of the first sections, which ended with the death of Cyrus. The latter is even mentioned explicitly (26.4), in the king's wish to prevent a recurrence of Cyrus' affair. Among the monarch's offspring, it would appear that Darius resembles young Artaxerxes, while Ochus is different from him. Darius is the elder among the brothers, as was his father (1.2), and for this reason should obtain the throne (26.1: ὡς ἔλαβεν αὐτός, οὕτως ἀπολιπεῖν πρεσβεῖα Δαρείῳ τὴν ἀρχήν). By contrast, Ochus is the younger (26.2), like Cyrus (cf. Xen. *Anab.* 1.1.1). Ochus even imitates Cyrus in nurturing desire for the throne. One may note the deliberate similarity drawn by Plutarch between the description of Ochus and that of Cyrus:

26.2: **ἤλπιζε** δὲ μάλιστα **κατεργάσεσθαι** τὸν πατέρα διὰ τῆς Ἀτόσσης (Ochus).
2.3: ἀνέβαινεν **εὔελπις** ὤν, ὡς **κατειργασμένης** ἐκείνης διάδοχον αὐτὸν ἀποδειχθῆναι τῆς ἀρχῆς (Cyrus).

In view of this similarity, the appointment of Darius to be the successor of Artaxerxes is understandable. The king himself plays a role identical to that of his father (known by the regnal name Darius), in frustrating the ambitions of a Cyrus surrogate. The ironic reversal of fate (which did not escape Plutarch and his source) is perfect: Darius [II] appointed his son Artaxerxes as an heir, and now Artaxerxes designates his son Darius as successor. The latter, however, is presented as someone who wishes to emulate Cyrus himself. Darius the prince asks for Aspasia, Cyrus' famous concubine, who is beloved by him. His ambition evokes that of Cyrus, rather than that of young Artaxerxes. The similarity between the brothers Ochus and Darius and Cyrus is visible through their attitude to the women in the late prince's life. As Cyrus relied on the support of his mother, Parysatis (Plut. *Art.* 2.3–4), so is Ochus assisted by his (step-)mother Atossa (who happens to be his sister). Darius requests the most significant woman in Cyrus' entourage to himself. This theme of imitation is one of the leitmotifs of the latter part of the biography.[2]

The aspirations of the characters are soon frustrated: the king, who desires Aspasia (27.3), Darius, who longs for Aspasia (27.1,

---

[1] See Pelling (1997) on closure.
[2] It is no wonder that in the *Pericles*, where imitation occupies one of the central ideas (see *Per.* 2.4, 13.9), this Aspasia appears again (*Per.* 24), in imitation of the well-known Aspasia. Cf. Stadter (1989: xxix–xxx, 3, 61). See Pelling (2002c: 30 n. 9), who interestingly insinuates that the narrator 'Plutarch' imitates here the well-read real Plutarch.

27.5), Aspasia, who chooses Darius (27.3), and Tiribazus, who hopes to marry Amestris or Atossa (27.7–8), are all incapable of satisfying their wishes. The desires of these four figures is curtailed not independently, but by each other: Aspasia disappoints Artaxerxes' hope (27.3), and the choice of Darius irritates the king (27); Artaxerxes suppresses Aspasia's desire (27.4) and frustrates that of Darius (27.5); the king's preference to wed his own daughters rather than give them away to Tiribazus causes a similar disappointment to the courtier (27.8–9).

In a symmetrical structure, the king competes with Darius over Aspasia and with Tiribazus over Atossa (see below). In both cases the king promises a woman to an important figure in court, and in both he does not keep his word, frustrating their desires. In response, Darius hatches an assassination plot, together with Tiribazus and others. The section dealing with Darius' revolt (*Art.* 29) begins with an attempted parricide and ends with an infanticide. In many respects it is the literary climax of the biography, a picture to which readers are led throughout the narrative. In two respects, it presents a reversal from the previous dramatic portrayal in which Artaxerxes does not punish his mother Parysatis (*Art.* 19). On the one hand, Darius conspires against his father, while Artaxerxes refrains from hurting his mother; on the other hand, the earlier clemency of the Persian king does not manifest itself again. Indeed, Artaxerxes' violence is underscored when juxtaposed with the executioner's reluctance to become a 'murderer of the king' (29.9). The executioner is finally forced into killing Darius, and this picture directs the reader, as it were, to the second version, in which the king himself takes the life of his son.

The last two sections employ conflicting images of the king, which are used by Ochus to get rid of his brothers and competitors for the throne. One image is that of Artaxerxes as one who has no compunction about killing his son (e.g. in the case of Darius), and another is that of the king as caring for his son (e.g. in the case of Arsames). Both are depicted as equally lethal: the first drives Ariaspes into madness; the other prevents Arsames from observing the trap. The first part of *Art.* 30 presents the king's success (the suppression of Darius' revolt) as a failure, with the death of Ariaspes. The latter part of *Art.* 30 may represent a tragedy (the killing of Arsames) as an ironic success: Cyrus' case will indeed not recur, since Ochus is the sole candidate for the throne. It would appear that each course of action adopted by the king costs him the life of another son: the execution of Darius terrifies Ariaspes so much that he takes his

Table 2

Plutarch	Justin
ἀνέδειξε τὸν Δαρεῖον βασιλέα (26.4)	*Darium ... regem vivus fecit* (10.1.2)
νόμου δ' ὄντος ἐν Πέρσαις δωρεὰν αἰτεῖν (26.5)	*contra morem Persarum ...* (10.1.2)
ἑάλω δὲ Κύρου πεσόντος ἐν τῇ μάχῃ (26.9)	*Occiso quippe Cyro fraterno bello ... Aspasian, pelicem eius,*
τότε δὲ τῷ βασιλεῖ παλλακευομένην (26.5)	*rex Artaxerxes in matrimonium receperat* (10.2.2)
ᾔτησεν Ἀσπασίαν ὁ Δαρεῖος (26.5)	*Hanc patrem cedere sibi sicuti regnum Darius postulaverat* (10.2.3)

own life, since he believes that the king will kill him as well. On the other hand, the clemency Artaxerxes shows to suspects of Ariaspes' murder leads to the death of Arsames, for the latter is not aware of the danger they pose.

In Plutarch's work, this section has an internal unity. Was it the same in his source? Some scholars believe that there are two stories recounted here and thus two respective sources involved: one is that of Aspasia and the plot of Darius, and the other is the ostensibly much later events of Ochus' machinations against his brothers and the death of Artaxerxes.[3] Manfredini, Orsi and Antelami (1987: 304), for instance, suggest a long temporal hiatus between Darius' plot and the occurrences surrounding Artaxerxes' death, because of the different types of behaviour the king displays in each case: at first, he energetically suppresses the conspiracy, but in the final episode he is feeble. However, this suggestion ignores the biographer's role in adapting an original account. Indeed, the impression one gets from reading Plutarch and other versions of the affair scattered in ancient literature is that there is a cetain connection between the two storylines.[4]

From the similarities between the stories of Plutarch and the Latin writer Justin (10.1), who abbreviated the first century BCE/CE author Gn. Pompeius Trogus, one can learn that Plutarch relied on one continuous account and that the different parts of *Art.* 26 (the question of succession and the appointment of Darius: 26.1–5; the story of Cyrus and Aspasia: 26.5–8) also appeared in the original version, and most importantly, in the same sequence (Table 2).

[3] See Forgazza (1970: 422).
[4] See Stevenson (1997: 49).

One can detect that the description of Aspasia was an essential component of the story in the account of the two authors. The likelihood that the two writers inserted this story independently of each other by using different sources is not great.[5]

Smith (1881: 23–5) argues that the differences between the two versions are too big to assume a common source for Plutarch and Justin (Trogus).[6] In his opinion, each of the authors used a different source. Similarly, Otto Neuhaus (1901: 274) believes that the conjecture that the two authors relied on the same source is 'ein grosser Irrtum' ('a great error'). This scholarly path should not be taken; the differences between the two authors are minor in character and can be explained as literary adaptations of the same story – perhaps even by a certain intermediary source. Thus, while Plutarch mentions a practice among the Persians, Justin (10.1.2) says that the appointment of Darius is done *contrary* to the Persian customs. The separate references by the two authors to Persian law at the very same point in the plot cannot be coincidental. Despite the apparent contradiction, it would seem that the two authors drew on an ultimate single source. Presumably Trogus believed that a more dramatic story would be to treat the very appointment of Darius rather than the failure to comply with Darius' wish as a behaviour opposed to tradition. In addition, Justin/Trogus (10.2.2) says that Aspasia is the wife of the king and not his concubine. This difference can be easily explained by simplification and abbreviation on the part of Justin or Trogus.[7]

Furthermore, only if we postulate the continued use of an unbroken source by both authors, describing the same story, can the persistent similarity between Plutarch's account (*Art.* 27) and the depiction of Justin (10) make sense (see Table 3). Again, Smith (1881: 23–5) highlights the variances. The obvious difference is that according to Plutarch, Aspasia is appointed high priestess of Artemis/Anaitis (*Art.* 27.4), while according to Justin/Trogus (10.2.4), she is appointed high priestess of the sun. It would appear that the description of Justin (Trogus) sought to make the plot more simplified and more stereotypically Persian. It is hard to imagine that the original version described a priestess to the sun, a situation that did not exist in Persia.[8] The portrayal of a priestess of Anaitis is more probable, and

[5] Cf. Stevenson (1985: 15).
[6] Cf. Binder (2008: 334).
[7] Or their tendency for rhetorical embellishment. Cf. Stevenson (1997: 36). For the differences see Smith (1881: 23–5).
[8] Cf. Thiel (1923: 412 n. 2), who assumes there were two different sources for Plutarch

Table 3

	Plutarch	Justin
The king gives	ἔδωκε μὲν ὑπ' ἀνάγκης τοῦ νόμου (27.3)	*primo facturum se dixerat* (10.2.3)
The king takes	δοὺς δ' ὀλίγον ὕστερον ἀφείλετο (27.3)	*mox paenitentia ductus, ut honeste negaret quod temere promiserat* (10.2.4)
The king appoints Aspasia as a priestess	τῆς γὰρ Ἀρτέμιδος ... ἱέρειαν ἀνέδειξεν αὐτήν (27.4)	*solis eam sacerdotio praefecit* (10.2.4)
Aspasia's position	ὅπως ἁγνὴ διάγῃ τὸν ἐπίλοιπον βίον (27.4)	*quo perpetua illi ab omnibus viris pudicitia imperabatur* (10.2.4)
The reaction of Darius	ὁ δ' ἤνεγκεν οὐ μετρίως, εἴτ' ἔρωτι τῆς Ἀσπασίας περιπαθὴς γεγονώς, εἴθ' ὑβρίσθαι καὶ κεχλευάσθαι νομίζων ὑπὸ τοῦ πατρός (27.5)	*hinc exacerbates iuvenis in iurgia primo patris erupit* (10.2.5)

the ascription of celibacy to a priestess of a goddess identified with Artemis is clearer.[9] The cumulative weight of evidence for resemblance between Justin (Trogus) and Plutarch (see more below) seems

and Justin and tends to believe Plutarch's version. He attributes the 'Error' to Justin/Trogus. One may note an ostensible resemblance with the cloistered *nadītu* women of the sun god Šamaš at Sippar of the Old Babylonian period (1900–1600 BCE), that is, a group which also included princesses and daughters of high officials. See Harris (1962; 1964; 1975: 303–16), Stone (1982), Jeyes (1983). But these women were apparently not priestesses (Harris, 1964: 108–9; 1975: 303) and the tradition was obsolete and disappeared in the first millennium BCE. This is true, even despite a solitary tablet, which contains a (Seleucid?) copy of Late Babylonian origin (before 800 BCE, Çağirgan and Lambert, 1991–3), which mentions a *nadītu* in a description of a New Year festival (l. 101). See Boiy (2004: 235, 276). Therefore, this correspondence is coincidental; it would be unimaginable that a Greek or a Latin author would know this obsolete tradition.

[9] It may be that the association of a priestess maintaining celibacy with the Persian Goddess of fertility Anahita involved a conflation of two types of temple priestess and presumably a confusion with the portrayal in which maidens were dedicated to the service of Anahita/Anaitis (associated with Ishtar) in certain places (like Armenia: Strab. 11.14.16). This service was largely imagined by the Greeks as sacral prostitution; see Yamauchi (1973). See, however, the criticism of modern scholars concerning the existence of sacral prostitution in Babylon: Fisher (1976), Goodfriend (1992: 507–10, with references), van der Toorn (1992: 512–13), Westenholz (1989, especially 260–5). Artemis was associated with virginity in myth (Callim., *Hymn.* 3.6; Ps.-Apollod. 3.8.2 [maintaining the virginity of maidens and punishing its loss]) and ritual (Burkert, 1985: 149–52). The identification of Artemis with Anahita, common in Asia Minor (see Wright, 1895: 64–6), perhaps caused this conflation of images. Brosius (1998) proposes that the basis for identification of the two goddesses Artemis and Anahita was affinity with water and responsibility for birth. It seems more likely that the 'pure' goddess (the meaning of the name 'Anahita') was easier to identify with the virgin goddess Artemis.

crucial towards a postulation of a shared source. Henceforth, we shall call it the 'common source'.

Moreover, Plutarch refers to Darius as 'young' (28.1: τῷ νεανίσκῳ). This is in disagreement with the depiction of Darius as being fifty years old (26.4: πεντηκοστὸν ἔτος γεγονότα). Stevenson (1987: 33 n. 17, 1997: 49) explains the use of the term by pointing out the fact that Darius was subordinate to Tiribazus,[10] yet this may have been an appellation by which Darius was called. We find the parallel epithet *iuvenis* in Justin's account (10.2.5), and since the word in Latin denotes a man till the age of forty-five (OLD s.v. 'iuvenis'[2] 1A), it cannot be applied to Darius unless used as a nickname. Alternatively, something should be said on the original narrative itself (see further below).[11] It is important to note here that both Plutarch and Justin have this peculiar feature in their accounts, and hence may derive it from the same source.

The same goes for *Art.* 29. Plutarch appears to be following the same single source he has already drawn upon for sections 26–8. The plausibility of this assumption may be established by a comparison to Justin (10.2.5–6), whose continuous narrative shows the same elements as those found in the biography (Table 4).

Not only do the same themes appear in the accounts of the two authors, but they are also more or less introduced in the same order. One should mention in particular the presence of the punishment of the children and the role of the gods, which are not essential to the plot, yet recur in both versions.

The resemblance is striking, all the more so since Plutarch and Justin/Trogus were not dependent on each other. Justin (M. Iunianus Iustinus) was indeed later than Plutarch (the scholarly views vary from the second to the fourth centuries CE),[12] but, as stated above, his work is an abridged version of an earlier one, of Pompeius Trogus, who was earlier than Plutarch.[13] In theory, Plutarch's account might have been dependent on Trogus, but that does not appear to be feasible. It is hard to imagine that Plutarch would use a Latin source

---

[10] Cf. Binder (2008: 346).

[11] One may wonder why Marasco (1994: 671) attributes here a 'notable contradiction' (*notevole contraddizione*) to Plutarch, since he addresses the passage in Justin as well (671 n. 64). Cf. Flacelière and Chambry (1979: 7).

[12] See Norden (1898: 300), Steele (1917: 144–5 n. 41), Kroll (1918: 957), Galdi (1922: 108), Castiglioni (1925: 88), Seel (1972: 346), Alonso-Núñez (1987: 61). Syme (1988b: 365), on the basis of the relevance of the Persian subject matter, the references to the work by the Church Fathers, and linguistic criteria, proposes to move the date further to the year 390.

[13] On the date of the writings of Pompeius Trogus, see Alonso-Núñez (1987), Syme (1988b: 367).

Table 4

	Plutarch	Justin
Plot against the king	πολλῶν ἤδη συνισταμένων ... τὴν ἐπιβουλὴν (29.1)	*mox facta ... coniuratione* (10.2.5)
Discovery of the plot in the act	ὀφθέντες ... οἱ σφαγεῖς ... φανεροὺς γεγονότας (29.6)	*deprehensus cum sociis* (10.2.5)
Punishment	καταγνόντων τοῦ Δαρείου θάνατον (29.9)	*poenas parricidii ... dedit* (10.2.5)
The role of the gods	ὁ μέγας Ὡραμάζης δίκην ἐπιτέθεικεν (29.12)	*diis paternae maiestatis ultoribus* (10.2.5)
Punishment to the children	τῷ δὲ Δαρείῳ μετὰ τῶν τέκνων ... καθίσας ... δικαστάς (29.8)	*coniuges quoque omnium cum liberis ... interfectae* (10.2.6)

when a Greek text was more readily available. Moreover, although Plutarch's statement (*Dem.* 2.1–2) that he is a latecomer in Latin is a *topos* (cf. Dion. Hal. *AR* 1.7.2–3) and has a literary significance internal to that biography, it may betray the truth that he did not feel comfortable in that language, at least not enough to make him prefer a Roman author over a Greek one.[14]

Do we have any clue as to the nature of the source which was at the basis of *Art.* 26–30 and of Justin (Trogus)? There are five passages outside the *Artaxerxes* that may shed some light on this question and on Plutarch's method of work.

(I) The story of Aspasia in *Art.* 26 may have been lengthier in the original version, if the largest section in Aelian's *Varia Historia* (12.1) is any guide. This is a rather long piece on Aspasia, in what is perhaps the closest we get to a written biography of a woman from the ancient world. The passage is not fully worked on or revised, and it is quite possible that it bears some similarity to the words that appeared in the original. The end point of Aelian is the moment when Aspasia is at the king's court, probably just before her status changes following the request of Darius (for she could not wait at the king's bedroom after her celibacy was decreed: *Art.* 27.4). It is

---

[14] See Jones (1971: 20, 28, 30, 84–6), who thinks that Plutarch used Greek translations of Latin works (even though he had a 'working knowledge' of Latin). Cf. Barrow (1967: 151), who assumes that the biographer read in the original, despite the scholar's awareness that Plutarch had no interest in Latin literature. Cf. Russell (1973: 54), Strobach (1997: 32–46), Zadorojnyi (2006), Pelling (2011: 43–4, 55–6).

therefore quite possible that the entire description is one continuous picture that came from the same source, and was included in it after the mention of Aspasia in Darius' request and before Darius' revolt.[15]

Neuhaus (1901: 277), however, does not believe that the versions of Aelian and Plutarch derive from the same source, and it would be interesting to address his arguments. The differences he mentions are two:

(a) In Plutarch' account Cyrus is depicted as having his meal (Κύρου δειπνοῦντος) when Aspasia first arrives in his presence, while in Aelian's version she appears to him for the first time in the course of a banquet after dinner (ἔτυχε μὲν ἀπὸ δείπνου ὢν καὶ πίνειν ἔμελλε ... μεσοῦντος οὖν τοῦ πότου).

(b) Plutarch has Aspasia, who declines Cyrus' invitation to sit next to him, threaten the men who approach her (the κατευνασταί, servants); Aelian has her threatening Cyrus himself.

But these slight changes, for which we can safely assume Plutarch is responsible,[16] are negligible, as even Neuhaus admits ('geringfügig'). Moreover, Neuhaus (1901: 276) shows that there is a strong similarity between the two accounts with relation to the following points: the origin of Aspasia, her upbringing, her behaviour towards Cyrus (which is markedly different from that of the other women), the words Cyrus utters to the person who brought Aspasia, and the description of the intimate connection between Cyrus and Aspasia after this incident.

The verbal similarity between Aelian and Plutarch may reflect the original version. Thus, Plutarch writes (26.6) that the women sit down and that when Cyrus proceeds to sport, touch and jest with them, they show no displeasure at his friendly advances (προσπαίζοντος αὐτοῦ καὶ **ἀπτομένου** καὶ σκώπτοντος, οὐκ ἀηδῶς ἐνεδέχοντο τὰς φιλοφροσύνας). According to Aelian, three of the women are instructed how to win Cyrus' attention; they learn not to turn away when he approaches or get angry when he touches them (**ἀπτομένου** μὴ δυσχερᾶναι). When Cyrus tells the women to sit next to him, they obey. When he starts to touch them (**ἀπτομένου** δὲ τοῦ Κύρου) and examine them, they submit to his conduct. Aspasia, by contrast, declines to accept it. In Plutarch's version, she shouts to

15 Cf. Judeich (1896: 1721), Stevenson (1997: 37).
16 Another argument of Neuhaus (1901: 277) is that the very word used by Plutarch, κατευνασταί, indicates that his source is a person who was acquainted with life in the Persian court. Since this particular word is absent in Aelian's story, the scholar believes that the latter had a different source at his disposal. It is conceivable, however, that Aelian omitted it from his description, especially if this word was not that common.

one of Cyrus' chamberlains: 'whoever lays his hands upon me shall regret this' (**οἰμώξεται** μέντοι τούτων … ὃς ἂν ἐμοὶ προσαγάγῃ τὰς χεῖρας: 26.7), while Aelian writes that when Cyrus himself touches Aspasia with his fingertip, she screams and says that he will be sorry (ἔφατο αὐτὸν **οἰμώξεσθαι** τοιαῦτα δρῶντα).

According to Aelian, Aspasia's reaction is pleasing to Cyrus (ὑπερήσθη τούτοις ὁ Κῦρος). He turns to the person who brought her (πρὸς τὸν ἀγοραστὴν) and says 'this is the only free and uncorrupted girl you have brought …' ('ταύτην μόνην' ἔφη 'ἐλευθέραν καὶ ἀδιάφθορον ἤγαγες'). This version is particularly close to the description of Plutarch (*Art.* 26.8), which appears as a question directed at the person who brought the women: 'Cyrus was delighted, and laughed, and said to the man who had brought the women: "Don't you see at once that this is the only free and unperverted woman thou hast brought me?"' (ὁ δὲ Κῦρος ἡσθεὶς ἐγέλασε καὶ εἶπε πρὸς τὸν ἀγαγόντα τὰς γυναῖκας 'ἆρ' ἤδη συνορᾷς ὅτι μοι μόνην ταύτην ἐλευθέραν καὶ ἀδιάφθορον ἥκεις κομίζων;').

Of course, the reverse possibility, namely, that Aelian embellished the account of Plutarch, is also plausible, but Aelian has details which are not found at all in Plutarch's depiction.[17] The hypothesis that Aelian included wholesale sections from the original in this crude and unpolished piece before he began editing and modifying them would appear more likely than the idea that Aelian found a skeletal depiction in Plutarch's work and began elaborating it (or else found an interim text that embroidered the version in Plutarch's biography). Another possibility would be that Aelian combined Plutarch and another source, but the most straightforward one would be to postulate that Aelian and Plutarch employed the same original account.

(II) The next external passage comes from a work attributed to Plutarch, the *De Superstitione* (*On Superstition*).[18] The accounts of the end of Tiribazus in the biography and in this work are wholly different. In the *Artaxerxes* (29.7), Plutarch describes the event in the following manner:

Tiribazus slew many of the king's guards as they arrested him, and at last was smitten by a spear at long range, and fell.

ὁ δὲ Τιρίβαζος **συλλαμβανόμενος** πολλοὺς ἀπέκτεινε τῶν βασιλέως δορυφόρων, καὶ μόγις **ἀκοντίῳ** πληγεὶς πόρρωθεν ἔπεσε.

---

[17] Furthermore, verbal similarity of Aelian's passage to other fragments of the probable author of this story, that is, Deinon (as we shall see below), makes it harder to maintain this position.

[18] On doubts concerning *De Superstitione*'s authenticity see Smith (1975).

Thus, a spear cast from far away, which no named person is said to throw, slays Tiribazus. In another place,[19] I argued that the image of a lance thrown by an unidentified agent, and in particular the words 'from afar', were probably inserted by Plutarch to form an association with a complementary previous scene within the biography, in which there is a thrower of a lance but no hit is mentioned. Earlier, Artaxerxes is said to throw his lance (10.2: **ἀκοντίῳ**), but it is not clear if he hits Cyrus. This association is thus made to link the eventual killing of Tiribazus with the previous attempt to halt Cyrus. In the other account (*De Sup.* 168e), however, the event is completely different:

> They say that Tiribazus, when the Persians arrested him, drew his sword, strong as he was, and fought. Yet when the men protested and shouted out that they were arresting him on the king's order, he immediately laid down his sword and held out his two hands to be chained.
>
> Τὸν Τιρίβαζόν φασιν ὑπὸ τῶν Περσῶν **συλλαμβανόμενον** σπάσασθαί τε τὸν ἀκινάκην, εὔρωστον ὄντα, καὶ διαμάχεσθαι· μαρτυρομένων δὲ καὶ βοώντων ὅτι συλλαμβάνουσιν αὐτὸν βασιλέως κελεύσαντος, αὐτίκα τὸ ξίφος καταβαλεῖν καὶ τὼ χεῖρε συνδῆσαι παρασχεῖν.

The resemblance between the openings of the two passages appears to exclude the option that these accounts designate dissimilar actions. The difference is perhaps to be explained in that one version is closer to the original tale, while the second is a reworked variant. It is more probable that the tale incorporated in the *De Superstitione* is the original, since it is quoted precisely so as to validate an argument. It casts Tiribazus' demeanour as undesirable, as an allegory for the conduct of the δεισιδαίμων (superstitious).[20] There is no necessity to suppose that Plutarch altered the story in his *Moralia* work in answer to certain needs, for he could have chosen an alternative anecdote with completely divergent features. Indeed, the version in the *Artaxerxes* appears to be the revised one, if only because of its remarkable similarity to the death of Cyrus by a spear (cf. *Art.* 11.5: **ἀκοντίῳ**). Apparently, Plutarch devised this allusion with the intention of associating the death of Darius, Tiribazus' accomplice, with that of Cyrus. One may also note this consideration: if the original story did have Tiribazus obediently yielding to the guards, this may account for the fact that his son was still alive after the revolt (*Art.* 30.8), a fact that suggests some sort of royal pardon to the family.[21]

---

[19] Almagor (2016a: 73–4).
[20] On this anecdote as displaying Tiribazus' character, see Meloni (1950: 333).
[21] Cf. Hdt. 3.15.

(III) The third passage is associated with the issue of the sequence of the *Art.* 29 and 30. Aelian's (*VH* 9.42) relates the following:

> After Artaxerxes executed his elder son Darius for conspiracy, the second son, on his father's orders, drew his sword and killed himself in front of the palace.
>
> Ἀρταξέρξου ἀποκτείναντος τὸν πρεσβύτερον υἱὸν Δαρεῖον ἐπιβουλεύοντα, ὁ δεύτερος ἀξιοῦντος τοῦ πατρὸς σπασάμενος τὸν ἀκινάκην ἑαυτὸν πρὸ τῶν βασιλείων ἀπέκτεινεν.

Manfredini, Orsi and Antelami (1987: 307) hold that this is another version of the end of the conspiracy and its aftermath. A closer examination, however, shows that there is no major difference between this description and Plutarch's biography. Aelian relates that Artaxerxes' son commits suicide, and that his father desired that. Plutarch's version has Ariaspes, Artaxerxes' son, being led to believe that the king wishes him dead by Ochus' murderous deception. It would seem that Aelian's version here is only an inadequate summary of the original description, with the omission of Ochus' plan. The only difference between the reports is the method of suicide. One possibility is that the dagger (ἀκινάκης), a typical Persian weapon[22], is a detail added in the process of embellishment, and that the suicide by poison was found in the original account. Alternatively, the drinking of poison was added by Plutarch, as another lethal beverage portrayed in the biography. An additional detail provided in Aelian's version is the location of Ariaspes' suicide – somewhere in front of the palace. Presumably the description of Themistius (32.362c), according to which 'of his sons, Artaxerxes had the throat of one slit and another he impelled to death of his own accord' (τὸν μὲν ἀπέσφαξε τῶν υἱέων, τὸν δὲ ἑκόντα ἀποθανεῖν κατηνάγκασεν), is based on a similar kind of poor abridgement. It is hard to believe that Themistius knew more details of the original story than those he included in this depiction. From these descriptions and the close proximity of the events in these brief epitomes, it would seem that the two incidents, namely, the death of Darius and the death of Ariaspes, belonged to the same source, and appeared one after the other.

(IV) Polyaenus (7.17) describes a stratagem he attributes to Ochus:

> When his father Artaxerxes died, Ochus knew that his father while alive intimidated his subjects, and that after his death he would be contemptible himself. Through an arrangement with the eunuchs, chamberlains, and the

---

[22] Cf. Hdt. 7.54, who defines it as a Persian weapon. Cf. Moorey (1985: 26–7). It appears in the *apadana* reliefs as the weapon of Persians and Medes (Miller, 1997: 46–8). See Schmidt (1953: pl. 27b, 65, 120), Roaf (1983: pl. 24).

Chiliarch, he concealed the death for ten months. Sending around letters in this period with the royal seal, he commanded in the name of his father that all proclaim Ochus king. After all made the proclamation and did obeisance, he acknowledged his father's death and he announced the mourning for the king according to Persian customs.

Ὦχος Ἀρταξέρξου τοῦ πατρὸς αὐτῷ τελευτήσαντος εἰδὼς, ὅτι περιὼν μὲν ὁ πατὴρ φοβερὸς ἦν τοῖς ὑπηκόοις, μετὰ δὲ τὴν τούτου τελευτὴν αὐτὸς εὐκαταφρόνητος ἔσοιτο, τοῖς εὐνούχοις καὶ κατακοιμισταῖς καὶ τῷ χιλιάρχῳ συνθέμενος ἔκρυψε τὸν θάνατον ἐπὶ μῆνας δέκα· ἐν δὲ τούτοις τὴν βασιλικὴν σφραγῖδα διαπέμπων ἐξ ὀνόματος τοῦ πατρὸς προσέταξεν Ὦχον ἀναγορεῦσαι βασιλέα. ἐπεὶ δὲ πάντες ἀνηγόρευσαν καὶ ὑπήκουσαν, τότε ὡμολόγησε τὸν θάνατον τοῦ πατρὸς καὶ τὸ βασίλειον πένθος ἐπήγγειλε κατὰ τοὺς Περσῶν νόμους.

In Plutarch's account, after the execution of the crown prince Darius, in one version even at the hands of Artaxerxes (*Art.* 29.11), the king seems to be descending into passivity and does not obstruct Ochus' actions to get rid of his brothers. In fact, the king appears to be so passive that in view of Polyaenus' account one is almost tempted to propose a morbid explanation for this inactivity. We may note the apparent similarities between Polyaenus' passage and Plutarch's depiction:

(a) In both descriptions, the same deceit is used. Polyaenus portrays Ochus as using the king's name and the king's seal, pretending that certain orders come from him. In Plutarch's version Ochus makes Ariaspes believe that certain instructions are the king's own.

(b) Both versions attribute the same motivation to Ochus, which is to secure his status as king. While in Polyaenus' account Ochus first holds power and then succeeds in gaining legitimacy, Plutarch presents his achievement as being made only through the removal of his opponents.

(c) The circumstances appear roughly the same for both accounts. In particular, the monarch's absence is notable. Ariaspes is not able to ascertain the king's true disposition towards him in *Art.* 30. This is understandable if Artaxerxes is no longer among the living.

Furthermore, it seems that there are significant verbal echoes between these two passages. For instance, compare the use of the words λόγους φοβεροὺς (*Art.* 30.4; 'terrifying words') with Polyaenus' φοβερὸς ἦν ('was intimidating'). Note the phrase εὐνούχους καὶ φίλους βασιλέως (*Art.* 30.4; 'eunuchs and friends of the king') and Polyaenus' τοῖς εὐνούχοις καὶ κατακοιμισταῖς καὶ τῷ χιλιάρχῳ ('the eunuchs, chamberlains, and the Chiliarch'). Plutarch concludes the biography (*Art.* 30.9) by saying that Artaxerxes had the reputation 'of being mild and caring for his subjects' (δόξας δὲ πρᾶος εἶναι καὶ φιλυπήκοος). This word, φιλυπήκοος, evokes Polyaenus' τοῖς ὑπηκόοις, and it is probably a compound created by Plutarch.[23]

It would not seem probable that Polyaenus draws upon the biographer for his information. While it is true that Polyaenus read Plutarch and relied on his works in other places,[24] here he adds the additional fact, not found in Plutarch's work, that Artaxerxes died and that his death was kept a secret for ten months. It would rather seem that Polyaenus' source is not Plutarch; yet, in view of the similarities between them, it may appear reasonable to conclude that both accounts depend on the same source.

Briant (2002a: 590, 1003) suggests that Polyaenus' text does not describe Artaxerxes III Ochus at all, but another Ochus, known as Darius II Nothos. According to a practice of using the same name in alternate generations, both kings whose given name was Ochus were sons of persons who assumed the regnal name Artaxerxes (the first and the second, respectively). Briant mentions the discrepancy between Plutarch's positive portrayal of Artaxerxes in *Art.* 30 and Polyaenus' overall unenthusiastic depiction. Thus, ostensibly, the phrase φοβερὸς ἦν τοῖς ὑπηκόοις found in Polyaenus' account is in stark contradiction to the portrait painted by Plutarch in the employment of φιλυπήκοος. Allegedly, one would have to conclude that these two authors refer to different kings and rely on different sources, and not on the same one, as is proposed here. This argument, however, can be contested.

For one thing, it could be shown that both accounts do seem to fit together. Note that according to Plutarch, the king's image is so terrifying that Ariaspes decides to take his own life. This description perfectly corresponds with the portrayal of the King as φοβερὸς ἦν τοῖς ὑπηκόοις in the description of Polyaenus. Indeed, it would also appear that the two accounts even complete each other. We can understand, for instance, the identity of the 'king's friends' (φίλους βασιλέως) mentioned together with the eunuchs in Plutarch's version as Ochus' collaborators; these are the chamberlains and the Chiliarch found in Polyaenus' report. Furthermore, it is not clear

---

[23] It is of special interest because the word is unique in the entire Greek corpus, and found only in Plutarch and the speeches of the twelfth century Byzantine teacher and rhetor Nicephorus Basilacius (*Or. In Joannem Comnenum*) – in the latter author as a noun (τὸ φιλυπήκοον).

[24] See Stadter (1965: 13–29).

how, according to Briant, Polyaenus' passage would agree with what is known of the circumstances which accompanied the rise of Ochus/ Darius II to power (Ctesias *FGrH* 688 F 15.47–50). In that account, there were two interim reigns of Darius' brothers, that is to say, Xerxes II (who ruled for one month) and Sogdianus (who ruled for six months). None of this tallies with the ten months mentioned by Polyaenus as a period during which the death of Artaxerxes was kept a secret.[25]

Weighing the evidence, therefore, one would have to agree with David Lewis (1977: 71 n. 141), hesitant though he was, in interpreting Polyaenus' passage as a description of Artaxerxes II and his son Ochus.[26] Other scholars, while acknowledging that both passages may speak of the same characters and about the same circumstances, assume nevertheless that the descriptions are to be taken in *sequential* order. Rüdiger Schmitt (1987: 658), for instance, puts the episode depicted in *Art.* 30 chronologically before Polyaenus' anecdote. According to Schmitt, Ochus came to power in 359 BCE, after Artaxerxes II died (Plutarch's version), and hid his father's death for ten months (Polyaenus' version) 'so that his official reign may only have begun in 358/7'. This view does not seem to be feasible. If Ochus succeeded in removing his competitors in the manner described by Plutarch, it is difficult to see why he should worry about his position as successor.

The story found in Plutarch is probably not totally unrelated to the original narrative in his source. After all, at some point Ochus had to announce the death of his father and to declare its cause. It would seem that the official version adopted by Artaxerxes III in that narrative was to concoct a connection between his father's end and the news of his son Arsames passing away. This royal propaganda would claim that the late king died out of grief and despair for the brutal and premature death of his son (which, we should recall, in reality was a death orchestrated by Ochus). Since there were no other rivals left to compete with for the throne, the only candidate to succeed Artaxerxes II would then be Ochus himself. Plutarch, according to this assumption, simply turned this tale, which was

[25] Briant (2002a: 590) continues and claims that 'what Ctesias and Polyaenus transmit, in their own way, is probably a scrap of the official version that circulated after Ochus' accession'. Yet it is hard to see this description as an official account, since Polyaenus' picture is not positive and essentially states that Ochus usurped the throne.

[26] 'Cf. Polyaenus VII.17, where Ochus conceals the death of his father Artaxerxes for ten months. I suppose the normal assignment of this to the accession of Artaxerxes III is correct, despite the attractive coincidences of name and dates'.

presented by his source as a piece of fabrication by Ochus, into his account of the *genuine* historical reality.

(V) Closely related to this point is our last external passage, a brief mention found in Plutarch's treatise *De fraterno amore* (*On Brotherly Love*) 480d:

> When Artaxerxes observed that his son Ochus conspired against his brothers, he lost hope and perished.
> Ἀρταξέρξης αἰσθόμενος Ὦχον τὸν υἱὸν ἐπιβεβουλευκότα τοῖς ἀδελφοῖς ἀθυμήσας ἀπέθανε.

Here, Artaxerxes seems to have passed away immediately upon discovery that Ochus schemed against his brothers. It is similar to what is recounted in the *Artaxerxes* but different from Polyaenus' passage. Assuming our hypothesis that Plutarch altered his source is correct, we could conclude that here, the biographer used an inaccurate summary of the episode (of the kind we saw above), which he read independently of the *Artaxerxes*.[27] This faulty summary may have given Plutarch the idea for his own presentation in the biography. Alternatively, it could be that the treatise *De fraterno amore* was composed after the *Artaxerxes*, and abridged its adapted report.[28]

SECTION (II): PLUTARCH, *ARTAXERXES*, 24–5

Let us move now to another section in Plutarch's biography, which again appears to form a closed unit in terms of content. The two sections concern a military campaign of Artaxerxes against the northern tribe of the Cadusians and its aftermath. *Art.* 24 depicts the course of the campaign and comprises three parts. In the first part, the king's army suffers hunger and great hardships (*Art.* 24.2–3), which force it to consume the beasts of burden. This picture evokes the adversities of Darius among the Scythians (Hdt. 4.123, 130), Cambyses in the desert on the way to Ethiopia (Hdt. 3.25) and Xerxes on his way back to Asia (Hdt. 8.115). Strabo's version (*Art.* 7.3.14) of the Scythian campaign has Darius and his soldiers almost dying of thirst.

In this great distress, the second section sees Tiribazus stepping in and saving the day. Tiribazus was known for his rhetorical and diplomatic abilities (in *Art.* 10.1 his words are significant in encouraging

---

[27] Cf. the mistake of a modern reader: Frye (1984: 131) writes that 'Artaxerxes II was murdered in 359', whereas there is no evidence for this in our sources.

[28] This work was probably written after the *Cato Minor*. See Brokate (1913: 17–24, 47, 58, 61). On the relative chronology see Ziegler (1951: 800). On Plutarch's use of his own earlier work see Pelling (2011: 54).

the king). Here he appears as devising a trick to end the war. It is a simple ruse by which both he and his son would turn separately to the two kings of the Cadusians, offer a peace treaty to both and cause each to finish hostility and reach the king first to sign a pact. Indeed, both kings arrive at the same time to sign the agreement (24.5–7):

> Since the Cadusians had two kings, and each of them was positioned separately, he [Tiribazus] met with Artaxerxes, told him what he intended to do, and proceeded himself to one of the Cadusian [leaders], sending his son in secret to the other. Each of them misled one [of the two kings], saying that the other [king] was dispatching an embassy to Artaxerxes and concluding friendship and alliance solely for himself, and that if he were sensible, he must meet him [Artaxerxes] first; [each of them] said he would assist in whatever he could. Both [kings] were convinced by these words, and thought they should anticipate one another; one sent delegates with Tiribazus, the other with the son of Tiribazus.

> (5) Ὄντων γὰρ δυεῖν ἐν τοῖς Καδουσίοις βασιλέων, ἑκατέρου δὲ χωρὶς στρατοπεδεύοντος, ἐντυχὼν τῷ Ἀρτοξέρξῃ, καὶ φράσας περὶ ὧν διενοεῖτο πράττειν, ἐβάδιζεν αὐτὸς πρὸς τὸν ἕτερον τῶν Καδουσίων, καὶ πρὸς τὸν ἕτερον κρύφα τὸν υἱὸν ἔπεμπεν. (6) Ἐξηπάτα δ’ ἑκάτερον ἑκάτερος, λέγων ὡς ἅτερος ἐπιπρεσβεύεται πρὸς τὸν Ἀρτοξέρξην, φιλίαν μόνῳ πράττων ἑαυτῷ καὶ συμμαχίαν· οὐκοῦν εἰ σωφρονεῖ, χρῆναι πρότερον ἐντυγχάνειν ἐκείνῳ, αὐτὸν δὲ συμπράξειν ἅπαντα. (7) Τούτοις ἐπείσθησαν ἀμφότεροι, καὶ φθάνειν ἀλλήλους νομίζοντες, ὁ μὲν τῷ Τιριβάζῳ συνέπεμψε πρέσβεις, ὁ δὲ τῷ παιδὶ τοῦ Τιριβάζου.

This image may call to mind Herodotus’ picture (4.118) that the Scythians had kings (τοὺς βασιλέας, in the plural); yet, in the latter case, the inner division is of a great advantage to the Scythians in their struggle against the Persians,[29] while in Plutarch’s depiction the Persians succeed in making the Cadusian kings yield as a result of this disunion. The stratagem Tiribazus uses is a familiar one, which causes people to act in a certain manner out of mutual suspicion.[30] It is close to the standard example analyzed in game theory, known as the ‘Prisoner’s Dilemma’, in which the perceived self-interest of two agents undermines their desire to cooperate with each other.[31] The outcome of this agreement between the king and the Cadusians is that the Persians are able to preserve their authority.[32] Part of

---

[29] Cf. Hartog (1988: 39).

[30] Cf. Polyaen. 2.1.33 (Agesilaus), 2.10.3 (Cleandridas). Cf. Diod. 16.49.7–8 (noted by Stevenson, 1997: 97 n. 97).

[31] See Tucker (1983), building on an example devised by Melvin Dresher and Merrill Flood at the RAND (= Research and Development) Corporation in 1950. See Poundstone (1992). For its use in the international diplomatic and political spheres see Snyder (1971: 68–9).

[32] See Briant (2002a: 576, 732, 766–7).

the agreement may have been that Cadusian forces would serve in Artaxerxes' army in the ensuing years; indeed, the expedition may have aimed to recruit forces.[33]

Plutarch begins this passage by stating that Tiribazus was at this time 'in disgrace and slighted' (τότε ταπεινὰ πράττων καὶ περιορώμενος: *Art.* 24.4). At the end of this section, Plutarch pictures Tiribazus as gaining glory and the triumphant king returning home with his army (*Art.* 24.9):

> After Tiribazus arrived, his son also came, both carrying the Cadusians, then peace and treaties were concluded with the two; and Tiribazus, now an eminent and glorious person, marched together with the king.
> Ἐπεὶ δ᾽ ἧκεν ὁ Τιρίβαζος, ἧκε δ᾽ ὁ υἱὸς αὐτοῦ, τοὺς Καδουσίους ἄγοντες, ἐγένοντο δὲ σπονδαὶ πρὸς ἀμφοτέρους καὶ εἰρήνη, μέγας ὢν ὁ Τιρίβαζος ἤδη καὶ λαμπρὸς ἀνεζεύγνυε μετὰ τοῦ βασιλέως.

Plutarch is toying in this section with the theme of rule of two against the rule of one. Before the Cadusian Campaign, Plutarch reports that Artaxerxes fails against Egypt, because the two separate commanders (Pharnabazus and Iphicrates) quarrel with each other (below). Next we have the two Cadusian kings. From a literary perspective, these two are in fact one, because they behave the same way and have the same fate (they even arrive at the same time to the king's camp: *Art.* 24.9). Each of them acts out of his own interest, and in this they resemble the previous pair, but nevertheless they are able to achieve a peace treaty. Next in appearance are Tiribazus and his son. Artistically, these are one who is actually two, since the son of Tiribazus is essentially his literary extension: he does not have his own personality (let alone a name, at this point) and he acts according to his father's plan; at the end, it is Tiribazus who receives the award (*Art.* 24.9). The coordination of these latter two lends them success.

It would seem that the key to understanding the metamorphosis in the king's fate in the two parts of *Art.* 24 lies in the component of φιλοτιμία (pursuit of honour or glory).[34] In the first segment it worked against him: the conflict of Pharnabazus and Iphicrates undermines the campaign against Egypt; the king, who tries to subdue the Cadusians himself, does not succeed and suffers hardship. Heading the expedition alone at the beginning (αὐτὸς ἐστράτευσε:

---

[33] Cf. Arr. *Anab.* 3.19.3: Darius III demands the Cadusians (and the Sacians) to provide him troops on the basis of a previous agreement. See Syme (1988a: 140), Briant (2002a: 767, 1036).

[34] See Duff (1999: 83–7).

24.2), Artaxerxes fails, but with the cooperation of Tiribazus he triumphs; it is the fact that he leads his army alone once more at the end (αὐτὸς ἐβάδιζε: 24.10) which may foretell us something about the next scene and foreshadow his following moral failure. In the second part, the honour-seeking characteristic works in favour of the king: Tiribazus, who wants to be relieved from a lowly status, succeeds, because of this trait, in saving the king and the army. The rivalry between the Cadusian kings leads them to a position in which they cannot cooperate with each other, and they are forced to arrive at an alliance with Artaxerxes.

Before Tiribazus' success, he is reported to be delayed in returning (24.8), a situation which causes suspicions to rise and slanders against him to be uttered before the king (ὑποψίαι καὶ διαβολαὶ κατὰ τοῦ Τιριβάζου τῷ Ἀρτοξέρξῃ προσέπιπτον). Artaxerxes himself loses confidence in his courtier and repents placing trust on him. It would appear that the king is especially concerned about his own name, since Artaxerxes regrets having provided the opportunity for his rivals to malign him. One could note that the suspicion Artaxerxes feels towards Tiribazus anticipates *Art.* 25, when the king is worried about his name and executes many of his commanders.

This is one connecting thread between the end of *Art.* 24 and the beginning of *Art.* 25. Another is the theme of the relations between the king and his soldiers (24.10–25.3). At the end of *Art.* 24, Artaxerxes appears so humble that he is ready to step down from his horse and walk on foot (24.10, essentially likening himself to a beast of burden),[35] marching as many as 200 stades daily on hilly roads.[36] His behaviour is ostensibly praised by Plutarch, since 'cowardice and softness (δειλίαν καὶ τήν μαλακίαν) are not the offspring of luxury' but of a 'base and ignoble nature (μοχθηρᾶς φύσεωςκαὶ ἀγεννοῦς)'. This may imply the king's ability to tolerate adversities and to prove a degree of self-discipline. Yet the description can be understood in another manner, and may be seen as completely sarcastic. The picture evidently suggests that Artaxerxes freely allows emotions such as vanity to control him because of his innate nature. This is visible in the reference to the twelve thousand talents' value of ornaments which he insists on wearing during his march (24.10: οὔτε γὰρ χρυσὸς οὔτε κάνδυς οὔθ'

---

[35] See Almagor (2014a: 8).
[36] This conduct evokes the belief of 'Cyrus' and his father that a good commander should encourage his soldiers with enthusiasm (Xen. *Cyr.* 1.6.19).

ὁ τῶν μυρίων καὶ δισχιλίων ταλάντων περικείμενος ἀεὶ τῷ βασιλέως
σώματι κόσμος ἐκεῖνον ἀπεκώλυε πονεῖν).³⁷

The next section begins with a memorable scene in the immediate
aftermath of the Cadusian Campaign (*Art.* 25.1–2):

> After he came down to a royal station, which had wonderful parks magnifi-
> cently arranged, in a land which was without trees and barren all around;
> because it was cold, he permitted his soldiers to chop the trees of the park
> and gather wood, and not to spare the pine or cypress. When they hesitated
> and refrained because of the great beauty and size [of the trees], he took an
> axe himself and chopped down the largest and most beautiful tree. After this
> they gathered wood, making many fires, and passed the night in ease.
>
> Ἐπεὶ δ᾿ εἰς σταθμὸν κατέβη βασιλικόν, παραδείσους ἔχοντα θαυμαστοὺς καὶ
> κεκοσμημένους διαπρεπῶς ἐν τῷ πέριξ ἀδένδρῳ καὶ ψιλῷ χωρίῳ, κρύους ὄντος
> ἐπέτρεψε τοῖς στρατιώταις ἐκ τοῦ παραδείσου ξυλίζεσθαι τὰ δένδρα κόπτοντας,
> μήτε πεύκης μήτε κυπαρίττου φειδομένους. (2) Ὀκνούντων δὲ καὶ φειδομένων διὰ
> τὰ κάλλη καὶ τὰ μεγέθη, λαβὼν πέλεκυν αὐτὸς ὅπερ ἦν μέγιστον καὶ κάλλιστον
> τῶν φυτῶν ἔκοψεν. Ἐκ δὲ τούτου ξυλιζόμενοι καὶ πολλὰ πυρὰ ποιοῦντες εὐμαρῶς
> ἐνυκτέρευσαν.

Some scholars perceive in the two sections a positive presentation
of Artaxerxes as moderate, brave and strong.³⁸ Yet this is probably not how Plutarch sees it. The biographer brings the image of
cutting plants/trees before that of killing people. This combination
evokes the memory of the way Thrasybulus the tyrant of Miletus
acts before the messenger from Periander the tyrant of Corinth (Hdt.
5.92). The tyrant cuts all the tallest ears (τῶν ἀσταχύων ὑπερέχοντα,
κολούων δὲ ἔρριπτε) in a wheat field, so that he destroys 'the most
supreme and prominent part of the harvest' (τοῦ ληΐου τὸ κάλλιστόν
τε καὶ βαθύτατον διέφθειρε). Whereas the messenger retorts that
Thrasybulos is destroying his own property, Periander understands
the metaphor well: he must destroy the prominent ones in the city.
Plutarch employs the same idea with some verbal echoes (κάλλιστον).
Immediately afterwards, Plutarch essentially terms the king a tyrant
(*Art.* 25.4: τυραννίσιν).

Plutarch makes *Art.* 25 a crucial part of the biography in terms
of the king's character by highlighting its violent aspect through
the garden imagery. In the first scene, the king is thoughtful of his
troops when he permits them to cut trees for timber, but in the
second, Artaxerxes suddenly slays numerous men in rage and out of
concern for his name, apparently stemming from the alleged fiasco

---

³⁷ Cf. Mossman (2010: 157), who claims 'environment and nurture, rather than nature,
have made of Artaxerxes what he is'.
³⁸ See Smith (1881: 11), Marasco (1994: 658), Briant (2002a: 237, 997).

of the campaign (25.3). The pictures that are juxtaposed here will cohere later on. In an anticipation of *Art.* 29, where Artaxerxes kills his own son Darius, the king now cuts down his own tree. Note that the axe anticipates the dagger (29.11) and the soldiers' hesitancy anticipates that of the executioner (29.9). In a digression, Plutarch elucidates the condition of despots in two circumstances. His assertion is that when anxiety (ἡ δειλία) directs tyrants, it is the most lethal (φονικώτατον), but once they are sporadically directed by their self-assurance (ἡ θαρραλεότης) they are gentle and unsuspecting (ἵλεων δὲ καὶ πρᾶον καὶ ἀνύποπτον).

Seemingly, Plutarch (*Art.* 24.1–2) brings the Cadusian Campaign after another campaign, which fails:

> He [the king] was unsuccessful in the war which Pharnabazus and Iphicrates waged for him against Egypt, because of their conflicts; against the Cadusians, then, he made an expedition himself, with three hundred thousand footmen and ten thousand horses.
> Πόλεμον δὲ πρὸς μὲν Αἰγυπτίους διὰ Φαρναβάζου καὶ Ἰφικράτους ἐξενεγκὼν ἀπέτυχε, στασιασάντων ἐκείνων. Ἐπὶ δὲ Καδουσίους αὐτὸς ἐστράτευσε τριάκοντα μυριάσι πεζῶν καὶ μυρίοις ἱππεῦσιν.

The sequence as presented by Plutarch is fairly simple: first, the campaign against rebellious Egypt, which is a complete failure, and then (note the particle δὲ) the expedition against the Cadusians, on which the biographer dwells in the rest of *Art.* 24. This very sequence of events appears also in a Latin source. It appears as the *prologus* (summary) of book 10 of Pompeius Trogus' lost *Philippica*:

> In the tenth volume Persian affairs are contained. How Artaxerxes Mnemon concluded peace with Evagoras, the Cypriot king, **and made arrangements for his war with Egypt in the city of Acre; [how he was] himself defeated among the Cadusians,** and [how] he oppressed his high officials who revolted in Asia, firstly Datames, satrap of Paphlagonia. The origin of the Paphlagonians is mentioned; then [punishment of] Ariobarzanes, satrap of the Hellespont; then, in Syria, [punishment of] Orontes, the satrap of Armenia. After all these were defeated, he [Artaxerxes] perished and was succeeded by his son, Ochus . . .
> *Decimo volumine continentur Persicae res. Ut Artaxerxes Mnemon pacifica-tus cum Evagora rege Cyprio* **bellum Aegyptium in urbe Ace conpararit, ipse in Cadusis victus,** *defectores in Asia purpuratos suos persecutus, primum Dotamen praefectum <Paphlagoniae>. Paphlagonon origo repetita: deinde praefectum Hellesponti Ariobarzanen, deinde in Syria praefectum Armeniae Oronten, omnibusque victis decesserit filio successore Ocho. . .*
> Paphlagoniae add. Bongars, Graevius

The beginning and end of the Egyptian Expedition can be determined by the careers of two Athenians: Chabrias and Iphicrates. Pharnabazus compelled Persia's ally, Athens, into calling back from

Egypt the mercenary-commander Chabrias and sending a different one to help the Achaemenid campaign there.[39] Chabrias was recalled and Iphicrates was sent to aid the Persians.[40] Diodorus (15.29.2–3) places both requests under the same year, 377/6 BCE, and the beginning of the Egyptian War in the summer of 374/3 BCE ('after many years [of preparation]': ἔτη δὲ πλείω).[41] Correspondingly, some scholars date the war to 374,[42] while others more convincingly place it in 373 BCE;[43] there are those who even opt for 372.[44] We gather from Diodorus (15.43) that the Egyptian Campaign proved a disaster mainly because of disputes between the Persian and Greek commanders, a point insinuated by Plutarch's arrangement. The Persian army retreated from Egypt, evidently to Acre. Pharnabazus sent messengers to Athens and blamed Iphicrates for the blunder. The Athenians replied that if they found fault with Iphicrates, they would punish him as he deserved, but a short time later (μετ' ὀλίγον χρόνον: 15.43.6) they appointed him as commander of the navy. In 373 BCE, we find Iphicrates defending the island of Corcyra against Sparta, deposing another Athenian, Timotheus, from the high command (Xen. *Hell.* 6.2.13; Diod. 15.47.7).[45] So the end of the Egyptian War would be 373 or 372 BCE at the latest. This should give us the upper limit for the Cadusian Campaign, if we follow the ostensible sequence in Plutarch and Trogus.

The chronology of the Egyptian Campaign seems thus to be firmly established.[46] Correspondingly, the scholar Robartus van der Spek (1998) suggests considering another piece of evidence as relevant for the event described in the Greek sources as the Cadusian War of Artaxerxes II. This is a Babylonian astronomical diary dated to the

[39] Cf. Nepos, *Chab.* 3.1. Chabrias helped Nectanebo I (Nakhtenebef, νεκτανεβώ, νεκτανέβης, νεκτάνεβις; founder of the last native dynasty, the 30th) ascend to the throne, according to Nepos, *Chab.* 2.1 (*Nectenebin adiutum profectus regnum ei constituit*), an event which occurred in 380 BCE. Cf. Dem. 20.76. For the year of Nectanebo's ascent to the throne see Traunecker (1979: 435–6).

[40] Cf. Nepos *Iph.* 2.4. Chabrias is reported to have engaged in the winter of 380/79 BCE on the Athenian border confronting the king of Sparta, Cleombrotus (Xen. *Hell.* 5.4.14). See Kirschner (1899: 2018). He was presumably selected as a *Strategos* in the spring of 379 BCE. See Beloch (1923: 3.2.229–30), Stylianou (1998: 259–30).

[41] This date cannot be correct for Chabrias. Furthermore, the beginning of Iphicrates' assistance to Persia is usually put in the year 379 BCE (see Hornblower, 1994: 83). See Ruzicka (2012: 100–6).

[42] See Parke (1933: 105–6).

[43] See Grote (1884: 9.348–91), Beloch (1923: 3.1.211–12), Bengtson (1969: 348), Gray (1980: 314–15), van der Spek (1998: 251–2), and Stylianou (1998: 337–8). See Ruzicka (2012: 114).

[44] See Marshall (1905: 64–71), Cawkwell (1963), Hammond (1959: 490–1).

[45] See Cary (1933: 77), Gray (1980: 316), Ruzicka (2012: 259 n. 18).

[46] For the campaign, see Ruzicka (2012: 114–21).

year 369 BCE (Sacks and Hunger, 1988: 369) which also describes an expedition against an eastern country (the land of Razaundu):

> Month XII (= 14 March – 12 April), 35 regnal year, Artaxerxes II (April 369 BCE)
> Rev. 8'. [The King] mustered his [troop]s for battle in the land of Razaundu
> Rev. 9'. [. . .]. . . from the end (of?) a far journey
> Rev. 10'. [. . .]. . . to
> Rev. 8'. [LUGAL ERIN.] MEŠ – *šú id-ke-e-ma ana şal-tu ina* KUR *Ra-za-un-du*
> Rev. 9'. [. . .] |x|-*nu-uḫ* TA TIL *ur-ḫu* SÙD-*tú*
> Rev. 10'. [. . .] |x| *nu* |xxx| *a-na*
> Rev. 11'. [. . .] |xx|

Van der Spek (1998: 252) argues that Razaundu is a location somewhere between Lake Urmia and the Caspian, identified as the Zaranda land, an Urartian district, known from the inscriptions of Sargon II.[47] Van der Spek links the expedition mentioned in the diary to Artaxerxes II's war against the Cadusians. Since the Egyptian War was in 373 BCE, this would certainty seem like the Cadusian Campaign that followed it. Apparently, we have a perfect match, and van der Spek's suggestion of identifying the event in the Babylonian diary with the Cadusian Campaign might be plausible. The proposal is accepted by many a scholar, presumably happy to discover an external corroboration of Greek literary texts.[48]

Yet there are some serious problems with this suggestion.[49] Firstly, Diodorus clearly places the Cadusian War *before* the Egyptian Campaign. He dates the Cadusian Expedition to the year 385/4 BCE (15.8.5, 15.10.1), and afterwards mentions the attempt to take Egypt in 374/3 BCE (15.41–3).

Secondly, and more devastating to this argument, the biographer Cornelius Nepos presents evidence that undermines it. In the biography of the satrap Datames, one of the satraps of Artaxerxes II, Nepos has the following two passages:

> Datames, performing military duty, first showed what sort of man he was **in the war which the king waged against the Cadusians;** for after several

---

[47] The so-called 'Letter to Asshur', 714 BCE, see Luckenbill (1926: 2.84). Stolper (1994: 239) identified the latter place as a Median city named Rhazounda (found in Ptolemy 6.2.12, east of Ecbatana). See Zadok (1997: 7/B.1), who suggests the name comes from Iranian *Raza-vant(a)*, 'provided with vines, vineyards'. See also Kuhrt (2007: 2.274).

[48] Briant (2001: 93) is one of the scholars who accept this proposal. Cf. Briant (2002a: 614).

[49] See Kuhrt (2007: 400, no. 67 n. 2), who is opposed to the very possibility of dating this campaign. Cf. Binder (2008: 317).

thousands of the king's men died, his action was of great benefit. It came to pass there, **that in this war Camissares died, so that he inherited his father's province.**
Datames, militare munus fungens, primum, qualis esset, aperuit in bello, quod rex adversus Cadusios gessit. Namque hic multis milibus regiorum interfectis magni fuit eius opera. Quo factum est, cum in eo bello cecidisset Camisares, ut paterna ei traderetur provincia (Dat. 1.2).

And

And thus, after giving splendid presents to Datames, he [the king] sent him **to the army which was then amassing, under the leadership of Pharnabazus and Tithraustes, for the Egyptian War,** and ordered that his authority should be equal to them. But later on when the king recalled Pharnabazus, the supreme command was given to him.
Itaque magnifice Datamen donatum ad exercitum misit, qui tum contrahebatur duce Pharnabazo et Tithrauste ad bellum Aegyptium, parique eum atque illos imperio esse iussit. Postea vero quam Pharnabazum rex revocavit, illi summa imperii tradita est (Dat. 3.5).

According to Nepos, first Datames' father is said to have died in the war against the Cadusians, and then Datames is made a satrap. Only later is Datames sent to prepare the expedition against Egypt. Preparations for an Egyptian campign (presumably in the 370s or 360s) are mentioned also in *Dat.* 4.1, 5.3.[50] Nepos and Diodorus, therefore, have the same order of events, which is the complete opposite to that of Plutarch and Trogus, namely, first the Cadusian War and then the Egyptian one. Van der Spek is aware of the difficulty, yet dismisses it in a footnote (1998: 249 n. 10): 'Nepos seems to have been mistaken, as he was more often than not.' It would appear that this explanation is not entirely convincing. It is not clear what the nature of Nepos' mistake was, nor how it was made. We should, I believe, accept the suggestion of Nicholas Sekunda (1988: 35) that in the biography of Datames, Nepos' longest surviving work, the biographer seems to be maintaining the chronological order of his source. Moreover, Nepos is not alone in making this mistake, as Diodorus seems to be independently following the same sequence of events.

Other scholars acknowledge the difficulty, yet propose to solve it in a manner that problematises matters even further. They suggest the occurrence of *two* Cadusian Campaigns, one before the Egyptian War and one after it, so that some of our sources (Nepos or Diodorus) speak about one early expedition and some (Plutarch or Trogus)

---

[50] Cf. Sekunda (1988: 41–2).

report a later one.[51] All our ancient sources, however, mention only *one* campaign led by Artaxerxes II;[52] hence, this suggestion does not have a high degree of probability. Furthermore, if it implies that both campaigns were described by the same ancient source, such a hypothesis is not very plausible. It is highly unlikely that there should be two descriptions of major military operations of the same Persian king in the same circumstances against the same group elaborated by the same writer. This certainly would weaken the dramatic and literary effect of each. With regard to this suggestion, we should completely agree with van der Spek (1998: 249), according to which it is a 'dubious procedure to create two Cadusian Wars, where the sources know of only one'. Furthermore, there is a close correspondence between these Persian stories in Plutarch, Trogus and Diodorus. In particular, both Diodorus and Plutarch appear to give an important position to the courtier Tiribazus in their account of the Cadusian Campaign. This is a strong argument in favour of the assumption that it is the same event rather than two separate Cadusian Campaigns.

Unless there are other interpretations or other compelling evidence, we should see the sequence of events as Nepos and Diodorus portray it: first the Cadusian War and then the Egyptian one. It would appear that all that van der Spek has shown is that Persia waged a war in the region between the Caspian Sea and Lake Urmia in the year 369 BCE, but that is probably not the expedition described in the ancient literature as 'Artaxerxes' Cadusian Campaign'.

If the foregoing assumption is correct, and the north-eastern war chronologically preceded the south-western skirmish in Egypt, the fact that Plutarch and Trogus both inverted the order of events is of great significance.[53] The existence of the same sequence of events in two authors, even though this order is not chronological, is singular and remarkable, and one has to conclude that such an arrangement of the material was already found in the common source used by Plutarch and Trogus.

---

[51] See Sekunda (1988: 38–9), Stylianou (1998: 153, 183), Briant (2001: 93; 2002a: 650), supposing that there was one expedition opposing the Cadusians in the 380s BCE (Stylianou: 382–380 BCE), but that in addition there was another after the year 373 BCE (according to the sequence of events of Plutarch). Before these scholars, Lachmann (1854: 2.351, 356) made a similar proposal. Cf. the error of Duff in Duff and Scott-Kilvert (2012: 5, 544): 'we know ... of several campaigns against the Cadusii'.

[52] Cf. Smith (1881: 22).

[53] Marasco (1994: 670) ascribes a chronological confusion ('confuse ... cronologico') to Plutarch, who places the Cadusian Campaign after the Egyptian one. However, this 'confusion' did not originate with Plutarch, but with his source. Similarly mistaken is Duff (2012: 7): 'Plutarch is arranging his material thematically.'

Let us examine the account of Diodorus. This author subsumes under a single year (385/4 BCE) all the following episodes:

(1) **The last phase of the war in Cyprus,** which Artaxerxes wages against Evagoras I. The king of Salamis negotiates with Artaxerxes the terms of peace. Tiribazus, the Great King's envoy, is presented in these negotiations as commanding the entire forces (ὁ δὲ Τιρίβαζος τῶν ὅλων ἔχων τὴν ἡγεμονίαν). The talks eventually fail because Evagoras does not agree to the clause by which he is to obey the Persian king as a slave would his master (ὡς δοῦλος δεσπότῃ).[54]

(2) **Orontes and Tiribazus.** After this diplomatic fiasco, Diodorus includes the following story, in which another Persian noble, Orontes, who is the deputy commander of the forces of the king in Cyprus (Ὀρόντης ὁ ἕτερος στρατηγός), envious of Tiribazus' high position, falsely accuses the latter before the king and lays charges of treason against him. Orontes accuses Tiribazus of collaborating with Evagoras (συλλαλεῖ περὶ κοινοπραγίας) and being an ally of the Spartans (πρὸς Λακεδαιμονίους συντίθεται συμμαχίαν ἰδίᾳ). Tiribazus is immediately arrested and sent to Persia.[55]

(3) **Cadusian War.** Diodorus intervenes and claims that this trial was postponed because of the campaign against the Cadusians.

(4) **Settlement in Cyprus.** In the meantime, the Cypriot front is settled, and a peace agreement is finally concluded between Evagoras and Orontes, who succeeds Tiribazus as commander of the forces.

(5) **Tiribazus' trial and acquittal.** At last, after the expedition against the Cadusians, Tiribazus is brought to trial. He is acquitted (mainly because of the favours he did to the king in the past: cf. Hdt. 1.137) and receives many honours; Orontes, who is found to have falsely libelled Tiribazus, is demoted and humiliated, and is removed from the circle of the king's friends (15.11.2).[56]

This picture is wrong for several reasons. Firstly, all these events cannot occur during one year. Diodorus himself (15.9.2) gives a period of ten years for the Cypriot War.[57] He even dates the beginning

---

[54] Cf. Spyridakis (1935: 66), Stylianou (1998: 181).
[55] Cf. Osborne (1973: 528–36).
[56] Cf. Osborne (1973: 537).
[57] See Shrimpton (1991b: 10), Tuplin (1996: 12). This information may not come from any source, but simply from his memory of Isocrates, *Evag.* 64: Εὐαγόρα δὲ πολεμήσας ἔτη δέκα). See Ruzicka (2012: 251 n. 10).

of the military operations in the war to 391/0 BCE (14.98.2–3).[58] Yet, in this portrayal, he packs all its occurrences into one year. If the war continued for ten years, placing its end in 385/4 is obvioiusly an error.[59] Secondly, if we combine the description in Diodorus with that of Plutarch, the picture does not make any sense. Yet it is the same event, as one may plausibly assume, if only because of the mention of Tiribazus as an important figure in both accounts. According to what Diodorus says, the Cadusian War took place between the negotiations in Cyprus and the trial of Tiribazus. However, if Tiribazus was suspected of treason and was imprisoned, is it conceivable that he would be taken to a military expedition and win the trust of the king in a private and secret mission, as Plutarch relates in the story? Although some scholars do not find it odd,[60] the question still remains: how could Tiribazus have enjoyed this freedom of action? As Sekunda aptly asserts (1988: 39):

> It is hard to see how a man awaiting trial on charges of treason could persuade the King that sending him and his son away to the rebel Cadusian kings was a good idea.

It would seem more probable that a man charged with high treason would be brought to justice rather than given any diplomatic mission in a military campaign. Moreover, Plutarch claims that Tiribazus obtains honour immediately after the campaign as a reward for the success of his ruse. Yet Diodorus asserts that Tiribazus only won respect after his acquittal. Lastly, Plutarch does not mention the trial, and does not have Tiribazus incarcerated as does Diodorus in his account (15.8.5: κατὰ μὲν τὸ παρὸν παρεδόθη εἰς φυλακήν).[61]

One option would be to consider the incompatibility of Plutarch's description with that of Diodorus as evidence that the same historical event was told by two different authors, and that Plutarch and Diodorus essentially employed different sources.[62] A more probable possibility would be to find here two different readings of ultimately

---

[58] See Judeich (1892: 120–1), Swoboda (1907: 825–6), Beloch (1923: 3.2.226), Olmstead (1948: 390), Costa (1974: 53), Cawkwell (1976: 274), Tuplin (1983: 178–82), Stylianou (1998: 143, 146–7). For other views, see Tuplin (1983: 178 n. 46). The war seems to have ended in 380 BCE: Theop. FGrH 115 F 103.10–11.

[59] See Ruzicka (1999: 27 n. 11). For various views on the dating of the main events in the Cypriot War, see Tuplin (1983), Shrimpton (1991b), van der Spek (1998: 240–51), Stylianou (1998: 143–54).

[60] See Shrimpton (1991b: 17), who assumes that Tiribazus in Plutarch's version proves that he was 'a man anxious to prove his loyalty and he was clearly under suspicion', cf. Stevenson (1997: 66).

[61] Stevenson (1997: 31) errs with regard to the agreement between the two classical sources as to Tiribazus' status.

[62] Cf. Binder (2008: 319–20).

the same story, taken from the same original source. In order to see this, and to comment on Plutarch's reading of the account, let us focus on the interpretation of Diodorus.

The fact that Diodorus includes so many diverse events in the same year 385/4 indicates that in all these episodes he is most likely following the same source. Presumably reading his source too closely, Diodorus does not attempt to divide up the description into separate sections matching discrete years (385/4 to 381/0); instead, he imparts it as a single unit. Diodorus connects the Cadusian Campaign and the Cypriot War through the trial of Tiribazus. It would make perfect sense to assume that he combines all these episodes together since Tiribazus was the hero and central figure of all these segments in the original version he was reading; we indeed know (from Plutarch's version) that Tiribazus was a prominent figure in his source's description of the Cadusian Campaign. The place in which Diodorus puts the whole Cadusian affair is completely wrong. We saw that it does not make sense to assume that just prior to his trial Tiribazus would have been taken on a military expedition and then employed on a secret mission. How could Diodorus have made such a serious blunder?

The answer has to do with the arrangement of the events in the original account and the reversal of the chronological sequence observed above in the works of Plutarch and Trogus. It is proposed here that the order of the Egyptian Campaign and the Cadusian affair as presented in the work read by Plutarch, Trogus, Nepos and Diodorus was not chronological but *thematic*. Only this unique arrangement, setting forth items according to topics rather than presenting events according to the temporal order of their actual occurrence, could explain Diodorus' failed attempt to place the event in its proper chronological place. Diodorus' source appears to have disregarded chronology, so that the expedition against the Cadusians was described in a manner which did not enable the reader to know the relationship of that event to others, i.e., it was presented in a way which was divorced from its context. Diodorus had to fathom the relationship of one event to others simply on the basis of reading the descriptions. Diodorus' sequence of events regarding the Cadusian Campaign, the Cypriot War and Tiribazus' trial seems to be based solely on the authority of his own interpretation, without any explicit statement to this effect in his source.[63]

Diodorus presumably placed the Cadusian Campaign at the

---

[63] On Diodorus as creating a historical tradition, see Stronk (2010: 64; 2017: 8, 11, 43).

moment he did (before Tiribazus' trial) in order to solve a pressing problem with which he was confronted in the texts he read. It may be hypothesised that something in the text compelled him to do so, and one could guess that this was the fact that the campaign was mentioned in the defence speech of Tiribazus during his trial. In Diodorus' account of the legal procedure (15.10.1–4), the Persian courtier defends himself by stating that he has served the king in the past, but the only incident by which he is explicitly made to substantiate this claim is that he once saved the monarch in a hunt. It is possible that there were other details in Diodorus' source which he did not include.[64] It would appear that what was deleted is hinted at in these words (15.10.4): 'in wars they say that he outshone in courage, and in advice he was so successful that when the king followed his guidance he was never wrong' (ἔν τε τοῖς πολέμοις ἀνδρείᾳ διενεγκεῖν φασὶν αὐτὸν καὶ κατὰ τὰς συμβουλὰς οὕτως εὐστοχεῖν, ὥστε τὸν βασιλέα χρώμενον ταῖς ἐκείνου παραγγελίαις μηδέποτε διαμαρτεῖν). If this is true, and in his defence Tiribazus mentioned his aid to the king during the war against the Cadusians,[65] we can perfectly understand why Diodorus decided to date the campaign before the trial (but at a totally erroneous point).

Diodorus' reasons for dating the campaign against the Cadusians are thus wrong because of the impossible situation in which Tiribazus would be. The date proposed by some scholars, i.e., around 380 BCE (between the Cypriot War and Tiribazus' trial) in an effort to reconcile Diodorus and Plutarch, is also erroneous.[66] The Cadusian War occurred after 387/6 BCE, when Tiribazus was involved in diplomatic actions to execute 'the King's Peace' in Greece.[67] One would assume that a plausible order would be that the Cadusian War came before Tiribazus' diplomatic efforts in Cyprus, and before the false charges against him, which immediately led to his arrest, trial and acquittal. Tiribazus began talks with Evagoras after the Battle of Citium, which Diodorus places as occurring in 386/5 BCE (15.3.6).

---

[64] Cf. Sekunda (1988: 39) and Ruzicka (1999: 36–7 nn. 26, 27). Just as Diodorus did not bring the details of the Cadusian Campaign, it is possible that he chose not to go into detail regarding the trial of Tiribazus.

[65] Indeed, see Stevenson (1987: 32), who claims that Tiribazus would have been more convincing had he mentioned his activities in the Cadusian Campaign.

[66] The year 380 BCE for the Cadusian Campaign was suggested by Meyer (1902: 5.316), Meloni (1950: 336–7), Syme (1988a: 139), Manfredi, Orsi and Antelami (1987: 300–1), Stevenson (1997: 96) and Ruzicka (1999: 36 n. 26: 381/0). Shrimpton (1991b: 2, 17) suggests 384/3.

[67] It appears that Tiribazus' involvement in this arrangement ended in 387, after the convening of the conference in Sardis in the autumn and the presentation of his terms to the Greek delegates (Xen. *Hell.* 5.1.30–1). In another conference, in Sparta, in the year 386, there were only Greeks. See Martin (1944: 19–20; 1949: 137).

Regardless of the date of the naval battle, it may be the case that Tiribazus was only present during the last phase of the Cypriot War, and after his role in establishing the King's Peace he was used elsewhere, perhaps pursuing diplomatic activity in the north-eastern front, against the Cadusians. Hence, the date of the Cadusian War could also be around 386/5 BCE.[68]

The settlement in Cyprus must precede the outcome of Tiribazus' trial and Orontes' fall. If the Cyprus affair ended in 381/0 BCE, a verdict in Tiribazus' trial was soon to follow. Although he was acquitted and received his honours back, Tiribazus' services were probably never used in delicate diplomatic negotiations again. The king was presumably still distrustful of this courtier (and justly so, as would eventually become apparent). Tiribazus' eventual involvement in a rebellion against the king for which he was probably executed (the story found in Plutarch's *Artaxerxes* 28–9), may be explained by this falling from grace. While some scholars denigrate Tiribazus' trial as an affair without any historical value,[69] its historiographic importance is immeasurable. The trial of the Persian noble and Diodorus' interpretation of it perhaps lead us closer to the character and content of the work consulted by Plutarch.

As mentioned above, the king is said to have conducted mass executions of his chieftains (25.3: καὶ πολλοὺς μὲν ἀνῄρει δι' ὀργήν, πλείονας δὲ φοβούμενος) because of the failure of his campaign. This picture is not known from any other source. Quite the contrary: the other sources do not relate that Artaxerxes displayed any extraordinary cruelty at this stage. Furthermore, the fact that Diodorus places Tiribazus' trial immediately after the campaign against the Cadusians shows that he himself is not aware of any portrayal of the king executing many without a trial. Contrary to Plutarch, who speaks of misfortune (ἀτυχία), the campaign does not seem to have been a failure. The king achieves what he desires, and from that perspective, the campaign is successful. Among the classical works, the only statement which summarises the events as a failure is that of Trogus, seen above (*Prol.* 10: *Ipse in Cadusis victus*); in other works, the king emerges victorious.[70]

---

[68] See Appendix I.

[69] See Stevenson (1997: 31–2, 34). Van der Spek (1998: 243) calls it 'a kind of novelistic digression'.

[70] As well noted by van der Spek (1998: 256 n. 15), the editions of Justin prior to the nineteenth century read *victor* and not *victus*. This can be clearly seen in the editions of Bongars (1581) and Graevius (1683). Presumably the change was influenced by the descriptions of Herodotus regarding Darius and the Scythians (cf. 4.123–42) or of Plutarch's *Artaxerxes* 25. Cf. Stevenson (1997: 96) and Briant (2002a: 732).

Some scholars accept this image of mass executions as true.[71] The event, however, probably did not occur.[72] Plutarch's πολλοὺς ἀνῄρει (25.3) is surely an overt hyperbole. Where did this image come from? As noted above, when the accounts of Plutarch and Trogus are compared, a fascinating correspondence between *Art.* 26–30, 24 and Justin 10 (with Trogus' *Prologus* 10) is revealed. A continuation of this comparison shows that at this point, the 'common source' should have described the stories of the rebellious satraps, or as Trogus has it, *Defectores in Asia purpuratos suos persecutus* (*Prol.* 10, 'he oppressed his high officials who revolted in Asia'). The stories mentioned as following are those of Datames (*Dotames*), Ariobarzanes and Orontes, all 'oppressed' by Artaxerxes. These segments are detailed by Diodorus (15.90.1–93.6).

Nepos describes the life and death of one satrap, Datames. A depiction of Datames' insurrection was present in the original account of Trogus as 'the first' (*Prol.* 10: *primum*), which implies that Datames' story was the first among the passages of the rebellious satraps to be recounted.[73] Diodorus, apparently dependent on the same source, relates the story of Datames (15.91.2–7) among the disobedient satraps. It is interesting that of this group of persons (including Ariobarzanes satrap of Phrygia, Mausolus satrap of Caria, Orontes satrap of Mysia and Autophradates satrap of Lydia), Diodorus tells at length only the story of Datames, and this satrap happens to be the only one to whom Nepos devotes a biography; he is the only one among these satraps whom Polyaenus mentions (7.29), assigning him seven different stratagems. It would be a plausible deduction to assume that in the so-called 'common source' there was a separate section devoted to Datames.

The events are collected together in the research literature under the erroneous name of 'The Great Satraps' Revolt', based on the false impression received from Diodorus' picture.[74] Modern scholars add their own hypotheses, which embellish these stories even further. Some maintain that there was a widespread and organised revolt by the satraps of Asia Minor in the 370s and 360s BCE;[75] Stevenson

---

[71] See Moysey (1992: 160), who writes that 'The fact that Artaxerxes executed important courtiers need not be doubted.'

[72] Cf. Manfredini, Orsi and Antelami (1987: 302).

[73] Cf. Sekunda (1988: 44–5).

[74] Diodorus seems to have added the detail about the revolt of the nations on his own (οἱ τὴν παράλιον οἰκοῦντες τῆς Ἀσίας ἀπέστησαν ἀπὸ Περσῶν: 15.90.1, cf. 15.90.3: πάντες οἱ παραθαλάσσιοι). Cf. Hornblower (1994: 86).

[75] See, especially, Judeich (1892: 190–209); Beloch (1923: 3.2.254–7) and Meloni (1951). Osborne (1973: 517 n.13, 540 n.119), regarding the numismatic evidence. See Hornblower

(1997: 107–10) even attributes an improbable motive to the revolt: the demand to appoint Darius as the heir apparent. The imagination of modern scholars combines the accounts of Diodorus and Plutarch to create formidable pictures. Thus, Robert Moysey (1992: 159–61) sees the executions mentioned by Plutarch as the *reason* for the revolt of the satraps. In accordance with his analysis, it was after the Cadusian Campaign that the king looked for scapegoats, whom he punished unjustly, but understandably.[76] As a result, the satraps suspected him and sought to be released from their subordinate, dangerous and lethal ties. Sekunda (1988: 43, 51) makes a similar proposal, whereby Artaxerxes tried to strengthen his position by these purges, which brought about the revolts of Datames and Ariobarzanes. This depiction, however, is not coherent: on the one hand, the satraps are said to be afraid of the strong king; on the other hand, the king is portrayed as feeble, and the weakness of the central government, made worse by the power struggle for succession, drives the satraps to attempt to exploit the situation and implement their desires.[77] The second picture perhaps has more probability, following a pattern known from earlier cases in Achaemenid history of rebellions at the periods of changes of rulers.[78]

Michael Weiskopf (1989) is correct in maintaining that there was no such large-scale and prepared revolt, as one might conclude from reading Diodorus, but only local unrest in the western part of the empire, which never threatened the monarch himself.[79] The executions mentioned by Plutarch were not the reason for the 'revolt of the satraps'. In fact, they are possibly *the very same* occurrences. It would seem that both Plutarch and Diodorus are referring to the identical stories, which they present as one major significant happening. The incidents were not presented chronologically by 'the common source', as we can learn from Trogus' sequence.[80] That being the case, it is difficult for us to date the events or to create any causal link between them. Diodorus, Trogus and Plutarch interpreted them in different ways. Once again we note the probable situation

---

(1982: 170–82, 1994: 84–7), who even divides it into four periods, and believes that at its peak it involved a planned pincer movement against the king by Datames, Orontes and Tachos. On Datames, see Sekunda (1988). See the bibliography found in Briant (2001: 93–5; 2002a: 993–8). See also Bing (1998), van der Spek (1998: 253–5). Cf. Binder (2008: 330–1).

[76] '[U]nderstandable ... warranted action' (160), which is justified to prevent the risk of Artaxerxes' own overthrow.

[77] Sekunda (1988: 51): he was a 'weak but well-intentioned monarch'.

[78] See, for example, DB 1.72–81; 2.5–8, 2.13–17, 2.78–91, 3.21–8, 3.76–83, 4.2–31. Cf. Hdt. 3.127.

[79] Cf. Briant (2002a: 656–75).

[80] Cf. Weiskopf (1989: 11).

of different interpretations of the same text by late authors.[81] It is
thus possible that the statements by Plutarch in *Art.* 25 are his own
understanding of the descriptions of the separate episodes, perhaps
available to him in the form of summaries.

DEINON?

The suggestion that the source of Plutarch's *Artaxerxes* 24–5, 26–30
was Deinon's *Persica* has already been proposed by scholars.[82] Let us
briefly view the main arguments for this attribution.

(1) The depiction that Artaxerxes lived till the advanced age of
ninety-four (*Art.* 30.9) is explicitly attributed to Deinon in Ps.-
Lucian's *Macrobioi* (15):

> Artaxerxes, who was called Mnemon, against whom Cyrus his brother
> fought, was reigning in Persia when he died of illness at the age of eighty-six,
> and Deinon reports ninety-four.
> Ἀρταξέρξης ὁ Μνήμων ἐπικληθείς, ἐφ' ὃν Κῦρος ὁ ἀδελφὸς ἐστρατεύσατο,
> βασιλεύων ἐν Πέρσαις ἐτελεύτησε νόσῳ, ἓξ καὶ ὀγδοήκοντα ἐτῶν γενόμενος· ὡς
> δὲ Δίνων ἱστορεῖ, τεσσάρων καὶ ἐνενήκοντα.

The work *Macrobioi* ascribed to Lucian is an awkward amalgam of
data, mostly dubious, as are some of its attributions to lost works.
But if this specific assignment to Deinon is true, then it may be
assumed with a high degree of probability that Deinon was Plutarch's
source for the detail mentioned at the end of the *Life*, and rightly set
by Jacoby as a fragment (*FGrH* 690 F 20a +b, respectively).[83] The
Greek tradition to describe the number of regnal years of Persian
kings appears in Herodotus (e.g. 1.214, 3.66, 7.4), and was conventional (Ctesias: *FGrH* 688 F 13.14, 13.23). If Deinon followed this
practice in the case of Artaxerxes, his text was also the origin of the
statement regarding the number of years of the king's rule, set by
Plutarch as sixty-two.

(2) The portrayal of Ochus as the villain in *On Isis and Osiris*,
attributed explicitly by Plutarch to Deinon (31.363c), corresponds
to the insinuation of his cruelty at the end of the *Artaxerxes*. It

---

[81] Cf. Stevenson (1997: 102), who is concerned with the omission of the descriptions of the
satrap revolts in the biography, and proposes that the king's direct involvement was perhaps
limited in these in Plutarch's account, or else that these episodes revealed less of the king's
character than was observed in other examples.

[82] Cf. Haug (1854: 98), Schottin (1865: 7), Smith (1881: 25–7), Mantey (1888: 20, 22–3),
Krumbholz (1889: 16, 22), Jacoby (1922: 2069), Stevenson (1997: 24–5). See, however, Binder
(2008: 332–5, 356).

[83] Cf. Smith (1881: 26), Manfredini, Orsi and Antelami (1987: 307), Moysey (1992: 166),
Marasco (1994: 667), Stevenson (1997: 24–5), Binder (2008: 355, 360).

would make sense to believe that Ochus was the villain in Deinon's original account. The rivalry between Ochus and Darius over the succession of Artaxerxes forms one of the key elements in the final sections of the biography. The competition between Artaxerxes and Ochus over Atossa is another central element in the plot, and links *Art.* 30 with the earlier narrative (*Art.* 26.2–3). We suggested above (Chapter 4) that Plutarch's mention (11.355c) of the killing of the Apis bull and the ensuing denigrating epithet 'the Knife' (μάχαιραν) used by the locals are details that most probably come from Deinon's work. We can add to these passages another section from Aelian (*VH* 2.17), in which the Magi predict Ochus' savagery and his murderous tendency towards his subjects, on the basis of the fact that he lays his hands first on one of the knives (τῇ μὲν δεξιᾷ τῶν **μαχαιρίων** τῶν παρακειμένων ἓν ἔλαβε). It is feasible to believe that this passage anticipated the Egyptian Campaign in the original work. The knife imagery and the pejorative nickname applied to Ochus may recur in Plutarch's wordplay (*Art.* 26.2) to introduce Ochus: (Ὦχος ὀξὺς, 'Ochus was sharp', i.e., 'keen, passionate', LSJ s.v. ὀξύς III).[84]

This attribution to Deinon is strengthened by the apparent use of this author by Aelian elsewhere in the same work (*VH* 4.8) to recount Ochus' sojourn in Egypt, a description which is close to that of Plutarch:[85]

> The Egyptians called Ochus an 'Ass' in their own language, scolding his dull-ness of mind by the weakness of that animal. Against them he sacrificed Apis with violence to an ass.
>
> Ὅτι τὸν Ὦχον οἱ Αἰγύπτιοι τῇ ἐπιχωρίῳ φωνῇ Ὄνον ἐκάλουν, τὸ νωθὲς αὐτοῦ τῆς γνώμης ἐκ τῆς ἀσθενείας τοῦ ζῴου διαβάλλοντες. ἀνθ' ὧν ἐκεῖνος τὸν Ἆπιν πρὸς βίαν κατέθυσεν Ὄνῳ.

Deinon is probably the ultimate source for these portrayals, whether Aelian made direct use of his work or not.

(3) Tiribazus is portrayed as a major figure in the last episodes of the *Artaxerxes* (27.6–9, 28, 29.1, 6–7). He also appears central in the Cadusian Campaign (*Art.* 24). As we saw from the match with the sections from Diodorus, his figure was prominent in the Cypriot affair, which ended in the trial. The internal links between the

---

[84] Another passage in Aelian's work (*VH* 6.8) recounts how Bagoas the eunuch killed Ochus (cf. Diod. 17.5.3–4) as a punishment for the slaying of the bull, and made a knife handle from the deceased king's thigh bone. This is again a reference to the same epithet (as well as an allusion to Herodotus' Cambyses), yet it is unclear whether this ultimately comes from Deinon, who may not have described Ochus' end, but rather from an author who used his account (Cleitarchus?).

[85] Cf. Stevenson (1997: 33, 36, 38) for the assumption that Deinon was ultimately the origin for the picture of Ochus in Egypt found in Diodorus and Aelian.

Cadusian Campaign and *Art.* 30 are also evident in the mention of
Tiribazus' son (30.8), presumably the same son who was employed
against the Cadusian kings. This would seem to correspond to
Tiribazus' pivotal role in *Art.* 10, which is attributed to Deinon.[86]
Tiribazus also appears in another of Deinon's fragments (Nepos,
Conon 5.2), where he is said to have arrested Conon. Tiribazus was
probably central in Deinon's account, as the chances of repeatedly
finding the same character in the few fragments we have are not high
if he were but a minor figure. The structure of Nepos' paragraph
would seem to suggest that he largely follows Deinon:

> a. Tiribazus ... summoned Conon. ... When he came and was present,
> because of this message, (Conon) was placed in chains, in which he was kept
> for some time.
> *Tiribazus ... Cononem evocavit ... huius nuntio parens cum venisset, in*
> *vincla coniectus est, in quibus aliquamdiu fuit*
> b. Some have left a written record that he was carried away to the king, and
> there died.
> *inde nonnulli eum ad regem abductum ibique [eum] periisse scriptum*
> *reliquerunt.*
> c. Against these accounts, Deinon the historian, whom we most trust on
> Persian matters, wrote that he [*scil.* Conon] fled. It is not clear whether it was
> done with knowledge of Tiribazus or whether he was ignorant of this.
> *Contra ea Dinon historicus, cui nos plurimum de Persicis rebus credimus,*
> *effugisse scripsit; illud addubitat, utrum Tiribazo sciente an imprudente sit*
> *factum.*

It seems evident that both of Nepos' references to Tiribazus here
(a, c) are part of the same narrative. The story of the *nonnulli* perhaps
did not involve Tiribazus at all, or, for all we know, it could have
been a brief and imprecise epitome of this episode, misinterpreting
Tiribazus' excuse to summon Conon (hinted by *ad regem eum se*
mittere velle magna de re (5.2), 'summoned Conon as if wishing to
send him on a matter of great importance to the king') and presenting
it as an actual occurrence. The closing insinuation that Tiribazus let
a potential enemy of the king flee unscathed may be reminiscent of
the charges brought against Tiribazus during the Cypriot expedition
(and presumably hinted during Tiribazus' absence in the Cadusian
War). In fact, Conon is known to have fled to Cyprus (to the same
Evagoras), and may have done so in Deinon's version as well.

(4) Since Plutarch admits having employed Deinon in the first

---

[86] Cf. Smith (1881: 12, 22, 25), Stevenson (1997: 36). Stevenson (1987: 29, 1997: 12–13,
cf. 73) even believes someone 'favourable and close' to Tiribazus was Deinon's principal informant for all the fourth-century material down to the late 360s. Cf. Lenfant (2009: 61, 72 n. 2).

two thirds of the *Artaxerxes*, it would seem probable that he also makes use of his work in the last part,[87] and hence that Deinon was the common source. Indeed, there may be some stylistic and thematic features as well as verbal echoes pointing to Deinon as 'the common source' referred to here. If what we said above about the arrangement of the episodes relating to the last part of the reign of Artaxerxes II in Plutarch's biography and the other parallel accounts (of Justin/Trogus, Diodorus and Nepos) is correct, the work used for these sections followed a thematic rather than a chronological order. This feature appeared in more than one instance (the Cadusian affair, the separate stories of the satraps). As we have seen in Chapter 4 above, this may have been one of the hallmarks of Deinon's work (cf. *Art.* 6.9).

Other features do not appear overwhelming, yet they should be noted as well. Aspasia's story in Aelian (*VH* 12.1) mentions a person who bought her (ἀγοραστής). Servants who fulfil this duty appear in a passage attributed explicitly to Deinon (τοῖς ἀγορασταῖς: Athen. 14.652c). Plutarch mentions the Persian crown in the last unit of the biography (*Art.* 26.4, 28.1), and we know that Deinon had special interest in the headcover of the Persian kings (Athen. 12.514a). Deinon also described the king's concubines and their presence beside the queen (Athen. 13.556b), a theme recurring in *Art.* 27.2. Stevenson (1997: 27) proposes that the reference to the carriages of the Persian women (*Art.* 27.1) comes from Deinon, for this detail also appears in the biography of Themistocles (*Them.* 26.4–5), where Deinon is mentioned as one of the sources (*Them.* 27.1). However, it is uncertain whether Plutarch read Deinon directly or extensively for the latter work. It is possible that the similarity between the biographies stems from Plutarch himself, his areas of interest and his style. If the *Artaxerxes* is later than the *Themistocles*, Plutarch could be referring to his own previous biography.

DEINON AND OTHERS

That there was a common source to the four later authors (Diodorus, Nepos, Justin/Trogus, Plutarch) and that this source may have been Deinon does not necessarily mean that Deinon was the ultimate

---

[87] For Deinon as the source of Plutarch for the section of 26–30, or at least the beginning of this segment, see Smith (1881: 22, 25), Mantey (1888: 22), Neuhaus (1901: 280–1), Thiel (1923: 413), König (1972: 91), Moysey (1992: 166) and Gera (1993: 213 n. 74 – as an option).

origin of the stories. In this section, we explore other scenarios which link the accounts of these four writers to other sources and contemplate the outcomes of these possibilities.

Tiribazus' ruse during the Cadusian Campaign calls to mind the diplomatic activity of Adusius (Ἀδούσιος) in Xenophon's *Cyropaedia* (7.4.1–11; cf. 8.6.7), which is meant to bring an end to the Carian Civil War.[88] Adusius concludes a treaty with each side, and asks each party to conceal this fact. After he summons both sides in the same night (νύκτα ... τὴν αὐτήν), each unbeknown to the other (λάθρᾳ ἑκατέρων), Adusius captures the fortresses of both. The next day, he succeeds in bringing peace between the leaders of both groups, who feel cheated (νομίζοντες ἐξηπατῆσθαι ἀμφότεροι). The stratagems in Plutarch and Xenophon are not absolutely identical, and what is striking is that an incidental element in one (the leaders leaving their own places and coming to the king at the same time) is an integral part of the other. Added to the similarity is the unique name of Adusius. His character seems to have been especially invented for the Carian episode,[89] and he was evidently named after the Cadusians.[90] This means one of the following three options:

(a) Xenophon was influenced by an earlier account, which described the Cadusian Campaign of Artaxerxes II and the employment of the same ruse.
(b) Xenophon was influenced by an earlier account, which described a Cadusian Campaign of a certain Persian king, and the employment of the same ruse.
(c) Xenophon was the origin of the depiction of this ruse, and a later writer invented a Cadusian Campaign based on this figure of Adusias.

Of the three, the third should be discarded immediately for obvious reasons.[91] It is inconceivable that the rare name Adusius would have been the inspiration for a description of a campaign against the Cadusians, who are more commonly found in literature (and preceded Xenophon, in Ctesias' work). Let us examine the first possibility. If the employment of this ruse in Artaxerxes' Cadusian

---

[88] See Stevenson (1997: 97).
[89] Gera (1993: 281).
[90] Syme (1988a: 150).
[91] Cf. Binder (2008: 320): 'Es ist nicht zu entscheiden, ob diese Passage Dinon als literarische Vorlage für seine Ausgestaltung des Kadusierfeldzuges gedient hat' ('It is unclear whether this passage has served Dinon as a literary model for his design of the Cadusian Campaign').

War belonged to the so-called 'common source' and was exclusively associated with it, it might seem that this account appeared before Xenophon's *Cyropaedia* (written during the 360s).[92] This 'common source' would then not be Deinon, since that would mean his work was composed and published over three decades (the last event recounted in it, as recalled, is Artaxerxes III's takeover of Egypt in 343/2 BCE). It is also difficult to accept (although this is not impossible) that Deinon included the reign of Artaxerxes II in a very early segment of his entire *Persica*, and before the actual end of this monarch's reign.

In that case, either the 'common source' was not Deinon or else option (b) would be the only possibility left. If option (b) is correct, then there was presumably an earlier story of a campaign against the Cadusians who were defeated by the employment of this ruse. This story inspired both Xenophon, who took it to his tale of the Carian civil war, and the author of the 'common source' (Deinon?), who integrated it in the reign of Artaxerxes II. Indeed, there seems to be evidence that this may have been the case. The only account that was popular and influential enough to shape the descriptions of his succesors was Ctesias' *Persica*. Ctesias probably addressed the relations between the Persians and the Cadusians as an important theme running from the early books (Medes and Cadusians: *FGrH* 688 F 1b = Diod. 2.33.1–6) to Cyrus' mission, found in the version of Nicolaus of Damascus (*FGrH* 90 F 66 = set by Lenfant as 688 F 6b.11–16). According to Nicolaus, the ruler (ἄρχων) of the Cadusians, Onaphernes, wished to shift to the side of the Median king and asked for a trustworthy man with whom he could negotiate the terms; the person sent by Astyages the Median was Cyrus. It may be that Nicolaus simplified the original account, which had two Cadusian monarchs and a depiction of the same ploy. If this is true, in Ctesias' account Cyrus played the role that the 'common source' (Deinon?) assigned to Tiribazus.[93] Against this background, Artaxerxes' suspicion of Tiribazus in the course of his diplomatic task is made understandable, given that Cyrus the Great began to entertain the thought of Persian rebellion during this very mission. We should note that Xenophon's adaptation transposes the use of this ploy to Caria, incidentally the homeland of Ctesias himself. If all this is true, then the elaboration of these Ctesian details within the

---

[92] See Gera (1993: 23–5).
[93] Thus playfully making Tiribazus echo both rebellious Cyrus the Great and Cyrus the Younger. Cf. Osborne (1973: 534). Cf. Ruzicka (2012: 94).

'common source' corresponds to the habit of Deinon we suggested above of adapting and adjusting the stories of his predecessor.

There may have been others, however, who could have revised Ctesias' description, and this leads us to explore briefly the possibilities of certain other authors whose texts may have been the 'common source', or who could have influenced it.

The traditional opinion, almost orthodoxy by now, is that Ephorus of Cyme was the sole source of Diodorus for the non-Sicilian parts of books 11–16. This suggestion was made by Christian Volquardsen in 1868, and is still accepted in many quarters of research today.[94] The idea behind this simple 'one source' hypothesis is the conception that Diodorus' *Bibliotheca* is an unsophisticated compilation derived from the works of his predecessors.[95] Assuming that this view is correct, Ephorus was also proposed as the source of Plutarch for *Art.* 24, as well as of the other authors, who wrote the parallel versions.[96] Marasco (1994: 669), for instance, directs the attention to a series of similarities between Diodorus and the sections of the biography discussed here (such as the campaign to Egypt in *Art.* 24).[97] Admittedly, there is no doubt that Diodorus used Ephorus, since he cites him in a few cases (e.g. 12.38.1–41.1, 13.41.1–3, 13.54.5, 13.60.5, 13.80.5, 14.11.1–4, 14.22.1–2, 14.54.4–6, 15.60.5, 16.14.3, 16.76.5). But was Ephorus Diodorus' only source for this part of his work?

Over the years, the hypothesis that Diodorus depended solely upon Ephorus was challenged in many ways, and several studies have proposed that Diodorus used other sources as well.[98] A reading

---

[94] Cf. Cauer (1847: 46–57). See Volquardsen (1868: 51–66), Collman (1869: 1–33), Holzapfel (1879: 1–25), Schwartz (1903a: 679–81), Herbert (1954: 37–8, 41–2), Drews (1962: 390) and Andrewes (1985: 189). See Stylianou (1998: 49–50), who claims that '[t]his was established long ago and requires no detailed argumentation', and who offers other arguments, related to the style and content, which are, however, not compelling. Stylianou (1998: 51–5) also claims that Diodorus relied on Ephorus for the western sections; cf. Barber (1935: 160–2). For another opinion, see Frost (1980: 32).

[95] On the work of Diodorus as an 'uncritical compilation', see Barber (1935: 21–2). According to Schwartz (1903a: 663), 'D.s Compilation – ein Werk kann man das Buch nicht nennen …' (D[iodorus'] compilation – one cannot call the book a work'). Compare to Stylianou's claim (1998: 132): '… the *Bibliotheca* is so obviously a work of compilation, one hastily and incompetently carried out …'.

[96] Haug (1854: 668–9). Cf. also Hornblower (1994: 84): 'Ephorus-derived material'. Yet Plutarch never mentions Ephorus in the *Artaxerxes* (Smith, 1881: 17).

[97] It would have been helpful to his view had he mentioned the Cadusian Campaign, which he curiously does not.

[98] See Stronk (2017: 45–6, 49, cf. 10, 17, 32). See Schwartz (1903a: 679–81), who places great weight on the chronographies in Diodorus' writings; cf. Stylianou (1998: 25–48), who speaks of a special source for the information on kings, literary works, the beginnings and endings of wars and the founding of cities. Stylianou (1998: 50, 108–9) even admits that some of the material is not from Ephorus, but tends to limit this dependency.

of Xenophon by Diodorus has already been suggested,[99] in particular for the sections dealing with the story of the Ten Thousand (14.19–31).[100] The work method of Diodorus accords with the suggestion that he used various authors. For example, with regard to the years 375–373 BCE, Vivienne Gray (1980: 320) holds that Diodorus inserts the episodic description of Ephorus into his particular framework in the following way: he preserves the original thematic description of Ephorus by dividing two regions (i.e., the Peloponnese and northwest Greece) into two different archon years (375/4, 374/3 respectively). Between them he introduces the Persian invasion of Egypt, taken, according to Gray, from a special book of Ephorus on eastern affairs. Rather than having Diodorus resort to a special book of Ephorus on Persia, whose existence is entirely conjectured,[101] a simpler interpretation would be to assume that Diodorus uses another author here, whose work specialised in the area of Persia (Deinon?).[102] Deinon appears to have been consulted for this purpose by some of Diodorus' rough contemporaries, like Cicero (*De div.* 1.23.46) or Nepos (*Con.* 5.2). Why not assume the same for Diodorus himself?[103]

Another form of the proposition of Diodorus' dependence on a single author is to claim that Deinon's work was the source of Ephorus' descriptions.[104] Alternatively, Deinon may have been dependent on Ephorus (so that Deinon's work was in fact passages culled from Ephorus).[105]

Details concerning the lives of these authors in fact seem to rule out the first option. We do not know much of Ephorus' life or the

---

[99] Barber (1935: 64–5, 125) points out differences between Diodorus and Xenophon; cf. Gray (1980: 326) who shows Diodorus' possible ultimate reliance on the latter.

[100] See Stylianou (2004).

[101] Except for the Persian Wars in book 10: *FGrH* 70 F 63, cf. FF 186–8, 191 and the story of the Ten Thousand in book 17: F 70. Cf. Drews (1973: 122, 203 n. 130) on books 8–9. See Stylianou (1998: 92).

[102] On Deinon's being the source for the revolt of the satraps, see Stevenson (1997: 101). Weiskopf (1989: 12) holds that Ephorus is the source for the descriptions of the revolts in Diodorus, since his descriptions show an echo of the Isocratic belief regarding the barbarians; but it appears to me that these characteristics are too general to be unique to the Athenian orator.

[103] See also Drews (1962: 384) on Diodorus' employment of popular sources. Cf. Stylianou (1998: 108–9), Stronk (2010: 66).

[104] See Hornblower (1994: 84), Stevenson (1997: 29–33), Binder (2008: 60). Stylianou (1998: 108–9) proposes that Deinon's work might be the basis for the romantic elements in the story of the life of Tiribazus, such as the trial. For the dependence of Ephorus on *Persica* works, see Barber (1935: 120). Jacoby (1926: 31) vehemently denies that Ephorus used Deinon regarding the confrontation of Artaxerxes and Cyrus.

[105] Cf. Krumbholz (1889: 24).

exact time in which he lived. The date of his *floruit* given in *Suda*, s.v. 'Ephippus', ε 3930 Adler (= *FGrH* 70 T 1)[106] is 'the year with no archons in Athens' (i.e., 404/3 BCE) 'in the 93rd Olympiad' (408–405 BCE), marking his birth year c. 440 BCE, but this date is surely too early, as we know Ephorus wrote about the siege of Perinthus in the year 341/0 BCE in book 27 (*FGrH* 70 T 10). Diodorus (16.75.5) states that Ephorus reached this point in his work himself (i.e., it was not a passage inserted later on by his son). The *Suda*'s description may be influenced by the entry of Theopompus (s.v., θ 172 Adler): 'Theopompus flourished when there was no archon in Athens during the 93rd Olympiad, as Ephorus also.'[107] It is possible that he was a student of Isocrates (436–338 BCE), in accordance with a common tradition among the ancients (*FGrH* 70 T 1, 2a, 3–5, 7–8, 27, 28).[108] Ephorus was also aware of Alexander's reign (*FGrH* 70 T 6, F 217). Clement of Alexandria (*Strom.*, 1.139.3 = *FGrH* 70 F 223) claims that according to Ephorus, 750 years elapsed from the campaign of the Heracleidae until the archonship of Euaenetus (335/4 BCE, the year of Alexander the Great's campaign against Asia).[109] If this sentence comes from the lost introduction to the history of Ephorus, then Alexander's campaign was apparently destined to be the end point of the work, since the Heracleidae were described at its beginning.[110] It is quite possible that Ephorus wrote the last section of the history after Alexander had ascended the throne, and at least following the death of Philip.[111] If that is the case, it is likely that Ephorus died in about 330 or 320 BCE, perhaps even later.[112] As mentioned above, the latest known event mentioned in Deinon's work is Artaxerxes III Ochus' conquest of Egypt (343/2 BCE), and he may not have continued further beyond this point. This fact would make Deinon and Ephorus close in the time frame of their subject matter, if not

---

[106] In reality an entry on Ephorus (s.v. ε 3953 Adler) but erroneously attributed to an Ephippus.

[107] See the suggestion of Parker (2014), that the *Suda* may have mistaken the date of birth for the *floruit*.

[108] See Volquardsen (1868: 49–51), Laqueur (1911: 204, 345) and Barber (1935: 2–4, 75–83). Jacoby (1926: 22) does not reject it. However, cf. Schwartz (1907: 1–2) against this connection.

[109] Cf. Volquardsen (1868: 5–13).

[110] Compare Tertullian *De anim.* 46 (= *FGrH* 70 F 217) on Philip's dream prophesying great things for his son.

[111] See Niese (1909: 170–1), Laqueur (1911: 336), Kalischek (1913: 13–15), Jacoby (1926: 24–5), Barber (1935: 1), Stylianou (1998: 110–12). See also the anecdote recounted by Plutarch (*De Stoic. rep.* 1043d = *FGrH* 70 T 6), that Ephorus rejected Alexander's request to join his campaign.

[112] Barber (1935: 9) writes that he did not outlive Alexander by much, because he was too old to write a world history.

in terms of the time of composition, which is not certain in the case of Deinon.[113] In order to contemplate the option that Ephorus used Deinon's *Persica* (or vice versa), we would have to assume that one writer's work was already published in the 330s or 320s for the other to consult, though even so it is a very strained hypothesis.

To think that all four authors (Diodorus, Nepos, Justin/Trogus, and Plutarch) used completely different sources while composing the relevant sections is hardly tenable, unless this is taken to mean that ultimately these distinct sources derive from the same account. Neuhaus (1901: 280–3) believes that for the Aspasia story, Plutarch used Deinon, while he considers Ephorus the origin of the version of Justin (Trogus). Neuhaus postulates that both Deinon and Ephorus borrowed the life story of Aspasia from Ctesias, and independently arrived at a similar narrative. This hypothesis is not probable. The coincidence that two authors would have used the literary device of flashback at the same point, as well as the overall conformity between the order of the details in the accounts of Plutarch and Justin (Trogus), is not conceivable, unless it relies on the content of the same shared source.[114]

Moreover, while the assumption that Ctesias wrote on the early life of Aspasia and her relationship with Cyrus the Younger is possible,[115] there is more likelihood that the entire story came from the same author who wrote about her importance to Artaxerxes II and Darius the crown prince,[116] events which postdated the time of the occurrences in Ctesias' *Persica*.[117] The source used by Plutarch and the parallel versions of the other authors associated this story with Darius' unfulfilled request and his revolt. Moreover, it should be noted that Xenophon also refers to Aspasia, and alludes to her capture during the Battle of Cunaxa. Xenophon mentions her, however, not by name but as 'the Phocaean' (*Anab.* 1.10.2). One may conjecture that had Xenophon known her name from Ctesias,

---

[113] On Deinon and Ephorus as being contemporaries, see Stevenson (1997: 10 n. 13).

[114] See also Thiel (1923: 412–13), Stevenson (1997: 36), Briant (2002a: 1002).

[115] Cf. Krumbholz (1889: 16, n. 12, 20–1).

[116] Stevenson (1997: 62, 50) holds that the story of Aspasia was invented (by Deinon) in order to fill a gap in the story he heard, where there was no real cause for the revolt of Darius. This does not seem to be correct because the story of Aspasia appears an essential part of the complete original story. On the tragic nature of this affair, see also Marasco (1988: 61–3).

[117] Note that in the depiction of Aelian, there is a eunuch called Tiridates who has recently died. Nicolaus (*FGrH* 90 F 66.23) mentions a Tiridates who was the οἰνοχόος (wine pourer) of Cyrus the Great. Ctesias may have been Nicolaus' source (Lenfant sets him as F 8d). Bearing in mind the physician's habit of taking names from his contemporaries and giving them to characters from previous times (cf. Schmitt, 2006: 202), seemingly, the reference to Tiridates the contemporary eunuch may also derive from his *Persica* as well. However, this is not necessary.

he would probably have mentioned it, and had he been familiar with her story, he would probably not have treated Aspasia on a par with an anonymous 'Milesian' (*Anab.* 1.10.3).

Some scholars tend to differentiate between the source of Plutarch and Trogus on the one hand and that of Diodorus on the other. Stevenson (1997: 32), for example, does so in relation to the description of the campaign against Egypt. She doubts whether the description of Diodorus comes from Deinon. The reason she gives is that according to Diodorus, when the commanders of the Persian army return from Egypt to Asia, and when the dispute breaks out between Pharnabazus and Iphicrates, the latter is afraid that he might be imprisoned and punished, like Conon before him (μὴ συλληφθῇ καὶ τιμωρίας τύχῃ, καθάπερ Κόνων ἔπαθεν ὁ Ἀθηναῖος,: 15.43.5), and therefore decides to secretly flee from the camp (15.43.5) to the port of Athens. In the version attributed to Deinon (Nepos, *Con.* 5.4), Stevenson continues, it is stated that the Greek commander actually escaped (as we saw above). According to Stevenson, Ephorus (Diodorus' source) used Callisthenes at this point. This argument is not decisive because even in the account assigned to Deinon by Nepos, Conon is evidently imprisoned before he flees. It would appear, on the contrary, that the description of Diodorus fills in the lacunae regarding the details of the dispute between Iphicrates and Pharnabazus, and is therefore completely in keeping with the short notes found in Plutarch and the extant *prologus* of book 10 in Trogus' work. Moreover, Stevenson (1997: 41) infers the nature of the original description of the Egyptian Campaign by Deinon from the remarks of Plutarch and Trogus. In her opinion, these notes are so brief that it appears strange that two authors would choose to delete these details on their own. She concludes that Deinon did not expand on this topic and that he ignored the defeat of the king's army. However, this conclusion is not necessary. Plutarch may have significantly abridged the original source, and it is hard to base any argument on the absence of details from the abridged *prologus* of Trogus.

In a similar vein, Smith (1881: 22) differentiates the sources of Nepos and Diodorus from those of Plutarch with regard to the Cadusian Expedition: the first two do not mention Tiribazus, while Plutarch does.[118] Smith considers Theopompus of Chios to be their source. However, Diodorus does not give any detail regarding the campaign against the Cadusians, so one cannot really deduce anything from his omission. Furthermore, Diodorus clearly creates a

---

[118] Cf. Ruzicka (1999: 36 n. 26).

link between the trial of Tiribazus and the operation against the Cadusians; thus, Tiribazus would seem to have appeared in Diodorus' source, as indeed suggested above.

The sources used by Pompeius Trogus are unknown.[119] The direct source of Trogus may have been the Greek work by Timagenes of Alexandria (first century BCE),[120] the historian and rhetor (*Suda*, s.v. Τιμαγένης, τ 588 Adler), who was notoriously hostile to Rome (Seneca, *Ep.* 91.13),[121] and whose interest in Persia of old may have resulted from his concern with contemporary Parthia.[122] If so, the relevant work to include anecdotes on the Persian monarchs may have been the lost *On Kings* (Steph. Byz. s.v. Μιλύαι = *FGrH* 88 F 1).[123] This does not preclude the possibility that the source of Timagenes was a different work. It would be plausible to propose that the ultimate origin of the stories in the first half of the tenth book of Trogus was Deinon. This was suggested by Hilarius Wolffgarten (1868: 73–8).[124] Curtius Rufus (9.5.21) ascribes the story in which Ptolemy I is said to have participated in the battle against the Mallians (and perhaps to have saved Alexander's life) to both Cleitarchus and Timagenes. Indeed, Timagenes may have cited Cleitarchus. Curiously, both the latter authors are mentioned by Quintilian (*Inst.* 10.1.74), who dates Cleitarchus to the period after Ephorus and a long time before Timagenes (*Inst.* 10.1.75). One would assume that both the grouping of Timagenes and Cleitarchus (in Curtius and Quintillian) and the relative chronology between them were based on explicit citations of sources by Timagenes. If this is true, then Timagenes certainly used Cleitarchus. There is a certain prospect that he also employed the text of Deinon, if what we said above on Cleitarchus' work as circulating together with Deinon's *Persica* is correct.

Trogus may have used the work of the historian Theopompus of Chios.[125] He evidently based the title of his work, *Historiae Philippicae*,

---

[119] See Forni (1958).

[120] See von Gutschmid (1882), Yardley and Heckel (1997: 22–8). Wachsmuth (1891) disagrees and proposes a range of other authors. See also Klotz (1913: 2305–8).

[121] The famous passage of Livy 9.18.6 on the *levissimi ex Graecis* ('silliest of the Greeks'), who prefer the Parthians over the Romans, is ascribed to Timagenes since Schwab (1834); see Yardley and Heckel (1997: 32). Cf. Laqueur (1936) and Atkinson (2002: 316). Cf. the saying that the Romans were good at giving what didn't belong to them (Justin 36.3.9), apropos of Rome's support of the Jews against the Seleucids; this gibe is attributed to Timagenes by Yaavetz (1998: 83–4). Cf. Bowersock (1965: 110).

[122] Cf. Sordi (1982).

[123] On this work see Alonzo-Núñez (1982) and Meister (1990).

[124] Cf. Drews (1973: 116, 200 n. 87), Lamarre (1907: 687–8), Stevenson (1997: 35–6).

[125] Cf. Heeren (1802: 53–6, 71), Hammond and Griffith (1979: 2.9–13) and Shrimpton (1991a: 120–5).

on that of Theopompus.[126] Theopompus died (shortly?) after Alexander the Great's death in 323 BCE (cf. Phot. *Bibl.* cod. 176 p. 120 b 19). Since Theopompus' work had a reputation for taking or elaborating the stories of others,[127] he may have borrowed items from the 'common source' or Deinon and altered them.[128] Thus, if one insists on differentiating Theopompus as the source of Trogus and the 'common source' or Deinon as the source of Plutarch, this would explain the minor modifications between the versions of the Darius/Aspasia story, which Theopompus could have made in his adaptation of the 'common source' or Deinon. Yet the fact that both authors were rough contemporaries makes the assumption of literary appropriation difficult (though not impossible) within the narrow bounds of chronology.

FRAGMENTS OF THE 'COMMON SOURCE'

The question of Deinon's ultimate authorship of the presumed narrative in the lost work which we call the 'common source' notwithstanding, there are some additional passages which should be added to it. These other texts appear to complete the remnants we have of the storyline, and thus increase our knowledge of the nature of the original work. We shall mainly discuss two passages coming from the works of Plutarch, and see how they shed light on his method of work. We will briefly mention three other sections from external works (one of which may come from Plutarch) that continue the plot in various points.

(I) Plutarch describes the aftermath of a hunting scene (*Art.* 5.3–4):

> During a certain hunt when Tiribazus showed him his torn coat, he [scil. Artaxerxes] asked him what he should do. When he [scil. Tiribazus] replied, 'Put on another, but give this one to me,' he [scil. Artaxerxes] did so declaring, 'I give this to you, Tiribazus, but forbid you from wearing it'. When Tiribazus

---

[126] See Gutschmid (1882: 549), Momigliano (1933: 994–5), Seel (1972: 267–8), Urban (1982: 82–4); Alonso-Núñez (1987: 58–9) on the title; see Devlin (1985: 115).

[127] E.g. the well known meeting of Agesilaus and Pharnabazus (Xen. *Hell.* 4.1.29–39). See Porphyry *ap.* Eus. *PE* 10.3.9–10 = *FGrH* 115 T 35, F 21), who asserts that Theopompus has changed much of Xenophon and that his theft (κλοπὴν) destroyed 'the energy and vigour of Xenophon'. See Flower (1994: 159–60). Porphyry claims that Theopompus 'has taken descriptions of actions from certain persons and transferred them to others' (πραγμάτων δ' ὑφαίρεσιν πεποίηται μεταθεὶς τὰ ἐπ' ἄλλων ἄλλοις). Moreover, it was not beyond Theopompus to elaborate on the accounts of his predecessors: see the case of Thucydides 8.103–5 and Anon. *Life of Thucydides* 5 (= *FGrH* 115 F 5).

[128] An obvious case would be thus Theopompus' description of the king's expenditure on meals in the cities (Athen. 4.145a), which is twenty or thirty talents. This information is unlike that attributed to Deinon (and Ctesias), namely, that on the king's dinner 400 talents were expended (Athen. 4.146cd). Deinon's account may be understandable without postulating the intermediate stage of Theopompus, while the latter's account may be an attempt to transfer to a different situation (during travel) the facts Deinon (or Ctesias) supplied for the court.

did not care for this order – he was no evil man, but rather light-headed and confused – and nonetheless immediately wore the king's garment, and put on himself golden ornaments and women's decorations of royal nature, everyone was outraged at this; for it was not allowed; but the king laughed, and said: 'I give you the ornaments to wear as a woman and the coat [to wear] as a madman.'
(3) Ἐν δὲ θήρᾳ τινὶ Τιριβάζου δείξαντος αὐτῷ τὸν κάνδυν ἐσχισμένον, ἠρώτησεν ὅ τι δεῖ ποιεῖν. ἐκείνου δ᾽ εἰπόντος 'ἄλλον αὐτὸς ἔνδυσαι, τοῦτον δ᾽ ἐμοὶ δός', οὕτως ἐποίησεν εἰπών· 'δίδωμι μὲν ᾧ Τιρίβαζε σοὶ τοῦτον, φορεῖν δ᾽ ἀπαγορεύω'. (4) Τοῦ δὲ Τιριβάζου μὴ φροντίσαντος – ἦν γὰρ οὐ πονηρός, ὑπόκουφος δὲ καὶ παράφορος – ἀλλὰ τόν τε κάνδυν εὐθὺς ἐκεῖνον ἐνδύντος καὶ δέραια χρυσᾶ καὶ γυναικεῖα τῶν βασιλικῶν περιθεμένου, πάντες μὲν ἠγανάκτουν· οὐ γὰρ ἐξῆν· ὁ μέντοι βασιλεὺς κατεγέλασε καὶ εἶπε· 'δίδωμί σοι καὶ τὰ χρυσία φορεῖν ὡς γυναικὶ καὶ τὴν στολὴν ὡς μαινομένῳ'.
καὶ γυναικεῖα om. Ziegler

Tellingly, two animals do not appear here. The first is the beast that probably tore the king's garment. The ancient Mesopotamian picture was of the king battling a lion, initially in order to confront the threat of predators to the community,[129] and later as symbolising the conflict of civilised life against forces aiming to destroy it.[130] In the ideological representations of the Neo-Assyrian monarchy, the figure of the king struggling with a lion was a favourite theme, as is evident in seals, inscriptions and reliefs from the ninth century BCE onwards.[131] Scenes depicting the Great King killing a lion are conspicuously non-existent in Achaemenid Persia, yet they are present in seals.[132] This absence perfectly matches the rest of *Art.* 5, where the king is oblivious of dangerous persons in his immediate surrounding (a Spartan, his mother and Tiribazus in this scene), who will in due course attempt to hurt him.[133] This unawareness also accords well with the fact that the king is unmindful of the peril posed by Cyrus, his brother, who in the intervening time gathers forces (*Art.* 4.3). Allegorically, this absence alludes to the king's unawareness of the flaws in his *psyche*, displayed in his passivity and tolerance towards Tiribazus.[134] The second animal is the horse. One would assume that the king was either mounted or in a carriage during the hunt,[135] but

[129] See Frankfort (1954: 78).
[130] See Strawn (2005: 141–50).
[131] See the well-known examples of the reliefs of Ashurnasirpal II (883–860 BCE) from Nimrud (northwest palace) and the staged scenes of hunting lions within an arena of Ashurbanipal (668–631 BCE) from Nineveh (north palace). See Albenda (1974), Weissert (1997).
[132] E.g. BM 89132 of Darius I. Some seals depict the 'royal hero' motif with lions or fantastic beasts, even though the figure has a royal crown. See Frankfort (1939: pl. XXXVII A, h, m, n), Schmidt (1957: pls. 2–5), Kuhrt (2007: 596) on Artystone's cylinder seal, PFS 38.
[133] See Almagor (2009/10: 10–11).
[134] See Plato's employment of the lion to signify passions of the soul (*Rep.* 9.588de, 589b, 590d).
[135] Xen. *Anab.* 1.2.7; cf. Strabo 15.3.18.

no stallion is mentioned in this scene. Again, this non-appearance may be allegorically interpreted as signalling a feature of Artaxerxes' soul,[136] namely, the absence of the trait of pursuit of honour, as can be seen in his unkingly lenience when dealing with Tiribazus' defiance.[137] Moreover, the fact that Artaxerxes is not mentioned as riding a horse proves right Cyrus' words in his letter to the Spartans (*Art.* 6.4, see Chapter 2) to the effect that his brother is not able to preserve his place in a chase or his throne facing danger. Finally, the absence of the lion and the horse where we expect them to be is part of Plutarch's play on the theme of the king's claim, to be made in the future, that he was present in a place where he was not, killing Cyrus; the reverse image anticipates the future official version, in which the persons really responsible for the deed are eliminated from it.

This scene may be the same one described by Diodorus (15.10.3),[138] as mentioned by Tiribazus in his trial:

> In the course of a hunt, while the king was in a chariot, two lions charged, ripped to shreds two of four chariot horses, and then attacked the king himself; but then Tiribazus emerged, killed the lions, and saved the king from the perils.
>
> κατὰ γάρ τινα κυνηγίαν ἐφ' ἅρματος ὀχουμένου τοῦ βασιλέως δύο λέοντας ἐπ' αὐτὸν ὁρμῆσαι, καὶ τῶν μὲν ἵππων τῶν ἐν τῷ τεθρίππῳ δύο διασπάσαι, τὴν δ' ὁρμὴν ἐπ' αὐτὸν ποιεῖσθαι τὸν βασιλέα· καθ' ὃν δὴ καιρὸν ἐπιφανέντα τὸν Τιρίβαζον τοὺς μὲν λέοντας ἀποκτεῖναι, τὸν δὲ βασιλέα ἐκ τῶν κινδύνων ἐξελέσθαι.

The mention of two lions attacking two horses is quite a rare one, and is surely meant to be linked with another dual danger,[139] most likely that of the two kings of the Cadusians, from which Tiribazus also saves the king. The scene may have adapted the famous picture in Ctesias (*FGrH* 688 F 14.43), mentioned above (Chapter 3), in which Megabyzus strikes a lion with his spear and thus saves the monarch. As opposed to the punishment that Megabyzus receives from Artaxerxes I, we gather from Diodorus that Tiribazus did not suffer at the hands of Artaxerxes II, and that in fact this deed saved him during his own trial. This lenience fits Artaxerxes' tolerance in *Art.* 5.[140]

---

[136] Cf. the Platonic imagery of the soul in the *Phaedrus* as a chariot driven by a team of winged horses: *Phaedr.* 246a–256de.

[137] See Stevenson (1997: 27, 78–9) on other improper requests from the Persian king, which ended in disaster.

[138] Cf. Briant (2002a: 321–2).

[139] It may also be a reversed allusion to the two whelps attacking a lion cub: see Hdt. 3.32.1.

[140] There may have been a sophisticated play in the original on the variance between words and deeds, displayed in the scene of *Art.* 5.3–4, since Tiribazus' words recount his deeds. The variance can also be seen in Diod. 15.41.2, in the dispute passage between Iphicrates and

If this is true, and the hunting scene in Plutarch's *Artaxerxes* is to be joined with that referred to by Diodorus, then two features of the original work may be seen:

(a) The hunting incident was probably introduced during Tiribazus' defence speech in his trial. It included not only a scene that would acquit Tiribazus for saving the king, but also a depiction of Tiribazus' defiance,[141] foreshadowing his open rebellion later on.

(b) The two love triangles of the king–Aspasia–Darius and the king–Atossa–Tiribazus (below) call to mind the Herodotean tale of the infatuation of Xerxes with his niece Artaunte, the daughter of Masistes, his brother, and the awareness of his wife, Amestris, of the matter (Hdt. 9.108–113), in which a request made to the king brings calamity. Artaunte's demand of the royal robe (9.109)[142] is echoed in Tiribazus' request here; he is indeed made to be represented as 'a woman': ὡς γυναικί).[143]

(II) Part of the story of the affair of the king and Atossa is the involvement of Parysatis (*Art.* 23.3–5):

... She [Parysatis] recognised that of his daughters, the king felt great passion to Atossa, and that he concealed it and contained his emotion not least because of her, as some say, although he had already consorted secretly with the maid. When Parysatis was apprehensive, she welcomed the girl more than before, and commended her beauty and her disposition to Artaxerxes, claiming that she was royal and outstanding. Eventually, she convinced him to wed the girl and make her his legal wife ...

(3)... ἤσθετο τῆς ἑτέρας τῶν θυγατέρων Ἀτόσσης ἐρῶντος ἔρωτα δεινόν, ἐπικρυπτομένου δὲ δι᾽ ἐκείνην οὐχ ἥκιστα καὶ κολάζοντος τὸ πάθος ὥς φασιν ἔνιοι, καίτοι γεγενημένης ἤδη πρὸς τὴν παρθένον ὁμιλίας αὐτῷ λαθραίας. (4) Ὡς οὖν ὑπώπτευσεν ἡ Παρύσατις, τὴν παῖδα μᾶλλον ἢ πρότερον ἠσπάζετο, καὶ πρὸς τὸν Ἀρτοξέρξην ἐπήνει τό τε **κάλλος** αὐτῆς καὶ τὸ ἦθος, ὡς βασιλικῆς καὶ μεγαλοπρεποῦς. (5) Τέλος δ᾽ οὖν γῆμαι τὴν κόρην ἔπεισε καὶ γνησίαν ἀποδεῖξαι γυναῖκα...

Pharnabazus, which perhaps also came from the same source (Pharnabazus is master of his words, but the king is master of his actions); cf. 15.41.5.

[141] Tiribazus' defiance in wearing the king's clothes may evoke Xen. *Cyr.* 8.3.13: ἄλλῳ δ᾽ οὐκ ἔξεστι μεσόλευκον ἔχειν and cf. 8.2.8 on jewellery (cf. Procopius *De bello Persico* 1.17.28).

[142] The king's robe was one of his exclusive regalia. See Eddy (1961: 45) and Sancisi-Weerdenburg (1983b: 29). Yet cf. Stevenson (1997: 78) on Artabanus and Xerxes (Hdt. 7.15–17).

[143] Indeed, in the preceding story Herodotus asserts (9.107.1) that this is the greatest insult in Persia (παρὰ δὲ τοῖσι Πέρσῃσι γυναικὸς κακίω ἀκοῦσαι δέννος μέγιστός ἐστι). Since this insult was thrown at the face of Artauntes, the male counterpart of Artaunte, as it were, the anecdote of Tiribazus seems to come full circle with this allusion.

The fictional story[144] echoes Ctesias' *Persica* in the portrayal of the dominant position of Parysatis in controlling the life of the king as well as evoking the physician's description of the power of the queen mother Amestris over the love life of her daughter Amytis (*FGrH 688 F 14.40*). It can also be seen as a clever and subtle allusion to Atossa's namesake in the account of Herodotus (3.31; below).

This story can be compared to a detail in the Aspasia section in Aelian (*VH* 12.1), providing some insights into the overall structure of the original narrative. Briefly described, Cyrus the Younger presents Aspasia with a necklace which, he claims, is worthy of the mother or the daughter of a king (ἄξιός ἐστιν οὗτος ἢ θυγατρὸς βασιλέως ἢ μητρός). Aspasia agrees with the evaluation, and declines to accept it. When Parysatis learns of this response, she is pleased in that Aspasia, notwithstanding Cyrus' love for her, does not wish to take her place (Παρύσατις ... ηὔφρανε γὰρ αὐτὴν μάλιστα ἐκεῖνο, ὅτι ... ἡ Ἀσπασία, ὅμως ἐν τῷ φιλεῖσθαι ὑπὸ Κύρου ἐβούλετο τῆς Κύρου τεκούσης ἡττᾶσθαι). Parysatis bestows gifts on Aspasia, which the Greek woman again refuses; forwarding them to Cyrus, she says that his love for her is her only ornament. Aelian's narrator intervenes to assert that Aspasia is admired for her external beauty as well as for her inner virtue (ἀναμφιλόγως ἐθαυμάζετο ἥδε ἡ γυνὴ καὶ διὰ τὸ **κάλλος** τὸ τοῦ σώματος καὶ ἔτι μᾶλλον διὰ τὴν εὐγένειαν τῆς ψυχῆς). One notes that the portrayal of Aspasia is roughly the same as that of Atossa in Plutarch's account. The relationship triangle (Parysatis–Cyrus–Aspasia) has the queen mother approving of her son's woman of choice and commending her behaviour in that she does not attempt to eclipse her. Both Cyrus and his mother give attention to Aspasia and bestow gifts upon her that she refuses. This section appears to echo (assuming it comes later in the same text, in a flashback) the relationship triangle of Parysatis–Artaxerxes–Atossa. Again, the queen mother supports her son's amorous choice, and the woman in question appears not to be strong enough to offer serious competition to her over status and position. Again, Parysatis and her son both show affection to the woman in question.[145] The two women, Aspasia and Atossa, would later on form different love triangles involving Artaxerxes

[144] Cf. Brosius (1996: 110), who believes that Parysatis truly desired to join her son with a young and inexperienced woman who would be under her control, and thus indirectly enable her own influence on Artaxerxes.

[145] The special relationship between the three figures was perhaps insinuated to be a love triangle (in a broad sense). It is interesting that the incestuous relationship was remembered differently by Agathias (2.24.4), who recounts that Artaxerxes refused Parysatis' advances since the act was unjust, not common and unnatural (οὐχ ὅσιον ὂν τοῦτό γε οὐδὲ πάτριον οὐδὲ τῷ βίῳ ξυνειθισμένον). See Cameron (1969–70: 92–3) and Bigwood (2009: 325).

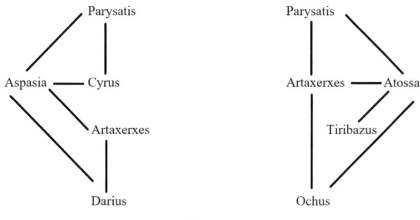

Diagram 2

(Diagram 2). Thus, the unfulfilled promise to give Atossa to Tiribazus and her marriage to Artaxerxes would provoke the future rebellion of the courtier, and the story of Darius coming between Artaxerxes and Aspasia would provide the spark needed to ignite this volatile situation. Atossa would later find herself involved in another triangle between Artaxerxes and Ochus, his other son.

The prominent place that Parysatis holds becomes apparent immediately after her reconciliation with Artaxerxes (*Art.* 23.2), an occurrence recounted in the 'common source'. There is some repetition of *Art.* 23.2 and 17.1. In both sections, Parysatis reconciles with the king (17.1: διαλυθεῖσα πρὸς αὐτόν; 23.2: διηλλάγη τῇ μητρὶ), is reported to be involved in his love life (17.1: τῶν ἐρωτικῶν ἐκοινώνει συμπράττουσα καὶ παροῦσα, 'by her presence and cooperation she took part in his love relationships; cf. 23.4–5) and brings about the death of a person (Tissaphernes and Masabates, respectively). The repetition seems to imply that Plutarch used the 'common source' twice. Once, it may be imagined, he was following his source closely; this appears to be *Art.* 23. Parysatis' involvement in Artaxerxes' love affairs seems particularly out of place in *Art.* 17, and the reconciliation appears to come too early. Both make more sense in *Art.* 23, *after* the murder of Stateira. The appearance of the same details in *Art.* 17, in a sequence coming from Ctesias (Chapter 2) shows that Plutarch transposed some elements from the 'common source' to Ctesias' narrative,[146] after his reading of the text of Ctesias was

---

[146] On transposing scenes in Plutarch, see Pelling (1979: 77, 79 n. 41; 1980: 129 n. 10; 2011: 57). Cf. Smith (1881: 16–17), Mantey (1888: 21–2), Binder (2008: 307–8).

Table 5

From the 'Common Source'	From Ctesias
[The relationship between Parysatis and Stateira till the murder of Stateira]	
End of the war (death of Cyrus)	End of the war (death of Cyrus)
Reconciliation of the king and Parysatis: execution of Tissaphernes, marriage with Atossa	Killing of the three persons: Masabates/Bagabates, the Carian, Mithridates
	Murder of Stateira

interrupted (see Chapter 2). It is suggested here that the basis for this transference of details is a certain overlap between the sequence of Ctesias and that of the 'common source'. A comparison of the two presumed sequences (Table 5) may show this clearly.

The death of Stateira was presumably told in different places in the respective sequences: in Ctesias' account it was right after the descriptions of the executions of the persons responsible for the death of Cyrus and the desecration of his body. In the 'common source' it was perhaps before the story of the war and the reconciliation of Artaxerxes and his mother. If this is true, then the sequence in this source matches perfectly what we proposed above (Chapter 4) concerning the thematic order in Deinon's work.

(III) In the work *The Sayings of Kings and Commanders* attributed to Plutarch, the last saying uttered by a person belonging to the 'Persian' section is attributed to Orontes (174b):

> Orontes, the son-in-law of Artaxerxes the king, falling from grace into dishonour and being reproached, said: as arithmeticians reckon occasionally tens of thousands on their fingers, sometimes only units; similarly, the kings' friends at times can perform everything with them, on occasion not much.
>
> Ὀρόντης, ὁ βασιλέως Ἀρτοξέρξου γαμβρός, **ἀτιμίᾳ** περιπεσὼν δι' ὀργὴν καὶ **καταγνωσθεὶς** ἔφη, καθάπερ οἱ τῶν ἀριθμητικῶν δάκτυλοι νῦν μὲν μυριάδας νῦν δὲ μονάδα ... δύνανται, τὸ αὐτὸ καὶ τοὺς τῶν βασιλέων φίλους, νῦν μὲν τὸ πᾶν δύνασθαι νῦν δὲ τοὐλάχιστον.

As may be recalled, in the narrative we examined, Orontes, who lays false accusations against Tiribazus, is condemned and disgraced when the latter is acquitted. In Diodorus' version the two consequences appear in roughly similar wording (15.11.2):

> Orontes, however, he [Artaxerxes] denounced as a person who had feigned a deceitful charge, banished him from his group of friends, and invested him with the greatest signs of humiliation.

τοῦ δὲ Ὀρόντου **καταγνοὺς** ὡς ψευδῆ κατηγορίαν πεπλακότος ἔκ τε τῶν φίλων
ἐξέκρινε καὶ ταῖς ἐσχάταις **ἀτιμίαις** περιέβαλεν.

The saying attributed to Orontes refers to the virtuality of the
honours given to the king's courtiers.[147] Later on in the original text
Orontes appeared as one of the rebels against Artaxerxes, as we see
in Diodorus' description (15.90.3, 15.91.1).

(IV) Valerius Maximus (9.2 ext. 7) continues to report the deeds of
cruelty (*crudelitas*) of Ochus once he assumes power: he buries alive
his sister/mother Atossa. His uncle (presumably Oxathres and his
branch of the family) and more than 100 sons and grandchildren he
encloses in an empty courtyard and kills them with arrows, although
they are innocent of any crime towards him. This description may
come from the same story.[148] Ochus thus seems to do what his
father did not dare to, namely, kill his mother. The contrast is surely
intended to be manifest, although it is clearly ironic, since Atossa
is not only Ochus' stepmother, but also his sister. Moreover, in an
allusion to Cambyses (Hdt. 3.31.6–32.4), which the figure of Ochus
in the descriptions of the author of the 'common source' is meant to
evoke in the minds of the readers, Ochus kills his own sister.

(V) Another segment to be considered seems to include all the passages where Diodorus describes Glos the Carian/Egyptian, Tiribazus'
son-in-law, during the Cypriot and Egyptian Campaigns.[149] First,
Glos appears as the leader of the Persian naval force (ὁ τῆς ναυτικῆς
δυνάμεως ἡγούμενος, Cf. Diod. 14.35.3), who puts an end to the
mutiny of the soldiers in Cyprus (15.3.2).[150] Next, he plays an essential part in the Battle of Citium (15.3.5–6).[151] Yet, since he is related
to Tiribazus (15.9.3) by being married to the latter's daughter, Glos

---

[147] Orontes' saying is present in two other versions in the extant Greek literature: Aelius
Aristides, *To Plato: in Defence of the Four*, 468, repeated by Photius (*Bibl.* cod. 248, p. 435
a–b), and the fourth century CE sophist and historian Eunapius (F. 84 Müller 1851: 4.51),
now extant in the *Suda* (s.v. Ἀρβαζάκιος, α 3752 Adler) apropos of the countless concubines
in the harem of Arbazacius the Isaurian. Polybius (5.26.12–13) does not attribute the idea to
any historical figure, and simply states that the men in the courts of kings are like counters
on a reckoning board.
[148] Curtius Rufus (10.5.23) refers to this mass murder committed by Ochus. Sisigambis,
Darius III's mother, recalls how in one day eighty of her brothers were killed by Ochus, the
most savage of kings (*saevissimo regum*), together with her father and six of her sons. Cf.
Justin 10.3.1.
[149] See Stylianou (1998: 148–9, 161). On Glos see also Ruzicka (1999). Cf. Briant (2002a:
631).
[150] Cf. Polyaen. 7.20.
[151] ὕστερον δὲ τοῦ Γλῶ μετὰ τοῦ βάρους ἐπενεχθέντος καὶ γενναίως ἀγωνισαμένου συνέβη φυγεῖν
τοὺς περὶ τὸν Εὐαγόραν καὶ πολλὰς τῶν τριήρων ἀποβαλεῖν, 'when Glos assaulted with a great
strength and fought in a noble manner, the outcome was that Evagoras escaped and squan-
dered numerous of his triremes'. Cf. Appendix I.

becomes fearful once Tiribazus is arrested. Glos then resorts to open revolt (15.9.3–4) by collaborating with the Egyptian king and the Spartans:

> Immediately, then, he [scil. Glos] dispatched envoys to Acoris, the king of the Egyptians, and made an alliance with him against the king. He also wrote to the Spartans and provoked them against the king, offering to give them a large amount of money and making other great promises. He took upon himself to be their ally in Greece and to assist them in establishing the hegemony of the city.
>
> εὐθὺς οὖν πρὸς μὲν Ἄκοριν τὸν βασιλέα τῶν Αἰγυπτίων διαπρεσβευσάμενος συμμαχίαν συνέθετο κατὰ τοῦ βασιλέως, πρὸς δὲ τοὺς Λακεδαιμονίους γράφων ἐπῆρε κατὰ τοῦ βασιλέως, καὶ χρημάτων πλῆθος ἐπηγγέλλετο δώσειν καὶ τὰς ἄλλας ἐπαγγελίας μεγάλας ἐποιεῖτο, ὑπισχνούμενος συμπράξειν αὐτοῖς τὰ κατὰ τὴν Ἑλλάδα καὶ τὴν ἡγεμονίαν αὐτοῖς τὴν πάτριον συγκατασκευάσειν.

Glos' address to the Spartans is similar to Cyrus' letter to the Spartans (from Ctesias?), recounted by Plutarch (*Art.* 6.3–4) and mentioned above.[152] Glos is eventually killed (Diod. 15.18.1) and Tachos (his son?)[153] attempts to renew operations; he too is killed (15.18.2), and the Spartans renounce their ambitions in Asia (15.19.1). Since the latter evidently happened before the conclusion of the Cyrpiot War, but is recounted after it, the sequence is not chronological.[154] This seems to correspond to the features which probably belonged to the original presentation of the 'common source', presumably employed by Diodorus here.

The fact that Diodorus mentions Glos within the story of the affairs of Tiribazus may lead us to infer that these two sections had some connection in the original arrangement. The tale of Glos appears to be a story of a person who was at the service of Cyrus the Younger (Xen. *Anab.* 1.4.16, 1.5.7, 2.1.3), like his father Tamos (Xen. *Anab.* 1.4.2, Diod. 14.19.5–6), and who was, however, apparently pardoned by the king and employed by him (cf. Xen. *Anab.* 2.4.24), especially in the naval battle near Citium.[155] There are parallels between the activity of Glos and that of Cyrus the Younger on the one hand, and with Tiribazus on the other. In all these cases, the king seems to be too merciful towards a person who later on becomes a real rebel, and whom Artaxerxes eventually has to suppress.

---

[152] See Chapters 2 and 3.
[153] See Beloch (1923: 3.1.99 n. 1), Hornblower (1982: 174–5), Ruzicka (1999: 31 n. 19, 41 n. 34).
[154] Cf. Stylianou (1998: 99, 149, 184–6).
[155] See Ruzicka (1999). Tamos fled to Egypt but was executed there: Diod. 14.35.3–5.

CONCLUSION AND FURTHER THOUGHTS: PLUTARCH'S USE OF DEINON AND THE 'COMMON SOURCE'

Let us examine Plutarch's method of reading and reworking his sources based on what we have suggested concerning both the lost text of Deinon and the source discussed here.

Reading

1. The reference to Deinon in the *Themistocles* merely lists him among other authors. It would be safe to believe that Plutarch had no direct knowledge of his work when he wrote this biography.

2. The reference to Deinon in the *Alexander* has a very brief mention taken out of context. As Deinon probably did not write on Alexander (as we can tell by the other fragments), he was not read by Plutarch specifically for the *Life* of the Macedonian king. The biographer most likely encountered the point attributed to Deinon in the *Alexander* in another work. It may be plausible to assume that Plutarch found this reference in a compendium of items or anecdotes related to Persia.

3. Another assumed reference to the text of Deinon in Plutarch's *Amatorius* may be dated to at least the period after 96 CE, as the end of the Flavian dynasty is mentioned in this work (771c).[156]

4. At some point, Plutarch seems to be familiar with the work of Deinon, especially the stories pertaining to Artaxerxes II and Artaxerxes III, as can be seen by the *Artaxerxes* and in the *On Isis and Osiris*.

5. Plutarch does not follow Deinon's arrangement in *Art.* 1–22. Concerning Stateira's death, he says so explicitly (*Art.* 6.9). He prefers to follow Ctesias (mainly for *Art.* 11–19) and occasionally to insert details from Deinon (based on notes or memory).

6. It would seem that Plutarch observed the broad similarities between Ctesias and Deinon and decided to follow the former's account.

7. Another reason for Plutarch's reluctance to use Deinon's arrangement may have to do with his thematic order. There are indications that Plutarch is not aware that Deinon's sequence is not chronological.

8. If this is the case, then this fact is telling. Plutarch would surely have been aware of the special character of Deinon's work

---

[156] See Ziegler (1951: 715–16), Jones (1966: 66, 72).

had he personally read it. In that case, it would appear that Plutarch's references to Deinon rely on notes taken from his *Persica*. These notes could have been composed by his assistants, slaves or freedmen.

9. In all probability, Plutarch follows mainly one source for the section of *Art.* 23–30 (apart from occasional sections he found in collections of anecdotes and included in *Art.* 22, 23). The stories in this section display internal links and therefore appear to be the same text. This text is also seen to be used by other ancient authors, and therefore was called here the 'common source'.

10. The original thematic order of the 'common source' at Plutarch's disposal is hard to fathom, but the following considerations should be taken into account:

(a) The Egyptian Campaign was placed before the Cadusian one;
(b) The Cypriot War, including the allegations against Tiribazus, was placed before the Cadusian Expedition;
(c) The affair of Glos is linked with the story of Tiribazus. It had therefore to come in its entirety (including the end of Glos) after the Cypriot War and Tiribazus' trial.[157]
(d) The story of Glos and his cooperation with the Egyptian Pharaoh probably marked the transition to the Egyptian arena. This section probably moved thematically to the story of the failed invasion of Egypt by Iphicrates and Pharnabazus. It was followed by the Cadusian War, in which Tiribazus was again prominent and saved the king.
(e) After the Cadusian War, there appeared disconnected portions relating the unrest of satraps in the western satrapies (especially Datames, Ariobarzanes and Orontes).

11. The portrayals of the affairs of the satraps could have appeared as follows:

(a) The revolt of Glos and his end (Diod. 15.18.1–3; he was betrayed) – this part was probably recounted in the story of Glos. It is worth noting that the end of the revolt belongs thematically to another section, the 'executions' after the section of the Cadusian War. In Diodorus' arrangement there seems to be some duplication, in that the end of Glos is divorced from the

---

[157] Cf. Ruzicka (1999: 32).

story of his rebellion. It may be that this incident was mentioned twice in the original.[158]

(b) The end of Datames (Nepos, *Dat.* 11.2.5; see Polyaen. 7.29.1; murdered treacherously). [Datames was the first among the satraps to be mentioned].

(c) The revolt in Cataonia, the end of Aspis (Nepos, *Dat.*, 4.4).[159]

(d) The struggle against Ariobarzanes and his end (Harpocration, s.v. Ἀριοβαρζάνης).

(e) The actions of Orontes (Diod. 15.90.3–91.1) and possibly his end.

12. There are signs that Plutarch is not aware of the thematic arrangement of the 'common source'. For instance, Plutarch's portrayal of a series of executions is probably to be expected, if the descriptions of the affairs of the satraps were presented to him succinctly in the manner of point 11. Without understanding the reasons for the outbreak of the revolts, and without understanding the temporal relationship between them, the descriptions appear to be a chain of killings of the king's satraps.

13. This may indicate that Plutarch had at his disposal only summaries of the 'common source'.

14. If the appellation of Darius the prince as a νεανίσκος (*Art.* 28.1; Justin 10.2.5: *iuvenis*) is to be taken literally, it may suggest that the device of flashback (*analepsis*) was used in the original. In that case, Darius desired Aspasia in his youth or relatively younger age and he was appointed heir at that time in his life. Darius' portrayal as fifty years old (*Art.* 26.4: πεντηκοστὸν ἔτος γεγονότα) may have been thus related to a different time, the date of his presumed revolt. This suggestion might explain some oddities in the depiction of Plutarch and Justin/Trogus, although it would not elucidate what actually triggered off the revolt, except for Tiribazus' persuasion.

15. If this is true, then again Plutarch is not aware of this fluctuation in the narrated time, and hence may have only seen summaries of the work.

Writing

16. Most of the details regarding the story of the Cypriot War and its conclusion, Tiribazus' trial and acquittal and the disgrace of

---

[158] Cf. Stevenson (1997: 126).
[159] Cf. Sekunda (1988: 43).

Orontes (as seen in Diodorus), are missing in Plutarch's biography. This section was presumably significant in the original narrative in portraying the rise, fall and comeback of Tiribazus the courtier. The allegations against Tiribazus proved to be false, and the king pardoned him, but he should have continued to distrust him, as evidenced by the future revolt he instigated. Plutarch only took the story of the hunting scene in which Tiribazus saved the life of the king. The importance of this scene (presumably within the entire original trial section) lies in the unawareness of Artaxerxes that Tiribazus would one day plot against him. Plutarch pushed this scene to the beginning of the *Life* in order to dissociate it even further from the eventual revolt and thus achieve a greater impact.

17. In order to simplify the story of Tiribazus' rise and fall, Plutarch eliminated traces of almost all other individual satraps and courtiers. He does not hesitate to embellish the account of the crushing of the revolts in a way pointing forward to *Art.* 29 (the execution of Darius) and in colours which are better suited to fit Ochus, in preparation for the comparison between the two in *Art.* 30.

18. If what we said above on the last scene of the biography is correct, Plutarch knowingly changed the original account of his source. Thus, instead of the story relating to the concealment of Artaxerxes' death which facilitated Ochus' rise to power, we seem to get a distorted view in the *Life*. While his source explicitly stated that Artaxerxes died, Plutarch presents the king as still living. He 'resurrects' him, as it were, only to have him pass away at a later point. Plutarch behaves exactly like Ochus in keeping the monarch alive even though he is already dead. Of course, to appreciate this subtle literary irony, Plutarch's readers would have to know the original text he was modifying, an assumption which cannot be taken for granted.

19. The probable last section of the 'common source' was the reign of Ochus, including a segment on the internal cruelty and his campaign against Egypt. Plutarch was most likely aware of this part of the work while composing the biography, but decided not to dwell on it. One of the reasons may be that the work did not relate the ending of Ochus, as suggested in Chapter 4 above.

6. Heracleides

Very little is known of Deinon and his writings; even less can be said of Heracleides of Cyme, the third *Persica* author who appears in Plutarch's corpus. In all, this figure appears about eight times in the extant Greek literature. It may be, however, that use was made of his work without explicit credit. Let us begin with the literary interpretation of the references to Heracleides in Plutarch's works, turn to what we know of his *Persica*, and on the basis of what we can conjecture about the structure of Heracleides' work, attempt to arrive at Plutarch's work method concerning this author.

PLUTARCH AND HERACLEIDES

The last third of the *Artaxerxes* does not name any source, apart from the mention of Heracleides apropos of the king's incestuous relationship with his daughter (*Art.* 23.6 = *FGrH* 689 F 7a):

> Some, however, relate, and among them in particular is Heracleides of Cyme, that Artaxerxes married, not only one of his daughters, but also a second, Amestris, on whom we shall report a little later.
>
> Ἔνιοι μέντοι λέγουσιν, ὧν ἐστι καὶ Ἡρακλείδης ὁ Κυμαῖος, οὐ μίαν μόνον τῶν θυγατέρων ἀλλὰ καὶ δευτέραν Ἄμηστριν γῆμαι τὸν Ἀρτοξέρξην, περὶ ἧς ὀλίγον ὕστερον ἀπαγγελοῦμεν.

Within the story of Artaxerxes' passion for and marriage to his own daughter Atossa (*Art.* 23.3–5) comes this information, which is admittedly from a different source than the rest of this section.[1] Mimicking the excess of the king who marries not only one, but two

---

[1] *Pace* Stevenson (1985: 16).

daughters, Plutarch finds evidence for this incestuous behaviour of Artaxerxes not only in one source (his main one), but in two (including Heracleides).

It would seem that *Art.* 23 has three parts: (a) In the first section (23.1–2) the king is portrayed positively, specifically favoured by the Greeks. He executes Tissaphernes the satrap and restrains his anger towards his mother by forgiving and appeasing her. (b) In the second segment (23.3–6), Artaxerxes is revealed as the complete opposite of Greek morality when he engages in an incestuous relationship with his daughter and adopts an arrogant attitude, believing that he is law incarnate and acts on behalf of the gods;[2] he is presented as taking two daughters in wedlock. (c) In the final third of *Art.* 23, Artaxerxes (23.7) is seen to be punished for his pride and excess. A skin disease, presumably inflicted by the gods, affects his daughter/wife, and the monarch suffers humiliation in having to prostate himself in prayer to a (Greek) goddess to have it removed. Some verbal echoes create the impression that the punishment fits the offence. Initially, the king sees himself as an arbiter from the god (and above human laws): ὑπὸ τοῦ **θεοῦ** (23.5), but when his daughter Attosa is sick, he prays to the goddess (τῇ **θεῷ**: 23.7). Correspondingly, the king's marriage bond(s) with his daughter(s) represent(s) his vanity: the excess in not marrying one offspring but two (οὐ μίαν **μόνον** τῶν θυγατέρων: 23.6) is answered by a prayer to one goddess alone (**μόνην** θεῶν ἐκείνην: 23.7); one notes the verbal play with the belief that Artaxerxes is the law given by the deities (**νόμον** αὐτὸν). In a similar vein, the author Heracleides (Ἡρακλείδης: 23.6) is mentioned in connection with the offence, Hera with the punishment (Ἥρᾳ: 23.7). The king is presented as someone doing obeisance (to the deity: 22.7), instead of others bowing before him.

In the transitions between the various parts of *Art.* 23, Parysatis plays an important role. The queen mother appears as a main player again, as she was prior to her banishment to Babylon. Plutarch

---

[2] Cf. Almagor (2017b). This followed an old Mesopotamian tradition, in which the king was seen as maintaining law and order on behalf of the gods, and the person who communicates their wishes. See Frankfort (1948: 252–74), cf. Cassin (1968: 65–82), Zandee (1971: 11–17), Kuhrt (1987: 30–40). Cf. 1 Kings 3:9, Isaiah 11:4; Jeremiah 23:5–6, 33:15–16, Psalms, 72:1–3. On assignment by the gods to administer justice on earth see Hammurabi's Code of Laws, 1.27–49 and the Assyrian kings (e.g. Tiglath-Pileser, I, *RIMA* 2 A.0.87.1: 1.15–25, 1.46–50, 7.36–41; A.0.87.2: 7–10; Ashurnasirpal II, *RIMA* 2 A.0.101.1: 1.9–17, 1.99–101, 3.118; A.0.101.2: 7–9; Shalmaneser III (*RIMA* 3 A.0.102.1: 3, 10, 11; A.0.102.5: 1.6, 11, 12). On Persian incest see Mandfredini, Orsi and Antelami (1987: 297–8), de Jong (1997: 424–32), Wiesehöfer (2001: 84–5).

reverts back to the year 395 BCE (the execution of Tissaphernes), after having already proceeded to events which occurred in the years 387 or 367 BCE in *Art.* 22. This structure highlights the rapid transition from Artaxerxes' political and diplomatic *acme* to one of his lowest moral points, and from a powerful position with respect to the Greek world to a weak and dependent one with regard to his mother. It is Parysatis who influences Artaxerxes to execute Tissaphernes and later on to marry his own daughter. The mention of the goddess Hera (who was also portrayed as a mother) seems to be an extension of Parysatis as a mother image, after she virtually disappears from the description after *Art.* 19. Artaxerxes' prostration before Hera to save his wife (and daughter) is reminiscent of his plea to his mother when Darius his father desires to execute his wife Stateira (*Art.* 2.2). The structure of *Art.* 23 thus shifts from the queen mother to the mother of the Olympian gods. In each section, the king exaggerates without restraint. While Nepos (*De Reg.* 1.4) shows the piety (*pietas*) of Artaxerxes towards his mother as evidence of the king's moral strength and justice (*iustitia*), Plutarch subtly presents these qualities as tokens of his weakness.[3]

Previously in the biography (*Art.* 16.2), Artaxerxes is concerned with his image in the eyes of the Greeks. He takes great pains so that all Barbarians and all Greeks will believe that he killed Cyrus. Now the king drifts away from the Greek world, and till the end of the biography gradually appears more and more like the 'Other'. Parysatis tells him to disregard Greek opinions and laws/customs (ἐάσαντα δόξας Ἑλλήνων καὶ νόμους: 23.5). This disrespect for (Greek) tradition anticipates the tyrannical demeanour of Artaxerxes.

The structure of the second part of *Art.* 23 evokes Herodotus' report (3.31) of Cambyses' behaviour when the Persian monarch desires to marry his full sister(s). The first of Cambyses' sisters is incidentally called Atossa (Hdt. 3.88), the name of Artaxerxes' first daughter/wife. The advice of Parysatis is comparable to that of Cambyses' royal judges, to the effect that the king can do whatever he wishes (τῷ βασιλεύοντι Περσέων ἐξεῖναι ποιέειν τὸ ἂν βούληται), and that no law or custom can restrict him (although this is presented by Herodotus as an instance of following another law). Cambyses' excess in marrying two sisters recurs in Plutarch's presentation of Artaxerxes in marrying two daughters. This is clearly Plutarch's own organisation, since he admits using two sources (at least) in constructing this account. The information he takes from

---

[3] Cf. Marasco (1994: 658) on *Art.* 19.

Heracleides thus fits in with the Herodotean framework. Similarly, the other daughter disappears from the story, just as in Herodotus the other sister is killed ('it was the younger, who accompanied him [to Egypt] whom he killed', τουτέων δῆτα τὴν νεωτέρην ἐπισπομένην οἱ ἐπ᾽ Αἴγυπτον κτείνει). There are more allusions to Herodotus in *Art.* 23. Of Atossa, the daughter Artaxerxes marries, nothing is known, apart from her depiction as παρθένον (23.3), παῖδα (23.4) and κόρην (23.5). Interestingly, when Darius the Great marries his own Atossa (and Cambyses') and her sister Artystone (Hdt. 3.88), the latter is described as παρθένον.[4]

As shown by Smith (1881: 22–3; cf. Mantey, 1888: 21), the mention of Amestris, the second daughter, disrupts the storyline and contradicts the rest of the details in the plot. Earlier (*Art.* 23.3–5), the king's affection towards his daughter, detected by the queen mother Parysatis, looks like an exceptional occurrence. Artaxerxes' conjugal union with his daughter seems to be an unusual act which requires extraordinary entreating from Parysatis to materialise it. Furthermore, the narrative continues (*Art.* 23.7) to stress Artaxerxes' devotion to Atossa, notwithstanding her skin illness. No hint is offered regarding the existence of an additional offspring of Artaxerxes. The mention of Amestris in *Art.* 23 as the second daughter (δευτέραν) to marry the king seems separated, consigned to the opinion of 'others', and is obviously deprived of any connection to the story since Plutarch pledges to address it only further on. Later (*Art.* 27.2) Plutarch persists in presenting Atossa as the one whom the king weds primarily or solely. These nuptials are described as ἔρωτι ποιησάμενος γυναῖκα παρὰ τὸν νόμον ('whom he made his wife out of passion, contrary to custom/law'). No intimation is given of Amestris. Yet, in *Art.* 27.7–8, Amestris is reported to be the first daughter whom the king married, i.e., before Atossa:

> The king had a number of daughters, and vowed to hand Apama in marriage to Pharnabazus, Rhodogune to Orontes, and Amestris to Tiribazus. He gave his [daughters] to the others, but lied to Tiribazus and wed Amestris himself, assuring Tiribazus instead his youngest daughter, Atossa. But shortly afterwards he became infatuated with Atossa also and married her, as has been reported, and then Tiribazus became a complete adversary to him . . .
>
> Πλειόνων οὐσῶν βασιλεῖ θυγατέρων, ὡμολόγησε Φαρναβάζῳ μὲν ᾽Απάμαν δώσειν γυναῖκα, ῾Ροδογούνην δ᾽ ᾽Ορόντῃ, Τιριβάζῳ δ᾽ ῎Αμηστριν. καὶ τοῖς μὲν ἄλλοις ἔδωκε, Τιρίβαζον δ᾽ ἐψεύσατο, γήμας αὐτὸς τὴν ῎Αμηστριν, ἀντ᾽ ἐκείνης

---

[4] Artaxerxes' story also evokes the infatuation of Xerxes with Artaunte, the daughter of Masistes (Hdt. 9.108).

δὲ τῷ Τιριβάζῳ τὴν νεωτάτην Ἄτοσσαν ἐνεγύησεν. Ἐπεὶ δὲ καὶ ταύτην ἐρασθεὶς ἔγημεν, ὡς εἴρηται, παντάπασι δυσμενῶς πρὸς αὐτὸν ὁ Τιρίβαζος εἶχεν. . .

In any manner one may choose to examine this situation, it would appear that there is some inconsistency between *Art.* 23 and 27. In the first passage (23.7), it is Artaxerxes' daughter Atossa who is designated as the king's wife, while Amestris is only mentioned in an additional account. In the second section (27.8), however, the sequence of marriages is reversed, and the monarch is portrayed as wedding Amestris prior to marrying Atossa. One could maintain Plutarch got the order of the two marriages wrong in his description.[5] It might make better sense, perhaps, to assume a different approach, in line with the content of the respective sections, and to hypothesise that Plutarch was not erroneous in his depiction, but purposely and of his own accord interwove his sources in a way that fashioned a new and confusing version of the data, to fit the aims of his fiction.

If we do not wish to consider Plutarch an inept author, a writer ignorant of the awkward position he puts his readers in, we may view this picture as tongue-in-cheek. In the first passage Plutarch pledges to mention Amestris in the future. In the second, Plutarch casually refers to Amestris, and asserts that the king guarantees her to the courtier Tiribazus, but breaks his vow and weds Amestris himself, promising his youngest daughter Atossa to Tiribazus instead. Shortly afterwards, however, Artaxerxes becomes infatuated with Atossa and weds her too, thus breaking his promise to Tiribazus twice. Like the king, Plutarch also makes a pledge but fails to keep his word. Although he refers to Amestris, he does it in a manner that makes her actual existence in the story problematic. In the initial section of *Art.* 27, when Darius requests Aspasia, Artaxerxes grants him his wish (27.3: ἔδωκε μὲν ὑπ' ἀνάγκης τοῦ νόμου), but then the king changes his mind and continues to cling on to her (27.3: δοὺς δ' ὀλίγον ὕστερον ἀφείλετο), breaking his promise to Darius. Mimicking the king, Plutarch takes Amestris back as soon as he brings her in, and is as untrustworthy as the king. Plutarch is thus not mistaken in his portrayal; instead, he purposely and autonomously introduces his sources in a way that generates a novel and deceptive portrayal of the facts, to match his literary goals.

The second (and final) reference to Heracleides by Plutarch comes from a passage we saw above in Chapter 4. Heracleides is one of

---

[5] Cf. Binder (2008: 313, 333–4). Cf. Mantey (1888: 21).

several historians mentioned in a passage from the *Themistocles* (27.1) on the Greek statesman's audience at the court of the Persian king: Thucydides and Charon relate that the meeting took place with Artaxerxes I, but a series of other historians ('Ephorus and Deinon and Cleitarchus and Heracleides and yet others more') maintain that it was Xerxes who met Themistocles.

For Plutarch, Heracleides may have been no more than a name. That the play on his name appears so blunt in the case of Hera may indicate this fact. The name 'Heracleides' has relation to Heracles and his descendants, the Heracleidae, who invaded the Peloponnese (Pind. *Pyth.* 5.69–72; Thuc. 1.9.2, Ps.-Apollod. 2.8; Diod. 4.57–8) after an initial stay in Athens (Paus. 1.32.6).[6] Heracleides the author came from Asia Minor (the Aeolian Cyme), where Themistocles finally stayed (Magnesia) after leaving Athens. Since Themistocles was partially a foreigner (and trained in the gymnasium of Heracles, where the *nothoi*, i.e., those born of foreign women, enrolled: *Them.* 1.3),[7] his arrival in Asia suggests he was ostensibly returning to the native country of some of his ancestors (Caria), like the Heracleidae arrived at their rightful inheritance.

HERACLEIDES AND HIS WORK

The impression we get from Plutarch's explicit mention of Heracleides is that this author was not significantly used for Plutarch's *Artaxerxes* or *Themistocles*. This may mean that Heracleides' text was not available to Plutarch. Alternatively, it may imply that Heracleides did not write a narrative, or else, if there was a narrative section in his work, it was not deemed very different from that of other authors.

Nothing is clear about the nature of Heracleides' work. In Athenaeus' allusions to Heracleides, we find that two titles are attributed to him: *Persian unique details* (Περσικὰ ἰδιώματα) and *Preparations* (Παρασκευαστικά). Jacoby (1913b: 470) and Drews (1973: 203 n. 127) are of the belief that the *Preparations* was the first portion of the *Persica*, encompassing two volumes, and was of an ethnographic nature, whereas the other books comprised stories

---

[6] Cf. Lys. 2.11–16; Euripides' *Heracleidae*.

[7] See Humphreys (1974). It was located in the deme Diomeia, not far from the south-east corner of the city walls; cf. Hdt. 5.63, 6.116, Schol. on Aristoph. *Ran.* 651, Liv. 31.24.17. Diog. Laert. 6.13. See Travlos (1971: 340), Kyle (1993: 84–7). Strictly speaking, Themistocles was perhaps a *metroxenos* rather than a *nothos*. See Ogden (1996: 55–7).

and narratives. Stevenson (1997: 16) regards the *Preparations* as a separate work, from the era earlier than Alexander (cf. Athen. 4.146d), and less celebrated than the *Persica*.[8] In her view (1997: 19), Heracleides composed a narrative of Persian history, pursuing the same pattern of his precursors, with occasional allusions to fascinating habits. However, if Heracleides was not an innovative writer, and if the substance of his work was merely a variety of particulars taken from other texts (below), it may be claimed that there was no great discrepancy in character between the alleged various segments of his work. Assuming this dependence on preceding works, his *Persica* may have been wholly comprised of digressions describing different subjects (e.g. concubines, or the king's dinner). Moreover, the very alternative title *Preparations*, used in plural form, seems to indicate an assortment of matters or tales. If this is true, it would seem that both titles were given as alternative names to his *Persica*.

There is also no evidence regarding any part of Heracleides' life. The latest chronological reference that may be attributed to him with some degree of certainty is the description of Themistocles at the court of Xerxes (c. 465 BCE), which comes from Plutarch. In addition, there is a reference to Xerxes and Amestris (below), and there may be another mention of Timagoras at the court of Artaxerxes II (367 BCE, below).

Among the fourteen persons called Heracleides, Diogenes Laertius (5.93–4) mentions 'a native of Cyme, who wrote of Persia (*Persica*) in five books' (Κυμαῖος, γεγραφὼς Περσικὰ ἐν πέντε βιβλίοις; the third one), a native of Cyme, orator, 'who wrote on (rhetorical) practice' (τέταρτος Κυμαῖος, ῥήτωρ, Τέχνας γεγραφώς; the fourth one); an Alexandrian (or from Callatis: Καλλατιανὸς ἢ Ἀλεξανδρεύς, the fifth) and lastly, 'an Alexandrian who wrote on Persian unique details . . .' (Ἀλεξανδρεύς, γεγραφὼς τὰ Περσικὰ ἰδιώματα, the sixth). Diogenes is interested in the author Heracleides of Pontus (c. 380–310 BCE), the person who was almost elected to be the head of the Academy after Speusippus.[9]

Following his usual custom, Diogenes enumerates homonyms at the segment's end. The third and fourth persons called Heracleides come from Cyme, but it is obvious that the third person mentioned is our writer. The fifth (who is the second century BCE author and

---

[8] Stevenson (1997: 20–1, 48–52); see, however, Lenfant (2009: 256, 258–61, 269).

[9] See Guthrie (1978: 483–9). According to Diogenes Laertius (5.86, after Sotion), Heracleides of Pontus was a student of Aristotle.

diplomat Heracleides Lembus, 'small boat')[10] and sixth persons are 'Alexandrian', and the sixth, like the third, referred to Persian matters. It was Müller (1848: 2.95) and Jacoby (1913b) who already considered the option that these two authors (the third and the sixth) may have been the same person. Jacoby, however, was not entirely certain of his identity, and therefore positioned the Alexandrian one as a different author in *FGrH* 696 F 30.[11]

If the sixth is not Heracleides of Cyme, there may be another possibility, bearing in mind that a work entitled *Zoroaster* is attributed to Heracleides of Pontus (cf. Plutarch *Adv. Col.* 1115a). Its contents are not stated, but Plutarch refers to this work within his recommendation to the Epicurean Colotes of Lampsacus (c. 320–c. 260 BCE) to consult books of Aristotle, Theophrastus and Dicaearchus, in order to see how much they diverge from Plato's natural philosophy. Most probably, this work is none other than the pseudoepigraphic composition *On Nature* (Περὶ φύσεως) which was already in circulation at the beginning of the third century BCE.[12] From the fifth century CE Neoplatonist philosopher Proclus (*In Remp.* 2.109–10 Kroll) we learn that, reproducing Plato's myth of Er (*Rep.* 10.614b–10.621), Zoroaster, 'son of Armenius, a Pamphylian by birth', Ζωροάστρης ὁ Ἀρμενίου Πάμφυλος) returns to life (after twelve days) and describes his experiences.[13] The *On Nature/ Zoroaster* might be seen as a work on 'Persian unique details', but no certainty can be achieved.

However, the third and sixth persons called Heracleides in Diogenes' list may be identical after all, and the titles of the respective books do indeed appear to be similar (Περσικὰ/ Περσικὰ ἰδιώματα). This duplicate entry may indicate that Diogenes is dependent on two catalogues: the third and fourth come from disparate registers, as are the fifth and sixth. The assumption that Diogenes Laertius used two different lists which duplicate the same persons seems to match Athenaeus' reference to two different titles, as noted above.

Why, then, is the writer from Cyme, the sixth on Diogenes' list, called 'Alexandrian'? Heracleides may have left Asia Minor to Egypt at one point and may have been part of the Alexandria intellectual milieu.[14] Alternatively, this epithet might just as well relate to the

[10] See Dilts (1971).
[11] See my *BNJ* entries 689, 696.
[12] Cf. Beck (1991: 518, 528–30).
[13] The opening is preserved also by Clement (*Strom.* 5.14.103.2–4), quoted by Eusebius (*PE* 13.13.30). Cf. Porph. *Vit. Pyth.* 12. See also Beck (1991: 530–1).
[14] See Lenfant (2009: 255 n. 3).

volume and not the person; Heracleides may have become at some point merely a library article, a work inseparably linked with the Alexandrian library and maybe completely affiliated with it. The very ascription of the composition to a Heracleides of Cyme might have had some relation to the Herodotean description (1.158) of a figure by this name. This person was the father of Aristodicus, who prevented the local people from handing the insurgent Pactyes the Lydian to the Persians (c. 546 BCE).[15] Assuming Heracleides' dependence on Herodotus, this idea may not be so fanciful. As Xerxes seems to appear in several passages, the reference may have something to do with Cyme as a stop Xerxes passed through on his way back (Hdt. 8.130). It might be safer to conclude that Heracleides is as shadowy a figure for us as he was for the ancients.

From the few fragments extant, it would indeed appear that Heracleides derived his information mainly and perhaps solely from other Greek literary sources (particularly from Herodotus and Ctesias).[16]

One long fragment discusses Persian feasts and expenditure (Athen. 2.145a–146a = *FGrH* 689 F 2). The extended and comprehensive record included in this section might create the notion that Heracleides is an innovative writer who knows the Persian court intimately. Alternatively, the list may be a compilation of items discovered by Heracleides in other Greek works. As far as the use of Herodotus and Xenophon as sources is concerned, more definite conclusions may be reached; regrettably, since the works of Ctesias and Deinon are not extant, it remains for us to speculate on their potential impact on Heracleides.

The section ascribed to Heracleides may be viewed as an explication or amplification of Herodotus 7.119, which relates how the Greek cities prepared food for Xerxes himself, his fellow diners and the soldiers ('for the enjoyment of the army', ἐς ὑποδοχὰς τοῦ στρατοῦ). Stevenson (1997: 147) suggests (and immediately withdraws this option), that Heracleides' account may have relied on Hdt. 1.133, which relates the birthday celebration of high-ranking Persians: they slaughter an ox, a horse, a camel and a donkey (βοῦν καὶ ἵππον καὶ κάμηλον καὶ ὄνον) to be consumed. In the said fragment of Heracleides, the items appear in almost an identical sequence,

---

[15] Cf. Brown (1978b), Briant (2002a: 37–8), Asheri, Lloyd and Corcella (2007: 181–3). Cyme did not appear in the story of Pactyes in Charon of Lampsacus' account according to Plutarch (*De Herod. malig.* 20.859ab).

[16] Cf. Lenfant (2009: 263).

though in the plural (ἵπποι καὶ κάμηλοι καὶ βόες καὶ ὄνοι), with deer
added to the list (καὶ ἔλαφοι).[17]

In a portrayal of the king's meal which is very similar to that
of Heracleides, Xenophon (*Cyr.* 8.2.2–4) relates how food placed
upon Cyrus' table is 'sufficient for a large number of people' (ἱκανὰ
παμπόλλοις ἀνθρώποις). Tellingly, among these are 'those whose services are on garrison duty or in service upon him (τούτοις οὓς ἀγασθείη
ἢ ἐν φυλακαῖς ἢ ἐν θεραπείαις)'. Then come servants the king favours
(ἐτίμα δὲ καὶ τῶν οἰκετῶν ἀπὸ τῆς τραπέζης ὁπότε τινὰ ἐπαινέσειε), and
they too are honoured with objects from the table; this detail appears
in Heracleides' account (δίδωσιν ἑκάστῳ τῶν οἰκετῶν, 'to the domestic
members').

Furthermore, the consent given to honourable Persians to be
exempted from joining dinner (Heracleides: ἵνα μὴ δὶς πορεύωνται,
'so that they do not appear twice') may come from Xenophon
(*Cyr.* 8.1.6): 'nobles must always be present at court and be ready
for whatever service Cyrus requests until he releases them' (ἔδοξε
τοὺς ἐντίμους ἀεὶ παρεῖναι ἐπὶ θύρας καὶ παρέχειν αὑτοὺς χρῆσθαι ὅ τι
ἂν βούληται, ἕως ἀφείη Κῦρος). Lastly, Xenophon (*Cyr.* 1.3.4) has
Mandane and her son dining with the Median king Astyages; this is
close to Heracleides' depiction (ἐνίοτε δὲ καὶ ἡ γυνὴ αὐτῷ συνδειπνεῖ
καὶ τῶν υἱῶν ἔνιοι, 'occasionally his wife and some of his sons are also
present').

Like Heracleides, Polyaenus (4.3.32), who details the items for
the king's dinner according to what was written on a bronze column
and revealed by Alexander in the king's palace,[18] mentions portions
provided to the troops (ταῦτα μὲν πάντα διαδίδωσι ταῖς στρατιαῖς).
Heracleides' demarcation of ἄριστον and δεῖπνον, translatable as
'breakfast' and 'dinner',[19] appears in Polyaenus (τὸ βασιλέως ἄριστον
καὶ δεῖπνον ... τῷ ἀρίστῳ καὶ τῷ δείπνῳ). The extent of the slaughter
is approximately similar: Heracleides' one thousand beasts slaughtered on a daily basis is matched by Polyaenus' eight hundred and
sixty. Almost half of the animals (four hundred) are sheep (list entry
twelve), like the assertion made by Heracleides that most of the beasts
are sheep. Heracleides adds two sorts of meat to those mentioned by

---

[17] Although in the Persepolis Fortification lists horses and camels do not appear as meat for
circulation or slaughter, but rather as recipients of food (horses: *PF* 1672, 1772–7; camels: *PF*
1711; for travel: 1418, 1786–7), they may nevertheless have been assigned for consumption.
See Lenfant (2009: 292 + n. 5, 293 + nn. 1–2). See more in Henkelman (2010).
[18] On this text see Lewis (1987), Briant (1989: 39–40, 2002a: 286–92), Stevenson (1997:
38–40, 144–8), Kuhrt (2007: 604–7), Lenfant (2009: 38, 191–5).
[19] See Lenfant (2009: 279 n. 1)

Polyaenus: he disregards the turtle-doves, but introduces cocks and ostriches. Whereas Heracleides refers to bread, Polyaenus incorporates wheat, barley, *olyra* (= rice-wheat?) and fine flour. Polyaenus also takes in fruits, oils and spices.[20] Even if ultimately grounded in some genuine Persian text, perhaps an official list, the description of Polyaenus appears to derive from some literary account.[21] In fact, Stevenson (1997: 39–40) supposes that Polyaenus relied on information coming ultimately from Deinon (in her opinion, via Cleitarchus).[22]

Heracleides' portrayal of the hidden presence of the king during the meal may be an attempt to explore passages like that of Xenophon, depicting the contrast between the behaviour of the Spartan king Agesilaus and that of the Persian king (*Ages.* 9.1–2). The Persian is said to think that 'his dignity requires that he should be seldom seen' (ὁ μὲν τῷ σπανίως ὁρᾶσθαι ἐσεμνύνετο). This is a recognisable theme in pictures of Persian monarchy.[23] His isolation and remoteness most probably originated from concerns for his safety and honour.[24] The point related to the separate wine consumed by the king surely has to do with the Chalybonian wine, as depicted by Ctesias (see Athen. 1.28d; cf. 4.145c; Strabo 15.3.22).[25]

Another case in point is the passage we mentioned from Plutarch's *Artaxerxes*. Devoid of clear context, the reference attributed to Heracleides (*Art.* 23.6) was perceived by Plutarch as relating to Artaxerxes' marriage with his daughter Amestris. This, however, may be a wrong interpretation, based most probably on inaccurate data. A copyist error might have altered 'Xerxes' into 'Artaxerxes' (a mistake most common and one that is also observed several times in other cases mentioned in the present volume). Presumably the blunder stemmed from an erroneous reading of Ὀτάνεα τὸν Ἀμήστριος πατέρα τῆς Ξέρξεω γυναικός ('Otanes the father of Amestris the wife of Xerxes': Hdt. 7.61). The first name Otanes (Ὀτάνεα) may have accidentally dropped from the text, forcing succesive changes to be made to the text, transforming (Arta)xerxes into the father of his wife. 'Several authors' (ἔνιοι μέντοι λέγουσιν), as claimed by Plutarch,

[20] See Stevenson (1997: 144–52).
[21] Cf. Briant (2002a: 288), who assumes it was Ctesias.
[22] Cf. Lenfant (2009: 291 n. 3). There is nothing to discard the idea that Polyaenus relied on a literary source. Cf. Athen. 4.146c for Ctesias and Deinon; cf. Athen. 11.503f.
[23] Cf. Ps.-Arist. *Mund.* 398a. See Plut. *Art.* 29.6, where the plotters are viewed by the king, but do not perceive him beyond a screen. Cf. Diod. 2.21.7; cf. Hdt. 1.99.
[24] See Manfredini, Orsi and Antelami (1987: 276), Lenfant (2009: 287).
[25] The protocol relating to the drinking of wine may concern his security. See Briant (1994: 59–60).

did actually mention Amestris as the wife of Xerxes (e.g. Herodotus, 7.61, 114, 9.104 and Ctesias, *FGrH* 688 F 13.24). Thus, this segment could have been in fact based on Herodotus (7.61).

Within the context of the known instances of luxury and effeminate ways, Athenaeus includes some scenes of court life as described by Heracleides (12.514bc = *FGrH* 689 F 1), which seem to be derived from Deinon and Herodotus. We know that Deinon (*ap.* Athen. 13.556b) mentioned the large number of royal concubines (πλῆθους τῶν παλλακίδων), and if *Art.* 27.2 comes from his account (see Chapter 5), then Deinon numbered the figure of the Persian monarch's concubines as 360.[26] Admittedly, Heracleides has τριακόσιαι γυναῖκες (300 women), but the addition of Meineke (ἑξήκοντα) is probably correct.[27] Heracleides' details concerning the 'apple bearers' (μηλοφόροι) presumably come from Herodotus (7.41), who distinguishes the spearmen (αἰχμοφόροι) accompanying Xerxes with apples at the butt-end of their lances (those who appear in the palace friezes of Susa and Persepolis), and the other soldiers (a thousand riders, and the ten thousand men on foot, called 'The Immortals', ἀθάνατοι; cf. 7.83). Heracleides seems to misunderstand Herodotus in that he makes the 'apple bearers' a division of the ten thousand, confusing them with the holders of golden pomegranate (ῥοιὰς ... χρυσέας), a unit of one thousand out of the ten thousand, according to Herodotus.

Furthermore, according to Heracleides in the same fragment, the king treads on rugs or is seated on a golden throne (ὁ δὲ θρόνος, ἐφ᾽ ᾧ ἐχρημάτιζεν καθήμενος, χρυσοῦς ἦν), ascends a chariot or mounts a stallion, but is never perceived outside the palace on foot (ἀνέβαινεν ἐπὶ τὸ ἅρμα, ἐνίοτε δὲ καὶ ἐφ᾽ ἵππον· πεζὸς δὲ οὐδέποτε ἐωράθη ἔξω τῶν βασιλείων). In one of the passages assigned to Deinon (*FGrH*

---

[26] Cf. Dicaearchus (*ap.* Athen. 13.557b) on Darius III, who had them escorting him on his expeditions. Cf. Curt. Ruf. 3.2.24 (cf. 6.6.8). Cf. Briant (2002a: 281) on this group of 360 as a restricted group among the numerous palace women. Cf. Widengren (1959: 255 n. 6). Diodorus (17.77.6) reports the identical figure for Alexander (after correction), associating it in particular with the number of the days of the year (cf. the rationale in Curt. Ruf. 3.3.10). Initally, the length of the year among the Persians was 360 days, of the lunar-solar year (a transitional stage between the 354 days of the lunar year and the 365 days of the solar year), as revealed by twofold calenders: the one pertaining to ritual in the Avesta, which was agricultural in nature (cf. *Yasna* 16.3–6) and the political one, grounded in the Babylonian model. See Taqizadeh (1938: 13–16). The ritual and traditional meaning of the number 360 is seen in many cases: Herodotus (3.90) remarks that 360 white stallions were sent yearly from Cilicia to the Great King, 'one for every day'; cf. 3.92 (360 talents), 3.94 (360 talents of gold-dust), 1.189–90 (360 canals of the river Gyndes). Cf. the banquet held in Esther 1:4 for 180 days (presumably half a year).

[27] This proposal was accepted by Jacoby (*ad loc.*) and Stevenson (1997: 18), but declined by Brosius (1996: 31) and Lenfant (2009: 271).

690 F 26), the king is said to descend from his chariot onto a golden stool (cf. Curt. Ruf. 5.2.13–15), which a royal chair-bearer accompanying him always brings.[28] The two passages complete each other; the word ἅρμα (chariot) is employed in both. Deinon's golden stool (*FGrH* 690 F 26: χρυσοῦς δίφρος) may be comprehended as a chair (see Hdt. 3.146 and 3.144, where the two words are used interchangeably).[29]

Athenaeus (12.517bc = *FGrH* 689 F 4), in a section which deals with instances of luxury, introduces the following passage after Persian (513f–515d) and Lydian (515d–517b) examples:

Heracleides of Cyme, the author of the *Persica*, having written in his *Preparations* that in the country which produces frankincense the king is independent, and subject of no one, he says the following: 'And he lives the life of luxury and ease, spending all his days in his palace and leading an extravagant life; and he does nothing and has no contact with people. Yet, he is the one to appoint the judges (over them), and if a man thinks that they have resolved unfairly, there is an opening at the uppermost part of the palace, which is affixed with a chain. The one who claims that an unjust decision has been made grips the chain, and pulls the window; and when the king hears it, he calls him, and adjudicates himself. And if the judges have made an undue verdict, they are executed; but if (the judges have determined) fairly, the man who has opened the window is put to death. And it is said that the sum of money expended on the king, his surrounding women and friends daily is fifteen Babylonian talents.'

Ἡρακλείδης δ' ὁ Κυμαῖος ὁ τὰ Περσικὰ συγγράψας ἐν τοῖς ἐπιγραφομένοις Παρασκευαστικοῖς εἰπὼν ὡς ὁ ἐν τῇ λιβανοφόρῳ χώρᾳ βασιλεὺς αὐτόνομός τέ ἐστι καὶ οὐδενὸς ὑπήκοος, γράφει καὶ ταῦτα· 'οὗτος δ' ὑπερβάλλει τῇ τρυφῇ καὶ ῥαθυμίᾳ· διατρίβει τε γὰρ αἰεὶ ἐν τοῖς βασιλείοις, ἐν τρυφῇ καὶ δαπάνῃ τὸν βίον διάγων, καὶ πράττει οὐδὲ ἓν πρᾶγμα, οὐδὲ πολλοῖς πλησιάζει, ἀλλὰ δικαστὰς αὐτο<ὺ>ς ἀποδεικνύει. Καὶ ἐὰν τις αὐτοὺς ἡγῆται μὴ δικαίως δεδικακέναι, ἔστι θυρὶς ἐν τῷ ὑψηλοτάτῳ τῶν βασιλείων, καὶ αὕτη ἁλύσει δέδεται· ὁ οὖν ἡγούμενος ἀδίκως δεδικάσθαι ἐπιλαμβάνεται τῆς ἁλύσεως, καὶ ἕλκει τὴν θυρίδα, καὶ ὁ βασιλεὺς ἐπειδὰν αἴσθηται, εἰσκαλεῖ, καὶ αὐτὸς δικάζει. Καὶ ἐὰν φαίνωνται οἱ δικασταὶ ἀδίκως δικάσαντες, ἀποθνήσκουσιν· ἐὰν δὲ δικαίως, ὁ κινήσας τὴν θυρίδα ἀπόλλυται. Τὰ δὲ ἀναλώματα λέγεται τῆς ἡμέρας εἰς τὸν βασιλέα καὶ τὰς περὶ αὐτὸν γυναῖκας καὶ φίλους γίνεσθαι τάλαντα πεντεκαίδεκα Βαβυλώνια'.

αὐτο<ὺ>ς Schweighäuser

The portrayal appears to be conflating accounts of Arabia and India. The description of the land which produces frankincense, that is,

---

[28] On the Persepolis depiction of the king's footstool, on which his feet rest, see Schmidt (1953: pls. 77–8 [east gate]; 112–19 [treasury]). The royal protocol contradicted the image of the 'royal hero', seen standing on the ground. See Briant (2002a: 221).

[29] Cf. Dem. 24.129; cf. Lib. *Dec.* 9.39. On the Persian throne see Jamzadeh (1991); cf. the golden throne on which Xerxes sits: Plut. *Them.* 13.1. Cf. Schmidt (1953: pl. 99), Lenfant (2009: 215).

Arabia, is close to what Herodotus describes (3.107: πρὸς δ᾽ αὖ μεσαμβρίης ἐσχάτη Ἀραβίη τῶν οἰκεομενέων χωρέων ἐστί, ἐν δὲ ταύτῃ λιβανωτός τε ἐστὶ μούνῃ χωρέων πασέων φυόμενος καὶ σμύρνη ... , 'Arabia, the furthest of inhabited countries in the direction of the midday, is the only one to grow frankincense and myrrh etc.'). This is also true with regard to its autonomy. Herodotus says that in Asia, all 'except the Arabians' are the Great King's subjects (οἱ ἦσαν ἐν τῇ Ἀσίῃ πάντες **κατήκοοι** πλὴν Ἀραβίων: 3.88). The impression is that Heracleides' claim that the local king is independent (βασιλεὺς αὐτόνομός τέ ἐστι καὶ οὐδενὸς **ὑπήκοος**) is his own interpretation.

The detail concerning the judges is surely a modified version of Herodotus' account of the royal judges (3.31.5.25, 7.194), who are executed if found to act unfairly. Lenfant (2009: 304–5) suggests that both Ctesias and Heracleides intend to address the Persian monarch but insinuate it through descriptions of phenomena distant in time and space. In fact, it could be that Heracleides' picture referred to some elements taken from Ctesias' picture (*FGrH* 688 F 45.31) concerning the administration of justice by the Indian king. In his pursuit of the truth, according to Photius' summary, the Indian king uses water from a spring, since it prompts the drinker to divulge everything. This is done in cases where allegations are made (ἐφ᾽ ὧν κατηγορουμένων); if the accused is found guilty, the sentence passed upon him is that he starves himself to death; if nothing is substantiated, the man is cleared. This description completes Heracleides' structure ostensibly referring to an appeal: if the judges appear to have decided unjustly, they are put to death; but if they appear to have decided justly, then the man who has moved the window is executed. Photius and Athenaeus may have stressed different features of a parallel portrayal.

Heracleides' account of the king's exclusive pleasures and his daily expenditure can be compared with Ctesias *FGrH* 688 F 39.[30] The reference to the 'Babylonian' unit implies that the author was acquainted with this weight system.[31] One should point to the appearance of Babylon in Ctesias' *Indica* as the setting to which he frequently refers in his reports.[32] Thus, the passage ascribed to Heracleides by Athenaeus could be ultimately derived from Ctesias (especially *FGrH* 688 F 45.31) and Herodotus (3.31, 5.25, 7.194 and 3.88, 107).

---

[30] Cf. Deinon *FGrH* 690 F 24. Lenfant (2009: 305).
[31] Darius I introduced the weight standard, which associated the silver tribute with the old Mesopotamian Shekel/Siglos (Hdt 3.89: the standard of the Babylonian talent, Βαβυλώνιον σταθμὸν τάλαντον ἀπαγινέειν; cf. 3.95); cf. Ael. *VH* 1.22. See Nau (1972: 6–7).
[32] See Chapter 2.

If all this is true, then Drews (1973: 121) is correct in supposing that Heracleides adopted data written in the books of Herodotus and Ctesias – although it is not evident whether Heracleides referred explicitly to his precursors. Moreover, whereas Deinon does not appear to be reliant on Heracleides, there may be indication of the latter's dependence on the former. Overturning the suggestion of Jacoby (1909: 94–5), Drews (1973: 116, 121) may also be correct in proposing that Deinon wrote before Heracleides.

The fact that Athenaeus could refer to the same work using two different titles and that Diogenes does not notice that he mentions the same person twice indicate that this work was not very popular in antiquity. There seems to be no sign that our two main writers attesting to its substance (Athenaeus and Plutarch) read it at first hand. Readers perhaps considered it too unoriginal,[33] although its conciseness was helpful for compilers of collection works of the sort Athenaeus apparently turned to.

HERACLEIDES AND TIMAGORAS

Heracleides may have referred to specific historical events that took place during the reign of Artaxerxes II Mnemon, if indeed one passage in Plutarch's *Artaxerxes* can be attributed to him. But the case is problematic. The text comes from Plutarch (*Art.* 22.9–11):

> with Timagoras the Athenian, who sent a secret written message through his secretary, Beluris, the king was so impressed that he granted him ten thousand darics, and eighty cows to follow him because he was ill and needed cow's milk; furthermore, he sent him a couch, with spreads and bed-makers (because the Greeks did not know how to make beds), and carriers to convey him down to the sea, for he was weak. While he was present at court, he sent him a most glorious dinner . . .
>
> Τιμαγόρα δὲ τῷ Ἀθηναίῳ, διὰ Βηλούριδος τοῦ γραμματέως εἰσπέμψαντι γραμματίδιον ἀπόρρητον, ἡσθεὶς μυρίους τε δαρεικοὺς ἔδωκε, καὶ γάλακτος βοείου δεομένῳ δι' ἀσθένειαν ὀγδοήκοντα βοῦς ἀμέλγεσθαι παρηκολούθουν· ἔτι δὲ κλίνην καὶ στρώματα καὶ τοὺς στρωννύντας ἔπεμψεν, ὡς οὐ μεμαθηκότων Ἑλλήνων ὑποστρωννύναι, καὶ φορεῖς τοὺς κομίζοντας αὐτὸν μέχρι θαλάσσης μαλακῶς ἔχοντα. παρόντι δὲ δεῖπνον ἐπέμπετο λαμπρότατον . . .

The royal gifts given to Timagoras were apparently part of the accusations brought against him upon his return to Athens. He was

---

[33] Cf. Stevenson (1997: 21), who suggests that the work was too brief, too exhaustive and too technical for it to be of use by writers of universal histories and therefore it was of no great concern to non-experts.

tried and executed in 367 BCE.[34] There are two diverse accounts with respect to the allegations against Timagoras: one is his unfaithfulness to his assignment and to his country (προδοσία), the other is the depravity and the acceptance of bribery (δωροδοκία). The gifts fall in the second category and smack of collaboration with Persia.[35]

Another text is Athenaeus (2.48c–49a = *FGrH* 689 F 5), who again mentions the 'bed makers' and explicitly ascribes this detail to Heracleides:

> The Persians, as Heracleides writes, were the first to discover the so-called 'bed makers', so that their layers might at all times have order and smoothness. Hence, Artaxerxes honoured Timagoras (the Cretan), or Entimos of Gortyn, as Phaenias the Peripatetic says, who came up to the king to imitate Themistocles, and gave him a tent exceptional in attractiveness and magnitude and a silver-footed couch; and he conveyed to him also luxurious bedspreads, and a person to organise them, saying that the Greeks did not know how to set a bed. And this Cretan was summoned to the meal of the relatives, by the king's kindness; this was never done to any Greek previously, and never has been subsequently, since the dignity was kept for (royal) kin. To Timagoras the Athenian, who made an obeisance before the king, and who was much honoured, this was not done. Of the items which were placed before the king some were dispatched to him from the (royal) table. To Antalcidas the Spartan he (Artaxerxes) sent his own wreath after he had immersed it in fragrance. But to Entimos he did many things and summoned him to the dinner of the relatives, which the Persians barely endured, since they believed it made the honour more regular and also because they supposed a military expedition against Greece was approaching. He gave him also a couch with silver feet and a bed, and a floral tent with a covering, a silver seat, and a gilded sunshade, twenty gold plates with valuable stones, a hundred big containers of silver, (a hundred) silver mixing bowls, and a hundred female slave girls, and a hundred male servants, and six thousand gold coins, apart from what was provided for him for his everyday needs.

> Πρῶτοι δὲ Πέρσαι, ὥς φησιν Ἡρακλείδης, καὶ τοὺς λεγομένους στρώτας ἐφεῦρον, ἵνα κόσμον ἔχῃ ἡ στρῶσις καὶ εὐάφειαν. Τὸν οὖν Κρῆτα Τιμαγόραν ἢ τὸν ἐκ Γόρτυνος, ὥς φησι Φαινίας ὁ Περιπατητικός, Ἔντιμον, ὃς ζήλῳ Θεμιστοκλέους ἀνέβη ὡς βασιλέα τιμῶν Ἀρταξέρξης σκηνήν τε ἔδωκεν αὐτῷ διαφέρουσαν τὸ κάλλος καὶ τὸ μέγεθος καὶ κλίνην ἀργυρόποδα, ἔπεμψε δὲ καὶ στρώματα πολυτελῆ καὶ τὸν ὑποστρώσοντα, φάσκων οὐκ ἐπίστασθαι τοὺς Ἕλληνας ὑποστρωννύειν. Καὶ ἐπὶ τὸ συγγενικὸν ἄριστον ἐκαλεῖτο ὁ Κρῆς οὗτος, τὸν βασιλέα ψυχαγωγήσας, ὅπερ οὐδενὶ πρότερον τῶν Ἑλλήνων ἐγένετο, ἀλλ᾽ οὐδ᾽ ὕστερον· αὕτη γὰρ ἡ τιμὴ τοῖς συγγενέσι διεφυλάττετο· Τιμαγόρᾳ μὲν γὰρ τῷ Ἀθηναίῳ τῷ προσκυνήσαντι βασιλέα καὶ μάλιστα τιμηθέντι τοῦτο οὐχ ὑπῆρξε. τῶν δὲ παρατιθεμένων βασιλεῖ τούτῳ τινὰ ἀπὸ τῆς τραπέζης ἀπέστελλε. Ἀνταλκίδα δὲ τῷ Λάκωνι τὸν αὐτοῦ

---

[34] See Hofstetter (1978: 183–4, no. 322).

[35] The two accusations are different, even though some scholars like Reincke (1936: 1073) claim that Timagoras was indicted and convicted of both bribery from the Persians and treason of his homeland. Cf. Xen. *Hell.* 7.1.38, Dem. 19.191.

στέφανον εἰς μύρον βάψας ἔπεμψε. τῷ δ᾽ Ἐντίμῳ τοιαῦτα πολλὰ ἐποίει, καὶ ἐπὶ τὸ συγγενικὸν ἄριστον ἐκάλει, ἐφ᾽ ᾧ οἱ Πέρσαι χαλεπῶς ἔφερον, ὡς τῆς τε τιμῆς δημευομένης καὶ στρατείας ἐπὶ τὴν Ἑλλάδα πάλιν ἐσομένης. Ἔπεμψε δὲ καὶ κλίνην αὐτῷ ἀργυρόποδα καὶ στρωμνὴν καὶ σκηνὴν οὐρανοφόρον ἀνθινὴν καὶ θρόνον ἀργυροῦν καὶ ἐπίχρυσον σκιάδειον καὶ φιάλας λιθοκολλήτους χρυσᾶς εἴκοσι, ἀργυρᾶς δὲ μεγάλας ἑκατὸν καὶ κρατῆρας ἀργυροῦς <εἴκοσι> καὶ παιδίσκας ἑκατὸν καὶ παῖδας ἑκατόν, χρυσοῦς τε ἑξακισχιλίους χωρὶς τῶν εἰς τὰ ἐπιτήδεια καθ᾽ ἡμέραν διδομένων.
εἴκοσι add. Olson

The only item associated with Heracleides is the claim that the Persians are the earliest to have a group of domestics whose task was to make the beds. This group of servants is known only in relation to different variations of this tale of the largesse granted to Timagoras[36] (Plut. *Art.* 22.9; *Pelop.* 30.10: στρώτας θεράποντας, and *Suda*, s.v. 'Timagoras', τ 591 Adler, adapted from Photius and hypercorrecting the latter to στρατιώτας θεράποντας, 'escorting soldiers').

Athenaeus' account appears to deal with two persons at the court of king Artaxerxes (but it is not clear whether it is the first or the second), namely, Timagoras or Entimos of Gortyn in Crete, and ascribes this detail to Phaenias the Peripatetic (Τιμαγόραν ἢ τὸν ἐκ Γόρτυνος, ὥς φησι Φαινίας ὁ περιπατητικὸς Ἔντιμον). Book 2 of Athenaeus is actually an epitome of the original,[37] and as a matter of fact, the text of the epitome is so muddled that its meaning is distorted. One needs only to observe the crude repetitions (which surely betray two stages of summary):

1. Invitation to the king's table twice:
   [a] **ἐπὶ τὸ συγγενικὸν ἄριστον ἐκαλεῖτο** ὁ Κρὴς οὗτος, . . .
   [b] τῷ δ᾽ Ἐντίμῳ τοιαῦτα πολλὰ ἐποίει καὶ **ἐπὶ τὸ συγγενικὸν ἄριστον ἐκάλει** . . .
2. The same items granted twice (a tent and silver-footed bed with covering):
   [a] τιμῶν Ἀρταξέρξης **σκηνήν** τε ἔδωκεν αὐτῷ διαφέρουσαν τὸ κάλλος καὶ τὸ μέγεθος καὶ **κλίνην ἀργυρόποδα** . . .
   [b] ἔπεμψε δὲ καὶ **κλίνην** αὐτῷ **ἀργυρόποδα** καὶ στρωμνὴν καὶ **σκηνὴν** οὐρανοφόρον ἀνθινὴν.

The fact that at some point in the transmission of the work, it was unclear to the reader of Athenaeus (or of the epitome) whether

[36] See Mosley (1972), Lenfant (2009: 306–8).
[37] See Zepernick (1921: 318–19) and Lenfant (2007: 51). The words ὥς φησιν Ἡρακλείδης perhaps indicate a rewording of a previous phrasing.

the hero of this story was Timagoras or a particular Crete named Entimos shows the complete uncertainty of this text.[38] The segment also comprises a seemingly unfitting depiction of Timagoras as one who did not have the dignity of sitting at the king's dinner, a description which clearly conflicts with Plutarch's picture in *Art.* 22.11.

This person called 'Entimos' is completely unknown. It would appear that in actuality the contrast referred to by our corrupt text of Athenaeus was not between Timagoras and an 'Entimos' at all, but rather between Timagoras and Themistocles, specifically mentioned at the start of the passage (ὃς ζήλῳ Θεμιστοκλέους ἀνέβη ὡς βασιλέα). The very existence of an Entimos of Gortyn in Crete is doubtful. It may be the result of a misunderstanding, based on the following: (1) the presence in the text of the word ἔντιμος, literally meaning 'honoured', cf. Ath. 4.146a: the ἐντιμότατοι, most honourable of the guests who come to the Great King's table for breakfast; (2) a (learned) reference to an Entimos who established the city of Gela in the early seventh century BCE, and whose origin was Cretan (cf. Hdt. 7.153.1, Thuc. 6.4.3, Diod. 8.23.1).[39]

This 'Cretan' (ὁ Κρὴς), who was summoned to eat at the royal table, and 'Entimos', who accepted presents from the king, are obviously the same person and they are most probably Timagoras, since the features relating to their respective descriptions by Athenaeus and Plutarch are almost identical. 'The Athenian' (τῷ Ἀθηναίῳ) who made the gesture of obeisance to the king is obviously Themistocles, who is probably also the one who obtained the honour of sitting at the king's table (cf. Plut. *Them.* 27.4–28.1).[40] The epitomator probably took the two Athenians – one who was the first to be invited to the king's table, and the other who was the last to be so honoured – and confused them with each other, as well as with the fictional 'Entimos'.

The appearance of this note inspired some scholars to hold that Heracleides, to whom the remark on the servants who make beds is assigned, is also the author of the entire Timagoras story, seen in both the works of Plutarch and Athenaeus.[41] Yet it would appear

---

[38] Cf. Smith (1881: 20). For a different view, see Zecchini (1989: 5–7) and Engels (1998: 340 n. 217).

[39] The mention of Gortyn could be the result of misreading a distorted text, whose condition one cannot establish, but which perhaps included the two forms TIM(O) and ΓOP. For 'entimos' see also Binder (2008: 296).

[40] The reference to the imminent expedition against Greece, if not transposed within the summary from one figure to the other, is perhaps an interpolation added to the unclear epitome, roughly based on the story of Themistocles (cf. Plut. *Them.* 31.3–4).

[41] See Bodin (1915: 266 n. 1); cf. Jacoby (ad 689 F 5), Kuhrt (2007: 637 n. 6), Binder (2008: 298).

more probable to assume that the brief quotation from Heracleides is set at the culmination of a list of citations, rather than as the commencement of a long depiction. One should observe that the sections in Athenaeus' text just before the Heracleides allusion quote some writers discussing beddings and coverings, among them Ephippus, Aristophanes, Sophron and Homer. That there is a common theme to the allusions may indicate the employment of a work which jointly assembled them, a work of the nature of a compendium of stories on this subject integrating Heracleides and the other authors.

Indeed, another name is thrown in by Athenaeus, the Peripatetic author Phaenias of Eresus (late fourth century BCE).[42] Phaenias was interested in Themistocles (Plut. *Them.* 1.2, 7.6, 13.3, 27.5, 29.7), and some scholars believe the complete section of Athenaeus comprising the Timagoras affair is a fragment of Phaenias' *Histories* (= Wehrli F 27).[43] Phaenias may have employed the work of Heracleides,[44] but the other way around is also possible, namely, that Heracleides used the work of Phaenias. Indeed, if we accept that the work of Heracleides apparently did not include a continuous narrative and was derivative in character, we could readily accept that he could have been later than Phaenias. Heracleides is only associated with one element of this story (the mention of the 'bed makers').[45]

It cannot be decided whether the contrast between Timagoras and Themistocles was created by Heracleides or Phaenias, or indeed whether any of them encompassed the Timagoras story at all. The comparison may have originated by Athenaeus himself, and set between the person of Themistocles as portrayed by Phaenias[46] and the character of Timagoras appearing in another work. There are no hints of any critical attitude towards Persian reality in Athenaeus' other references to Heracleides.[47] Therefore, the appearance here of this pejorative approach, stressing the deference gesture to the king as appalling, may come from a later hand (Athenaeus himself or his epitomator).

Johannes Engels (1998: 341) supposes that Phaenias gathered historical instances of well-known Greeks in the Persian court.

---

[42] On Phaenias' date see Engels (1998: 290).

[43] Cf. Schottin (1865: 8), Mantey (1888: 17), Westlake (1939: 14).

[44] See Zecchini (1989: 7).

[45] It would seem that Heracleides culled only the sections that were of interest to him, namely, the class of bed makers, in accordance with his interest in the imperial personnel of the Persian kingdom (cf. *FGrH* 690 FF 1, 2). The beds could be related to dining couches, another known interest of Heracleides. See Lanfant (2009: 307).

[46] See Zecchini (1989: 6, 12) on Athenaeus' reading of Phaenias at first hand.

[47] As rightly noted by Lenfant (2009: 308).

Apparently, concurring with this supposition is the speculation of some scholars that for these same particulars told in his *Pelopidas* version, Plutarch used Phaenias.[48] Equally plausible, however, is the consideration that the portrayal of Phaenias was incorporated into this kind of collection (alongside the anecdote of Heracleides?), a collection which was employed by certain authors afterwards (like Plutarch and Athenaeus).

A clue may be found in the following facts: Athenaeus mentions Timagoras twice, each time in combination with a different tale. The two occurrences are that of Antalcidas and a wreath granted to him by Artaxerxes at a banquet (2.48e), and the jest of the statesman and ambassador Epicrates that the Athenians should elect nine envoys to the Persian king rather than nine archons (6.251b). All three anecdotes are manifest in Plutarch's *Pelopidas* 30. Only the stories of Antalcidas and Timagoras are found in Plutarch's *Artaxerxes* (22.2 and 22.9–13). One can infer that Plutarch discovered both stories in the same text, which may explain their combined reappearance in two of his works. There are negligible differences between the variants in the two biographies. Athenaeus was not reliant on any of them – especially not on Plutarch's *Pelopidas* for the sixth book of his *Deipnosophistai*, since Athenaeus refers to Hegesander (of Delphi) as the origin of the Epicrates story, a detail not seen in Plutarch's corresponding depiction.

As Henry D. Westlake (1939: 14 n. 3) comments, there appears to be no accident in the continuing joint recurrence of these tales. Perhaps they all ultimately come from the same work. This composition, one may suppose, was either posterior to Hegesander, whose Ὑπομνήματα (*Commentaries*) must belong to the middle third century BCE onward, since this writer alluded (Athen. 9.400d) to Antigonus II Gonatas (d. c. 239 BCE)[49] – or it could *be* the work of Hegesander itself. Athenaeus appears to have been dependent on Hegesander widely for strings of citations, especially in books 2–4, 6–10, 12–14. Thus, either Hegesander or a compilation that used his work referred to Timagoras and cited Heracleides (and Phaenias).[50] The reason for the presence together of these stories dealing with Persian decadence (in Hegesander or in a later work) may be that these themes were typical of Persia in Greek imagination.

If all this is true, in what manner did the description of Heracleides

---

[48] Cf. Schottin (1865: 8), Georgiadou (1997: 178 n. 5).
[49] See Müller (1851: 4.412–22).
[50] Cf. Mantey (1888: 18).

reach Plutarch? As suggested here, Plutarch and Athenaeus may have encountered the relevant passages or points ascribed to Heracleides in popular collections of anecdotes and apophthegms. This kind of work had circulated since the Hellenistic period, usually abridging and excerpting tales from larger compositions. In the two other cases, Plutarch may have found the name of Heracleides mentioned in several compendia, once in a list (together with Ephorus, Deinon and Cleitarchus), and once as an author describing (Arta)xerxes and Amestris. Similarly, he may have found the entire Timagoras tale (along with the stories of Antalcidas and Ismenias) in such a compendium, where the name of Heracleides may or may not have been mentioned in that source.[51]

PLUTARCH'S USE(S) OF HERACLEIDES

We are now able to express some ideas concerning Plutarch's employment of Heracleides. Since the information assigned to Heracleides in the *Artaxerxes* disrupts the whole storyline in which the king falls in love with his own daughter Atossa and marries her, Heracleides is obviously different from the source of the main storyline of *Art.* 23, 24–5, 26–30 of the biography which form a closed and coherent unit (above).[52] Moreover, for this very reason, the source used for this unit did not use Heracleides and could not have been mentioned by Heracleides.

In fact, this case offers us a rare glimpse at Plutarch's work method. It appears to show two distinct stages in the composition of the work. We can see this by comparing the information in *Art.* 23 and 27 of the *Artaxerxes*:

(a) Atossa: 23.3–5: ἤσθετο … Ἀτόσσης ἐρῶντος ἔρωτα δεινόν … τέλος δ' οὖν γῆμαι τὴν κόρην ἔπεισε … ('… he was desperately in love with one of his two daughters, Atossa … At last, then, she persuaded the king to marry the girl and proclaim her his lawful wife').

(b) Amestris: 23.6: οὐ μίαν μόνον τῶν θυγατέρων, ἀλλὰ καὶ δευτέραν Ἄμηστριν γῆμαι ('… married, not one of his daughters only, but also a second, Amestris').

(c) Amestris, 27.7–8: ὡμολόγησε … Τιριβάζῳ δ' Ἄμηστριν … Τιρίβαζον δ' ἐψεύσατο, γήμας αὐτὸς τὴν Ἄμηστριν ('he promised …

---

[51] Cf. Mantey (1888: 22).
[52] Cf. Marasco (1994: 667), Bigwood (2009: 326 n. 89) and confusedly Smith (1881: 25).

[to give] Amestris to Tiribazus. He broke his word to Tiribazus and married Amestris himself').

(d) Atossa: 27.8–9: ἀντ' ἐκείνης δὲ τῷ Τιριβάζῳ τὴν νεωτάτην Ἄτοσσαν ἐνεγύησεν. ἐπεὶ δὲ καὶ ταύτην ἐρασθεὶς ἔγημεν ... ('... betrothing in her stead to Tiribazus his youngest daughter Atossa. Soon, however, he fell enamoured of Atossa also and married her ...').

This portrayal suggests that there were (at least) two stages in the composition of this segment in the biography: one which followed the main source, the so-called 'common source' (Deinon?), which we saw in Chapter 5, and another which inserted material from a different source. Browsing through his sources, Plutarch presumably came across this detached note (already erroneously referring to Artaxerxes), and inserted it at the appropriate places in the biography. In *Art.* 23, Plutarch introduces the marriage to Amestris *after* that to Atossa, keeping in one piece the main storyline and the innovation in this betrothal. In *Art.* 27 he adds Amestris *before* Atossa, preserving the significant feature that the king's marriage to Atossa is the event that principally insultes Tiribazus. At this stage, Plutarch includes internal cross-references (23.6: περὶ ἧς ὀλίγον ὕστερον ἀπαγγελοῦμεν, 'of whom we will speak a little later'; 27.9: ὡς εἴρηται, 'as said').[53] Plutarch thus both amplifies the description of Artaxerxes' wrongdoing and intensifies his intemperance. Placing this disconnected note on Amestris in the story of Atossa forced Plutarch to invent a double affront to Tiribazus, which most probably did not appear in the original source he was using. Plutarch was thus able to fit Artaxerxes into the framework of Cambyses and his sisters. In order to achieve these literary effects, Plutarch had therefore to manipulate his sources.

*

The two occasions in which Plutarch uses Heracleides are similar. In both, we see that the information provided is sparse and taken out of historical context. In the two examples, there is a conflation between Xerxes and Artaxerxes. In one case this confusion is explicit – in the case of the identity of the king that Themistocles met – and in the other case it is implied, as the reference to Artaxerxes is probably meant to indicate Xerxes. These facts indicate that Plutarch did not

---

[53] For this type of cross-reference in Plutarch's *Lives*, see *Thes.* 29.2, *Rom.* 21.3, *Fab. Max.* 21.3, *Pelop.* 35.4, *Flam.* 12.13, *Luc.* 4.5, 29.8, *Ant.*, 16.1, 60.5, *Brut.* 13.3, *Arat.* 30.6.

read a narrative account by Heracleides, and did not have the work of this author at his disposal.[54]

EXCURSUS: CHARON OF LAMPSACUS

In the same passage mentioned above (*Them.* 27) on Themistocles' interview at the Persian court, Plutarch accepts the version of Thucydides and Charon that the king in question was Artaxerxes I and not that of the four other historians mentioned (Ephorus and Deinon and Cleitarchus and Heracleides) 'and others more' (ἄλλοι πλείονες), according to which it was Xerxes. As the mention of Deinon and Heracleides was already studied, let us examine briefly the reference to Charon,[55] who also wrote a *Persica*, the content of which is entirely obscure to us.[56]

When we first explored the use of the names of Deinon and Heracleides in this passage, we chose the road not taken by Plutarch. It is most telling that Plutarch opted for the variant espoused by only two historians, as opposed to that of the majority of writers, in direct correspondence to Themistocles' leaving the Athenian democratic customs, and to the choice he made to dwell among the Persians. Plutarch's choice thus anticipates Themistocles' adoption of barbarian customs.

Plutarch follows those historians who are numerically in the second place, and this evokes Herodotus' portrayal of Themistocles, who received only 'second honours' for valour (8.123: τὸν δεύτερον) in the Battle of Salamis, a passage referred to in the biography (*Them.* 17.1). Among the Greeks, Themistocles was denied the first place and was obviously insulted, being as he was overly ambitious and passionate for glory (φιλοτιμία: *Them.* 3.4, 5.3, 5.5, 6.3, 10.5, 18.1: φιλοτιμότατος), desirous to be the first (*Them.* 3.1: πρωτεύειν).[57] Plutarch believes Thucydides and Charon should be chosen, and thus be first. Indeed, he places them first in the section. This may insinuate that, like Themistocles, who regarded himself as possessing merit which is not justly appreciated, Plutarch's choice is made because the historical writings of Thucydides and Charon have more value for him than those of the others he mentions. Put differently, when it comes to Greek history writing

---

[54] Cf. Marasco (1994: 667). *Pace* Binder (2008: 72).

[55] On this passage see Frost (1980: 213–14), Marr (1998: 149–50).

[56] See Schwartz (1899a: 2179) who believes the following reference is not from the *Persica*. See Lenfant (2009: 15–16).

[57] See Wardman (1974: 115–24), Larmour (1992: 4183–4), Duff (2010: 46–7, 49, 52).

(unlike Greek politics), it is not the quantity, but the quality that matters.

Or does it? The mention of Charon's birthplace, as opposed to all the other historians in *Them.* 27, implies the outcome of Themistocles' choice (*Them.* 29.11):[58] he receives from the king three cities, Magnesia, Lampsacus and Myus (respectively, for bread, wine and meat), so that artistically, Plutarch's choice may even allude to the (material) benefits derived from Themistocles' decision.

Furthermore, the impression is that Charon disappears in the course of the paragraph. Plutarch not only places Thucydides' name at the beginning of the entire passage, but mentions it twice. If we follow our way in making the historiographic reference stand in allegorically for the political sphere, Plutarch moves from the dominance of the few to the supremacy of one, corresponding to the way Themistocles says he will augment the king's renown and influence (ἀλλ' ἐγὼ τὴν βασιλέως ... φήμην καὶ δύναμιν αὐξήσων: *Them.* 27.6).

Finally, Thucydides' version is chosen despite the fact that the chronological records are not fixed (οὐδ' αὐτοῖς ἀτρέμα συντατομένοις). The impression is that regardless of the stress on the *nomos* in this section, Greek historiography has no laws or fixed criteria. The gradual turn away from Greek practices, of both Plutarch and Themistocles, moves them closer to the whimsical demeanour stereotypical of the east.[59]

Not much is known of Charon (see Chapter 1), but several points are worthy of mention. Plutarch's appreciation of his description, as hinted above, is indeed visible in the way he employs his depictions against Herodotus' narrative (*De Herod. malig.* 20.859ab, 24.861ad). His mention of Charon in another place (*Mul. virt.* 18.255ae ~ Polyaen. 8.37) may indicate that Plutarch was familiar with his work at first hand.[60] Yet Charon's descriptions in the *De Herodoti malignitate* (*On the malice of Herodotus*) appear extremely pithy.[61] They might be epitomes of his work, or else Charon's depic-

---

[58] Cf. Thuc. 1.138.5, Diod. 11.57.7, Nep. *Them.* 10.3, Strab. 13.1.12, 14.1.10, Amm. Marc. 22.8.4. See Frost (1980: 220 n. 220) for further references. This picture presents a problem, in that Lampsacus was apparently not the king's to give, but the association of Themistocles and the city is attested (in an annual festival). See Gomme (1945: 292), Frost (1980: 220–3), Hornblower (1991: 224), Marr (1998: 226–8).

[59] But the east is made to look more stable, as the same adjective is used to describe the chiliarch's complaint (*Them.* 29.2: ἀτρέμα στενάξας, 'groans calmly').

[60] See Stadter (1965: 98) on the last passage.

[61] They could be verbatim quotations; cf. the Ionism of βασιληίου in *De Herod. malig.* 24.861cd (= *FGrH* 687b F 5).

tions might even be epitomes of Herodotus,[62] as they do not really present contradictions to the Halicarnassian,[63] despite the fact that Plutarch employs them as such. This suggestion of a work which is derivative in nature may explain its disappearance; it can certainly explain the disappearance of Charon's name in the second reference to the 'Artaxerxes variant' in the *Themistocles*. Indeed, the parallel version of Nepos, *Them.* 9.1 (quoted in Chapter 4) only has Thucydides, whom the Roman biographer believes because he was closer in time to Themistocles and of the same city. If Charon indeed presented a similar opinion, it was not considered relevant to Nepos.

[62] This suggestion would explain the similarity of the Astyages dream story as found in Herodotus and Charon (Tert. *De Anim.* 46).

[63] See Jacoby (1940: 17–18): the fundamental facts and the line of narrative coincide.

7. Conclusions

The attempt to arrive at Plutarch's method of work through a literary reading of his *Lives* and other treatises has yielded some interesting results in the case of the fourth century BCE *Persica* volumes. Let us start with our understanding of these works and conclude with Plutarch's manner of composition.

THE *PERSICA*

Some of the features which can be attributed to the lost works used by Plutarch and to their authors were probably those that the biographer presumed to be common knowledge and regarded as information shared by his intended readers. This inference is feasible due to the fact that Plutarch seems to have worked with the assumptions and anticipations of his audience, and therefore had to postulate their beliefs and the degree of their familiarity with texts or portrayals in order for his imagery and messages to be successfully decoded. However, our study has shown that certain other traits appear to be unknown to Plutarch.

Ctesias

A fundamental distinction that recurs in Plutarch's text is that between Ctesias as a historical agent spending time in Persia and acting as the king's physician and Ctesias as an author, depicting, among other stories, his own activity. Plutarch testifies to the extent that Ctesias mentioned himself in the last books of his *Persica* as a significant agent acting in the circles of the king and of his mother, mediating between the king and Clearchus and his Greeks, between

Clearchus and Parysatis and between Artaxerxes and Conon and Evagoras in Cyprus. Ctesias also emphasised his role in saving the king when he was injured. The fact that Ctesias was a figure in his own narrative enabled the physician to allude to the circumstances in which his own work was created.

Plutarch seems to stress an element in Ctesias' work which is not noticed in other passages ascribed to him and is hardly ever discussed in connection to his work. This is the feature of subtle and elusive *metapoetic* references to Ctesias' own historical writing and his awareness of the methods and imagery employed, including awareness of the question whether, and to what extent, historical reports can be truthful. Thus, Ctesias himself probably referred to his relations with other contemporary characters on two levels, ostensibly the historical and subtly the literary. As a real person, he was dependent on these figures; as an author, they (as literary constructs) were dependent on him. Plutarch conveys this sophisticated aspect, while Photius (and ancient authors referring to Ctesias) do not. Ctesias, as can be revealed in Plutarch's passages, seems to have been conscious of the readers and of the reception of his writings. He perhaps expected his audience to be mindful of the ironies presented in overt fabrications and tall stories, but most ancient (and some modern) readers have completely misinterpreted his reports. Plutarch is cognizant of Ctesias' inventiveness, but also of the negative view of him held by unreflective readers.

Similarly, in a way that does not appear in Photius' skeletal epitome, Plutarch communicates another feature of Ctesias' text, and this is its polyphonic richness, through which the physician was able to express diverse opinions and attitudes. This element served Plutarch in his employment of certain voices of the characters of Ctesias' narrative world, which the biographer masked as independent historiographic accounts – a suggestion we proposed here.

Our study has discovered one stylistic feature of Ctesias' work, and this is explicit internal references. At least one case has to be assumed, and this is a reference in book 19 or 20 of the *Persica* back to the punishment of Aspamitres in book 17. Many other traits of Ctesias' writing shown or commented upon by Plutarch, such as verbosity, excessive digressions, dubious descriptions, bias and the stress on autopsy, are also evidenced by other ancient authors.

Deinon

The portrayals of the obscure author Deinon are presented by Plutarch as possessing two traits: one is being derivative, and based on other accounts or testimonies, especially Ctesias and Herodotus. Plutarch may even have assumed that Deinon is known to his readership for this quality. The other feature of Deinon's work is the imaginative elaboration of previous reports, by extending the same description to other areas or periods of time. We have proposed that this dual nature of Deinon's work is comparable to the variance in Xenophon's writing, between accounts which appropriated material from other authors (in *Anabasis* 1) and new descriptions with complete fictional characters, albeit built on the basis of the works of others (*Cyropaedia*).

It would appear from Plutarch's biography that Deinon's work was mainly of a narrative character, dealing with historical events, and had less of the character of an ethnographic compendium of dissociated details, as might appear from its presentation in some ancient sources referring to it. Notwithstanding this feature, Deinon is seen to have arranged his description in an unpredictable manner. We have suggested that this order was *thematic*, and not chronological. The arguments for identifying Plutarch's source for *Art.* 23–30 as Deinon were put forward. The complete original sequence in that source was again thematic.

Deinon's work is obliquely presented by Plutarch as belonging to the period before Alexander, either in its subject matter or in the time it was composed. At least, this is how he was perceived by Plutarch, and presumably by his readers.

Heracleides

Plutarch gives the impression that his references to Heracleides are always an after-thought, and hence it would seem that he did not employ a narrative text of this author. Presumably there was none available to him. The two brief explicit occurrences in which Heracleides is mentioned by Plutarch display a conflation of Xerxes and Artaxerxes. One may assume that the details ascribed to Heracleides circulated devoid of any historical or chronological context. A reasonable conjecture we proposed was that Heracleides' work was entirely derivative, but did not elaborate upon earlier accounts in an innovative manner like Deinon's writing. It may be the case that Heracleides' work was actually a series of items from Persia culled from other authors and (mis)interpreted.

PLUTARCH'S WORK METHOD

Ctesias

We have suggested that the appearances of Ctesias in Plutarch's work suggest that there were two different stages. The first involved Plutarch's reading of anecdotes detached from his work and gathered in some collections; one such compendium was probably of stories relating to animals (employed in the *De sollertia animalium*). The second stage was reading done especially for the *Artaxerxes*. Since Plutarch uses Ctesias almost exclusively for *Artaxerxes* 11–19, it would seem realistic to assume that at least at one stage of the composition, this was the main book scroll open before him.[1] This proposal does not exclude the possibility that Plutarch simultaneously used notes previously taken from Ctesias,[2] as there seems to be some break in his reading in the transition from *Art.* 16 to 17 and since *Art.* 19 contains some oddities which may result from a misunderstanding of written notes. It is impossible to know whether Plutarch used an abridged version of Ctesias' work, although it is probable that he did, bearing in mind the popularity and accessibility of the epitomes of Ctesias. We found some verbal correspondences with Photius' text, which might suggest that both were roughly the same adapted version. If we can estimate on the basis of several form names, the quality of Ctesias' MS which Plutarch had was better than that of Photius. Plutarch does not show any sign of acquaintance with the *Indica*, but since the subject matter of this work is irrelevant to the lifetime of Artaxerxes II it is hard to conclude whether Plutarch's edition of the *Persica* circulated together with it or not.

Apart from explicit censure of certain stylistic peculiarities of the physician's work associated with deviations from the truth – like lengthy descriptions, digressions, and abundance of mythic and marvellous details – Plutarch himself uses an array of literary devices that underscore the physician's descriptions as lies or untrustworthy fictitious accounts. These devices include indirect speech, insinuation

---

[1] See Haug (1854: 90–4), Schottin (1865: 4–5), Smith (1881: 32–5), Mantey (1888: 13–14), Krumbholz (1889: 3).
[2] Cf. Stadter (2014: 673, 683).

of *metalepsis* (i.e., violations of the registers of narrative between the author and his fictional world) or inconsistent use of logical or epistemic criteria. In particular, Plutarch stresses divergent versions, or even creates them where none were found, by presenting Ctesias' narrative in two variants (each introducing different elements), by treating the same action from the point of view of two agents (Ctesias and the king), by introducing the voices of figures within the fictional narrative world as real historiographic reports of the events, and so forth.

An interesting yet ironic device used by Plutarch to check Ctesias' account is his playing on the expectations of the readers and on their acquaintance with the more popular description of Xenophon. Thus, in reverse to the chronological order of things, Ctesias' report is made to answer that of Xenophon, and is even implied to be a misquotation or a falsification of his text.

Yet, in view of what this study has shown, a great deal of text manipulation is to be attributed to Plutarch himself. When it comes to Ctesias, this practice is almost necessitated by the hyperbole and fantasy of the physician; it almost seems natural when it is remembered that Ctesias perhaps manifestly tried to improve certain descriptions of his predecessors (specifically Herodotus). Furthermore, the devices used by Plutarch are designed to highlight the feature mostly associated with Ctesias (especially his *Indica*), namely, his unreliability. Plutarch artistically connects this trait of Ctesias' writing to the content of the relevant books of his *Persica* dealing with Artaxerxes' false version of the death of Cyrus the Younger. The doubt in Ctesias' trustworthiness is also channelled through Plutarch's general Platonic skepticism towards the written word. Plutarch underscores the difficult (if not impossible) way of reaching the truth through textual or artistic measures. While Plutarch's manipulation of the text is opposed to any tradition of faithfulness to the original, it is done in the effort to arrive at a greater truth, and is grounded in the Platonic belief that truth exists beyond the text.

Deinon

Similar conclusions seem to apply to Plutarch's use of Deinon's text. Here too, there appear to have been two phases in Plutarch's acquaintance with this author. The reference to Deinon in the *Themistocles* merely lists him as one among other authors. The one in the *Alexander* has a very brief mention taken out of context, since Deinon probably did not write on Alexander. We mentioned several other passages repeated in collections of anecdotes or sayings, of the sort used by Athenaeus, which may indicate that all these items spread independently from the work of Deinon, and were presumably found in this form by Plutarch. At another phase, Plutarch shows acquaintance with the work of Deinon, though only with those sections concerned with Artaxerxes II and Artaxerxes III. This reading is visible in the *Artaxerxes* and in the *On Isis and Osiris*, where Plutarch seems to know a relatively continuous section from Deinon's work concerning Artaxerxes III Ochus' campaign against Egypt. In these two latter works, first-hand knowledge of Deinon's work can be deduced. It would be reasonable to assume that the two phases of reading Deinon were sequential. An assumed use of Deinon in Plutarch's *Amatorius* can be dated to after 96 CE, while the citation in the *On Isis and Osiris* would be later, in c. 115 CE. If the knowledge displayed in the *On Isis and Osiris* postdated the gathering of material for the *Artaxerxes*, then the biography may be seen to have been written before or simultaneously with this work, although more precise dating is probably impossible.

Above we suggested, basing our hypothesis on the observation that Plutarch does not recognise the particular thematic order of Deinon's work, but instead ascribes to him a chronological error, that the biographer did not do the reading of Deinon and the ensuing annotation himself; this act was presumably done by his assistants.[3] In the *Artaxerxes* Deinon is not cited frequently, and his book is apparently not used as the default scroll for the first two thirds of the biography. This may have to do with Plutarch's comparison between his work (perhaps as presented in notes) and Ctesias' *Persica* and his deduction that Deinon's account is derivative. Indeed, in almost all the references to Deinon, he is compared with Ctesias. This appears to be an important point in the analysis of Plutarch's work method, namely that very early in the composition of his work he characterised the authors and works he was to deal with and, playing with this characterisation, he arranged and altered his material.

We proposed the existence of a text used by later authors, including Plutarch, which we termed 'the common source'. We presented some arguments for the claim that this text is to be identified with Deinon.

---

[3] See Russell (1963: 22), Jones (1971: 87 n. 35); cf. Pelling (1979: 95; 2002: 24), especially with regard to 'the more recherché sources'. Deinon's work might well fall into that category of sources. On the copying of rolls by slaves, see Cic. *Ad Fam.* 16.21.8. One may assume that if Plutarch's assistants were those who epitomised the work, they were given a clear guideline in advance on how to summarise it and what to take from the text. Yet cf. Pelling (2011: 38) on Quint. *Inst.* 10.1.128 (Seneca misled by his assistants).

Leaving this question aside, it is clear that in *Art.* 23–30 it is the turn of notes taken from this work to be consulted throughout as the main source employed.

Plutarch uses several devices in order to streamline the stories in this work and fit them to the material presented in the first parts of the *Artaxerxes*. These devices embrace condensing and grouping events together, the omission of others, and in an artistic manipulation of the text, the presentation of a fabricated story from this source as true (the circumstances of Artaxerxes' death). Plutarch also bridges this section with the portions he adapted from Ctesias, in a series of verbal echoes that create a sense of closure between scenes, transposition of scenes from one text into the sequence derived from another (e.g. the hunt scene of Artaxerxes and Tiribazus), and repetition (e.g. *Art.* 17.1 and 23.4–5). In fact, the device of repetition may reveal that in some cases Plutarch did not have enough material, and had to rework the same notes; it also insinuates that Plutarch only had summaries of some texts at his disposal.

Heracleides

Plutarch's play on Heracleides' name in both of the texts where he mentions him implies that for the biographer, this author was perhaps no more than a name. Plutarch may have found the reference to Heracleides in several compendia, once in a list (together with Ephorus, Deinon and Cleitarchus), and once as an author describing Amestris. Since the information attributed to Heracleides disrupts the entire narrative sequence of *Artaxerxes* 23–9, his work was probably not consulted for this unit except for this one detail, apparently falsely attributed to Artaxerxes. If this is so, it would appear that Heracleides was added at a later stage in the composition of the work.[4] Ostensibly, he was chosen because he undermines and problematises the prevailing account in the last third of the *Artaxerxes*. If the source used in this section is Deinon, then Heracleides fulfils the role of Deinon's own Deinon, as it were, comparable to the alternative which Deinon establishes with regard to Ctesias in the early part. Heracleides is thus the third *Persica* author to be used in the biography in a way that casts doubt on the very notion that a written work leads to the truth.

*

---

[4] Cf. Pelling (2011: 41): '... some last-minute integration of material that came to mind as he wrote'.

In Achaemenid scholarship Plutarch is still seen as an author who largely copies his sources or echoes royal propaganda reflected in the Greek texts he uses. Yet one cannot dissociate the information in Plutarch's texts from their author, his aims and work method. He did not merely duplicate passages from his source material. Therefore, some of the fragments commonly regarded as such by scholars are not really fragments of the *Persica* works but rather sections which Plutarch composed himself, using several works while twisting them around, omitting and adding details. Indeed, several 'fragments' are the result of his work method, which involved interpretation and manipulation of his sources. In certain cases he is intentionally ironic, a fact unfortunately misunderstood by many readers.

In this volume I have tried to present these aspects of Plutarch's technique, claiming that his work method and the issue of the content of his sources are closely knit questions in research and have to be dealt with together. The inferences in one field are related to deductions in the other. The methodology employed can be used to advance us further along the road to grasp the character of the lost works on Persia. It thus enables us to appreciate the historical value of these *Persica* works, not lost on Plutarch himself.

The methodology proposed here is indeed hampered by the absence of the sources Plutarch used, but the fact that the works studied form a closed unit and are approximately similar with respect to content, date and approach allows the research to be more focused. Fortunately for our study, it seems that in classical antiquity only a handful of contemporary authors narrated court stories of ancient Persia. Due to Plutarch's employment of these lost works throughout his *Artaxerxes*, this biography offers a rare opportunity to examine Plutarch's method of work in composing a biography of a statesman. It is possible to observe the visible seams, as it were, between their manifestations in the *Life*. This employment of sources also makes it possible to trace, to a certain extent, the several phases of the composition of the *Life*.

Through a close reading of the text and, more importantly, by appreciating the predominance of the literary aspect of Plutarch's works, we are in a better position to understand the character of the *Persica* works Plutarch used. We comprehend the extent of Plutarch's manipulation, as we see the way he lets these texts (as well as Xenophon's *Anabasis*) check and balance each other. This facet relates to the question of character and the restraints placed upon passions. Plutarch allows some descriptions to get out of hand, as it were, and proceed into improbable fantasy, but he also curbs them, sometimes by reasonable arguments and occasionally simply by other textual allusions. This structure resembles the Platonic scheme where passions are controlled by reason or by other passions. It is because of these features that even when Plutarch describes real scenes from the past, his work is not strictly speaking historical, but more of a work of art with a philosophical message, which the reader has to find out. Hopefully, the methodology proposed here can be an important tool to comprehend what Plutarch is doing in the *Lives* and other works as well, while appreciating them as great artistic achievements.

Appendix I:
Two Notes on the Cypriot War

WAS TIRIBAZUS PRESENT AT THE BATTLE OF CITIUM?

The question whether Tiribazus was present at the scene of the naval Battle of Citium, in which Artaxerxes defeated Evagoras of Salamis, has bearing on the issue of his presence in another place where he may have been employed for his diplomatic skills, namely, the Cadusian Campaign. One notes that there is something interestingly disconcerting about the accounts we have of the battle.

Diodorus (15.2.2) first calls Tiribazus 'a commander of the fleet' (στρατηγοὺς δ' ἀπέδειξε τῆς πεζῆς δυνάμεως Ὀρόνταν κηδεστήν, τῆς δὲ ναυτικῆς Τιρίβαζον; 'as commanders he [Artaxerxes] chose for the land force his son-in-law Orontes, and for the naval Tiribazus'). Soon, however (15.3.2), it is Glos, Tiribazus' son-in-law (cf. 15.9.3), who is called the 'naval commander' (ὁ τῆς ναυτικῆς δυνάμεως ἡγούμενος, ὀνομαζόμενος δὲ Γλῶς; 'leader of the naval armament, known as Glos')[1] and who suppresses a mutiny. Again, Tiribazus is the supreme commander after the Battle of Citium (15.8.1: τῶν ὅλων ἔχων τὴν ἡγεμονίαν). Some scholars believe that this discrepancy can be solved by postulating that there was a division of powers between the two persons.[2]

Nevertheless, there may be a different interpretation. The two were probably commanders, but not at the same time; Tiribazus was not at all present during the preparations leading to the sea battle of Citium, and during the actual clash.[3] He only arrived in Cyprus after

---

[1] Cf. Aen. Tac. 31.35.
[2] Ruzicka (1999: 27): 'Glos ... seems to have been the real fleet commander'; (28): 'the fleet, apparently commanded operationally by Glos'. Cf. Ruzicka (2012: 87–93). Cf. Stevenson (1997: 121 n. 5), Stylianou (1998: 155–7).
[3] Ruzicka (2012: 88) claims that when mutiny occurred, 'the Persian commanders, Tiribazus and Orontes along with Glos, restored order', but Diodorus mainly speaks of Glos.

the defeat of Evagoras to negotiate the terms of capitulation, and then assumed supreme command.[4] This may be gathered from the other source we have of this event, namely Thopompus, or rather the summary made by Photius to book 12 of his *Philippica* (*FGrH* 115 F 103 = *Bibl.* cod. 176 p. 120 a 25–34):

(6) how he began to make war more vigorously against Evagoras, and about the sea-fight at Cyprus ... (9) how Tiribazus made war, how he plotted against Evagoras, and how Evagoras denounced him to the king and got him arrested with the complicity of Orontes.

(6) ὅπως τε πρὸς Εὐαγόραν ἐπικρατέστερον ἐπολέμει, καὶ περὶ τῆς ἐν Κύπρῳ ναυμαχίας... (9) καὶ ὡς Τιρίβαζος ἐπολέμησεν, ὅπως τε Εὐαγόρᾳ ἐπεβούλευσεν, ὅπως τε αὐτὸν Εὐαγόρας πρὸς βασιλέα διαβαλὼν συνέλαβε μετ' Ὀρόντου.

First we have the Battle of Citium, and *only afterwards* is Tiribazus mentioned. One explanation for the two odd details we have in our sources could be that Tiribazus only arrived later in the scene. While admittedly Theopompus' section in its entirety may not follow strict chronological order and is partially thematic,[5] there is no denying that Tiribazus appears in these passages separated from the sea battle, and within the context of Orontes' charges. The verb ἐπολέμησεν ('made war') may relate to the siege of Salamis after the naval battle (Diod. 15.8.1: τὴν Σαλαμῖνα πολιορκουμένην ἐνεργῶς; cf. Isoc. *Paneg.* 134).[6] It is patent that Theopompus' account has to be taken together with the description of Diodorus (15.8.3–4, discussed above) of the accusation against Tiribazus, brought by Orontes, with regards to the collaboration with Evagoras.[7] This fact is important, since in this section Diodorus is following the 'common source' for the Cypriot War, a sequence which Theopompus also appears to follow.[8]

Diodorus has Tiribazus going up to the king to announce the victory and request money to continue the campaign (15.4.2).[9] This

---

[4] Cf. Spyridakis (1935: 66), who speaks of a command reshuffle among the Persians after the naval battle and Tiribazus' arrival from the king. Stylianou (1998: 156) also points at some absence of Tiribazus: 'while still in Ionia Tiribazus had probably appointed Glos nauarch of his fleet'.

[5] Milns and Ellis (1966), Tuplin (1996: 14–15), Stylianou (1998: 151).

[6] See Ruzicka (1999: 28). This could be Diodorus' 'two years of continuous fighting' (15.9.2: διετῆ χρόνον τὸν ἐπὶ πᾶσι συνεχῶς πολεμηθείς). The period may be his own interpretation, with no sign for this periodisation in his source, as indeed suggested by Stylianou (1998: 147): 'Diodoran improvisation'. Could this temporal designation be the result of corrupt MSS? See Stylianou (1998: 184).

[7] Cf. also Polyaen. 7.14.1. Photius may have missed the exact nuances, in that Tiribazus was charged of having conspired *with* Evagoras and Orontes was the one who libelled him before the king. See Osborne (1973: 528–9), Shrimpton (1991b: 17), Stylianou (1998: 181–2, 183–4).

[8] Diodorus may have also used Ephorus for the battle itself (cf. Polyb. 12.25f.1) in 15.2–4. If this is so, then there may be a case here of combining two reports. According to the main one, however, Tiribazus is not mentioned during the battle.

[9] καὶ Τιρίβαζος μὲν μετὰ τὴν ναυμαχίαν διαβὰς εἰς Κιλικίαν, κἀκεῖθεν πορευθεὶς πρὸς τὸν βασιλέα,

description parallels Diodorus' account of the actions of Evagoras, who asks assistance from the king of Egypt (15.4.3, 15.8.1).[10] The schematic neatness of the comparison makes this depiction appear doubtful, and may in fact be Diodorus' attempt to grapple with his source and explain why Tiribazus is described as arriving in Cyprus *after* the battle.[11]

These considerations lead us to conclude that Tiribazus' activities in the Cadusian and Cypriot fronts were presented in different sections of the original source, and perhaps not in chronological order, as outlined above.

THE BATTLE OF CITIUM AND THE 'EGYPTIAN WAR'

According to the prevailing view (since Meyer 1902: 5.312–13 and Beloch, 1923: 3.2.226–8), the Battle of Citium occurred close to the termination of the war; the date suggested according to this view (381/0 BCE) was challenged by Gordon Shrimpton (1991b), who preferred to place it in 386/5, immediately after the conclusion of the King's Peace.[12] Not all are convinced.[13]

Most of the arguments of Christopher Tuplin (1996: 9–15) against Shrimpton's date concern the failed Persian War against Egypt, which Isocrates mentions as occurring *before* the Cypriot War (*Paneg.* 140). The difficulty is to find a reasonable timeframe for both campaigns, and to include in it the incidents of famine and mutiny in the Persian army, the first mention of Egyptian assistance rendered to Evagoras (Diod. 15.3.1–3) – before the Egyptian War, one would assume – and the 'devastation of Phoenicia and Syria' or rebellion in Cilicia, as related by Isocrates (*Paneg.* 161, *Evag.* 62).[14] Tuplin's arguments are cogent, especially in view of Shrimpton's belief that the Persian

---

τήν τε νίκην ἀπήγγειλε καὶ δισχίλια τάλαντα πρὸς τὸν πόλεμον ἀπεκόμισεν. 'Meantime Tiribazus crossed over to Cilicia after the sea-fight and continued thence to the king, reported the victory, and brought back two thousand talents for the prosecution of the war' (trans. C. H. Oldfather).

[10] Εὐαγόρας μὲν ὁ τῶν Σαλαμινίων βασιλεὺς ἧκεν εἰς Κύπρον ἐξ Αἰγύπτου, κομίζων χρήματα παρὰ Ἀκόριδος τοῦ βασιλέως Αἰγύπτου ἐλάττονα τῶν προσδοκηθέντων, 'Evagoras, the king of the Salaminians, came to Cyprus from Egypt, carrying money from Acoris, the king of Egypt, but not as much as he had anticipated' (15.8.1; trans. C. H. Oldfather). Stylianou (1998: 180) makes the comparison.

[11] Diodorus may have creatively changed the direction of Tiribazus, who arrived in Cilicia on his way *to* Cyprus (15.2.2).

[12] This is in a way a return to the chronology noted first by Judeich (1892: 119–31). Cf. van der Spek (1998: 241–7).

[13] See Tuplin (1996: 9–15). Stylianou (1998: 152–4) dates the naval battle to 384 BCE. See Ruzicka (1999: 27–8 n. 11). Cf. Osborne (1973: 526–7).

[14] Isocrates' oration *Panegyricus* was delivered before the end of the Cypriot War, perhaps in 380. See Tuplin (1983: 179–82; 1996: 10), Stylianou (1998: 143–4).

attack on Egypt followed or was simultaneous with the invasion of Cyprus (that is, in 387/6 BCE).

Yet what if there was no actual war against Egypt? It is suggested here that the rhetorical hyperbole of Isocrates, who is our sole source for this campaign, is misread.[15] Isocrates was no historian (Shrimpton 1991b: 19), and his utterances are not to be judged by historical standards.[16] Isocrates' oration was meant to persuade the public, and his exaggerated depictions were intended to harp on Greek derision of the Great King. Isocrates claims (*Paneg.* 140):

> First is the revolt of Egypt: what has he accomplished against those holding it? Did he not send to this war the most celebrated of the Persians, Abrocomas and Tithraustes and Pharnabazus, and did not they, after remaining three years and receiving more evils than they effected, finally wished to be delivered in such a manner so that the insurgents are no longer pleased with their freedom, but are already seeking to expand their control over their neighbours as well?
>
> Καὶ πρῶτον μὲν ἀποστάσης Αἰγύπτου τί διαπέπρακται πρὸς τοὺς ἔχοντας αὐτήν; Οὐκ ἐκεῖνος μὲν ἐπὶ τὸν πόλεμον τοῦτον κατέπεμψεν τοὺς εὐδοκιμωτάτους Περσῶν, Ἀβροκόμαν καὶ Τιθραύστην καὶ Φαρνάβαζον, οὗτοι δὲ τρί' ἔτη μείναντες καὶ πλείω κακὰ παθόντες ἢ ποιήσαντες, τελευτῶντες οὕτως ἀπηλλάγησαν ὥστε τοὺς ἀφεστῶτας μηκέτι τὴν ἐλευθερίαν ἀγαπᾶν, ἀλλ' ἤδη καὶ τῶν ὁμόρων ζητεῖν ἐπάρχειν;

By whatever standard we choose to interpret his portrayal of this campaign, stating that the Persian force 'remained' (μείναντες) for three years is hardly suitable to describe an ongoing expedition (especially one that involved hardships).[17] It is more fitting as a description of a force that was assembled in order to leave for an expedition, but did not actually depart. This is the exact picture we find in Nepos, *Dat.* 3.5, of a force assembling, but due to other considerations, never setting out on its course. The mention of Pharnabazus and Tithraustes by both Isocrates and Nepos implies that they refer to the assembling of the same force. Another source should perhaps be added here, *Prologus* 10 of Trogus' lost *Philippica*, which has the king 'preparing' for war against Egypt (*bellum Aegyptium in urbe Ace conpararit*).[18]

In *Paneg.* 142, Isocrates asserts that the king allows his navy of

[15] Influenced by his *Phil.* 101?

[16] Cf. Briant (2002a: 650): 'Isocrates' chronologically rather imprecise presentation certainly need not be taken absolutely literally.'

[17] Cf. Ruzicka (2012: 74–6).

[18] If this is the same campaign, one should note that it follows the Cypriot War in the order of the *Prologus*. Cf. Binder (2008: 318).

only a hundred ships to be blockaded for three years,[19] and this theme of inactivity recurs also in the portrayal of the Cypriot War (141).[20] It would appear that the same goes for the Egyptian front. The argument is that nothing has been done for three years, not that the king invaded Egypt. The mention of 'war' here is not free from irony, and surely was understood as such by Isocrates' audience.

Isocrates places the Egyptian Campaign before the Cypriot one, and this sequence is indeed temporal, as rightly claimed by Tuplin (cf. Shrimpton 1991b: 18). But we should not make much of this order, since Isocrates groups together both the force assembled by Abrocomas (in 401 BCE) and that gathered by Pharnabazus and Tithraustes.[21] The fact that they are indistinguishable in the eyes of Isocrates (and his audience) perhaps alludes to the fact that both expeditions did not materialise. Isocrates' timeframe in this passage is from the Egyptian revolt (404 BCE) onward, which allows him to place all events together and create an impressive rhetorical picture.[22] Bearing in mind this fact, there is nothing that would hinder placing the assembling of the forces headed by Pharnabazus and Tithraustes after the battle of Citium, or at least after the King's Peace (as Shrimpton has it).

Furthermore, as Panico Stylianou (1998: 150) rightly comments, we know that Chabrias the Athenian mercenary-commander was in Egypt (Diod. 15.29.1–2, hired by Acoris) until he was recalled (see Chapter 5), but there is no evidence of a Persian campaign against Egypt at the time of his sojourn there. This does not mean that the war preceded his stay, but rather that there was none.

Equally hyperbolic is Isocrates' description of the extension of the rebel dominion to neighbouring peoples. This probably refers to the Egyptian alliance with Evagoras (Diod. 15.2.3) and the Pisidians (Theop. F 103.13). The references to Phoenicia, Syria and Cilicia (*Evag.* 62) are surely exaggerated, since the Persian king used Cilicia as a base for operations against Cyprus (Diod. 15.2.2, 15.3.3, 15.4.2),[23] and Acre (Acco) as a base for the planned expedition against Egypt (if Trogus' *Prologus* 10 indeed refers to this Persian

---

[19] ... τρία μὲν ἔτη περιεῖδε τὸ ναυτικὸν τὸ προκινδυνεῦον ὑπὲρ τῆς Ἀσίας ὑπὸ τριήρων ἑκατὸν μόνων πολιορκούμενον.

[20] τοιαῦται βραδυτῆτες ἐν ταῖς πράξεσιν ταῖς βασιλέως ἔνεισιν, 'there are actions of such slowness among the king's operations'.

[21] These are clearly two separate forces and two separate commands. Cf. Ruzicka (2012: 64, 72, 76). On Abrocomas see Xen. *Anab.* 1.4.3, 1.4.5. Shrimpton (1991b: 7).

[22] Shrimpton (1991b: 18) raises this as a possibility.

[23] See Kuhrt (2007: 1.387).

army).²⁴ Isocrates may refer to the impact of Evagoras' attack on the Persian supply line (Diod. 15.3.1).²⁵ The evidence brought in support of Isocrates' claim, i.e., inscriptions and altar base bearing the name of Acoris found in Tyre, Sidon and Acre,²⁶ really attests to the influence of Egypt in Phoenicia, and has nothing to do with Isocrates' hyperbolic 'seized' (κατείληπται) by the Great King's enemies (*Paneg.* 161), in particular when in the *Evagoras* he speaks of Tyre as taken by the king of Salamis and his son.²⁷

Lastly, Isocrates' phrase 'six years' refers to the entire period of the expedition against Evagoras (surely, counted from the King's Peace),²⁸ and not to the time passed since the Battle of Citium. He certainly refers to this battle, in a phrase which downplays its importance (141: κατὰ μὲν θάλατταν προδεδυστύχηκεν, 'with regard to his navy he has been unfortunate'), but it is difficult to date this event with accuracy. The overall impression is that the king is unable to defeat Evagoras.

The preparations for an Egyptian Campaign probably began after the King's Peace,²⁹ and were halted for various reasons; Pharnabazus was temporarily taken away for some other business (Nep. *Dat.* 3.5).

With the phantom of an 'Egyptian War' in the 380s out of the way, it is possible to believe the Cypriot campaign began in c. 386 and that the battle occurred c. 384 or even slightly later – although preparations may have taken several years before the actual campaign began,³⁰ thus making Isocrates' claim of a 'ten-year war' approximately true. Either date suggested for the battle can fit in with the hypothesis that Tiribazus was not present at the battle, but was employed in the simultaneous Cadusian Campaign, around 386/5 BCE, and only appeared in Cyprus after this north-eastern expedition ended and after the Battle of Citium.

---

²⁴ Ruzicka (2012: 84) may not be right in saying '[w]ith Tyre's defection came also the loss of many mainland sites ... belonging to Tyre, chief among them Acco, the Persian staging ground for attacks on Egypt.' This function of Acre/Acco has not changed since Cambyses' assault (Strab. 16.2.25).
²⁵ Stylianou (1998: 161). The claim may have been embellished afterwards, to correspond to *Phil.* 102, which may refer to the political unrest in the 360s and 350s.
²⁶ Stylianou (198: 160) and Ruzicka (2012: 83, 254 n.1) citing Stern (1982: 205, 254-5, 278).
²⁷ Indeed, see Ruzicka (2012: 254 n. 5).
²⁸ Cf. Judeich (1892: 121-2), Ruzicka (2012: 87); cf. Stylianou (1998: 149).
²⁹ Cf. Diod. 14.110.3.
³⁰ In this case, Isocrates does not think of the Autophradates/Hecatomnus campaign of 391/0 BCE (Diod. 14.98.3-4) as the same one as that of the 380s. Cf. Ruzicka (2012: 69). Perhaps that campaign never materialised either: Spyridakis (1953: 57), Stylianou (1998: 534).

Appendix II:
Plutarch, the Persica *and the* Regum et Imperatorum Apophthegmata

Discussion on the difficult issue of the relationship between the Persian material within the *Regum et Imperatorum Apophthegmata* (*The Sayings of Kings and Commanders*) and the *Persica* works has been postponed to this point and relegated to a mere appendix for the simple reason that we are not certain whether this work is indeed Plutarch's own and whether the material in it comes exclusively from Plutarch. Yet this question cannot be ignored completely, despite the fact that full justice to this issue could not be done in this brief analysis, focusing on its Persian section.

The work itself is listed as no. 108 in the Lamprias Catalogue (ἀποφθέγματα ἡγεμονικά, στρατηγικά, τυραννικά, cf. no. 125: ἀπομνημονεύματα), and was evidently attributed to Plutarch already in late antiquity.[1] It has the character of a *facta/acta et dicta* (words and deeds) collection, used by orators and rhetorically inclined historians.[2] There would seem to be three available options concerning this work:

(1) Plutarch composed this work and intended it to be circulated more or less in its present format, with its introduction.[3]

(2) Plutarch prepared the material which ended up in this work during his lifetime, presumably with the purpose of incorporating it in other works.[4] The task of the arrangement and presentation of this material as a work encompassing 'sayings' of notable persons was taken by a later hand. In this sense, the work is a posthumous treatise of Plutarch.[5]

---

[1] Photius mentions it in *Bibl.* cod. 161, p. 104 b. The work was suspected as spurious already in the days of Wilhelm Xylander (1570). On the work and its relation to Plutarch see Schmidt (1879).

[2] See Russell (1973: 46), Cf. Saller (1980: 72, 74), Beck (2002: 169) on Quint. *Inst.* 1.1.35–6, 12.2.29–30 and Plut. *Praec. ger. reip.* 802f–803e.

[3] Cf. Pelling (2002b: 70, 85), Stadter (2014: 675).

[4] See Ziegler (1949b: 226–8), Babbit (1931: 7), Fuhrman (1988: 3–15), Stadter (1989: xlv).

[5] Cf. Gasparov (1980).

(3) Plutarch did not prepare any of the material found in this work. The treatise was composed after Plutarch's death by culling passages from his works and from other volumes, most likely collections of anecdotes bearing the same character as this very work.[6]

Of these options, (2) and (3) – with some variation – can peacefully coexist side by side with each other. There is no contradiction in the hypothesis that even though Plutarch prepared some of the material found in the work, another part came from a different source after his death. By contrast, (1) and (2) both postulate that Plutarch prepared material which he deliberately did not intend to use in his biographies, and preferred either to leave it out or include it in another work.

The question at hand is one of great importance:[7] does this collection in fact present some form of the notes (*hypomnemata*)[8] Plutarch says he was composing, as mentioned in Chapter 1? There are two schools of thought here, as described by Christopher Pelling (2002b): (a) the *hypomnemata* are basically the notes taken during reading (Stadter, 2014: 669–70, 677; 2015b: 128–9), (b) they are roughly completed and finished penultimate drafts, either as a cluster of ideas (Van der Stockt, 1999, 2004) or already containing a full train of thought visible in the biography (Pelling, 2002b). The collection *Regum et Imperatorum Apophthegmata* would thus seem to be composed, respectively, from these notes as a self-standing work,[9] or culled from the rough drafts prepared for the *Lives*. The first possibility does not need Plutarch to gather all these notes into a collection; the second requires it.[10]

1. Let us begin this brief examination by commenting on the introduction to the work, dedicated to Trajan himself (172b–d):

> Artaxerxes, king of the Persians – O Caesar Trajan, greatest Emperor – thinking it is no less kingly and kind to receive small gifts favourably and willingly than to give great presents, when he rode by along the road, and a simple day labourer, having nothing else, took water from a river with his two hands and offered it to him, received it joyfully and smiled, determining the favour not by the use of the thing given but by the goodwill of the giver.
> Ἀρτοξέρξης ὁ Περσῶν βασιλεύς, ὦ μέγιστε αὐτόκρατορ Τραϊανὲ Καῖσαρ, οὐχ ἧττον οἰόμενος βασιλικὸν καὶ φιλάνθρωπον εἶναι τοῦ μεγάλα διδόναι τὸ μικρὰ λαμβάνειν εὐμενῶς καὶ προθύμως, ἐπεὶ παρελαύνοντος αὐτοῦ καθ᾽ ὁδὸν αὐτουργὸς

---

[6] Wyttenbach (1810: 6.2.1039–42): gleaned from Plutarch's *Lives* (and other sources); cf. Volkman (1869: 1.210, 218–34), Jones (1971: 79). Cf. references in Fuhrmann (1988: 3).

[7] *Pace* Babbit (1931: 5).

[8] Cf. the term 'records' (ἀπομνημονευμάτων) very close to Plutarch's *hypomnema*.

[9] Stadter (2014: 677): from a more extensive anecdotal collection.

[10] Pelling (2002b: 85): 'the person who knows his way best about his notes and draft is always the author himself'.

ἄνθρωπος καὶ ἰδιώτης οὐδὲν ἔχων ἕτερον ἐκ τοῦ ποταμοῦ ταῖς χερσὶν ἀμφοτέραις ὕδωρ ὑπολαβὼν προσήνεγκεν, ἡδέως ἐδέξατο καὶ ἐμειδίασε, τῇ προθυμίᾳ τοῦ διδόντος οὐ τῇ χρείᾳ τοῦ διδομένου τὴν χάριν μετρήσας.

Lycurgus made the sacrifices in Sparta cheap, so that they would always be able to revere the gods easily and from whatever is present. With the same judgement, when I offer to you my supplicatory and friendly gifts, the common first fruits of philosophy, that you accept the benefit of these records with favour, if they offer anything to the exploration of the customs and conducts of leaders, observable in their words more than in their deeds.

ὁ δὲ Λυκοῦργος εὐτελεστάτας ἐποίησεν ἐν Σπάρτῃ τὰς θυσίας, ἵνα ἀεὶ τοὺς θεοὺς τιμᾶν ἑτοίμως δύνωνται καὶ ῥᾳδίως ἀπὸ τῶν παρόντων. τοιαύτῃ δή τινι γνώμῃ κἀμοῦ λιτά σοι δῶρα καὶ ξένια καὶ κοινὰς ἀπαρχὰς προσφέροντος ἀπὸ φιλοσοφίας ἅμα τῇ προθυμίᾳ καὶ τὴν χρείαν ἀπόδεξαι τῶν ἀπομνημονευμάτων, εἰ πρόσφορον ἔχει τι πρὸς κατανόησιν ἠθῶν καὶ προαιρέσεων ἡγεμονικῶν, ἐμφαινομένων τοῖς λόγοις μᾶλλον ἢ ταῖς πράξεσιν αὐτῶν.

[My] work has the lives of the famous leaders and law makers and emperors among the Romans and Greeks. Most of the actions have a mixture of fortune, while the spoken reactions and the utterances against the deeds, experiences and the chance happenings provide, as in a mirror, the [opportunity] to examine the thoughts of each person in a pure manner. Therefore Seiramnes the Persian, to those who wondered how, when his words are sensible, his actions are not successful, said that he was the master of his words, but fortune and the king are masters of his actions.

καίτοι καὶ βίους ἔχει τὸ σύνταγμα τῶν ἐπιφανεστάτων παρά τε Ῥωμαίοις καὶ παρ' Ἕλλησιν ἡγεμόνων καὶ νομοθετῶν καὶ αὐτοκρατόρων· ἀλλὰ τῶν μὲν πράξεων αἱ πολλαὶ τύχην ἀναμεμιγμένην ἔχουσιν, αἱ δὲ γινόμεναι παρὰ τὰ ἔργα καὶ τὰ πάθη καὶ τὰς τύχας ἀποφάσεις καὶ ἀναφωνήσεις ὥσπερ ἐν κατόπτροις καθαρῶς παρέχουσι τὴν ἑκάστου διάνοιαν ἀποθεωρεῖν. ᾗ καὶ Σειράμνης ὁ Πέρσης πρὸς τοὺς θαυμάζοντας, ὅτι τῶν λόγων αὐτοῦ νοῦν ἐχόντων αἱ πράξεις οὐ κατορθοῦνται, τῶν μὲν λόγων ἔφη κύριος αὐτὸς εἶναι, τῶν δὲ πράξεων τὴν τύχην μετὰ τοῦ βασιλέως.

There [in that work], the spoken reactions of men are mixed with actions and require leisure of the reader. Here, however, I believe that since the words themselves are collected together as examples and seeds of the lives, they will not be annoying to your time, since they supply in brief words an exploration of the many men worthy to be remembered.

ἐκεῖ μὲν οὖν ἅμα αἱ ἀποφάσεις τῶν ἀνδρῶν τὰς πράξεις παρακειμένας ἔχουσι σχολάζουσαν φιληκόϊαν περιμένουσιν· ἐνταῦθα δὲ [καὶ] τοὺς λόγους αὐτοὺς καθ' αὑτοὺς ὥσπερ δείγματα τῶν βίων καὶ σπέρματα συνειλεγμένους οὐδὲν οἴομαί σοι τὸν καιρὸν ἐνοχλήσειν, ἐν βραχέσι πολλῶν ἀναθεώρησιν ἀνδρῶν ἀξίων μνήμης γενομένων λαμβάνοντι.

καὶ del. Hartman

Despite recent attempts to rehabilitate the authenticity of this dedicatory introduction,[11] the arguments of Richard Volkmann (1869: 1.211–34) are mostly persuasive; the introduction does not seem

---

[11] See Flacelière (1976), Fuhrmann (1988: 5–10), Beck (2002), Roskam (2014: 190–1).

authentic for many reasons.[12] One notes the crude style,[13] the reference to 'Imperators' (αὐτοκρατόρων) describing the protagonists of the biographies[14] or the mention of the *Parallel Lives*, Plutarch's most popular work, without any reference to *Lives* in general, especially to the solitary *Artaxerxes*, in which the example given recurs.

Yet the most important point to be considered is the appeal to Trajan to learn from the example of Artaxerxes. It is inconceivable that Plutarch would make this subtle comparison of the emperor and the Persian king (also by placing the name of Artaxerxes before that of Trajan), wary as he was of the prospect of any wrong inference being made by his audience from the mention of Greek and Persian interaction in conjunction of Greek and Roman relations (see Chapter 1). Such innuendo was a play of the sophists and the rhetorical schools, as Plutarch was well aware; it was never displayed in this direct manner by him. This is especially true of Trajan, even if the dedication could possibly have been made prior to his planned campaign against the successors of the Persians, the Parthians. Trajan's father, M. Ulpius Traianus, received triumphal insignia for holding against the Parthians as governor of Syria (76 CE; Plin. *Paneg.* 16.1).[15] Pliny the Younger (*Paneg.* 14.1, 100 CE) even goes on to say that under Traianus' command, Trajan won this glory for his father.[16] This claim was certainly not unpleasing to Trajan, and the confrontation with the east appears to have been part of the emperor's formative background. One would appear to be stretching plausibility to assume that in his address to Trajan, Plutarch would put forward two examples from the Persian past (and not the Roman), with one of them of a king notoriously known for his decadent court – and not, for instance, of Cyrus the Great.[17]

If this scepticism is in place, the introduction was written after Trajan and after Plutarch, and was presumably composed by inter-

---

[12] See Ziegler (1951: 658, 864), Jones (1971: 30–1).

[13] Note the repetitions φιλάνθρωπον . . . ἄνθρωπος, προσφέροντος . . . πρόσφορον, the cases of hiatus μέγιστε αὐτόκρατορ, ἅμα αἱ.

[14] Cf. Volkmann (1869: 1.217). This word has to be understood in the same way as the dedicatee αὐτοκράτωρ. For another view, see Beck (2002: 171 n. 11).

[15] Ulpius Traianus was deified, but not immediately after his death (cf. Plin. *Paneg.* 89.2). It was probably in connection with the dedication of Trajan's new forum complex (Jan. 112 CE, cf. Dio Cass. 68.16.3); cf. Beckman (2000: 127–9, 2007: 79–80). He was celebrated in a new series of coins from Trajan's sixth consulate (112 CE), bearing his image, signaled as DIVI NERVA ET TRAIANVS PAT(er) [facing busts with Nerva] on the reverse (BMC 498–9); in another coin type (BMC 506–8) he appears alone with the legend DIVVS PATER TRAIAN on the reverse. See Bennett (1997: 186, 191), Beckman (2000, 2007).

[16] See Roche (2002: 46–7).

[17] Yet cf. Beck (2002: 165): '[t]he mention of this Persian ruler here, and later of the Persian Seiramnes, may allude to the Emperor's expedition to Parthia.'

weaving two *exempla* into a fictional dedication.[18] Ostensibly, that the introduction was added later does not entirely exclude the possibility that Plutarch arranged this collection himself (perhaps with a different introduction), but the probability for this option is low. This point is made even clearer when we note that the introduction has a special relationship with the collection's structure. Thus, the prominence of the Persian examples in the introduction is not divorced from the fact that Persians appear at the beginning of the work. The two portions go hand in hand and reflect each other thematically: for instance, an anecdote of Artaxerxes II also relates his acceptance of small gifts (174a). There are even verbal echoes between the two sections. The epithet 'kingly' (βασιλικόν) on receiving gifts echoes a saying attributed to Artaxerxes I (173d: βασιλικώτερον), though with the opposite meaning. Cyrus the Great is made to say (172f) that the seeds of plants and the lives of men resemble the soil they occupy (τῶν φυτῶν τὰ **σπέρματα** καὶ τῶν ἀνθρώπων οἱ **βίοι**); the same components appear in the introduction (τῶν **βίων** καὶ **σπέρματα**).[19] It would be fair to say that they belong to the same stage of editing.

2. One important feature of the collection is its structure: it begins with the barbarians (Persians, Egyptians, a Paphlagonian, Thracians, Scythians), moves on to the Greeks and concludes with the Romans. Such structure might conform to the threefold division of humanity observed in Plutarch's works (Chapter 1), but the arrangement also appears to be geographic, as it progresses from the Persian east to the Roman west. Now, the inclusion of the Rhodian Memnon, Darius Codomannus' commander of Greek mercenaries, in the Persian section (174b) would not appear to be have been made by Plutarch. It would seem to correspond to a Roman division of mankind into Romans and *externi*.[20]

3. Let us examine the structure of the Persian section of the work. It has the sayings of ten persons (Cyrus the Great, Darius I, Semiramis, Xerxes, Artaxerxes I, Cyrus the Younger, Artaxerxes II, Parysatis, Orontes, Memnon), beginning with the word Πέρσαι (which is the first after the introduction) and ending in Alexander

[18] With adaptations of the Plutarchisms of *Alex.* 1.2, *Cat. Mai.* 7, *Aem. Paul.* 1.2 (but see Roskam, 2014: 190–1), *De gar.* 510e–11a, *Adv. Col.* 1117d, *Dem.* 2.2 (Beck, 2002: 166–7, 173), *De e* 384de (Flacelière, 1976: 102–3) and many other places. The format was influenced by examples such as the beginning of Valerius Maximus' dedication to Tiberius (praef.).
[19] Cf. Beck (2002: 168) on *De cur.* 516c.
[20] For instance, Valerius Maximus includes under this designation both Alexander (1.1.ext.5, 3.3.ext) and Darius (5.2.ext.1, 6.9.ext.5). One extant passage from Nepos' work is *De Regibus Exterarum Gentium* (On the Kings of the Foreign Nations), which embraces both Greeks and barbarians, not to mention his *De excellentibus ducibus exterarum gentium* in general.

(Ἀλεξάνδρῳ). The sequence is largely chronological, apart from the places of Semiramis and Parysatis (the latter located after her sons), but these two exceptions create a chiastic scheme (nos. 3 and 8).[21] If Memnon is left out (because he is Greek), Artaxerxes I becomes the central figure (in a 4–1–4 structure). One can hardly see the point of such an arrangement in a note which is not intended to be published. So either the work was indeed intended by Plutarch to be circulated in its present form, or else some later hand intervened to arrange the names in this order. The second option is more likely, as this sequence is too schematic and forced, and does not demonstrate Plutarch's sophistication.[22]

4. There are twenty-three sayings in the Persian section. Most of them do not appear elsewhere in Plutarch's oeuvre. Four of them are repeated in other works of the *Moralia*. Two facts are interesting with regard to these four: (a) each of them belongs to a different figure (Cyrus, Darius, Xerxes, Cyrus the Younger), (b) they appear as the first or sole saying of that person in the collection (172e ~ *Praec. ger. reip.* 821e, 172f ~ *An seni* 792c, 173c ~ *De frat. am.* 488df, 173e ~ *QC* 6.4.620c). These facts would suggest, according to the 'rough draft' approach, that the four anecdotes were in Plutarch's *hypomnema*, although there is hardly any narrative connecting them. Alternatively, since each of these four anecdotes represents a different king, it might also be the case that they were taken from Plutarch's known works in order to increase the volume of this Persian section.

5. One anecdote of Artaxerxes I which is related to mild punishment recurs in two works of the *Moralia*, but is unattributed to him (173d ~ *De aud. poet.* 35e, *De Sera* 565a). This would lend support to the theory that Plutarch had a fuller *hypomnema* and only used part of it. Since the anecdote does not involve a saying at all, one would assume that this *hypomnema* was arranged around the theme of 'Persian Kings'.

The manner in which Artaxerxes II is compared with his grandfather in *Art.* 4.4, alluding to the removal of the sadistic pleasure from punishments (κολάσεως δὲ πάσης ἀφαιρῶν τὸ ἐφυβρίζον καὶ ἡδόμενον) while refraining from specifying exactly what Artaxerxes I did in his own mild form of penalty, would suggest again that Plutarch had

---

[21] Wyttenbach (1810: 6.2.1044) believes Semiramis' place is dictated by the Herodotean origin of the anecdote related to Darius.

[22] See, however, Pelling (2002b: 71, 84–5), who believes the stories (in the Roman section) are carefully ordered and display 'artistry'.

a fuller *hypomnema*. Similarly, the fact that Artaxerxes II appears to emulate his grandfather when giving more honours and favours than deserved (περὶ τὸ τιμᾶν καὶ χαρίζεσθαι τὸ κατ᾽ ἀξίαν ὑπερβάλλων) seems to hint at another saying in the collection (173d) assigned to Artaxerxes I, according to which it is more kingly to add than to take away (τὸ προσθεῖναι τοῦ ἀφελεῖν βασιλικώτερόν ἐστι). If this is true, it would appear that both anecdotes belong to a certain *hypomnema* and that while composing the *Artaxerxes* Plutarch transferred these stories from Artaxerxes I to the protagonist of the biography, using the comment on the 'imitation' of Artaxerxes I (*Art.* 4.4: ζηλοῦν ἔδοξε τὴν Ἀρτοξέρξου τοῦ ὁμωνύμου πραότητα) to justify this transference.

6. It is a different case with the other two other anecdotes associated with Artaxerxes I. Using our knowledge of the content of the *Persica* works (especially of Ctesias), we see that both involve mistakes. One saying (173e) involves the person Satibarzanes, described as the κατακοιμιστής (chamberlain) of the king. This is surely an error (see Chapter 3), since Satibarzanes was one of the courtiers of Artaxerxes II, apparently described by Ctesias. Plutarch is unlikely to have made this mistake if he found the name of Satibarzanes in his reading of the physician (*Art.* 12.4). This has to be a later addition from another source, or a misplacement of Plutarch's notes by a reader unfamiliar with Ctesias' text.

The same goes for the second anecdote (173d), in which Artaxerxes I allows those who hunt with him, if they are able, to throw their spears before him (Πρῶτος δὲ πρωτοβολεῖν ἐκέλευσε τῶν συγκυνηγετούντων τοὺς δυναμένους καὶ βουλομένους). It is the complete opposite of Ctesias' story of this king and Megabyzus (*FGrH* 688 F 14.43, see Chapter 3), and could have been handled by someone completely ignorant of Ctesias' description. This person deliberately altered the note to make it correspond with other portrayals – most likely, Xenophon's (*Anab.* 1.9.6: 'the man who was the first to help him [i.e., Cyrus the Younger, attacked by a bear] he made an object of envy to many'); cf. *Cyr.* 1.4.14).[23]

The evidence concerning Artaxerxes I would seem to suggest that there were two different stages in the handling of the anecdotes. In one case the editor appears to divulge less than he knows, in the second he seems to know less than he should. It may be safe to conclude that there were at least two persons involved in the collection or arrangement of material for the collection. The first is Plutarch

[23] But cf. Kuhrt (2007: 315).

himself, who had some fuller *hypomnemata*, perhaps even narratives; the second is a later editor, who struggled to make sense of these *hypomnemata*.

7. In the second part of this section, three sayings (out of seven) of the last five persons are repeated in the *Artaxerxes* – two of Artaxerxes II himself (173f ~ *Art.* 5.6, 174a ~ *Art.* 4.5) and one of Cyrus the Younger (the same one mentioned above, 173ef ~ *Art.* 6.3–4). If there was one rough draft comprising these sayings, it was probably meant to be employed mainly in this biography. Moreover, the figure of Artaxerxes II dominates the second part of the Persian section, as four of the last five persons are introduced interacting with him: Cyrus talks of his brother, Parysatis is presented as his mother and Orontes as his son-in-law. Yet, Memnon was not conceivably part of this note related to Artaxerxes II. So we are left with two options: either this second half of the Persian section embraced two *hypomnemata* which are different from the one used for the first half, or the rough draft on which both parts were based underwent several phases of composition.[24]

8. The sayings attributed to Cyrus the Younger parallel *Art.* 6.3–4, but in the reverse order: Cyrus' self-praise comes before the promises made to the Spartans. The first part (Cyrus' self-praise) recurs elsewhere in Plutarch's works (*QC* 6.4.620c) and so may indicate that at some point Plutarch had this section in his *hypomnema*. Indeed, since this part concerns regal behaviour, the chances are that Plutarch included it in his 'Persian kings' note suggested above. The part concerning Cyrus' promises to the Spartans was thus found in this *hypomnema* but not used in the *Moralia* work, and the order changed when it reached the biography for artistic reasons.

9. The first anecdote (again, not a saying) attributed to Artaxerxes II (173f) concerns his permission to his wife to be accessible to the public, paralleling *Art.* 5.6. The version in the *Artaxerxes* is fuller and includes the name of Stateira. One option would be that this anecdote is later than the biography; another would suggest that there was a fuller *hypomnema*, several of whose items were left out.

We find some unclarities concerning the other two sayings. The anecdote of the person giving a fruit to the king (174a) parallels *Art.* 4.5, but with one major difference: in the biography it is a pomegranate (**ῥόαν** μίαν ὑπερφυῆ μεγέθει προσενέγκαντος), while in the collection it is an apple (**μῆλον** ὑπερφυὲς μεγέθει προσενέγκαντος). There is another version presented by Aelian (*VH* 1.33), which is even fuller

[24] Cf. Mossman (2010: 147).

and is probably not derived from Plutarch.[25] In that version we have a pomegranate again. Another anecdote told of Darius (173a: Ῥοιὰν δὲ μεγάλην ἀνοίξας) has a pomegranate, repeating Hdt. 4.143 (ῥοιὰς τρώγειν). Most chances are that a pomegranate appeared in the original story, which Plutarch knew.[26] One option would be that Plutarch decided to change the fruit to an apple in the collection, for whatever artistic reasons he may have had. But would it not be simpler to assume that the apple (μῆλον) version is later than the biography and involved a misreading of the biography's μίαν? If this is true, the entire anecdote was taken from the biography and inserted into the collection at a later stage. Furthermore, one should recall that the story of the person giving water to the king, found in the biography in close proximity to this anecdote (*Art.* 5.1), appears in the introduction to the collection. We noted that the introduction is probably later than Plutarch; this seems to be true also of the apple variant.[27]

The story of Artaxerxes given dry figs (ξηρὰ σῦκα: 174a) and exclaiming that he never enjoyed such a pleasure is clearly another variation of Ctesias' story of water given to Artaxerxes (*Art.* 12.5–6, see Chapter 3).[28] Indeed, one might think that Plutarch had in his rough draft three stories, the two used in the *Artaxerxes* and this version, and that he included all three without noticing their similarity. But, again, would it not be simpler to assume that Plutarch did notice their similarity and that the three variants were separate notes at his disposal? One of them may have involved some misreading in the transmission.[29]

10. An interesting case is that of the saying of Parysatis (174a), according to which anyone who intends to discourse with the king freely (τὸν βασιλεῖ μέλλοντα μετὰ παρρησίας διαλέγεσθαι) should use 'linen phrases' (βυσσίνοις χρῆσθαι ῥήμασιν). The context is not given, but it is surely a piece of advice offered by the queen mother to someone who wishes to communicate with the king. The point here, I would assume, is not the softness of the linen but rather their

[25] On the relationship between Aelian and the *Reg. et Imp. Apophth* see Ziegler (1951: 864–5).

[26] Cf. Wyttenbach (1810: 6.2.1043).

[27] The two also appear in Aelian's work in proximity (*VH* 1.32–3), albeit in reverse order. The fact that both stories are repeatedly found together may indicate that originally they formed part of the same anecdote. Aelian is not dependent on Plutarch, since his version is richer and even provides the name of the person who gives water (Σιναίτης).

[28] See Wyttenbach (1810: 6.2.1046–7), Babbit (1931: 21 n. e).

[29] In this case, dried fig (ἰσχάς) may have originally been a distorted ἰσχνόν, in the sense of 'light' (*LSJ*, s.v., A.5), (mis)rendering Ctesias' κουφότατον, describing water, now in assimilation to the adjacent anecdote in 173c (from Deinon). Both anecdotes probably circulated together. See Chapter 4.

covering function, i.e., the way words conceal more than they reveal,[30] and what attracted Plutarch was probably this precise contradiction between open discourse and camouflaging words. There are several candidates for the person whom Parysatis could have addressed, the main ones being Ctesias, perhaps in the context of handling the incarcerated Clearchus, or Cyrus, at the moment it served his purpose to veil his plans from his brother before setting on his campaign against him. Although this saying did not find its way to the biography, it has a special relationship with it, if the medical overtones of βύσσινος (a linen bandage treating wounds: cf. Hdt. 7.181) are taken into consideration. Thus, this saying could be at the background of Plutarch's use of θεραπευτικός, 'submissively' (*Art.* 4.3),[31] said of Cyrus' approach to his brother or ἰάσασθαι 'deal with the matter' (*Art.* 18.3, where there is also an allusion to concealment), said of Ctesias; both words are plays on medical treatment. In this case, the elaboration of the *hypomnema* would seem to involve less the use of a rough draft, but rather a certain rudimentary note, with a clever insinuation, which was never employed in the biography.

11. The rest of the anecdotes have no parallel in Plutarch's work. Some contain interesting alterations of Herodotus. The story of Megabyzus (Megabazus, Hdt. 4.143) is transferred to Zopyrus (173a), his son. Since there is another anecdote involving Darius and Zopyrus (173a), one would assume that Plutarch was presumably writing a *hypomnema* intended to form a basis for a narrative that never materialised. Similarly, Plutarch[32] may have transferred the revolt of Babylon from Darius (Hdt. 3.150) to Xerxes (173c), and attributed Cyrus' measures against the Lydians (Hdt. 1.156) to Xerxes' dealings with the Babylonians. This may have been prepared for the unwritten biography of Leonidas (*De Herod. malig.* 32.866b). While it is possible that Plutarch also made the transference of the story of Nitocris (Hdt. 1.187) to Semiramis, this may have also been done by a careless reader of Herodotus (Semiramis is mentioned in Hdt. 1.184) or in a flawed epitome of the Halicarnassian.

12. Let us return to our initial possibilities. Nothing precludes the option that Plutarch composed *hypomnemata* either as rudimentary

---

[30] Cf. Gera (2007: 453): 'deceptive and flattering softness', which is entirely in Parysatis' character.

[31] Here the queen mother alleviates the king's suspicions, βασιλέως δ' ἥ τε μήτηρ παροῦσα τὰς ὑποψίας ἀφῄρει.

[32] Not strictly following Ctesias *FGrH* 688 F 13.26 since the physician transferred to Megagyzus the story of Zopyrus (Hdt. 3.153–60) his son. Cf. Diod 10.19.2 for the ensuing confusion.

notes or as fuller rough drafts, or that he used both methods. The question remaining is how these notes ended up in the collection of sayings. Once the authenticity of the dedicatory introduction is discarded, there is little to recommend the assumption that Plutarch was responsible for the format of the collection as we have it now. There was clearly some later editing involved.

Pelling (2002b: 70) is right to assume that the introduction insinuates the procedure involved in the creation of the collection. The mention of the *Lives* as already published in a book (τὸ σύνταγμα: 172c), as well as the metaphor 'seeds of lives' (172d), imply that the sayings were procured from some texts, including the *Lives*. This inference corresponds to the impression we noted above, that the editor seems to be interpreting Plutarch's text, either his primary notes or his biographies. If the purpose of the editor was to present material that had not appeared before (see point 10 above), he would have been obliged to compare Plutarch's rough drafts with his extant writings, a difficult task, technically speaking, verging on the impossible. It is more likely to believe that the editor would turn to rudimentary notes and the known biographies[33] rather than delve into Plutarch's unfamiliar rough drafts.

A case in point is the first *exemplum* in the introduction. Resembling the anecdote of *Art.* 5.1, it is introduced by a rationale absent from *Art.* 5, and yet is composed of a description and a principle present in *Art.* 4.4 and 4.5. The anecdote itself does not involve a saying at all, and in fact the authorial intervention of Plutarch in *Art.* 4.4, that Artaxerxes *appeared* gracious and kind (φαινόμενος εὔχαρις καὶ φιλάνθρωπος) to the givers no less than in his giving to the receivers, becomes in the introduction to the collection Artaxerxes' own philosophy. This slight change could not have been made by Plutarch himself, aware as he was of all the nuances and subtleties of Artaxerxes' character, but by a reader of the biography.

We have to assume that there was relatively little effort involved on the part of the editor in finding sayings, if we accept that Plutarch's *hypomnemata* used for the collection were mostly these rudimentary notes left behind by the biographer.[34] In this manner, for instance, the reverse order of the saying attributed to Cyrus the Younger is to be explained by an addition to Plutarch's initial note (Cyrus' self-praise) through a revision of a section from the biography. But if this is true,

---

[33] Cf. Tritle (1992: 4287–90) in the case of *Phocion* in the same collection.
[34] And here a selection was probably made, but not like the one envisaged by Stadter (2014: 679), of one collection out of a larger collection.

and the responsibility of the editor was greater than initially assumed, how can we be sure that the notes are indeed Plutarch's? One such note may derive ultimately from Deinon (173c, see Chapter 4), but it is not a detail from a section read for the *Artaxerxes*. The saying of Orontes after he is disgraced (174b) ultimately comes from what we termed the 'common source'. While it is related to the material which Plutarch read for the *Artaxerxes*, the fact that it is found as an anecdote in various authors (see Chapter 5), lends some likelihood to the possibility that it circulated independently, and was inserted into the work by the later editor of the collection. We have to admit, therefore, the possibility that some of the material in the collection (at least in the Persian section) could be alien to Plutarch.

There are a great number of questions that must be explored with relation to the collection *Regum et Imperatorum Apophthegmata*, and which this brief examination, focusing on the Persian section, could not deal with. However, it seems that the work was not intended by Plutarch to circulate in the form it is extant now. We have seen that there are at least two layers in the sections of the work we explored, one that is most likely Plutarch's notes, which were never meant to be published,[35] and another that involves the introduction which is most probably not authentic and passages rewritten from the *Artaxerxes*.

[35] Cf. Van der Stockt (1999: 579): 'Plutarch's hypomnemata were private, written documents, made by himself and for himself.'

Bibliography

The following abbreviations are used in the bibliography:

AC	*L'antiquité classique*
AchHist	*Achaemenid History*
AION	*Annali dell'Istituto universitario orientale di Napoli*
AJN	*American Journal of Numismatics*
AJPh	*The American Journal of Philology*
AMI	*Archäologische Mitteilungen aus Iran*
ANRW	*Aufstieg und Niedergang der Römischen Welt*
AncSoc	*Ancient Society*
APQ	*American Philosophical Quarterly*
ASNP	*Annali della Scuola Normale Superiore di Pisa*
BIFAO	*Bulletin de l'Institut Francais d'Archéologie Orientale au Caire*
BSOAS	*Bulletin of the School of Oriental and African Studies*
BTB	*Biblical Theology Bulletin*
CAH	*Cambridge Ancient History*
CCJ	*Cambridge Classical Journal (formerly PCPhS)*
CJ	*Classical Journal*
CPh	*Classical Philology*
CR	*Classical Review*
CQ	*Classical Quarterly*
CW	*Classical World*
DNP	*Der Neue Pauly*
DOP	*Dumbarton Oaks Papers*
EI	*Encyclopedia Iranica*
G&R	*Greece & Rome*
GLB	*Graeco-Latina Brunensia*
GRBS	*Greek, Roman and Byzantine Studies*
HPQ	*History of Philosophy Quarterly*
HSPh	*Harvard Studies in Classical Philology*
HTR	*Harvard Theological Review*
IA	*Iranica Antiqua*
ICS	*Illinois Classical Studies*

JAAC	The Journal of Aesthetics and Art Criticism
JANES	Journal of the Ancient Near Eastern Society
JbAC	Jahrbuch für Antike und Christentum
JCR	The Journal of Conflict Resolution
JCS	Journal of Cuneiform Studies
JESHO	Journal of the Economic and Social History of the Orient
JHS	Journal of Hellenic Studies
JNES	Journal of Near Eastern Studies
JRS	Journal of Roman Studies
LCM	Liverpool Classical Monthly
MDOG	Mitteilungen der Deutschen Orient-Gesellschaft zu Berlin
MH	Museum Helveticum
NC	Numismatic Chronicle
OLZ	Orientalistische Literaturzeitung
Op. Ath.	Opuscula Atheniensia
OSAP	Oxford Studies in Ancient Philosophy
P&P	Past & Present
PACA	Proceedings of the African Classical Association
PCPhS	Proceedings of the Cambridge Philological Society
PdP	Parola del Passato
QS	Quaderni di storia
QUCC	Quaderni urbinati di cultura classica
RA	Revue Archéologique
RE	Pauly-Wissowa-Kroll, Realencyclopedie des klassischen Altertumswissenschat
REA	Revue des Études Anciennes
REG	Revue des Études Grecques
RhM	Rheinisches Museum für Philologie
RHR	Revue de l'Histoire des Religions
RIL	Rendiconti/Istituto Lombardo, Accademia di Scienze e Lettere, Classe di Lettere, Scienze morali e storiche
RSA	Rivista storica dell'Antichita
SIFC	Studi Italiani di Filologia Classica
TAPhA	Transactions of the American Philological Association
VDI	Vestnik drevnej istorii
WS	Wiener Studien
ZDMG	Zeitschrift der Deutschen Morgenländischen Gesellschaft
ZA	Zeitschrift für Assyriologie und verwandte Gebiete
ZPE	Zeitschrift für Papyrologie und Epigraphik

*

Aalders, G. J. D. (1982), *Plutarch's Political Thought*, Amsterdam: North-Holland Publishing Company.
Accame, S. (1982), 'La leggenda di Ciro in Erodoto e Carone', *Miscellanea greca e romana* 8: 1–43.

Albenda, P. (1974), 'Lions on Assyrian wall reliefs', *JANES* 6: 1–27.

Almagor, E. (2005), 'Who is a Barbarian? The Barbarians in the Ethnological and Cultural Taxonomies of Strabo', in D. Dueck, H. Lindsay and S. Pothecary (eds), *Strabo's Cultural Geography: The Making of a Kolossourgia*, Cambridge: Cambridge University Press, 42–55.

Almagor, E. (2009), 'A "Barbarian Symposium" and the Absence of *Philanthropia* (*Artaxerxes* 15)', in J. R. Ferreira, D. F. Leão, M. Tröster and P. B. Dias (eds), *Symposion and Philanthropia in Plutarch*, Coimbra: Classica Digitalia, 131–46.

Almagor, E. (2009/10), 'Characterization Through Animals: The Case of Plutarch's *Artaxerxes*', *Ploutarchos* n.s. 7: 3–22.

Almagor, E. (2010), 'The King's *Daimon* Reconsidered', in L. Van Der Stockt, F. Titchener, H. G. Ingenkamp and A. Pérez Jiménez (eds), *Gods, Daimones, Rituals, Myth and History of Religions in Plutarch's Works: Studies Devoted to Professor Frederick E. Brenk*, Logan: Utah State University Press/Málaga: Universidad de Málaga, 31–40.

Almagor, E. (2011), 'Plutarch on the End of the Persian Empire', *GLB* 16: 3–16.

Almagor, E. (2012), 'Ctesias and the Importance of his Writings Revisited', *Electrum* 19: 9–40.

Almagor, E. (2013a), '"But This Belongs to Another Discussion": Ethnographic Digressions in Plutarch', in E. Almagor and J. Skinner (eds), *Ancient Ethnography: New Approaches*, London: Bloomsbury, 153–78.

Almagor, E. (2013b), 'Two Clandestine Readers within Plutarch's *Lives*: The Narrator and the Implied Author', in G. Pace and P. Volpe Cacciatore (eds), *Gli scritti di Plutarco: Tradizione, traduzione, ricezione, commento. Atti del IX Convegno Internationale della International Plutarch Society*, Naples: D'Auria, 19–28.

Almagor, E. (2014a), 'Hold Your Horses: Characterization through Animals in Plutarch's *Artaxerxes*, Part II', *Ploutarchos* n. s. 11: 3–18.

Almagor, E. (2014b), 'The *Aratus* and the *Artaxerxes*', in M. Beck (ed.), *A Companion to Plutarch*, Malden, MA: Wiley-Blackwell, 278–91.

Almagor, E. (2015), 'Health as a Criterion in Ancient Ethnological Schemes', in R. Futo Kennedy and M. Jones-Lewis (eds), *The Routledge Handbook of Identity and the Environment in the Classical and Medieval Worlds*, London: Routledge, 75–92.

Almagor, E. (2016a), 'Parallel Narratives and Possible Worlds in Plutarch's *Life* of Artaxerxes' in K. de Temmerman and K. Demoen (eds), *Writing Biography in Greece and Rome*, Cambridge: Cambridge University Press, 65–79.

Almagor, E. (2016b), '"This is What Herodotus Relates": The Presence of Herodotus' Histories in Josephus' Writings' in J. Priestley and V. Zali (eds), *Brill's Companion to the Reception of Herodotus in Antiquity and Beyond*, Leiden: Brill, 83–100.

Almagor, E. (2017a), 'The Empire Brought Back: Persianism in Imperial Greek Literature', in R. Strootman and M. J. Versluys (eds), *Persianism in Antiquity*, Stuttgart: Franz Steiner, 327–43.

Almagor, E. (2017b), 'The Political and the Divine in the Achaemenid Royal Inscriptions, in T. Howe, S. Müller and R. Stoneman (eds), *Ancient Historiography on War and Empire*, Oxford: Oxbow, 26–54.

Almagor, E. (2017c), 'Plutarch and the Persians', *Electrum* 24: 123–70.

Alonso-Núñez, J. M. (1982), 'L'opposizione contro l'imperialismo romano e contro il principato nella storiografia del tempo di Augusto', *RSA* 12: 131–41.

Alonso-Núñez, J. M. (1983), 'Die abfolge der Weltreiche bei Polybios und Dionysios von Halikarnassos', *Historia* 32: 411–26.

Alonso-Núñez, J. M. (1987), 'An Augustan World History: The *Historiae Philippicae* of Pompeius Trogus', *G&R* 34: 56–72.

Alpers, K. (1969), 'Xerxes und Artaxerxes', *Byzantion* 39: 5–12.

Alt, K. (1993), *Weltflucht und Weltbejahung. Zur Frage des Dualismus bei Plutarch, Numenios, Plotin*, Mainz: Akademie der Wissenschaften und der Literatur.

Anderson, G. (1976), *Lucian: Theme and Variation in the Second Sophistic*, Leiden: Brill.

Anderson, G. (1989), 'The *Pepaideumenos* in Action: Sophists and their Outlook in the Early Roman Empire', *ANRW* 2.33.1: 79–208.

Anderson, G. (1993), *The Second Sophistic: A Cultural Phenomenon in the Roman Empire*, London: Routledge.

Anderson, G. (1994), 'Lucian: Tradition Versus Reality', *ANRW* 2.34.2: 1422–47.

Anderson, J. K. (1974), *Xenophon*, London: Duckworth.

Anderson, R. D., Jr. (1999), *Ancient Rhetorical Theory and Paul*, revised ed., Leuven: Peeters.

Anderson, R. D., Jr. (2000), *Glossary of Greek Rhetorical Terms Connected to Methods of Argumentation, Figures and Tropes from Anaximenes to Quintilian*, Leuven: Peeters.

Andrewes, A. (1985), 'Diodorus and Ephorus: One Source of Misunderstanding', in J. Eadie and J. Ober (eds), *The Craft of the Ancient Historian: Essays in Honor of C. G. Starr*, Lanham, MD: University Press of America, 189–97.

Annas, J. (1985), 'Self-Knowledge in Early Plato', in D. J. O'Meara (ed.), *Platonic Investigations*, Washington, DC: Catholic University of America Press, 111–38.

Archie, A. (2015), *Politics in Socrates' Alcibiades: A Philosophical Account of Plato's Dialogue Alcibiades Major*, New York: Springer.

Arnott, W. G. (1987), 'In Praise of Alexander of Myndos', in A. Bonanno (ed.), *Laurea Corona: Studies in Honour of Edward Coleiro*, Amsterdam: Grüner, 23–9.

Arnott, W. G. (2007), *Birds in the Ancient World from A to Z*, London: Routledge.

Ash, R. (1997), 'Severed Heads: Individual Portraits and Irrational Forces in Plutarch's *Galba* and *Otho*', in J. Mossman (ed.), *Plutarch and his Intellectual World*, London: Duckworth, 189–214.

Asheri, A. B. Lloyd, and A. Corcella (2007), *A Commentary on Herodotus: Books I–IV*, Oxford: Oxford University Press.

Asmonti, L. (2015), *Conon the Athenian: Politics and Warfare in the Aegean, 414–386 BC*, Stuttgart: Franz Steiner.

Atkinson, J. (2002), 'Originality and its Limits in the Alexander Sources of the Early Empire', in A. B. Bosworth and E. J. Baynham (eds), *Alexander the Great in Fact and Fiction*, Oxford: Oxford University Press, 307–25.

Auberger, J. (1991), *Ctesias: Histoires de l'Orient*, Paris: Les Belles Lettres.

Averincev, S. S. (1965), 'Podbor geroev v 'Paralel'nykh Zhizneopisaniyakh' Plutarkha I antichnaya biograficheskaya traditsiya' ('The Choice of Heroes in Plutarch's 'Parallel Lives' and Ancient Biographical Tradition'), *VDI* 92: 51–67 (in Russian).

Babbitt, F. C. (1931), *Plutarch's Moralia III*, Loeb Classical Library, Cambridge, MA: Harvard University Press.

Babut, D. (1969), *Plutarque et le Stoïcisme*, Paris: Les Belles Lettres.

Babut, D. (1983), 'La doctrine démonologique dans le "De genio Socratis" de Plutarque: cohérence et function', *L'Information Litteraire* 35: 201–5.

Badian, E. (1965), 'The Date of Clitarchus', *PACA* 8: 5–11.

Bähr, J. C. F. (1819), *Specimen Observationum in Plutarchi Vitam Artaxerxis*, Leipzig: Hahn'sche Buchhandlung.

Bähr, J. C. F. (1824), *Ctesiae Cnidii Operum Reliquiae*, Frankfurt am Main: in officina Broenneriana.

Baldwin, B. (1978), 'Crepereius Calpurnianus', *QUCC* 27: 211–13.

Baltes, M. (2000), 'La Dottrina dell'Anima in Plutarco', *Elenchos* 21: 245–70.

Barber, G. L. (1935), *The Historian Ephorus*, Cambridge: Cambridge University Press.

Barbieri, G. (1955), *Conone*, Rome: Angelo Signorelli Editore.

Bar-Kochva, B. (2010), *The Image of the Jews in Greek Literature: The Hellenistic Period*, Berkeley: University of California Press.

Barnes, J. (1995), 'Rhetoric and Poetics', in J. Barnes (ed.), *Cambridge Companion to Aristotle*, Cambridge: Cambridge University Press, 259–86.

Barnett, R. D. (1963), 'Xenophon and the Wall of Media', *JHS* 83: 1–26.

Barrow, R. H. (1967), *Plutarch and His Times*, London: Chatto and Windus.

Bartley, A. (2003), 'The Implications of the Reception of Thucydides within Lucian's "Vera Historia"', *Hermes* 131: 222–34.

Bassett, S. R. (1999), 'The Death of Cyrus the Younger', *CR* 49: 473–83.

Bassett, S. R. (2002), 'Innocent Victims or Perjurers Betrayed? The Arrest of the Generals in Xenophon's *Anabasis*', *CQ* n.s. 52: 447–61.

Batten, L. (1913), *A Critical and Exegetical Commentary on the Books of Ezra and Nehemiah*, Edinburgh: T. & T. Clark.

Baynham, E. (2003), 'The Ancient Evidence for Alexander the Great', in J. Roisman (ed.), *Brill's Companion to Alexander the Great*, Leiden: Brill, 3–29.

Becchi, F. (2000), 'Irrazionalitá e Razionalitá degli Animali negli Scritti di Plutarco (Ovvero: Il paradosso della superioritá razionale ed etica degli animali)', *Prometheus* 26: 205–25.

Becchi, F. (2001), 'Biopsicologia e giustizia verso gli animali in Teofrasto e Plutarco', *Prometheus* 27: 119–35.

Beck, M. (2002), 'Plutarch to Trajan: the Dedicatory Letter and the Apophthegmata Collection', in P. Stadter and L. Van der Stockt (eds), *Sage and Emperor: Plutarch, Greek Intellectuals, and Roman Power in the Time of Trajan (98–117 A.D.)*, Leuven: Leuven University Press, 163–74.

Beck, M. (2007), 'Plutarch', in I. J. F. De Jong and R. Nünlist (eds), *Time in Ancient Greek Literature: Studies in Ancient Greek Narrative*, Leiden: Brill, 397–411.

Beck, R. (1991), 'Thus Spake Not Zarathustra: Zoroastrian Pseudepigrapha of the Greco-Roman World', in M. Boyce and F. Grenet, *History of Zoroastrianism*, vol. 3, Leiden: Brill, 491–565.

Beckman, M. (2000), 'The Early Gold Coinage of Trajan's Sixth Consulship', *AJN* 12: 119–56.

Beckman, M. (2007), 'Trajan's Gold Coinage AD 112–117', *AJN* 19: 77–129.

Belfiore, E. (2009), 'The Elements of Tragedy', in G. Anagnostopoulos (ed.), *A Companion to Aristotle*, Malden, MA: Wiley-Blackwell, 628–42.

Beloch, K. J. (1923), *Griechische Geschichte*, vol. 3, Leipzig, Berlin: Teubner.

Bengtson, H. (1969), *The Greeks and the Persians*, London: Weidenfeld & Nicolson.

Bennett, J. (1997), *Trajan, Optimus Princeps: A Life and Times*, London: Routledge.

Benveniste, E. (1929), *The Persian Religion According to the Chief Greek Texts*, Paris: Librairie Orientaliste.

Benveniste, E. (1966), *Titres et noms propres en iranien ancien*, Paris: Klincksieck.

Bequignon, Y. (1940), 'Le breuvage du Grand Roi', *REA* 42: 20–4.

Bianchi, U. (1987), 'Plutarch und der Dualismus', *ANRW* 2.36.1: 350–65.

Bichler, R. (2007), 'Ktesias "Korrigiert" Herodot', in R. Bichler, *Historiographie – Ethnographie – Utopie. Gesammelte Schriften, Teil 1: Studien zu Herodots Kunst der Historie*, Wiesbaden: Harrassowitz, 229–45.

Bidez, J., and F. Cumont (1938), *Les Mages hellenistes: Zoroastre, Ostanès et Hystaspe, d'après la tradition gecque*, 2 vols, Paris: Les Belles Lettres.

Bigwood, J. M. (1964), *Ctesias of Cnidus*, diss., Harvard University.

Bigwood, J. M. (1976), 'Ctesias' Account of the Revolt of Inaros', *Phoenix* 30: 1–25.

Bigwood, J. M. (1978), 'Ctesias as Historian of the Persian Wars', *Phoenix* 32: 19–41.

Bigwood, J. M. (1980), 'Diodorus and Ctesias', *Phoenix* 34: 195–207.

Bigwood, J. M. (1983), 'The Ancient Accounts of the Battle of Cunaxa', *AJPh* 104: 340–57.

Bigwood, J. M. (1986), '*POxy* 2330 and Ctesias', *Phoenix* 40: 393–406.

Bigwood, J. M. (1989), 'Ctesias' *Indica* and Photius', *Phoenix* 43: 302–16.

Bigwood, J. M. (1993a), 'Aristotle and the Elephant Again', *AJPh* 114: 537–55.

Bigwood, J. M. (1993b), 'Ctesias' Parrot', *CQ* n.s. 43: 321–7.

Bigwood, J. M. (1995), 'Ctesias, His Royal Patrons and Indian Swords', *JHS* 115: 135–40.

Bigwood, J. M. (2009) '"Incestuous" Marriage in Achaemenid Iran: Myths and Realities', *Klio* 91: 311–41.

Binder, C. (2008), *Plutarchs Vita des Artaxerxes*, Berlin: De Gruyter.

Binder, C. (2011), 'Plutarch und Ktesias. Beobachtungen zu den Quellen der. Artaxerxes-Vita', in J. Wiesehofer, R. Rollinger and G. Lanfranchi (eds), *Ktesias' Welt/ Ctesias' World*, Wiesbaden: Harrassowitz, 53–68.

Bing, J. D. (1998), 'Datames and Mazaeus: The Iconography of Revolt and Restoration in Cilicia', *Historia* 47: 49–76.

Birley, A. R. (2000), 'Hadrian to the Antonines', in A. K. Bowman, E. Champlin and A. Lintott (eds), *CAH*² XI, Cambridge: Cambridge University Press, 132–90.

Biltcliffe, D. A. W. (1969), '*P.Ox.* no. 2330 and its Importance for the Study of Nicolaus of Damascus', *RhM* 112: 85–93.

Bivar, A. D. H. (1961), 'A "Satrap" of Cyrus the Younger', *NC* n.s. 1: 119–27.

Bivar, A. D. H. (1983), 'The Political History of Iran under the Arsacids', in E. Yarshater (ed.), *Cambridge History of Iran*, 3, Cambridge: Cambridge University Press, 21–99.

Boardman, J. (1970), *Greek Gems and Finger Rings*, London: Thames and Hudson.

Bodin, L. (1915), 'Histoire et biographie: Phanias d'Érèse (1)', *REG* 28: 251–81.

Bodin, L. (1917), 'Histoire et biographie: Phanias d'Érèse (2)', *REG* 30: 117–57.

Boiy, T. (2004), *Late Achaemenid and Hellenistic Babylon*, Leuven: Peeters.

Booth, W. C. (1983 [1961]), *The Rhetoric of Fiction*, Chicago: University of Chicago Press.

Bos, A. P. (2001), 'The Distinction between "Platonic" and "Aristotelian" Dualism Illustrated from Plutarch's Myth in *De facie in orbe lunae*', in A. Pérez Jiménez and F. Casadesús (eds), *Estudios sobre Plutarco: Misticismo y religiones mistéricas en la obra de Plutarco*, Madrid: Ediciones Clásicas and Málaga: Charta Antiqua-Distribución Editorial, 57–70.

Bosworth, A. B. (1992), 'History and Artifice in Plutarch's *Eumenes*', in P. A. Stadter (ed.), *Plutarch and the Historical Tradition*, London: Routledge, 56–89.

Bosworth, A. B. (1997), 'In Search of Cleitarchus. Review of Luisa Prandi, *Fortuna e realtà dell' opera di Clitarco* (Historia Einzelschriften 104)', *Histos* 1: 211–24.

Bowden, H. (2013), 'On Kissing and Making Up: Court Protocol and Historiography in Alexander the Great's "Experiment with Proskynesis"', *BICS* 56: 55–77.

Bowersock, G. W. (1965), *Augustus and the Greek World*, Oxford: Clarendon Press.

Bowie, E. L. (1970), 'The Greeks and their Past in the Second Sophistic', *P&P* 46: 3–41.

Bowie, E. L. (1997), 'Hadrian, Favorinus, and Plutarch', in J. Mossman (ed.), *Plutarch and His Intellectual World*, London: Duckworth, 1–15.

Bowie, E. L. (2008), 'Plutarch's Habits of Citation: Aspects of Difference', in A. G. Nikolaidis (ed.), *The Unity of Plutarch's Work*, Berlin: De Gruyter, 143–57.

Boyce, M. (1957), "Some Reflections on Zurvanism", *BSOAS* 19: 304–16.

Boyce, M. (1975), *A History of Zoroastrianism vol. 1*, Leiden: Brill.

Boyce, M. (1982), *A History of Zoroastrianism vol. 2: Under the Achaemenians*, Leiden: Brill.

Boyce, M. (1990), 'Some Further Reflections on Zurvanism', in D. Amin, M. Kasheff and A. S. Shahbazi (eds), *Iranica Varia. Papers in Honor of Professor Ehsan Yarshater*, Leiden: Brill, 20–9.

Boyce, M. (1996), 'On the Orthodoxy of Sasanian Zoroastrianism', *BSOAS* 59: 11–28.

Boyce, M., and F. Grenet (1991), *History of Zoroastrianism*, vol. 3, Leiden: Brill.

Breitenbach, H. R. (1967), 'Xenophon (6): Xenophon von Athen', *RE* 9 A 2: 1567–1928, 1982–2052.

Bremer, J. (2004), 'Plutarch and the "Liberation of Greece"', in L. de Blois, J. Bons, T. Kessels and D. M. Schenkeveld (eds), *The Statesman in Plutarch's Works*, Leiden: Brill, 2.257–67.

Brenk, F. E. (1977), *In Mist Apparelled: Religious Themes in Plutarch's Moralia and Lives*, Leiden: Brill.

Brenk, F. E. (1987), 'An Imperial Heritage: The Religious Spirit of Plutarch of Chaironeia', *ANRW* 2.36.1: 1248–349.

Brenk, F. E. (1992), 'Plutarch's *Life* "Morkos Antonius": a Literary and Cultural Study', *ANRW* 2.33.6: 4347–468.

Brenk, F. E. (2005), 'The Barbarian Within: Gallic and Galatian Heroines in Plutarch's *Erotikos*', in A. Pérez Jiménez and F. Titchener (eds), *Historical and Biographical Values of Plutarch's Works: Studies Devoted to Professor Philip Stadter*, Logan: Utah State University Press/Málaga: Universidad de Málaga, 93–106.

Briant, P. (1989), 'Table du roi. Tribut et redistribution chez les Achéménides', in P. Briant and C. Herrenschmidt (eds), *Le Tribut dans l'Empire Perse*, Leuven: Peeters, 35–44.

Briant, P. (1994), 'L'eau du Grand Roi', in L. Milano (ed.), *Drinking in Ancient Societies: History and Culture of Drinks in the Ancient Near East*, Padua: Sargon srl, 46–65.

Briant, P. (2001), *Bulletin d'Histoire Achéménide II*, Paris: Thotm.

Briant, P. (2002a), *From Cyrus to Alexander: A History of the Persian Empire*, Winona Lake, IN: Eisenbrauns. (English translation of *Histoire de l'empire perse: De Cyrus à Alexandre*, Paris: Fayard, 1996.)

Briant, P. (2002b), 'History and Ideology: The Greeks and "Persian Decadence"', in T. Harrison (ed.), *Greeks and Barbarians*, Edinburgh: Edinburgh University Press, 193–210.

Briant, P. (2015), *Darius in the Shadow of Alexander*, trans. T. M. Todd, Cambridge, MA: Harvard University Press.

Brokate, C. (1913), *De Aliquot Plutarchi Libellis*, diss. inaug., Göttingen.

Brosius, M. (1996), *Women in Ancient Persia, 559–331 BC*, Oxford: Oxford University Press.

Brosius, M. (1998), 'Artemis Persike and Artemis Anaitis', *AchHist* 11: 227–38.

Brosius, M. (2011), 'Greeks at the Persian Court', in J. Wiesehöfer, R. Rollinger, and G. Lanfranchi (eds), *Ktesias' Welt/Ctesias' World*, Wiesbaden: Harrassowitz, 69–80.

Brown, T. S. (1949), 'Alexander and Callisthenes', *AJPh* 70: 225–48.

Brown, T. S. (1978a), 'Suggestions for a Vita of Ctesias of Cnidus', *Historia* 27: 1–19.

Brown, T. S. (1978b), 'Aristodicus of Cyme and the Branchidae', *AJPh* 99: 64–78.

Bruce, I. A. F. (1967), *An Historical Commentary on the 'Hellenica Oxyrhynchia'*, Cambridge: Cambridge University Press.

Brust, M. (2005), *Die indischen und iranischen Lehnwörter im Griechischen*, Innsbruck: Institut für Sprachen und Literaturen der Universität Innsbruck.

Buckler, J. (1977), 'Plutarch and the Fate of Antalcidas', *GRBS* 18: 139–45.

Bürchner, L. (1921a), 'Kaunos (1)', *RE* 11.1: 85–8.

Bürchner, L. (1921b), 'Kolophon (2)', *RE* 11.1: 1114–8.

Burkert, W. (1985), *Greek Religion*, transl. J. Raffan, Cambridge, MA: Harvard University Press.

Burn, A. R. (1962), *Persia and the Greeks*, London: Edward Arnold.

Bury, J. B. (1913), *A History of Greece*, New York: Modern Library.

Büttner-Wobst, T., and A. G. Roos (1906, 1910), *Excerpta historica iussu imperatoris Constantini Porphyrogeniti confecta*, vol. 2: *excerpta de virtutibus et vitiis*, 2 pts, Berlin: Weidmann.

Çağirgan, G., and W. G. Lambert (1991–3), 'The Late Babylonian Kislīmu Ritual for Esagil', *JCS* 43/45: 89–106.

Calmeyer, P. (1977), 'Vom Reisehut zur Kaiserkrone: B. Stand der Archaeologischen Forschung zu den Iranischen Kronen', *AMI* 10: 168–90.

Cameron, A. (1969–70), 'Agathias on the Sassanians', *DOP* 23–4: 67–183.
Cary, M. (1933), 'The Second Athenian League', in J. B. Bury, S. A. Cook and F. E. Adcock (eds), *CAH* VI, Cambridge: Cambridge University Press, 57–79.
Cassin, E. (1968), *La splendeur divine*, Paris: La Haye.
Castiglioni, L. (1925), *Studi Intorno alle 'Storie Filippiche' di Giustino*, Naples: Rondinelli.
Cauer, E. (1847), *Quaestiones de fontibus ad Agesilai Historiam Pertinentibus*, Breslau: Trewendt.
Cawkwell, G. L. (1963), 'Notes on the Peace of 375/4', *Historia* 12: 84–95.
Cawkwell, G. L. (1972), 'Introduction', in R. Warner (trans.), *Xenophon: The Persian Expedition*, 2nd ed., Harmondsworth: Penguin, 9–43.
Cawkwell, G. L. (1976), 'The Imperialism of Thrasybulus', *CQ* n.s. 26: 270–7.
Cawkwell, G. L. (2004), 'When, How and Why did Xenophon Write the *Anabasis*', in R. Lane-Fox (ed.), *The Long March: Xenophon and the Ten Thousand*, New Haven, CT: Yale University Press, 47–67.
Chaniotis, A. (2005), 'The Great Inscription, its Political and Social Institutions and the Common Institutions of the Cretans', in E. Greco and M. Lombardo (eds), *La Grande Iscrizione di Gortyna. Centoventi anni dopo la scoperta*, Athens: Scuola Archeologica Italiana di Atene, 175–6.
Chatman, S. (1978), *Story and Discourse: Narrative Structure in Fiction and Film*, Ithaca, NY: Cornell University Press.
Cherniss, H. (1954), 'The Sources of Evil according to Plato', *Proceedings of the American Philosophical Society* 98: 23–30.
Cherniss, H. (1976), *Plutarch. Moralia. Volume XIII, Part I, with an English Translation*, Cambridge, MA: Harvard University Press.
Chlup, R. (2000), 'Plutarch's Dualism and the Delphic Cult', *Phronesis* 45: 138–58.
Christensen, A. (1944), *L'Iran sous les Sassanides*, Copenhagen: E. Munksgaard.
Chugg, A. (2009), *Alexander the Great in India: A Reconstruction of Cleitarchus*, AMC Publications.
Clarke, K. (1999), *Between Geography and History: Hellenistic Constructions of the Roman World*, Oxford: Oxford University Press.
Clermont-Ganneau, C. S. (1886), 'Mané, thécel, pharès et la festin de Balthasar', *Journal Asiatique* 8: 36–67.
Cole, T. (1983), 'Archaic Truth', *QUCC* 42: 7–28.
Colledge, M. A. R. (1967), *The Parthians*, London: Thames and Hudson.
Collman, W. (1869), *De Diodori Siculi fontibus commentationis criticae*, Leipzig: Teubner.
Cook, J. M. (1961), 'Cnidian Peraea and Spartan Coins', *JHS* 81 (1961): 56–72.
Cook, J. M. (1983), *The Persian Empire*, London: Dent; New York: Schocken Books.

Cooper, J. M. (1984), 'Plato's Theory of Human Motivation', *HPQ* 1: 3–21.

Costa, E. A. (1974), 'Evagoras I and the Persians, ca. 411 to 391 B.C.', *Historia* 23: 40–56.

Coste, D., and J. Pier (2009), 'Narrative Levels' in P. Hühn, J. Pier, W. Schmid and J. Schönert (eds), *Handbook of Narratology*, Berlin: De Gruyter, 295–308.

Cowley, A. (1923), *Aramaic Papyri of the Fifth Century B.C.*, Oxford: Clarendon Press.

Croiset, M. (1899), *Histoire de la littérature grecque*, vol. 5.2: période romaine, Paris: Fontemoing.

Daryaee, T. (2002), 'Mind, Body, and the Cosmos: Chess and Backgammon in Ancient Persia', *Iranian Studies* 35: 281–312.

de Blois, L. (1992), 'The Perception of Politics in Plutarch's Roman *Lives*', *ANRW* 2.33.6: 4568–615.

de Boor, C. (1905), *Excerpta historica iussu imp. Constantini Porphyrogeniti confecta, vol. 3: excerpta de insidiis*, Berlin: Weidmann.

de Jong, A. (1997), *Traditions of the Magi: Zoroastrianism in Greek and Latin Literature*, Leiden: Brill.

de Jong, I. J. F. (2004), *Narrators and Focalizers: The Presentation of the Story in the Iliad*, 2nd ed., London: Bristol Classical Press.

Debevoise, N. C. (1938), *A Political History of Parthia*, Chicago: University of Chicago Press.

Del Corno, D. (1962), 'La lingua di Ctesia (POx. 2330)', *Athenaeum* 40: 126–41.

Delebecque, E. (1957), *Essai sur la vie de Xenophon*, Paris: Klincksieck.

Denyer, N. (2001), *Plato: Alcibiades*, Cambridge: Cambridge University Press.

Descat, R. (1995), 'Marché Tribut: l'approvisionnement des Dix-Mille', in P. Briant (ed.), *Dans les pas des dix-mille: Peuple et pays du Proche-Orient vus par un grec* [= *Pallas* 43], Toulouse: Presses Universitaires du Mirail, 99–108.

Dillon, J. (1977), *The Middle Platonists*, London: Routledge.

Dilts, M. R. (1971), *Heraclidis Lembi Excerpta Politiarum*, Durham, NC: Duke University Press.

Dodds, E. R. (1945), 'Plato and the Irrational', *JHS* 65: 16–25.

Dorati, M. (1995), 'Ctesia falsario?', *QS* 41: 33–52.

Dörrie, H. (1967), 'Xenocrates', *RE* 9 A 2: 1512–28.

Drews, R. (1962), 'Diodorus and his Sources', *AJPh* 83: 383–92.

Drews, R. (1963), 'Ephorus and History Written *kata genos*', *AJPh* 84: 244–55.

Drews, R. (1973), *The Greek Accounts of Eastern History*, Cambridge, MA: Harvard University Press.

Drews, R. (1974), 'Sargon, Cyrus and Mesopotamian Folk History', *JNES* 33: 387–93.

Drews, R. (1976), 'Ephorus' *kata genos* history revisited', *Hermes* 104: 497–8.

Drost-Abgarjan, A. (2006), 'Ein neuer Fund zur armenischen Version der Eusebios-Chronik', in M. Wallraff (ed.), *Julius Africanus und die christliche Weltchronistik*, Berlin: De Gruyter, 255–62.

Due, B. (1989), *The Cyropaedia: Xenophon's Aims and Methods*, Aarhus: Aarhus University Press.

Duff, T. (1999), *Plutarch's* Lives: *Exploring Virtue and Vice*, Oxford: Oxford University Press.

Duff, T. (2010), 'Plutarch's *Themistocles* and *Camillus*', in N. Humble (ed.), *Plutarch's Lives: Parallelism and Purpose*, Swansea: The Classical Press of Wales, 45–86.

Duff, T. (2011), 'Plutarch's "Lives" and the Critical Reader', in G. Roskam and L. Van der Stockt (eds), *Virtues for the People: Aspects of Plutarch's Ethics*, Leuven: Leuven University Press, 59–82.

Duff, T. and I. Scott-Kilvert (2012), *Plutarch: The Age of Alexander*, London: Penguin.

Dürrbach, F. (1893), 'L'apologie de Xénophon dans l'*Anabase*', *REG* 6: 343–86.

Eck, B. (1990), 'Sur la vie de Ctésias', *REG* 103: 409–34.

Eddy, S. K. (1961), *The King Is Dead*, Lincoln: University of Nebraska Press.

Eddy, S. K. (1973), 'The Cold War between Athens and Persia', *CPh* 68: 241–58.

Ehrhardt, C. (1970), 'Xenophon and Diodorus on Aegospotami', *Phoenix* 24: 225–8.

Ehtecham, M. (1946), *L'Iran sous les Achéménides*, Fribourg: Saint-Paul.

Eilers, W. (1935), 'Das Volk der karka in den epichorischen Alphabeten Kleinasiens', *OLZ* 38: 201–13.

Eilers, W. (1940), *Iranische Beamtennamen in der keilschriftlichen Überlieferung*, Leipzig: Brockhaus.

Else, G. (1965), *Aristotle's Poetics*, Cambridge, MA: Harvard University Press.

Engels, J. (1998), 'Phainias of Eresos', in G. Schepens (ed.), *Felix Jacoby. Die Fragmente der griechischen Historiker Continued IV: Biography and Antiquarian Literature. IVA: Biography*, Fasc. 1: *The Pre-Hellenistic Period*, Leiden: Brill, 266–351.

Erbse, H. (1956), 'Die Bedeutung der Synkrisis in den Parallelbiographien Plutarchs', *Hermes* 84: 398–424.

Farrell, W. J. (1961), 'A Revised Itinerary of the Route Followed by Cyrus the Younger through Syria, 401 B.C.', *JRS* 81: 153–5.

Fensham, F. C. (1982), *The Books of Ezra and Nehemiah*, The New International Commentary on the Old Testament, Grand Rapids, MI: Eerdmans.

Ferrari, G. R. F. (1987), *Listening to the Cicadas: A Study of Plato's Phaedrus*, Cambridge: Cambridge University Press.

Ferrari, G. R. F. (2007), 'The Three-Part Soul' in G. R. F. Ferrari (ed.), *The Cambridge Companion to Plato's Republic*, Cambridge: Cambridge University Press, 165–201.

Fiechter, E. (1919), 'Karyatides', *RE* 10.2: 2247–52.

Fisher, E. (1976), 'Cultic Prostitution in the Ancient Near East? A Reassessment', *BTB* 6: 229–36.

Flacelière, R. (1963), 'Rome et ses Empereurs vus par Plutarque', *AC* 32: 28–47.

Flacelière, R. (1976), 'Trajan, Delphes et Plutarque', in F. Chamoux (ed.), *Études sur l'antiquité grecque offertes à André Plassart par ses collègues de la Sorbonne*, Paris: Les Belles Lettres, 97–103.

Flaceliére, R., and E. Chambry (1979), *Plutarque, Les vies XV*, Paris: Les Belles Lettres.

Flower, M. A. (1994), *Theopompus of Chios: History and Rhetoric in the Fourth Century* BC, Oxford: Oxford University Press.

Fludernik, M. (1996), *Towards a 'Natural' Narratology*, London: Routledge.

Fludernik, M. (2009), *An Introduction to Narratology*, trans. P. Häusler-Greenfield and M. Fludernik, London: Routledge.

Forgazza, G. (1970), 'Aspasia Minore', *PdP* 25: 420–2.

Forni, G. (1958), *Valore storico e fonti di Pompeo Trogo*, Urbino: STEU.

Fowler, R. L. (1996), 'Herodotus and his Contemporaries', *JHS* 116: 62–87.

Fowler, R. L. (2006), 'Herodotus and his Prose Predecessors', in C. Dewald and J. Marincola (eds), *The Cambridge Companion to Herodotus*, Cambridge: Cambridge University Press, 29–45.

Fowler, R. L. (2013), *Early Greek Mythography. Vol. 2: Commentary*, Oxford: Oxford University Press.

Frankfort, H. (1939), *Cylinder Seals*, London: Macmillan.

Frankfort, H. (1948) *Kingship and the Gods*, Chicago: University of Chicago Press.

Frankfort, H. (1954), *The Art and Architecture of the Ancient Orient*, London: Penguin.

Fraser, P. M., and E. Matthews (1987), *A Lexicon of Greek Personal Names*, vol. 1, Oxford: Oxford University Press.

Fraser, P. M., and E. Matthews (1997), *A Lexicon of Greek Personal Names*, vol. 3a, Oxford: Oxford University Press.

Fraser, P. M., and E. Matthews (2000), *A Lexicon of Greek Personal Names*, vol. 3b, Oxford: Oxford University Press.

Friedländer, P. (1964), *Plato: An Introduction, Vol. II*, trans. H. Meyerhoff, Princeton: Princeton University Press.

Frisk, H. (1960), *Griechisches etymologisches Wörterbuch*, vol. 1, Heidelberg: Winter.

Froidefond, C. (1987), 'Plutarque et le platonisme', *ANRW* 2.36.1: 184–233.

Froidefond, C. (1988), *Plutarque: Euvres morales, V.2: Isis et Osiris*, Paris: Les Belles Lettres.

Frost, F. J. (1980), *Plutarch's Themistocles: A Historical Commentary*, Princeton: Princeton University Press.

Frye, R. N. (1959), 'Zurvanism Again', *HTR* 52: 63–73.

Frye, R. N. (1962), *The Heritage of Persia*, London: Weidenfeld and Nicolson.

Frye, R. N. (1972), 'Gestures of Deference to Royalty in Ancient Iran', *IA* 9: 102–7.

Frye, R. N. (1984), *The History of Ancient Iran*, Munich: Beck.

Fuhrmann, F. (1988), *Plutarque: Oeuvre morales II: Apophtegmes de rois et de généraux – apophtemet Laconiens*, Paris: Les Belles Lettres.

Funck, B. (1981) 'Studie zu der Bezeichnung *bárbaros*', in E. C. Welskopf (ed.), *Soziale Typenbegriffe im alten Griechenland und ihr Fortleben in den Sprachen der Welt*, Bd. IV, Berlin: Akademie-Verlag, 26–51.

Gabelmann, H. (1984), *Antike Audienz- und Tribunalszenen*, Darmstadt: Wissenschaftliche Buchgesellschaft.

Galdi, M. (1922), *L'epitome nella letteratura latina*, Naples: Federico e Ardia librai editori.

Gardiner-Garden, J. R. (1987), *Ktesias on Early Central Asian History and Ethnography*, Bloomington: Indiana University Press.

Garrison, M.B. and Root, M.C. (1998), *Persepolis Seal Studies: An Introduction with Provisional Concordances of Seal Numbers and Associated Documents on Fortification Tablets 1–2087*, AchHist 9.

Gasche, H. (1995), 'Autour des Dix-Mille: Vestiges archéologiques dans les environs du "Mur de Médie"', in P. Briant (ed.), *Dans les pas des dix-mille: Peuple et pays du Proche-Orient vus par un grec* [= *Pallas* 43], Toulouse: Presses Universitaires du Mirail, 201–16.

Gasparov, M. L. (1980), 'Scripta Moralia *Regum et Imperatorum Apophthegmata*', *VDI* 153: 237–53 (in Russian).

Geiger, J. (1975), 'Zum Bild Julius Caesars in der Römischen Kaiserzeit', *Historia* 24: 444–53.

Geiger, J. (1979), 'Cornelius Nepos, *De Regibus Exterarum Gentium*', *Latomus* 38: 662–9.

Geiger, J. (1981), 'Plutarch's *Parallel Lives*: The Choice of Heroes', *Hermes* 109: 85–104.

Geiger, J. (1985), *Cornelius Nepos and Ancient Political Biography*, Stuttgart: Franz Steiner.

Geiger, J. (1988), 'Nepos and Plutarch: From Latin to Greek Political Biography', *ICS* 13: 245–56.

Geiger, J. (2008), '*Lives* and *Moralia*: How Were Put Asunder What Plutarch Hath Joined Together', in A. G. Nikolaidis (ed.), *The Unity of Plutarch's Work*, Berlin: De Gruyter, 5–14.

Genette, G. (1980 [1972]), *Narrative Discourse: An Essay in Method*, trans. J. E. Lewin, Ithaca, NY: Cornell University Press.

Genette, G. (1988 [1983]), *Narrative Discourse Revisited*, trans. J. E. Lewin, Ithaca, NY: Cornell University Press.

Gentili, B., and G. Cerri (1988), *History and Biography in Ancient Thought*, Amsterdam: Gieben.

Georgiadou, A. (1988), 'The *Lives of the Caesars* and Plutarch's Other *Lives*', *ICS* 13: 346–59.

Georgiadou, A. (1997), *Plutarch's Pelopidas*, Stuttgart and Leipzig: Teubner.

Georgiadou, A., and D. H. J. Larmour (1994), 'Lucian and Historiography: "*De historia conscribenda*" and "*Verae Historiae*"', in *ANRW* 2.34.2: 1448–509.

Gera, D. (1993), *Xenophon's* Cyropaedia: *Style, Genre and Literary Technique*, Oxford: Oxford University Press.

Gera, D. (2007), 'Themistocles' Persian Tapestry', *CQ* n.s. 57: 445–57.

Gershevitch, I. (1964), 'Zoroaster's Own Contribution', *JNES* 23: 12–38.

Gerson, L. P. (2003), *Knowing Persons: A Study in Plato*, Oxford: Oxford University Press.

Giangrande, G. (1976), 'On an Alleged Fragment of Ctesias', *QUCC* 23: 31–46.

Gilmore, J. (1888), *The Fragments of the* Persika *of Ktesias*, London: Macmillan and co.

Gnoli, G. (1963), 'Ax^varətəm x^varənō', *AION* n.s. 13: 295–8.

Gnoli, G. (1979), 'Sol Persice Mithra', in U. Bianchi (ed.), *Mysteria Mithrae*, Leiden: Brill, 725–40.

Goldingay, J. (1989), *Word Biblical Commentary: Volume 30: Daniel*, Nashville: Thomas Nelson Inc.

Gomme, A. W. (1945), *A Historical Commentary on Thucydides, vol. 1: Introduction and Commentary on Book I*, Oxford: Oxford University Press.

Goodfriend, E. A. (1992), 'Prostitution (OT)', in D. N. Freedman (ed.), *Anchor Bible Dictionary*, New York: Doubleday, vol. 5: 505–10.

Gowing, A. (1990), 'Dio's Name', *CPh* 85: 49–54.

Grant, M. (1980), *Greek and Roman Authors 800 BC – AD 1000: A Biographical Dictionary*, New York: H. W. Wilson.

Gray, V. J. (1980), 'The Years 375 to 371 BC: A Case Study in the Reliability of Diodorus Siculus and Xenophon', *CQ* n.s. 30: 306–26.

Gray, V. J. (2003), 'Interventions and Citations in Xenophon, *Hellenica* and *Anabasis*', *CQ* n.s. 53: 111–23.

Gray, V. J. (2017), 'Xenophon's Language and Expression', in M. A. Flower (ed.), *The Cambridge Companion to Xenophon*, Cambridge: Cambridge University Press, 223–40.

Grayson, A. K. (1975), *Texts from Cuneiform Sources V. Assyrian and Babylonian Chronicles*, Locust Valley, NY: J. J. Augustin.

Grenfell, B. P., and A. S. Hunt (1922), *Oxyrhynchus Papyri*, vol. 15, Oxford: Oxford University Press.

Gribble, D. (1999), *Alcibiades and Athens: A Study in Literary Presentation*, Oxford: Oxford University Press.

Griffiths, A. (1987), 'Democedes of Croton: a Greek Doctor at Darius' Court', *AchHist* 2: 35–71.

Griffiths, G. (1970), *Plutarch's* De Iside et Osiride, Cardiff: University of Wales Press.

Grote, G. (1884), *A History of Greece*, vol. 9, London: J. Murray.

Gruber, M. I. (1980), *Aspects of Nonverbal Communication in the Ancient Near East*, Rome: Biblical Institute Press.

Gugel, H. (1971), 'Die Aufstellung von Kyros' Heer in der Schlacht von Kunaxa', *Gymnasium* 78: 241–3.

Gutmann, J., and D. Sperber (1971), 'Angaria', *Encyclopedia Judaica* 2: 115–8.

Guthrie, W. K. C. (1978), *History of Greek Philosophy*, vol. 4, Cambridge: Cambridge University Press.

Guyot, P. (1980), *Eunuchen als Sklaven und Freigelassenen in der griechisch-römischen Antike*, Stuttgart: Klett-Cotta.

Hägg, T. (1973), 'Photius at Work: Evidence from the Text of the *Bibliotheca*', *GRBS* 14: 213–22.

Hall, E. (1989), *Inventing the Barbarian*, Oxford: Oxford University Press.

Hall, J. (1981), *Lucian's Satire*, New York: Arno Press.

Hall, J. M. (1997), *Ethnic Identity in Greek Antiquity*, Cambridge: Cambridge University Press.

Hallock, R. T. (1969), *Persepolis Fortification Tablets*, Chicago: University of Chicago Press.

Hamilton, J. R. (1961), 'Cleitarchus and Aristobulus', *Historia* 10: 448–58.

Hamilton, J. R. (1969), *Plutarch, Alexander: A Commentary*, Oxford: Oxford University Press.

Hammond, N. G. L. (1959), *A History of Greece to 322 B.C.*, Oxford: Clarendon Press.

Hammond, N. G. L. and G. T. Griffith (1979), *A History of Macedonia, vol. 2, 550–336 B.C.*, Oxford: Clarendon Press

Hanson, A. E. (1991), 'Continuity and Change: Three Case Studies in Hippocratic Gynecological Therapy and Theory', in S. B. Pomeroy (ed.), *Women's History and Ancient History*, Chapel Hill: University of North Carolina Press, 73–110.

Hardie, P. (1997), 'Fifth-Century Athenian and Augustan Images of the Barbarian Other', *Classics Ireland* 4: 46–56.

Hardie, W. F. R. (1964–5), 'Aristotle's Doctrine That Virtue Is a "Mean"', *Proceedings of the Aristotelian Society* n.s. 65: 183–204.

Harris, R. (1962), 'Biographical Notes on the *naditu* Woman of Sippar', *JCS* 16: 1–12.

Harris, R. (1964), 'The *naditu* Woman', in R. D. Biggs and J. A. Brinkman (eds), *Studies Presented to A. Leo Oppenheim*, Chicago, University of Chicago Press, 106–35.

Harris, R. (1975), *Ancient Sippar: A Demographic Study of an Old-Babylonian City (1894–1595 BC)*, Istanbul: Nederlands Historisch-Archaeologisch Instituut te Istanbul.

Harrison, G. M. W. (1991), 'The Critical Trends in Scholarship on the Non-Philosophical Works in Plutarch's *Moralia*', *ANRW* 2.33.6: 4646–81.

Hartman, J. J. (1887), *Analecta Xenophontea*, Leiden: van Doesburg.

Hartman, J. J. (1911), 'Annotationes Criticae ad Plutarchi Opera (Continued)', *Mnemosyne*, 39: 68–105, 195–222, 293–331.

Hartog, F. (1988), *The Mirror of Herodotus*, trans. J. Lloyd, Berkeley: University of California Press.

Haug, M. (1854), *Die Quellen Plutarchs in den Lebensbeschreibungen der Griechen*, Tübingen: F. Osiander.

Hazzard, R. A. (1992), 'Did Ptolemy I Get His Surname from the Rhodians?', *ZPE* 93: 52–6.

Hazzard, R. A. (2000), *Imagination of a Monarchy: Studies in Ptolemaic Propaganda*, Toronto: University of Toronto Press.

Heckel, W. (2008), *The Conquests of Alexander the Great*, Cambridge: Cambridge University Press.

Heeren, A. H. L. (1802), *Commentatio de Trogi Pompeii eiusque epitomatoris iustini fontibus et auctoritate*, Göttingen: Typis Dieterichianis.

Heeren, A. H. L. (1833), *Historical Researches into the Politics, Intercourse, and Trade of the Principal Nations of Antiquity; Asiatic Nations, vol. 1*, trans. D. A. Talboys, Oxford: Talboys and Browne.

Held, G. J. (1935), *The Mahābhārata: An Ethnological Study*, Amsterdam: Uitgevermaatschappij Holland.

Helm, P. R. (1981), 'Herodotus' *Medikos Logos* and Median History', *Iran* 19: 85–90.

Helmbold, W. C., and E. N. O'Neil (1959), *Plutarch's Quotations*, Baltimore: American Philological Association.

Henkelman, W. (2003), 'An Elamite Memorial: The *šumar* of Cambyses and Hystaspes', *AchHist* 13: 101–72.

Henkelman, W. (2010), '"Consumed before the King": The Table of Darius, that of Irdabama and Irtaštuna, and that of his Satrap, Karkiš', in B. Jacobs and R. Rollinger (eds), *Der achaimenidische Hof/ The Achaemenid Court*, Wiesbaden: Harrassowitz, 667–776.

Henkelman, W. (2011), 'Cyrus the Persian and Darius the Elamite: A Case of Mistaken Identity', in J. Wiesehöfer, R. Rollinger and G. Lanfranchi (eds), *Ktesias' Welt/Ctesias' World*, Wiesbaden: Harrassowitz, 577–634.

Herbert, K. B. J. (1954), *Ephorus in Plutarch's Lives*, PhD diss., Harvard University.

Hershbell, J. P. (1977), 'Plutarch and Heraclitus', *Hermes* 105: 179–201.

Hershbell, J. P. (1997), 'Plutarch's Concept of History: Philosophy from Examples', *AncSoc* 28: 225–43.

Herter, H. (1967), 'Xanthos der Lyder', *RE* 9: 1354–74.

Herzfeld, E. (1931), 'Die Magna Charta von Susa, I. Text und Commentar', *AMI*, 3: 29–81.

Hewitt, J. W. (1919), 'The Second Phase of the Battle of Cunaxa', *CJ* 15: 83–93.

Hinz, W. (1974), 'Tiara', *RE Suppl.* 14: 794–6.

Hinz, W. (1975), *Altiranisches Sprachgut der Nebenüberlieferungen*, Wiesbaden: Harrassowitz.

Hinz, W., and H. Koch (1987), *Elamisches Wörterbuch*, 2 vols, Berlin: Dietrich Reimer.

Hirzel, R. (1895), *Der Dialog: Ein literarhistorischer Versuch*, vol. 1, Leipzig: S. Hirzel.

Hirzel, R. (1912), *Plutarch*, Leipzig: Dieterich.

Hofstetter, J. (1978), *Die Griechen in Persien*, Berlin: Dietrich Reimer.

Höistad, R. (1948), *Cynic Hero and Cynic King: Studies in the Cynic Conception of Man*, Uppsala: C. W. K. Gleerup.

Holford-Strevens, L. A. (1982), 'Fact and Fiction in Aulus Gellius', *LCM* 7: 67.

Holford-Strevens, L. A. (1988), *Aulus Gellius*, Oxford: Oxford University Press.

Holzapfel, L. (1879), *Untersuchungen Über die Darstellung der Geschiente von 489 bis 413 v.Chr. bei Ephoros, Theopomp und anderen Autoren*, Leipzig: Hirschfeld.

Homeyer, H. (1965), *Lukian: Wie man Geschichte schreiben soll*, Munich: Wilhelm Fink.

Homolle, T. (1917), 'L'origine des Caryatides', *RA* ser. 5, 5: 1–67.

Hood, D. C. (1967), *Plutarch and the Persians*, PhD diss., University of Southern California.

Hopfner, T. (1940), *Plutarch über Isis und Osiris*, Darmstadt: Wissenschaftliche Buchgesellschaft.

Horky, P. S. (2009), 'Persian Cosmos and Greek Philosophy: Plato's Associates and the Zoroastrian Magoi', *OSAP* 37: 47–103.

Hornblower, S. (1982), *Mausolus*, Oxford: Oxford University Press.

Hornblower, S. (1991), *A Commentary on Thucydides, vol. I: Books I–III*, Oxford: Clarendon Press.

Hornblower, S. (1994), 'Persia', in D. M. Lewis et al. (eds), *CAH*[2] VI, Cambridge: Cambridge University Press, 45–79.

Horst, J. (1932), *Proskynein*, Gütersloh: Bertelsmann.

House, H. (1956), *Aristotle's Poetics*, London: Hart-Davis.

Humphreys, S. C. (1974), 'The Nothoi of Kynosarges', *JHS* 94: 88–95.

Hunter, R., and D. A. Russell (2011), *Plutarch: How to Study Poetry (De Audiendis Poetis)*, Cambridge: Cambridge University Press.

Huyse, P. (1990), 'Persisches Wortgut in Athenaios' "Deipnosophistai"', *Glotta* 68: 93–104.

Instone-Brewer, D. (1991), '*Mene Mene Teqel Uparsin*: Daniel 5.25 in Cuneiform', *Tyndale Bulletin* 42: 310–16.

Irigoin, J. (1986), 'Le Catalogue de Lamprias, tradition manuscrite et éditions imprimées', *REG* 99: 318–31.

Isaac, B. (2004), *The Invention of Racism in Classical Antiquity*, Princeton: Princeton University Press.

Jacobs, B. (1987), 'Das Chvarnah – Zum Stand der Forschung', *MDOG* 119: 215–48.

Jacoby, C. (1874), 'Zur Beurtheilung der Fragmente des Nikolaus von Damaskus', in *Commentationes philologae: Scripserunt Seminarii philologi regii lipsiensis*, Leipzig: Giesecke and Devrient, 193–211.

Jacoby, F. (1909), 'Über die Entwicklung der griechischen Historiographie und den Plan einer neuen Sammlung der griechischen Historikerfragmente', *Klio* 9: 80-123.

Jacoby, F. (1913a), 'Hellanikos', *RE* 8: 104–55.

Jacoby, F. (1913b), 'Herakleides (42)', *RE* 8: 469–70.

Jacoby, F. (1921), 'Kleitarchos (2)', *RE* 11: 622–54.

Jacoby, F. (1922), 'Ktesias', *RE* 11: 2032–73.

Jacoby, F. (1926), *Die Fragmente der griechischen Historiker, Teil 2, Zeitgeschichte – C. Kommentar zu Nr. 64 – 105*, Berlin: Weidmann.

Jacoby, F. (1930), *Die Fragmente der griechischen Historiker, Teil 2, Zeitgeschichte. – D. Kommentar zu Nr. 106 – 261*, Berlin: Weidmann.

Jacoby, F. (1938), 'Charon von Lampsakos', *SIFC* 15: 207–42.

Jacoby, F. (1940), *Die Fragmente der griechischen Historiker Teil 3, Geschichte von Städten und Völkern. Teil 3, Geschichte von Städten und Völkern. – A. Autoren über einzelnde Städte (Länder), Nr. 262–296*, Leiden: Brill.

Jacoby, F. (1954), *Die Fragmente der griechischen Historiker, Teil 3, Geschichte von Städten und Völkern. – B (Suppl.), A commentary on the ancient historians of Athens. – Vol. 1: Text, Vol. 2. Notes, Addenda, Corrigenda, Index*, Leiden: Brill.

Jacoby, F. (1955), *Die Fragmente der griechischen Historiker: Teil 3, Geschichte von Staedten und Voelkern. – B, Kommentar zu Nr. 297 – 607. Text – Noten*, Leiden: Brill.

Jacoby, F. (1958), *Die Fragmente der griechischen Historiker: Teil 3, Geschichte von Staedten und Voelkern. – C, Autoren ueber einzelne Laender. – Bd. 1. Aegypten – Geten [Nr. 608a – 708]*, Leiden: Brill.

Jamzadeh, P. (1991), *The Achaemenid Throne: Its Significance and Its Legacy*, PhD diss., University of California, Berkeley.

Jeyes, U. (1983), 'The Naditu Women of Sippar', in A. Cameron and A. Kuhrt (eds), *Images of Women in Antiquity*, London: Croom Helm, 260–72.

Johnson, F. (1952), *A Dictionary of Persian, Arabaic and English*, London: W. H. Allen & Co.

Jones, C. P. (1966), 'Towards a Chronology of Plutarch's Works', *JRS* 56: 61–74.

Jones, C. P. (1971), *Plutarch and Rome*, Oxford: Oxford University Press.

Jones, C. P. (1986), *Culture and Society in Lucian*, Cambridge, MA: Harvard University Press.

Jones, P. J. (2005), *Reading Rivers in Roman Literature and Culture*, Lanham, MD: Lexington Books.

Jouanna, J. (1974), *Hippocrate a l'Ecole de Cnide*, Paris: Les Belles Lettres.

Judeich, W. (1892), *Kleinasiatische Studien*, Marburg: Elwert.

Judeich, W. (1895), 'Ariaios (2)', *RE* 1.3: 811.

Judeich, W. (1896), 'Aspasia (2)', *RE* 1.4: 1721–2.

Jung, M. (2006), *Marathon und Plataiai. Zwei Perserschlachten als leux de memoire im antiken Griechenland*, Göttingen: Vandenhoeck & Ruprecht.

Justi, F. (1895), *Iranisches Namenbuch*, Marburg: Elwert.

Kaemmel, O. (1875), 'Die Berichte ueber die Schlacht von Kunaxa und den Fall des Kyros am 3 September 401 vor Chr.', *Philologus* 34: 515–38, 665–96.

Kahn, C. H. (1987), 'Plato's Theory of Desire', *The Review of Metaphysics* 41: 77–103.

Kalischek, A. E. (1913), *De Ephoro et Theopompo Isocratis discipulis*, diss., Münster.

Karst, J. (1911), *Eusebius' Werke 5: Die Chronik aus dem Armenischen übersetzt mit textkritischem Kommentar*, Leipzig: J. C. Hinrichs.

Keller, W. J. (1911), 'Xenophon's acquaintance with the History of Herodotus', *CJ* 6: 252–9.

Kent, R. G. (1953), *Old Persian: Grammar, Text, Lexicon*, New Haven, CT: American Oriental Society.

Kindt, T., and H.-H. Müller (2006), *The Implied Author: Concept and Controversy*, Berlin: De Gruyter.

King, H. (1998), *Hippocrates' Woman: Reading the Female Body in Ancient Greece*, London: Routledge.

Kingsley, P. (1995), 'Meetings with Magi: Iranian Themes among the Greeks, from Xanthus of Lydia to Plato's Academy', *Journal of the Royal Asiatic Society* 5: 173–209.

Kirk, G. S. (1954), *Heraclitus, The Cosmic Fragments*, Cambridge: Cambridge University Press.

Kirk, G. S., and J. Raven (1957), *The Presocratic Philosophers*, Cambridge: Cambridge University Press.

Kirschner, J. (1899), 'Chabrias (1)', 3.2: 2017–21.

Kohl, R. (1915), *De scholasticarum declamationum argumentis ex historia petites*, PhD diss., Münster.

Kollesch, J. (1989), 'Knidos als Zentrum der frühen wissenschaftlichen Medizin im antiken Griechenland', *Gesnerus* 46: 11–28.

Klotz, A. (1913), 'Pompeius (142) Trogus', *RE* 21.2: 2300–13.

König, F. W. (1972), *Die Persika des Ktesias von Knidos*, Graz: Weidner.

Konrad, C. (1994), *Plutarch's Sertorius: A Historical Commentary*, Chapel Hill: University of North Carolina Press.

Krappe, A. H. (1933), 'Solomon and Ashmodai', *AJPh* 54: 260–8.

Kroll, W. (1918), 'M. Iunianus Iustinus', *RE* 10: 956–8.

Kronenberg, A. J. (1927), 'Ad Plutarchi *Vitas*', *Mnemosyne* n.s. 55: 66–78.

Kronenberg, A. J. (1933–4), 'Ad Plutarchi *Vitas*', *Mnemosyne* 1: 161–74.

Krumbholz, P. (1889), *De Ctesia Aliisque Auctoribus in Plutarchi Artaxerxis Vita Adhibitis*, Eisenach: Hofbuchdruckerei.

Kühn, C. G. (1823), *Claudii Galeni opera omnia, vol. 6*, Leipzig: Knobloch.

Kühn, C. G. (1827), *Claudii Galeni opera omnia, vol. 14*, Leipzig: Knobloch.

Kuhrt, A. (1987), 'Usurpation, Conquest and Ceremonial: from Babylon to Persia', in D. Cannadine and S. Price (eds), *Rituals of Royalty*, Cambridge: Cambridge University Press, 20–55.

Kuhrt, A. (1988), 'Earth and Water', *AchHist* 3: 87–99.

Kuhrt, A. (2003), 'Making History: Sargon of Agade and Cyrus the Great of Persia', *AchHist* 13: 347–61.

Kuhrt, A. (2007), *The Persian Empire*, 2 vols, London: Routledge.

Kuhrt, A. (2009), 'Review of C. Binder, *Plutarchs Vita des Artaxerxes*', *Gymnasium* 116: 174–6.

Kuhrt, A., and H. Sancisi-Weerdenburg (1997), 'Artaxerxes', *DNP* 2: 47–8.

Kuntz, M. (1994), 'The Prodikean "Choice of Herakles": A Reshaping of Myth', *CJ* 89: 163–81.

Kyle, D. G. (1993), *Athletics in Ancient Athens*, Leiden: Brill.

Lachmann, K. H. (1854), *Geschichte Griechenlands von dem Ende des Peloponnesischen Krieges bis zu dem regierungsantritte Alexanders des Grossen*, Leipzig: Dyk.

Lacocque, A. (1976), *Le livre de Daniel*, Neuchâtel/Paris: Delachaux et Niestlé.

Lamar, H. (1927), 'Lusoria Tabula', *RE* 13: 1900–2029.

Lamarre, C. (1907), *Histoire de la littérature latine au temps d'Auguste*, vol. 3, Paris: J. Lamarre.

Lamberton, R. (2001), *Plutarch*, New Haven, CT: Yale University Press.

Laqueur, R. (1911), 'Ephoros 2: Die Dispositionen', *Hermes* 46: 321–54.

Laqueur, R. (1936), 'Timagenes (2)', *RE* 6 A.1: 1063–71.

Laqueur, R. (1938), 'Phainias aus Eresos', *RE* 19.1: 1565–91.

Larmour, D. H. J. (1992), 'Making Parallels: *Synkrisis* and Plutarch's "Themistocles and Camillus"', *ANRW* 2.33.6: 4154–200.

Lausberg, H. (1998), *Handbook of Literary Rhetoric*, trans. M. T. Bliss, A. Jansen, and D. E. Orton, Leiden: Brill.

Lehmann-Haupt, K. F. (1902), 'Zur Geschichte und Überlieferung des ionischen Aufstandes', *Klio* 2: 334–40.

Lehmann-Haupt, K. F. (1921), 'Satrap und Satrapie', *RE* 2.3: 82–188.

Leisegang, H. (1950), 'Platon', *RE* 20.2: 2342–537.

Lemerle, P. (1986), *Byzantine Humanism*, trans. H. Lindsay and A. Moffat, Canberra: Australian Association for Byzantine Studies.

Lendle, O. (1986), 'Xenophon in Babylonien: Die Märsche der Kyreer von Pylai bis Opis', *RhM* 129: 193–222.

Lendle, O. (1995), *Kommentar zu Xenophons* Anabasis, Darmstadt: Wissenschaftliche Buchgesellschaft.

Lenfant, D. (1996), 'Ctésias et Hérodote, ou les réécritures de l'histoire dans la Perse achéménide', *REG* 109: 348–80.

Lenfant, D. (2000), 'Nicolas de Damas et le corpus des fragments de Ctésias. Du fragment comme adaptation', *AncSoc* 30: 293–318.

Lenfant, D. (2004), *Ctésias de Cnide. Edition, traduction et commentaire historique des témoignages et fragments*, Paris: Les Belles Lettres.

Lenfant, D. (2007), 'Greek Historians of Persia', in J. Marincola (ed.), *A Companion to Greek and Roman Historiography*, Malden, MA: Wiley-Blackwell, 200–9.

Lenfant, D. (2009), *Les histoires perses de Dinon et d'Héraclide*, Paris: De Boccard.

Lenfant, D. (2010), 'Le médicin historien', in G. Zecchini (ed.), *Lo storico antico: mestieri e figure sociali*, Bari: Edipuglia, 231–47.

Lenfant, D. (2011), 'À propos d'un commentaire récent de l'Artaxerxès de Plutarque', *Histos* 5: 306–15.

Lenfant, D. (2012), 'Ctesias and his Eunuchs: A Challenge for Modern Historians', *Histos* 6: 257–97.

Lenfant, D. (2014), 'Greek Monographs on the Persian World. The Fourth Century BCE and Its Innovations', in G. Parmeggiani (ed.), *Between Thucydides and Polybius: The Golden Age of Greek Historiography*, Washington, DC: Center for Hellenic Studies, Trustees for Harvard University, 197–210.

Lenschau, T. (1921), 'Klearchos (3)', *RE* 1.21: 575–7.

Leo, F. (1901), *Die Griechisch–Römische Biographie nach ihrer Literarischen Form*, Leipzig: Teubner.

Lepper, F. A. (1948), *Trajan's Parthian War*, Oxford: Oxford University Press.

Lerouge, C. (2007), *L'image des Parthes dans le monde gréco-romain*, Stuttgart: Franz Steiner.

Lesky, A. (1971), *Geschichte der griechischen Literatur*, Bern/Munich: Francke.

Lévy, E. (1984), 'Naissance du concept de barbare', *Ktema* 9: 5–14.

Lewis, D. M. (1977), *Sparta and Persia*, Leiden: Brill.

Lewis, D. M. (1987), 'The King's Dinner (Polyaenus 4.3.32)', *AchHist* 2: 79–87.

Lewis, D. M. (1997), 'Persians in Herodotus', in P. J Rhodes (ed.), *Selected Papers in Greek and Near Eastern History*, Cambridge: Cambridge University Press, 345–61.

Lincoln, B. (2007), *Religion, Empire and Torture: The Case of Achaemenian Persia, with a Postscript on Abu Ghraib*, Chicago: University of Chicago Press.

Lintott, A. W. (1972), 'Imperial Expansion and Moral Decline in the Roman Republic', *Historia* 21: 626–38.

Llewellyn-Jones, L., and J. Robson (2010), *Ctesias' History of Persia: Tales of the Orient*, London: Routledge.

Lommel, H. (1930), *Die Religion Zarathustras nach dem Awesta darges-tellt*, Tübingen: Mohr.

Longden, R. P. (1931), 'Notes on the Parthian Campaigns of Trajan', *JRS* 21: 1–35.

Lonie, I. M. (1978), 'Cos Versus Cnidus and the Historians', Part I and II, *History of Science* 16: 42–75 and 77–92.

Lonsdale, S. H. (1990), *Creatures of speech: Lion, Herding, and Hunting Similes in the Iliad*, Stuttgart: Teubner.

Lord, C. (1969), 'Tragedy without Character: *Poetics* VI.1450a24', *JAAC* 28: 55–62.

Lorenz, H. (2006), *The Brute Within: Appetitive Desire in Plato and Aristotle*, Oxford: Oxford University Press.

Losin, P. (1987), 'Aristotle's Doctrine of the Mean', *HPQ* 4: 329–41.

Lucas, D. W. (1968), *Aristotle Poetics*, Oxford: Clarendon Press.

Luce, T. J. (1977), *Livy: The Composition of His History*, Princeton: Princeton University Press.

Luckenbill, D. D. (1926), *Ancient Records of Assyria and Babylonia*, Chicago: University of Chicago Press.

McDonald, A. H. (1953), 'Review of *Realencyclopädie der Classischen Altertumswissenschaft* by Pauly Wissowa and K. Ziegler', *JRS* 43: 162–3.

MacLaren, M., Jr., (1934), 'Xenophon and Themistogenes', *TAPhA* 15: 240–7.

MacLeod, M. D. (1991), *Lucian: A Selection*, Warminster: Aris and Phillips.

MacLeod, M. D. (1994), 'Lucianic Studies since 1930', *ANRW* 2.34.2: 1362–421.

Manfredini, M., D. P. Orsi and V. Antelami (1987), *Plutarco, Le Vite di Arato e di* Artaserse, Milan: Fondazione Lorenzo Valla/Mondadori.

Mango, C. (1975), 'The Availablity of Books in the Byzantine Empire, A.D. 750–850', in *Byzantine Books and Bookmen: a Dumbarton Oaks colloquium*, Washington, DC: Dumbarton Oaks, 29–45.

Mansfeld, J. (1992), *Heresiography in Context*: *Hippolytus' Elenchos as a Source for Greek Philosophy*, Leiden: Brill.

Mantey, O. A. (1888), *Welchen Quellen folgte Plutarch in seinem Leben des Artaxerxes*, Greifenberg in Pommern: Lemcke.

Manton, G. R. (1949), 'The Manuscript Tradition of Plutarch Moralia 70–7', *CQ* 43: 97–104.

Marasco, G. (1988), 'Ctesia, Dinone, Eraclide di Cuma e le Origini della Storiografia Tragica', *SIFC* 6: 48–67.

Marasco, G. (1994), *Vite di Plutarco*, vol. 5, Turin: Unione Tipografico-Editrice Torinese.

March, D. A. (1997), 'Konon and the Great King's Fleet, 396–394', *Historia* 46: 257–69.

Marcovich, M. (1967), *Heraclitus, editio maior*, Mérida, Venezuela: Andes University Press.

Marcus, R. (1937), *Josephus, VI: Books 9–11*, Loeb Classical Library, Cambridge, MA: Harvard University Press.

Marincola, J. (1997), *Authority and Tradition in Ancient Historiography*, Cambridge: Cambridge University Press.

Marincola, J. (1999), 'Genre, Convention, and Innovation in Greco-Roman Historiography', in C. Shuttleworth Kraus (ed.), *The Limits of Historiography: Genre and Narrative in Ancient Historical Texts*, Leiden: Brill, 281–324.

Marincola, J. (2017), 'Xenophon's *Anabasis* and *Hellenica*', in M. A. Flower (ed.), *The Cambridge Companion to Xenophon*, Cambridge: Cambridge University Press, 103–18.

Marr, J. L. (1998), *Plutarch: Life of Themistocles*, Warminster: Aris and Phillips.

Marshall, J. (1905), *The Second Athenian Confederacy*, Cambridge: Cambridge University Press.

Martin, H. M., Jr. (1960), 'The Concept of *Praotes* in Plutarch's *Lives*', *GRBS* 3: 65–73.

Martin, V. (1944), 'Le traitement de l'histoire diplomatique dans la tradition littéraire du IVᵉ siècle avant J.-C.', *MH* 1: 13–30.

Martin, V. (1949), 'Sur une interprétation nouvelle de la "Paix du Roi"', *MH* 6: 127–39.

Mayer, K. (1997), 'Themistocles, Plutarch, and the Voice of the Other', in C. Schrader, V. Ramón and J. Vela (eds), *Plutarco y la Historia. Actas del V Simposio Español sobre Plutarco*, Zaragoza: Prensas Universitarias de Zaragoza, 297–304.

Mayrhofer, M. (1973), *Onomastica Persepolitana*, Vienna: Österreichischen Akademie der Wissenschaften.

Means, T. (1947/8), 'Plutarch and the Death of Cyrus', *CW* 41: 39–41.

Meijer, F. J. (1984), 'Cato's African Figs', *Mnemosyne* 37: 117–24.

Meister, K. (1990), *Die griechische Geschichtsschreibung von den Anfängen bis zum Ende des Hellenismus*, Stuttgart: W. Kohlhammer.

Meloni, P. (1950), 'Tiribazo Satrapo di Sardi', *Athenaeum* n.s. 28: 292–339.

Meloni, P. (1951), 'La grande rivolta dei Satrapi contro Artaserse II', *Rivista Storica Italiana* 63: 5–27.

Mendels, D. (1981), 'The Five Empires: A Note on a Propagandistic *Topos*', *AJPh* 102: 330–7.

Meyer, E. (1902), *Geschichte des Altertums*, vol. 5, Stuttgart: Cotta.

Millar, F. (1964), *A Study of Cassius Dio*, Oxford: Clarendon Press.

Miller, F. D. (1998), 'Plato on the Parts of the Soul', in N. D. Smith (ed.), *Plato: Critical Assessments, vol. 3: Plato's Middle Period: Psychology and Value Theory*, London: Routledge, 48–65.

Miller, M. C. (1997), *Athens and Persia in the Fifth Century BC: A Study in Cultural Receptivity*, Cambridge: Cambridge University Press.

Milns, R. D., and J. R. Ellis (1966), 'Theopompus, fr. 103 Jac', *PdP* 21: 56–60.

Mitford, T. B. (1980), 'Cappadocia and Armenia Minor: Historical Setting of the *Limes*', *ANRW* 2.7.2: 1169–228.

Moggi, M. (1972), 'Autori greci di *Persika* I: Dionisio di Mileto', *ASNP* 2: 433–68.

Moggi, M. (1977), 'Autori greci di *Persika*, II: Carone di Lampsaco', *ASNP* 7: 1–26.

Momigliano, A. (1931), 'Tradizione e invenzione in Ctesia', *Atena e Roma* n.s. 12: 15–44.

Momigliano, A. (1933), 'La valutazione di Filippo il Macedone in Giustino', *RIL* 66: 983–96.

Momigliano, A. (1958), 'The place of Herodotus in the History of Historiography', *History* 43: 1–13.

Momigliano, A. (1971), *The Development of Greek Biography: Four Lectures*, Cambridge, MA: Harvard University Press.

Momigliano, A. (1975), *Alien Wisdom: The Limits of Hellenization*, Cambridge: Cambridge University Press.

Momigliano, A. (1990), *The Classical Foundations of Modern Historiography*, Berkeley: University of California Press.

Montgomery, J. A. (1927), *A Critical and Exegetical Commentary on the Book of Daniel*, Edinburgh: T. & T. Clark.

Moorey, P. R. S. (1985), 'The Iranian Contribution to Achaemenid Material Culture', *Iran* 23: 21–37.

Morris, C. D. (1881), 'Review of C. F. Smith's *A Study of Plutarch's Life of Artaxerxes*', *AJPh* 2: 236–37.

Mosley, D. J. (1972), 'Timagoras' bed-makers', *CR* n.s. 22: 12.

Mossé, C. (1996), 'Plutarque, historien du IVe siècle', in P. Carlier (ed.), *Le IVe Siècle av. J.-C.*, Nancy: A.D.R.A.; Paris: De Boccard, 57–62.

Mossman, J. M. (2010), 'A Life Unparalleled: Plutarch's *Artaxerxes*', in N. Humble (ed.), *Plutarch's Lives: Parallelism and Purpose*, Swansea: Classical Press of Wales, 145–68.

Moysey, R. A. (1992), 'Plutarch, Nepos and the Satrapal Revolt of 362/1 B.C.', *Historia* 41: 158–68.

Müller, C. (1844), *Ctesiae Cnidii et chronographorum, Castoris, Eratosthenis, etc. fragmenta dissertatione et notis illustrata*, [= Anhang zu] Dindorf, W., *Herodoti Historiarum libri IX*, Paris: Didot.

Müller, C. (1848), *Fragmenta Historicorum Graecorum*, vol. 2, Paris: Didot.

Müller, C. (1849), *Fragmenta Historicorum Graecorum*, vol. 3, Paris: Didot.

Müller, C. (1851), *Fragmenta Historicorum Graecorum*, vol. 4, Paris: Didot.

Müller-Goldingen, C. (1995), *Untersuchungen zu Xenophons Kyrupädie*, Stuttgart and Leipzig: Teubner.

Münscher, K. (1920), *Xenophon in der griechisch-römischen Literatur*, Philologus Suppl. 13/2, Leipzig: Dieterich.

Murray, O. (2001), 'Herodotus and Oral History', in N. Luraghi (ed.), *The Historian's Craft in the Age of Herodotus*, Oxford: Oxford University Press, 16–44.

Nadon, C. (2001), *Xenophon's Prince: Republic and Empire in the Cyropaedia*, Berkeley: University of California Press.

Nau, E. (1972), *Epochen der Geldgeschichte*, Stuttgart: Württembergisches Landesmuseum.

Neuhaus, O. (1901), 'Die Uberlieferung uber Aspasia von Phokaia', *RhM* 56: 272–83.

Newmyer, S. T. (1992), 'Plutarch on Justice Towards Animals: Ancient Insights on a Modern Debate', *Scholia* n.s. 1 (1992) 38–54.

Newmyer, S. T. (2008), 'The Human Soul and the Animal Soul: Stoic Theory and Its Survival in Contractualist Ethics', in A. Alexandridis, M. Wild, and L. Winkler-Horaček (eds), *Mensch und Tier in der Antike: Grenzziehung und Grenzüberschreitung*, Wiesbaden: Reichert, 71–80.

Newmyer, S. T. (2014), 'Animals in Plutarch', in M. Beck (ed.), *A Companion to Plutarch*, Malden, MA: Wiley-Blackwell, 223–34.

Nichols, A. (2008), *The Complete Fragments of Ctesias of Cnidus: Translation and Commentary with an Introduction*, PhD diss., University of Florida.

Nichols, A. (2011), *Ctesias: On India, and Fragments of His Minor Works*, London: Bristol Classical.

Niese, B. (1907), 'Eukleidas (18)' *RE* 6.1:999.

Niese, B. (1909), 'Wann hat Ephoros sein Geschichtswerk geschrieben?' *Hermes* 44: 170–8.

Nikolaidis, A. G. (1986), 'Hellenikos-Barbarikos: Plutarch on Greek and Barbarian Characteristics', *WS* 20: 229–44.

Nikolaidis, A. G. (ed.) (2008), *The Unity of Plutarch's Work*, Berlin: De Gruyter.

Norden, E. (1898), *Die antike Kunstprosa*, Leipzig: Teubner.

Nünlist, R. (2009), *The Ancient Critic at Work: Terms and Concepts of Literary Criticism in Greek Scholia*, Cambridge: Cambridge University Press.

Obermeyer, J. (1929), *Die Landschaft Babylonien in Zeitalter des Talmuds und des Gaonats*, Frankfurt am Main: Kaufmann.

Occhipinti, E. (2016), *The Hellenica Oxyrhynchia and Historiography: New Research Perspectives*, Leiden: Brill.

Ogden, D. (1996), *Greek Bastardy in the Classical and Hellenistic Periods*, Oxford: Oxford University Press.

Olmstead, A. T. E. (1948), *History of the Persian Empire*, Chicago: University of Chicago Press.

Opelt, I./Speyer, W. (1967) 'Barbar', *JbAC* 10: 251–90.

Opsomer, J. (2004), 'Plutarch's *De animae procreatione in Timaeo*: Manipulation or Search for Consistency?', in P. Adamson, H. Baltussen and M. W. F. Stone (eds), *Philosophy, Science and Exegesis in Greek, Latin and Arabic Commentaries,* London: Institute of Classical Sudies, 137–62.

Opsomer, J. (2012), 'Plutarch on the division of the soul', in R. Barney, T. Brennan, and C. Brittain (eds), *Plato and the Divided Self*, Cambridge: Cambridge University Press, 311–30.

Orsi, D. P. (1979–80), 'Tracce di tendenza anticirea (Plutarco, *Vita di Artaserse*, capp. 1–19)', *Sileno* 5–6: 113–46.

Orsi, D. P. (1988), 'La rappresentazione del Sovrano nella *Vita di Artaserse* Plutarchea', *AncSoc* 19: 135–60.

Osborne, M. J. (1973), 'Orontes', *Historia* 22: 515–51.

Osborne, M. J., and S. G. Byrne (1994), *A Lexicon of Greek Personal Names*, vol. 2, Oxford: Oxford University Press.

Pade, M. (2007), *The Reception of Plutarch's Lives in Fifteenth-Century Italy*, Copenhagen: Museum Tusculanum Press.

Pangle, T. (ed.) (1987), *The Roots of Classical Political Philosophy: Ten Forgotten Socratic Dialogues*, Ithaca, NY: Cornell University Press.

Parke, H. W. (1933), *Greek Mercenary Soldiers*, Oxford: Clarendon Press.

Parker, R. A., and W. H. Dubberstein (1956), *Babylonian Chronology 626 B.C. – A.D. 45*, Chicago: University of Chicago Press.

Parker, V. (2005), 'Pausanias the Spartiate as depicted by Charon of Lampsacus and Herodotus', *Philologus* 149: 3–11.

Parker, V. (2009), 'Source-Critical Reflections on Cleitarchus' Work', in P. Wheatley and R. Hannah (eds), *Alexander and His Successors: Essays from the Antipodes*, Claremont: Regina Books.

Parker, V. (2014), 'Ephoros (70)', in Ian Worthington (ed.), *Brill's New Jacoby*.

Pearson, L. (1939), *Early Ionian Historians*, Oxford: Clarendon Press.

Pearson, L. (1960), *The Lost Histories of Alexander the Great*, New York: American Philological Association.

Pechter, E. (1975), *Dryden's Classical Theory of Literature, Vol. I*, Cambridge: Cambridge University Press.

Pelegrín Campo, J. (1997), 'La noción de barbarie en las *Vidas Paralelas* de Plutarco de Queronea', in C. Schrader, V. Ramón and J. Vela (eds), *Plutarco y la Historia: Actas del V Simposio Español sobre Plutarco*, Zaragoza: Prensas Universitarias de Zaragoza, 367–78.

Pelling, C. B. R. (1979), 'Plutarch's Method of Work in the Roman *Lives*', *JHS* 99: 74–96.

Pelling, C. B. R. (1980), 'Plutarch's Adaptation of his Source-Material', *JHS* 100: 127–40.

Pelling, C. B. R. (1985), 'Plutarch and Catiline', *Hermes* 113: 311–29.

Pelling, C. B. R. (1986), '*Synkrisis* in Plutarch's *Lives*', in F. E. Brenk and I. Gallo (eds), *Miscellanea Plutarchea* (Atti del I convegno di studi su Plutarco), Ferrara: Giornale Filologico Ferrarese, 83–96.

Pelling, C. B. R. (1989), 'Plutarch: Roman Heroes and Greek Culture', in M. Griffin and J. Barnes (eds), *Philosophia Togata*, Oxford: Oxford University Press, 199–232.

Pelling, C. B. R. (1990), 'Childhood and Personality in Greek Biography', in Pelling, C. (ed.), *Characterizaionand Individuality in Greek Literature*, Oxford: Oxford University Press, 213–44.

Pelling, C. B. R. (1995), 'The Moralism of Plutarch's *Lives*', in D. Innes, H. Hine and C. B. R. Pelling (eds), *Ethics and Rhetoric*, Oxford: Oxford University Press, 205–20.

Pelling, C. B. R. (1997), 'Is Death the End? Closure in Plutarch's *Lives*', in D. H. Roberts, F. M. Dunn and D. Fowler (eds), *Classical Closure: Reading the End in Greek and Latin Literature*, Princeton: Princeton University Press, 228–50.

Pelling, C. B. R. (2002a), 'Plutarch and Thucydides', in Pelling, *Plutarch and History*, Swansea: Classical Press of Wales, 117–42.

Pelling, C. B. R. (2002b), 'The *Apophthegmata regum et imperatorum* and Plutarch's Roman Lives', in Pelling, *Plutarch and History*, Swansea: Classical Press of Wales, 65–90.

Pelling, C. B. R. (2002c), *Plutarch and History*, Swansea: Classical Press of Wales.

Pelling, C. B. R. (2007), '*De Malignitate Plutarchi*: Plutarch, Herodotus, and the Persian Wars', in E. Bridges, E. Hall and P. J. Rhodes (eds), *Cultural Responses to the Persian Wars: Antiquity to the Third Millennium*, Oxford: Oxford University Press, 145–64.

Pelling, C. B. R. (2011), *Plutarch: Caesar*, Oxford: Oxford University Press.

Penfield, W. (1957), 'The Asclepiad Physicians of Cnidus and Cos, with a Note on the Probable Site of the Triopion Temple of Apollo', *Proceedings of the American Philosophical Society* 101: 393–400.

Perry, B. E. (1962), 'Demetrius of Phalerum and the Aesopic Fables', *TAPhA* 93: 287–346.

Petermann, J. H. (1866 [1865]), 'Über die bis jetzt vorhandenen Texte und Übersetzungen der armenischen Chronik des Eusebius', *Monatsberichte der Königlich Preußischen Akademie der Wissenschaften zu Berlin*, Berlin: Buchdruckerei Der Königlichen Akademie der Wissenschaften, 457–62.

Petrucci, F. M. (2016), 'Argumentative Strategies in the "Platonic Section" of Plutarch's *De Iside et Osiride* (chapters 45–64)', *Mnemosyne* 69: 226–48.

Plant, I. (2004), *Women Writers of Ancient Greece and Rome: An Anthology*, Norman: University of Oklahoma Press.

Plommer, H. (1979), 'Vitruvius and the Origin of the Caryatids', *JHS* 99: 97–102.

Poralla, P. (1913), *Prosopographie der Lakedaimonier*, Breslau: J. Max.

Porteous, N. W. (1965), *Daniel: A Commentary*, London: SCM Press.

Porter, W. U. (1937), *Life of Aratus*, Dublin and Cork: Cork University Press.

Poundstone, W. (1992), *Prisoner's Dilemma: John von Neumann, Game Theory and the Puzzle of the Bomb*, New York: Anchor Books.

Poutsma, A. (1912), 'Ad Vitam Artaxerxis', *Mnemosyne* n.s. 40: 209–12.

Prandi, L. (1996), *Fortuna e realtà del'opera di Clitarco*, Stuttgart: Franz Steiner.

Prandi. L. (2012), 'New Evidence for the Dating of Cleitarchus (*POxy* LXXI. 4808)?', *Histos* 6: 15–26.

Puchstein, O. (1895), 'Artasyras', *RE* 2: 1308.

Puech, B. (1992), 'Prosopographie des amis de Plutarque', *ANRW* 2.33.6: 4831–93.

Pyankov, I. V. (1971), 'Ancient Sources on the Struggle of Cyrus II against Astyages', *VDI* 117: 16–37 (in Russian).

Rabel, R. J. (1997), *Plot and Point of View in the Iliad*, Ann Arbor: University of Michigan Press.

Rahe, P. A. (1980) 'The Military Situation in Western Asia on the Eve of Cunaxa', *AJPh* 101: 79–96.

Rajabzadeh, H. (1993), 'Daftar', *EI* 6: 563.

Ravazzolo, C. (1998), 'Clitarco e il suo tempo', *Patavium* 6: 31–44.

Regenbogen, O. (1949), 'Pamphila (1)', *RE* 18.3: 309–28.

Reinach, T. W. A. (1890), 'La Dynastie de Commagène', *REG* 3: 362–80.

Reincke, G. (1936), 'Timagoras (2)', *RE* 6 A.1: 1073.

Rengakos, A. (2011) 'Historiographie, vii. 1 (Gattungsgeschichte) – 2 (Die Anfänge der Historiographie', in B. Zimmermann (ed.), *Handbuch der griechischen Literatur der Antike, I: Die Literatur der archaischen und klassischen Zeit*, Munich: Beck, 328–30.

Rettig, H. C. M. (1827), *Ctesiae Cnidii vita cum appendice de libris quos Ctesias composuisse fertur*, Hannover: Hahn.

Reuss, E. (1887), *Kritische und exegetische Bemerkungen zu Xenophons Anabasis*, Wetzlar: Schnitzler.

Rezania, K. (2010), *Die zoroastrische Zeitvorstellung. Eine Untersuchung über Zeit- und Ewigkeitskonzepte und die Frage des Zurvanismus*, Wiesbaden: Harrassowitz.

Richards, D. (2001), 'Reciprocity and Shared Knowledge Structures in the Prisoner's Dilemma Game', *JCR* 45: 621–35.

Richards, H. (1903), 'Critical Notes on Plutarch's *Lives*', *CR* 17: 333–9.

Richter, D. S. (2001), 'Plutarch on Isis and Osiris: Text, Cult, and Cultural Appropriation', *TAPhA* 131: 191–216.

Rigsby, K. (1976), 'Teiresias as Magus in *Oedipus Rex*', *GRBS* 17: 109–14.

Rimmon-Kenan, S. (1983), *Narrative Fiction: Contemporary Poetics*, London: Routledge.

Roaf, M. (1983), 'Sculptures and Sculptors at Persepolis', *Iran* 21: 1–164.

Robinson, J. V. (1990), 'The Tripartite Soul in the *Timaeus*', *Phronesis* 35: 103–10.

Roche, P. A., 'The Public Image of Trajan's Family', *CPh* 97: 41–60.

Rosivach, V. J. (1984), 'The Romans' View of the Persians', *CW* 78: 1–8.

Roskam, G. (2014), 'ἀποθεωρεῖν / ἀποθεώρησις: a Semasiological Study', *Glotta* 90: 180–91.

Rowland, I. D., and T. N. Howe (eds) (1999), *Vitruvius: Ten Books on Architecture*, Cambridge: Cambridge University Press.

Rung, E. (2015), 'The Language of the Achaemenid Imperial Diplomacy towards the Greeks: The Meaning of Earth and Water', *Klio* 97: 503–15.

Russell, D. A. (1963), 'Plutarch's *Life* of Coriolanus', *JRS* 53: 21–8.

Russell, D. A. (1966), 'On Reading Plutach's *Lives*', *G&R* 13: 139–54.

Russell, D. A. (1968), 'On Reading Plutarch's *Moralia*', *G&R* 15: 130–46.

Russell, D. A. (1973), *Plutarch*, London: Duckworth.

Rutherford, I. (1998), *Canons of Style in the Antonine Age: Idea–Theory and Its Literary Context*, Oxford: Clarendon Press.

Ruzicka, S. (1985), 'Cyrus and Tissaphernes, 407–401 BC, *CJ* 80: 204–11.

Ruzicka, S. (1999), 'Glos, Son of Tamos, and the End of the Cypriot War', *Historia* 48: 23–43.

Ruzicka, S. (2012), *Trouble in the West: Egypt and the Persian Empire, 525–332 BCE*, Oxford: Oxford University Press.

Rykwert, J. (1996), *The Dancing Column: On Order in Architecture*, Cambridge, MA: MIT Press.

Sachs, A. J., and H. Hunger (1988), *Astronomical Diaries and Related Texts from Babylonia*, vol. I, Vienna: Österreichischen Akademie der Wissenschaften.

Sachsen-Meiningen, F. (1969), 'Proskynesis in Iran', in F. Altheim (ed.), *Geschichte der Hunnen*, vol. 2: *Die Hephthaliten in Iran*, Berlin: De Gruyter, 125–66.

Saïd, S. (2001), 'The Discourse of Identity in Greek Rhetoric from Isocrates to Aristides', in I. Malkin (ed.), *Ancient Perceptions of Greek Ethnicity*, Cambridge, MA: Harvard University Press, 275–99.

Saller, R. P. (1980), 'Anecdotes as Historical Evidence for the Principate', *G&R* 27: 69–83.

Sancisi-Weerdenburg, H. (1983a), 'The Zendan and the Ka'bah', in H. Koch and D. N. Mackenzie (eds), *Kunst, Kultur und Geschichte der Achämenidenzeit und ihr Fortleben*, Berlin: Dietrich Reimer, 145–51.

Sancisi-Weerdenburg, H. (1983b), 'Exit Atossa', in A. Cameron and A. Kuhrt (eds), *Images of Women in Antiquity*, London: Croom Helm, 20–33.

Sancisi-Weerdenburg, H. (1987), 'Decadence in the Empire or Decadence in the Sources? From Source to Synthesis: Ctesias', *AchHist* 1: 33–46.

Sancisi-Weerdenburg, H. (1994), 'The Orality of Herodotus' *Medikos Logos*', *AchHist* 8: 39–55.

Sandbach, F. H. (1969), *Plutarch's Moralia in Sixteen Volumes, vol. XV, Fragments*, Loeb Classical Library, Cambridge, MA: Harvard University Press.

Sansone, D. (2004), 'Heracles at the Y', *JHS* 124: 125–42.

Saunders, T. J. (1962), 'The Structure of the Soul and the State in Plato's *Laws*', *Eranos* 60: 37–55.

Schepens, G. (1975), 'Some Aspects of Source Theory in Greek Historiography', *AncSoc* 6: 257–74.

Schepens, G. (1977), 'Historiographical Problems in Ephorus', in C. Prins (ed.), *Historiographia Antiqua: Commentationes Lovanienses in honorem W. Peremans septuagenarii editae*, Leuven: Leuven University Press, 95–118.

Schibli, H. S. (1993), 'Xenocrates' Daemons and the Irrational Soul', *CQ* n.s. 43: 143–67.

Schironi, F. (2009), *From Alexandria to Babylon: Near Eastern Languages and Hellenistic Erudition in the Oxyrhynchus Glossary (P.Oxy 1802 + 4812)*, Berlin: De Gruyter.

Schleiermacher, F. D. E. (1836), *Introductions to the Dialogues of Plato*, trans. W. Dobson, Cambridge: J & J.J. Deighton.

Schmid, W. (2010), *Narratology: An Introduction*, Berlin: De Gruyter.

Schmidt, C. (1879), *De apophthegmatum quae sub Plutarchi nomine feruntur collectionibus*, diss., Greifswald.

Schmidt, E. F. (1953), *Persepolis I: Structures, Reliefs, Inscriptions*, Chicago: University of Chicago Press.

Schmidt, E. F. (1957), *Persepolis II: Structures, Reliefs, Inscriptions*, Chicago: University of Chicago Press.

Schmidt, E. F. (1970), *Persepolis III: The Royal Tombs and Other Monuments*, Chicago: University of Chicago Press.

Schmidt, T. S. (1999), *Plutarque et les Barbares: la rhétorique d'une image*, Louvain: Peeters.

Schmidt, T. S. (2002), 'Plutarch's Timeless Barbarians and the Age of Trajan', in P. A. Stadter and L. Van der Stockt (eds), *Sage and Emperor: Plutarch, Greek Intellectuals, and Roman Power in the Time of Trajan (98–117 A.D.)*, Leuven: Leuven University Press, 57–71.

Schmidt, T. S. (2004), 'Barbarians in Plutarch's Political Thought', in L. de Blois, J. Bons and T. Kessels (eds), *The Statesman in Plutarch's Works*, vol. 1, Leiden: Brill, 227–35.

Schmidt, T. S. (2011), 'Sophistes, barbares et identité grecque: le cas de Dion Chrysostome', in T. S. Schmidt and P. Fleury (eds), *Perceptions of the Second Sophistic and its Times/Regards sur la Seconde Sophistique et son époque*, Toronto: University of Toronto Press, 105–19.

Schmitt, R. (1967), 'Medisches und Persisches Sprachgut bei Herodot', *ZDMG* 117: 119–45.

Schmitt, R. (1977), 'Thronnamen bei den Achaimeniden', *Beiträge zur Namenforshung*, N. F. 12: 422–5.

Schmitt, R. (1979), 'Die Wiedergabe iranischer Namen bei Ktesias von Knidos im Vergleich zur sonstigen griechischen Überlieferung', in J. Harmatta (ed.), *Prolegomena to the Sources on the History of Pre-Islamic Central Asia*, Budapest: Akadémiai Kiadó, 119–33.

Schmitt, R. (1982), 'Achaemenid Throne-names', *AION* 42: 83–95.

Schmitt, R. (1983), 'Achaimenidisches bei Thukydides', in H. Koch and D. N. MacKenzie (eds), *Kunst, Kultur und Geschichte der Achämenidenzeit und ihr Fortleben*, Berlin: Dietrich Reimer, 69–86.

Schmitt, R. (1987), 'Artaxerxes II', *EI* 2: 656–8.

Schmitt, R. (2002), *Die Iranischen und Iranier-Namen in den Schriften Xenophons*, Vienna: Österreichischen Akademie der Wissenschaften.

Schmitt, R. (2006), *Iranische Anthroponyme in den Erhaltenen Resten von Ktesias' Werk*, Vienna: Österreichischen Akademie der Wissenschaften.

Schottin (1865), *Observationes de Plutarchi Vita Artaxerxis*, Budissin: Ernst Moritz Monse.

Schreiner, J. H. (1984), 'Historical Methods, Hellanikos, and the Era of Kimon', *Op. Ath.* 15: 163–71.

Schwab, G. (1834), *Disputatio de Livio et Timagene, historiarum scriptoribus, aemulis*, diss., Stuttgart.

Schwartz, E. (1899a), 'Charon (7)', *RE* 3.2: 2179–80.

Schwartz, E. (1899b), 'Quellenuntersuchungen zur griechischen Geschichte', *RhM* 44: 161–93.

Schwartz, E. (1903a), 'Diodoros (38), Diodoros von Agyrion', *RE* 5.1: 663–704.

Schwartz, E. (1903b), 'Dinon (2)', *RE* 5.1: 654.

Schwartz, E. (1907), 'Ephoros', *RE* 6.1: 1–16.

Schwartz, J., (1949), 'Les conquérants perses et la littérature égyptienne', *BIFAO* 48: 65–80.

Seager, R. (1967), 'Thrasybulus, Conon, and the Athenian Imperialism 396–386 B.C.', *JHS* 87: 95–115.

Seager, R. (1980), '*Neu sinas Medos equitare inultos*: Horace, the Parthians and Augustan Foreign Policy', *Athenaeum* 58: 103–18.

Seel, O. (1972), *Eine römische Weltgeschichte*, Nuremberg: Hans Carl.

Segal, C. (1971), *The Theme of the Mutilation of the Corpse in the Iliad*, Leiden: Brill.

Seidl, U. (1976), 'Ein Relief Dareios' I. in Babylon', *AMI* 9: 125–30.

Seidl, U. (1999), 'Ein Monument Darius' I. aus Babylon', *ZA* 89: 101–14.

Sekunda, N. V. (1988), 'Some Notes on the Life of Datames', *Iran* 26: 35–53.

Shannahan, J. (2014), 'Two Notes on the Battle of Cunaxa', *Ancient History Bulletin*, 28: 61–81.

Shayegan, M. R. (2011), *Arsacids and Sasanians: Political Ideology in Post-Hellenistic and Late Antique Persia*, Cambridge: Cambridge University Press.

Sherk, R. K. (1988), *The Roman Empire: Augustus to Hadrian*, Cambridge: Cambridge University Press.

Shipley, D. R. (1997), *A Commentary on Plutarch's Life of Agesilaos: Response to Sources in the Presentation of Character*, Oxford: Oxford University Press.

Shrimpton, G. S. (1991a), *Theopompus the Historian*, Montreal: McGill-Queen's University Press.

Shrimpton, G. (1991b), 'Persian Strategy against Egypt and the Date for the Battle of Citium', *Phoenix*, 45: 1–20.

Shorey, P. (1933), *What Plato Said*, Chicago: University of Chicago Press.

Sirch, P. B. (1974), 'Tiara', *RE Suppl.* 14: 786–94.

Smith, A. N. D. (2004), 'Did Plato Write the *Alcibiades* I?', *Apeiron* 37: 93–108.

Smith, C. F. (1881), *A Study of Plutarch's Life of Artarxerxes*, PhD diss., Leipzig.

Smith, M. (1975), '*De Superstitione* (Moralia 164E–171F)', in H. D. Betz (ed.), *Plutarch's Theological Writings and Early Christian Literature*, Leiden: Brill, 1–35.

Smith, W. D. (1973), 'Galen on Coans Versus Cnidians', *Bulletin of the History of Medicine* 47: 569–85.

Snyder, G. H. (1971), '"Prisoner's Dilemma" and "Chicken" Models in International Politics', *International Studies Quarterly* 15: 66–103.

Sordi, M. (1982), 'Timagene di Alessandria: uno storico ellenocentrico e filobarbaro', *ANRW* 2.30.1: 775–97.

Soury, G. (1942), *La Démonologie de Plutarque*, Paris: Les Belles Lettres.

Spawforth, A. J. (1994), 'Symbol of Unity? The Persian-Wars Tradition in the Roman Empire' in S. Hornblower (ed.), *Greek Historiography*, Oxford: Oxford University Press, 233–47.

Sperber, D. (1969), 'Angaria in Rabbinic Literature', *AC* 38: 164–8.

Spyridakis, K. (1935), *Evagoras I von Salamis*, Stuttgart: Kohlhammer.

Stadter, P. A. (1965), *Plutarch's Historical Methods: An Analysis of the Mulierum Virtutes*, Cambridge, MA: Harvard University Press.

Stadter, P. A. (1989), *A Commentary on Plutarch's Pericles*, Chapel Hill, NC: University of North Carolina Press.

Stadter, P. A. (2000), 'The Rhetoric of Virtue in Plutarch's *Lives*', in L. Van der Stockt (ed.), *Rhetorical Theory and Praxis in Plutarch*, Leuven: Peeters, 493–510.

Stadter, P. A. (2002), 'Plutarch's *Lives* and Their Roman Readers', in E. Ostenfeld (ed.), *Greek Romans and Roman Greeks*, Aarhus: Aarhus University Press, 123–35.

Stadter, P. A. (2004), 'Plutarch: A Diplomat for Delphi', in L. de Blois, J. Bons, T. Kessels and D. M. Schenkeveld (eds), *The Statesman in Plutarch's Works*, Leiden: Brill, 19–31.

Stadter, P. A. (2012), '"Staying up Late": Plutarch's Reading of Xenophon', in F. Hobden and C. J. Tuplin (eds), *Xenophon: Ethical Principles and Historical Enquiry*, Leiden: Brill, 43–62.

Stadter, P. A. (2014), 'Plutarch's Compositional Technique: The Anecdote Collections and the *Parallel Lives*', *GRBS* 54: 665–86.

Stadter, P. A. (2015a), 'Revisiting Plutarch's *Lives of the Caesars*', in P. A. Stadter, *Plutarch and His Roman Readers*, Oxford: Oxford University Press, 56–69.

Stadter, P. A. (2015b), 'Before Pen Touched Paper', in P. A. Stadter, *Plutarch and his Roman Readers*, Oxford: Oxford University Press, 119–29.

Stausberg, M. (2002), *Die Religion Zarathustras*, 2 vols, Stuttgart: Kohlhammer.

Steele, R. B. (1917), 'Pompeius Trogus and Justinus', *AJPh* 38: 19–41.

Steele, R. B. (1921), 'Clitarchus', *AJPh* 42: 40–57.

Steingass, F. (1963 [1892]), *A Comprehensive Persian–English Dictionary*, London: Routledge & Kegan Paul in association with Iran University Press.

Stern, E. (1982), *The Material Culture of the Land of the Bible in the Persian Period, 538–332 BC*, Warminster: Aris and Phillips.

Stevenson, R. B. (1985), *Fourth Century Greek Historical Writing about Persia in the Period Between the Accession of Artaxerxes II Mnemon and That of Darius III (404–336 B.C.)*, DPhil Diss., Oxford.

Stevenson, R. B. (1987), 'Lies and inventions in Deinon's *Persica*', *AchHist* 2: 27–35.

Stevenson, R. B. (1997), *Persica: Greek Writing About Persia in the Fourth Century BC*, Edinburgh: Scottish Academic Press.

Stocks, J. L. (1915), 'Plato and the Tripartite Soul', *Mind* 94: 207–21.

Stokes, M. (2012), 'Three Defences of Socrates: Relative Chronology, Politics and Religion', in F. Hobden and C. Tuplin (eds), *Xenophon: Ethical Principles and Historical Enquiry*, Leiden: Brill, 243–67.

Stolper, M. W. (1994), 'Mesopotamia, 482–330 BC' in Lewis et al. (eds), *CAH* ² VI, Cambridge: Cambridge University Press, 234–60.

Stone, E. C. (1982), 'The Social Role of the Nadῑtu Women in Old Babylonian Nippur', *JESHO* 25: 50–70.

Strauss, B. S. (1983), 'Aegospotami Reexamined', *AJPh* 104: 24–35.

Strauss, B. S. (1986), *Athens after the Peloponnesian War*, London: Croom Helm.

Strawn, B. A. (2005), *What Is Stronger than a Lion*, Fribourg: Academic Press and Vandenhoeck & Ruprecht.

Strobach, A. (1997), *Plutarch und die Sprachen. Ein Beitrag zur Fremdsprachenproblematik in der Antike*, Stuttgart: Franz Steiner.

Strobel, K. (1994), 'Zeitgeschichte unter den Antoninen: Die Historiker des Partherkrieges des Lucius Verus', *ANRW* 2.34.2: 1315–60.

Stronach, D. (1978), *Pasargadae*, Oxford: Oxford University Press.

Stronk, J. P. (2004–5), 'Ctesias of Cnidus. From Physician to Author', *Talanta* 36–7: 101–22.

Stronk, J. P. (2007), 'Ctesias of Cindus. A Reappraisal', *Mnemosyne* 60: 25–58.

Stronk, J. P. (2010), *Ctesias' Persian History: Introduction, Text, and Translation*, Düsseldorf: Wellem Verlag.

Stronk, J. P. (2011), 'Ctesias the Poet', in J. Wiesehöfer, R. Rollinger, and G. Lanfranchi (eds), *Ktesias' Welt/Ctesias' World*, Wiesbaden: Harrassowitz, 385–402.

Stronk, J. P. (2017), *Semiramis' Legacy*, Edinburgh: Edinburgh University Press.

Stylianou, P. J. (1998), *A Historical Commentary on Diodorus Siculus Book 15*, Oxford: Clarendon Press.

Stylianou, P. J. (2004), 'One *Anabasis* or Two?', in R. Lane-Fox (ed.), *The Long March: Xenophon and the Ten Thousand*, New Haven, CT: Yale University Press, 68–96.

Swain, J. S. (1940), 'The Theory of the Four Monarchies: Opposition History Under the Roman Empire', *CPh* 35: 1–21.

Swain, S. (1989), 'Plutarch: Chance, Providence, and History', *AJPh* 110: 272–302.

Swain, S. (1991), 'Plutarch, Hadrian, and Delphi', *Historia* 40: 318–30.

Swain, S. (1996), *Hellenism and Empire*, Oxford: Oxford University Press.

Swoboda, E. (1907), 'Euagoras (8)', *RE* 6.1: 820–7.

Swoboda, E. (1922), 'Konon (3)' *RE* 11.2: 1319–34.

Syme, R. (1988a), 'The Cadusii in History and in Fiction', *JRS* 108: 137–50.

Syme, R. (1988b), 'The Date of Justin and the Discovery of Trogus', *Historia* 37: 358–71.

Taqizadeh, H. (1938), *Old Iranian Calendars*, London: Royal Asiatic Society.

Tarn, W. W. (1933), 'Persia, From Xerxes to Alexander' in J. B. Bury, S. A. Cook and F. E. Adcock (eds), *CAH* VI, Cambridge: Cambridge University Press, 1–24.

Tarn, W. W. (1948), *Alexander the Great*, 2 vols, Cambridge: Cambridge University Press.

Tatum, J. (1989), *Xenophon's Imperial Fiction*, Princeton: Princeton University Press.

Taylor, T. (1821), *Iamblichus on the Mysteries of the Egyptians, Chaldeans, and Assyrians*, Chiswick: Whittingham.

Thiel, J. H. (1923), 'De Dinone Colophonio Nepotis in Vita Datamis Auctore', *Mnemosyne* 51: 412–14.

Thompson, S. (1957), *Motif-Index of Folk-Literature*, Copenhagen: Rosenkilde and Bagger.

Tietz, P. (1896), *De Nicolai Damasceni fontibus quaestiones selectae*, PhD diss., Marburg.

Toye, D. L. (1995), 'Dionysius of Halicarnassus on the First Greek Historians', *AJPh* 116: 279–302.

Traunecker, C. (1979), 'Essai sur l'histoire de la XXIXe dynastie', *BIFAO* 79: 395–436.

Travlos, J. (1971), *Pictorial Dictionary of Ancient Athens*, New York: Praeger.

Treadgold, W. T. (1977), 'The Preface of the *Bibliotheca* of Photius: Text, Translation, and Commentary', *DOP* 31: 343–9.

Treadgold, W. T. (1980), *The Nature of the Bibliotheca of Photius*, Washington, DC: Dumbarton Oaks.

Treu, M. (1873), *Der sogenannte Lampriaskatalog der Plutarchschriften*, Waldenberg in Schlesien: Gymnasium.

Treu, M. (1967), 'Xenophon (6): Ps.-Xenophon D. πολιτεία Ἀθηναίων', *RE* 9 A 2: 1928–82.

Tritle, L. A. (1992), 'Plutarch's "Life of Phocion": An Analysis and Critical Report', *ANRW* 2.33.6: 4258–97.

Tucker, A. W. (1983), 'The Mathematics of Tucker: A Sampler', *The Two-Year College Mathematics Journal* 14: 228–32.

Tuland, C. G. (1966), 'Josephus, *Antiquities* Book XI: Correction or Confirmation of Biblical Post-exilic Records?', *St. Andrews University Seminary Studies* 4: 176–92.

Tuplin, C. J. (1983), 'Lysias XIX, the Cypriot war and Thrasyboulos' naval expedition', *Philologus* 127: 170–86.

Tuplin, C. J. (1996), *Achaemenid Studies*, Stuttgart: Franz Steiner.

Tuplin, C. J. (1997), 'Education and Fiction in Xenophon's *Cyropaedia*', in A. H. Sommerstein and C. Atherton (eds), *Education in Fiction*, Bari: Levante Editori, 65–162.

Tuplin, C. J. (1999), 'On the Track of the Ten Thousand', *REA* 101: 331–66.

Tuplin, C. J. (2004), 'Doctoring the Persians: Ctesias of Cnidus, Physician and Historian', *Klio* 86: 305–47.

Tuplin, C. J. (2007), 'Treacherous Hearts and Upright Tiaras: on the Head-gear of Persian Kings', in C. J. Tuplin (ed.), *Persian Responses*, Swansea: Classical Press of Wales, 67–97.

Tuplin, C. J. (2011), 'Ctesias as Military Historian', in J. Wiesehofer, R. Rollinger, and G. Lanfranchi (eds), *Ktesias' Welt/ Ctesias' World*, Wiesbaden: Harrassowitz, 449–88.

Urban, R. (1982), '"Historiae Philippicae" bei Pompeius Trogus. Versuch einer Deutung', *Historia* 31: 82–96.

Urmson, J. O. (1973), 'Aristotle's Doctrine of the Mean', *APQ* 10: 223–30.

Van der Spek, R. J. (1998), 'The Chronology of the Wars of Artaxerxes II in the Babylonian Astonomical Diaries', *AchHist* 11: 239–56.

Van der Stockt, L. (1992), *Twinkling and Twilight: Plutarch's Reflections on Literature*, Brussels: Paleis der Academiën.

Van der Stockt, L. (1999), 'Plutarchan Hypomnema on Self-Love', *AJPh* 120: 575–99.

Van der Stockt, L. (2004), 'Plutarch in Plutarch: The Problem of the Hypomnemata', in I. Gallo (ed.), *La biblioteca di Plutarco. Atti del IX Convegno plutarcheo*, Naples: D'Auria, 331–40

Van der Toorn, K. (1992), 'Cultic Prostitution', in D. N. Freedman (ed.), *Anchor Bible Dictionary*, New York: Doubleday, vol. 5: 510–13.

Vander Waerdt, P. A. (1985), 'The Peripatetic Interpretation of Plato's Tripartite Psychology', *GRBS* 26: 283–302.

Van Herwerden, H. (1880), 'Ad Plutarchi Vitas', *RhM* 35: 456–68, 529–42.

Vanotti, G. (2007), *Aristotele. Racconti meravigliosi. Introduzione, traduzione, note e apparati*, Milan: Bompiani.

Verdegem, S. (2010), *Plutarch's Life of Alcibiades: Story, Text and Moralism*, Leuven: Leuven University Press.

Vickers, M. (1985), 'Persepolis and the Erechtheum Caryatids: The Iconography of Medism and Servitude', *RA* ser. 6, 64: 3–28.

Vlassopoulos, K. (2017), 'Xenophon on Persia', in M. A. Flower (ed.), *The Cambridge Companion to Xenophon*, Cambridge: Cambridge University Press, 360–75.

Volkmann, R. (1869), *Leben, Schriften und Philosophie des Plutarch von Chaeronea*, Berlin: Verlag S. Calvary & Co.

Volquardsen, C. A. (1868), *Untersuchungen über die Quellen der griechischen und sicilischen Geschichten bei Diodor, Buch xi bis xvi*, diss., Kiel.

von Christ, W. (1912), *Geschichte der griechischen Literatur*, vol. 1, Munich: Beck.

von Geisau, H. (1919), 'Karyai (2)', *RE* 10.2: 2245–6.

von Gutschmid, A. (1882), 'Trogus und Timagenes', *RhM* 37: 548–55.

von Möllendorf, P. (2001), 'Frigid Enthusiasts: Lucian on Writing History', *PCPhS* 47: 117–40.

von Voigtlander, E. N. (1978), *The Bisitun Inscription of Darius the Great: Babylonian Version, Corpus Inscr. Iran., pt. I, vol. II: Texts I*, London: Lund Humphries.

Vullers, I. A. (1864), *Lexicon Persico-Latinum Etymologicum*, Bonn: Adolph Marcus.

Wachsmuth, C. (1891), 'Timagenes und Trogus', *RhM* 46: 472–5.

Wardman, A. E. (1971), 'Plutarch's Methods in the *Lives*', *CQ* n.s. 21: 254–61.

Wardman, A. (1974), *Plutarch's Lives*, Berkeley: University of California Press.

Waters, M. (2017), *Ctesias' Persica in its Near Eastern Context*, Madison: University of Wisconsin Press.

Weiser, W. (1989), 'Die Eulen von Kyros dem Jüngeren. Zu den ersten Münzportäts lebender Menschen', *ZPE* 76: 267–96.

Weiskopf, M. (1989), *The So-Called 'Great Satraps' Revolt', 366–360 B.C.*, Stuttgart: Franz Steiner.

Weissert, E. (1997), 'Royal Hunt and Royal Triumph in a Prism Fragment of Ashurbanipal (82-5-22, 2)' in S. Parpola and R. M. Whiting (eds), *Assyria 1995, Proceedings of the 10th Anniversary Symposium of the Neo-Assyrian Text Corpus Project*, Helsinki: The Neo-Assyrian Text Corpus Project, 339–58.

Weizsaecker, A. (1931), *Untersuchungen über Plutarchs Biographische Technik*, Berlin: Weidmann.

Wellmann, M. (1892), 'Alexander von Myndos', *Hermes* 27: 389–406.

Westenholz, J. G. (1989), 'Tamar, Qedesha, Qadishtu, and Sacred Prostitution in Mesopotamia', *HTR* 82: 245–65.

Westlake, H. D. (1938), 'The Sources of Plutarch's *Timoleon*', *CQ* 32: 65–74.

Westlake, H. D. (1939), 'The Sources of Plutarch's *Pelopidas*', *CQ* 33: 11–22.

Westlake, H. D. (1987), 'Diodorus and the Expedition of Cyrus', *Phoenix* 41: 241–54.

Whitmarsh, T. (2001), *Greek Literature and the Roman Empire: The Politics of Imitation*, Oxford: Oxford University Press.

Whitmarsh, T. (2002), 'Alexander's Hellenism and Plutarch's Textualism', *CQ* n.s. 52: 174–92.

Whitmarsh, T. (2005), *The Second Sophistic*, Oxford: Oxford University Press.

Whitmarsh, T. (2011), *Narrative and Identity in the Ancient Greek Novel*, Cambridge: Cambridge University Press.

Widengren, G. (1959), 'The Sacral Kingship of Iran', *La regalità sacra. Contributi al Tema dell'VIII Congresso internazionale di Storia delle Religioni*, Leiden: Brill, 242–57.

Wiesehöfer, J. (2001), *Ancient Persia from 550 BC to 650 AD*, trans. A. Azodi, London and New York: I. B. Tauris.

Wilken, U. (1906), 'Hellenen und Barbaren', *Neue Jahrbucher für klassische Altertum* 17: 457–71.

Will, F. (1960), 'Aristotle and the Question of Character in Literature', *The Review of Metaphysics* 14: 353–9.

Wilson, N. G. (1983), *Scholars of Byzantium*, London: Duckworth.

Wiseman, T. P. (1993), 'Lying Historians: Seven Types of Mendacity', in C. Gill and T. P. Wiseman (eds), *Lies and Fiction in the Ancient World*, Exeter: University of Exeter Press, 122–46.

Wolffgarten, H. (1868), *De Ephori et Dinonis historiis a Trogo Pompeio expressis*, diss., Bonn.

Wolski, J. (1993), *L'Empire des Arsacides* (= Acta Iranica 32), Leuven: Peeters.

Wood, J. L. (2009), 'Is There an "Archê Kakou" in Plato?', *The Review of Metaphysics* 63: 349–84.

Wright, J. H. (1895), 'A Votive Tablet to Artemis Anaitis and Men Tiamu in the Boston Museum of Fine Arts', *HSPh* 6: 55–74.

Wylie, G. (1986), 'What really happened at Aegospotami?' *AC* 55: 125–41.

Wylie, G. (1992), 'Cunaxa and Xenophon', *Acta Classica*, 61: 119–34.

Wyttenbach, D. (1810), *Plutarchi Chaeronensis Moralia*, vol. 6, Oxford: Clarendon Press.

Yaavetz, Z. (1998), 'Latin Authors on Jews and Dacians', *Historia* 47: 77–107.

Yamauchi, E. M. (1973), 'Cultic Prostitution' in H. A. Hoffner (ed.), *Orient and Occident: Essays Presented to Cyrus H. Gordon on Occasion of his Sixty-Fifth Birthday*, Kevelaer: Butzon and Bercker, 213–22.

Yardley, J. C., and W. Heckel (1997), *Justin: Epitome of the Philippic History of Pompeius Trogus*, vol. 1, Oxford: Oxford University Press.

Zadok, R. (1997), 'Some Iranian Anthroponyms and Toponyms', *Nouvelles Assyriologiques Brèves et Utilitaires* (1): 6–7.

Zadorojnyi, A. (2006), 'King of his Castle: Plutarch, *Demosthenes* 1–2', *CCJ* 52: 102–27.

Zaehner, R. C. (1955), *Zurvan: A Zoroastrian Dilemma*, Oxford: Oxford University Press.

Zambrini, A. (2007), 'The Historians of Alexander the Great', in J. Marincola (ed.), *A Companion in Greek and Roman Historiography*, Oxford: Oxford University Press, 210–20.

Zandee, J. (1971), 'Le Messie. Conceptions de la royauté dans les religions du Proche-Orient ancien', *RHR* 180: 3–28.

Zecchini, G. (1989), 'Entimo Di Gortina (Athen. II 48d–f) e le Relazioni Greco-Persiane durante la Pentecontetia', *AncSoc* 20: 5–13.

Zeitz, J. F. T. (1854), 'Observationes Criticae in Plutarchi Artaxerxem', in *Miscellanea Philologa*, Utrecht: Kemink et Filium, 21–35.

Zepernick, K. (1921), 'Die *Exzerpte* des Athenaeus in den Dipnosophisten und ihre Glaubwürdigkeit', *Philologus* 77: 311–63.

Ziegler, K. (1908), 'Plutarchstudien I. Der "Brief des Lamprias". II. Die alteste Sammlung der Biographien Plutarchs', *RhM* 63: 239–53.

Ziegler, K. (1927), 'IV. Noch einmal der "Brief des Lamprias". V. Zur Geschichte des Seitenstettensis. VI. Erläuterungen zu Band III 2 der Biographien', *RhM* 76: 20–53.

Ziegler, K. (1949a), 'Paradoxographoi', *RE* 18.3: 1137–66.

Ziegler, K. (1949b), *Plutarchos von Chaironeia*, Stuttgart-Waldsee: A. Druckenmüller.

Ziegler, K. (1951), 'Plutarchos von Chaironeia', *RE* 21: 636–962.

Ziegler, K. (1952), 'Polykritos (7)', *RE* 21.2: 1760–1.

Ziegler, K. (1972), 'Zenon (20)', *RE* 10 A: 214.

Index

fragments, 4, 16, 58, 64–5, 70n, 73, 83, 105, 109, 118, 141, 148, 151–2, 154, 157–8, 161, 165, 168, 204, 206, 216, 225, 237, 240, 247, 261
Frankincense, 241–2

Gela, 246
Gellius, Aulus, 63, 69
genre, 12–15, 28–9, 63, 148
Gigis, 53–4, 128–31, 140
Ginge, 129; see also Gigis
Glos, 110n, 223–4, 226, 263
Gobryas, 121
gods, goddesses, 23, 51–3, 83, 104, 107, 116, 124, 156, 162, 177n, 178–9, 230–1, 271
Gorgus, 147–8
Gray, Vivienne, 211
Great King, the, 16n, 18, 28n, 55, 64, 78, 87–8, 115, 135, 140–2, 145, 167, 197, 217, 240n, 242, 266
absence, 239
bravery, 41, 93, 191
conference with, 15, 143, 145, 251
divine (?), 145–6
king's table, king's meal/dinner, 13, 19, 21, 154–5, 216n, 235, 238, 243–6
uninhibited, absolute, 19, 20
whims, 252
Great Satraps' Revolt, 202, 226–7
Greek symposium, 21n, 123

Hadrian (Caesar Publius Aelius Traianus Hadrianus Augustus), 24n, 27
Hamilcar, 27
Hannibal, 27
Haug, Martin, 105
headdress, 95–6, 207
Hecatomnus, 268n
Hector, 52
Hegesander of Delphi, 248
Hellanicus of Lesbos, 13–15
Hellenocentric perspective, 26, 29
Hera, 230–1, 234
Heracleidae, 212, 234
Heracleides Lembus, 235–6
Heracleides of Cyme, 13, 32, 154, 229–53, 256–7
absence of narrative, 234, 247, 251, 256
association with Alexandria, 236–7

derivative, 237, 247, 256
Persica, 234–5, 241
Preparations, 234–5, 241
Heracleides of Pontus, 235
Heracles, 42, 234
Hermesianax, 148
Hermione, 142, 167
Herodotus, 1, 13–15, 19–20, 29, 37, 46, 57–8, 62–3, 69n, 70–1, 102, 117, 122, 126n, 145, 151, 153–61, 168, 188, 204, 219–20, 231–2, 237, 240, 242–3, 251–3, 256, 278
Herzfeld, Ernst, 114
Hesiod, 24n
Hippocrates of Cos, 61
historiography, 41–2, 112, 137, 141, 145, 201, 252
historiographic debate, 37, 40, 46–7, 54–5, 107, 133, 135, 138–40, 144, 166, 258
Homer, 52, 108, 247
honey, 124, 142
Horomazes, 23; see also Ahura Mazda
horseman, horsemanship, 41, 155
horses, 41, 64, 94–6, 113, 137, 190, 217–18, 237, 238n, 240
hunt, hunting, 39, 41n, 93, 200, 216–19, 228, 260, 275
hypomnema, -ta (note/s, draft/s), 3–4, 270, 274–6, 278

Idernes, 100
implied author, 7–8, 10
imprisonment, incarceration, 49–50, 97, 106–8, 129, 158, 197–8, 206, 214, 224, 278
Inarus, 65n, 84
incestuous relationship, 172, 174, 219–22, 229–33, 249–50
India, Indians, 62–3, 89, 105, 241–2
indirect speech, 50, 52, 55, 257
infanticide, 174
innuendo, 8, 45, 64
Intaphernes, 101n
interpolations, 78, 80, 91, 95n, 111n, 246n
Ionia, 147, 158
Ionic dialect and forms, 12–13, 69–70, 74
Iphicrates, 189, 192–3, 214, 218n, 226
irony, 8, 80, 95, 99, 103, 108, 110, 115, 121, 127, 139, 228, 255, 261, 267